WHAT OTHERS ARE SAYING ABOUT THIS BOOK AND JUDY KERR:

"A wonderful introduction to the world of show biz." Jerry Seinfeld

"Informative and to the point. She knows the roads that every actor must walk on." Michael Richards

"This is good, Judy, this is good!" Julia Louis-Dreyfus

"A first rate primer, an excellent refresher course... Judy's work is a sound guide down the bumpy road of show biz." Jason Alexander

"If show biz had a good mother...it would be Judy!" Jennifer Grey

"A must for anyone thinking of getting into show business. It is more than a guidebook...it is a bible." Jonathan Silverman

"Judy is an inspiration and a love. Every set should have a Judy." Maureen McCormick

"When I first came to Los Angeles, this book could have saved me from getting ripped off many times." Ernest Borgnine

"I wish I'd had this book when I was first starting out. In all the years I spent studying acting, I was never taught about the business." Susan Blakely

"Judy Kerr's book will help you get jobs and grow as an artist." Joan Darling, Director/Acting Coach

If you really want to know how to make it in Los Angeles, this book is a must."
Bill Macy, Actor

"An actor's roadmap to the ins and outs of what truly is a business."
Dee Wallace Stone, Actress

"Very informative—a must for all actors."
Lou Ferrigno, Actor *(The Incredible Hulk)*

"It took me fourteen years to discover the Hollywood secrets that Judy Kerr gives you."
Dianne Kay, Actress *(Eight Is Enough)*

"The best reference book of its type on the market."
Steven Nash, Personal Manager

"Offers more real help per page than stacks of other books on the subject!"
Al Burton, Producer

"Rich with the wisdom of a dedicated professional."
Eve Brandstein, Producer/Director

"Don't make the mistake so many actors make. Read this book."
Dan Gauthier, Actor

"Excellent. Helpful and direct."
Bud Cort, Actor

"Practical information and sound advice. I use it myself."
Joel Asher, Acting Coach/Director

"A great handbook for every actor, beginner or pro!"
Beverly Long, Casting Director

"A must-read for actors who are serious about a career."
Eric Morris, Acting Coach/Author/Director

"For any actor who wants to know the who's, what's and where's of L.A."
Deborah Kurtz, Casting Director

Completely New and Revised 9th Edition
Custom collection of resources
Expert Interviews
L. A. Hangouts

Yes, You Can Live Your Life As An Actor!

Acting Is Everything you do, you are,
you have been or hope to be in your life.

If your dream is to live your life as a professional actor, your first tool is your basic acting craft. Good training helps you discover the power, control and confidence to act. Once you have confidence and know how to interpret a script and develop a character, then the business side of acting begins. It takes desire, guts, preparation, discipline, talent and luck to have an acting career.

Welcome to *Acting Is Everything*. In this ninth edition, I will guide you toward fulfilling your dreams, giving you important information about developing the actor inside you. I share ideas, facts and many special secrets for establishing your career. This advice has helped bring a great deal of success to countless readers and many of my students over the years.

I hope it will do the same for you.

Judy Kerr,
Studio City, California

ACTING IS EVERYTHING

An Actor's Guidebook for a Successful Career in Los Angeles

by Judy Kerr

Ninth Edition, Completely Revised

September Publishing
Studio City, California, USA

Distributed By:
SCB Distributors
15608 South New Century Drive
Gardena, California, 90248, USA
310/532-9400

ACTING IS EVERYTHING

An Actor's Guidebook for a Successful Career in Los Angeles by Judy Kerr

Published by: **September Publishing**
Studio City, California, USA
www.actingiseverything.com

Distributed by: **SCB DISTRIBUTORS**
15608 S. New Century Dr., Gardena, CA 90248, USA
310/532-9400

All rights reserved. No part of this publication may be reproduced or transmitted in any form or by any means, electronic or mechanical, including photocopying and recording, or by any information storage or retrieval system without prior permission in writing from the author or publishers, except for the inclusion of brief quotations in a review. Requests for permission must be in writing.

Copyright © 1981, 1989, 1992, 1994, 1997, 2000

1st Edition 1981
2nd Edition, 1983, updated
3rd Edition 1988, updated
4th Edition 1989, completely revised
5th Edition 1990, updated
6th Edition 1992, completely revised and expanded
7th Edition 1994, completely revised and expanded
8th Edition 1997, revised, updated and expanded
9th Edition 2000, completely revised and expanded, first printing

Publisher's Cataloging in Publication Data
Kerr, Judy
Acting Is Everything: An Actor's Guidebook for a Successful Career in Los Angeles/ by Judy Kerr.
—9th edition, completely revised.
Bibliography: k.
Includes index
1. Acting—Guidebooks, handbooks, manuals, etc.
2. Career—Guidebooks, handbooks, manuals, etc.
Library of Congress Catalog Card Number: 99-60713
ISBN: 0-9629496-4-7

Buckets of gratitude to my husband Ron Gorow—without his love and support you would not be reading this; my daughters, Christina, Cynthia and Catherine for their encouragement and enthusiasm; my friend Robin Gee for her time, inspiration and start-up skills; my teacher, Joan Darling, for her continued guidance and all my students over the years for whom this was written.

Cover Design: Thomas Cobb

SECTION ONE

Developing Your Talent

SECTION TWO

Breaking Into The Biz

SECTION THREE

Places To Work As An Actor

SECTION FOUR

Career Team

SECTION FIVE

Career Tools

SECTION SIX

Personal Tools
Creating Your Style and Image

SECTION SEVEN

Acting Is Everything

SECTION EIGHT

Child Actors

SECTION NINE

Becoming Geographically Desirable

SECTION TEN

Reference Section

ABOUT THE AUTHOR

Photography and Makeup Michael Maron

Accomplished acting coach/actress/director Judy Kerr brings over 25 years of experience to this edition of *Acting Is Everything.*

Judy is recognized in Hollywood for her unique gift of nurturing talent and helping actors succeed. She used that gift brilliantly as the dialogue coach on the hit series *Seinfeld*, working with all of the cast members, as well as guest stars. Rehearsing one-on-one with some of the top names in the business, Judy works to enhance the artistry and technical skill necessary to create top notch television programming.

Judy's recent credits include dialogue coach on *It's like, you know...*, *The Single Guy*, and *Alright Already.*

Her cable television show in Los Angeles, *Judy Kerr's Acting Workshop,* is in its 15th season. She is the bestselling author of eight previous editions of *Acting Is Everything*, contributing to the success of thousands of readers.

With this Ninth Edition, Judy opens the doors of Hollywood to a new generation of acting hopefuls with a straightforward road map for breaking into the business. Judy Kerr continues to coach on sets, teach acting workshops, coach privately and conduct seminars worldwide.

How To Use This Book

• **You are holding a workbook.** It is meant to be studied, highlighted, marked in and pages turned down. Using this book as a guide, many actors and potential actors have traveled from all over the country to fulfill their dreams by seeking their fame and fortunes in Los Angeles. I love to see their well-used copies of *Acting Is Everything.* Discover your own favorite people and services.

• **This book is big—think of each section as almost a seperate book.** This is not necessarily a book to be read cover to cover. Read and take the appropriate actions for what is most important to you. I've tried to give you some information on most aspects of the acting/entertainment business.

• *Acting Is Everything* is protected under copyright law but you have my permission to make copies of pages you need to keep with you and to share with your friends. I think they'll need and want a book of their own.

• **I can't resolve the he/she pronoun issue** so I have broken the rules; I use *they* and *their* as singular pronouns meaning *he* or *she.*

• **I love beginnings and helping you make your dreams come true.** Now is the time to turn your dreams into goals and to aim your heart toward them.

• **William Shakespeare** said, "Our doubts are traitors, and make us lose the good we oft might win by fearing to attempt."

• **Anthony Hopkins,** when asked if he had doubts, replied, "Yes, but you can't let them get in your way. Just do it, be bold. Mighty forces will come to your aid."

• **Let the fears and doubts be there** and still go for your dreams. You deserve it.

ABOUT THE RESOURCES LISTED IN *ACTING IS EVERYTHING*

All of the resources for actors included in *Acting Is Everything* have been personally researched by me. I have used most of the services myself or have had excellent reports from my students and friends who have used them.

In this ninth edition, the resources have been reviewed and updated and new ones added. In Los Angeles, phone area codes change fairly often; we do our best to have the latest ones for you. When you reach a wrong number, try using one of the newer area codes. If you have a problem with any of the businesses listed please let me know by Fax: 818/505-9311 or on my web page www.actingiseverything.com

I provide resources to help you begin your own list of special people and services. Always research all your contacts carefully; prices and integrity have been known to change. This book will point you in the right direction and help you get the maximum value for every dollar spent.

This book is about doing all you can to build your artistic acting career and living your life as an actor... so the journey begins...

SECTION ONE

WHAT IS ACTING?

Acting is living your life, then using those experiences to enable the audience to experience their own lives and emotions.

• **Richard Dreyfuss** said, "An actor's job is not to feel things, it is to make the audience feel them."

• **Emmy Award-winning Director Joan Darling** says, "Acting, when it is done at its best, is behaving as if you were alive in a set of given circumstances that are different from your own given circumstances."

• **Acting *in the moment*** is always the goal. The *moment* is that instant in time when the actor's imagination and talent create a flash of truth. The audience recognizes and identifies with this truth and is transported and moved.

• **Robert De Niro** said, "Sometimes I get moments I know are right on the head, almost an epiphany, knowing you're exactly there; you're in the moment, in character. Most of the other times it's just a struggle to get through it and hope that it's right."

• **Meryl Streep** when asked about spontaneity said, "It's the only thing worth looking at, what nobody expected to happen. In a play, when somebody drops something, forgets a line, suddenly it all becomes electric, alive, it all feels real. The spontaneous is what you dream of, wish for and hope appears."

• **Actors cannot always depend** on this *spontaneous moment* happening by accident or luck. By learning the craft of acting, you can *deliver the goods* on demand, whether you feel like it or not. In acting classes, you can learn the craft of using your own life experiences as your acting tools.

• **Acting is a physical, athletic event.** As you are always in a changing, growing process, you need to develop an awareness of what is going on in your life at all times, be aware of every emotional and physical fiber in your body.

• **Your face, body, voice and spirit** are your billboards—what sells you—they are what the casting directors who interview you notice first. You cannot have the right *look* for every role, nor can you figure out what each director, producer or writer has in mind for each role. However, you can make the best of every casting meeting by figuring out who you are and giving of your whole self at each and every meeting.

• **To discover the *inner you*** takes time spent thinking, reading and soul searching. Finding the physical you takes honesty when looking at yourself in the mirror and on camera. Presence, vocal quality, hair, makeup, clothes, weight, height, and your spiritual development are all important aspects of the presentation of your unique self. Only you can decide who you are and then make the commitment to perfect and fine-tune your acting instrument—you.

• **The best part** about all this self-discovery is that it makes you an actor every minute of the day. Even though it may have been a long time since a job or interview, you are still working, studying, preparing all the time. Actors usually don't work as much as they would like, so it is very important to enjoy the process, the privilege of living an actor's life. If you become discouraged and unhappy, the great destroyer—negativity—sets in.

• **Nicholas Cage** said about shooting *The Rock* with Sean Connery, "It's like playing cops and robbers in the backyard." This is the ideal for every actor to reach in every role; each line and movement will be absolutely believable.

• **Leonardo DiCaprio**, says: "I don't really understand the process. The main thing is just getting into the reality of what the character is, finding all the suitable things to go along with it. I often look at a situation from the outside, like I was a camera."

• **John Malkovich**, says: "Acting is a job; if it's not fun, why do it?"

• **Sally Field** says, "being an actor is both wonderful and horrible...you never know what's next. After my children, acting's the love of my life, my best friend, my lover, my companion."

• **Harrison Ford**—when speaking of why acting is fun—said, "There is a certain foolish pleasure in having these experiences."

• **Richard Gere** said, "This is what we do in acting—we embarrass ourselves all the time. You have to be able to make a fool out of yourself regularly to do this, otherwise it is not going to be any good."

• **Anthony Hopkins**, says, "My goal, principally, is to always get into the technical relaxation that Stanislavski talks endlessly about in his books and just listen."

• **Willliam H. Macy** told *Back Stage West,* "I think an actor's task is to read the script, figure out the action—the objective—and do that and let everything else go hang. We can never forget acting is a big fat trick that we play on the audience. You're standing in a set. It's not real, but it's real enough, and the audience is willing enough to suspend disbelief that there you are in the setting and you're wearing somebody's else's clothes that have been designed. So it's the actor's job to figure out what his character wants and to do something that's similar to that so that it looks like you're making it up as you go along. The emotions will follow; they will be there as you need them."

• **Steve McQueen** said, "Acting was hard; playing a role was like reaching inside you and pulling out broken glass." He "treated every script like an enemy."

• **Kimberly Jentzen,** acting coach, film director and director of Living The Art Institute, says: "Acting is an art form of compassion. It is an act of courage. Great acting will move the audience from thinking to feeling, from judging to identifying—giving us subtle but sacred permission to feel when we are too proud to release our own fears, laughter and tears, creating a pathway to experience our connection to each other. When this occurs, a performance is truly memorable."

• **Choices are where the real talent lies**. If you choose to love the process, life can be so much easier. You can learn and grow through pleasure as well as pain; both are simply choices. Try to choose pleasure whenever you can; it's more fun. Acting is fun and easy; getting the job is tough, but possible. Lots of actors get roles each and every day.

• **Acting is an art and a craft**. Some people make a living at acting while others act and make their living doing other things. Both ways are valid and artistic. Being an actor takes dedication, desire and ambition beyond reason. Most actors are gamblers—there is something about gambling with your life and your security that is attractive to you. An actor must be a survivor, must persevere.

ACTING TECHNIQUE

• **This is the most important section of this book.** A solid acting craft or technique is what makes a career possible.

• **You will probably remember your first acting class session.** Mine was at El Camino College in Redondo Beach. I took a basic acting class as a fluke, I thought. In my first class the teacher presented a scene from *Applause,* with experienced actors. When I saw those actors on stage my life changed. I knew I had to learn to act so I could *try* to move an audience like I was moved. That moment in time led me on this adventure.

• **In basic acting class, you learn specific acting tools**—how to develop characters and how to interpret a script. You can decide where to study by going to watch different classes or interviewing teachers to discover who might teach the best techniques for you. There are many acting coaches to choose from. I would encourage you to pick a coach who is supportive, not abrasive or negative. There is no reason to be humiliated in order to learn.

• **If you can afford it**, study basic craft, improvisation, voice and scene study at the same time. Four classes a week and all the homework in between for a year or two would give you a solid foundation. If you could also work in the theater and do student films, you would gain actual experience too. I know this isn't possible if you have to make a living at the same time. If you are not one of those actors who are lucky enough to be funded for a year or two, take on as much as your time and money will allow.

• **Scene study classes** are often taken after you've honed your basic craft. The actors prepare scenes and present them to the teacher for critique. It takes personal motivation and homework.

• **Jason Alexander** (*Seinfeld*) when being interviewed by Rob Kendt of *Backstage West/DramaLogue* gave the most understandable explanation of what acting technique is:

- **Technique for me is:** How do I do enough crafting so that I can rehearse intelligently, and how do I then make choices that will sustain me for a run? That's all it is. It's nothing that a studied actor has not heard before; it's just very clear-cut. You have to answer four questions: Who am I speaking to? What do I want from them? How am I going to get it? and What is standing in the way of what I want?

- **But it's not just answering the questions**—you have to answer them so incredibly specifically that it can take weeks to come up with answers for these things. You not only have to make choices that are smart but fit the material. And ideally you're making choices that once you get them, they make your instrument do things so that you don't have to manufacture a performance—they're so strong that when you plug in the right thought, or the right word, or whatever it is, your instrument starts to respond. And that's hard.

- **That's the difference between a craftsman and a non-craftsman.** Actors have to take the responsibilty that any artist makes in going, "I choose that color, that stroke, right there. Right or wrong, there it is." Actors have to go, "I'm not winging it, I'm not waiting to see what happens; I'm making this choice right here with my intelligence and with my instrument."

- **It's especially good when you're preparing stuff for auditions.** No one's gonna tell you different; no one's gonna direct you out of it. So you have to be able to craft this material so that it shows you in a great light, shows your range, shows your ability, and shows your everything. How do I walk into that room and be undeniably more masterful than anyone that's walked in before me? It can't just be cockiness, it just can't be, "I know I'm good." It has nothing to do with me being good or not. It's that I'm doing things that the average schmo on the street is not doing. They don't know how. I craft, and they hope. That's the difference.

• **Director Martha Coolidge** said, "Acting is an art form and is probably one of the toughest. You need to learn as much about it as any musician knows about their instrument. Ironically, it's a career chosen by people who need to be loved, people who will probably receive 98% rejection in their lives. Without a craft to back you up, you're riding for a fall."

• **Brad Pitt** worked as an extra in 1989 on *Cutting Class*. He says, "I am the living testament that you can learn anything, because I was so bad."

• **Jason Alexander** was doing a scene on *Seinfeld* about why he had to postpone his wedding. It wasn't getting the laughs. The writers changed a line to include the name of the hall the reception was to be held in. On the next take Jason got a huge laugh. I asked him how he did that so fast. He said he immediately identified the reception hall with a place he knew that was specific, eventful, truthful and full of history. The audience couldn't help but identify with his wedding dilemma, believe it, and laugh at his uncomfortableness.

• **Lisa Kudrow** of *Friends* says about her character, Phoebe: "She's operating out of a huge amount of denial; so many horrible things have happened to her that she would not be able to even breathe another breath if she took it all in. She's in search of whatever feels good. I think Phoebe thinks she's a very talented, struggling artist, but she's just not." When you know the truth of the character you are playing, it will make your acting choices specific and identifiable for the audience.

• **Richard Dreyfuss** played the character Boy Wonder in *Inserts*. Writer John Byrum says through Boy, "The ability to steal from the thoughts of others is merely an indication of industry... What passes for genius is the ability to steal from your own (thoughts). If you want to reach your peak you better learn how to rob yourself blind."

• **Director Martin Scorsese says about Harvey Keitel** whom he has worked with five times, "He pays scrupulous attention to the smallest detail of a role. I've seen him get deeper and deeper into himself. Harvey travels into very forbidding regions of his soul for his work, and he's able to have that experience and put it on the screen in an absolutely genuine way I find very touching."

• **Laurence Fishburne**, Oscar nominee, says about acting, "I want to startle people in a subtle kind of way—the way people are startled when they catch sight of themselves in a mirror. That's the goal of my work: communicating with people on a much deeper level than whatever is obviously going on. It's not so much about finding the truth as *revealing* it. Getting to the truth requires a tremendous amount of patience because things are only revealed to you when you're ready to deal with them."

• **Sally Field** said in a *Bravo Actors' Studio* interview, "Anyone who isn't terrified of acting is a liar. I'm always terrified when I know I have to be emotional."

• **Dinah Manoff** says: "My process is to use whatever works. I studied method and it is wonderful. And sometimes I have an onion in my purse in case I have to cry."

• **Dustin Hoffman's** colleague, Jessica Lange said, "Dustin has obsessive curiosity." Meryl Streep said, "His mantra is specificity, specificity, specificity."

• **Danny Glover** in an *Actor's Studio* interview, said, "Listening is the key (to acting). Listening and relaxing, because if you're not relaxed you can't listen."

• **Joan Allen** in *Back Stage West*, said, "If you lose your focus when acting, you can regain it by turning outward, by really listening.

• **Billy Wilder**, legendary director, said about an actor's preparation, "You can tell how good an actor is by looking at his script. If he's no good, the script will be neat as a pin. Charles Laughton's script was so filthy it looked like a herring had been wrapped in it."

• **Anthony Hopkins** told Ed Bradley on *60 Minutes* that Katharine Hepburn gave him his most valuable piece of advice on his first movie, *The Lion In Winter.* She said, "Don't do anything; don't act. Just be what you are. Acting is reacting; just listen."

• **Jessica Tandy** told Bob Krakower, when he begged her to talk to the actors at Actors Theatre of Louisville, that she really didn't have anything to say. "After all, all I do is read the play every day."

• **Joan Darling, my teacher**, has been nominated for an Emmy, three times as a director and once as an actor. She won for directing. She was the original director of *Mary Hartman, Mary Hartman*—one of the first women to direct film and television in the 1970s. She is a legendary acting teacher in Los Angeles, New York and Sundance.

Q: Can acting be taught?

- **It is possible** to teach someone the techniques of how to wake up different portions of their own personality in order to create a set of given circumstances inside the actor that are similar to what the character is experiencing. That is a craft that can be taught to anybody; everybody knows how to be alive. It is easier for some people to immediately understand and process this craft almost innately without thinking about it and to be able to do it right away.

- **People tend to think** that actors who can do it right away, because it is easy for them, are talented and other people who can't do it right away aren't talented. I've taught long enough to see that if people work hard enough they will learn everything they need to learn to really be wonderful. I think the measure of whether a person can do it or not is totally dictated by how much they want it.

Q: What are some specific acting tools you teach?

- **Acting is a sport** and you have to learn the tools and techniques in your body. Everything that you know and understand is stored in your body through information you got from your five senses. There is an acting technique called "sense memory" which teaches you how to evoke that memory. When you let yourself remember the different sensory stimulus surrounding a particular event, it wakes up the memory of that event and makes it present for you to use in an acting scene. While people know how to do this by just thinking about an event that is similar to the event in the play, "sense memory" is a real craft technique that wakes up the information of the event for you in a much deeper and much more reliable way.

- **Another acting technique** is called "personalizing." If the other actor on stage is your sister in the play and it is a sister your character hates, then you might "personalize" that other actor as someone you hate, meaning you would deal with them as if they were that person you hate.

- "**Relaxation**" is one of the single most important acting techniques. You really need "relaxation" because when you have impulses come into and go out of your body, any physical tension you have will prevent that flow. Just so you don't make a mistake: "Relaxing exercise" in acting is not like Yoga or meditating. You are not trying to calm yourself down; you're simply trying to get your body to let go, relax and be curious about what emotionally is going on with you and to not meddle with it. Don't think you are supposed to become calm when you are "relaxing."

Q: What does "being in the moment" mean?

- **Briefly, "being in the moment"** means that not only does the actor deal with all the stuff they have awakened, with whatever acting technique they use that makes them similar to the play, or allows them to function as if they were in the play, but the actor is also relating to themselves at that moment in time on stage. The actor that allows himself or herself to be totally conscious of their experience at a given moment on stage, along with the work they created as an actor, is much more compelling to watch.

Q: What should new actors focus on?

- **I think new actors should read a lot of plays**, get acquainted with what their appetite is, what parts they love, the little child in them that really wants to be the princess or the athlete in the story.

- **If you are really serious about acting** you need to gather information. Try all kinds of acting techniques. I strongly recommend that new actors be insistent that their teachers are not punitive (punishing) and that their teachers have real information for them. If teachers ask you to do something, they have to be able to tell you how to do it. If they can't tell you how, then they are not teaching you.

- **Look around and see the actors you admire**. Make it a quest to find out how they do whatever you can't do and teach yourself how to do it.

Q: Is acting magic?

- **Yes and no.** I believe there is something magical in acting; in the communication between a person standing on a stage and the people sitting in the audience. An actor can stand on stage in a 1500 seat auditorium and have a wave of jealousy go through her and somebody from the back of the audience will say, "Oh, she's jealous," without the actor saying anything or making a face to show it. That is kind of magical.

- **In terms of learning to act**, there are very pragmatic things you can learn to do. If you do them like a recipe, you will be able to act a scene and act it well. So in that regard, I don't think it's magical at all. The magical question relates back to: do some people have talent and others not? I don't believe that's the case: I believe anybody can learn anything about acting that they need to know to be a good actor.

• **Kim Darby**, veteran actress, three-time Emmy and two-time Golden Globe nominee.

Q: In your view point, what is most important in acting?

- **You must learn a technique** that doesn't involve playing the words, the emotions or the feelings. Actors are afraid the audience won't feel or understand that conflict is going on. You have to play the action in the scene and deal with the resistance you are getting from the other character. When you put the action and obstacle on the other person then the drama and conflict come out of trying to change that person. Acting is not self-absorbed, it is the interaction that is important.

- **This technique shouldn't be academic and complicated;** what do I want and what is keeping me from getting it? There is always preparation. How do I feel at the top of the scene, what am I thinking about, what is my rhythm? You do your preparation and when the scene starts you drop the preparation and play the action again. If you play the results it will not be truthful and the audience will not be involved.

• **Larry Moss** is the acting teacher Helen Hunt thanked when she accepted her Golden Globe, SAG, and Academy Award for *As Good as It Gets.* When Karen Kondazian asked him in a *Back Stage West* interview about acting techniques, he replied:

- **The three things that actors need the most** are relaxation, imagination and the ability to analyze a script.

- **I work enormously with intentions.** And to find those, you need to know who the character is. You've got to understand their background. I'm a great believer in building a character's biography, because once you've done that, you walk into the play or screenplay with a full life. Things like the character's education, religion, relationship to parents, past events that were troubling or exciting, politics, dreams, etc. And what you create should be a combination of your own experiences and your imagination. If you just use yourself and not your imagination or you just use your imagination and not yourself, you're going to come off half-baked. I think it's absurd for any teacher to say that an acting student could just walk in and be themselves in any play. It's almost sophomoric and it's very, very destructive to the actor.

- **Film acting is all about containment**, but you have to have something to contain. The problem that some people have is they have nothing to contain and that's when you see bad acting. All good film and television acting has an enormous volcano in it that's being held back.

• **Janice Lynde, prominent Emmy-nominated,** Obie Award-winning actress and acting coach for actors as well as faculty members at the American Film Institute, teaches directors how to work with actors.

Q: How do you create a character that is very different from yourself?

- **Do research; it grounds you in authenticity.** Choose personalizations, where you may have behaved in a similar way as the character, imitation and sense memories to support the imitation. I find animal exercises enormously valuable. Imitate someone you know who is like the character. Dress like them, I always insist on the right shoes. How do they move? What mannerisms are keys to their psychology? Then personalize the other characters and each "event."

- **Example: When I played Marilyn Monroe,** I watched films and newsreeels and read everything I could about her life. I began to imitate her physicality. Then I found a sense memory of a feather tickling my lips, which not only made me look "as if" I were her, but gave me an inner glow. My secret "acting work" tickled me which resulted in giving me an incandescent sparkle. I also did an animal exercise of Kitty, the brown skunk, who lived next door. She would taunt my dog, brushing her tail in his face and moving in a slow luxurious, sensual way. Then from scene to scene, I personalized the other characters as people with whom I was very sensual, or vulnerable. My "event" was to get them to love me, including the audience.

- **Example: A heroin addict.** I found a drug rehab center, watched someone in withdrawal and talked to people who had been addicted. I chose a sense memory of an itch I couldn't scratch and a migraine headache for when the character was in need of a "fix." For right after a "fix" I chose a smell from a place remembering thunderous applause and a specific smell after orgasm. For the "high" state I also did an animal exercise of a gorilla after a nap.

- **Once you have the craft to support your ideas,** your artistry guides you in your choices. It's fun. To me, character work takes me to the edges and depth of my own spiritual being. As a result I "own" more of myself, I am more whole. The process of becoming whole is the most fulfilling aspect of acting.

• **John Kirby, acting coach, director,** teaches classes as well as privately coaches many top industry actors, including international and Broadway personalities.

Q: What are the mistakes you see in actors' work?

- **One of the biggest problems** actors make in their work and especially what they do on auditions is to *suggest* the work! They suggest the character and the events of the script, but never reveal a life—a true living person. They go on automatic and stay in the *event* of the audition. The actor is so caught up on being good or not being bad that they forget these thoughts are of no concern to their character and have nothing to do with what their character wants or is happening in their character's life. The greatest lesson an actor can learn is to own the room and make the place safe to live in!

• **Anita Jesse, acting coach, author** of *Let The Part Play You: A Practical Approach To The Actor's Creative Process* and *The Playing Is The Thing: Learning to Act Through Games and Exercises.*

Q: What would you say is the best method for improving an actor's concentration?

- **It takes time and patience** to master concentration. However, you can learn to choose a mental target, place it at the center of your awareness, and hold it there regardless of distractions. Script exploration, remembering lines, audition pressures, staying in character—all these become manageable only if you master concentration.

- **Sometimes you consciously order your mind** to focus on a particular mental target, then struggle to screen out distractions. Other times it's almost as if the mental target chooses you and everything else seems to automatically fade from awareness. For example, you effortlessly become enthralled by an appealing movie or book, a person you find attractive or your favorite music. It's almost as if you have *unconsciously* hit the switch that focuses attention on a particular object or train of thought.

Q: Would you explain how to do one of the concentration exercises from your book, *Let The Part Play You?*

- **A favorite seems to be**, "Doing My Job:" While driving, make that activity the center of your awareness. When your mind wanders, refocus. When you find yourself thinking about what you will do when you get to your destination or replaying past events, gently redirect your attention to *this* moment—to what is happening right now. Pay attention to the cars around you, the feel of your car, everything happening on the road and exactly how it relates to you. Use variations of this exercise anytime during the day—while reading, eating, talking to a friend, or washing dishes.

• **Eric Morris, actor, acting coach** and author, travels the world giving seminars on acting.

Q: What is your approach to teaching technique?

- **I do something that Lee Strasberg** was terrified about, which he would have called "therapy." Psychotherapy it isn't. It's a behavioral-modification therapy. The circle of the work is the instrument, which is the actor—his mind, body, voice, and his emotions. Truth can only come from a place of truth, and unless you accomplish your "being" state, your place of truth, you cannot act from an organic place. So largely the instrumental emphasis of my work is to eliminate obstacles and liberate the actor to be free, to be who he or she is.

- **I ask actors to do the hardest things** for them to do first. To people who are very proper and socially obligated, I give exercises that break down that propriety, antisocial exercises. My work is profoundly life-changing because an actor is liberated to be a free person, to enjoy life on an impressive and expressive level.

- **I teach actors to be professional experiencers.** Your responsibility as an actor is to fulfill the author's intentions, obligations and responsibilities. You have to be able to really experience, from your own frame of reference and inner, organic fabric of emotions, what the character is experiencing. You become, not an actor who acts, but an experiencer who really experiences. You have to be able to discover the next moment of behavior in the next moment, at exactly the same moment the audience does. That's true acting, true experiencing.

• **Joel Asher, well-respected acting coach** and director of film and television, has produced three training videos for actors.

Q: What acting techniques do you teach?

- **I use many techniques.** Just as a carpenter wouldn't go to a job carrying only one tool, an actor can't do that either. If an actor uses the same technique to audition for a soap opera as a situation comedy, it's not going to work. So I give actors different scenes with different styles, different challenges, so they can constantly be expanding their techniques. I teach weekly technique, professional and master scene study classes. We do exercises and improvisations that grow out of the scene work. These are improvisations that are done to isolate a specific skill and work on that issue.

• **In Don Richardson's book**, *Acting Without Agony: An Alternative to the Method,* he has an extensive list of emotions that may help you when making your acting choices. Here are a few he lists: admiration, amazement, anger, awe, boredom, curiosity, desire, desperation, disbelief, disgust, embarrassment, envy, expectation, fascination, fear, grief, hatred, hope, anger, horror, hysteria, indignation, jealousy, loneliness, lust, panic, pity, pride, relief, remorse, respect, serenity, shame, suspicion and terror. It is absolutely essential to figure out what your character is thinking and feeling. As an exercise, pick any sentence and try using a different emotion each time you say the sentence. This will help you to realize it is the acting that is most important, not the words.

• **On the set of *Seinfeld*** one day, Jerry, Julia and Jason were playing around, thinking of all the ways you can say *alright* or *okay* and which one should be used in specific circumstances. During the laughter, Jerry said, "Hey, Judy, that would be a great exercise for your actors." It is a great exercise. Try it with your friends.

ACTING TRAINING: COACHES AND TEACHERS

The mediocre teacher tells. The good teacher explains. The superior teacher demonstrates. The great teacher inspires. William A. Ward

Great teachers have always been measured by the number of their students who have surpassed them. Don Robinson

• **It takes many teachers** in life to develop an actor. Following are teachers, tools, suggestions and recommendations that have helped me and others to develop lives and careers. There are countless paths, and part of an actor's job is to keep exploring new ones.

• **You should always be studying.** Your training will be a constant expenditure so don't skimp in this area. Your technique and acting knowledge will make you more employable.

• **Choosing an acting coach** is an important choice, but it is not a life or death one. Choose one, take a month's classes, give it your all and then evaluate what you have learned. If you've improved and others in class have grown and improved, then stick with it.

• **William H. Macy** in *Back Stage West,* when asked about what kind of teachers actors should seek out said, "I believe that an actor is held in better stead if he doesn't rely on his talent. What you rely on is technique. Talent is given by God and there's no negotiating. Technique is something anybody can learn, and for a technique to be a valid technique, it's got to be scientific. It's got to be repeatable. It's got to be testable. That's what they should look for in a teacher."

• **Eve Brandstein, Casting Director, Producer, Career Coach,** says about choosing an acting coach, "I think you have to see a teacher work. You could have heard that this is the greatest teacher in the whole world and they've taught some of the biggest names in the business, but if there's no chemistry, forget it. Some actors are better off in a negative situation and others in a positive one. One teacher says, 'Why do you bring that piece of s--- into class? You're a terrible actor; who ever said you could act?' And this inspires the actor to greatness. Another teacher says, 'That was beautiful work, but what about this?' And that works for that actor. You have to find out if the teacher and you are magical together."

• **Joan Darling, legendary acting teacher:**

Q: Should working actors still go to class?

- **If you find yourself starting to be disappointed** after you finish a job instead of feeling that you grew and things are wonderful and you can't wait to act again—then you should get into a class where the working on one's art is respected and you have fun. If you don't exercise your acting muscles at top capacity, you'll lose them.

Q: What if an actor can't afford to study?

- **Find a teacher that you can apprentice yourself to.** Or get other actors with the same desire and meet in your living room once a week. Ask a friend who knows about acting to conduct this workshop for you.

• **Larry Moss, respected acting coach,** in a *Back Stage West* interview when asked about acting teachers said:

- **I believe that the aim of a teacher** should be to help the individual students find the tools to realize their greatest potential. When you try to teach from a singular point-of-view or method, you're going to hurt the student.

• **About the expense of acting classes.**

- **I have actors who hold down two jobs** in order to take class. I think that your education as an actor is something that you pay for because you care about it. It's like therapy. I had a therapist who once said to me, "If you don't think enough of yourself to pay for therapy, how do you think you're going to get well?" I don't think the classes would be as productive for the students if they weren't making some sacrifices. I don't think that life is about getting it easy. I don't think being an artist is easy. I think you get to earn things in life.

• **Cherie Franklin, actress, acting coach** and well known dialogue coach, on feature films and television:

Q: What should an actor gain by working with a coach?

- **The value of working** with an acting coach on an ongoing basis is this: they can offer a safe environment that can allow you to reveal your fears and bring your work to a place where you can face your truths. This work state will invite you to trust in yourself, creating confidence and steering you clear of self-sabotage throughout your journey as an actor.

Q: Who is your ideal student?

- **One who is committed to excellence**, to daily homework, to investigating his emotional levels, to understanding his blocks, and understanding what he does and doesn't do well. Someone who wants to be the best actor they can be, who is willing to do all that it takes to get what they want. Homework might include journal work to discover emotional blocks, practicing cold reading, vocalizing, the reading of a play, seeing a TV show or a new director's work and so on. Bottom line, an actor should remember that perfect is an end state. Therefore, as actors we have the priviledge of becoming a better craftsman with each new day whether working on set or at home. We can continue learning and advancing as the business changes.

• **Anita Jesse, acting coach and author:**

Q: How can actors make the most of class?

- **Be professional.** Be on time. Be prepared. Be "present." Fully commit all your energies to learning. I'm amazed at how many actors throw away their time and money. If you aren't ready to commit to the training, save your money and wait until you are.

- **Learn to listen.** Learn to take what you can from every comment given you and don't waste time arguing with the teacher. If you disagree with the majority of what a particular coach has to say, you are in the wrong workshop.

- **No one can teach you to be an artist.** Whether or not you become an artist must be left to you and your creative spirit. You hope to find a workshop where you can learn your craft.

- **Eric Morris, actor, acting coach and author says:**

  - **My ideal student** is a person who commits himself to acting on a level of artistry. Somebody who is so committed to the work that it becomes a way of living. Unless you must act, because it's a calling, something you need to do, forget it! It'll break your heart.

- **Joel Asher, well-respected acting coach describes his ideal actor.**

  - **Someone who is so hungry to grow** constantly that they will be eating, sleeping, breathing acting 24 hours a day. When an actor is walking down the street, it's a sense memory exercise. You can constantly be training yourself as an actor by being alive in the space that you inhabit. Preparation is the key to spontaneity.

- **John Kirby, popular acting coach** makes observations regarding actors studying:

  - **In Los Angeles** it feels like there is a breed of young actors who want a "quick fix approach" to learning their craft. They run to any cold reading class or gimmick to keep themselves from doing the real kind of work that's going to raise their abilities to greatness. This can be very detrimental to anyone who does not already have a strong foundation in training. Their work becomes automatic, cranked out and extremely technical. Although they feel they may have given a great audition, what they have produced is slick, and may appear perfect because they did not drop a line or held their sides [script] correctly, but they have revealed nothing in the room that could blow anyone away with their performance. Their audition will lack dimension and effective moments. I love the actors who are in acting for the long run, who invest themselves in the work and take all the time necessary to be truly great.

- **Terrance Hines, acting coach and personal manager,** Hines and Hunt Entertainment, explains why he thinks training is so important.

  - **Whether you are one of the Three Tenors,** a member of the Bolshoi Ballet, an Iron Man in baseball, an Olympic swimmer or a waiter at Denny's, you have a coach and a trainer who warms you up, guides you and prepares you for the physical and emotional struggle that lies ahead that day. For an actor it is important to be in a class so that your instrument stays flexible and focused. Unlike a violinist who plays an instrument, you the actor are the instrument you play. It is as wrong to mistreat your body with alcohol and smoke as it is to deny this same instrument the opportunity to be nurtured by exposure to good writing, risk taking and the emotional communion that happens with other artists in a safe landscape. Class offers you the opportunity to share your losses and gains with others who will understand. Compliments or criticism from a fellow artist you trust is the highest form of support and sharing.

• **The following list of teachers are experts** and have good reputations. These few are just a small representation of what is available in Los Angeles. Extensive lists of teachers are in the *Working Actor's Guide*, *The Selective Hollywood Acting Coaches and Teachers Directory* and in special issues of *Back Stage West.* Follow your instincts on choosing a teacher and also trust your intuition when it is time to move on. I've been studying with my teacher, Joan Darling, over 20 years. Some actors change teachers every few months. You will find the way it is best for you to study and grow.

• **If you are reading this outside of Los Angeles,** use these guidelines to pick your teachers in preparation for your move to a bigger market. Good and bad acting coaches teach all over the country.

Resources

FOUNDATION, BASIC TECHNIQUE AND SCENE STUDY TEACHERS

Judy Kerr's Acting Workshop, 818/505-9373. $450 for a 12-week class. Basic, auditioning and camera techniques. I use the camera in every class so you can see how your acting tools are working. You keep and review your tape copy each week. Many students appear on my cable television show, gaining three-camera experience. For the group class I only take actors who are working on professional careers, have their headshots, resume and some experience. A very strong commitment is expected. I usually teach one 12-week class in the spring. The remainder of the year, I work with actors privately and on-set. Call to discuss the classes, schedule a time to audit and to get on my mailing list. I coach privately and do career counseling. Privately, I take actors at all levels and I love beginners.

Joan Darling's Acting Class, 323/964-3410. $300 for four weekends, from 8-5. She is a master teacher, director, actress. Living in New Mexico, she usually teaches scene study, Shakespeare and improvisation classes four times a year in Los Angeles. Don't miss out on the opportunity to have at least one session with her. Very supportive and insightful. Her scene study classes are great for beginners because she incorporates her very valuable basic exercises. She is also great for working professionals who have been beat up on their jobs; she will help you heal. Lots of homework in this fast paced class. Auditing permitted.

West Coast Actors Studio, 323/654-7125. West Hollywood. Anyone over 18 can audition and it takes three votes to get in. Sydney Pollack, Martin Landau and Mark Rydell are the executive directors in Los Angeles. Arthur Penn is New York president. The combined membership in both venues is 950.

Catlin Adams Acting Lab, 323/851-8811. Strasberg trained director. All levels, improv, cold reading, sensory work, scene study. $235 a month for one class per week, $385 for 2 classes per week. Endorsed by Melanie Mayron, Lee Grant, Ellen Burstyn, Dinah Manoff, Joe Bologna and Lily Tomlin. Located on the Paramount Pictures lot. Auditing is allowed

Janet Alhanti Studio, 323/465-2348. She and her associate, Iris Klein, teach two 20-week session professional technique classes a year. Students must be recommended by agents, managers, casting directors or actors who have studied with them. Janet also teaches a poetry monologue class and a master class. She is one of the most respected teachers in the business.

A Noise Within, 323/224-6420. Seven-week classes are $300. This classical theater company offers conservatory classes in Shakespeare. Introduction to Acting Shakespeare, Acting Shakespeare I and II. Classical Scene Study, Movement and Private Coaching. The company is extraordinary.

Joel Asher, 818/785-1551. His informative video tapes are *Getting the Part,* all about cold readings; *Casting Directors "Tell It Like It Is"* and *Agents "Tell It Like It Is."* He has a great little theater in the valley which he designed and built. Uses video in classes. $195 a month, one class a week plus unlimited private work at no charge. Takes beginners. Four ongoing, different level, scene study classes. He incorporates as many techniques as possible with an emphasis on film and television work. His on-camera cold reading class is $150 a month. He also offers Jeff Doucette's "Acting on Instinct" improvisation class, $150 a month alone or $100 a month if taken with a scene study class. Private coaching $55-$85 an hour.

Tony Barr's Film Actors Workshop, 310/442-9488. Taught by Eric Klein, held in a three-camera video studio. Students cold read, rehearse and tape scenes from feature films. Emphasis is on the listening technique Barr developed in his book, *Acting for the Camera.* Actors must interview for the class and no auditing is permitted. Ongoing beginning and advanced classes, $165 per month.

Ron Burrus, 323/953-2823. Emphasizes imagination as an actor's primary tool and stresses the ability to live in the present. The only technique teacher personally trained by Stella Adler. Beginning acting technique is in two formats: the day program is six weeks, four times a week, 3 hours a day, $775. The evening program is three months, twice a week, 6 hours a week, $225 a month. The intermediate class does scenes, cold readings and performances, meeting twice a week for $250 a month. The advance class is $250 a month, with script interpretations and character development, culminating in a showcase production after two months. "It is up to the actor to convey what language cannot. The technique I teach pushes the actor beyond words." Admittance by interview. Interview before auditing.

Gary Carter, 213/448-5533. $200 per month; for people reading this book, $150 a month. Actor and filmmaker, he has taught for 15 years. Small weekly classes, Stanislavski and Meisner, mostly on-camera. "The Judo of acting for the camera." His classes embody inner technique and choices, characterization, cold reading, improvisation, overcoming fear and blocks. Beginners accepted. Also teaches at Greenway Court Theatre through the Fairfax Adult High School. Classes are extremely reasonable.

Diana Castle, 323/936-6818. Scene study, stressing imagination over knowledge. Limited to 20 students and costs $200 a month. She occasionally played Mrs. Zanfino (Joey's mom, Jerry's neighbor) on *Seinfeld.*

Ivana Chubbuck, 323/935-2100. Scene study, beginning, advanced and master classes. I have had several students who have studied with her organization and they gave glowing reports.

Kim Darby, 818/985-0666. $175 a month. Scene study and cold reading, actors work in every class on camera. All levels and beginners are very welcome. She is a veteran actress, three-time Emmy and two-time Golden Globe nominee. To keep a "safe atmosphere," she limits the class size and requires auditions for admittance. "My class is based on a listening process, always honoring the author by learning the words but not letting the words tell you how you feel; you learn to listen to full implication."

Wayne Dvorak, 323/913-9563. Ongoing classes for all levels, incorporating techniques from Meisner to marketing, $125 a month. Interview, audition and free audit are required for admittance. Class sizes are limited. The highly selective professional networking class showcases in front of top casting directors and agents on a regular basis. This class offers the next step, once you have done serious training.

Howard Fine Studio, 323/951-1221. 12-week basic technique class for $650, taught by Howard. A 12 week introductory scene study class for $220 a month with another teacher and ongoing intermediate and advanced classes for $220 a month. Other teachers and classes are available. An audit, referral and audition are required. Check out their web site at www.howardfine.com

Cherie Franklin, 323/650-4796. Cherie is a very inspirational coach. She teaches classes for feature films, comedy and the situation comedy, dramady and episodic television. In addition, she teaches privately and on set, emphasizing confidence, pacing, behavior, developing a character and how to remove fear. Her on-camera awareness classes include audition technique and most especially how to identify the emotional arc of the character and how to nail those emotions throughout the filming process of shooting out of sequence. Classes are $175 to $250 a month, all levels. She travels giving seminars world wide.

Kathleen Freeman, 818/761-5181 or 818/781-5096. She is a wonderful actress and teacher; been in the business forever. Samantha Eggar says about Kathleen, "She's the essence of theatre in her knowledge, tenacity, and truth, and the soul of the actor in her clarity, humor and heart." She teaches several types of classes within various time frames. Serious beginners welcome, basic techniques included.

Clu Gulager's Film Acting, 310/451-1800. I admire Clu as an actor and have a feeling this could be a very good experience. He teaches a six-week "on location" film acting class in which students pair off, block and rehearse a scene at a location, then shoot and evaluate it later in class. Clu teaches with his son John and associate Diane Goldner. He says they "try to help actors find their quality as film actors, their physical type and what characters they communicate best. $300, admission by interview.

Brad Heller, "The Acting Without Agony School," 310/275-4277. Brad was a long-time protege of the late director Don Richardson, who wrote *Acting Without Agony: An Alternative to the Method.* I don't know Brad but I was a big fan of Don's and am glad to see his work carried on.

Darryl Hickman, 818/344-5796. He's been in this business since he was a child. His classes are emotionally involving. "Out of control in full command." Introductory acting classes for $350 per 10 weeks. Three scene study classes held at different times, $350 for 10 weeks.

Lorrie Hull, Ph.D. and Dianne Hull Acting Workshops, 310/828-0632. Her workshops offer intensive training in a broad spectrum of acting tools. Techniques of relaxation, concentration, sense memory, affective memory, emotional recall, improvisation, cold reading, preparing and learning the role, motivating and justifying behavior. Auditing allowed for a fee. Author of *Strasberg's Method: As Taught by Lorrie Hull A Practical Guide for Actors, Teachers and Directors* and video *The Method.*

Laura James, 818/562-3075. Ongoing acting workshop, "A safe place for the novice to learn, develop and practice your craft. And the experienced actor to be challenged and grow in your craft." Exercises, improvs, scenes, monologues, cold reading and audition technique. Small classes with individual nurturing attention. First class is free.

Kimberly Jentzen, 818/509-1311. Award-winning director and acting coach, creator of audio tapes *Fearless Acting* and *Coming From Love.* "My goal is to create a safe place for actors to take risks, explore and develop skills, stretch their emotional range and learn how to make choices that allow their own individuality, depth and power to emerge." Training covers: scene study, monologues, cold reading, improv, concentration, imagination, audition technique and film acting. On going classes as well as *the cold reading weekend intensive, the comedy intensive, the essence weekend intensive* and *fear day.* Admission by interview/audition. Beginning-master classes. Auditing available.

Anita Jesse Studio, 323/876-2870, author of *Let The Part Play You: A Practical Approach To The Actor's Creative Process* and *The Playing Is The Thing: Learning to Act Through Games and Exercises.* "Our mission is to give actors techniques that will enable them to find fulfillment in their art while competing successfully for jobs in the film and television industry." *Memorized scenes, cold readings, camera technique. The tools: concentration, imagination, listening, silencing the inner critic, reclaiming your emotions, script exploration, relaxation.* For actors who are serious about their craft. Seven ongoing classes, all levels. Interview and audition required, no auditing. The other teachers at the studio are Nick Granoski and James Ingersoll. Classes meet twice a week. Brochure available.

KD Studio Actors Conservatory of the Southwest, 214/638-0484. Dallas, Texas. They have a four semester program where you can earn an AA degree. Includes every phase of actors development including opportunities for gaining actual working experience. They have evening and weekend classes for actors not involved in the Conservatory program. My daughter, Cynthia Kerr, loved this conservatory and was able to pay her way through it with the acting jobs and commercials she landed while studying there.

John Kirby, 323/939-5284. "Hollywood's prominent acting coach." $425 for a 12-week commitment, classes ongoing. Intensive scene study classes for the professional, as well as newcomer. Classes are extremely disciplined and require a strong committment. No gimmicks, exercises or class member critique. Homework and rehearsals required. Uta Hagan fundamentals. Auditing, five dollars.

M.K. Lewis Workshops, 310/826-8118. Author of *Your Film Acting Career.* Teaches an ongoing "Acting for the Camera" class. Also a 10-week film technique for professional and mid-level performers. All classes are $180 per month. Auditing permitted.

Joanne Linville, 323/656-2040. She teaches a twice-weekly ongoing intensive basic technique and scene class for $550 per three months. No auditing. Michael Richards, Kramer on *Seinfeld,* had Joanne coach him for many of the episodes. He says, "She has helped me earn two Emmys." You can gain a good solid acting technique with this type of committed class. She also moderates at the Actor's Studio West.

Janice Lynde, 323/650-0515. $150 a month on an ongoing basis. She is the only other teacher besides myself teaching Joan Darling's technique. Working with all levels of actors she teaches exercises and scene study in a loving, safe environment. Class limited to 15 actors so everyone works every week. She also teaches an audition formula involving three simple acting choices that helps actors book the jobs. Janice is a working, two-time Emmy nominated actress and director. She is also on the faculty at the American Film Institute teaching "Directing the Actor" for directors, screenwriters and producers. Also private coaching.

Ned Manderino, 323/860-8790. The author of *All About Method Acting* teaches a method technique that blends Strasberg, Adler and Stanislavski. "I believe an acting talent should first be technique-honed."

Allan Miller, 818/907-6262. Author of *A Passion for Acting* and instructional video *Auditioning.* Ongoing classes in techniques to refresh the creative imagination. Professionals only, by interview. $120 a month. A very passionate, experienced teacher and accomplished director.

Eric Morris Actors Workshop, 323/466-9250. He offers three ongoing weekly classes focusing on group exercises, instrumental work, craft work, scenes and monologues. $250 for four classes. He has developed his own system and has written some excellent books about how acting works: *No Acting Please, Being & Doing, Irreverent Acting, Acting From The Ultimate Consciousness, Acting & Imaging.*

Larry Moss, 310/393-3801. Very famous acting coach from New York, he taught at Juilliard Studio and Circle in the Square. Helen Hunt thanked him when she accepted her Academy Award! Many well-known professionals study scene work with him. He teaches a professional class and an intermediate/advanced class; both are $325 a month.

His partner, Michelle Danner, teaches a basic technique and scene study class and an advanced class, both for $175 a month. Her on-camera cold reading class is $160 a month. No auditing; acceptance is by interview. Jason Alexander of *Seinfeld* says that classes with Larry Moss are what made his acting career. Highly recommended!

Judy Pioli, 818/760-2428. Extensive experience in episodic television. She studied with the late Roy London and incorporates much of his approach. All levels, free audit. I like her ads in *Backstage West* and her first name.

Primetime Actors Studio, Mary Lou Belli & Phil Ramuno, 323/874-4131. $525 for 12 weeks. These veteran sitcom directors teach individual sitcom technique scene study classes.

Stuart K. Robinson, 310/558-4961. $140 for four sessions, on Monday evenings and Saturday afternoons. As a commercial teacher he is a genius, so I am sure his theatrical classes are very special too. He teaches a motivating, positive acting philosophy, very focussed on actors landing the jobs. His classes always have waiting lists—good luck.

Sal Romeo, 323/665-6360. A workout for working and intermediate actors. Based in Stanislavski, classes focus on relaxation, self exploration, voice and speech, camera technique, cold reading, improvisation and building the character. Sal has 25 years of experience in stage, television and film directing, as well as professional teaching. $150 a month. I really like the way Sal thinks and talks about acting. One of his "team teachers" is Michael Nehring, who also teaches at Chapman University. This is definitely a class to check out!

Diane Salinger, 310/966-1917. She has worked with Woody Allen, Clint Eastwood and Tim Burton. She offers beginning, intermediate and advanced classes in technique, scene study and how to audition. "Greatest gift you have to offer is yourself. Bring yourself to the work and become fearless."

Candace Silvers Studios, 323/856-6275. She was a student of Roy London, and teaches based on his technique. Three main classes: a Foundation Workshop, Scene Study with Script Analysis, and Designing your Career. "I help actors to stop focusing on the outcome and begin to build their own process for choosing the highest, most imaginative stakes that let their characters come alive." She offers a very valuable free audio tape *Tools Tape for Auditions.* Call to request it.

Tom Todoroff, 310/281-8688. His actors use primarily classical text (anything written pre-1900 or translated from another language) in class, unless they have an audition. He believes that if you learn to use language properly with great writing, you can easily work your way through any contemporary script. After training at Juilliard he specialized in voice placement and dialects for many years. Tom says, "It's my belief that whenever the voice is blocked it is always emotional, witness that babies have big voices. Teaching is deeply gratifying as it transforms people's lives; suddenly their work is free because their life is." He is now producing films (seven in the last four years). Six of his class students were in his last two films. Some of Tom's famous clients are: Liam Neeson, Lolita Davidovich, Jimmy Buffett, Tony Goldwyn, Robert Wagner, Roma Downey and Bob Hoskins.

UCLA Extension, 310/825-9064, www.espa.unex.ucla.edu Many weekend intensives and weekly evening clases, a typical 12-week course is $465. Classes taught by working professionals. It is good to get on their mailing list just to see the wide array of classes.

Warren Vanders, The Actors Lab, 323/256-6800. Classes or private coaching. Colleague of Daniel Mann, Oscar, Tony, Emmy award winning director. A technique for inspiration! Scene work and selected exercises, small classes. Video taping scenes periodically gives actors a personal library as a reference to monitor individual growth. Actors' Survival Kit, free audit and brochure.

Doug Warhit, 310/479-5647. Author of *Warhit's Guidebook for the Actor.* Casting Director Junie Lowry-Johnson of NYPD says, "I wish I could see actors trained by him at every casting session." My student, David Roth, felt he learned a lot from his class and found the showcasing to be very valuable. Ongoing scene study and cold reading classes, beginning through advanced.

Caryn West, 818/785-2392. She regularly teaches at Michael Howard's studio in New York, also teaches and coaches privately in L.A. "There is emphasis on script analysis, breath, presence and spontaneity." She offers six to 12-week classes on audition skills. Privates are $75 for 75 minutes.

Yale Drama Grad Workshop, 310/712-1601. A group of graduates of the prestigious Yale School of Drama are offering classes and private coaching on audition preparation, scene study and cold readings. I do not know them but it sounds like it could be very good, I certainly love the actors from this school.

Zephyr Theatre, 323/653-4667. I understand Paul Linke, a very fine actor, is teaching an ongoing intermediate/advanced level scene study class there.

COLD READING AND AUDITION TECHNIQUE TEACHERS

On actual auditions you should never be asked to cold read because SAG guarantees we get our sides the day before. Where cold reading comes in very handy is for auditioning for student films and for casting director and agent showcasing. You must be excellent at cold reading when you attend these showcases—you are putting your talent on the line. The casting directors' jobs depend on them calling in good actors to read. They may believe if you can cold read you are a good actor. There are actors who can cold read well but deliver poorly on the set. I would suggest you get your basic acting technique first then learn this type of instant acting so you can cover all bases.

Judy Kerr, 818/505-9373. $80-$100 an hour. Private coaching for film and television. We work with the audition material and decide how you want to portray your character. Special $40 half hour fee. We put it on camera and if it looks great we don't fix it.

Joel Asher, 818/785-1551. Teaches a cold reading class for $150 a month, all on camera.

Lori Cobe-Ross, CSA, 818/757-3020. Film and television casting director. Lori has a small class once a week in Brentwood, 8-10 people in the class. You work with the sides, put it on camera, she critiques it and you tape it again.

Cherie Franklin, 323/650-4796. $75-$150 an hour private coaching for cold reading. Cherie is a very inspirational teacher and on-set coach. She teaches seminars, classes and privately, emphasizing confidence, pacing, behavior, developing a character and how to remove fear.

Sandy Holt, 310/271-8217. She is a *Second City* alumni, has a looping group (voice casting) and teaches on-camera improvisation. $400 for 10 weeks. She will point out what is working or not working in the characters you create. She teaches how to take care of yourself at auditions, how to switch gears in a second, "how to be interesting and specific, get to the heart of the character, and audition with power." Hones in on what is special about you so you can totally rely on yourself. She has guided some of my students into creating characters they can use in selling themselves to agents and casting directors. "80% of the actors who work with me are landing the jobs. They're prepared, open to taking risks and committed to going full out with their characters.

They make an impression; they stand out." She also teaches weekend seminars on voiceover/looping and produces voiceover demos. Private, $75 on camera.

Kip King, 818/784-0544. One of the original Groundlings. Private coaching $75 for nonstudents, $50 for students. Helps you bring yourself to each character you play. Especially helpful with comedy. *See Commercials & Improv sections.*

L.J. Lane, 310/826-0624. Five-weeks, $200. She is a Paramount casting associate. She takes actors through the actual casting process from the first meeting with a casting director to the producer's callback and then how to test for the part. This seems like a very worthwhile class.

M.K. Lewis, 310/826-8118. Author of *Your Film Acting Career.* Teaches a 12-week cold reading and interview technique workshop for $180 per month. On camera. Auditing permitted.

Joey Paul, 818/ 784-6500. On the staff at TVI. She is a casting director, and teaches basic technique, cold reading, improv, scene study, all geared toward getting the job or the audition process. On camera.

Primetime Actors Studio, Mark Malis, 323/874-4131. He offers a 12-week cold reading workshop for $550. Mark was VP of casting at Universal Television and has developed a great course. Primetime offers other classes including Joseph Hacker's 12-week "Audition Solution" for $595. Daniel Travis has an eight week cold reading course for $350 and sitcom directors teach sitcom technique for $525 for 12 weeks.

Melissa Skoff, 818/760-2058 or VM: 310/262-8651 for her assistant, Larry Woods. $150 a month. She is a very respected casting director for films and television. There are industry guests at the workshop, $37.50 for a paid audit.

Clair Sinnett, 310/470-8641. Casting director for films and television. Audition workshop includes: marketing, interview techniques, survival, cold reads, making choices, taking risks, director and producer auditions, getting in the door.

PRIVATE ACTING COACHES

• **Many actors routinely use an acting coach** when they are auditioning for an important role. The time to get your coaching is before your first reading. If they call you back, they liked what you did. Sometimes, though, the casting director or director will ask you to take the script and bring a character back with a whole different attitude. Your coach can help you discover a new way to approach the character.

• **Actors when working on projects** will often hire their coach to prepare them for the role before shooting starts. They will work on the whole role so when they are shooting out of sequence the actor will know and remember the work they had planned for each scene. Often on a film or a single-camera television show, you may shoot the first and last scene the same day. You may be shooting the nude love scenes, your first day on the project, even the first day of meeting your partner. For several seasons of *Seinfeld,* Michael Richards worked with his coach, Joanne Linville, for each show.

• **Working with an acting coach** privately will help you progress faster, as every moment will be concentrated on you. However, there is no audience to work off of, as there is in an acting class.

• **Your first consideration** will probably be the cost. The average price is $50 to $100 per hour and at least twice that much if you are being coached on the set or for a role you're being paid for.

• **A beginning actor** who is very shy may want to have private sessions before joining a class.

• **You may need coaching** if you are a new actor and have been given a job as a result of your fame in another field, such as sports or modeling. When I was Joan Darling's assistant, she coached, among many others,

Joe Namath, for his first film after his football career. Some of the personalities I've worked with are Catherine Oxenberg when she was on *Dynasty;* Miss America, Debbie Maffett, when she landed her first television job hosting *P.M. Magazine* and Thea Vidale, a successful stand-up comic, who had her own ABC television show, *Thea.*

• **A good time to seek a coach** is when you are getting lots of callbacks but not landing the jobs. The coach may be able to give you that extra edge of confidence to put you over the top.

• **The time to go to an acting coach** for an auditon is before the original interview. If you have a callback, you did something right. You wouldn't want to change your performance that much by working with a coach. The exception would be if they said something like, "We like your look but want a stronger performance," or if they asked you to read for a different role.

• **I usually video tape when coaching.** I believe actors learn faster if they are able to see their work and observe their own strong and weak points. They also take the tape home and continue to learn from their work and my notes.

• **Some of the coaches** listed below are also written about in greater detail under the Acting Coaches section. (See page 18)

Private Coaches

Judy Kerr, 818/505-9373. All levels, acting techniques and audition work, $80-$100 an hour. I teach one 12-week class a year, usually in the spring. The remainder of the time I work privately with actors. I give the actor a script ahead of time; they work on it and bring it in as a finished piece of work. I coach on video and ask the actors to bring their own tape so they keep a copy of their acting along with my notes. This way they can review their work at home and learn more. Also a one time only one-and-a-half hour career coaching/guiding meeting for $100.

Rae Allen, 310/396-6734. Tony Award winning actress and director. $125 per session on camera.

Joel Asher, 818/785-1551. $55 - $85 an hour.

Sandra Caruso, 310/476-5113. Private coaching and audition preparation. $40 an hour. Author of three books, and teaches a UCLA Extension course, "What's Funny, What's Not."

Cherie Franklin, 323/650-4796. $75-$150 an hour.. Cherie is an inspirational teacher and on-set coach.

Nina Foch Studio, 310/553-5805. $200 an hour for consulting and coaching for actors and directors. She is an Oscar and Emmy nominee, a working actor since 1942, a professor at USC and a director of documentaries and MOWs.

Kathleen Freeman, 818/761-5181 or 818/781-5096. $75 an hour.

Sandy Holt, 310/271-8217. $75 an hour.

Janice Kent, 818/906-2201. A very experienced actress, director and coach. She specializes in sitcom, but coaches everything. She emphasises taking the risks to make bold choices.

John Kirby, 323/939-5284. $60 an hour, unless paid by a studio or agency. Works privately on auditions, bookings and onset coach. Also does career consulting.

Joanne Linville, 323/656-2040. $100 an hour.

Janice Lynde, 323/650-0515. $75-$150 an hour. Teaches a wonderful, fast, simple audition technique, as well as coaching for a specific role you have been cast in.

Allan Miller, 818/907-6262. $125 an hour.

Mike Muscat, 818/904-9494. He works as an on-set film coach. He coaches on-camera for $50 an hour and offers a money back guarantee. He is especially good at helping stage actors adjust to film acting.

Joe Scully, 818/705-0620. He has been a casting director for 45 years. He trained as an actor at the prestigious Goodman Theatre of the Arts in Chicago.

Cynthia Szigeti, 818/980-7890. $50-$75 an hour. Former head of the Groundlings' training program, now head of Acme Comedy Theatre's improv workshops. Students have included Lisa Kudrow, Conan O'Brien, Alex Borstein and Julia Sweeney. Coaches actors and standups.

Galen Yuen, 818/769-4909. $50 per session, often runs longer than an hour. He had a successful acting career, then owned a management company, now is a working writer/ director. He was the resident director in my class for several years. Many actors credit him with emotional and career breakthroughs.

IMPROVISATION

• **I believe every actor** should have some improvisational training. Many casting directors look for the ability to improvise on your resume. I have been hired for several acting jobs solely because I knew how to improvise. In television it is almost essential because you have very little rehearsal time; nor is there time for the director to tell you how to play a scene.

• **Improv is also good** for breaking down barriers you might have in revealing yourself, so it is helpful to study it at the beginning of your acting career—you get off to the right start.

• **Jeff Doucette**, founding member of the ongoing "Improv at the Improv" and veteran of Chicago's Second City.

Q: How does improvisation help actors?

- **There is a common misconception** that improvisation is about being funny. When actors are working on their feet, they often make the more comic choice, but that is not by any means the only valid one. Wonderful improvisations often center on more dramatic situations and emotions. Improvisation is a technique of acting. Acting is playing. As actors, we play parts in plays, screenplays, or teleplays. Spontaneity is the natural by-product of play. Improvisation opens the door to spontaneity by focusing on playing and solving problems in the moment. Through the process of improvisation, actors learn their own acting technique naturally by learning how to push their own buttons. They learn scene structure and character development. They unlock their creativity and open their imagination.

- **Learning the lines and breaking down a scene** can only give an actor a game plan. Once the camera is rolling, once the lights come up on the stage, the actor must trust his choices and find the truth in the moment. He must play the part. Improvisation teaches an actor to trust his instincts. An actor trained in improvisation learns to love being out on a limb. He's not afraid because he knows that if the branch gives way, there will either be a net to catch him or he will discover that he can fly.

- **Improvisation also helps the actor in everyday life** and in almost any audition situation. By learning to play with people and trust his instincts, an actor can overcome fear and learn to project his personality in a positive and constructive way.

Q: How should an actor pick an improv teacher?

- **First of all, the actor has to decide what he wants.** There is comedic-performance oriented improv and there is improv aimed more at the acting process. Both are good, but many actors are intimidated by the comedic improv classes. They feel that they have to be clever, quick and funny, or are intimidated by the competitiveness of the class.

- **Obviously you should talk to the teacher.** But ask specific questions and listen carefully for the answers. The more you know what you want out of a class the more specific you can be with your questions. You're not going to "get" the whole course in an interview, but how you relate to the teacher will give you a feeling of how it might be in the class.

- **Take advantage of an audit.** You can get a feel for the teacher, the class and the other students. If auditing isn't permitted, try to talk to as many students as possible. Most will say they love it, but try to pin them down and find out why they love it. See if you can get them to be specific. This will give you a better idea of what it is they look for in a class. It may or may not be what you are looking for.

• **Sandy Holt improv/cold reading teacher,** acting coach, actress, comedy writer and co-owner of a voice casting company, began her career performing with *Second City.*

Q: Why is improvisation important for the actor?

- **Improvisation is the springboard to your imagination**. I get actors to unlock the part of their brain where the creativity is, to break through the cliches. Improv is like jazz—you pick up on the riff that's happening and go with the dance and bring your magic to it. I get actors to find their own magic. Sandra Bernhard told me when doing *King Of Comedy*, she used all the skills she learned in class. She got the part because she brought her own excitement to the work, her own stamp.

- **Improvisation is also valuable for writers and stand-ups.** If a writer is having trouble with a script, we improvise to see what isn't working. Is it the action? Too wordy? Are the characters authentic? I had writers from *Cheers* come to my class. They were having trouble pitching ideas. By getting them into improvising and playing different roles, they really increased their pitching skills. Stand-up comedians find out what's funny about them and what makes them special.

Q: How would you describe your ideal student?

- **Someone who wants to play**, is willing to take direction, wants to participate, loves to get up and is willing to work through resistance. Actors should use their improv class as a safe place to make mistakes, work through blocks, get their courage up, take risks, go through their discomfort, and move through fear, so they can tap into the most wonderful, craziest part of themselves. When I interview actors wishing to join my classes I ask what they need to work on. Some people say, "I'm going up for auditions but I don't nail the job." So we work on how to nail the job. I work with actors on camera because this is a film business. I work on appearance and image. When you walk into a room, what do they see?

Resources

Acme Comedy Theater, **Cynthia Szigeti**, and others 323/525-0233. 135 N. La Brea Ave., Los Angeles. Former teacher at the *Groundlings,* she has taught most of the *Groundling* players who are now performing and many television personalities. Audition for 12-week basic class, $350.

Jeff Doucette, 818/782-0762. Founding member of the ongoing "Improv at the Improv" and veteran of Chicago's *Second City.* He is the winner of the Drama Critics Circle Award for best lead performance, appeared in hundreds of TV shows, over 30 films, 70 stage productions. Acting on instinct, scene structure, character development, sense memory, all levels. Jeff says about his class, "through the various acting/improv exercises actors learn to trust their instinctual voice and develop their own workable acting technique." I have heard very good things about Jeff's work with actors in helping them to release their inhibitions and fly. Auditing is welcome, and brochures are available. I highly recommend his classes to all my students.

Andy Goldberg, 310/479-1498. Author of *Improv Comedy* as well as member of the Off the Wall improv group since 1975. Ongoing class applying improv techniques to character development.

The Groundlings, 323/934-4747. 7307 Melrose Ave. in Hollywood, 90046. A performing group producing many working actors specializing in comedy. Go see a performance and get an idea of what is possible in improvisation. A four-tiered training program, students audition for the basic level, then are invited to the intermediate class, the writing lab and finally the ongoing advanced workshop. 12-week classes are $395. A pre-beginning-level class called Funshop is also available for $200. Auditions are not required and often include non-actors. Great place to think on your feet.

Sandy Holt, 310/271-8217. See the Cold Reading section, page 30. She combines improv with cold reading.

Kip King, 818/784-0544. $350 for 10 weeks, returning students $300 for 11 weeks. One of the original Groundlings. Helps you bring yourself to each character you play. Especially helpful with comedy. Uses improv with commercials and comedy.

Improv Underground, 310/451-1800. Based on *Second City* school of comedy. Classes and live performance. Games, scene work, character development and long-form improv. $300 for eight weeks.

Harvey Lembeck Comedy Workshop, 310/271-2831. Scott Baio says, "The workshop broke the boundaries for me. It taught me how to be more creative, how to be more free." Robin Williams said, "I looked around the class and said I'm home, they can't hurt me now, forget therapy. This is a home, someplace real special. I felt safe. It gave me freedom." Using improv as a method to teach comedy. Three levels of ongoing classes showing actors how to play comedy in scenes.

Brian Lohmann, 800-938-7572. Taught at A.C.T. and worked as a coach for Francis Ford Coppola. His class promotes truthful characters in unpredictable situations. He says they are "a fun, safe environment to develop technique, hone instincts and exercise your imagination."

Mark Lonow, 323/936-9550. Mark is an actor/writer/director and co-owner of The Improv. He teaches two 10-week classes, one on acting and one on standup comedy point of view—which culminates with a performance at the Improv.

Dee Marcus, 310/395-1830. Founder of performing improv groups, *Off the Wall* and *The Illegitimate Theatre.* She also runs a voice casting looping group, *Super Loopers.* She is a busy lady and teaches at different times of the year in different locations, each session culminates with a showcase. Free audit. Improv comedy workshops for actors, writers, directors and producers.

Marsha Meyers, 818/846-3559. She is a founding member of the improv troupe War Babies and artistic director of Improvicide. She has weekly improv workshops for beginning, intermediate and advanced levels. She places an emphasis on "freeing the imagination and nurturing confidence in what you offer as an actor." No audits but you can observe the work at the workshop's periodic showcases.

Brian Mulligan Improv Workshop, 323/960-2075. A 15-year member of Theatresports International. His workshop is suitable for all levels, acceptance by interview.

VOICE AND VOICE TEACHERS

To an actor a word is not just a sound, it is the evocation of images. Your job is to instill your inner visions in others... and convey it in words. Constaintin Stanislavki

The voice is the audio reflection of your soul. Expanding the voice opens the artist and the soul. Bob Corff

• **Acting is a vocal art**; our voices are used to interpret and depict scripts. Most actors need voice training in order to have complete control of their speaking voice. In many plays, actors need to use their voice for a considerable length of time. In film and TV, a big yelling scene may come after 12 or 16 hours of work; your voice should last through all of that. Another skill that must be in the actor's tool kit is the ability to speak with a general American accent; without it you will be very limited in the roles you will be considered for. You can add other accents and dialects for even more versatility. Of course, speaking other languages helps too.

• **Sal Romeo, a popular acting coach says:**

- **As an actor it is necessary to free one's natural voice** so the truth of feeling comes through. Much of what is done in film and television today is shot in close up and really all you've got is your voice to bring the nuance and emotional truth to the work. Vocal relaxation and use of language enhances and brings truth to one's performance. Many of us have been raised with tension in our voices, we put on a nice personality that hides our feelings in order to please. Often that voice is pitched from two or three notes to even an octave higher than our real, natural, true voice. When you learn to relax the tension in the voice, the emotional truth rings out in a richer, more resonating sound.

- **Tom Todoroff, film producer, acting, dialogue and dialect coach, says:**
  - **Basically, all you have to act with is your breath.** If you're not connected to your breath, it's possible to speak but you are saying words that don't come from where you feel things. I can understand you, but I'm not receiving your words where I feel things. The breath sends off vibrations that the other actor and the audience feels.
- **Gary Catona, voice builder, says:**
  - **The voice is a character**, as identifiable as your physical appearance. Your voice should be an expression of who you are, as an actor and as a person. When a person acts and a singer sings, they are indulging in an athletic activity. It is athletic because you are using muscles. In a sense, an actor is somebody who is a vocal athlete and you have to look at his or her voice in that light. Vocal exercises are important; exercise is necessary to improve your voice.
- **Bob and Claire Corff, well known voice teachers, say:**
  - **Enriching and improving your voice alters the way you feel** about yourself and the way people respond to you. Voice is the purest representation of you, revealing levels of confidence and attitude. The voice is one of the first and most powerful characteristics people respond to. A strong and self assured voice commands attention and respect.
  - **Developing an effective voice is as important** to a person and an artist as developing a toned and healthy body. Practicing the proper exercises from one to three weeks can make a striking improvement in any actor's voice. This can have as dramatic an effect on their performance and confidence as having plastic surgery.
- **Godeane Eagle, speech pathologist and voice teacher, says:**
  - **Actors are their own instruments**, and in order to play that instrument, it has to be in tune. Some of the problems are: not using the voice to the fullest, lack of confidence, vowel shapings or vowel projection, and the sound of the voice. If, at the end of a performance or rehearsal, the performer is feeling strain or pain in the throat area, he or she is doing something incorrectly. Voices can be stressed to the point where they simply stop.
- **Kate Devine, voice and dialect or accent adjustment teacher, says:**
  - **Our voice is what gives color to a word**, shading it with feelings, painting it with vivid emotional images. To expand your palette,

vocal range, texture and to become aware and fine tune your intonation, diction, articulation, pronunciation and breath is invaluable. This type of awareness will give you the security to trust and thus liberate your voice. A voice that is free is always interesting, honest and alive. You will have the capability of rising to a new level of expression and have the flexibility to convey endless possibilities of emotions with conviction, color and passion.

• **Ben D'Aubery, dialect and accent coach, explains the difference between dialects and accents.**

- **Dialect is regionalism**—as far as emphasis on the words and pronunciations as used in language. You have an accent when you use your own language regionalisms on someone else's language. For instance: a German learning to speak English would be speaking with an accent. But if a Californian goes to the South and speaks as a Californian, it would be considered a dialect. If English is your native language and you go to another country where English is spoken, you would be speaking a dialect, because your "English" would be a regional difference on that country's "English"—Irish, Scottish, Australian, etc. If you take on a foreign language, you're speaking with an accent—Spanish, Italian, Russian, etc.

• **When listing dialects and accents** on your resume, make sure you list them correctly.

• **Godeane Eagle,** when working with accents, believes ear training is the first step.

- **It's necessary to take the actor to the piano** and check how he or she recognizes pitches; it must be known if they can match a pitch, or even hear a pitch. Ear training makes people aware of fine-tuning differences in sound, such as between 'pen' and 'pin.'

• **Larry Moss, a popular dialect teacher**, (not the acting teacher) recommends getting recordings of plays or videos of movies with excellent performances, then listening to those well-trained actors. You can train your ear for the proper language or dialect you wish to use. Another good source is Dove Books on tape. The books are read by well known actors and authors. If someone says they want you to play an Elizabeth Ashley or Tom Hanks type, you can get a tape of that actor reading a book or parts of a book and pick up some of what their essence is.

• **Shopping for the right voice teacher** is important because working with your voice is extremely intimate and personal.

• **Godeane Eagle believes:**

- **It's necessary** that the voice teacher be someone with whom you feel comfortable, someone who cares about you and is interested in your voice. The speaking voice is very sensitive, delicate, and will respond negatively to negative teaching. Actors can learn both privately and in small classes, though beginners frequently need one-on-one because they need total attention.

• **Tom Todoroff recommends:**

- **Meet with three different coaches** and take a class with each—see who you connect with.

• **He also spoke of the discipline required for voice work:**

- **Your voice is a series of muscles** like other muscles in your body and it responds to exercise. When you go to the gym or take a dance class, your body becomes more elastic, more coordinated; your voice is the same way. If you don't work on it, it doesn't take care of you. An actor needs to work 20 minutes each and every day on their voice. To be an actor and not work on your voice is akin to being a dancer and saying, "I don't go to dance class" or a pianist who says, "I don't believe in scales or practicing." So much of what I teach beginners in the first classes has to do with the benefits of discipline. Discipline allows you incredible freedom.

• **For information on work in voiceovers,** read Voiceover Work in Section 3. For extended information and demonstrations, check out www.voicedatabase.com

Resources

• VOICE TEACHERS

Bob Corff, 323/851-9042, www.minusa.com/corff $75 a half hour, if you mention this book he will give a special rate of $65 a half hour. For actors and singers, works on giving your voice color, strength and stamina. Working on breathing, diction, accents and accent reduction, sibilant "s" and other speech problems, proper placement, lowering your voice and widening your range. Small group classes and private sessions. Author of the tape, *The Bob Corff Voice Method.* Some of his famous clients include Antonio Banderas, Glenn Close, Heather Locklear, Jenna Elfman, Faye Dunaway, Sally Field and Salma Hayek.

Claire Corff, 323/969-0565. $35 to $45 and up. She teaches the Bob Corff method. Singing, speaking and accent reduction. She's fun and easy to be with. Many of my students have improved greatly while working with her.

Sam Chwat, In New York, 212/242-8435. (Pronounced schwah.) People Magazine says: "Speech pathologist to the stars, accent-uates his celebrity clients." Adam Sandler in *The Waterboy;* Julia Roberts in *Mystic Pizza;* Leonardo DiCaprio in *The Basketball Diaries;* Robert De Niro in *Cape Fear.* He's recorded three audio books about accent elimination. They can be ordered through New York Speech Improvement Services, 1/800/SPEAKWELL.

Ben D'Aubery, 818/783-1951. $45 to $60 an hour. Private and group lessons, specializing in accent reduction and acquisition. I worked with him at the West Coast Ensemble Theatre to develop a North Carolina accent; he was excellent. He can deliver a crash course to get you ready for an audition in a short amount of time. Standard English, Cockney, Scottish, Irish, Aussie, French, German, Russian, Italian, Spanish, Yiddish, American Southern, New England, New York and Caribbean. On *Seinfeld* he helped the Jamican jogger (who Elaine fouled up) create his accent.

Bill Dearth, 818/761-1051. www.Sqlman.com/SpeechMech $55 per session, $275 for six lessons. Specializes in learning and losing accents and developing speaking voices. "Your voice is as important as your picture!" Highly recommended by commercial teacher Carolyn Barry.

Brian Drillinger, 310/828-9107. $45 an hour for private coaching. $35 a week for the group class. Recommended by acting coaches Larry Moss and Michelle Danner and actress Jode Edwards. Brian begins by working privately. You learn to connect with your full breath and work through a series of exercises that become a vocal warm-up you can use the rest of your career. Once you've learned the warm-up, you join the advanced class and work on acting material from a vocal perspective. In class you will work to create a clear channel of breath, emotion, and voice. Brian believes, "You must have an emotionally connected, fully expressive voice; it is the primary connector between you and the audience."

Kate Devine, 323/550-8942, VM:213/504-2844. $40-$80. Discount packages available. She focuses mainly on accent and dialect adjustment by guiding you through developing, strengthening and fine tuning Standard American speech. Finds the balance of keeping your own voice yet being flexible, articulate and versatile. Working with recorded evaluations, phonetic symbols, phonics and lips, tongue and breath placements. You are directed to create natural sounding speech. "To act is to tell a story. Learn to communicate it clearly with confidence and make a huge difference in the way you express yourself as an actor without the accent becoming an obstacle!"

Godeane Grace Eagle, 310/450-5735. $50 to $75 an hour. Godeane holds an M.A. combination in music, theatre, and clinical speech. She teaches singers and actors who want to sing. She teaches stage voice, projection, and is very mindful regarding voice and throat protection. She works with students of all ages, including young children and is trained in speech defect correction and accent reduction. She was my special teacher and helped me find my real voice. I am eternally grateful.

Dr. Lillian Glass, 310/274-0528. Your total image. Diction, accent/dialect, stuttering, voice projection, public speaking and vocal disorders. Julio Iglesias, Dustin Hoffman and Marlee Matlin have studied with her. She is the author of *Talk to Win.*

Libby Jordan, 310/428-2992. Sliding scale starting at $60. American dialect coach, she works almost exclusively with Australian, English, and New Zealand actors who require a natural-sounding American accent. She also works with American actors who need to perfect a new dialect. Her technique focuses on how the breath, tongue, lips, placement of the jaw and intonation all determine how our dialects sound. Libbys says this method quickly teaches you how to physically change your speech patterns effortlessly so you can slip into any American dialect easily.

Larry Moss, (the dialect/accent coach not the famous acting coach) 310/395-4284. Prefers not to have his price quoted. Private coaching and classes on acting with a dialect; helps students be credible in any accent, including mainstream American. The goal is to achieve truthful performance without the dialect getting in the way.

Elizabeth Sabine, 818/761-6747. email: lizsabine@aol.com $95 a session. Voice strengthening specialist. She teaches at the Lee Strasberg Theater Institute and UCLA Extension. She also specializes in heavy metal and rock 'n roll artists, including Axl and Steve Adler of Guns N' Roses; Megadeth's Dave Mustaine; Men at Work's Colin Hay and Paula Abdul. Some of her celebrity actors are Kathy Griffin, Chuck Norris, Elisabeth Shue and Priscilla Presley. She trains her students to replicate the physical and emotional manifestations of extreme emotions by taking short breaths and holding their abdominal muscles tight, the same as they would if they were yelling at someone in anger, or like a hungry infant when it cries for a bottle.

Tom Todoroff, 310/281-8688. See Acting Coach section.

Nadia Venesse, The Venesse Voice Accent Reduction Classes. $395 for classes, 8-weeks on Accent Reduction or 6-weeks on Voice/Speech/Dialect; locations in Pasadena and Santa Monica. Studio rate is $300 an hour. Individual coaching rates are variable, call for details. She's worked on hundreds of projects. They include: *Flintstones II; Any Given Sunday; Stuart Little; Dance With Me; Twister; Amistad; People vs Larry Flynt; Nixon.*

• VOICE AND DIALECT TAPES

The Bob Corff Voice Method, www.mnusa.com.corff *Bob Corff Speaker's Voice Method* and *Voice Method for Singers.* Sold at Samuel French Booksellers, The Singing Store, Hollywood Sheet Music and other music stores. "With the confidence that comes from having a strong, powerful voice there are no limits to what you can achieve in your career." Casting director Ruben Cannon says, "Your success as an actor or singer will be greatly determined by your vocal skills. Study with a master - Bob Corff."

Sam Chwat's SPEAKUP! Programs, 1/800-SPEAKWELL, M-F 9-6 EST. Three different tapes: *American regional accent elimination; Spanish regional accent elimination; Asian Middle Eastern, Hindi-Indian-Pakistani, Chinese, Japanese, Vietnamese, & Pacific.* Call for more information.

Jerry Blunt audio tapes of accents and dialects available at theatrical bookstores. These tapes are very conversational and easy to learn from.

David Alan Stern, 800/753-1016. He teaches from a very academic point of view on these tapes, but many actors use them. His books and audio tapes are available at theatrical bookstores or by mail order. Call for their catalogue; they will probably have a tape for any dialect or accent you need.

• SINGING TEACHERS

Morgan Ames, well known composer, singer and producer, recommends the following two voice coaches to the professional and studio session singers she produces and arranges for. They work strictly with the singing voice.

Lis Lewis, 323/460-2486. She produces a newsletter for singers titled *Angel City Voice.*

Rosemary Butler, 818/907-SING.

Jennifer Haworth, 310/557-1939. USC graduate in classical vocal performance. $40 an hour, $5 discount for actors. She teaches classical, pop, rock and musical theatre singing for singers and for actors who want to sing. Her specialty is vocal problems and breathing. She incorporates physio-synthesis into the teaching. She helps "screamers" perfect their hard rock techniques so they protect their vocal chords. Also available to come to your location if you have a piano.

• BOOKS AND MATERIALS

"The Total Singer" by Lisa Popeil, 800-BEL-VOCE
"The Secrets of Singing" by Jeffrey Allen, 800/644-4707 ext. 22.
Tom Todoroff's recommended reading list: "Voice and the Actor" and "The Actor and the Text" by Cicely Berry; "Freeing the Natural Voice" by Kristen Linklater; and "Speak With Distinction" by Edith Skinner.
The Brand Library, 818/548-2051. 1601 W. Mountain Street, Glendale, 91201, at the top of Grandview Ave. Hours: T & Th 1-9, W & F 1-6, Sa 1-5; W 1-5. They have a vast supply of records, tapes, CDs, print music and art books available for loan-out.
Theatrical bookstores sell books and tapes to help you with standard American speech as well as dialects.
Travel Stores, for tapes of people instructing how to speak other languages. Usually the instructor on the tape has the accent of the language they are teaching.
Working Actors' Guide lists voice teachers for speech and singing.

• **Tongue Twisters** can sometimes be a very good warm-up for your voice on the way to auditions or before getting ready to act in class, on the stage or set. Memorize your favorite ones to be able to use them anytime. Godeane Eagle gave me these two favorites of mine: "Blueberry pie with peach ice cream" and "Strawberry shortcake with whipped cream." Really move your mouth, pucker and smile. Tom Todoroff's favorite is: "Eleven benevolent elephants." Try some of the following twisters. Use a tape recorder to make sure your pronunciation is correct.

TONGUE TWISTERS

- The lips, the teeth, the tip of the tongue.
- Which witch, what watt?
- A big black bug bit a big black bear.
- Loving Lucy likes light literature.
- Some shun sunshine, do you shun sunshine?
- Bad blood (ten times very quickly.)
- The sun shines on shop signs.
- Six long, slim, slick Sycamore saplings.
- Flesh of freshly dried flying fish.
- Betty Blue blows big black bubbles.
- Seven slick, slimy snakes sliding slowly southward.
- The soldier's shoulder strap slipped from the soldier's shoulder.
- Fanny Finch fried five flounders.
- Double bubble gum bubbles double.
- Toy boat, toy boat, toy boat, toy boat, toy boat, toy boat.
- Red leather, yellow leather, red leather, yellow leather.
- Rubber baby buggy bumpers.
- Around the rugged rock the ragged rascal ran.
- I slit a sheet, a sheet I slit. Upon a slitted sheet I sit.
- Lemon liniment, lemon liniment, lemon liniment.

STAGE PRESENCE

• **The moment you step on stage** or in front of a camera, you must become larger than life. This ability comes from the control you have over your body. We are born with the capacity to use our bodies perfectly but somewhere along the way, many of us learn bad body habits. I don't think there is an acting institution or acting teacher who does not recommend some type of body movement class. We act through our bodies; acting is an athletic event.

• **In the beginning of my career**, an acting coach told me I would never be able to work as an actress because I was "sunk into myself," I had no presence. I had spent a great deal of my life trying not be seen—very detrimental for an actor. Your presence, your appearance, really does make the difference in getting jobs. It is the way you present your *package* when you walk in the door that will make a lasting impression.

• **He was the right kind of acting teacher** because he not only told me the problem but gave me the solution: The *Alexander Technique.* It took me about four lessons before I began to get an understanding of how to hold my body properly. Once you learn the technique, it is yours. I studied constantly for two years because I was in bad shape, but then it became mine.

• **It is now a habit**, just like the bad posture was. This technique has helped me in everything I do, whether it's yoga, ballet or weight lifting. It is a specific, unique body technique that will increase the amount of space you take up in a room and what you *radiate* in person, on the stage, or in front of a camera.

• THE ALEXANDER TECHNIQUE

• **F. M. Alexander was an Australian actor.** When he lost his voice while performing, he went to specialists and was told there was no solution. He decided to look for the cure himself. He spent many months in front of a three-way mirror to try and detect the exact reason for the hoarseness in his voice. He discovered the hoarseness came as a result of vocal misuse and an overall pattern of body misuse. He could clearly see it in his mirror but he couldn't feel it. It became clear he could not correct his voice without changing his mental concepts and the way he used his whole body. He noticed the muscles at the back of his neck pulled his head down and caused a chain reaction of pressure down his spine. This created tension throughout his entire body.

• **Alexander then developed a technique** to help himself and over the years trained many actors and taught others to teach his technique. The changes he noticed in himself and his students included: a release of excess tension in the body, a lengthening of the spine, greater freedom and flexibility in movement, more efficient breathing, elimination of vocal problems and improved posture and appearance. His most famous directive and one his teachers give over and over again is: "Let my neck be free to let my head go forward and up, to let my back lengthen and widen." When you learn to move in this fashion you will acquire better posture, grace of movement, better balance and coordination in your body for all of your activities.

• **The *Alexander Technique* is taught** at many institutions, including The Julliard School in New York, ACT in San Francisco, SMU in Dallas, UCLA and USC in Los Angeles. Julliard graduate Kevin Kline says, "The many obvious benefits that the technique afforded us as actors included minimized tension, centeredness, vocal relaxation and responsiveness, mind/body connection and about an inch and a half of additional height." Andre Rotkiewicz, movement teacher at KD Studio Acting Conservatory in Dallas, says, "It makes you, the actor, aware of your mannerisms so you can control and change your actions. You will become more neutral and able to take on more characters. The connection with the mind and body will let you become more universal." Alexander said, "Every man, woman and child holds the possibility of physical perfection; it rests with each one of us to attain it by personal understanding and effort."

- **Lyn Charlsen, certified *Alexander* instructor says:**

  - **Performers need to be conscious of what they're doing** with their bodies, because that is their means of expression. It really becomes the tool for the expression of their art—whether that's somebody holding a violin, an actor on stage, or a singer. The way that we are using our body translates into the sound of the guitar, the sound of the voice, or the expression of the face.

  - The *Alexander Technique* can increase an actor's physical coordination and allow him to express himself fully. The elements of choice and consciousness enliven performance skills and make it possible for people to do what they intend. What's so wonderful for actors to know is that their instrument is so finely tuned that they can really be spontaneous.

- THE SIKE TECHNIQUE

- **Dr. Mallory Fromm and Therese Baxter of the SIKE Institute** explain this unique body work, which is a healing art and a means of correcting poor body behavior, harmful to the quality of presence, movement and voice.

  - **The *SIKE Technique* combines two healing and alignment techniques.** The first one is *Physio-Synthesis*, created by an osteopathic physician to restore structural balance in order to improve the body's contour, grace in movement, circulation and breath control. The second technique comes from Japan and is based on the precise use of Ki (or Chi) Energy to send energy directly into the nervous system to command muscles and ligaments to move and shift bones and organs.

  - **This technique relaxes the upper body, head and neck** by strengthening the actor's body from the ground up. Inner core muscles extend the spine which lifts and supports the head up and off the top of the neck, producting a "floating" sensation. The body is grounded and light at the same time. Application of Ki Energy to the head and solar plexus produces mental clarity and heightened concentration. Thus a unity of mind and body is achieved. In this way stage presence is enhanced through the natural projection of character, substantiality, and intensity.

  - **The *SIKE Technique* for actors** is a series of weekly or bi-weekly treatment and instruction that, as the actor gains confidence, tapers off to seasonal treatments ito maintain an integrated body structure. The ultimate goal is to make the actor independent of the practitioner.

Resources

North American Society of Teachers of the Alexander Technique, 800/473-0620. www.alexandertech.com This is the only organization of authorized or certified teachers of the technique in the United States. You can call this number, leave your name and address, and they will send you a list of all certified teachers. Teachers can only be a member of this society if they have gone through a three year, rigorous, approved training course. The booklet also includes societies in other countries.

Dr. Mallory Fromm and Therese Baxter of the SIKE Institute, 818/992-0713, www.sikehealth.com $45 per treatment. Workshops are announced on the website. Mallory is the author of "The Book of Ki: The Healing Principles of Life Energy." Therese has experience with Feldenkrais Technique, Alexander Technique and is a certified practitioner of *Physio-Synthesis.*

Lyn Charlsen, Alexander Technique, 818/786-3944, Van Nuys. $50 per private class. She is my special teacher and has worked with many actors.

Debby Jay, Alexander Technique, 818/769-9171. She teaches an introductory course on the Alexander Technique at the Howard Fine Acting Studio. Open to all actors. Privates available in Studio City. Call to get on her mailing list to receive her very informative newsletter.

Bruce I. Kodish Ph.D., P.T.Life Moves, 626-441-4627. Specializing in self-care methods for pain and performance problems. Individual sessions, groups and workshops offered. Get on the mailing list for his interesting newsletter.

Larry White, Alexander Technique, 310/394-3177. Santa Monica. Specializes in scoliosis.

UCLA, USC, Howard Fine Acting Studio and many other colleges offer group classes.

MATERIAL FOR WORKSHOP SCENES

Choosing the work you want to do in class takes effort but it is very rewarding; you get to act the roles that attract you, roles you may not otherwise have the opportunity to portray.

Take chances! Stretch! Can't hurt! It also really helps you to read scripts. Even if you read 15 scripts to find one scene, you will have learned something.

Videotapes are a great source for scenes, as are books. When you pick a scene from a book, chances are no one has seen it before, which is a big plus.

Resources

Academy of Motion Pictures Library, 310/247-3035 for general information 310/247-3020 for general reference 9AM-3PM. 333 S. La Cienega, at Olympic, West Hollywood. M,Tu,Th,F 10-5:30; Closed Wednesday and weekends. You must present a valid ID such as a passport or driver's license. No personal belongings are permitted, but they provide storage lockers. For film scripts: read the scene into a tape recorder or hand-copy and take home to type—there is no photocopying unless the script has been published. Great place to go.

The American Film Institute, Louis B. Mayer Library, 213/856-7654. 2021 N. Western Ave., north of Franklin, Hollywood. M-F 9:30-5:15; W till 7:15; Sa 10-4:30. Library is closed during the summer and odd hours during Christmas and Spring breaks. No copying of unpublished scripts but you can copy published ones. Books, periodicals, clipping files, festival files, motion picture collections, seminar transcripts, oral history transcripts, special collections.

Movie World, 818/846-0459. 212 N. San Fernando, Burbank, 91502. Everyday 11-6. Books, posters, magazines, photos, autographs, memorabilia and scripts.

Script City, 323/871-0707, out of California (800) 676-2522. Ask them for a catalogue. It's all mail order. They have thousands of movie and TV scripts, directories, guides, books, audio/video seminars, etc.

Samuel French Theatrical Bookstores, 323/876-0570 or 818/762-0535. For plays; get their free catalogue. They also sell many published film and television scripts.

Dramatists Play Service, 212/683-8960. 440 Park Ave. South, New York, NY 10016. Call, ask for a catalogue; they will mail it.

• SCENE AND MONOLOGUE BOOKS

It's a good idea to buy two of the scene books; then you and a partner can read all the scenes together—good practice.

99 Film Scenes For Actors edited by Angela Nicholas. The interview with acting coach Mark Monroe on how to pick scenes for class is worth the price of the book.

The Ultimate Scene and Monologue Sourcebook: An Actor's Guide to Over 1000 Monologues and Scenes from More Than 300 Contemporary Plays by Ed Hooks. This reference book should be on every actor's and acting teacher's bookshelf.

The Monologue Index: A guide to 1,778 Monologues from 1,074 Plays edited by Karen Morris.

The Perfect Monologue by Ginger Howard Friedman. Forward by Michael Shurtleff.

Contemporary Movie Monologues: A Source Book for Actors edited by Marisa Smith and Jocelyn Beard. Over 95 monologues from contemporary films.

50 Great Scenes For Student Actors edited by Lewy Olfson.

Film Scenes For Actors edited by Josha Karton.

Neil Simon Monologues: Speeches from the works of America's Foremost Playwright edited by Roger Karshner.

One Hundred Men's Stage Monologues From the 1980's edited by Jocelyn A. Beard. One of a series of stage monologues and scenes books. Also available in women's roles and in more current years.

One on One: The Best Women's Monologues for the Nineties edited by Jack Temchin. Presents examples of well known actor's auditions and cautions actors to choose monologues carefully and to choose ones that "fit."

Scenes, Acting and Directing by Samuel Elkend. 29 scenes compiled from well known plays for both students and teachers.

Scenes and Monologues From the Best New Plays edited by Roger Ellis. A sampling of the more recent works of playwrights.

The Actor's Book Of Classical Monologues collected by Stefan Rudnicki.

The Actor's Book Of Contemporary Stage Monologues edited by Nina Shengold.

The Actor's Book Of Movie Monologues edited by Marisa Smith & Amy Schewel.

Words of Women by Dianne Luby. Monologues.

The Actor's Scenebook, Vol. I & II edited by Michael Schulman & Eva Mekler.

The Best Stage Scenes for Men From the 1990s edited by Jocelyn A. Beard and Kristine Graham. Also available is a 1990s book for women.

The Best Stage Scenes of 1992 edited by Jocelyn A. Beard. Forty-five audition pieces for men and women.

By Actors For Actors: A Collection of Original Monologues and Scenes edited by Catherine Gaffican.

Uptown Character Monologues for Actors: Powerful original audition pieces by Glen Alterman.

The Book of Scenes for Acting Practice by Marshall Cassady. Presents a variety of scenes from classical to modern. Presents time, setting and background information to aid in understanding the characters.

The Scene Book For Actors & Great Monologues & Dialogues From Contemporary & Classical Theatre edited by Norman A. Bert.

Many screenplays are in book form—usually several scripts by the same writer or director.

How to Rehearse and Prepare for Scenes, Monologues, Audition Material and Acting Jobs

• **Never start to memorize lines until you have chosen your acting work.** If you memorize the words before choosing the work, it will tie you up so you won't be able to really investigate all that is waiting to be discovered.

• **Read the whole script** (if available) to discover the given circumstances. *Given circumstances* are all the things the story (script) tells you about the events taking place and the characters taking part. Such as: What happened right before and after this scene? What was I doing? What was I saying? How old am I and the other characters? What is my relationship to the other people in the scene and to the people mentioned in it? How do I feel physically? Emotionally? What do I want? What is standing in the way of my getting what I want? Where is the event taking place? What is the place like? Is it home? Is it a place that is uncomfortable and why? Are the ceilings high or low? Is it hot or cold? Ask and answer every possible question you can think of.

• **Nina Foch, famous actress, director** and private acting coach who charges $200 an hour says, "I never tell people what to do. But I ask them every possible question and I get them to ask themselves every possible question. When they leave me, it's unlikely they'll be asked any questions they're not prepared to answer. They're prepared." Be as thoroughly prepared as if you were paying $200 an hour. It may help you to write the given circumstances on your script as you discover them.

• **If all the given circumstances** aren't in the script, you'll have to create them with your imagination. Your choices should be *hot* ones: passionate, filled with feeling. You either *love or hate* yourself, the situation and the other characters. Be specific: this character is afraid of the dark, has hot flashes, is sexually aggressive, shows affection by teasing, feels betrayed by his sister, etc.

• **Now in order to *personalize* the lines** (make them mean something to you personally), go through the script and decide who you would be talking to from your real life in these type of circumstances and what you would like to be saying in those situations (when you were, for instance, insecure, macho or afraid). Then use the lines of the scene as a *code* for what you would say, did say or wished you had said. You must figure out what the author means in each and every line so you know how to personalize it, or relate it to your own life. Occasionally, when a line or two is impossible to figure out, then just simply say it.

• **Next, choose sensory work** to make the given circumstances and your personalizations of the piece very specific and unique to your own life. The way to choose sensory work is: if the character is insecure, macho or afraid, think of a *real* time in your own life when you felt insecure, macho or afraid. Then *make an effort* to wake up the memory of that time through one or more of your five senses: the *smell* of the room; the *touch* (what your fingers remember) of an object from that place or a piece of clothing you were wearing; the *sound* of music that was playing or a horn honking; the *taste* of food you had eaten; the *pain* in your heart or foot; the butterflies in your stomach; how the moon *looked*; from that specific event in *your life* when you felt insecure, macho or afraid.

• **Rehearse the scene** a few times, trying some of the pieces of sensory work you've chosen; see how each piece can change the way the scene plays. Try several different pieces. Then when you're ready to perform the scene, monologue or audition material, you'll have an idea of what works best. You still must remain free enough to act *in the moment* when everything is working beautifully and you are living the scene; or free enough to choose a new piece at the last moment because you had a wonderful flash (driving in your car) of what the scene is really about. Trust your instincts.

• **Eli Wallach, talking of creating the reality** in acting, said: "If I ask you to sing *Happy Days Are Here Again,* the same words but I change the circumstances—If I say to you, 'Sing it like you've just been given a raise or won the Academy Award,' you'll sing one way; if I say to you, Your wife of 30 years just died—now sing *Happy Days Are Here Again.* You sing it without me prompting you as how to sing it... and that's one of the secrets of good acting."

• **If this is a scene for an audition piece** or acting class, now is the time to get with your partner to rehearse. Discuss and agree on the given circumstances that are the same for your two characters. Remember, the events that you are personalizing from your own life will be very different from your partner's and you should never discuss them; you can defuse your personal choices by talking about them. Your choices are your tools, your treasures, your actor's secrets; they can't possibly help anyone else and the only way you can lose them is to discuss them. Next, cut the scene. An audition or showcase scene should be four minutes or less and a class scene five or six minutes (acting minutes not reading minutes) with a beginning, middle and end. Do not add lines or words unless they are necessary to set up or end a scene.

• **Rehearse in a professional way**. Be considerate of your partner—never be late. Arrive with your homework done. Scene partners may find it very useful to improvise scenes that could have happened outside of the script. Such as: when they first met, last Christmas, two years later, when they were caught in a snowstorm, etc.

• **Harvey Keitel, speaking of *acting as if*:**

- **Improvisation was always a very good tool for me to use.** It helped to bring me closer to the role; to find the role in me. To learn about the life of a pimp *(Taxi Driver)*, I found myself a pimp and we improvised. I played the girl and he the pimp, and he showed me how a pimp would treat one of his girls and then we would reverse the roles. So first I had to research what a pimp is; then I can play it *as if* I'm a pimp. The notion of improvisation, the notion of *as if* is very simple: to do it as if I'm your brother, as if I'm your father, as if I'm your husband—sort of a jumping-off spot, the *as if.*

- **Sally Field says:**

  - Rehearsal is a most exciting time for me, delving into what you can create, and when the director calls 'Action,' you take flight, leave your body, and are no longer on this planet.

- **Never give or ask another actor for acting notes. It is most unprofessional, and will not be appreciated by anyone.** Community theater actors are famous for this. You may discuss the scene or script endlessly but you must make your own choices. Tell your partner, "I'm going to try something different this rehearsal." Never ask anyone for a line reading and decline when someone wants to give you one—these are choices *you* must make. That is what being an actor is all about. If you need some help thinking of choices to make, call your coach or an actor friend and ask for help. I still have to do that, even though I'm hired as a coach to help actors make their choices. Sometimes you need that outside perspective.

- **Find an activity to be doing during the scene or monologue.** *Never pretend* to do something. One time when I was directing a very important show, an actress during rehearsals always pretended to be embroidering. I had assumed that during performances she would really be doing it. On opening night she was still pretending and I sat in the audience dying. There is so much pretending in acting; anything you can really do—do it. Pick an activity that is logical for the character. Fix food, cut up an apple or cheese, find an article you really want to read in the paper or magazine, repair your radio, polish your nails, clean your gun, wax the furniture, shave, put makeup on, etc. Again, try several different things; never settle on the first one. Always investigate.

- **Next, memorize the lines.** The work above will give you a good idea of what the scene is about and what you are talking about; it will make the memorization much easier. *The lines are not the important part of the scene; the relationships are what is most important.* Yes, you learn the lines word-perfect; that is the only way to be professional. The lines are more like the costume; they are just tools to help get the story across, but not the whole story. The actors who bore us are the ones who are just saying or reading the lines. Anyone seven years old can read or memorize lines. It is all the other work that makes it an acting piece.

• When you have been *hired* for an acting job, *always* show up on the set or sound stage with your lines memorized. That is your job as a professional actor. The exception is a stage play where you have the opportunity to rehearse and grow in the character before you learn lines. This luxury is what makes working in a play so much fun. You are allowed to discover your character.

• **Memorize word-perfect: it is a valuable habit.** (See the next section for more details on memorizing.)

MEMORIZING

• **If it is hard for you to memorize—never, never mention it.** No one wants to hear it. Actors who memorize easily may not understand and think you are a fool. You'll hate them because it seems they'll have an advantage. Other actors who have trouble learning lines will resent you for bringing it up. They also won't trust you to learn yours because they know what the fear is like. So for your own sake, keep it to yourself how hard or easy it is for you to memorize. It is the *ultimate* actor's secret. Discussing it does nothing but damage. Assume that other actors memorize and you can too; it just takes practice, time and effort. Being a good actor has nothing to do with how easy or difficult it is to learn lines.

• **Some actors go through torment memorizing.** So what! We really do not care. You go through this trial alone or with a loved one at home who will hold book for you. Memorizing is just a mundane part of your acting craft that must be conquered silently, without complaint.

• **William H. Macy** says, "It should look as if you're making up the words and you've never said them before and it's happening in real time right before your eyes, even though it's not. It's scripted."

• **An industry insider** said he wished actors would conduct themselves like Richard Gere—who arrives on the set at the beginning of a project with "two suitcases and the script memorized."

• **Memorize lines in a flat monotone.** Do not memorize in an acting way or you'll be stuck with that rehearsed line reading. You won't be free to add sensory work and personalizations to change the meaning of the piece. The writer's words are a code for what *you* are feeling and experiencing from your own life. The actor gives the piece meaning by using specific, personal acting choices. When a director asks you for a different reading of a line, be able to change your acting choice immediately. Make several choices before settling on one so you'll be prepared. Keep trying different acting work with the same words to see what unique things, what new insight, you can bring to the script.

• **Highlight your lines in yellow** and draw a dark line underneath so they stand out. Memorize the writer's lines word-perfect. This is professional. No one is holding book in acting class but on the set, the script supervisor is watching each word.

• **Set aside blocks of 15 to 20 minutes** of solid, concentrated memorization time. Hold a piece of paper over everything but the first line. Say the line, then look to see if it's right. When it is, add the second line and do both together until they're memorized, then add the third line, etc. Memorize your cue line also; if you don't know the cues you won't know when it's your turn to speak. Another good way (to augment the above) is to tape-record the piece in a *flat monotone* voice. You can record all the parts; just change your voice for each one. You can act the other roles if you want but, again, yours is spoken in flat monotone. Now play the tape over and over—in your car or while you're doing the dishes. When you have the lines down, record a tape leaving a blank space for your lines, then say your lines with the tape; you'll learn the cues this way.

• **When I was the dialogue coach on *Seinfeld*,** Jerry used to love to be tested. He felt the key was learning all the cues. So if I could give him a cue from any place in the script and he knew the line—he won. He would also take Ginkgo Biloba (said to be a memory enhancing herb) in the afternoon on show day and then right before we started shooting the show.

• **Still another technique**—write or type out all the lines except yours. Just type the character's name where your lines go. Have a bunch copied, then write in your lines like filling in the blanks. Then check to see how accurate you are. Writing the lines in long hand helps get them in your memory.

• **Speed drills are good—on your own or with your scene partner.** This is Joan Darling's "bla bla" exercise. Say the lines as fast as you can, NO ACTING. If you can't think of the line, say "bla bla bla" till you do or it's the other actor's line, then jump back in with yours. The secret is: the words tumble out of your mouth with no meaning—then you are free for acting.

• **Get the words into your body.** Set up a rehearsal space similar to where you'll be acting. Move around the space as you are doing the lines.

• **To practice, memorize something every day** until you perfect the memorization craft. Soap opera actors have to memorize a new script every night.

• **Look for books on memorizing** and learn other people's techniques. All is fair in the pursuit of learning lines, more tools for your tool kit.

• **I also believe it helps** to put your script under your pillow when sleeping.

• **Not knowing your lines can stop you from being an actor—toughen up!**

Resources

Vicki Mizel, "Brainspouts," 213/963-1275. www.artnewmedia.com/brainspouts She offers a three week, 12 to 16 hour acting intensive class called "Off Book...in Minutes." $300. She also teaches privately, $50 an hour. "Through stimulating and strengthening your mind you will turn the main ideas into tangible pictures allowing you to memorize, retain, and recall monologue and script copy easily. You will be able to get off book in minutes for auditions or once you've landed the part." She says, "Using the combination of the three-week class and the audio tape program, you can integrate all the techniques necessary to use these methods of memorization forever."

ACTING BOOKS
AND
TAPES

All of the following theatrical books may be purchased or ordered through Samuel French and other theatrical bookstores 323/876-0570 or 818/762-0535.

• ACTING BOOKS AND TAPES

Acting For The Camera by Tony Barr. Excellent.

Acting In Film by Michael Caine. Excellent—I quote him all the time in my classes.

Acting Is Believing by Charles McGaw.

Acting Truths and Fictions: Straight Talk about the Many Myths, Myth-Conceptions and Mistakes that Affect Actors' Development and Professional Careers Today! by Lawrence Parke. This is several books in one, a wealth of practical knowledge. Treat yourself.

Acting Without Agony: An Alternative to the Method, 2nd Edition by Don Richardson. Mr. Richardson passed a few years ago. Thankfully, he left us this wonderful book as a legacy.

The Actor's Improvisation Book by Sandra Caruso.

Audition by Michael Shurtleff. Memorize this book. He is a fabulous teacher!

Call Back: The Complete Guide To Preparing And Performing The Audition That Will Get You The Part! by Ginger Howard Friedman.

Cold Reading Advantage: New Tools For Those Who Perform (**Actors, Athletes, Musicians and Mountain Climbers**) by Guy Stockwell.

The Craft of Acting: Auditioning. A video tape by Allan Miller. The next best thing to reading is watching. Very practical tape.

How To Audition by Gordon Hunt. Helen Hunt's father.

If You Don't Dance They Beat You by Jose Quintero.

Instant Acting by Jeremy Whelan.

Laurence Olivier On Acting by Laurence Olivier.

Let The Part Play You by Anita Jesse. She is a teacher, famous for her audition techniques. Her exercises will make you a better actor and give you an understanding of what the acting process actually is.

Method or Madness? by Robert Lewis. Explores what the method is and is not as a workable theory of stage techniques.

New School Acting: Rules Tools Reasons by Jeremy Whelan. Featuring: The Dictionary of the Emotions, The Thesaurus of the Emotions.

No Acting Please by Eric Morris. This is the best explanation of relaxation and preparation for an actor that I've seen. Author of **The Craft Of Acting** and **The Meg Approaches.**

On Acting by Sanford Meisner.

A Passion for Acting: Exploring the Creative Process by Allan Miller. Innovating acting exercises to help the actor develop his or her craft. I love this book!

The Playing Is The Thing: Learning to Act Through Games and Exercises by Anita Jesse. "These games and exercises thrust actors into situations where they are inclined to interact naturally, and without self-consciousness.

A Practical Handbook For The Actor by Melissa Bruder, Lee Michael Cohn, Medeleine Olnek, Nathaniel Pollack, Robert Previto, Scott Zigler. Introduction by David Mamet. He says, "This is the best book on acting written in the last twenty years."

Screen Acting: How to Succeed in Motion Pictures and Television by Brian Adams. A broad range, practical guide to film and television acting.

Sense Of Direction by Bill Ball. San Francisco's ACT longtime artistic director's book for actors and directors.

Stanislavski's Legacy by Constantin Stanislavski.

Strasberg's Method, As Taught by Lorrie Hull: A Practical Guide for Actors, Teachers and Directors by S. Lorraine Hull. Comprehensive and detailed guide to Strasberg's work. She also has a two hour video tape examining the acting techniques. Included are relaxation techniques, four basic sensory and concentration exercises and scene critiques. To order: 310/828-0632 or 805/682-0638.

The Technique Of Acting by Stella Adler.

Towards A Poor Theater by Jerzy Grotowski.

Your Film and Acting Career: How to Break Into the Movies and TV and Survive in Hollywood by M. K. Lewis and Rosemary R. Lewis. M. K. Lewis is a prominent Los Angeles acting teacher whose career spans 25 years in theater, TV and films. Rosemary Lewis has worked in the print media as well as TV and films.

• BOOKS LISTING TEACHERS

The Selective Hollywood Acting Coaches and Teachers Directory by Acting World Books. Detailed information.

Working Actors Guide, published every year.

Back Stage West/Drama-Logue ads. Request their latest back issue featuring the workshops and teachers in Los Angeles. They also feature some Northern California teachers. There are issues with all the college training programs and summer training opportunities.

• GUIDE BOOKS, HOW-TO BOOKS AND TAPES

The Actor: A Practical Guide To A Professional Career by Eve Brandstein with Joanna Lipari. Excellent. It really gives you immediate advice.

The Actor's City Sourcebook by Andrea Wolper. If you are new to one of the 11 cities she has profiled or are thinking of moving to one, this is a jewel. (Also see section 9, *Cities Outside of L.A.)*

The Actor's Guide to Getting The Job, An Audio Tape, By Carolyne Barry and Kevin E. West. $24.95. www.carolynebarry.com.

Actor's Interview Log*: Where Am I Going! Where Have I Been!* This is a great way to keep track of all your interviews, location, what you wore, tax information, etc.

The Actor's Picture/Resume Book by Jill Charles with photographer Tom Bloom. Very good advice and illustrations.

An Actor Succeeds by Terrance Hines and Suzanne Vaughan. This is a most valuable book; they have a real working knowledge of the business.

An Actor's Workbook: Get The Agent You Need And The Career You Want by K Callan.

The Agencies: What the Actor Needs To Know by Acting World Books. If you don't have this guide, you aren't really looking for an agent. This is the authentic, well-researched agent guide. There are other publications that look like this one—don't be fooled.

Agents "Tell It Like It Is!" a video tape by Joel Asher. See actual agents in their offices. Great tape.

The Audition Book by Ed Hooks. The Rolls Royce of audition information. I think any actor who has not read this book is not doing everything possible to get work.

The Backstage Guide To Casting Directors by Hettie Lynne Hurtes. 56 top casting directors interviewed here offer convincing evidence that the more you know about their jobs, the closer you'll come to your dreams.

Back To One: How To Make Good Money As A Hollywood Extra by Cullen Chambers. This is the book you must have if you want to work as an extra. He gives all the answers, the agencies, tells you what to do on the set.

The Camera Smart Actor by Richard Brestoff. You must have this book. It clearly explains what it takes to act in front of a camera. This book is like a good friend; take it on the set with you.

Casting Directors "Tell It Like It Is." video tape. Famous acting coach Joel Asher has produced this informative tape all about casting directors. $19.95. Get $5.00 off by calling 800-652-7437 and mentioning this book.

Confidence & Clarity: The Complete Guide to Instant Line-Learning by Russ Weatherford. Explanation of a technique with exercises to help you learn lines.

Discover Yourself in Hollywood by Lilyan Chauvin. The ins and outs of coming to Hollywood. Mail order 323/877-4988.

Dreams Into Action: Getting What You Want by Milton Katsellas.

From Agent to Actor by Edgar Small. A well informed perspective from both sides. Tells how careers are established and nourished.

Getting The Part, video tape by acting coach Joel Asher. There are actual casting meetings and interviews. Very informative. The tape is very well produced and filled with information. $29.95. Get $5.00 off by calling 800-652-7437 and mentioning this book.

The Glam Scam: Successfully Avoiding the Casting Couch and Other Talent and Modeling Scams by Erik Joseph. Glam scams occur everywhere—beware.

Hollywood Agents & Managers Directory by Hollywood Creative Directory. Over 1000 talent, literary agencies and managers in L.A., N.Y. and across the nation.

Hollywood, Here I Come!; An Insider's Guide to a Successful Acting and Modeling Career in Los Angeles by Cynthia Hunter. This is a great book, very helpful.

Hollywood Scams and Survival Tactics by Lilyan Chauvin. She tells of all the scams!

How To Be A Working Actor: The Insider's Guide to Finding Jobs in Theater, Film and Television by New York casting director Mary Lynn Henry.

How To Conquer Hollywood, a video tape by Associated Artists Video. Great overview of what it takes to develop a career. Jason Alexander (*Seinfeld*) is featured.

How To Get Publicity by William Parkhurst.

How To Make It In Show Biz by June Walker Rogers.

How To Sell Yourself As An Actor by K Callan. How to merchandise your craft after you've learned it. K was Superman's mom on *Lois & Clark.*

The Job Book: 100 Acting Jobs For Actors edited by Glenn Alterman.

Life is a Contact Sport: Ten Great Career Strategies That Work by Ken Kragen with Jefferson Graham. Ken has managed careers of Kenny Rogers, Lionel Richie, Harry Anderson, Burt Reynolds, Travis Tritt, Trisha Yearwood; he does know what works.

The Los Angeles Agent Book: Get the Agent You Need For the Career You Want by K Callen.

Ross Reports: TV Commercial Casting guide, Comedy Casting Guide and Personal Managers Directory are among the great ones. Subscriptions only, 800/817-3273. Special Directories, 212/536-5170. Check out all these reports.

Seminar Books by Acting World Books. I love these and recommend all of them: **The Selective Holywood Acting Coaches and Teachers Directory, The Agencies, Publicizing Yourself**, etc.

Survival Jobs, 118 Ways To Make Money While Pursuing Your Dreams by Deborah Jacobson.

Voice and the Actor by Cicely Berry. Speaking is an expression of inner life and of emotion.

The Working Actor's Guide edited by Karin Mani. If you live in LA or are planning to move here, you must have it! Lists all the services available.

Working in Hollywood by Alexandra Brouwer & Thomas Lee Wright. It describes the jobs of everybody you see in the credits. Great!

Fake Cigarettes and Fake Tears

CIGARETTES

Ben's Smoke Shop, 323/467-5000. 6423 Hollywood Blvd., Hollywood, 90028. M-Sa 11-6. If you have to smoke in a play or film, use herbal cigarettes; they are nonaddictive. Even if you are a smoker it is wise to use the herbals for take after take. Many health food stores also sell the herbals.

TEARS

For tears, you learn in acting class how to reach the emotions where the tears are likely to come from but if they don't come and the director wants them you will have to create them however you can.

Some actors tell me they learn to look out of their eyes in a certain way that the tears just flow. On a sitcom you can get away with giant sobs and putting your hand over your eyes and make it look like you are wiping away the tears.

Ammonia Inhalants, by North Health Care, at most drugstores, can help. They are for reviving people when they have fainted. One sniff makes your eyes water.

Also try liquid Binaca loaded up on your finger or knuckle. Rub your eye with it to start tears.

A fresh cut onion in a plastic bag in your pocket can help. Get the juice all over your hand and rub it in your eye.

Section Two

Preparing For Success and Living Your Dream

• **Whatever your acting career dreams and goals are**, creating a successful business to support and propel your career is necessary and exciting. Simply speaking, an acting career consists of three components: the acting, (which is the art) the business and your dream. As you begin to develop your career, you are in fact setting up a small business in which you are the president and CEO. When setting up your business, you'll be making many decisions and purchasing quality goods and services for, hopefully, the best price. This book will guide you as you make these decisions. The best career choices are made when you follow your instincts and use your own good judgment, based on who you are and what your values are.

• **To be an actor you must act**. Study, always study, but find places to express your art; act for audiences and for the camera. Lucille Ball, in speaking of why she succeeded: "I acted anywhere and everywhere they would let me." If you have the business but not the art, you are likely to feel something is missing in your life. Discover the ways to satisfy the artist within your soul. You must develop the art and the business to have a well-rounded, enduring acting career. Labors of love (usually jobs without financial reward) often lead to life changing career paths.

• **Lili Taylor** (*The Haunting*) when asked by *Backstage West* what she would say to actors trying to break into the business, said: "Have faith and trust. And know that there are no rules. Knock down rules."

• **Robert Ellenstein—actor, director, teacher and artistic director of the Los Angeles Repertory Company:**

- **We must rearrange the priorities.** Namely, put the god of our art first and our career second. It means we must pursue our craft every day. We must learn a new speech every day. We must keep our voice and body in shape every day. We must live our lives alert for how we can use it for our craft. We must dedicate ourselves to what we feel is the highest, not the best paying. We must work at it despite self doubts, disdainful smiles, approval or disapproval from others, showbiz expediency—dedicating ourselves to the perfection of our craft, with faith that this will give us life.

- **Such purposeful, active dedication is so rare** that we will stand out of the crowd of toadies to the system almost immediately and become a choice morsel that the buyers would like to have—thus satisfying our material needs.

• **Joan Darling, Emmy-award winning director, acting coach and actress:**

Q: What does it take to be a success in this business?

- **There are two things** you have to make a delineation between. One is to succeed in the business, which takes one set of skills, and the other is to succeed for yourself as an artist, which is another kettle of fish altogether.

- **To succeed in the business**, you have to come to where the business is happening, which is either New York or Los Angeles. Get yourself into an acting class; that is how you meet people and begin to network. You need a resume, good pictures and an audition scene, three minutes long, that shows you off. Show the scene to anyone who will let you. Go to all the open calls and start to get used to auditioning; work breeds work.

- **If you can't get in the door** anywhere, then get together a little showcase, rent a theater and invite as many people as you can. Start networking, which is why class is very helpful—any kind of class that gets you in touch with other actors, because that's where you begin to get the information about how to do it. Learn everything you don't know; study body movement, voice and speech. The more skills you have, the more chances you have to succeed.

- **Make a list** of anyone you or your parents know who is connected with the business. Contact them all and see if there is anyone they can introduce you to, so you can start making your own connections in the business. Keep performing someplace and get people in to see you. And the rest of it is: pray a lot.

• **Jay Bernstein, manager, writer, publicist, producer** taught a course called *Stardom, the Management of, the Public Relations for, and the Survival and Maintenance In.* He has managed careers for Mary Hart, Linda Evans, Suzanne Sommers, Bruce Boxleitner, Stacey Keach, Jamison Parker, etc.

Q: What does it take to be a star?

- **To be a star,** everything has to be 100% with your talent, your representation and your presentation. For example, if you're talented and you present yourself well but you don't have an agent, it's going to be pretty hard to get a job—so your representation is failing. If you're very talented and the representation is the best you can get but you dress like a rock star, they're probably not going to hire you to play a nun—so that's your presentation.

- **If your presentation** and your representation are wonderful, maybe you need some work on your talent. If talent is a problem, maybe there won't be stardom. There's nothing you can do with just representation and presentation. I think that talent is 35% of making it. The other 65% is having the right team with you.

- **The team** is the right agent who gets you the jobs, the right personal manager who gives you direction, the right business manager who makes sure your money grows as your career grows, the right entertainment attorney because there's an awful lot of small print in Hollywood, and the right public relations person that will help you maximize what you've done.

Q: What if actors are shy about asking for help?

If you don't ask, the answer is already no. The worst thing that will happen if you ask is, the answer will still be no.

• **What success can look like. Tom Cruise's** filmography: 1981: *Taps, Endless Love.* 1983: *All the Right Moves, Losin' It, The Outsiders, Risky Business.* 1985: *Legend.* 1986: *The Color of Money.* 1988: *Young Guns, Cocktail, Rain Man.* 1989: *Born on the Fourth of July.* 1990: *Days of Thunder.* 1992: *Far and Away.* 1993: *The Firm.* 1994: *Interview With A Vampire.* 1996: *Mission: Impossible, Jerry Maguire.* 1998: *Eyes Wide Shut.* 1999: *Mission: Impossible II.*

• **Another way it can look: Guba Gooding Jr.**, Oscar-winner for *Jerry Maguire,* when growing up in Orange County, lived for a while in a U-Haul trailer. He was paid $32,000 for *Boyz N the Hood,* $100,000 for *Gladiator,* $400,000 for *Outbreak,* $500,000 for *Lightning Jack,* $600,000 for *Jerry Maguire,* $250,000 for *As Good as It Gets,* $1.5 million for *What Dreams May Come.* At 30 years old, he was paid $2.5 million for *Instinct.* Looks like the sky is the limit.

• **Show business** is the most exciting business in the world and no one can keep you out of it, because no matter how big your dreams are, how long it takes or what paths there are to follow, you are willing to do it. Why?—for the THRILL of putting yourself on the line, wonderful close-ups and actors you respect telling you they enjoy your acting work. Money and fame are only a phone call away; don't let anyone convince you differently. Make your choices and commit. You can have everything you *intend* to have.

• **Abraham Lincoln** said, "Always bear in mind that your own resolution to succeed is more important than any other one thing."

How To Take Great Acting Pictures

• **Your 8x10 pictures put you into the acting business**; they are your most important career marketing tools. An 8x10 picture is usually your first introduction to the people who will be calling you in for interviews and auditions, and casting you in their productions. You must have pictures, they must look like you, and you must like them so you never have to apologize when handing them out.

• **Agents, casting directors, producers and directors** will pick up the telephone to arrange to meet you because of something they see in your eyes, attitude, look or style. An actor always brings an 8x10 picture to every interview; the people you meet need it in order to remember you.

• **As your collection of pictures grows**, you will be able to show the interviewer a portfolio of different looks: body and stunt shots, glamour looks, character shots of you working on a set or in a play, riding a motorcycle, with or without a mustache, lighter, darker, shorter or longer hair, etc.

• **Mark Malis, former head of Universal Casting.** "I tell actors they must look like their pictures on a daily basis. Otherwise they are wasting the casting director's time. They should attempt to find a photographer who can capture their personality. If they can accomplish those two things, they will get what they need."

• **Having your pictures taken** is an important acting assignment, one in which you will be investing a great deal of money, time and energy. Preparation is the key. Research various looks, characters and attitudes you can play, watch TV shows, commercials and rent movies. Make a list of looks and attitudes you would like the photographer to capture. Gather the appropriate clothes for these aspects of yourself from your wardrobe, thrift stores, new purchases or friends; have them repaired, altered, cleaned, ironed and ready. These will also serve as your audition clothes.

• **Get your hair cut, colored, permed and restyled** at least a week before the shoot. The exception is men doing long and short hair looks in the same photo session; they will shave and get their hair cut in the middle of the session. If you are planning on doing your own makeup, have a makeup designer show you how to do it and purchase the right products. Do this a couple of weeks ahead and practice, practice, practice. This also applies to having a facial; do it at least one week before the shoot. *See Age Defying Techniques in Section Six, page 366.*

• **To look as good as you can on the day of your shoot**, get two weeks of vigorous exercise and three or four nights of rest. You don't want a tan on your face for B&W pictures, so wear sun block. Avoid foods that darken your blood: meat, carrots, beets, sugar. They darken the circles under your eyes. Be alcohol and drug free for at least a week before the shoot. Train for the session as a highly competitive athlete would.

• **One of your most important steps** in preparation is shopping for a photographer. It is good business to interview at least three.

• **Popular photographer Suze Lanier suggests:**

> • **Take the time to interview several photographers**; you don't want to rush having your pictures taken. Look at their books. Look at their proof sheets to see the ratio of good shots. Every photographer can luck out and get one great shot. Look for the technical quality of the photograph. What kind of energy and expression is coming out in the face?
>
> • **The most important thing** in the photograph are the eyes. Make sure they are saying something. I like the fun and warmth to come out in the shot. Look at pictures of people in your age range with your similar hair, skin and eye coloring so you can see how that person was lit. If you have blue eyes, find somebody in the book with blue eyes so you can see how those eyes look. Some photographers will make the eyes dark.

- **The photographer's personality** is very important—someone you can trust and feel comfortable with. You need to be relaxed to have a good time. Certain personalities will completely click in and be magic, and then sometimes you find someone you don't feel comfortable with. Go for the magic.

• **Tom Lascher also advises ways to choose your photographer.**

- **The goal of the head shot is to suspend the disbelief** of the casting director, so that he or she sees beyond the photograph and feels the presence of the person/actor it represents.

- **The three issues to consider when choosing a photographer are:** first, look at the pictures and imagine whether you would fit in this photographer's style. The second factor is whether you and the photographer want to go in the same direction. If you're thinking femme fatale and he's thinking ingenue or you're thinking villian and he's thinking leading man, you may spend the whole session tugging in different directions. Third and most important is whether or not you can have enough of a relationship with the photographer to be able to use the photographer not just as a technician but as a scene partner.

• **The price for a photo shoot** is usually $100 to $500 plus makeup for women and also men who need it, though some photographers do their own. The price seems to be based on reputation and what the market will bear. My students and I have obtained good pictures from photographers in all price ranges. If the picture helps you get interviews, it has done its job. In your teens and 20s, you may need new pictures every year; after that, every two to five years. Pictures are one of your biggest expenses and greatest payoffs. This is the place to use a good percentage of your available promotion dollars.

• **The most important thing about your picture** is that you are looking straight into the lens, eyes open. Pretend or personalize the camera as someone you are eager to talk to, for a specific reason. Let your guard down, no defenses; be at your most vulnerable. Let the camera see inside you and let it see you project the attitudes you and your agent, acting coach or the photographer think are appropriate for you to portray—the characters you will be cast to play. The focus should be *very sharp.*

- **Glamour photographer Michael Maron says:**

  - **Actors are used to having a character** to hide behind so they freeze up in front of the camera when they have to be themselves. The key is to let everything go, just be present, be who you are. Use your acting abilities, your technique. Think of a role you enjoyed playing, the time somebody did something wonderful for you or a funny situation that happened. Be in that moment so you won't be self-conscious.

- **Casting director Clair Sinnett says:**

  - **Don't just do smiling and non-smiling looks.** What you need in a picture is attitude, feeling, thought behind the eyes. Actors should have two monologues prepared when they go to a photographer. One, a dramatic piece that really touches them, makes them angry, hurt or even makes them cry. And second, a comedic monologue that makes them laugh. When actors don't have monologues, as a short cut they can think of the worst day they've ever had, for theatrical pictures; the best day, for commercial pictures.

  - **Do your own hair and makeup** the way you do them on a day-to-day basis. You want to look like your picture when you walk into the casting director's office.

- **Well-known photographer Mary Ann Halpin says:**

  - **Actors arrive at my studio under pressure** from their agents, managers, mothers and the world to get the perfect photograph. They are carrying so much weight on their shoulders that it is hard for them to just be themselves. I see portraiture as an emotional dance. When an actor lets go and goes with the dance, it can be magical. I'm convinced that when someone reacts positively to a photograph it's because of the actor's energy rather than just the aesthetic beauty of the photograph.

  - **The casting directors all want "slice of life" photos.** What is the actor feeling, not what do they look like. The most interesting shot wins. I shot an actress from New York sitting on the floor barefoot in jeans; we created a look. She called to tell me she got cast because they loved her feet. The producers, after seeing the picture, restyled the character on the soap to reflect the way she looked in the photograph.

• **Here is Mary Ann's list of clothes** to wear for different styles of pictures. She says, "Bring everything."

Wardrobe List

Men

- **Sporty Look:** Tennis shirts, Izod shirts, T-shirts with white collars, sweat shirts and jackets, ski jackets, zip-up cotton jackets are great; stripes and colored patterns work fine.
- **Rugged Outdoor Look:** Plaid shirts, woolen Pendelton shirts, blue denim shirts and jackets, down jackets or vest, sheepskin, leather or big old funky jackets, safari shirts and jackets are good too. Also, big bulky sweaters like ski and fisherman knits.
- **Street Look:** Tight black T-shirts or shirts. Black, navy, or gray sweat shirts. Again, denim or rough looking jackets, undershirts.
- **Clean-Cut Look:** Cotton dress shirts in lighter colors and patterns, V-neck sweaters, crew-neck sweaters, sports jackets in lighter colors, casual ties, light leather or suede jackets. Also a couple of pairs of good fitting jeans or pants with a belt to finish off the look.
- **Businessman/Executive Look:** Three piece suit, pin stripe, tuxedo and tuxedo shirt for a dressier look. Dress shirts, vests, and a variety of ties. Also, bring some tie clips/pins and cuff-links to finish off the look.

Women

- **Casual/Earthy:** Men's shirts: cotton type dress, denim, Pendleton, plaids. Patterned blouses if they're not too busy. Sweaters: textured, lacy, angora, V-necks, crew necks, boat necks, and turtle necks. Vintage clothes are unusual and interesting. Bring a pair of jeans or leggings and an assortment of belts.
- **Business/Spokeswoman:** Business suits and jackets: tweeds patterned or plain: dark or light colors are great. Blouses: silk, lacy, or tailored; interesting colors. Vest with a tie or suspenders are fun. Bring interesting tailored pants or skirts.
- **Upscale/Sexy/Dramatic:** Silk shirts, men's shirts, tuxedo shirts, lacy things. Black sweaters and dresses, off the shoulder or low necklines. Romantic dresses: vintage, flowered or lacy. Lacy camisoles and romantic lingerie. Bring earrings, pins and bracelets. It is preferable to work with texture, pattern, style and design. Avoid plain fabrics in medium reds, blues and greens that rely purely on color for their effect.

• **The first picture you need** is a commercial or theatrical B&W head shot (currently, that means from the waist up) that looks just like you will look when you walk in the office. Your next picture may be a ¾ shot (down to at least your knees), usually with a little more projection of your personality by the clothes you are wearing and your attitude. In pictures there are really no hard, fast rules; you and your photographer can be creative in designing the shots you wish to have. I'm giving you the following descriptions and photo examples as guidelines to opening your own imaginations. Styles in photos change; research what are the most current, up-to-date shots and figure out if they fit your style. Sometimes the most interesting shot is one where rules have been broken.

• **A theatrical head or 3/4 shot** is used for film and television auditions and for seeking a theatrical agent. This shot, in general, should not have a full smile; often quite an intense look is required, such as the soap opera bitch or the gang leader, if that's how you will be cast. All pictures need attitude. Look in the camera lens, let the camera see inside of you, and then imagine you are talking to someone you know who would make you say things like:

"I want you."	"You make me angry because..."
"Come here."	"I'm so embarrassed."
"Get out of here!"	"I'm ready."
"I hate you."	"I love you."
"You devastated me."	"You feel so good."
"I'll pay you back."	"You're so sexy."
"I'm bad."	"You're so cute."
"Please forgive me."	"Come on, let's play."
"You are so bad."	"Let's party!"
"I'll never forgive you."	"Where's the party?"

• **Your commercial B&W head or 3/4 shot** will be used in seeking a commercial agent and on commercial auditions. This picture should be honest and upbeat, usually a smile that looks happy, perky, in love with life, with lots of energy in your eyes. When looking in the lens, say things like,

"Hey!"	"This is the best!"
"Oh!"	"Yummy!"
"What a great day!"	"What a bargain!"
"What a surprise!"	"I got the job!" etc.

- Do whatever it takes to get your energy up. Talk to your puppy or pet bird; find what works for you and then do the acting.

For much more about commercial shots, go to Section Three, page 160, where we have examples and more information.

• **After you have these basic shots**, you will want to add pictures of characters you can play. Some I always have are businesswoman, waitress, tough madam-hooker, country grandma, prison warden, quirky commercial, and soap-opera glamour looks.

• **Makeup artist Rita Montanez** designed the following list for photographer Alan Weissman to give to his clients.

Clothing List

Bring a lot of clothing so we can play and figure out what works best!

- Solid colors work best (no prints, patterns or stripes), we've been using more white, texture works well.
- Long sleeves are best for headshots, short sleeves can work for 3/4 shots, never wear short sleeves if you are uncomfortable with your arms.
- Mock turtlenecks, nothing bulky.
- White, black and gray t-shirts work well under denim shirts, sport jackets, etc.
- Dark blue and black jeans as well as regular blue jeans.
- For women, jewelry is simple, studs and small earrings. No watches or rings.

Commercial

- Think The Gap, Banana Republic, J.Crew, etc. Casual and comfortable. I also like layered looks.

Theatrical

- Dark colors are inherently more dramatic. We love black.
- For women: bodysuits, simple shirts with clean lines. Cleavage is not always appropriate. if a suit has been suggested, again, simple clean lines. Large shoulder pads are out.
- For men: blazers with collared shirts or t-shirts. Suits for an upscale look. Ties are good for a detective, a cop and a business look.

• **If you have a great body,** male or female, and like to show it off, you will need a body-shot picture. Consider tennis, bike riding, dance, work-out clothes or one of your own personal skills that require body-fitting clothes. If you do stunts, you need pictures of you doing martial arts, jumping from a building, firing a gun, whatever your specialty is. If you want to be considered for sexy roles where nudity or partial nudity is required, take pictures in a tiny bathing suit or an outfit that plays up your body. Do not mail these shots. Give them out personally when it is appropriate to the role.

Daring photographer Michael Lamont tells of how breaking the rules can work:

- **Ten years ago I met Lolita Davidovich** (*Play It To The Bone, Mystery Alaska, No Vacancy)* at a wrap party. She presented herself in a very sensual, sexual, daring, low cut, 20 year-old way. For three years she insisted I shoot her in various ways of cute and adorable. After not being able to get any response from the pictures, she booked one more session; she wanted to do another mailing, and if it didn't work she was going to move back home to Toronto. I said I'm not shooting cute and adorable. I want the Lolita I met at the party, half-naked, comfortable and sensual. We got a 3/4 shot, which was not in style at that time, with a hot look in her eyes, a thong bathing suit and open jean jacket. She used the shot as a mailer, which got her an agent and a manager. She finally marketed who she was. You put those eyes on that body and how could you not stop and look at the picture. I received a card a year later saying, "I'm on my fourth film, still haven't had to take my clothes off, pictures are working." The rest is Hollywood history.

• **The above descriptions** of pictures are for the Los Angeles market. If you are in another city, research the trends in your area. If you are moving to Los Angeles, plan on having your professional pictures taken here. If your pictures are from New York, chances are they will work. If they are from San Diego, San Francisco, Seattle or your home town, they almost certainly will not be useable.

• **If you want to work as an extra**, you'll need 3x5 waist-and-knee length color snapshots taken on a white background. The extra casting people need to get an idea of your size and weight.

• **For commercial interviews in some parts of the country** (not Los Angeles), your agent may want a composite. These can be three or four shots on one side or a commercial head shot on one side and several commercial-type situation shots on the back: horseback riding, grocery shopping, selling fast-food, cheerleading, holding a baby, playing baseball, doing laundry, typing, etc. When my martial artist daughter, Cynthia Kerr, lived in Dallas, she used a one-sided composite made up of two pictures—one wearing a tank top and karate pants, doing a perfect side kick, the other a glamour head shot. Composites always have your name, your agent's name and oftentimes your measurements. *See commercial shots, page 164.*

• **When you have your first pictures** taken and your funds are limited, contact art schools and colleges and investigate how to become a model for the photography students in exchange for photos. *See the Art Center under the Photographer listings in this section.*

• **Or ask a talented friend with a good 35mm camera** to shoot a B&W trial roll in an outdoor setting with nice light. You can rent an appropriate lens from a camera supply store. A good lens is a 105mm F-2.5 Nikon portrait lens. In Hollywood, try Samy's Camera at 200 S. La Brea, Los Angeles, 90036. 323/938-2420. *See Hank Tovar's directions for amateur photographers, page 472.*

• **Have the roll developed and printed** onto an 8½x11 or 11x14 proof sheet at a photo lab. A proof sheet can have up to 36 exposures on it. *See the photo lab section.* Purchase a photographer's loop for a few dollars at a camera store. It is the only way to look at your proof sheets. You must have these professional tools. Look at the proofs with the loop to check lighting and focus. You can have all the shots done in 4x6 proof prints cheaply at Isgo's Lab at the time of developing. Pick a few shots and have them made into 3x5s or 8x10s to see the real quality. All this can be done cheaply and may result in a fine head shot to get you started.

• **When you have the money** to invest in professional pictures, choose the right photographer for you. Ask your friends, look at ads in the trades, and check out the ones I've listed here. Although I've worked with all of the following photographers, I have never found one that everyone has been satisfied with. This could be a reflection on the actor as well as the photographer. Make sure the photographer you choose guarantees their work. This means if you and your agent did not get the shots you need, they will reshoot for the price of the film and makeup artist only.

• **Try not to be discouraged** if it takes more than one photo session to get an 8x10 you love. It is unusual to have a truly successful first shoot. Use these picture-taking events as a time to learn something about acting in front of the camera. Your personal preparation and ease with the photographer will make all the difference in the success of the shoot. It can be very tough not to have your pictures come out as you dreamed they would. I have been though some agony myself and with my daughter, Cynthia, and many of my students. It can be a situation where you spend a great deal of money and have a product that you hate or that your agent says won't work for you. Try to diagnose what didn't work. This isn't to look for blame, but to educate yourself. Blame will not solve anything and can lead to self-pity, which can kill your spirit. Pick yourself up, save more money and go for it again.

• **UCLA anthropologist Mari Womack**, an expert in self-image says, "As far as photos are concerned, no one likes the way they look. We can never really see ourselves from the outside; we see ourselves from *inside.* It's not just vanity, it's the shock of the image."

• **The next step is choosing the right shots** from your proof sheets, 3x5s or 4x6s to be blown up to 8x10 masters. Ask your photographer to pick their favorite choices. They will mark these with a grease pencil, which easily wipes off with a Kleenex. Equipped with your grease pencil and loop, ask three or four people their opinions of which pictures look most like you. It's best to ask someone in the business: your acting coach, a working actor, an agent or casting director. Keep track of each person's picks and then make your choices.

• **I suggest you choose last** so you can see how others perceive you. If you have selected a lot of shots, see if your photographer can save you money by having 3x5s blown up and making your final choices for 8x10 masters from those. Blow up your selections into 8x10 borderless (four-way bleed) matte finish masters or use interesting, artistic borders your photographer, agent or photo lab may suggest. The rejects can be gifts to your family members.

• **Now you are ready to reproduce your master picture**. Again, take the masters to three or four people and ask their opinions. Some pictures will be eliminated right away because of flaws that were not perceptible when looking at the proof sheet or 3x5s. Many flaws can be corrected by retouching; a good picture is worth the expense. If there are some pictures you hate, you have my permission to destroy them no matter how much they cost. You don't want a picture you hate to be anywhere in this world; you never know when it will turn up to embarrass you. Next, look at the masters chosen most by your people and see if you agree. Then have them retouched if necessary and reproduced. *See Photo Retouching, page 98.*

•**Hugh Grant** says, "I'm terrible at having my picture taken. I'm always furious and unpleasant."

• **The following pictures are presented here** to demonstrate different types of 8x10s used for theatrical interviews and auditions. I thought it might be informative to show you pictures taken of me; actressess Janice Allen, in her 20s and my daughter, Cynthia Kerr, in her 30s; actors Anthony Christiansen, in his 20s and Ben Dewell in his 30s, by four different photographers. Each photographer chose the photo to be used, the makeup artist, and decided if retouching should be done. Notice how each shot tells a different story. Imagine how many stories your pictures will tell.

CHECKLIST FOR A SUCCESSFUL PHOTO SHOOT

Before the shoot:

- Pick photographer.
- Makeup artist.
- Cut, curl and color hair.
- Get in shape.
- Gather clothes and makeup.
- Drink water and rest.

After the shoot:

- Purchase photo loop and grease pencil, black, red or green.
- Pick up proof sheets.
- Make picture choices, blow up 3x5s or 4x6s
- Blow up 8x10s.
- Retouching.
- Reproduction.
- You are now in show business

On the next few pages are samples of theatrical headshots. The same actors appear in commercial shots on Pages 164-166.

My special thanks to the photographers,

makeup artists and retouchers for their

time, energy and creativity.

Business Theatrical Head Shot

Photographer
Michael Helms

Makeup
I did myself from Rita's chart, page 353

Retouching
Nichan
Blown up from a $3/4$ Shot. It got fuzzy, Nican fixed it.

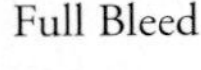

Full Bleed

Theatrical Shot

Photographer
Nancy Jo Gilchrist

Makeup & Hair
Robert Raphael

Retouching
Ray the Retoucher

Black Line Border

'40s Look

Photographer
Alan Weissman

Hair and Makeup
Rita Montanez

Clothes
Dino Designs

Retouching
none

Sloppy Border

Grandma

Photographer
Bob Bayles

Publicity still from a play. Shot at the West Coast Ensemble Theatre.

Makeup
none

Retouching
none

Theatrical
¾ Shot

Anthony
Christiansen

Photographer
Carrie
Cavalier

Full bleed

Headshot

Photographer
Rich
Hogan

Rich's
Computer
Custom
Border

Photographer
Sean Kenney

Anthony Christiansen

Retouching
Sean Kenney

Full bleed

Dramatic Headshot

Photographer
Suze Lanier

Retouching
none

Horizontal Print

Theatrical

Janice Allen

Photographer
Mark Husmann

Hair and Makeup
Brett Freedman

Retouching
none

Black Line Border

Theatrical

Photographer
Sean McCall

Hair and Makeup
Rita Montanez

Retouching
none

Photographer
Carrie Cavalier

Makeup
Laura Connelly

Retouching
none

Horizontal Print

Theatrical

Janice Allen

Photographer
Mara

Hair and Makeup
Mara

Retouching
Mara

Full Bleed

Headshot unshaven

Ben Dewell

Photographer **Bob Bayles**

White Borders

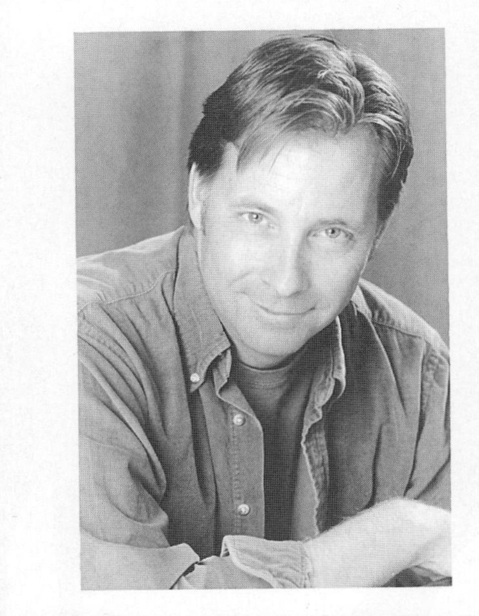

Headshot after shaving

Photographer **Bob Bayles**

White Borders

Theatrical

Ben Dewell

Photographer
Kevin Merrill

White Borders

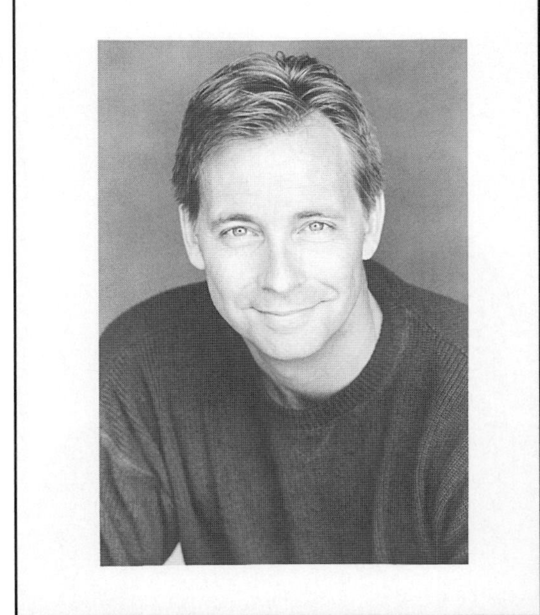

Theatrical

Ben Dewell

Photographer
Raffi Alexander

Spiderbox Photography

Theatrical

Cynthia Kerr

Photographer
Alisha Tamburri

Makeup & Hair
Alisa Chompupong

Retouching
none

Theatrical

Cynthia Kerr

Photographer
Michael Lamont

Makeup
Michael Lamont

Retouching
none

Theatrical

Cynthia Kerr

Photographer
Diana Lannes

Makeup & Hair
Rela Martine

Retouching
Nichan

Full bleed

Theatrical

Cynthia Kerr

Photographer
Mary Ann Halpin

Makeup & Hair
Sandy Williams

Retouching
Nichan

He removed a shadow above her knee.

Photographers

The Art Center, Model Office, 818/396-2250. They will send you information on how to register in their film and print work files. Located in Pasadena, their students are always looking for subjects. You usually pay for supplies only. Great way to learn about print modeling.

Raffi Alexander, Spiderbox Photography, 818/244-2291. Web Page: www.spiderbox.com $250 for two rolls, includes two 8x10s. Each additional roll, $125, includes one 8x10. Extra 8x10s, $20 each. Makeup available $75-$100. *See theatrical shot of Ben Dowell on page 91.*

Bob Bayles, 818/997-8518. $85 for one roll, $50 for each additional roll. $8 for additional 8x10s. Shoots in the studio or on location. Use your own makeup artist. He guarantees a proof sheet in two days and 8x10s in two more days. He has shot many of my students. *See photos of me in my Grandma shot on page 85 and Ben Dewell, theatrical shots (unshaven and clean shaven) on page 90.*

Carrie Cavalier of Cavalier Photography, 818/840-9148 and 818/566-8291. www.cavalierphotography.com. Her specialty is creative outdoor location shots, $150 for one roll and $240 for 2 rolls. In studio it is $135 for one roll, two changes; $225 for two rolls, 4 changes; $290 for three rolls, five changes. Makeup and hair extra, starting at $35. Includes negatives, but no 8x10s. Charge for 8x10s is $12.50 to $16 each. Carrie also shoots color 3x5 or 4x6 extra photos: 36 prints, $150, including negatives. *See Anthony's theatrical shot on page 86. See Janice Allen's horizontal shot on page 89 and her commercial photo on page 166.*

Nancy Jo Gilchrist, 818/780-0803. One roll, $200; $375 for two rolls, up to five looks; $75 for an additional role. Makeup and Hair, $50 - $125. Stuart Stone top commercial casting director recommends her. Alexandra Paul, Sharon Lawrence, Samuel Jackson are some of the celebrities she's worked with. Her speciality is in shooting someone who wants to make it to the next level, someone who's ready to escalate their career. Relaxation exercises and an organic atmosphere. Loves working with children, 1 roll, $200; 2 rolls, $300. *See my theatrical shot on page 84, and commercial shot on page 165.*

Rod Goodman, 818/760-0733. He advertises in *Back Stage West.* 36 exposures and proofs for $35. Photographer Mark Husmann and agent Bonnie Howard thinks his photos are good.

Mary Ann Halpin/Halpin-Croyle Photography, 323/874-8500. $650 including sales tax for four rolls and negatives, three different looks in a three to four hour session; B&W Polaroid shots before each look. Options for hair and makeup: they provide a stylist $150; you bring a stylist you like; you can do your own styling. A $200 nonrefundable deposit, contact sheet in two to three days. She says, "If an actor says, 'This is the most fun I've ever had having my pictures taken,' then I feel I've done my job!" The music and snacks are great. She is the author of a coffee table book, *Pregnant Goddesshood: A Celebration of Life,* check out her web site at www.goddesshood.com. *See photos of Cynthia Kerr, theatrical shot on page 93, commercial shot on page 164 and on commercial resume, page 170.*

Terri Hanauer, 310/452-4968. $490 including sales tax for three rolls the negatives and proofsheets. $380 for two rolls and you keep the negatives. Commercial and theatrical head and 3/4 shots. Makeup, $100. She is a talented actress and works well with actors. She is on many top agents' photographers lists. Terri says, "Being an actress, I shoot people the way I need to be photographed with a great deal of attention to the inner spirit. I try to bring out what is unique, real and authentic in the person I photograph." Terri is a very loving, fun, supportive person to be with.

Michael Helms, 818/353-5855; www.active-media.com/helms. Two rolls, $250; three rolls, $300, cash only. Proof sheets and negatives are paid for at the lab, and you are responsible for printing the 8x10s. For makeup, you can do your own, bring a makeup artist or choose one from his list. He does a preview black & white Polaroid for your approval. He was recommended to me by Stuart K. Robinson, famed commercial acting teacher and by agent Neil Kreppel of Commercial Talent. He is very easy and laid back and gives you specific instructions for your shoot. *See theatrical shot of me on page 84 and commercial shot on page 165.*

Rich Hogan, 323/467-2628. $135-$175 for one roll, one 8x10, wardrobe change included. You keep the negatives. $135 is a special price for people who have this book. Rich registers non-union extras for Sunset Casting for a $25 package, which includes the pictures for Sunset. He does extras' 3x5 shots on a white background, ask for price. He's shot Tina Turner, Magic Johnson, Big Boy of Power 106, Jay Thomas, Playboy and Penthouse models of the year. He does a good job, along with his special makeup artist Ali Finnie. He does computer imaging with over 400 different borders available to enhance your 8x10 and is capable of printing out a master in about an hour. *See theatrical photo of Anthony Christiansen, on page 86 and commercial shot on page 166.*

Mark Husmann, 213/680-9999. $395 for 3 rolls, 4x6 test prints are $1.95, master 8x10s are $18.50. Makeup and hair artist is $150. He shoots inside a studio, using the natural light that comes in through the windows. Mark meets people prior to shooting so they will feel comfortable with him on the day of the shoot. "I tell people to try and keep the pictures as simple as possible; the photographs should be about them, not the clothing, the makeup, or the background." *See theatrical photo of Janice Allen on page 88.*

Diana Lannes Photography 213/427-8096. $250 for 3 rolls and 2 8x10s, $75 for each additional roll including 1 8x10, you keep the negatives. Professional hair and makeup available, $75 or she will help the actor do their own makeup. Diana's been shooting for 10 years in New York and L.A. She shoots in natural light in her garden or in the studio. She specializes in commercial and ultra-glamorous shots. She loves working with young children. *See theatrical photo of Cynthia Kerr on page 93, commercial photo on page 165 and Jackson Tovar's child photo on page 168.*

Sean Kenney, 800/505-7698. For adults $250 for one roll, three changes, two 8x10s including minor retouching; $350 for two rolls, five changes and four 8x10s. Guarantees to have 8x10s back in five to seven working days. Extra 8x10s are $25 each. Rush orders are available. You can buy your negatives for $75 per roll. Works with adults and children. Note the savings here because he does minor retouching. Sean travels to other parts of the country, bringing the Los Angeles style. *See Anthony Christiansen's theatrical photo on page 87, commercial photo on page 166 and child photo of Austin Tovar on page 169.*

Michael Lamont, 818/506-0285. Variable rates from $300. All rates include makeup and grooming, which Michael does himself. "I work moment to moment. The shots come out of an emotional life and a conversational reality. If we get the first setup in 8 to 12 frames, I change the lighting and background and we move on. Each person is lit differently, according to their own range, including commercial, theatrical head and 3/4 shots. In working moment to moment, if it is not in the eyes, we don't shoot. Hopefully, they will walk away with 36 out of 36 usable shots." Michael is a member of IATSE 600 International Cinematographers Guild. As director of photography he shoots feature films as well as music videos. *See theatrical photo of Cynthia Kerr on page 92, commercial photo on page 165.*

Suze Lanier Photography, 818/508-7116. $175-$500 depending on client's needs. Some packages include 8x10s. Makeup: no charge for men and $60 for women. 16x20 proof sheets available, negatives are negotiable. Suze shoots every person differently and likes to shoot to music. "It's important to have a good time at the session." Specializes in 3/4 and head shots, as well as zeds, high fashion, bands, publicity and magazine assignments. She also has a studio in Dallas, 214/373-2226, and does location shooting everywhere. *See horizontal theatrical head shot of Anthony Christiansen, page 87.*

Tom Lascher, 310/581-1980. $250 session fee plus cost of film at about $5 per roll. Actor takes the exposed film to lab of their choice for processing and selecting their masters. "I'm committed to meeting my clients before we shoot in order for us to get to know each other and to better plan a potential shoot. Some of my favorite clients are actors who truly detest having their pictures taken. When things work right we can use the rehearsal process of shooting to create a really strong final 8x10." Acting coaches Sal Romeo and Michael Nehring give Tom the highest of recommendations.

Mara, 818/781-8933. $250 for three rolls, including makeup; $6.50 for each 8x10, you keep the negatives. She's been a photographer for 25 years. Mara loves working with new people and thinks getting the best pictures is the photographer's responsibility. An agent said, "She is the only photographer who is consistently good with my clients." Mara was a New York model for many years; she is beautiful herself and makes you feel beautiful while she's shooting you. *See photos of Janice Allen, theatrical shot, page 89, commercial shot, page 166.*

Kevin McIntyre, 213/212-4277. $135 for one roll, $225 for two rolls, $300 for three rolls, negatives included. Travels to a location (i.e. the beach) for an additional minimal charge. Proof sheets in 24 to 36 hours. Kevin shoots headshots, fashion and music bands. "His ability to adapt to any pace and personality is complimented by his easygoing manner, the product intensely and simplistically captures the honest essence of a client." He is a natural light devotee and is recommended by many top agents.

Kevin Merrill, 818/508-4533. Three rolls $295, negatives included, two to four "looks"with clothing changes. $50 for extra roll at time of shoot. Uses natural and studio lighting. Black and white Polaroids. Make up, $100. Prints, $18. Works with many celebrities and familiar faces. I was very impressed by his proof sheets of Ben, there was not a bad shot on them. *See theatrical photo of Ben Dewell on page 91.*

Sean McCall, 310/820-4995. $250 for three rolls, three changes; 8x10s are at the lab's cost; you keep the negatives. Makeup is $75-$100. Sean specializes in fashion and commercial print, zed cards, catalogues, editorials and works as director of photography on commercials and features. If you are looking for an artistic 8x10, something different, talk to him. *See Janice Allen's theatrical shot, on page 88.*

Pamela Springsteen Photography, 323/874-9188. $500 for three rolls, no prints included; you keep the negatives. Each 8x10 is at lab cost. Makeup artist available. She shoots many celebrities and CD covers, works in a studio and starts with Polaroids. Pamela also directs music videos and short films. She's taken pictures of me and many of my students; her work is good, and she is fun to be with.

Alisha Tamburri, 818/998-8838. $295-$495. Makeup, $95. She begins with relaxation, your choice of music and a Polaroid. She directs, leads improvs and keeps the energy flowing so there's always something "going on" in the eyes. Her background in casting and personal management enhances her work, great with new people as well as celebs. Jae Ross of 20th Century Artists says, "Alisha Tamburri is the best!" Commercial agent Hugh Leon says, "My actors are getting more auditions after shooting with Alisha." I was impressed with the photography video she has produced; she will arrange for you to view it when meeting with her. *See Cynthia Kerr's theatrical shot on page 92 and commercial shot on page 164.*

Alan Weissman, 818/766-9797. 11288 Ventura Blvd., #G, Studio City, 91604. Web site: www.alanweissman.com. $350 + tax for two rolls, one 8x10. Additional 8x10s are $17. Makeup, $100. One roll is for sitcoms, comedic features and commercials. The second roll is for a more serious film and television look. Additional rolls are $125. The $125 roll is a "contempory film noir" look, flavor of the '40s. Alan lights everyone individually, using B&W Polaroids to get the right look. His mellow dog Rex welcomes everyone to the studio. He shoots many celebrities. I think he really serves the working, experienced actor; he can capture the look you want. *See photo of me with his '40s film noir look, page 85.*

Other Photographers With Good Reputations

Michael D'Ambrosia	310/444-7391
Elliot Photography	323/876-8821
Erin Fiedler	323-341-1897 - $200 for 3 rolls, including negs.
Bader Hower	310/472-8584
Robert Kazandjian	323/957-9575 - $125 a roll.
Harry Langdon	310/859-4900 Very high end, but spectacular.
Michael Papo Photography	818/760-8160
Cari Pike	310-288-6620
Marina Rice	310/859-4687
Maggie Smith	800/836-8678, a lovely person.
Adam Sheridan Taylor	323/954-1770

Waitress

Photographer
Charles Fretzin

Hair and Makeup
Rita Montanez

This is an unretouched photo. However, a retoucher can change the effect dramatically.

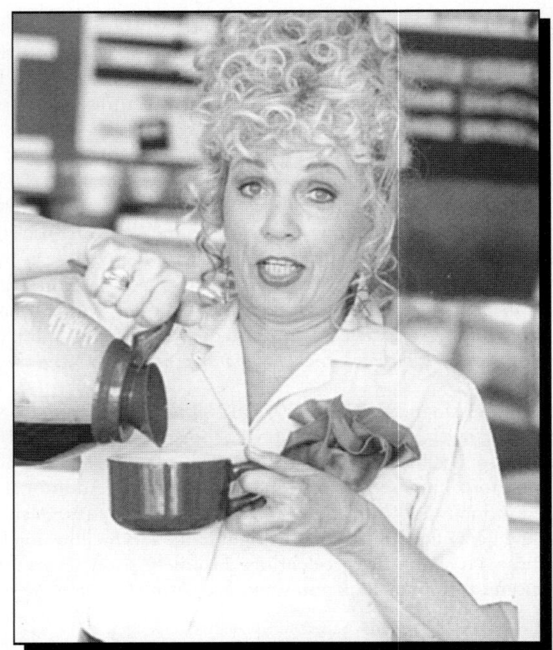

Nichan demonstrates. Notice the
- background
- face
- neck
- eyes
- coffee pouring out of the pot.

Photo Retouching

• **The photos you use for your head shot** should closely represent you. As you mature, your wrinkles will get you roles, but as a young person lines and shadows on your photos that look like wrinkles will hurt your chances of being called in for your age appropriate roles. Your retoucher can advise you according to what your specific needs are; the cost can range from $10 to $50 for an uncomplicated job. As always, get an estimate of the cost before proceeding.

• **I like to work personally with a retoucher**, for them to see me and for us to discuss my needs. Many photo labs offer retouching services but usually the clerk marks it and puts it in a stack, then you aren't a real person to the retoucher.

• **Nichan, master artist, retoucher.**

Q: Why get pictures retouched?

- **Once you convert the color reality** to a black and white print, blotches appear on the face which copy light and dark. There are shadows of light under the eyes exposing the depths of the wrinkles. We clean the shadow inside the line or wrinkle. We remove any blemishes or undesirable marks.

- **If the mouth is in-between** opening and closing we restore it to normal.

- **When a picture is out of focus,** we sharpen the eyes by adding more lashes and by adding white to the eye, and on the edge of the pupil.

- **If the hair looks thin** because the light hits it very strongly, we can add more detail. We can remove hair that is out of proportion or in the wrong place.

- **When the background is too distracting** or there's something missing, we can change it—even remove the whole background and put in a new one.

Q: How do you shop for a retoucher?

- **The best way is to see the retoucher's work and get the prices.** Your picture is something you are going to use for a couple of years. Five or 10 dollars over a two year span is not going to affect you that much.

Resources

Nichan Photographic Services, 323/467-5638. 5851 Melrose Ave., L.A., 90038, near Vine. M-F 10-6. Minimum is $25 a picture, some services available while you wait. Complete retouching services, his techniques are etching, bleaching, dyeing and airbrushing. Average is $40, unless there is a great deal of work to be done. He is indeed an artist and has been retouching for many years, the favorite of many photographers. *See examples: Michael Helm's photo of me on page 84, Diana Lannes shot of Cynthia Kerr on page 93 and Mary Ann Halpin's shot of Cynthia on page 93. See Diana's shot of Jackson, page 168.*

Mary Morano, 323/466-4079. 424 N. Larchmont, L.A., 90004. M-F 10-1 & 2-5. Minimum $25 for head shots. Call for appointment.

Multi Image, Gail Rudy, 323/466-1266. 1760 N. Hillhurst Ave. Suite E, Los Angeles, 90027. $12 minimum, free consultation. 2 day turnaround. Color, B&W retouching on head shots and any photos used for reproduction. Old photos restored. In business since 1977.

Cameron Murley, 818/760-6756. Flexible hours and turnaround time. Prices start at $10, average is $20 to $40. Full service retoucher, art background. Works on color, B&W; glossy and fiber based papers. Digital retouching available. Full satisfaction guaranteed. Can reconstruct bodies and faces. Restores and builds old photographs. Treats each picture as an art project.

Ray The Retoucher, 323/463-0555. 1330 N. Highland, Hollywood, 90028. M-F 8:30-7, Sa 10-4. Other locations in Studio City and Burbank. They use a bleach and dye technique for a natural photographic look. Airbrushing and digital imaging are used for extensive work such as adding a part of a shoulder or removing a background. $25 minimum, one to three day turnaround. *See Nancy Jo Gilchrists' theatrical photo of me on page 84 and her commercial photo on page 165.*

The Retouching Company, 818/842-4790. 3412½ W. Magnolia Blvd., Burbank, 91505. M-F 9-5. Very caring people, good work at a good price. $20 per hour for retouching; $40 per hour for air brushing. No minimum.

RJG Photo Retouching, Rodney Gottlieb, 310/202-0150. Los Angeles. B&W $55 an hour, color $60 an hour. $28 to $75 for the average 8x10. Airbrushing. For changing the background, taking fat off the face, removing flyaway hairs, the range is slightly higher. He will quote the price before he does the work. 20 years experience.

PHOTO LABS

For developing your film to proof sheets and 4x6 proof prints and to produce your border or borderless matte 8x10 masters, plus many other services. All of these labs except Xibit do multiple prints; see the picture reproduction section for that information. All labs listed take mail orders.

Resources

Isgo Lepejian Custom Photo Lab, 818/848-9001. 2411 W. Magnolia Blvd., Burbank, 91506, 1/2 block east of Buena Vista. M-F, 9-6. This place is my absolute favorite for the service. Orders may be taken at their smaller location, (323) 323/876-8085. 1145 N. La Brea Ave. Hollywood, 90038, 1/2 block north of Santa Monica. M-F, 10-6, Sa 11-4. Processing and 8 1/2 x11 proof sheet, $11, with 4x6 proof prints, $13-$17; in by 1:00 back by 4:30 same day. All 8x10 masters, 4-way bleed, white or sloppy borders are $11, if from a color negative, $15; back in 3 days. B&W and color digital imaging. They can repair or restore any photo. For instance, retouching can't remove tattoos but digital imaging can. They can tone prints sepia or any custom color. B&W print made from color slide is $25. Many of the photographers listed in the photography section say they are the best.

Nardulli, 323/882-8331. 1720 La Brea, Hollywood, 90046. M-F 8-10, Sa 9-4. Processing and proof sheet in 5 hours, $8. 11x14 proof sheet, $25.50. 16x20 proof sheet, $30.50. 8x10 master in three days, $13. All work is custom including bleeds, sloppy borders and border with lines. Top of the line.

Producers and Quantity Photo, 323/467-6178. 6660 Santa Monica Blvd., Los Angeles, 90038, two blocks east of Highland. M-F 8-5:30. B&W processing, $2.60 per roll; 8x10 proof sheet, $2.60; 11x14 proof sheet, $8; 16x20 proof sheet, $12; 20x24 proof sheet, $16. (They can make the larger proof sheets from your already developed negatives.) They say same day processing if you bring in before noon; after noon you get it the next day. Call to make sure they can deliver that day; my order took several days due to overload. 8x10 master, bleeds or borders, $6.50. They also do color processing.

Photo Impact, 323/461-0141. 931 N. Citrus Ave., Hollywood, 90038, north of Melrose & 1 block west of Highland. M-Th 8:30AM-9PM, Fr 8:30-6:30, Closed Sa, Su 1-9PM. Second location 310/449-8655. 2938 Nebraska, Santa Monica, 90404. M-F 9-7; closed between 12-1. Developing and proof sheet, $9.50. 11x14 proof sheet, $26, 16x20 proof sheet, $45. Film in by 8:30AM, out by 2:30PM; in by 12, out by 6; in by 4PM out by 8:45PM. Master 8x10, borders or borderless prints, $16, in 2 days. Premium enhanced masters, $26 in 2 days. "One-of-a-kind" print category.

Richard's Photo Lab, 323/939-8893. 7161 Beverly Blvd., Los Angeles, 90036, one block west of La Brea. M-F, 9-6. Processing and 8½x11 proof sheet, $7. In before 6, ready by 1 next day. 11x14 proof sheet, $7, next day by 3. Master for reproduction with border or any bleeds, $7.

Xibit Photo Lab, 323/933-2777. Michel Karman, 745 N. La Brea., Los Angeles, 90038. M-F 9-6PM. Creative gallery type prints toned. Their pictures are hand done, one at a time. This would be for a very special marketing tool, top of the line expense. An artist in what he does; art exhibitions in his lab.

PICTURE REPRODUCTION

• **Your original 8x10 master picture** must be of excellent quality. When you mass-produce the picture, quality is always lost; you cannot avoid it. Go to a duplication lab that specializes in photo reproduction. Most pictures will need to be retouched at least a little before you bring them in to be reproduced. *See Photo Retouching, page 98.* Always photocopy a few copies of your master so you will have something to give an interviewer, should the occasion arise before the lab is finished.

• **Take very good** protective care of your master and negative. If they get bent you will have to pay for another one. I keep each of mine with a piece of cardboard in an 8x10 labeled envelope, in a labeled folder in my file drawer. I am able to find my master and negative at a moment's notice.

• **Your 8x10 head shots** should be B&W and printed on photographic paper. The photographic paper choices are glossy, matte or pearl, with or without borders. Your duplication lab will show you what's available. The cheapest is glossy with borders which is definitely acceptable, though it doesn't fax well. Make a color photocopy to fax. The most expensive is pearl and borderless. Sometimes fancy borders cost more, especially the "sloppy" or "full frame" borders. These borders have the actual sprockets of the film showing and usually must be on your master when you take it to the reproduction house. Use what your agent wants or what you think will sell you and the picture best. Be creative, stand out.

• **Your next decision** is how many prints to run. If you have an agent, they will tell you how many they need. If you are looking for an agent, you may need two different photos reproduced, perhaps 50 of each. A new agent may want new pictures or new shots mastered and reproduced. Have enough run off to be able to submit yourself for jobs while shopping for an agent. Any picture is better than no picture.

• **If you are using great quantities** of 8x10s and are short on cash, then lithographs are an alternative to photographic paper. Lithographs can wash the master out and weaken your picture; they also fade over time, so shop for a lithographic printing place very carefully—their quality seems to be inconsistent. I have seen a few lithos that I thought were photographic paper. Have at least a few copies of your best head shot reproduced on photographic paper. Use these shots on special occasions when lithos or 3/4 shots are not the best choice for promoting yourself. Perhaps in the lobby of the theatre where you are in a play or doing a showcase. You will find uses for them when you are promoting yourself.

• **If you are very low on cash**, there are a couple of ways to photocopy your master. Go to a fine copy service and have a velox or halftone made of your master. You can use a small computer generated printout of your name and glue it in the corner of your master with nonpermanent paste. If you have had your master duplicated make the velox from one of the reproductions. This should cost $10. You can photocopy the velox on plain paper for five cents or card stock at 10 cents each. If you find a good deal on a color Xerox (used on the B&W setting) they make great copies. Trim the picture to 8x10 and attach your 8x10 resume with double stick tape or, less desirable, staples. If you copy the picture on card stock, you can copy your resume on the other side and trim as usual. There are some high quality copying machines that can give you a pretty good copy (when set for copying photos) straight from the master, if you can't afford the velox. Another low cost method: copy your master or reproduction on photographic paper— Simpson's Tahoe Gloss 100 lb., available at Kelly Paper, 323/957-1176, 844 N. La Brea, Los Angeles (and other locations). Have a caring person at a good copy place run the picture off. Then trim.

• **You will be able to use these copies** of your pictures when submitting through *Back Stage West/Drama-Logue* for plays, student films and nonunion productions, and your more expensive reproductions when submitting to an agent or director you want to impress. This technique is also a good way to reproduce a picture that you will seldom use because it is a very different look for you: with a beard, on a motorcycle, bungee jumping.

• **Some of my favorite copy places** for this process are Charlie Chan on Sunset 323/850-5407, and on Santa Monica near Crescent Heights 323/650-7699; Henry's at Gower & Sunset 323/464-7228; and Pink Copy Center 818/762-8100, Studio City and 818/783-4900, Sherman Oaks.

• **Your professional pictures** must have your name on the front. The photo reproduction service will do this for you. Don't put your agent's name on your pictures because if you change agents the pictures become obsolete. Your agent's and manager's information is always on your resume, which will be securely attached to the back of your picture. I believe it is important to write your phone number in pencil on the back of each of your pictures in case it gets separated from your resume.

• **When you pick up your pictures**, always carefully inspect the negative and prints before accepting them. I believe it's best to keep the master negatives in your possession. Labs have a way of going out of business or burning down. You will take better care of your negatives than anyone else. Of course, if you are not good at keeping things, let the lab store the negative.

• **Go to the places listed here and others.** Look at the papers and finishes and collect samples. Write the name of the lab and prices on the back of the sample picture and keep this in your picture reproduction file. This knowledge will be valuable because you will have pictures run for different uses. Have the reproduction lab do test shots. Test shots are several samples of what the finished reproduced picture will look like. Proof the shots and pick the exact skin tone and look you want. Your educated instinct will tell you which of the test shots is best. Doing test shots usually doubles the delivery time.

Photographic & Reproduction Terms

- **Border:** 1/4" or more of white around the picture.
- **Sloppy Border or Full Frame:** Shows sprockets of the film around the picture.
- **Bleed:** Picture covers all the paper.
- **Black Line:** Added to border around the picture.
- **Overlay:** White name on dark area or black name on white area of picture.
- **Litho Line:** Your name, or other information.
- **Line Negative:** Name in border of picture.
- **Copy Negative:** Negative made from master print.

Resources

FOR PHOTOGRAPHIC PAPER

These labs will all do mail order work for actors in other areas of the state and country. Call for details.

Argentum Photo Lab, 323/461-2775. 1050 Cahuenga Blvd., Hollywood, 90038. $70 for 100 prints plus $22 set up fee, borders and full bleed same price. I've heard very good reports about their work.

Duplicate Photo Lab, 323/466-7544. www.duplicate.com.1522 N. Highland Ave., Hollywood 90028. North of Sunset. M-F 9-6; Sa 9-1. Second location, 818/760-4193. 12606 Ventura Blvd., Studio City, 91604. 310/475-7531. 2180 Westwood Blvd., #2B, Los Angeles, 90025. Allow three working days for reproduction. For 200% more, they'll do it in one day. Get 8x10 border or full bleed with name. Border negative, including your name, $22.50. For 100 prints glossy $51; pearl $62. Borderless or full bleed negative with name overlay $27. For 100 prints of full bleed master: glossy $69; pearl $73. Pictures with a border are: glossy $51, pearl $62. Usually they can use negatives other labs have made especially with the glossy paper. $10 to run a test; add two days to the delivery time. Quality and service very good; I've used them for years.

Isgo Lepejian Photo-Digital Lab, 818/848-9001. 2411 W. Magnolia Blvd., Burbank, 91506, 1/2 block east of Buena Vista. M-F 9-6. Smaller location, 323/876-8085. 1145 La Brea, Hollywwod, 90038. M-F 10-6, Sa 11-4. Copy negative and name border or bleed is $22. For custom multiples of bleed, bordered prints on pearl or glossy paper, 100 for $75; 150 for $100; 200 for $130. If you get 200 or more, the copy negative and name price is $11. The quality is top of the line, I love them.

Photo Impact, 323/461-0141. 931 N. Citrus Ave., Hollywood, 90038, north of Melrose Blvd. and one block west of Highland. M-Th 8:30AM-9PM, F 8:30-6:30, Su 1-9. Second location 310/449-8655. 2938 Nebraska, Santa Monica, 90404, M-Th 9-7, F 9-6:30. When you bring in 8x10 master, copy negative is $25, your name is $8 with borders; borderless multiples are not available. On matte or glossy, 100 for $90; over 250, 60 cents each; over 500, 55 cents each. Tests are free of charge on all orders. Top of the line multiples.

Photo Farm, 323/650-5446. 903 N. Fairfax Ave., West Hollywood, 90046. M-F 10-5. You bring in your master to be reproduced; they do not develop film. Copy negative is $15, name plate with borders $7, name plate borderless $15, plus $70 to print 100 on pearl, matte and glossy papers. New orders take five working days, reorders three days.

Nardulli, 323/882-8331. 1720 N. La Brea, Hollywood, 90046. M-F 8-10, Sa 9-4. All work is custom. 10% discount for repeat customers. The tests are free and ready in three days, then two days to complete the run. Copy negatives with borders $12. Full bleed is $16.50. 100 copies on pearl or glossy are $70. Name overlay for borders is $10 and for bleed is $15. Total for first time run 100 border prints is $100; for 100 bleed prints, $106.50. Top of the line reproductions.

Producers and Quantity Photo, 323/467-6178. 6660 Santa Monica Blvd., Los Angeles, 90038, two blocks east of Highland. M-F 8-5:30. They do an average job for the price, but they are the fastest. If you are going there for the speed, call to make sure they guarantee to deliver them on time. Recently I was testing their quality and it took them five days to do reproductions for me. I have used them in the past to get pictures in an emergency. Leave your picture before noon one day and pick the reproductions up after 4:30 the next day. Copy negative and name with borders, $24. Full bleed and name overlay negative, $38. For 100 glossy prints with borders, $42; pearl, $52. Borderless glossy prints, $62; pearl $72. Test shots with borders glossy, $5, pearl, $5.50.

Quality Custom Photo Lab, 323/938-0174. 142 N. La Brea Ave., Los Angeles, 90036. M-F 9-6. You must bring in your 8x10 master print or 35mm negative. Negative with or without border is $20. Name on border picture is $10, overlay in the photo image is $17. Test run is $8. Test takes four days, two more days for the run. Great work on pearl or glossy medium weight paper. $70 per 100 prints.

Ray The Retoucher, 323/463-0555. 1330 N. Highland, Hollywood, 90028. M-F 9-7, Sa 10-4. Other locations in Studio City and Burbank. Free test prints, three day turnaround. Copy negative with name, $26. Can add a black line or sloppy borders for $11. $79 per 100, pearl, matte, glossy, border or borderless prints.

Richard's Photo Lab, 323/939-8893. 7161 Beverly Blvd., Los Angeles, 90038, one and a half blocks west of La Brea. M-F 9-6. For copy negative and your name, $18; to add a black line on border, $10. They only print pictures with borders. For 100 reproductions on pearl, $80, on glossy $70. They will do test prints at no charge when you order 250, otherwise test is $5. Test prints take two working days, prints two working days after test is okayed.

FOR LITHOGRAPHS:

Many lithograph companies do poor quality work. Shop around, look at their samples, ask for test shots. You must do this to assure the quality you need in order to present yourself as a professional. Those actors who put the extra effort and money into their careers are the ones who get the interviews.

Anderson Graphics, 818/909-9100. 6037 Woodman Ave., Van Nuys, 91408. Head shots or postcards are 100 for $55, set up is free. For each additional 100 add $15; this includes your name. They have been in business for years and have many services including 8½ x 11 composites with up to five pictures, two sides, $135 for 500. Cash, Master Charge or Visa at time of ordering. Takes 5 working days, including returning to proof your order before it's run. They do beautiful work but it is very important to proof your picture before it is run. When you are proofing the test shot, cross out their company name on the side of your picture. I don't believe in crediting them unless they will give you a price break to advertise them. They insist on keeping the copy negative; ask them to keep it indefinitely.

Image Starter, 310/854-0443. 1145 S. Sherbourne, Los Angeles, 90035. www.imagestarter.com. 100 for $65, 300 for $85, 500 8x10s for $99, 500 business cards for $50, 4x6 postcards, 300 for $50 500 for $60; 5x7 postcards 300 for $85, 500 for $99. Free name, negative and border. I love the unique resumes this company designs. I have seen the examples of their lithos and they look great. I have not used them myself but I have a feeling they are good. I will be giving them a try.

Final Print, 323/466-0566. 1958 N. Van Ness Ave., Los Angeles, 90068. One block north of Franklin, between Gower and Western. Other locations: 323/466-5404. 6305 Yucca at Vine, Suite 401, Los Angeles, 90028. 818/780-6467. 6308 Woodman Ave., Ste. 113, Van Nuys 91401. 310/306-1154. 4560 Admiralty Way, Bldg. 110, Ste. 7, Marina Del Rey 90291.M-F 9:30-4:30. Joycelyne Lew is the owner. $77.50 for 250 8x10s, includes the copy negative and borders of your choice. For 500 it's $99. Postcards are $65 for 500, and 500 business cards are $55. Visa, Mastercard, American Express, Discover and ATM. Work is guaranteed, they do not do any proofing. Many actors, managers and photographers have recommended them to me. Joycelyne is very proud of the quality she delivers, using state of the art equipment. She doesn't put her name on the side of the picture. They will keep your masters on file and mail out your work to you. They do Fan-grams for celebrities, pictures that talk.

Grand Prints, 818/763-5743. M-F 9;30-5:30. 100 for $60, 250 for $75, 500 for $105, 1000 for $165. Composites: add $15 for each additional picture. For back side resume printing $30 plus $15 per picture. The prices include negative, borders or bleeds, any lettering required, cropping, enlarging, reducing, color to B&W conversion and UPS delivery to your door. They charge $15 for adding a black line around the picture. For rescreening, which means if you've lost your master they are able to use a lithograph for a master, $10. 100 postcards, $60; 250, $75; 500, $100; 1000, $125. Picture business cards are 100 for $60; 500 for $70; 1000 for $110. Good prices and quality for picture cards. Husband and wife Jeff and Aviva Heston are actors and understand your needs; they are especially nice and very creative. Standard delivery time is two weeks, but rush orders are available. **If you request, they will not print their name on the picture.** They do not provide test shots but stand behind their quality and will redo your order if necessary. They keep the negative so your reorder will take just one week, or you can take the negative. You must pay for the pictures at the time of ordering. They think they have the lowest color prices in town; call for figures.

Signature, 323-962-8159. 1624 Cahuenga Blvd., Hollywood. For headshots: 200, $59; 300, $68; 500, $95. 500 post cards for $65. Prices includes set-up, border and name. They are the very fastest in town, nice owner. Photographer Rich Hogan highly recommends them.

Resumes

• **First and foremost,** your resume is selling you and it should represent you in a professional way. The purpose of your resume is to give the reader a brief description of you and your professional experience. You must have one to go along with your picture when you are seeking interviews and auditions.

Resume Form

- **At the top**, centered, put your name in bold letters
- **On the left side** of center in a column put
  Weight:
  Height:
  Hair: (color)
  Eyes: (color)
- **In the center** of the page under your name, include any union affiliations: SAG, AFTRA, AEA.
- **On the right side**, how to contact you: your agent's name and telephone number; if no agent, your home number with a machine or pickup type message service.
- **Do not** put your home address or age range on your resume.

Now comes the fun part—your experience and training. Always list the latest project first, then the others in chronological order.

- **List films first.** First column: film title; center column: billing, starring, supporting or featured; third column: the director. If you list a student film, put the name of the school instead of the director.
- **Television.** Left column: title of show; center column: billing; star, co-star, guest star, featured; right column: director.
- **Stage or Theater.** Left column: play; center column: character name (lead or supporting in parenthesis); right column: the name of the theater—unless the director is famous, then list both.
- **Training.** First, the teacher you are studying with currently; then any other acting teachers. You can list any speciality class, such as voice or commercials, and the teacher's name. Last, your degree and from what college.
- **Special skills**, including any foreign language, accents, dialects, any sports or training that might make you special—computers, medical lab, sharpshooting, pilot's license, CPR, etc.

• **You must have some type of message arrangement; if there is no answer, they will not call again.**

• **Also have call-waiting** on your phone; they will not call back if the line is busy. If call-waiting is unavailable or you don't like to interupt your calls, have two phone lines that ring on a rotary when one line is busy. Telephone companies offer a digital voice mail system that will answer the line while you are talking on it. The caller will never hear a busy signal. Then list your home phone number or what will sound like your home number (when it is answered) to your caller. You can also put a cell phone or pager number on your resume, but be sure to identify it as such. (P:, B:, VM:, CELL, etc)

• **If you have not acted professionally**, in place of Film/Television/Stage, put Acting Workshop Scenes and list scenes and characters you have performed in acting class. Now look for credits to put on your resume; student films and plays are a way for your resume to grow rapidly.

• **It can take two years** (after obtaining your union cards and agent) for your resume to reach a fairly comfortable professional place. It does grow! The process is fun.

• **Sylvester Stallone's** pre-Rocky resume credits: *A Party at Kitty and Stud's,* 1970; *Bananas* (unbilled bit), 1971; *The Lords of Flatbush,* 1974; *The Prisoner of Second Avenue* (bit), 1975; *Capone,* 1975; *Death Race 2000,* 1975; *Farewell My Lovely,* 1975; *Cannonball,* 1976; *No Place To Hide,* 1976; *Rocky* (writer and actor), 1976. No wonder he had nothing in the fridge. The legend goes that he turned down $250,000 for his *Rocky* script and got very little for it in order to act in the movie. The reason he wrote the script was to get a break as an actor in the biz, and he didn't sell out.

• **Harrison Ford's early resume**: *Dead Heat on a Merry-Go-Round,* 1966; *Long Ride Home,* 1967; *Luv,* 1967; *Zabriskie Point,* 1970; *Getting Straight,* 1970; *American Graffiti,* 1973 (memorable but too small to lead to anything other than more character work); *The Conversation,* 1974 (just a few moments but very daring); *Heroes,* 1977; *Star Wars,* 1977—this is the role that led to his many leading man roles.

• **Michael Keaton**: *Night Shift,* 1982; *Mr. Mom,* 1983; *Gung-Ho,* 1986; *Batman,* 1989; and then the big time.

• **Some copy services will typeset** and laser-print your resume. There are many services that advertise in *Back Stage West/Drama-Logue*; I've listed a couple in the resources on page 113. If you are computer savvy, typeset and laser print your own resume. Your resume must be trimmed to 8x10 to fit on the back of your 8x10 picture.

• **Have just a few resumes** photocopied each time (you'll be adding things often) unless you're sending out a large mailing. Copy places charge more to use color paper, if you are using color paper it is cheaper if you provide your own. Ask them to charge you the rate for white copies. *See resources, page 112 for paper.*

• **Always have your resumes cut** to 8x10 so they will fit on the back of your 8x10 picture. Attach the resume back to back to your picture, facing out. Use double-stick tape, spray glue or staples. When you staple, do it from the picture side and hide the staples in the borders so they won't draw the viewer's eye away from your face. Place two on top and two on the bottom about two inches from the left side so when a three-hole punch is used, the picture and resume will go into the punch easily. *Never submit a resume that is not cut-down to the exact size of the picture.*

• **When submitting your package** for a particular role, put a post-it note on your picture with the name of the role you want to audition for. Also put the name of the role on the outside of the envelope. A cover letter is not necessary, unless there is particular reason why you are right for the role.

• **At all times keep pictures**, resumes, and a roll of double-stick tape or stapler in a zippered briefcase in your car! You may get a job because your pictures and resumes are with you.

• **Alex Stone, a 25 year veteran of film and TV**, talks about picture and resume submission packages.

Q: What are some tips to help actors gain interviews?

- **The casting person** will get a huge stack of submissions, so you have about a second for your photo to grab their eye. The choice of a good photographer is crucial: the money you spend there is never wasted. After that, good reproductions. The resume is important. It should be truthful, factual, neat, clean, and the same size as the picture.

- **Some resumes are almost unreadable** because of poor typewriters, exotic computer typefaces or faded xerox copies. One actor listed a special skill as "requitball." Typos or misspellings are not acceptable. You must have a professional looking resume. Duplicate your resumes on light colored paper. Avoid bright orange, red or green; a casting person may need another copy of your resume and these colors won't fax or copy well.

- **A lot of people use the "special skills" as icebreakers.** It's an excellent technique because the more odd skills you have, the more chance you get to talk to the casting person.

- Fine art
- Sign language
- Canoeing
- Baton twirling
- Nursing
- Wire welding
- Skydiving
- Bartending
- CPR
- Dog showing
- Sculpture
- Trampoline
- Chainsaw and wood splitting
- Accents and weird noises
- California State Champion Cheerleader
- Beijing opera dance techniques (If I had this person in the office, I'd say, "Tell me about Beijing".)

- For *Dracula,* they were casting people who could speak a middle-eastern language, not just put on the accent. An actress got a role because she knew enough words to string together and they liked the sound.

Resources

Xpedx Paper & Graphics, M-F 7:30-5. 818/409-0077. 1220 Air Way, Glendale, 92101. 818/785-4237. 6947 Hayvenhurst Ave., Van Nuys, 91406. 310/478-4026. M-F 7:30-5; Sa. 8-1.They have a great selection of papers. I like to pick out my own and not be restricted to just what the copy service provides.

Kelly Paper, M-F 7:30-5. Sa 9-1. Many locations, local and out of state, some are: 323/957-1176. 844 N. La Brea, Los Angeles, 90038. 818/843-0393. 724 Flower St., Burbank, 91502. 818/764-0850. 12641 Saticoy St., No. Hollywood, 91605. 310/452-7590. 1601 Olympic Blvd., Los Angeles, 90404.

Staples Office Superstore, 800/333-3330 for locations. Many stores in the L.A. area.

Staples stores provide business services: photocopying, printing, faxing, envelopes and paper.

RESUMES

See Working Actor's Guide and Back Stage West for many other places.

Imagestarter Resume Design, specializing in Photo Resumes, 310/854-0443. Standard resume, $54; photo resume, $89. Michael Barak developed this unique style of using a photo on the resume—I love it. Works equally well for newcomers and seasoned professionals. Their guarantee: "We're so sure you'll like our work that we offer unlimited proofs to ensure you get the results you paid for, plus our exclusive 100% money back guarantee, which means that if you're not completely satisfied, you pay nothing!" They accept mail orders.

- *See the examples of the photo resume on page 117 and in the commercial section on page 170.*

Smart Girl Productions, 323/850-5778. Melody Jackson creates resumes and other marketing tools for actors and writers. $25, walk out with it in 1/2 an hour.

BOOKS

Order through Samuel French Bookstore 323/876-0570.

Actor's Resumes, The Definitive Guidebook by Richard Devin.
The Actor's Picture/Resume Book by Jill Charles with photographer Tom Bloom.

JODE LEIGH EDWARDS

SAG

METROPOLITAN TALENT AGENCY 323.857.4500

VOICE MAIL/PAGER: 818.000.0000

FILM		DIRECTORS
Sour Grapes	Supporting	Larry David (CastleRock)
What Do Women Want?	Lead	Guy Shalem (Exposure Films)
Tropic of Oz	Lead	Richard Bailey (Compone Prod)
Sometime Girl	Lead	Roye Segal (USC)
TELEVISION		
Beverly Hills, 90210	Guest-Star	Kim Friedman (FOX)
Touched By An Angel	Guest-Star	Sandor Stern (CBS)
Fired Up	Co-Star	Jeff Melman (NBC)
Tornado (Mow)	Co-Star	Noel Nosseck (FOX)
Weird Science (2 episodes)	Featured	David Grossman (USA)
THEATRE (Touring*)		
Sleeping Beauty*	Little One*	Dallas Children's Theatre*
A Clearing in the Woods	Ginna	Theatre 3 Below
Tapes	Mercedes	KD Studio
Weekend Comedy	Jill	Prairie House
Caution: Deaf Children at Play	Jenny	Main Street Theatre
The Effect of Gamma Rays on Man-in-the-Moon Marigolds	Beatrice	KD Studio
A Funny Thing Happened on the Way to the Forum	Philia	CRT
This Property is Condemned	Willie	CRT
Naomi in the Living Room	Johnna	University of Texas

COMMERCIAL

Conflicts Available Upon Request

TRAINING

Scene Study: Michelle Danner (Larry Moss Studio)
Judy Kerr's Acting Workshop
Commercial: Beverly Long
KD Studio Actor's Conservatory of the Southwest
Associate of Applied Arts (Scholarship)
Scene Study, Film Technique, Stage Combat, Voice/Diction, Commercial Technique, Shakespeare, Mime, Script Analysis

SPECIAL SKILLS

Kickboxing, Volleyball, Basketball, Softball, Hiking, Cycling, Jogging, Swimming, Southern Accent

*1/2" demo tape available

Jode Leigh Edwards has been in Los Angeles a couple of years. She studied and worked in Dallas, Texas before moving here. See Diary: Actress Living Her Dream in Los Angeles, on page 231, for her daily acting career activities for the first three months in Los Angeles and then a two-week sample of her current activities. Jode designed this resume on her computer.

ELI SCHWARTZ

HEIGHT: 5'3"
WEIGHT: 108
HAIR: Brown
EYES: Brown

213/ 555-5555

Films

SNAPSHOTS	Supporting	USC

Theater

THE MIRACLE WORKER	Helen Keller	Fl., Katy Award
WATER ON THE MOON	Leading	F.A.T.E. Theatre
LOVERS & OTHER STRANGERS	Leading	Florida
BYE BYE BIRDIE	Leading	Florida
THE SOUND OF MUSIC	Leading	Maine
YOU'RE A GOOD MAN CHARLIE BROWN	Leading	Maine
THE PRIME OF MISS JEAN BRODIE	Leading	Maine
OLD JED PROUTY OF BUCKSPORT MAINE	Leading	Maine
LETTERS TO KELSO	Leading	Maine
BRIGHTON BEACH MEMOIRS	Supporting	Florida
110° IN THE SHADE	Supporting	Maine
THE MIRACLE WORKER	Supporting	Maine
OLIVER!	Supporting	Maine

Industrial Films

CHILD ABUSE PREVENTION
CPR TRAINING
CAR/BIKE ACCIDENTS

Training

Judy Kerr's Acting Workshop, Class Assistant

Special Skills

Competitive Gymnastics: Bars, Floor, Tumbling
Unicycle Riding, Snow & Water Skiing
Firearms
Drawing, Painting, Singing, Piano
Bartending and Waitressing
Various Southern Dialects, New York accent, British accent

Eli Schwartz, 22 years old, new to Los Angeles and just starting to get film work. Meanwhile, she stresses her theater background and her leading roles in major shows out of town. Designed on home computer.

Will Estes

Don Buchwald & Associates
323/655-7400

Feature Films

		Directors
Terror Tract	Lead	Clint Hutchison
U-571	Lead	Jonathan Mostow
Blue Ridge Fall	Lead	James Rowe
The Road Home	Lead	Dean Hamilton
Dutch	Supporting	Peter Fairman

Television

Kelly Kelly	Series Regular	WBN/Caplan/LaPan/Kendall
Diagnosis Murder	Guest Star	CBS/Viacom
Meego	Series Regular	CBS/Miller/Boyette/Warren
Secret World of Alex Mack	Guest Star/5 episodes	NICK/Lynch Ent.
Kirk	Series Regular	WBN/Bickley/Warren
Full House (2 episodes)	Guest Star	ABC/Miller/Boyette
Boy Meets World (2 episodes)	Guest Star	ABC/Disney Studios
Step By Step	Guest Star	ABC/Bickley/Warren
It Had To Be You	Series Regular	CBS/Lorimar

Training

Kevin McDermott, Center Stage L.A.
Judy Kerr, Private Coaching
Diane Hill Hardin's Young Actors Studio
Improvisational Theatre, Music Center ON TOUR Program

Special Abilities

Gymnastics, Surfing, Motorcycling,
Swimming (Ocean Jr. Life Guard), Sailing,
Basketball, Baseball
Brazilian Jiu Jitsu

Will Estes is now 21, he started working in commercials at age 9 and has made the transition from child to adult actor. See his interview in *Child Actors, Section Eight.* His resume looks low key but he has a powerful mid-level agent and has had several starring roles in movies. He recently spent several months on location in Italy.

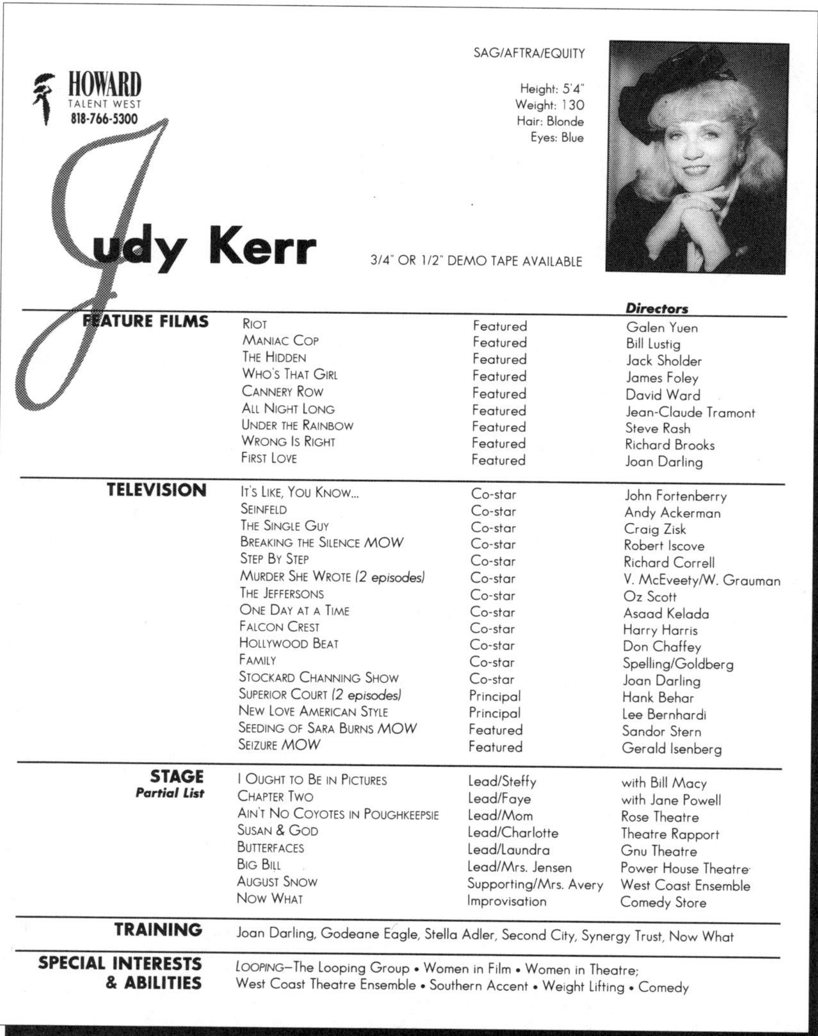

HOWARD
TALENT WEST
818-766-5300

SAG/AFTRA/EQUITY

Height: 5'4"
Weight: 130
Hair: Blonde
Eyes: Blue

Judy Kerr

3/4" OR 1/2" DEMO TAPE AVAILABLE

			Directors
FEATURE FILMS	Riot	Featured	Galen Yuen
	Maniac Cop	Featured	Bill Lustig
	The Hidden	Featured	Jack Sholder
	Who's That Girl	Featured	James Foley
	Cannery Row	Featured	David Ward
	All Night Long	Featured	Jean-Claude Tramont
	Under the Rainbow	Featured	Steve Rash
	Wrong Is Right	Featured	Richard Brooks
	First Love	Featured	Joan Darling
TELEVISION	It's Like, You Know...	Co-star	John Fortenberry
	Seinfeld	Co-star	Andy Ackerman
	The Single Guy	Co-star	Craig Zisk
	Breaking the Silence *MOW*	Co-star	Robert Iscove
	Step By Step	Co-star	Richard Correll
	Murder She Wrote *(2 episodes)*	Co-star	V. McEveety/W. Grauman
	The Jeffersons	Co-star	Oz Scott
	One Day at a Time	Co-star	Asaad Kelada
	Falcon Crest	Co-star	Harry Harris
	Hollywood Beat	Co-star	Don Chaffey
	Family	Co-star	Spelling/Goldberg
	Stockard Channing Show	Co-star	Joan Darling
	Superior Court *(2 episodes)*	Principal	Hank Behar
	New Love American Style	Principal	Lee Bernhardi
	Seeding of Sara Burns *MOW*	Featured	Sandor Stern
	Seizure *MOW*	Featured	Gerald Isenberg
STAGE *Partial List*	I Ought to Be in Pictures	Lead/Steffy	with Bill Macy
	Chapter Two	Lead/Faye	with Jane Powell
	Ain't No Coyotes in Poughkeepsie	Lead/Mom	Rose Theatre
	Susan & God	Lead/Charlotte	Theatre Rapport
	Butterfaces	Lead/Laundra	Gnu Theatre
	Big Bill	Lead/Mrs. Jensen	Power House Theatre
	August Snow	Supporting/Mrs. Avery	West Coast Ensemble
	Now What	Improvisation	Comedy Store

TRAINING Joan Darling, Godeane Eagle, Stella Adler, Second City, Synergy Trust, Now What

SPECIAL INTERESTS & ABILITIES *Looping*–The Looping Group • Women in Film • Women in Theatre; West Coast Theatre Ensemble • Southern Accent • Weight Lifting • Comedy

This is my resume, created by Michael Barak of Imagestarter Resume Design. The industry response to these photo resumes has been excellent. (See the commercial resume on page 170.) I chose this '40s style picture by Alan Weissman, makeup and hair by Rita Montanez, to show a different look from my usual 8x10s.

PRINTING AND PHOTOCOPYING

• **A valuable relationship** can be built with your reproduction people. They will be very helpful in the promotion of your career.

• **In the printing department**, you can have postcards printed with your picture and a space for a message. Have five hundred or a thousand printed blank and then when you want to print a message, you can just run off five or a hundred, whatever you need, or handwrite short "thank you for the interview" notes. Let people on your mailing list know what you are doing or wish them a "merry new TV season" or any other idea you come up with. Print your picture and resume on book mark size cards or on cards the size of business envelopes. I believe its best to mail these in envelopes so they don't get messed up in the mail. They are opened and look good lying on the desk. Agent Bonnie Howard loves these.

• **Have picture business cards made up**. I always keep the masters in case I want to use the small velox (picture) on flyers and other pieces of advertising.

• **When you do a play or showcase**, send out flyers or cards to let casting directors know you are acting somewhere. Even if they never attend, your name and picture cross their desk. It is good to send something to all the casting directors once or twice a year. The best times, I believe, are mid-July, the beginning of the television shooting season, and mid-January, the start of pilot season.

• **A very clever actress** printed 8½ x 11 white mailing envelopes with an inch and a half by three inch imprint of her eyes in the lower right hand corner with "look into my eyes..." underneath them.

• **You can design your own note cards** with a picture on the front and then open it up to write inside. Christopher Paul Ford sent my favorite. It was a great picture of him printed vertically, his name and phone number in black in the bottom border. In the left corner, in white, it says, *The journey of ten thousand miles begins with a single phone call.—Confucius Bell.* Clever, fun and inventive.

Resources

Alpha Printing & Graphics, 310/273-9460. 9030 West Sunset Blvd., West Hollywood, 90069. They scanned my resume and put my agent's logo on it, printed 200 copies and trimmed them for $9.65. Seemed like a good bargain, and it only took ten minutes with validated parking.

Bob The Printer, 818/754-0081. 11002 Magnolia Blvd., North Hollywood, 91601. 818/754-0081, 3760 Cahuenga Blvd. West, Universal City, 91608. Complete business printing, script copies, color copies, full and self serve copying, faxing, mail boxes. Very helpful, big busy place.

Charlie Chan, 323/650-7699. 8267 Santa Monica Blvd., West Hollywood, 90046. Also 3233/850-5407. 7402 Sunset Blvd., L.A. 90046. M-F 8:30-6, Sa 9-5. Self or full-service copying, offset printing, computers and laser printers for customer's use. Friendly, helpful, fast service. Talk to general manager, Alex, for your special printing needs and designs; postcards, business cards, flyers, velox and halftones, etc.

Copymaster, 323/467-6111. 1553 Cahuenga Blvd., Hollywood, 90028. M-F 9-6. Printing only, no photocopying. Very helpful. Great postcards and business cards.

Copymat, 323/461-1222. 6464 Sunset Blvd., Hollywood, 90028. At Wilcox.M-F 8-Midnight, Sa & Su 9-7. Color, oversize and laser copies; high-speed duplicating; professional binding; self-service typing and worldwide fax service.

Henrys, 323/ 464-7228. 6110 Sunset Blvd., Hollywood at Gower Gulch. M-F 8:30-6, Sa 9-5. Self or full-service copying, offset printing, Friendly, helpful, fast service.

Input/Output, 323/654-0707. 7313 Sunset Blvd., Hollywood. MAC or IBM Computers to rent $25 an hour. $25 an hour to scan photos or copy with a 15 minute minimum. They help you input to their printers; help beyond that is $60 an hour. 1800 DPI laser prints up to 11x17.

Kinko's, Many locations. Open 24 hours, 7 days a week. I find, in general, their photocopying work is not up to my standards but with their 24 hours, in an emergency, they have saved me. Where I find they do have excellent services is in their computer departments. The employees are knowledgeable and helpful, the computers work well. In the largest stores they can print out 11 x 17 Canon Firey prints which will give you an idea of what your Pantone colors will look like. You can design there or bring in your disks with the fonts loaded and print out the work you've done on your computer. The computer department is not open 24 hours. All of the locations do not have big departments; my favorite store is on Ventura Blvd., in Encino next to Jerry's Deli.

Legal Source, 310/837-7707. 3000 S. Robertson Blvd., Suite 135, West Los Angeles, 90034. 24 hours a day. They specialize in large copy projects, microfilming, exhibit-board design and enlargements.

New Image Copy Printing, 323/876-1102. 7109 Sunset Blvd. at La Brea, Hollywood, 90046. M-F 9-7; Sa 9-6. Also lithos.

Pink Copy Center, 818/762-8100. 12080 Ventura Place #2 (Laurel Canyon & Ventura Blvd.) Studio City, 91604. 818/783-4900. 14762 Ventura Blvd., Sherman Oaks, 91403. Copying, printing, color copying, digital (Fiery) output, digital b/w copying. They give a discount to actors. They will copy a message on your picture postcards at a cheaper cost than having them printed. Very helpful.

Staples Office Superstore, 800/333-3330 for locations. Many stores in the L.A. area. Many are open 24 hours a day.

UNIONS

• **Until you join a union**, there are no restrictions. There are many opportunities for work that are nonunion. They may not be under the best conditions, and the pay will certainly be lower, but take a look at the ads for work in *Back Stage West/Drama-Logue* and see if you are really ready to give up all these opportunities of gaining audition experience, the possibility of getting good film on yourself, building a reputation, and networking.

• **Don't be persuaded by other actors'** impatience to join a union. You have your priorities for yourself; you are building a career. That means study, developing an audition tape, and having a resume with legitimate credits and experience on it.

• **When you are starting out** and don't have an audition tape, in all likelihood you will not be able to land an agent even if you are in the Screen Actors Guild. It is easier to get a job on a nonunion project than on a SAG film. Do your nonunion work and your nonsignatory student films now. Those young film makers are trying to get into their respective guilds too. A few years down the line the producers and directors who hire you for student and nonunion productions will be hiring you for union productions.

• **When you are SAG eligible**, you can put SAG on your resume. You will be in the SAG computer as a "must join." When you land a SAG speaking role you will have to go in and pay your initiation fee and dues. Make sure you have that $1,200 available or you will lose the part.

• **When you have your experience, tape and resume**, your next goal will be to join SAG and there are several ways to do that, described below under the SAG listing.

• **I want to warn you** about some schemes actors have used to get into SAG using false credentials. These unlawful plans can get you barred from the union forever, besides costing you a lot of money.

• **Make it a habit** to call all the union hot lines. Even if you are not a member, there may be the perfect job you could fill. If you know about the job, try to get an interview and possibly get the job. The hot lines are recorded information and operate 24 hours a day. It's good to get in the habit of checking them once or twice a week.

• **If you have decided** you must live your life as a professional actor, there are benefits for joining the American Federation of Television and Radio Artists, AFTRA, as soon as you can afford it. *See the AFTRA listing below.*

• **If you plan to do game shows**, get your AFTRA card first so you will be paid for appearing. The shows don't seem to mind at all if you are union and you'll receive union scale payment for your appearance. The real bonus is: after belonging to AFTRA for one year, that work on the game show will make you eligible for SAG.

• **Most people reading this book** are not concerned with the SAG employment status known as "financial core," but I want to talk about it for a moment to dispel some rumors I've heard. Call the union if you have any questions. If you live in a right-to-work state and are not a member of the union, you may work both union and nonunion jobs. If you are a member of SAG you may not do nonunion work even in a right-to-work state. Taking a financial-core status means you pay 80% of your dues but you are not a member of the union and you can't put it on your resume. It is a very drastic step and you cannot rejoin. Investigate carefully what your advantages may be. I would strongly advise against it.

• **Thoughts** on actors being Taft-Hartleyed into SAG.

  • **Taft-Hartley is a labor law** that basically says that you cannot force a person to join a union just because they did one job. If you go for a second union job, you are saying to everyone, "Hey, I'm interested in this as a profession." Now you have to join the union.

- **It is a catch-22.** You have to be in the union to get a job, and you have to have a job to join the union. SAG rules say that as long as they read 25 actors for a role, the production company will not be fined for giving a nonunion actor a job. If you are on a set and the director decides someone has to say a line and there is no time for casting, they can give you the line, a SAG contract and wages for the day. It is done through the Taft-Hartley Law. You can get your SAG card as soon as the paperwork is in the computer at the union.

Screen Actors Guild

Screen Actors Guild, SAG, 323/954-1600. www.sag.com. 5757 Wilshire Blvd., Los Angeles, 90036. (between Fairfax and La Brea) M-F 9-5. *See Out of State Resources for listings in other states.*

• **SAG covers motion pictures,** filmed television and most commercials, regulating working conditions and processing residual payments for reuse. SAG also franchises agents, who must sign an agreement that requires ethical conduct. They must also agree to a maximum of 10% commission on an actor's salary. There are more than 500 agents nationwide.

Requirements to join SAG: 323/549-6772
• **An actor must present a letter** from a SAG producer stating that the applicant is wanted for a principal or speaking role in a specific film or commercial.
• **If the actor is a paid-up member** of AEA, AFTRA, SEG, AGVA or the American Guild of Musical Artists (AGMA) for one year or longer and has worked as a principal performer in that union's jurisdiction at least once, he/she may join or "cross over" to SAG.
• **An actor, being paid** with a SAG voucher, who accumulates three days of employment as an extra on SAG projects, becomes eligible to join.

• **The cost to join** SAG is around $1,200. You must pay all of this with cash, money order, cashier's check or credit card. Yearly dues are $100 minimum, then charged on a sliding scale depending on your earnings. Also after hitting that magical $7,500/ $12,500 levels, you will become eligible for health insurance and begin earning your retirement benefits after paying in for 10 years.

• SAG **pay scale:**
These rates are all for an 8-hour day;
after that there is time-and-a-half and double-time.
- **Film:** day player $596; weekly $2,070.
- **Low-budget features:**
Day player $466; weekly $1,620.
- **Television** 3-day rate:
30 or 60-minute TV show $1508;
90-minute or 2-hour show $1776.
- **Commercial** pay scale is $480 weekdays
- **Extra rate** to 6/30/00 $95, then to 6/30/01 $100, then to 2002 $105, 2003 $110, 2004 $115. ; stand-ins make $115, by 2004 $130.
Commercial extras and stand-ins make $260.

You can find much of the information you may want on line at: www.sag.com.

Agents List, 323/549-6733.
Child Actor Hotline, 323/549-6030.
Hot Line, for casting information, 323/937-3441.
Casting Seminars and Showcases, 323/549-6540.
Online: www.sag.com or www.sag.org. Check whether your name is available when you are ready to join.
Membership Services, 323/549-6778.
SAG **Agency Department**, 323/549-6737. Locate actors' agents here.

• AFTRA-SAG **Credit Union**, 323/461-3041. Join as soon as you become a member of an actors' union. You might as well start building your credit with them. They have savings, checking and a Visa cards.

• **There is an important bulletin board** in the lobby of the SAG building. Actors find scene partners, roommates, sublets, housesitters, used cars, rides to New York, Chicago and other destinations and news about special events and discounted theater tickets. Recent postings saw the formation of a running club and a Shakespeare Reading Circle.

• **Franchised Agent List** is free to members and costs $3 in check or money order payable to SAG for nonmembers.

• SAG **Conservatory**, 323/856-7736. $10 a year for SAG members. Free classes and seminars. Your pictures are put in their casting books for student films at the American Film Institute.

American Federation of Television and Radio Artists

American Federation of Television and Radio Artists, AFTRA, 323/634-8100. 5757 Wilshire Blvd., Suite #900, Los Angeles, 90036. M-F 9-5:30. *See Out of State Resources, page 500 for offices in other cities.*

• AFTRA **covers** radio, live and taped television shows including daytime soaps. Actors, dancers, news people, singers, disc jockeys, sports casters, announcers, specialty acts, phonograph recordings and stunt people are covered.

• **To join**, you have to sign the application for membership and pay in cash, cashier's check or credit card, about $1000. The dues are $100 minimum a year, then a sliding scale depending on your earnings.
Some of the shows that use AFTRA actors are *The Bold and the Beautiful, Days of our Lives, General Hospital, Port Charles, Sunset Beach, The Young and the Restless, City Guys, Hang Time, Malibu, One World, Saved By The Bell, The New Class, Rude Awakening, Mad TV.*

• **After being a member** of AFTRA for a year and after having a role with lines on an AFTRA show, you are eligible to join SAG. When you join AFTRA, you will receive a list of all the AFTRA shows you'll be eligible to work on, as well as a list of agents who are franchised by AFTRA.

• **You can send for a "Show Sheet"** which lists the television shows that work under an AFTRA contract. Send a self-addressed stamped envelope (55 cents) and put on the outside envelope Attn: Show Sheet.

AFTRA union scale pay rates:

- **On-camera day player on network sitcom or stunt performer:**
  $576 for one day
  $1,457 for three days
  $2,000 for five days
- 30 minute soap opera daily $466
- 60 minute soap opera daily $621
- **5 lines or less**
  60 minute program $321
  30 minute program $260
  30 minute daytime $235
  60 minute daytime $288
- **Extra daily rates:**
  - **General extra** network sitcom $80; 30 minute serial $99, 60 minute serial $128

AFTRA/SAG Credit Union, 323/461-3041. 6922 Hollywood Blvd., Hollywood, 90028. M-F 9-4. Have your residuals automatically deposited in your savings account.

AFTRA Extras Casting File. This is a file of pictures and resumes of paid-up members of the L.A. local who are available to do extra and stand-in work on AFTRA programs. Producers and Casting Representatives call and request names and home telephone numbers from the file. To submit, send your picture and resume to Extra File, c/o AFTRA or drop them off at the Membership counter.

AFTRA Roster of Franchised Agents, Nationwide, is available to all members. To receive one write to: Agency Department, AFTRA National Office, 260 Madison Avenue, 7th Floor, New York, NY 10016.

Actors Equity Association

Actors Equity Association, AEA, also called Equity, 323/634-1750. www.actorsequity.org. 5757 Wilshire Blvd., Los Angeles, 90036. *Other cities in Out of State Resources.*

• **Equity covers** principals, dancers, singers, chorus and stage managers in live theater. The initiation fee is $800. Dues are $39 twice a year—$5 less if you belong to another union.

• **To join Equity**, you have to have an Equity contract job. They will give you the papers to sign up on your first day of rehearsal for an Equity show and deduct the initiation fee from your pay. Even if you aren't a member, check the hot line because it sometimes is easier to get an interview for an Equity job than it is for the other unions, and they do see non-union people.

• **Union members** interested in access to Equity auditions may receive an eligibility card by applying through the Equity office well in advance.

• **You may wonder why actors would run for office to serve in their union.**
SAG top salaries for fiscal year ending 8/31/95.

Ken Orsatti, National executive director	$219,231
John McGuire, Associate national director	$178,366
Leonard Chasman, Hollywood director	$142,692
John Sucke, New York director	$132,500
Mel Karl, Southeast director	$117,212

NETWORKING: CHARITIES, CHURCHES AND ORGANIZATIONS

• **Increase your friendship circles** and social involvements. If you are not naturally a socially involved person, then this will be another thing you will have to learn to do. Look for places within the show biz community where you can feel comfortable networking. Clubs or restaurants you frequent, tennis courts, such as Plummer Park, gyms, acting class, dance classes, charity volunteer, baseball or bowling teams, seminars, workshops, etc.

• **The more people you know in the business**, the more likely you are to get a phone call from someone who wants you to work on a project. We all like to work with people we know and who are fun to be with. Also, by talking about the business, you pick up news and hints that will help you with your acting and career.

• **Publicist Joyce Schwarz** suggests attending or working at one charity event each month. Choose a charity that is close to your heart.

Resources

• **CHARITIES**

AIDS Project Los Angeles, 323/993-1600. They offer legal, medical, financial and psychological aid.

Actors and Others for Animals, 818/971-7059.

Heal the Bay, 800/Heal-Bay. Memberships start at $25. Fighting for a swimmable, fishable, surfable Santa Monica Bay.

Los Angeles Society For The Prevention Of Cruelty To Animals, 323/730-5300. Bathe, groom and play with animals; general help.

Meals On Wheels, 310/208-3439. Provides meals to the elderly.

PAWS (Pets Are Wonderful Support), 323/876-7297. Provides pet care for ill people with pets.

Portals, 213/387-1129. Helps lead mentally ill homeless back into the mainstream through permanent housing and job training.

Project Angel Food, 323/845-1800. Provides meal delivery to incapacitated people with terminal illnesses.

Union Rescue Mission, 213/628-6103. Provides food, shelter and clothing to the homeless. Need servers for Thanksgiving and Christmas.

• CHURCHES

Bel-Air Presbyterian Church, 818/788-4200. 16221 Mulholland Dr., L.A., 90049. Many programs for all ages of people, great singles groups, spectacular location and building.

Church On The Way, 818/779-8000, 14300 Sherman Way, and 14800 Sherman Way, Van Nuys. At Sherman Way and Van Nuys Blvd., Pentacostal Christian.

First Baptist Church of Beverly Hills, 310/276-3978. 9025 Cynthia St., Beverly Hills, 90210. Lots of actors and people in the business; very active membership.

First Presbyterian of Hollywood, 323/463-7161. 1760 N. Gower, Hollywood. 90028. Pastor Lloyd John Ogilvie is very well known. Great Choir. Lots of programs.

Grace Community, 818/782-5920. 13248 Roscoe Blvd., Sun Valley, 91352. Between Coldwater and Woodman. Fundamental Christian.

Kabbalah, 310-657-5404. 1062 South Robertson, Los Angeles, 90035. Tuesdays, 7PM, What is Kabbalah?

North Hollywood Church of Religious Science, 818/762-7566. 6161 Whitsett Ave., North Hollywood, 91606.

Performing Arts Synagogue, Wadsworth Hall, UCLA. First Friday of every month.

Self-Realization Fellowship, 323/661-8006. 4860 W. Sunset Blvd., Hollywood. 310/454-4114. 17190 Sunset Blvd., Pacific Palisades.

St. Ambrose Catholic Church, 323/656-4433. 1281 N. Fairfax Ave., Los Angeles.

• ORGANIZATIONS

The Actors' Network, 818/509-1010. "Where the Serious Actor Does Business." They are a professional, unique, business networking organization, created by actors. This an organization I have a great deal of respect for. I believe dedicated actors can make a difference in their careers by working in this group.

Academy of Television Arts and Sciences, 818/754-2800. 5220 Lankershim Blvd., North Hollywood, 91601. They will send you requirements to join; they are less stringent for non-voting members.

Actresses @ Work, 818/299-8700. They try to help women realize their mid-career potential. Their cinematic inspiration was "The First Wives Club."

Audience Unlimited Inc., www.tvtickets.com, 818-753-3470. Free tickets to live TV comedy and drama show taping sessions (no game shows). Hours and availability vary, at mostly Valley locations. Details also available online.

IPF/West, Independent Feature Projects West, 310/475-4379. 1964 Westwood Blvd., #205, Los Angeles, 90025. Annual membership $85. "This non-profit membership organization is one of the largest and most dynamic groups supporting quality independent filmmaking today." They offer seminars, top level contacts, member gatherings, luncheons and the Breakfast Series.

On The House, 310/399-3868. Yearly membership fee of $149 for two. This is a "papering service" which means they help fill theater seats. The members call a hotline and hear what shows are available, reserve two tickets and show up at the theater. This is another tip from Geri Cook in Friday's L.A. Times.

Showbiz Softball League, 909/336-9750. Vic Puglisi. Play, but also go to games!

The Actors Studio, Inc. 323/654-7126. 3341 Delongpre Ave., West Hollywood, 90069. The is the West Coast branch of New York's Actors Studio. No dues or tuition. Actors are admitted on the basis of talent; previous training is essential.

Women In Film (for men too), 323/463-6040. 6464 Sunset Blvd., Suite 530, Hollywood, 90028. You need two members to sponsor you. Dues: $125 a year. You can volunteer to work in the office in order to meet people who later may sponsor you.

• EVENTS

Back Stage West's yearly Actorfest is an event to meet people and to see many booths with services for actors. New York also has a yearly event like this.

THE ACTORS' NETWORK

• **This is the organization for actors who are really serious** about getting work in this industry. I tell all of my students, as do many other acting coaches in town, to join. It is the best show biz bargain in existence.

• **Actors Kevin E. West and Paulo Andres** are making the effort to build a true acting community in our spread-out, industry-driven town. This is not an acting school, it is a group of information-sharing, working actors interested in the business side of their careers. They share trade publications, job leads, resources, tips, scams they've run across and general moral support and encouragement.

• **Their resource library is vast.** Most actors could not afford to own all the books and guides here, and they are certainly not available at the public libraries. They teach how to use these resources to make effective submissions for jobs.

• **The Network invites unpaid industry guests,** including casting directors, agents, producers and acting coaches, to come in each month for Q & A sessions. They have no problem filling these spots with top people, proof of how respected and well thought of they are in the industry. They have activities such as improv workouts, cold reading workouts, demo reel review nights. The members sign up for these events. Talking to some of my students, they say the competition is tough to get in; you have to be there to sign up soon after events are announced.

• **The Actors' Network offers free orientation meetings** three times a month for actors to come in and listen to what they do. It is two hours of what can be overwhelming information.

• **Membership is $40 a month with a six month commitment.**

• **In *Backstage West's* column on The Actors' Network**, Karen Konadazian quoted their philosophies. Paulo Andres: "Our philosophy is to help actors help themselves. Learning from each other can save them five years of struggling, of listening to the wrong people, and of going down the wrong roads." Kevin E. West: "One of our biggest mottos here is a quote of Margaret Mead's: 'Never doubt that a small group of thoughtful, committed citizens can change the world. Indeed, it is the only thing that ever has.' This is what I believe very strongly and why I started this place. It's how we feel."

Check out Jode Leigh Edwards diary in *Section Three, page 231,* to see all the things she did at The Actors' Network her first three months in town.

Resources

The Actors' Network, 818/509-1010. "Where the Serious Actor Does Business." They are a professional, unique, business networking organization, created by actors. This is an organization I have a great deal of respect for. I believe dedicated actors can make a difference in their careers by working with this group.

SECTION THREE

FILM AND TELEVISION INTERVIEWS, AUDITIONS AND CALL BACKS

• **If auditions scare you**, get *Back Stage West/Drama-Logue* each Wednesday afternoon, Thursday morning, or be really on top of it and subscribe on-line at www.backstagewest.com. Send out your pictures and resumes, and go on every reading you can. You will be more comfortable doing interviews only after doing a lot of them. Give the interview and reading all of your attention and focus at the time. Then let go of the audition. The casting person or director will either hire you or not. You may get a few jobs to build your resume.

• **To some actors**, *interview* and *audition* are two of the most terrifying acting words. To others, they are very exciting words because they are the actions that lead to landing acting roles. Perhaps with more understanding, you will realize how the other people involved (agents, casting directors, directors, producers) do their jobs and what exactly *your* job is as an actor. The fact is, auditions cause stress; it's how we handle the stress that makes the difference in landing the jobs.

• **Get your script or sides ahead of time.** SAG guarantees that you can get them at least the day before your interview. Often, though, in the case of episodic television, the script is still being written. In this situation, make arrangements with the assistant at the casting office to pick up your script as soon as it's available. This may be only an hour or two before the interview.

Castnet, Showfax or *Actor Fax* are great companies that, for a fee, will fax your audition sides to you. You can also get your sides on-line 24 hours a day by signing up with the above organizations. *See Resources, page 142.* This can really help you when working or auditioning across town and you can't get to the casting director's or production office to pick up sides in person. Sometimes your agent has the script and will fax the sides to you.

• **Whenever you walk into an office** for an interview, whoever you are meeting is hoping 100% you are wonderful and will:

- **Make them a lot of money,** as in the case of an agent.
- **Make an impression on the producer or director** that a casting director is having you meet. Casting directors' reputations depend on introducing new discoveries (you) to their employers.
- **Fit the concept of the role** the director or producer has.

They are all rooting for you!

• **This is absolutely true.** I have worked many hours in casting sessions as assistant to director Joan Darling. Directors hire excellent casting directors so they will screen out the bad actors and thus save them a lot of time. The casting directors' reputations depend on the caliber of actors they bring in. However bad, untrained and scared, actors do end up coming in for readings. They are usually friends of the producer or director, the director's assistant, someone the network thinks is up and coming, a waiter at Canter's because he has been so nice and has a good look, etc. When you get an opportunity to read, be prepared and take full advantage of it.

• **So if you've met the casting director** and they've called you in to read for the director, you are a good actor or have a great look. That is not in question. If your agent has obtained the reading without your meeting the casting director first, you are a good actor represented by an agent with a good reputation. If you've obtained the interview in one of the other ways, say "thank you very much" and enter the office knowing that you have acting work to do. Let the fear be there—let it be part of the character.

• **Commit to the acting choices** you made when you read the script. Be open and vulnerable, and you will do a good acting job. Listen without any defenses to directions you may be given and deliver them to the best of your ability. This is your job as an actor. You may not get the role (most of the time you won't) but this is not proof of whether or not you did a good job. It may be proof they are not doing a terrific job by not hiring you, or there may have been another actor who was better suited to the role.

• **Mira Sorvino said the first time she auditioned** for the hooker role in Woody Allen's *Mighty Aphrodite,* she didn't get the part. Woody thought she wasn't sensual enough. Then, while she was in London, she found out he was there and still auditioning. She went to King's Road, bought trashy clothes and mules with plastic flowers, fluffed out her hair, dredged up a cartoon voice, went to see Woody and wowed him. She eventually won the supporting actress Oscar for the role.

• **Ned Bellamy**, character actor, played the role of Eddie, Elaine's psychotic employee, on *Seinfeld.* He made the character choice to use a raspy, creepy voice. I asked Jerry if he used that voice at the audition. He said, "Yes, and I was quite surprised when he showed up at rehearsal and that wasn't his real voice." I asked Ned about it. Moments before the audition, he decided on the voice and asked casting director Marc Hirschfeld if he should use it. Marc said, "Why not?" Ned had a couple of questions to ask about the role and used the same voice to ask them because he didn't want to break the illusion of the character. Besides being a wonderful actor and looking the part, his choice of using that voice may have been what gave him the edge over the other actors auditioning.

• **Katie Holmes** (*Dawson's Creek)* is from Cleveland, Ohio. She had done some school plays and then, in her junior year, she and her mother went to a talent convention. She did a monologue, they liked her, sent her to Los Angeles. She auditioned for the film *Ice Storm* and got it. After shooting it and returning home, she auditioned for pilots by recording her reading on video tape and sending it to her agent. Her mother read the other characters off camera. She said she kidded James Van Der Beek, saying he was good but her mom really knew how to play Dawson.

• **Luke Perry** (*90210*) had 216 auditions before landing his first job.

• **Gail O'Grady** auditioned for the part of the secretary on *NYPD Blue*, wearing a '60s hairdo, false eyelashes, a tight angora sweater, bright stirrup pants and adding a heavy New York accent. She was inspired by characters in the film *Working Girl.* She said, "I know this woman, she's very physical. And I knew nobody else would show up like that." They auditioned over 100 actors for the part. The three-episode role turned into a regular role with Gail receiving an Emmy nomination.

• **David Schwimmer** (*Friends*) wanted the part in *The Pallbearer* from the moment he read the script. He was obsessed. A dozen actors were up for the role. One morning the film's director, Matt Reeves, found a tiny coffin on his desk. The message inside: "I'd kill to be in this movie!" It was signed by David Schwimmer. Persistence paid off.

• **Debi Mazar** *(L.A. Law, GoodFellas, Jungle Fever),* in an interview, spoke of her audition with Spike Lee for *Malcolm X.* She wore a blond wig, 1940s makeup, platform shoes, and landed the part of Malcolm's friend, Shorty's girlfriend. She said, "I thought Spike would like to see the character the minute I walked in the door. It was a great audition."

• **Hiep Thi Le's** sister didn't want to go to the casting call alone, so **Hiep** went along to keep her company. With life's quirky fate, Hiep ended up being cast in the leading role of Le Ly Hayslip in Oliver Stone's film *Heaven and Earth.*

• **Casting Director Tom McSweeney** says, "We love actors; they're our livelihood. We love to find new people. There's nothing more fun than giving an actor a break. I don't want to see actors suffer; I want to see them work; I want to see them happy."

• **Tuesday Knight** was working as a receptionist at Orion Television. "Somebody from the show *Fame* saw me. They were looking for a combination Deborah Harry/Madonna–so they had this big cattle call. I saw it on TV, about 3,000 girls. Then the next day they saw me in the office and they hired me. It was like a dream. I was a regular for a while."

• **Director Ron Shelton's original plan** for Woody Harrelson's date in *White Men Can't Jump* was to be a snooty Ivy League girl. Rosie Perez showed up for an interview and blurted out to him, with feeling, "I can't audition today! I'm having a bad hair day!" That grabbed his attention; she got the role.

• **Alan King** said that when he got the starring role in *Just Tell Me What You Want* with Ali MacGraw, Sidney Lumet called him and said, "Remember, 15 years ago. We were driving across the Whitestone Bridge to the Bronx and I promised you that someday I would find a movie for you to star in?..."

• **Danny DeVito** was fearless in his audition for the television role on *Taxi.* He jumped up on the desk and started hopping up and down to make his point.

• **Katharine Hepburn** said, "Show me an actor with no personality and I'll show you an actor who isn't a *star.*"

• **Regina Taylor** auditioned for *I'll Fly Away.* She felt she was very different from the part until she started thinking of her grandmother and her family. "When I finally sat down to audition to a room full of suits in Los Angeles, I told them I wasn't ready to do the scene, that I felt like talking. They said, 'Sure, talk.' I told them about where I came from, about the faces of the people who raised me. When I was done talking, no one said anything. Someone thanked me. I got up and left." A month later she was in Atlanta filming the part of Lily Harper.

• **Anna Maria Horsford** *(Amen)* says when she went to audition for the part of Sherman Hemsley's ditsy daughter, she wore a pink bathrobe, a pair of little-girl teddy bear slippers and carried a supermarket tabloid under her arm. Her reasoning was: if the character doesn't work, then what does she do? She watches soap operas and reads the gossip sheets.

• **Mariska Hargitay** auditioned for the TV series *Tequila & Bonetti.* The executive producer, Donald Bellisario, said, "I vividly remember the day she auditioned and gave a sly twist to a tragic monologue about a dead husband. The other actresses played it straight, but Mariska played it with laughter. She told this horrible story as if it were a joke, and as she continued, tears started to streak past her smile. She got the part."

• **Edward Norton** brought the stutter into the audition for *Primal Fear.*

• **Susan Ruttan** *(LA Law),* referring to every character she auditioned for said: "You can get away with anything you are comfortable with. If you think you're pushing it, then you are. Never hit a casting director. Never touch them. Commit, commit, commit. I know that whenever I fully commit to a choice, I either get the job or get a chance to do it another way."

When talking about her *LA Law* audition, she said:

- **There was a clue in the script**: "She would chew off her right arm for Arnie." I took that and committed to that part of the personality. I didn't know anything else about her. There were four little scenes. One was where she came in, in the morning, and there was this big smell in the office. I brought an empty spray can with me and I sprayed it around the room and used it. I'm not sure props are always right, but they were right for this moment. As I was leaving, Greg Hoblit said, "You made us laugh." They didn't know she was funny. I made a choice; I risked—but you have to do it. Otherwise when you go in to read and just do what the stage directions say, you're doing what everyone else is doing.

- **It takes guts to go with your instincts** like that; but in these cases, the actors ended up launching their careers with long-running television series. It certainly was worth it. I'm sure there were times these actors didn't get jobs using outrageous choices, but the few successes are worth the many failures.

- **One stunt that didn't work**: when Annette Bening announced that she wouldn't be able to play Catwoman in Batman II because she was having Warren Beatty's baby, Sean Young dressed up in a Catwoman outfit, hired a limo, got through the gates at Warner Bros. by saying she was Annette Bening and went to the office of director Tim Burton to try to win the part. A few days later, it was announced that the role went to Michelle Pfeiffer.

- **Casting Director Cathy Henderson** says:

  - **I think the actor who usually gets the part** will be someone who walks in and does it as if they were walking on the set, somebody said "Action" and they did it. Making it their own and making it real.

  - **A great deal of the reason** why one person will continually get a job and someone else won't is very often not how talented someone is, but more that they grasp what the director and producer are doing that day, which is trying to hire several people for specific roles, and not that they're waiting for someone to come in and blow them away. I mean, it's great if that happens, if the part calls for it. But lots of times your part doesn't call for you to come in and blow somebody away. They want somebody natural, somebody who has good chemistry with the rest of the cast and somebody who makes it real.

- **Casting director Clair Sinnett** says actors should ask, "Would you like to see what I've prepared or is there something specific you would like to see?"

• **If you know any directors or casting directors**, you might ask if you can volunteer to be a reader for them. As a reader, you will read all the other roles with feeling to the auditioning actor. You will be a partner to play off of. The time you spend in a casting office will be a real eye-opener to the casting business.

• HOW TO PREPARE FOR THE INITIAL AUDITION

• **How to make the choices for your interpretation** of the script is your "acting work." How you choose your acting work comes from your own life experience, your own reality.

• **First, read the script,** then read your scenes; or, if you don't have the script, read the copy or sides over many times—everyone's role, not just your lines. Read it out loud so you can hear the words. Don't use any acting at first. Decide what the given circumstances of the script are. This means what, when and where are the circumstances of the script? Look for every clue possible. It's important what the other characters say about your character. If the role is a day player part with just a few lines, then you may have to make up your given circumstances. For instance: this is an accountant who loves his job, a bank teller who has a hangover, a garbage collector who is an opera buff, a doctor who is very proud of his education, a socialite who has a drinking problem, a musician who is afraid of becoming deaf, a ballerina who is obsessed with her feet. For most day player roles you will be the only one who knows these things about the character.

• **Now decide who you are talking to** and what you are talking about. If it is like a situation that you have experienced in your life, it's fairly easy and there won't be much acting work involved. If it is different from your own life, then choose a similar or parallel situation. Remember where the event took place in your life. To personalize, recall who you were talking to: sister, father, lover, person you hated, someone you betrayed, who betrayed you, and so on. Think of a piece of sensory work appropriate to any of these people and *use the first one that comes to your mind.*

• **Now read or say the lines**, thinking of these pieces of acting work. Try several different ways and personalizations; if the director gives you some direction during the audition, you will not be fixed on just one way of acting the role. Now you can highlight your lines, saying them as you are highlighting. Underline your cues. Sometimes it is not a line, it is a phone ringing or a kiss or a doorbell. You want to memorize those cues so you have a reaction planned, even though they don't actually happen in the audition room.

• **Remember**: the lines are not the most important thing; they can get 50 people off the street to simply read the lines letter-perfect. They are looking for a *relationship* between you and the person you are reading with. Most of the time you are not reading with an actor so you will usually have to create the whole relationship yourself. You can do this by being very specific about the choices you have made. Even if you are reading with an actor who may be good or not so good, keep your work specific.

• **Play in the moment**. You may have a better grasp of your character than the other actor does; don't pick up that energy unless it fits with yours. You may get the call back and they won't. If the auditioners are matching you with an actor already cast for the project, then that is the most fun because you can play more in the moment with what is really going on between the two of you.

• **Be real. Know who you are talking to from your real life** and what you are talking about. Again, you determine this by the given circumstances provided for you in the script.

• **I believe you must memorize the script** for an audition and only look down at the script once or twice during the interview. (Always hold the script—even if it's memorized.) I know for some actors this skill isn't easy to acquire, but to compete, you must give a full performance of the material. Anything less and someone else gets the job. Do not memorize until you have done your script analysis and chosen your acting work. Memorize in a flat monotone, saying the lines over and over but not using the acting work. By using a flat monotone to memorize, the words will just be instruments to get across the script's meaning and you will never get stuck doing just a line-reading audition.

• **Absolutely, do not look at the script when you are talking or listening.** I can not say this strongly enough. It could determine whether you get the job. The time to look down is when the other person reading with you has finished their line and you don't know what your next one is. Start your reaction to what has been said to you and then look down and "grab" the words. Look at the other person and take the time to play the lines. Don't just say them. Use all your acting work and choices. Remember, the lines are not important.

• **Kathleen Freeman**, character actress and teacher, taught me a very valuable exercise for quickly learning to pick up your lines from a page. Read out loud from a newspaper. Hold your thumb near the copy. Look down, pick up words. Look up in a mirror or into the room and try and make real conversation with those stiff kind of words. Newspapers work better than magazines, because they are written in a dryer form. If you do this 10 minutes every day for three months, you will become very good at picking up words off the script.

• **Joe Reich, casting director**, when asked how an actor should hold a script during an audition replied, "I only care that the actor does hold the script. It is axiomatic that when you memorize the script you will always forget a line, usually at the most crucial point (and usually at an important audition). So even if you do memorize, please carry the script and spare yourself that agonizing moment."

• **Wallis Nicita, producer** and former vice president of Warner Bros. Casting, says, "In casting, it is a new person every 10 minutes, eight hours a day, five days a week. You get one take to hit your emotional level and then, good-bye, thank you very much."

• **There is nothing to be afraid of.** You are a business person, a career person, a professional dealing with other professionals. Take up your full space, ask questions if you don't know something. It is okay not to know.

• **Take care of the people interviewing you.** Interviews are also difficult for some of these people; they are shy too. The reason they ask a question is to find out about your personality and who you are, not necessarily what your credits are.

• **Come to love the question** "What have you been doing?" If you can love that question and come up with an entertaining, positive, happy answer you've got the interview 90% down.

• **Don't list your credits**; try to talk about anything else. Even if you don't get to tell any stories, you will still be full of them and you will get the feeling that in some way you have already been talking to these people and you will feel some kinship, as though they aren't total strangers. You are both after the same thing: work, money, and a successful project.

• **Casting director James F. Tarzia speaks of general interviews.**

- During a general, I'll read the actor's resume and ask them to tell me about themselves. I don't want them to tell me what's on the resume, I can read what's there. I want to know if there is a well-rounded human being here, or are you one-minded and focused on just being an actor? If you're not a well-rounded human being, then there are no dimensions to you. I want people to be three-dimensional.

• CALL BACKS

• **When you go back for another reading,** wear the same clothes, hair style and make the same acting choices, unless you have been asked to read for another part. The time to use an acting coach is before the first audition, not for the call back. They have called you back because they liked how you looked and what you did. The exception would be if they told your agent they didn't like your acting and wanted you to play the role in another way. At this point, a coach could be of great help to open your mind to another point of view in choosing your work.

Casting director James F. Tarzia says,

> Of course, we all know about actors on call backs—they never seem to do it the same way they did it when they came in. There must be this thing about it: "I got a call back, I think I'll rework this totally differently from what I did the last time." But I liked what you did, don't change it, please don't change it, because I'm going in before you and saying to my director, "This is the most brilliant reading I've seen, I mean he was just absolutely great," and the actor will come in and do something *totally* different, and I'm like, "What are you doing?" My director is looking at me going "Uh huh, okay." It's a surprise and we don't want to be too surprised. So leave it, don't change it.

• **There are enough acting jobs** to go around, and you will get yours. This is your career path and you must take each one of the steps. There is a natural progression. Yes, some people seem to get luckier breaks. *Yeah!* They will get there faster and help us. Everyone likes to have their friends working with them. It makes for a happier family on the set.

• AFTER THE INTERVIEW

Most important, have an appointment in your book to go to afterwards: facial, dance class, rehearsal, movie, lunch, etc., so the interview becomes just another event in your day. Write down the people you've met, put them on your networking address list, send thank you notes if appropriate and forget it. Look forward to the next audition. Remember the things that you did right and let go of the things you think you might have done better; you will remember next time. For the most part, don't talk about your auditions.

Resources

Mobile Mailbox, 323/969-9853. 1514 N. Formosa Avenue, Los Angeles, 90046. Biff Yeager is the actor/owner of the company. This is a way actors can submit themselves for projects they hear or read about that are currently casting. To quote the brochure, "We are a unique messenger service developed several years ago as a twice-a-day, fast pickup and delivery service. Similar to the postal service but much faster. Our service is simple: We pre-sell our own special delivery stamps as low as $.90 each. Anything that fits in a 10 x 13 inch envelope may be sent by affixing the required amount of stamps and depositing the envelope into one of our conveniently located drop boxes around the Los Angeles, Hollywood, Century City, Beverly Hills, North Hollywood and Burbank areas!" Biff has come up with an unique way to get a leading role in a movie. Check it out at: www.ultimatewishgift.com.

Actor Fax, 310/652-9425, 877-228-6732. www.actorfax.com. 1017 N. La Cienega Blvd. #309, West Hollywood, 90069. Hours: 9AM-10PM. Automated and on-line sides available 24 hours a day. Faxed sides are $1.25 a page with a maximum cost of $10. On-line cost is $38 a year for unlimited sides. They sound like they really are trying to help actors reduce their costs of getting sides. I am signing up for this service too.

Castnet, 323/777-0715. www.castnet.com. They have sides for actors on-line plus many, many other actor services. See much more about them in *Section Five, Career Tools.* I feel they are very valuable and have been with them since my agent told me about them.

Showfax, 310/385-6920. www.showfax.com. 1110 S. Robertson, Los Angeles, 90035. Hours: M-F 8-10, S & S 10-2. Web Site, three shows a day, $68 a year. "The service for faxing sides." Showfax starts at $1.75 per page, with a price cap that never exceedes $12. No charge for cover page or any non-dialogue pages, such as maps or character descriptions included by the casting director. I'm on-line with them.

The Casting Workbook, 310/207-5660. www.castingworkbook.com. 11925 Wilshire Blvd., 3rd Floor, L.A. 90025. Basic membership is $42 a year which includes free sides.

Conquering Fear

• **John Wayne** said,

  • **Courage** is being scared to death and saddling up anyway.

• **If you haven't** already thought of your own ways to get through some or all of your interview, audition and performing fears, here are some tried and true ones. Use them all and add your own until you can walk through your fears. These are *not* the most important moments in your life; they are just simply moments.

• **Jeremy Irons**, Oscar winner for *Reversal of Fortune,* says about acting,

  • **A lot of it is like hang gliding**—you just hold on and hope it works. When I talk to acting students, I always read them this poem: "Come to the edge, it's too high, come to the edge, you might fall, come to the edge—so they came. And they flew." I want to keep coming to a high edge. That's why I've made the choices I have. Sometimes I will fall, and sometimes, please God, I will fly. But I wouldn't want to get so scared that I come to a low edge I can just step off easily.

• **Meryl Streep** said,

  • **Characters that are in precarious life and death circumstances** are dangerous characters to visit with your body and soul. It's dangerous to go there. We spend our whole lives as real human beings trying to get beyond the fears and the terrors that are there, everywhere, for us. To be an actor is to want to visit those dark places, the scary parts.

• **Patrick Swayze**, when he was still studying, out of work and broke, used to tell himself over and over,

  • **I'm a winner and my life works.**

• **Time.** When you know the time and location of your interview, start planning backwards. You want to arrive and park your car one half-hour before your scheduled appointment time. That means checking the address in your Thomas Guide and figuring your exact route and leaving for your destination in plenty of time to find it. As a rule, on your way to the audition, the traffic will be the worst it has ever been in history. Always give yourself a break and allow the most time it could take—not the least.

• **Bill Macy**, (mature character actor) was doing a presentation of a scene from *Maude* at the Television Academy to honor Norman Lear. Three days before the event we were talking and he casually mentioned he had just come back from a trial run to make sure he knew exactly where the Academy was, where he would park and how long it would take him to get there. Now this is from an ex-New York cab driver who starred in his own TV series for seven years and has worked decades in films, television and on stage. Still, this veteran is clocking how long it will take him to get to his destination for this important event. He says, "It makes me feel secure to know where I'm going." He gets secure so he can walk on the edge of the cliff in his acting. He loves taking risks, that's why he's so funny!

• **Keep a coin purse** in your glove compartment so you'll always have quarters and dimes for parking. I also keep a few coins in my appointment book.

• **Keep a magnetic lock box** hidden on the outside of your car with your car key and house key in it—never be locked out of your car or home before an audition or set call. If you haven't already done this, please put this book down and do it right now. You can get the lock box at Rite Aid, Sav-on, Target, Pep Boys, etc. and keys can also be made at most of those stores.

• **In getting ready to leave the house**, whatever preparation it takes to turn you on to yourself, do it. This may involve some of your *actor's secrets* or simply deciding what to wear, ironing it, primping, playing positive tapes or music, reading something inspirational.

• **If you have an early appointment** and you aren't any good in the morning till you've been up for three hours and have had four cups of coffee, it means you are up $3^1/_2$ hours before the appointment. Luckily, when you work in film and TV and your call is for 6 or 7AM, you can just take a shower, wash your hair and go to work. The hair and makeup people take care of the rest and give you a chance to wake up.

• **Okay. You are prepared**, parked in your car one half-hour ahead of time. Now relax. Just sit with any fears, tears, giggles, anger or whatever comes up; you may start to cry or laugh. Experience all of it because beyond those feelings and tensions are the knowledge of who you are and the energy to use all of yourself. Allow plenty of time for this, then take down all of your defenses, be willing to let whatever happens to you happen. Go into the office, sign or report in with the secretary, and check to make sure there aren't changes of dialogue in the sides you are reading today or pick up your copy or sides if you don't already have them.

• **If for some insane reason you weren't able to get your script ahead of time,** find the bathroom so you can say all your lines out loud. Figure out what the scene or copy is about (the situation), who the characters are and to whom they are talking. Find similar experiences and characters in your own life and act as if you were talking to them under these given circumstances. Memorize as much of the material as you can—at least the first couple of lines.

• **Then back to the office**, relax, observe everything going on but don't expend your energy playing with the other actors until you have read and are on your way out.

• **Practice these *being ahead of time* muscles** by being at class on time to get ready to act—whatever that takes for you: coffee, socializing, talking to your teacher, etc. Also practice this with any appointments that have to do with your career. This will build your muscles in finding out what it takes for you to be at your most comfortable, relaxed, unique best.

• **On your drive to the interview** or before, start thinking of your stories. Have an answer to "What have you been doing lately?" It is very important to have a wonderful story to tell about each entry on your resume, as the interviewer might use it as a guide for conversation.

• **Stories.** These are *positive* stories about your life, your career, the weather; it doesn't matter. If anyone mentions the smog, you haven't noticed because of some other positive thing you *have* noticed. If it's raining—isn't it grand how fresh it smells.

• **Make the stories short**, interesting and geared to show off who you are. You just got back from a great vacation, skiing, surfing, Las Vegas. You're taking a class in anthropology and are going on a dig next week. You can use things that happened a few months back as if they were last week; a story is more exiting if it sounds like it just happened. Funny incidents entertain. The most trivial information can be made humorous. Show biz gossip stories are good: shows you've worked on, stars you've worked with. Just make sure the story revolves around *you* and not who or what you are talking about.

• **List of questions.** Joan Darling taught me this one. Write out five questions—to find the answers to during the interview—on a piece of paper and put it in your pocket or purse. Find out the answers in the meeting without asking the questions, of course, but by observation. I love sex questions because they entertain me the most. Such as: Who in the room gets the most sex? Who lost their virginity first? Last? Other questions: Who's most ambitious? Who's most in control of the situation? etc. Always include yourself—it is answered between you and the rest of the people in the room. You talk about whatever is appropriate but you are also thinking about finding the answers to the questions you have written down. This device is to keep you involved with the people and uninvolved in your fear.

• **William James** said, "If you want a quality, act as if you already had it." Try the "as if" technique.

• **Love of yourself.** Give yourself the *permission* to be wonderful. Your uniqueness is the gift, yes gift, you are giving the audience, whomever they may be. Keep putting yourself on the line; don't be afraid to be outrageous, or to be willing to just say the lines. Most of the time you are going up for parts that are exactly like you.

From Nelson Mandela's 1994 Inaugural Speech

Our deepest fear is not that we are inadequate.

Our deepest fear is that we are powerful beyond measure.

It is our light, not our darkness, that most frightens us.

We ask ourselves: Who am I to be brilliant, gorgeous, talented and fabulous?

Actually, who are you not to be?

You are a child of God. Your playing small doesn't serve the world.

There's nothing enlightening about shrinking so that other people won't feel insecure around you.

We were born to make manifest the glory of God that is within us.

It's not just in some of us; it's in everyone.

And as we let our own light shine, we unconsciously give other people permission to do the same.

As we are liberated from our own fear, our presence automatically liberates others.

I've asked my students to make a copy of this speech on a bright colored piece of paper and put it in their wallet. Everytime they take out some money, they see the bright color and think of not being afraid.

DEALING WITH REJECTION

• **Through my spiritual work and inner growth,** I have found positive ways to accept not getting an acting job I've wanted. I don't forget the jobs and I still wish "they" had wanted me, but I have come to accept the fact that they didn't.

• **I hate dealing with rejection** but I can tolerate it, even though it hurts. Sometimes I do stew about it, rationalize that somehow it's for my own good, get angry and/or feel sorry for myself. I've learned, if I'm really in self-pity, to give myself a time limit, whether it's 15 minutes or two days. It usually doesn't last the full time but sometimes it does and then time is up and I let go of it. I really do believe I have a choice in my thoughts.

• **There have been times in my life** when I have allowed the depression to take over for longer periods, but not anymore. Time seems too precious to me now; I've got so many things in my life that fulfill me. I still don't have enough acting jobs. When I do get one, I really celebrate the whole event.

• **Dr. Sherie Zander** instructs actors on ways to deal with rejection.

  • **Everyone must face rejection**, but for the actor rejection is a constant companion. It cannot be avoided. No one is immune. It not only affects the beginner, but the seasoned actor as well. Success, fame and fortune don't keep the experience and pain of rejection away. Rejection must be faced and dealt with so that it will not destroy the motivation and self-esteem that are necessary in order to maintain an acting career.

  • **No one likes rejection**. It can be discouraging and hurtful. It may lead to insomnia, depression and despair. Because it is so prevalent and so destructive, it is critical that you, as an actor, discover how to detach from its harmful effect. But, how is that possible? You are told not to take rejection personally, but how do you differentiate who you are from what you do?

- **When I work with actors who are struggling** with this issue, I begin by taking a look at possible sources of rejection in childhood. Often the healing of early emotional wounds will provide the emotional stability that is required to move through rejection with less pain and stress. You may need to get to a good therapist.

- **I work with attitude and perspective**. Because every success will be preceded by many rejections, it may be helpful to view each rejection as a stepping stone rather than a set back. Remember that every rejection brings you one step closer to success.

- **There are many practical things** you can do to keep rejection from getting you down. Finding a safe way to release feelings of anger, sadness, hurt, fear and guilt is a good place to start. You may need to cry or yell, hit a punching bag or pour out the feelings on paper. This will serve to clear your mind and body and prepare you to carry on in spite of disappointment.

- **You may find a creative outlet** for all of that rejection energy—write a poem, write an article, draw, paint or sculpt. Physical exercise will help. Get the sleep you need and eat regular, healthy meals. Take this opportunity to do things that are fulfilling and refreshing.

- **Turn your focus away from thoughts of failure** and onto improvement. Take time to study and explore your craft. This is the time to continue the mechanics of finding new work—phone calls, mailings, photos, networking. Make a decision to learn what you can from this rejection by doing the following:

  - **Make an effort to find out why you were turned down.**
  - **Notice any positive things that came out of this incident.**
  - **Make two lists:**
    Things I can change.
    Things I can't change.
  - **Utilize the practice of meditation and prayer.**
  - **Decide to go for the next opportunity and try again.**

- **I would encourage you to prepare now for that day**. You can do so by making sure you are living a full life. Take time to develop deep and lasting friendships. Nurture and enjoy family relationships. Involve yourself with other actors in study or support groups. These are the persons who will help to lift your spirits when discouragement and despair threaten to bring you down.

- **You have many choices**. Refuse to allow rejection to ruin your day or your future.

CASTING DIRECTORS

• **Casting directors are mentioned all through this book** because they are usually the people who bring you in to meet the producers and directors of film and television projects. *(For commercial casting directors, see the Commercial Section, Page 160.)* Below I have interviewed several casting directors with many years of experience. Almost every week *Back Stage West/Drama-Logue* runs an interview with a casting director. Save these articles. Keep them in an alphabetized file so when you have a meeting with someone you will know a little about them.

• **There is so much valuable information** that can help you with your career, including books with nothing but interviews with casting directors. When you go to showcases, take notes of what the casting director says so you will be able to mention it in your thank you letter or when you have an interview two years later. You can, for instance, inquire whether their child won his Little League championship or not.

• **When you see a film or television** show you especially like the casting of, write the casting director telling them what you liked in particular. Their addresses can always be obtained through Breakdown Services.

• **Joey Paul, film, television and stage casting director:**

Q: How should the actor approach a *general interview,* when you are just meeting with the casting director?

- **For the most part, actors take the wrong psychological approach.** If they walk into a general interview and a casting director has to say to them, "So, tell me about yourself," they're not off to a good start. Part of the reason that a general interview might go very well is that a real dialogue of action and response occurs between two people, just like in a regular scene. If a general interview is one where the casting director is just asking questions and then passively sits there and listens to the actor talk about their life or their day, etc., it is not very conducive to making a long-lasting impression. Everybody likes to talk about themselves, particularly people in show business, who are oriented toward, and proud of their accomplishments. The goal of a general interview should be to find a common bond, something that both people can jointly discuss. The actor should be asking questions, too.

- **Questions like**, "I am familiar with some of your work, it's amazing what you do. Is casting everything you thought it would be and is it a creative and fun process for you?" or "I was curious; how did you first get started as a casting director?" I think that if an actor seems interested in the casting director, they'll have a better chance of the casting director being interested in them. People always respond well when somebody says, "You know, I saw such and such film that you cast and I felt... How long have you been casting this project? Are you still looking for such and such? I notice the artwork in your office is of a southwestern taste..." Coming from a business point of view, I don't think of that as flattery. That kind of discussion lends itself to being able to remember the actor better, but only if it comes from a real and genuine place.

- **For me, there's nothing worse** than when actors come in, sit in my office and don't say a word. Nothing, not even bad small talk like, "Boy, the traffic was busy getting here today. What was it like for you after the earthquake?" To me a general interview is kind of like a blind date; you have hopes that maybe this time it might work out. You hope there's a possibility that you could make a friend. Maybe this person will like you and remember you. If you were to go on a blind date and all the person did for 20 minutes was talk about himself, you'd walk away saying he couldn't care less about me. All the regular things also apply: be yourself, don't be somebody you're not, be real and honest, have a sharing dialogue. If they ask a question, you ask a question, or start off the conversation with a question.

Q: So you're really talking about personality development?

- **Yes, because ultimately if an actor becomes a major, major star**, one of the reasons may be because they have an incredible personality in addition to their talent. Robin Williams is a perfect example of that. I tell students of mine that they should see a general interview in their mind the same way they would if they were going to appear on David Letterman or Jay Leno. If they aspire to be a celebrity someday, then that aspiration has to be with them today. The reason that kind of success happens is because that's who they are now.

- **Actors who are shy and would rather do the acting work** than be in situations where their personalities must carry them, shouldn't do general interviews. Whoever represents them or is helping them to promote their careers should put the emphasis on trying to get them the audition. Let the actors do their magic in the reading and leave.

Q: When going in for an audition, should the actor immediately start to do the audition or try to get a general conversation going first?

- **I have never been impressed by an actor**, regardless of whether it's a call back or an initial meeting, who wants to try to create a general interview situation prior to their audition. Particularly if they assume that we're going to sit down and talk before they read. I firmly believe that less is more. There are ways actors can develop a certain kind of control over auditions, rather than coming in like victims. One of the ways they can do this is by truly looking at the audition as a journey.

- **With the entrance into my office they have the opportunity** to take me on a little fantasy journey that will be created by what they do. If actors are in control of this journey, they will have a better chance of my going along fully for the ride. When they come in and decide they want to talk, tell stories, do whatever before they read, they've put a heavier burden on themselves. They hope that I am following them, am attentive and they are holding my interest for that entire story, talk or whatever. After we're done with that, they've got to go back to a somewhat neutral place, so they can get into the character that they're reading.

- **Look at that audition as if it were a bunch of line to line dots** on a piece of paper. They have to take me along from dot to dot to dot to dot on this journey, which is comprised of their story and all the points of interest. Once they've finished the story there's another dot they've got to carry me to, back to that neutral place so they can be the artist. Then they've got to take me to the next dot when they begin to perform, and all the little dots that are within that performance. They hope for that entire journey, I'm with them. It's a much heavier burden doing all of that, because if they say anything that's the least bit of interest to me, it's going to be much more difficult to get me back on track and hold my attention. Whereas, if they simply come in and just begin to do their magic, the role, it's like the curtain comes up, they do the audition, the curtain comes down and they leave the stage or my office, as it were. They have a greater chance of maintaining my attention and now that they're gone and I was so enraptured with what they did, I have the potential of thinking, "Wow, I want more. That was great." The only way I can get more is by bringing them back.

• **Tony Shepherd was the Vice President of Talent** for Aaron Spelling Productions for 14 years.

Q: What do you see when an actor is entering the casting meeting?

- **If you're in the business of buying talent**, a casting director, producer or director, you can see the talent in the actor in 30 seconds or less; it's that indefinable something. You feel it, you know it. I look for a twinkle in the eye. You can't create that, it comes from within. I think the best actors are people who understand what they are about, understand what is going on in the world around them and how they relate to that world.

Q: How can an actor make the best impression?

- **Boring people make boring actors**. Work on yourself, process your life, examine how you relate to other people, how you communicate. Learn how to work with and motivate yourself and use that person from within. Acting is just a little bit bigger than real life. You are going to use who you are in everything you do. If you aren't focused, centered, honest, a risk-taking person, what kind of an actor can you ever expect to be? What you do in your daily life is directly reflected in what you do as an actor.

- **80 percent of jobs are lost**, not because the actor is right or wrong for the role or they can't act, but because something has gone wrong and they come in less than 100% focused. You don't know why, it's just that the person isn't right. In casting sessions, listen to what we say about actors: "He's cold, he has an edge, he has no warmth, he has no vulnerability, he has no strength." We're not talking about the person's acting ability, we're talking about the person, what they bring of themselves to the role they are playing or reading for. If an actor sits in a room with me and is interesting, exciting and there is a sparkle, a twinkle, an energy and a vitality about them, I can tell you right now they are going to work; it's only a matter of time.

- **Finally, in your auditions** and acting work, find tragedy in the comedy and humor in the drama.

• **Richard DeLancy casts, among other things, *Unsolved Mysteries*.** He is also a personal manager representing about 15 actors.

Q: Does *Unsolved Mysteries* call for a particular type of casting?

- **I call it "reality based" casting.** I deal with people who can use their training as an actor to be natural. It seems that those are the types of shows that people call me to do. All of the shows that I do have re-creations involved.

Q: What's important to you on the resume?

- **Theater. I find that stage actors**, even if it's community theater, are able to continue on, even though something may not be working the way they think it's supposed to. I also look at the resume to see what kind of stuff they've done. Most of the shows I deal with contain a great depth of drama; there's not a lot of laughter in them. I often call upon people that I know can deliver that. I let people know the first time I meet them that, if the role requires it, they had better be in touch with their emotions in order to cry—whether they are a six-year-old girl or a 65-year-old man. If you've seen the variety of shows that I've cast, you'll notice that we use a great deal of that sort of thing.

Q: Are a lot of the auditions for *Unsolved Mysteries* improvisation?

- **Our show is done on an improvisation basis.** There is rarely a script written; only when there is precise wording that has to be said.

- **We've maintained a good rating** because our actors do quite a good job. We demand a lot because we give the actors the ability to create a character. They're given the information from an outline and they sit and talk and sometimes view tapes. There have been times when the information given me was a tape of Christmas morning and Christmas dinner, watching the real person.

Q: How many pictures do you receive for each role?

- **I can get 600 pictures at any given time.** Sometimes I see 30 people for each role, usually 20 or 25. I usually take five of those actors to meet with the directors, sometimes just three.

Q: What will cause an actor to lose a job or not be called in again?

- **Being late. That's my number one pet peeve.** I believe that an actor's job is the interview. If you can't make the interview, then... A lady was late for her interview with producers. She was so perfect for the role but if she's going to be late for her interview with the producers, I cannot guarantee she is going to be at work on time. In New York, if you are late for your audition, you are no longer going to be considered for that role. That's the discipline I like.

- **Lori Cobe-Ross, CSA, is an independent feature film casting director.**

Q: What does a casting director do?

- **I read the script**, with the director or writer, work up the breakdowns of the characters and specifically what we want or what we need. I submit the descriptions to the Breakdown Service, they send this information over computer or fax to all of the agents. From that, the agents submit actors. That same day, particularly on a feature, I receive hundreds of pictures and resumes. I don't interview all of the actors, but I look at everything.

Q: Do you prefer seeing actors through agents?

- **Unfortunately, 99 percent of the time, I have to say no to the actors.** If I see a hundred people, only one is going to get the role. So it's a lot easier to talk to the agents, without saying directly to the actor why they weren't right. Also, actors without agents would be at a disadvantage making their own deals because they're not really equipped to do that, whereas, agents are.

Q: Is making the deals the most important part of your job?

- **For the producer it is**; for the director it's getting the right actor for the part. I work for the producer and the director. To me they are of equal importance, though I would think getting the right actor is more important.

Q: Do you think there's a stigma about doing extra work?

- **It isn't something you need to put on your resume**, but it's certainly a way to get your SAG card. Lots of films I've worked on, people have been upgraded to a speaking role and get their SAG card, or at least get Taft-Hartleyed, so the next time they work, they can get their card. It's also important to be comfortable around a set. When people only have theater training, I'm very nervous about hiring them for a series, or for a feature. When you work on sets and meet directors or producers that think you're terrific, they may give you a shot at a job; it happens all the time. I think you need to do whatever you can to meet the people that can get you work.

Q: How about getting the audition?

- **There's so much competition, even when you get an audition**, it's a victory. If you get the part, it's a miracle. There are so many wonderful actors who are just dying to work. I think that auditioning is acting. Actors lose sight of that. Someone said, "I had five auditions today and I didn't get a call back." Five Auditions! That's unbelievable. I know a girl that's auditioning for three pilots and a feature in one day. Who knows if she's going to get any callbacks, but that alone is fantastic. She's acting, she's out there, she's meeting people.

Q: How valuable are the cold reading, casting director workshops?

- **At the end of the day**, if I can go to a workshop, bring sides, sit for two hours and meet 20-25 actors, especially when I was doing *Divorce Court*, it saved me time. When I do a showcase I am always very specific with the type of actors I want to see. I don't want them wasting my time and their money.

Q: When actors are reading together for a role with kissing and such, should they do it for the audition?

- **People are afraid to ask questions about physical movement.** Some actors are afraid to look each other in the eyes. You really need to act physical. You should talk about it ahead of time. You could say to the actor, "Is it okay if we kiss?" or "What do you want to do?" Make sure you are both willing to do it. Then ask the auditioners what they would like to see.

• **Lori wrote a letter to the editor of *Back Stage West* recently**, I thought it was a great perspective for all actors. She gave me permission to print it here for you.

- I thought it was time to remind actors that casting is a business—that we casting directors do our part and that actors need to do the same.

1. Always bring a picture and resume with you to every audition; I cannot tell you how many actors don't have their pictures with them. Come on—keep some in your car.

2. Get a contact number (voice mail/pager) with a Los Angeles area code and keep that number. Yes, I know that you are willing to drive in for an audition from Orange County, San Diego, or Mars, but there are so many new area codes that we don't know if some are local or not. And some casting directors might not want to make a long distance call. Why risk losing an audition?

3. Don't call a casting office unless you are running late for an audition or it is some emergency. We get a huge amount of phone calls and it is really difficult to find the time to chat with actors about what we are working on or if we remember meeting them two years ago, or if we got their new pictures in the mail.

   Remember, our job is to find the best actor for the job. We are not career counselors. We know how important it is for you the actor to get feedback, but please realize that after talking to agents and managers to schedule, negotiate, and book actors, auditions, preparing and approving sides, and dealing with our producers and diretor, there is little or no time left in the day.

4. Don't make excuses once you are in for an audition. If you aren't prepared, *don't audition.* Ask for more time. I'd much rather give you time than see you stumble through the material. Get the sides as soon as you get the audition appointment. Now that it is so easy to get sides, *get them.* And remember, we don't know who has had the sides for an hour or for a week; we assume you've spent time on the material.

5. Be kind to the casting assistants. I don't need to say more.

6. It's fine to ask questions in an audition. If you have unanswered questions about your character, you cannot do a good job.

7. One last hint that I learned from my best friend, casting director Mark Paladini: If you go to an audition and you know the casting director, and it is just the two of you in the room, it is fine to chat, reminisce, schmooze...*but* if there are others in the room just do your audition and answer any questions you're asked. You don't want the producers, director, or others to think that you were brought in as a favor. You want them to think you're there because you are one of the best choices for the role.

   Remember, we casting directors want you to do a good job. We really, *really* are on your side. We want you to be great. We love to call and say "He/she got the job!"

• **Clair Sinnett, independent casting director,** casts features, industrials, infomercials and television. She is also an accomplished actress, director and teacher.

Q: What do you need to make it in an acting career?

- **It's show business, not show-art.** Actors should realize that they are promoting and marketing themselves just as they would in any other business. Take it from the point of view that you are now self-employed. You have established your own corporation. Many actors have borrowed money for pictures, resumes, classes, etc. That's like selling shares of stock. In our corporation we need to have print advertising, which is your resume, a good solid commercial, which is your interview. The marketing is knowing who the buyers are.

- **See at least one feature film a week,** if that's the area that you want to go into. Watch television. What are some of your favorites? Who does the casting of those shows? That's the "business of the business." Learn the business. You need to know who the casting directors, directors and producers are in television as well as feature film. Once you know who they are, try to find out a little bit about them so you can send them a personal cover letter that accompanies your picture and resume every time you write them. Remember, your picture and resume is your liaison between their desk and you.

Q: How can new young actors meet casting directors?

- **Being young is certainly an advantage.** Television is youth oriented so find out who casts those shows. When you meet new acquaintances try to find out four things about them: their hometown, alma mater, children and pets. No matter how long someone has been out of your home town, there's still an alliance there, a camaraderie, and roots. They will always have memories about their alma mater. I have never met anyone that when I said, "Do you have children?" and they said, "Yes" that they didn't immediately go on and on about them, whether they're boys or girls, or how old they are... The same thing with pets. This type of information opens up whole areas of conversation and it also gives you more information to include in your follow up cover letters to them.

Q: What should actors talk about on their initial interviews?

- **There are two questions that come up in interviews**, "So tell me about yourself." and, "What have you been doing lately?" The second question is very easy to answer if you've been doing any theater, working on a set, on TV, commercials, or anything of that nature because it's current and it's probably not on your resume yet. All actors are actively pursuing their careers. They're seeking auditions, working on their audition skills, getting to networking meetings, meeting new people, getting new pictures, working on their craft. These are things that you should be doing, so that becomes a very easy question. When they say, "Tell me about yourself," we freeze up. We can never think of a thing to say, and yet, it's the one thing that we know more about than anything else. Think of five interesting things about yourself. What makes you different, unique, and special?

- **If you sing, include that on your resume.** Most of the theater in Los Angeles that pays is musical or dinner theater and many of the Equity theaters do musicals, so you have an advantage.

Resources

The publications below are at theatrical bookstores.

Breakdown Service, (310) 276-9166. 1120 S. Robertson Blvd., 3rd floor, Los Angeles, CA 90035. $45 a year for a subscription to the **Casting Directors Directory** and updates. Casting directors move around very fast, this directory is updated every two weeks. $80 to deliver your play flyers to all the casting directors.

Casting directors mailing labels (300) for $16, so you can send out notices of a film, television show or play that you would like to have them see you in. Again, your name crosses their desks.

Casting By, is a book of CSA casting directors with 10 of their credits.

I asked my daughter to write this section because I thought it would be educational for readers who are interested in a commercial career. She is including a diary of the steps she took to launch her commercial career in Los Angeles, and examples of the tools she is using. As this goes to print, she has an agent and she is nailing her auditions in class. There are also commercial shots of the other actors you saw in the Photography Section.

THE BUSINESS OF COMMERCIALS

BY CYNTHIA KERR

• **I love commercials. Working in commercials** can change your life. One good national commercial is worth roughly $35,000 a year. If you were to book three or four nationals in the next year, just imagine how much your financial world might change. After booking a couple of national commercials, while living in Dallas, Texas, I was able to finance my childhood dream of attending an acting conservatory and provide my family with additional health insurance. The security of having money in the bank gave me the confidence to continue pursuing the career of my dreams.

• **A commercial career is a tough, competitive**, ever-changing specialty career. In commercials, you must have an agent in order to get auditions. It is rare to find student or non-union opportunities to gain experience. Commercial acting classes are essential. You will also benefit from taking improvisation classes, as well as basic acting craft.

• **Hugh Leon, successful commercial agent with Coast to Coast Talent Group says:**

> • **If you are not in class, you're not serious about making a living** working in commercials. I don't care how many commercials you book, you still need to study, to get in there and practice. You are always going to learn something new by looking over new copy, getting in front of the camera and staying current. When you take classes from various casting directors, you are no longer just a face on a picture. You learn what is going to get you a call back when you audition for them.

• **If you want a commercial career, be an expert in commercials**. Watch commercials at different times of the day and night. Where are you going to make your money? Figure out what your type is. Are you the spokesperson, young mom or dad, fast-food counter guy or girl, granny or gramps, blue collar worker, executive, athlete, model type, the comedian? Maybe you fit several types. Knowing your types and the spots you will be cast in will help you sell yourself when you start interviewing with agents.

• **Keep a notebook; study the actors who look like you** and are in the same age category. What is the product, the style of campaign, the type of people, what was their behavior, why did they book the job? Write down the copy (dialogue in commercials) and practice doing the commercial yourself. What type of clothes are they wearing? Clothing terms are usually:

- **Casual**, meaning what you might wear to clean your house or mow your lawn, dockers and T-shirt. No jeans or denim shirts.
- **Nice casual**, which is what you would wear out to dinner and a movie with friends—dockers with a nice shirt or sweater.
- **Upscale casual**. This look is casual and classy.
- **Upscale**. Dressy and classy.
- **Business/Spokesperson**, suit and tie for men, tailored dress or suit for women.
- **Hip/trendy look** means the latest fashion trend.

• **Your notebook will help you when you get an audition** for Coke, Xerox, IBM, Folgers, Citibank, etc. You will have a sense of what the campaign is and what the client might be looking for when they are auditioning you.

•Stuart K. Robinson, respected and sought-after commercial coach, who teaches the skills, techniques and philosophy of how to book the job, says:

- **The reason most actors are not successful** is that they don't know what the client (the person/people who represent the product which is being advertised) wants. The client will tell you what they want you to do, but they do not tell you what they need. Stuart adds that in order to be competitive in the commercial business, the actor must be an expert at three things.

- **First, you must be able to diagnose what the client needs without being told.**
- **Second, you must be able to create the behavior to answer that need.**
- **Third, you must be able to execute that need before the camera.**

• **Once you have an idea of the type of characters** you can play and you have taken enough commercial classes to be consistently good, it is time to shop for an agent. You now need a promotional package. This consists of a great head shot, a resume, and a powerful cover letter.

• **Your commercial head shot is the most important tool** in your promotional package; it is your ticket in the door. Your picture will be one in a thousand that passes the desk of a casting director or agent in any given week. The competition is fierce. In order for an agent or casting director to open their door to you, you must grab their attention in the millisecond they spend looking at your picture. If your head shot does not do that, then your picture will end up in the trash.

• **What is a good commercial head shot?**

• **Commercial agent Hugh Leon says:**

- **I like personality shots.** I should be able to say 10 things about who that person is, whether this person is a smart-ass, intelligent, crazy, warm and loving or shy—something about that person. A commercial actor can have multiple pictures—a business shot, a casual shot, an athletic shot if you are athletic and a zany/crazy shot if you are a character.

• **Stuart Stone, top commercial casting director**, likes pictures that have great energy. He adds:

- **Your picture should look like you do** at any given moment of the day. I want to know what I am getting when I call you in. I like natural shots, messy hair is great.

- **Beverly Long, respected commercial casting director and commercial teacher, recommends:**

  - **A fairly loose head shot, very natural.** It doesn't have to be big teeth, just has to be pleasant with energy. The 3/4 shot gives a lot more sense of the person. I would have a head shot and 3/4 shot.

- **Stuart K. Robinson says:**

  - **Anytime I look at a head shot and I know what the person is thinking,** that is a great photo. A photograph is not meant to capture a look on your face. A photograph has to capture your quality, a specific feeling.

- **How do you get a great head shot?**

- **In Stuart K. Robinson's five-week commercial class, he teaches:**

  - **To take a great shot you have to have a thought.** "I am so happy to be here." "It is good to see you!" "It's my birthday!" You have to have a feeling about what is going on, so the photographer can capture that feeling. That thought will be real joy, true pride, warm love, real power, great satisfaction, or whatever it is you are trying to capture.

  - **Thoughts create great photos; posing creates portraits.** Let the picture show your acting ability. Bad pictures do not come from bad photographers. Bad pictures come from bad acting.

  - **To get a great shot you have to prepare for your photo shoot.** Interview photographers. Do not just pick one because someone tells you to go to them. Meet them, make sure you feel comfortable in their company. Look at their work, see what they think a good shot is. Do the eyes talk to you? Are the pictures saying anything? You want a photographer that gives you the motivation, freedom and comfort so you can have specific thoughts. One who knows when to snap the photo.

  - **Before the shoot, decide what categories you want to capture**, what thoughts to have in your head in order to do that. Bring to the shoot your favorite music and photographs from your life that can help you trigger the moods you want to feel. Do not rush your session—take all the time you need. Remember, this picture is going to open up the doors to your career.

• **I have been in and out of this business for 25 years** and I've had hundreds of pictures taken. When Stuart shared this information, I finally understood what my responsibility is during my photo shoots. In the past, I would go to the shoot with the right clothes and knowing the looks I wanted, but I had general, not specific, thoughts from my life. Stuart's advice makes all the difference.

• **When I get proof sheets, I find it helpful to scan the shots** I like and enlarge them on my home computer. I print them out using photographic copy paper. This gives me a better look at the pictures. Then I choose several shots and have 4x6 copies made. I show the 4x6s to my acting teachers, casting directors I know and agents to help me decide which is the best shot to use for my 8x10 master. From the master, I ran off 100 reproductions. Quality lithographs are acceptable for commercial agents and casting directors.

As you will see from reading Cynthia's diary (page 179), this was not a fast process.

Cynthia Kerr

Photographer: **Alisha Tamburri**
Makeup/Hair: **AlisaChompupong**

Photographer: **Mary Ann Halpin**
Makeup & Hair: **Sandy Williams**
Retouching: **Nichan**

Photographer: **Dianna Lannes**
Makeup & Hair: **Rela Martine**
Retouching: **Nichan**

Photographer: **Michael Lamont**
Makeup: **Michael Lamont**
Retouching: **Michael Lamont**

Judy Kerr
Photographer: **Michael Helms**
Makeup: **Rita's Makeup Chart**
Section Six, page 353.

Photographer: **Nancy Jo Gilchrist**
Makeup & Hair: **Robert Raphael**
Retouching: **Ray The Retoucher**

Anthony Christiansen
Photographer: **Rich Hogan**
Custom Computer Border

Photographer: **Sean Kenney**

Janice Allen
Photographer: **Mara**
Hair & Makeup: **Mara**
Retouching: **Mara**

Photographer: **Carrie Cavalier**
Hair & Makeup: **Laura Connelly**

From The Child Actors' Section, Page 456.

Photographer
Hank Tovar

Cynthia and the boys, Austin and Jackson Tovar.

Hank's directions of how he took these two photos are on Page 472.

Cynthia used this picture on a 5x7 postcard as a marketing tool. She listed their names, agents and phone numbers under each of their faces.

Photographer
Hank Tovar

Austin Tovar

From The Child Actors' Section, Page 456.

Photographer
Doreen Stone
See Page 473

Jackson Tovar
Age 4

Photographer
Diana Lannes

Retouching
Nichan

There was a loose string on the button, it was distracting so Nichan took care of it.

FROM THE CHILD ACTORS' SECTION, PAGE 456.

Photographer
Doreen Stone

Austin Tovar
Age 10

Cynthia used these two pictures on a 5x7 postcard, sent to casting directors to show two sides of Austin's personality.

Photographer
Sean Kenney

• **The resume is the second tool** in your promotional package. What should be on your commercial resume? Special skills and commercial training are closely looked at. *More details and resume examples in Section Two, pages 109-117.*

Cynthia's commercial resume was designed by Image Starters. They used photographer Mary Ann Halpin's 3/4 shot.

CYNTHIA KERR

FEATURE FILMS

Buffy the Vampire Slayer	Martial Arts Stunts	Fran Kuzui
Bionic Man Trilogy	Lead	Ron South
Three People	Featured	Willard Rodgers

TELEVISION

The Facts of Life	Recurring	Assad Kelada
Diff'rent Strokes	Guest	Herbert Kenwith

THEATRE

Pizza Man	Julie	Red Barn Nashville
Ladies in Waiting	Kate	S.T.A.G.E. Dallas
Search and Destroy	Lauren/Jackie	KD Studio Dallas
The Heidi Chronicles	Heidi	KD Studio Dallas
Reckless	Rachel	KD Studio Dallas
Fallen Angels	Julia	KD Studio Dallas
Julius Caesar	Portia	KD Studio Dallas
Vanities	Kathy	Westwood Playhouse

COMMERCIALS

List Upon Request

INDUSTRIALS

Mary Kay Cosmetics	Lead	Quin Matthews
Centex Homes	Lead	Peter Polce
Dynamic Kata	Lead	Sidekick Productions
Explosive Kicks	Lead	Sidekick Productions
IBM	Featured	Vision West
Mortgage Network	Featured	IBC Productions
Crime Re-enactment	Featured	David Orr

SAG/AFTRA

Hair: Blonde

Eyes: Blue

Height: 5'6"

Weight: 125

TRAINING

Acting	Judy Kerr Acting Workshop
	Joan Darling Technique and Scene Study
Commercials	Stuart K. Robinson On-Going Semi Private Workouts
	Workshops w/ Stuart Stone, Megan Foley, Terry Berland
Education	KD Studio Actor's Conservatory of the Southwest
	Associate of Applied Arts/Acting Performance

Gold Marshak Liedtke Associates
Talent and Literary Agency
3500 West Olive Avenue, Suite 1400
Burbank, California 91505
tel 818 972 4300 fax 818 955 6411

SKILLS & INTERESTS

Martial Arts/Tae Kwon Do (Blackbelt, Kickboxing), Weight and Exercise Machines, Spinning, Cycling, Hiking, Camping, Horseback Riding, Softball, Photography, Real Estate, Reading, Soccer Mom

- **Casting director Stuart Stone says:**

  - **Put everything you can on your resume** and be proficient in everything you list under special skills. I look under training to see if you have taken commercial workshops. Do you have theatre credits? List plays you have done, no matter how long ago or how small the venue. We want to see on your resume that you are studying and working.

- **The third tool in your package is a powerful cover letter.**

- **Stuart K. Robinson says:**

  - **A strong cover letter will tell me why I need to respond** to this right now. Cover three points in your letter.

  - **First, what is great about you?** Do not wait for them to discover it. If it is that you just finished two major motion pictures, your career is about to unfold and you are looking to get into commercials, tell them that. It could be that you have just finished the greatest commercial class and you feel like, "Ahhh, I know my calling now." Tell them that. It could be as simple as, "Everywhere I go, people ask me if I am an actor." Anything that will make them go, "oooh."

  - **Second, tell them why you do not have an agent.** Is it because you just moved here from another market? Or you have been in another business for a while and you are just getting started now as an actor. Or you have been with a smaller agency, or an agency that did not quite work for you and you want to move somewhere more proactive. Tell us why, if you are so great, no one has scooped you up before me.

  - **Third point, where you are going to make money.** Why are you going to book young mom spots or why you are going to book any spot that has soccer in it? Tell them the sure thing. Tell them why money is going to come in if they respond to this submission.

  - **Cover these three points in three very short paragraphs.** Add some personality, that is a big plus, and you will have a strong cover letter. Some cover letters are very colorful and some are right to the point. Either way, you want to catch their attention and give them the good news right away.

- **My cover letter read like this:**

  I have just finished the greatest commercial class in the world with Stuart K. Robinson. I am continuing to work with him in his semiprivate classes. Having revived and sharpened my commercial acting tools, I am ready to go out and be competitive.

I recently moved to Los Angeles after having a successful commercial career in Dallas, Texas. I have booked many national commercials, including Mc Donald's, Chevrolet, Southwest Airlines and Applebee's Restaurants, to name a few.

I book young mom spots, teacher, part of a couple, housewife, lady next door and business woman. I am also a champion black belt martial artist, so any spots in that category are mine.

I am looking forward to meeting with you at your earliest convenience.

• **Now your package is together.** How do you get a commercial agent, or at least an appointment to meet with one?

• **There are three ways to get an appointment with an agent.**

1) **The standard way**. Mail your head shot, resume and cover letter to agencies. This method is not very effective unless your materials are so dynamic that they just have to see you as soon as possible.

• **Beverly Long, casting director and teacher says:**

• **There are books with the names of agents** and a little blurb about each agent in the city. There are probably 200 commercial agents in Los Angeles. You can't send your picture out to every agent, but with some help you can narrow it down. That is what I try to do in my classes—narrow it down, and give you maybe 10 to 12 choices of agents who will be likely to represent you.

2) **The scenic route way**. Doing theater or showcases and hoping someone sees your work, that you impress them and they suggest a meeting.

3) **Referrals, the most effective way**. When an agent is told by someone they respect that they should see you, they will. How do you get referrals? You ask! If you know someone who has an agent or who knows an agent, ask him to introduce you. Make it known that you are looking for an agent.

• **When you get an interview with an agent, you want to go in there** and really sell yourself. What usually happens is, we try to be on our best behavior and answer the agent's questions without letting our personality out. The agent then wonders what is so special about this person? Go into that office knowing exactly where you are going to make your money, act and look your type, dress your type. Be extremely clear about the roles you are going to book and the categories you are going to work in. Talk about commercials you love. Talk about what their part is in the business; you are an expert too.

• **Tell stories about yourself.** Look around the office and learn about them. Try to find a common denominator and establish a relationship. Most agents will take you on because they like you and like being around you. It is not always about your acting ability.

• **Neil Kreppel, long time, respected commercial agent from Commercial Talent Agency.**

Q: How do you build a relationship with an agent? Should you ask them to lunch?

- **Make an appointment,** come in and just talk so we can get to know each other. As for lunch, at this time in the agency, we are really too busy to go out to lunch. If someone wants to bring in something for us to have lunch together that would be all right.

Q: What is the actor's responsibility?

- **They should always have pictures here** with their resume stapled on the back. They should immediately confirm with us the information we have given them about an audition. They should always arrive early for their appointment times and of course, they should book some jobs.

Q: How can the actor help the agent?

- **We expect clients to be very professional.** We want them to have trust in us. It is all right if occasionally you fax or call about a casting that you have heard about and wonder if you have been sent out. Sometimes you have been submitted and sometimes you may not be what the casting director has asked for. We don't like people to be annoying, calling every day about submitting them for projects because they have seen the breakdowns.

• **Commercial agent Hugh Leon** talks about what he expects from the actors he represents.

- **I expect the actor to give me the right pictures**; I need the marketing tools to get you out there. I don't want to hear, "I don't have the money to get better pictures." Once I have called you with an audition, don't ask me to rearrange the audition time to meet your schedule. Don't miss an audition— this is not a hobby, this is a career; it should be the number one priority. If it is not, get out! Do the best you can, be professional and go into your audition prepared. Don't call me 20 times a day. Keep good records, write down the audition information, who you saw, where you went, what you wore, so if I call you a week later with a call back you are ready to go. Have a Thomas Guide in your car— I'm not a map. Confirm auditions. Be grateful that I got you an audition. Remember, I work for free until you book a job.

• **Once you have signed with an agent,** it is a good idea to start marketing yourself to casting directors. They are the ones who will call you in to audition.

Stuart Stone, casting director, talks about marketing:

- **Postcards with your picture on it are a great marketing tool.** I don't have to open an envelope, your picture is right there. Write a note, let me know you just signed with such and such agency, or you will be on a TV show (with date, time and channel) so I can watch, or that you are in a play. You can send postcards or fliers every few weeks. I will become familiar with your face, so when your agent submits your picture to me, I think to myself, "I know her" and I'll call you in. You can also knock on my door and say, "Hey, I just wanted to introduce myself." I don't mind an actor doing that, because most actors do not take the initiative.

• **When my agency took me on, this is the card I sent out.** My picture is on the left; under it my name and under that SAG. The message was on the right with my agent's logo under it. "I'm ready to work! Just signed with Gold Marshak Liedtke Associates for commercial representation. Looking forward to auditioning for you soon!"

• **Commercial auditions.**

• **Danny Goldman, casting director, director and teacher, describes his job:**

- **The function of the casting director** is to show the director, the agency and the client a variety of people—the types they ask for and some alternatives. We have seen as many as 200 people for one part. The final decision is made by the client, the agency and the director when the director is a star director. The casting director has no say whatsoever. If the dialogue is really bad, those actors that can come in and solve the problems of the dialogue are the ones who get the job.

• **When your agent calls you with an audition,** they are going to give you some valuable information. They will tell you the date and time of your call, the casting person/company and their location, as well as the product, the wardrobe you should wear and the type of character they are looking for (i.e. young mom, clerk, spokesperson etc.). You must write all this information down and use it to help prepare yourself for your audition.

• **Plan your wardrobe** based on the information your agent gave you and from your own research on the product and type of character they are looking for. Dress for the part. Don't forget your head shot and resume.

• **Use your Thomas Guide** to map out your route to the location and plan to arrive at least 15 minutes before your call time to go over any copy you will need to rehearse.

• **When you arrive at the audition, check the storyboard** (a series of hand drawn pictures showing each scene of the commercial) and see if there is any copy you need to prepare for the audition. Diagnose the script quickly with the techniques you have learned from your commercial training. Don't worry about memorizing the copy.

• **Once you feel prepared to audition, sign in** on the Exhibit E SAG/AFTRA Commercial Audition Report, (sign-in sheet). Print your name, social security number (SAG membership number can be used instead of social security number for security purposes), agent, time of actual call, time you arrived, your initials, whether it is your first call or a call back. The sex, age, and ethnicity questions are optional; the unions use these to track casting trends. Upon leaving, always be sure you sign out. If the audition runs longer than an hour, you may be entitled to compensation from the production company.

• **Next, fill out the size card if one is available.** This is used for call backs to help size up groups or pairs and also for the wardrobe people when you book the commercial, so be accurate. You do not have to put your address or Social Security number on the card. After you complete the size card, the casting director will probably take a Polaroid of you. These usually look pretty bad—don't get upset over it. The casting people say they only use them as a reference to help match you up with your video audition.

• **When the paper work is done, continue to work** on the audition copy. Rehearse out loud, get comfortable with the words and your actions. Make the material about you. Own it! Keep a positive attitude; do not let other actors in the room distract you. Compete for the job.

• **Carolyne Barry, commercial actress, teacher and casting director says:**

  • **Good commercial acting is good acting, only speeded up**; it is the pauses that are tightened up. When auditioning, you must spend time with the copy as you would a cold reading. You must motivate the copy, know who you are talking to and determine your objective.

Casting director Stuart Stone suggests:

- **Always know what has happened in this character's life** the moment before you start talking and what is going to happen after the last moment of the scene. Make the piece real to you, then it will be real to us. Give the most feeling you can to the copy and still be honest. This is the ideal in commercial acting.

• **You are auditioning when you enter the audition room.** Be in character. Your behavior, body language, tone of voice and emotions should reflect the situation in the commercial scenario.

• **There will be a mark on the floor where you should stand.** Most likely it will be a piece of tape in the shape of a T. Stand on your mark with the T between your feet and look into the camera. If a cue card (the copy written in large print placed near the camera) is provided, look it over. Some words may be different from your script. Get familiar with the sentence structure so you know where to look when you need to read the next line.

• **Not all auditions have copy**. Many times you are asked to improvise a scene or tell a funny joke, or the casting director will ask you a question like, "Name three people living or dead that you'd like to have dinner with and why?" Do not panic, just say the first thing that pops in your mind. If the question does stump you, keep a constant connection with the camera. This will allow your personality to show and remember, you can always make something up. The people looking at the tape are looking at your personality and how you will fit it with their product. Many times they watch these tapes with the sound turned off.

• **The casting director or the camera operator will give you directions.** As you listen to them, look into the camera and picture someone you know in the lens and let the camera see inside you.

• **You will be asked to slate your name.** Slating is your introduction and your opportunity to let the clients know, within the first three seconds, you are what they are looking for. After you slate your name, the casting director or camera operator will often ask for profiles. This means they want to see your face from different angles. The operator will then say "action" and you start the scene. Go for it!

• **The casting director is not always in the room** during the first call audition, but don't think they are not watching. Most casting facilities have video feed from the audition room to the casting director's office down the hall. Listen to all directions given to you and work them into your audition. You must be flexible; they are also looking to see if you are able to take direction.

• **After the audition say to yourself,** "I just took a shot at a $35,000 job today," and then forget about it. You may hear from your agent in a couple of days that you have a call back. Congratulations. A call back means you are a finalist for the job and you get to audition again, this time for the clients, the director, producer and advertising agency. When you go to the call back, dress and look the same way you did for your first audition unless your agent tells you differently. Figure out why they called you back, so you can give them more of the same behavior. The director will most likely be directing your audition. One of the things they will be looking for is how flexible you are, how well you take direction and how easy you will be to work with.

• **After your call back, your agent may call you to say** you are on "avail/first refusal" or they have put you on "hold." "Avail/first refusal" means the casting director wants to know if you are available to work on a certain date. It is not legally binding; the actor can accept other work. When the actor is put on "hold" they are asked to schedule a specific day to work. The actor and employer have made the commitment, it is legally binding and payment must be made whether or not the actor works on that day.

• **You booked the job!**

•**Your agent or someone from the production company** will call you with the days you will need to be available for the commercial shoot and the time and date of your wardrobe fitting. You will be paid hourly with a one-hour minimum for the fitting. At your fitting appointment you will be given the date, time and location shoot for the commercial.

• **When you arrive on the set, find the second** AD (assistant director), who will have your SAG contract and let you know where you need to be. I suggest asking them for today's call sheet. It will have the names of everybody who is working that day. I also find it helpful when writing my thank you notes because the addresses of the advertising agency and production company are usually on the call sheet. You want to file this away. You may need to refer to it years later when you are working with some of the same people again. Make sure you read your contract carefully. If you are unsure about anything, call your agent before signing. Have the production company fax a copy to your agent.

• **Always be professional, polite, prepared and eager to work.** Stay relaxed and comfortable. If you are not working on a shot, stay close by and let the AD know where you are at all times. When they call for you, be ready to work. Have fun; this is what you have been working so hard for.

• **When and how much do we get paid?**

• **An on-camera principle actor gets paid a session fee** for each day of work or for each commercial produced, whichever is greater. Currently the session fee is $478.70 for an eight-hour workday, excluding mealtime. The ninth and tenth hour are paid at time and a half ($89.76 per hour). The eleventh hour and beyond is known as golden time and is paid at double-time ($119.68 hour). The session fee must be paid within 12 working days.

• **The session fee allows the advertising agency** the right to use the commercial for 13 weeks. The actor cannot work for a competitive product during the same period of time.

• **Holding fees or fixed payment fees** are paid every 13 weeks to maintain the rights to the commercial and the actor's exclusivity to the product. The amount is equal to the session fee. If you do not get a holding fee after 13 weeks it means you have been released and then you can book another commercial with a competing product.

• **When the commercial is aired, you are due residual payments.** There are several different types of residual payments and they are paid on different scale levels depending on how the commercial is used. Some of the different categories are: network use, cable use, national, regional, local, wild spot, dealer use.

• **It is not uncommon in commercials to receive a "buyout" payment.** This means you will be paid a single fee for the shooting and airing of the commercial. No residuals. These are usually commercials that are sold to foreign markets.

• **Your pay checks usually get mailed to your agent** and they will take out their 10 percent of the session fees, holding fees and residuals. The agent then mails you a check. When you have a good national commercial running, it is fun to go to the mailbox.

Cynthia's Diary: Launching a Commercial Career

Wed.Feb 17	Took pictures for Mom's book with Diana Lannes. It was fun, kind of gave me the acting bug a little bit.
Wed. March 24	Took a commercial intensive workshop with Stuart K. Robinson. Got inspired to act again. Jackson is close to four years old. I feel the time is right to start my commercial career in L.A.
Fri. March 26.	Enrolled in Stuart Robinson's five-week commercial class.
Tue. March 30	Started updating resume.
Tue. April 6	Called photographers Mary Ann Halprin and Michael Lamont to set up photo sessions.
Wed. April 7	Started Stuart's commercial class.
Sat. April 10	Interviewed commercial agent Hugh Leon on cable show (*Judy Kerr's Acting Workshop*).
Mon. April 12	Met photographer Michael Lamont, set photo session.
Wed. April 14	Stuart's commercial class.
Tue. April 20	Photo shoot with Mary Ann Halprin.
Wed. April 21	Stuart's commercial class. We bring pictures next week.
Mon. April 26	Photo shoot with Michael Lamont.
Wed. April 28	Stuart's class—what it takes to get a great headshot.
Thu. April 29	Interviewed casting director Stuart Stone on cable show.
Sat. May 1	Contact sheets on scanner to pick shots to make 4x6s.
Wed. May 5	Last class—how to write a powerful cover letter. Decided to continue in his semi-private classes.
Thu. May 6	Started writing cover letter to submit to agents.
Fri. May 7	Set photo session with Alisha Tamburri for May 28.
Wed. May 12	Semi private workout with Stuart Robinson.
Fri. May 28	Photo shoot with Alisha Tamburri.
Mon. June 2	Jackson turns four years old.
Wed. June 4	Pick up contact sheets from Alisha, scanned on computer.
Mon. June 7	Meet with casting director Stuart Stone. He picked out a a couple of shots from scanned copies of my contact sheets.
Wed. June 9	Ordered 4x6s.
Tue. June 15	Picked up 4x6s.
Wed. June 23	Stuart Robinson's class, he picked out best shot from 4x6s.
Tue. June 29	Began Stuart Stone's four-week commercial workshop. Stuart Stone picked same shot as Stuart Robinson.
Wed. June 30	Ordered 8x10 master.
Tue. July 6	Stuart Stone's commercial workshop.
Wed. July 7	Stuart Robinson semi private.
Thu. July 15	Met with Emily at Acme Talent and Literary agency, set up by Stuart Stone. Emily liked my commercial shot. Ordered lithos at Andersons.
Fri. July 16	Called Acme Talent, they have too many in my category.
Tue. July 20	Stuart Stone's commercial workshop, third class.
Wed. July 21	Stuart Robinson's class. He read my cover letter, said, "I'ts great, who wouldn't want to call you in."
Thu. July 22	Picked up lithographs. Made copies of resume and cover letter.
Mon. July 26	Mailed submissions (headshot, resume, cover letter) to the top 12 agencies.

Tue. July 27	Abrams Artists called, received my submission, set interview. Stuart Stone's final class in this series.
Wed. July 28	Interview at Abrams Artists. Set appointment with Gold Marshak Liedke—Stuart Stone referral.
Thu. July 29	Interview with Gold Marshak Liedke.
Fri. July 30	Called Abrams Artists, left message.
Tues. Aug. 3	Called Seana at Gold Marshak Leitke. She would like to take me on.
Wed. Aug. 4	Dropped off 100 pictures and resumes to new agent. She liked Jackson's picture and will try him out. Get her pictures. Putting addresses of commercial casting directors in computer to make mailing labels.
Thu. Aug. 5	Ordered 100 postcards from Anderson Graphics to send to commercial casting directors announcing my new agent.
Thu. Aug. 12	Picked up postcards from Andersons'. Miscommunication resulted in 300 postcards announcing my new agents, so I will be sending to advertising agencies and commercial production companies listed in the Ross Reports TV commercial guide. Input addresses in computer for mailing labels. Mailed postcards to commercial casting directors.
Wed. Aug 18	Stuart K. Robinson's class 11-12:30. Began another four-week Stuart Stone workshop.
Thu. Aug 19	Delivered Commercial Section for the ninth edition to Mom.

COMMERCIAL CLASSES Recommended by Judy Kerr

Stuart K. Robinson, Class Line: 310/558-4961. He teaches a $70 one-night introduction to commercials. Five-week commercial class is $300. Semi-private classes $35 each, private $80 an hour. Cynthia and I continue to study with him in his semi-private hour-and-a-half workouts. He is the only teacher who has this type of on-going classes where you can get a chance to work on audition copy on a weekly basis. Stuart is recommended by most agents and casting directors. He usually has a waiting list but it is worth the effort to get into his classes. Also check out his acting classes.

Carolyne Barry's Commercial Acting Workshops, 323/654-2212. www.carolynebarry.com. All workshops are divided into beginner, intermediate and advance levels. Including: Improvisation, Improv for Commercial Auditions, Performance Improv I & II, Intro Commercial, Intermediate Commercial, Advanced Commercial Technique and the unique Agent Showcase Tape Class. Classes range in price from $315 to $425 for eight-week sessions. Recommended by agents. **Carolyne and Kevin E. West of Actor's Network have produced an audio tape: *The Actor's Guide to Getting The Job.*** Great to listen to on your way to auditions.

Terry Berland, casting director, 310/571-4141. Author of *Breaking Into Commercials: Complete Guide to Marketing Yourself.* Six-week on-camera, $325. She teaches how to apply your unique personality and develop a confident approach. Learn on camera how to create dimension in this one minute commercial medium. Class includes meeting an agent.

Pamela Campus, casting director, 310/398-2715 or 818/897-1588. Has cast over 3,000 commercials and taught over 10,000 adults and children. Adults and teens, beginners and advanced. six-week classes at Westside Studios. Children starting at age three. They are always taught personally by the casting directors. Very highly recommended by agents.

Divisek Casting, casting directors, 818/506-6868. Children and adults, always taught personally by the casting directors. Very highly recommended by agents.

Megan Foley, casting directors, 818/755-9384. $150. Teaches a commercial intensive, a one day, eight-hour class on camera, that covers all aspects of the commercial audition.

Kip King, 818/784-0544. Commercial copy and improvisation. Successful actor, over 400 movies, TV shows, commercials and voice-overs. One of the original Groundlings; only class of its kind. On camera improv for TV and commercials. Guest casting directors, agents, celebrities and voice-over pros. On-going, 11 weeks: $350. Private coaching, $75 for non-students, $50 for students.

Lien/Cowan, Michael Lien and Dan Cowan, casting directors, 323/937-0411. www.liencowancasting.comTheir office casts hundreds of commercials a year. Associates Jan Bina and John Smet teach one day, four-hour, seminars. 15 to 20 actors per class. They critique pictures and have the actors read actual copy from commercials they've cast. They show the call back tapes of people who got the commercials they've read for. $75 for the class .

Beverly Long, casting director, 818/754-6222. I took my first commercial class with Beverly over 20 years ago. She is very knowledgeable, fun and a great teacher. Many of my students have taken their first classes with her.

Stuart Stone, casting director, 323/932-6330. "Everything you need to know to book the job!" Copy reading techniques, overcoming obstacles and working with props. Four week classes, $275.

BOOKS & TAPES

Order from Samuel French Bookstore 323/876-0570 (Hollywood) or 818/762-0535 (Studio City.)

The Actor's Guide to Getting The Job, an audio tape, by Carolyne Barry and Kevin E. West. $24.95. www.carolynebarry.com.
The Agencies: What the Actor Needs To Know by Acting World Books.
The Actor's Picture/Resume Book by Jill Charles & Tom Bloom.
An Actor's Workbook: Get The Agent You Need And The Career You Want by K. Callan.
Acting In Television Commercials by Squire Fridell.
Acting In the Million Dollar Minute by Tom Logan.
Breaking Into Commercials: Complete Guide to Marketing Yourself by Terry Berland.
Commercials, Just My Speed!! by Vernee Watson-Johnson.
Word of Mouth, a Guide to Commercial Voice-Overs, by Susan Blu & Molly Ann Mullin.
Hollywood Agents & Managers Directory by Hollywood Creative Directory.
Ross Reports Television and Film: Agents, TV Commercial Casting Guide By Backstage

COMMERCIAL PRINT MODELING

BY CYNTHIA KERR

• **Print work is an additional source for actors to gain experience** and make extra money. Commercial print is a still picture of a commercial. It is the type of advertising you see in newspapers, magazines, on billboards and buses. Print models get paid by the hour. In the Los Angeles market models are paid between $150 to $200 an hour. There are no residuals, but depending on the format and product identification, it is not unusual to be paid a bonus on top of the hourly rate.

• **Aaron Marcus is an actor, commercial model and author** of *How to Become a Successful Commercial Model.* He says:

- **A lot of very successful commercial models are actors.** Photographers love hiring actors because they can take direction, and provide a variety of believable emotions.

Q: What is the difference between commercial modeling and fashion modeling?

- **Everyone knows about the fashion model**—tall, thin, very unusual and exotic looking. To even be considered as a fashion model, you must have very specific physical requirements. For commercial print work they hire everybody; there are no height, weight or age requirements. Fashion models normally promote high-end designer clothes; commercial models advertise everything else.

Q: How can someone get started in the commercial print business?

- **The most basic way would be with an 8x10 head shot.** Call the agents in your city and find out if they handle commercial print. Ask if they have open calls, or if you should submit by mail. Once you get an agent you will need to get a composite sheet. This is a collection of photographs that shows a variety of ways you can look and the different categories you can play. The agent can help you decide on the categories that would be marketable for you. The composite is your calling card. It is what the agent submits to a photographer or an art director in order to get you work. It is not uncommon to get hired from your composite, without having to audition.

Q: How do you audition for print work?

- **The audition for commercial print modeling is called a go-see,** because you go and you are seen. When your agent calls you with the audition information, make sure you find out what they are looking for, and dress the part. When you walk in the room you want them to say, "Yeah, that is the person for this job." Before signing in, look over the layout of the ad (copy of ad). It shows what the clients are looking for. Study it. What does this person look like? What are their facial and body expressions? Is there any copy, any words to the ad? Know the kind of expressions you want to show. When you feel prepared and ready, sign in. In most situations you will have a Polaroid shot taken and they will staple it to your composite sheet.

- **When you book the job, it is important that you understand the ad** and how it needs to be delivered. I view commercial print work as any other acting job. I say words or sounds that will allow me to feel the emotion that I need to present. It will make the shots look very powerful. When you are in touch with your expressions and emotions, there is believability in your eyes and your body will move naturally. Some photographers might say, "I really don't want to see any kind of talking," then you need to do an internal monologue. The key is to have some life going on in your brain.

Q: When do you get paid?

- **The client pays the advertising agency,** the advertising agency pays the photographer, the photographer pays the agent. Once the check clears, the agent takes out their 20% commission and then the model gets paid. In most cases it takes 90 days to get paid.

- **At the shoot there are two forms you need to fill out.** One is a voucher and the other is a model release form. The voucher is the contract that you sign at the end of every job. You get a copy, your agent gets a copy and the person paying you gets a copy. The other form is the model release form. Basically it says the photographer can use your image any way he wants to. You must get familiar with these forms, learn to fill them out correctly and make the necessary changes. If the changes are not made, you could lose a tremendous amount of money.

• **While researching the print modeling business,** I talked to several actors who supplement their acting income as "fit models." Fit modeling is basically a garment industry job. Every company that manufactures clothing uses fit models to make their patterns. The fit model goes to the factories and works with the designers. They drape their designs on them and decide what trim to use or what buttons would be best. Then the model goes to the fit room and tells the pattern maker what is uncomfortable, what is too tight or too loose.

• **The hours are flexible;** the manufacturers will work with your schedule if you are the size they need. The required size is "average" but one company's average might be a size eight for women, another's a size two. You do have to be well proportioned. The pay is $75 to $85 an hour minus the agency commission which is 15 to 20%. Models can work for several manufacturers; many fit models work non-stop.

• **Natasha at Peak Models, Inc., says her company handles many actors** that add to their acting income by fit modeling, print modeling or working conventions as hosts and hostesses. You can send a picture and resume along with snapshots, your measurements and the type of work you are interested in, to Peak Models, Inc., 25852 Mc Bean Parkway, PMB 190, Valencia, CA 91355.

Resources

How to Become a Successful Commercial Model, by Aaron Marcus www.howtomodel.com. 410/764-8270.
Ross Reports Television & Film: Commercial Casting Guide, by Back Stage West.
The Agencies: What the Actor Needs To Know by Acting World Books. Use this guide to look for an agent. Their listing will specify if they do print or not.
The Working Actor's Guide, L.A., Aaron Blake Publishing.

Voice-Over for Commercials and Animation Acting

This takes a special acting energy, coming from a different perspective. You should be a well-trained actor before studying voice-overs; it is a *very* lucrative field to get into. You must have an agent for this work; there are several of them in town. This is another very tough field to break into—you need a very special voice and talent. I would take classes with casting directors. Look in *Back Stage West/Drama-Logue* for ads. If you get in the circle of people who are doing voice-overs, you will learn a lot about it.

Voice-Over Classes

Susan Blu, contact 818/783-9130. Great classes, she knows the business. Studio: 818/501-1BLU for voiceover demos. Susan is the author of *Word Of Mouth, A Guide To Commercial Voice-Overs.*

Michael Bell's Voice Animation Workshop, 818/784-5107. Six-week classes. "In my class, you will learn to paint the picture with your voice, test the limits of your pipes and your imagination and rediscover the fun of eating the scenery! Above all discover who's hidden inside, let them out and make them pay!"

Dolores Diehl, The Voiceover Connection Inc. 213/384-9251. Teaches workshops in all phases of voiceovers, commercial, narration and animation, from basic to advanced levels. Agents, casting directors and performers teach the intermediate to advanced levels. 8 sessions, $350.

Joni Gerber, 323/654-1159. Private classes $65 per hour, semiprivate $80 ($40 each). One of the top working voice-over people.

Sandy Holt, 310/271-8217. Teaches voiceover/looping workshops and produces voiceover demos.

Nova Productions, Nicholas Omana, 323/969-0949. $65 per hour private. Beginners and intermediate classes, $350 for 6 weeks. Advanced, $250 for 4 classes. Professional workout, $80 a month. Nicholas also produces demo tapes.

Voice-over is What We Do, 800/871-2828. Word of Mouth Productions. Classes taught by working voice-over pros!

National Voice Database, www.voicedatabase.com. 310/278-9292. 9399 Wilshire Blvd., Suite 105, Beverly Hills, 90210. Go to their website and listen to the demo tapes. They say you can live anywhere in the country and do voice-overs. This website is full of information for voice-over actors.

BOOKS

The Agencies: What the Actor Needs To Know by Acting World Books. This is the authentic, well-researched agent guide. There are other publications that look like this one—don't be fooled. You will find agents who specialize in voice-overs.

Take It From The Top! How to Earn Your Living in Radio & TV Voice-Overs by Alice Whitfield, available on audio cassette. I would advise every actor to listen to these tapes. Yes, you hear all about voice-overs but you also hear the proper way to conduct business in your whole acting career.

Word Of Mouth, A Guide To Commercial Voice-Overs by Susan Blu.

Voice and the Actor by Cicely Berry. This is not necessarily about voice-overs, but about using your correct voice.

Voice-Overs: Putting Your Mouth Where the Money Is, by Chris Douthitt.

Agencies

Abrams Artists & Assoc. 310/859-1417, 9200 Sunset Blvd., 11th fl., L.A., 90069.
Abrams-Rubaloff & Lawrence, 323/935-1700, 8075 W. 3rd St., #303, L.A., 90048.
Artist Management Agency, 949/261-7557, 180 E. Garry, #101, Santa Ana, 92705.
Brand Talent & Model Agency, 714/850-1158, 1520 Brookhollow Dr., #39, Santa Ana.
CL Inc., 323/461-3971, 843 N. Sycamore Ave., L.A., 90038.
Cunningham, Escot, Dipene, 310/475-2111, 10635 Santa Monica, #130, L.A., 90025.
Sandie Schnarr, 310/360-7680, 8500 Melrose Ave., #212, W. Hollywood, 90069.
The Sun Agency, 310/888-8737, 8961 Sunset Blvd, #V, L.A., 90069.
Sutton, Barth & Vennari, 323/938-6000, 145 S. Fairfax, #310, L.A., 90036.
Talent Group, Inc., 323/852-9559, 6300 Wilshire Blvd., #900, L.A., 90048.
Arlene Thornton & Assoc., 818/760-6688, 12001 Ventura Pl., #201, Studio City, 91604.
Tisherman Agency, 323/850-6767, 6767 Forest Lawn Dr., #101, L.A., 90068.
The Wallis Agency, 818/953-4848, 1126 Hollywood Way, #203A, Burbank, 91505.

LOOPING

• **Looping is another acting tool** to add to your tool box. Many actors have never heard about this lucrative work. Looping is done on a post-production sound stage; the actors replace or add voices to film and television productions after they have been edited. Loopers need strong improvisational skills because the main function is to supply the voices of the extras that are seen in the background. There are a few looping groups but they are very hard to break into. In general, TV shows may use just five actors and films may use six to 12 actors for all the voices.

• **There are several different modes** of looping such as "Wall to Wall," "Doughnut," "Pass By's" and others. You will be taught these in a workshop or you may get the chance to observe a looping group in action.

• **The most important tool is your looping notebook.** This is where you write down sentences you might use in conversations at an airport, hospital, bowling alley, boxing match, nightclub, singles joint, computer lingo, dance studio, etc. You look for potential dialogue everywhere. Cut out the *L.A. Speak* page of the *Los Angeles Times Magazine* in the Sunday *L.A. Times* each week, and add it to your notebook. It gives lingo or jargon of different occupations. One week it was Disc Jockey Discourse. You must do extensive research on each job you do, depending on the situation of the film. This all adds information to your notebook. Long time, experienced loopers arrive on the sound stage with several huge notebooks.

• **Toby Stone of *Sounds Great* looping group:** "When I worked on *Backdraft* I needed to find out all about Chicago, including street maps. Then I called the burn unit ward at Sherman Oaks Burn Hospital to find out what the vitals are on a burn victim. What kind of drugs they would give, what kind of salve they would use." This information went into her looping notebook to be used for that job, and saved for any other project involving burn victims. This authentic type of conversation is what makes looping believable.

• **When you take a workshop,** the teacher will hand out sheets to begin your looping notebooks, including Police Codes and Traffic Violations, Police Dispatch, Police Precinct, Phones, General Conversation, Forensics/Crime Scene, Airport Pages and Airport Terminal Conversation.

• **In looping, the conversation can't be all that interesting** because the audience doesn't want to be aware what the background voices are saying. There's a fine line between not being boring and having new things to say, something with a little spin to it. It's like walking and chewing gum at the same time. There are different kinds of restaurant conversations; it may be a Denny's kind of lunch place or it may be a very fancy upscale dinner kind of place. Depending on what you are seeing on the screen, you may change your voice or the type of attitude you have. If there are only six loopers on the sound stage, you have to be able to sound as if you are everyone in every situation.

• **Even if you are not planning** to seek actual looping work, I think all actors will find taking a workshop helpful because you could be called in to revoice or loop your own lines on film and television projects due to sound or other technical problems. With the experience you gain in a looping workshop, you can go on any sound stage knowing looping etiquette, what will be expected of you and what terms are used. Self-confidence is a real key to looping.

• **Sandy Holt** owns a looping group, *Loop Ease,* and runs looping workshops. "Sometimes we have to revoice a main character. We may do a teenage or baby's voice, also different dialects. All the actors in the company are incredible at improvisation. We're quick and creative on the spot; you have to be able to improvise while you're looking at the scene on the sound stage screen."

• **Loopers make Screen Actors Guild minimum and residuals.**

Resources

LOOPING WORKSHOPS

Loop Ease, Sandy Holt at 310/271-8217 is a voice casting director. She holds weekend looping seminars on a professional sound stage.

Contact SAG for current list of Looping Groups.

EXTRA WORK

• **All actors should do** at least several days of extra work at the beginning of their careers. New actors have no idea what it is like to be on an actual film or television set. No person or book can explain what it is like to be working on location or on a sound stage. As an extra, you are part of the action and become familiar with studios and locations. If you are working part-time jobs to support your career, why not include these extra jobs?

• **Keep a very low profile on the set** if you are already a trained actor; that way no one will really remember you as an extra. There is still a bit of a stigma attached to being an extra in Los Angeles; in New York it is not unusual to be an extra one day and a principle the next. If you are at the very beginning of your training, it is okay to be seen on camera and to be a stand-in.

• **There is a strict on-the-set protocol**. Never go on the set until you have read *Back To One: The Movie Extras' Guidebook*, see resources. As an extra you are the lowest in the pecking order, so your needs will be barely considered. Bring water, snacks, sun screen, chair and reading material with you. Have anything you might need packed in your car—clothes to layer, sun glasses, loose change and small bills; what you need to be comfortable.

• **Your best friend on the set is the second assistant director** (2nd AD). Report in as soon as you arrive and always let the AD know when you are stepping away from the set. When you are called, answer immediately in a loud voice that you are on your way and start walking with haste to where you are needed. The AD will most likely tell you where to move and what to do during the filming. Just recently, I overheard a second assistant director tell the third AD that she never wanted to see a certain extra on the set again because he wasn't cooperative. Everywhere you work, you are building a reputation; make sure you can be proud of it.

• **There is a possibility of getting your SAG card.** When you get three SAG vouchers, you are eligible to join SAG. A voucher is your pay record and is a three-page multicolored form. Or, if they decide they need someone to say something like, "Hey, pull that truck over here," there is no time to go out and hire an actor, so they point to one of the extras. That means you get paid SAG minimum ($596) and are eligible to join SAG. Plus, you'll get residuals on that work for many years.

• **Rob Morrow** (*Northern Exposure)* had been on *Saturday Night Live* in 1980 as an extra, playing juror #11 in a skit with Jane Curtain, Bill Murray and Garrett Morris. 12 years later, he guest-hosted the show.

• **Judith Light** *(Who's The Boss)* began her career with a five-year role on *One Life To Live.* She landed that role after being an understudy on the soap. She took the understudy role—which is not even on-camera—because she was broke. Lucky for her.

• **Bruce Willis** in 1990 was on a TV show honoring Frank Sinatra's 75th birthday. He said in 1980 he was a photo-double and stand-in (extra) on Frank's movie, *First Deadly Sin.* Bruce said Frank had been such an inspiration on the set, talking to the actors and extras, telling stories of working on *From Here To Eternity.* Bruce went from a film extra to a multimillion dollar superstar in those 10 years.

• **Casting director Marvin Paige**, who cast *General Hospital* for years, said in an interview:

> • **I don't refer to our people in that category as "extras."** I refer to them as atmosphere people. The point is, I want every cast member to be an actor. I don't just want a body standing there because, among other things, if they aren't actors, there's always a chance they'll trip over the scenery. People who have the training and background respond much better to direction so I prefer to have people who really are pursuing acting careers even in small roles. For example, we have an actor who plays a bartender, sometimes he has dialogue and sometimes not. But he's been working with us three or four years and that's an actor's number one goal—getting work.

• **Other actors who worked as extras** at the beginning of their careers are Ben Affleck, Matt Damon, Sharon Stone (Woody Allen movie), Bruce Willis, *(The Verdict),* Brad Pitt (*Cutting Class),* Anjelica Huston, Dustin Hoffman, Kevin Costner, John Wayne, Bette Midler, Gary Cooper, Marlene Dietrich, Clark Gable, Robert Mitchum, Jean Harlow and Sophia Loren.

• **Cullen Chambers, actor, background artist, author,** has helped tens of thousands of people work as extras over the years. His best selling book, *Back To One: The Movie Extras' Guidebook*, is a manual with step by step instructions.

Q: Why would an actor want to work as an extra?

- **It's the first step toward an acting career.** It's like starting in the mail room and working your way up. You gain knowledge, experience and technical insight into the film making process. I've had to do more acting in the background on certain films than in principal roles; as a fireman, fighting fires, rescuing people in earthquakes, warping across the galaxy on the bridge of Starship Enterprise. You become aware of where the camera is and how to make a cross very precisely take after take so you won't block an actor who's delivering lines.

Q: How does a person get started?

- **By registering with one or more of the extra casting agencies.** I've listed over 100 agencies in my book and rated them. You'll also find agencies advertised in trade publications. Some agencies charge a fee. Scams abound in this business—don't register with any agency that charges more than $20 or insists on expensive photos. You can have your extra pictures taken for $25 by the best in the business.

Q: What tools does an extra need?

- **Here are a few: 3x5 color photos, telephone, an answering machine** or service and/or a pager, dependable transportation, Thomas Brothers Guide Mapbook, and wardrobe which can be picked up at yard sales or thrift shops. Put together a business and formal look and some period outfits from the '50s, '60s, '70s etc. It's all tax-deductible.

Q: What are some of the rules for an extra when on the set?

- **Number one rule is listen.** The director or assistant director's job is to tell you exactly what to do. Be on time. Bring three changes of wardrobe, pen and paper, book, small change, snack, and a folding chair. Sign in and out with the assistant directors or their assistants. Don't talk to or bother the principal actors—those with lines.

Q: How much does a nonunion extra make and how often can they work?

- **If they hustle, five to seven days a week.** The lowest pay is $40 a day plus overtime and bumps which are for special bits. On many shoots you do work overtime.

Q: How can you work on your favorite TV show?

- **The end credits list the Unit Production Manager**, Stage Manager or Assistant Director, and where the show is taped or filmed. Call the studio. Ask for the show's production office and ask for the production manager or AD. Say you're interested in working as a background actor and ask what extra casting agency they use. Then contact that agency and follow up as instructed in my book.

- **Wardrobe designer and costumer Tom Baxter gives a few hints to extras:**

  - **If you are working as an extra the best thing to do is to be polite** to the wardrobe person. A lot of times they can get you silent bits, sometimes they can even get you a line if you fit into a costume they have. I can't tell you how many times an extra who fit the mailman or cop uniform has gotten lines because I said that's who fits the costume. If you are wearing wardrobe from the studio's department, take care of it, watch where you put it down and never leave it lying around. We lost a jacket on a show that was loaned to an extra and he won't be back on the show again. The jacket cost more than he made. Make sure all of the clothes you bring to wear are clean and ironed perfectly.

- **I spoke with Judi Keppler of Judi's Casting.**

Q: What do you think it takes to be an extra?

- **People have no conception of the discipline and hard work it takes.** A lot of people aren't used to getting up early. When we were doing a two-day commercial shoot, our call time at the Johnny Rocket Cafe was 5:30 in the morning. It takes money. You need money to survive when you're not working. There's no guarantee you're going to work next week.

Q: Do you have any special advice for extras?

- **If an extra is really intent on getting ahead**, they should not only register with the different agencies, but they should learn how to network a little bit so they are not just a photo on a piece of paper. They have to get an identity and a reputation with the agency and that takes time. And yet, it's a fine line because they can't be a pest. I've had actors who would call me up in the morning and say, "Do you need any cigarettes? Do you want a cappuccino?" They were very smart. You can't bring people flowers and

> booze, it's too tacky. But little things like, "I've got a half a day free. Can I come by and do some filing or something?" Those people you remember, obviously, and try to take care of them. It's a matter of perseverance, which means you don't give up.

•**Stand-in.** The stand-in takes the place of the principal actor. It frees the actor from tedious hours of lighting and camera blocking. They also are there to protect and take care of the actors they replace—by showing them any blocking changes. The stand-ins tend to get more respect on the sets they work on because they are there week in and week out. They are part of the crew.

• **Extra casting agencies** are listed in *Back Stage West/Drama-Logue*; I've listed a few here to get you started. All agencies require two forms of identification: social security card, driver's license, passport or birth certificate and either a 3x5 or 4x6 color picture of you against a white background.

• **Call-in Services.** Most of the people I know who are doing extra work say they have to use calling services to get their jobs. The service calls the agencies for you and books your work for the next day. They call your machine or beep you to tell you where to report. There is usually a fee for starting the service and then a monthly fee of around $50.

• **On *It's Like, You Know, Seinfeld, Single Guy, Alright Already* and** some of my best friends on the set are the stand-ins. They are a great asset to the production and are hired year after year. Shows have several extras over and over again also, but there have been people who have come on the shows and behaved in a way that they will never be asked back. The actors are always pleasant but they are, in fact, working and can't be visiting with everyone. Never ask for an autograph or picture unless you are on the set as a guest.

• **At this writing, SAG is investigating** the call-in services and the easy accessibility of SAG vouchers. As in all areas of the business, changes can happen very fast. Investigate everything thoroughly.

Resources

Cullen Chambers, 323/969-4897, *Back To One: Movie Extras' Guide*. www.cullenchambers.com. The book can be purchased through theatrical bookstores and many newsstands in Los Angeles, or you can call and get the book through mail order.

Rich Hogan's Photos for Extras, 323/467-2628. 1680 Vine at Hollywood Blvd. in the Taft Building, Suite 722, Hollywood, 90028. The best. Prices start at $25 for 3x5 color photos. He has printed instructions to tell you exactly what to do and how to register for several of the extra casting agencies.

Thomas Warner, Extra Photographer, 818/769-9377. $35 for 3x5s.

Screen Actors Guild Extra scales: to 6/30/00 $95, then to 6/30/01 $100, then to 2002 $105, 2003 $110, 2004 $115.; stand-ins make $115, by 2004 $130. **Commercial extras and stand-ins** make $260.

AFTRA Extra daily rates are: **General extra** network sitcom $80; 30-minute serial $99. 60-minute serial $128.

AFTRA Extras Casting File. This is a file of pictures and resumes of paid-up members who are available to do extra and stand-in work on AFTRA programs. Producers and casting representatives call and request names and home telephone numbers from the file. To submit: send your picture and resume to Extra File, c/o AFTRA, or drop them off at the membership counter. Sometimes you may be hired without being in AFTRA. You can work 30 days without being a member and after that they will deduct the union payments from your paycheck. Two of my daughters worked on *Facts of Life* as extras, joining this way. Some situation comedies hire AFTRA members as extras or "under 5s" (under five lines). Pick up an AFTRA show sheet (printed monthly.) Then contact the production companies and find out who casts the extras. Call the person, ask if you can send a picture and/or come in for a meeting. Soap Opera Casting Directors do cold reading showcases, so you can meet them that way. You can also send in a picture, etc. They will be listed on the show sheet.

EXTRA CASTING AGENTS

People registering for extra work must bring two original ID's: driver's license, passport, voter registration card, birth certificate or social security card. If in a union, bring union card. Also, bring exact cash or money order.

Central Casting, 818/562-2888, ext. 3200. 1700 W. Burbank Blvd. Burbank, 91505. Fee: $20 union only, cash only, exact change. Current union card. Registration: Tu, Th 2-3:30.

Cenex Casting West, 818/562-2888, ext. 3219. 1700 W. Burbank Blvd., Burbank, 91505. Fee: $20 nonunion, cash only, exact change. Registration: M,W,F 10-11:30. 18 and older. They will take two pictures; don't wear black or white. They charge a 5% fee when you work.

For Children: Academy Kids, 818/769-8091, 4942 Vineland Ave., North Hollywood. www.academykids.com. Top Hollywood children's managers T.J. Stein and Bethany Constance have an extra casting company for children. Parents and children can get a good feel of what the business really is by working at least a few days as an extra; there is a $139 charge to join.

Anna Miller Casting, 323/957-4696. Screenland Studio, 10501 Burbank Blvd. (east of Cahuenga). Fee: $0 union, $20 nonunion. Call for registration time. Pictures: 3x5 full-body color, 4x6, three 8x10s, 3x5 or $5 for photo. Very small agency, doesn't seem to cast many projects.

Background Players, 323/692-1783. 7301 Melrose Ave., #D, L.A. 90046.

Bill Dance Casting, 323/878-0668. 3518 W. Cahuenga West, Suite 210, Los Angeles, 90068. Fee: $2 Union, $20 Nonunion. Registration: Walk-in M-Th. Be there promptly at 12 noon. Pictures: 3x5, 4x6, 8x10, or $2 for a Polaroid. Join. Everyone says good things about them.

Idell James Casting, 310/394-3919. 626 Santa Monica Blvd., POB 315, Santa Monica, 90401. Pictures: send 8x10 with resume. Union members for commercials. Likes beautiful young people. Very selective.

Messenger Casting, 818/760-3696, 10806 Ventura Blvd., #5, Studio City, 91604.

Producers Casting, 310/364-2300. Fee: $20 for photos twelve 4x6s. Registration: Call for SAG registration times. Casts for commercials. Very selective.

Rainbow Casting, 818/377-4475. 12501 Chandler Blvd. Suite 204, North Hollywood, 91607. Jeff Olan and Terry Zarchi, great people. Fee: $20 computer imaging. Registration: M-Th, 11-2. Pictures: 3x5 or $3 for photo. They will call you in; they prefer not to work with a call-in service.

Sunset Casting Registration: Call Rich Hogan 323/467-9326; he gives full information on the machine, so grab a pencil before you call. Nonunion commercials.

CALL-IN SERVICES

Direct Line, 818/223-3590 Fee: $75, $45 a month. Union and nonunion.18 color 3x5s.

Extra Effort, 818/981-1144. 14431 Ventura Blvd., #277, Sherman Oaks, 91403. Fee: $25 registration fee, $55 monthly, send photo. Union/nonunion.

Extra Phone, 818/972-9474. 1723 Burbank Blvd., Burbank, 91506. Fee: $50 per month; pay first and last plus $10 for a digital picture. Union/nonunion. Call for appointment. Photos: ten 3x5s, one 8x10, six 8x10s plus resumes.

Studio Phone, 310/202-9872. 10624 Regent St., Los Angeles, 90034. P.O.B. 34481, L.A. 90034. The oldest and most respected calling service. 10 3x5s, 10 head shots and resumes. Fee: $110 first and last month, $55 monthly. Union only. Registration Tu,W,Th by appointment. They do take some nonunion extras and will try to help you get your three vouchers. Send a headshot, resume, cover letter, Atten: Jennifer. If they accept you their fee is $220, then you have to call twice a day. It could take months to get your vouchers. SAG vouchers have become increasingly hard to get, so their policy may change.

FREE REGISTRATION EXTRA CASTING COMPANIES

To register at the following agencies, send a 3x5 color snapshot along with your general information.

Sande Alessi, 818/623-7040, P.O. Box 4577, Valley Village, 91617.
Cast of Thousands, 818/985-9995, P.O. Box 1899, Burbank, 91507.
Creative Extras Casting, 310/203-7860, 2461 Santa Monica Blvd., #501, Santa Monica, 90404.
Extras Network Casting, 323/692-8289, P.O. Box 93549, Hollywood, 90092.
On Location Casting, 310/558-6856, 322 Culver Blvd., #348, Playa Del Rey, 90293.
Raquel Osborne Casting, 323/257-8601, 235 E. Colorado, Box 189, Pasadena, 91101.
Tammy Smith, 310/364-3521, 520 Washington Blvd., PMB 402, Marina Del Rey, 90202.
Debe Waisman, 310/558-3916, 11664 National Blvd., #368, L.A., 90064.
Webster-Davis Casting, 818/503-7474, 859 N. Hollywood Way, #217, Burbank, 91505.
Xtraz Casting, 818/781-0066, P.O. Box 4145, Valley Village, 91617.

GRADUATE AND STUDENT FILM PROJECTS

• **Acting in student films** and projects can be your gateway to an acting career. It is not always easy to get the tape copy—you can probably expect a 50/50 chance of getting it and that is with a great deal of persistence on your part. Student films are not always shot under the best of circumstances; the directors are learning too. But if you are lucky and end up on a director's reel, you could be seen by every producer and agent in town, and possibly many film festivals. There is a possibility of being spotted and cast in a major production because of your acting work in a promising graduate director's reel.

• **If you are a beginner, you will gain valuable experience** in front of a camera—experience you cannot get in acting class or anywhere else. If you are a seasoned actor, you may get the chance to play a leading role, portraying the type of character that you may not be cast as in a commercial film. Circulating that tape or being seen at the screening may have casting people thinking of you for a wider variety of roles.

• **USC, UCLA, AFI** (American Film Institute), Cal Arts and Loyola Marymount are the finest film schools in the world and their students need actors for their projects. They advertise in *Back Stage West/Drama-Logue* most heavily at the beginning of each semester or quarter. Crew work is also available. It is valuable to meet these future filmmakers when they are starting out. I wonder who acted in George Lucas' first films at USC.

• **When working on a student production** expect long delays, expect mistakes. You will learn how to size up a situation and to pick and choose the projects that you think will benefit you. Often student directors want actors to rehearse scenes from well known films to take into their directing classes. I feel it is a value to do this; their professors are working directors who may be in the process of casting a film you would be perfect for. You must open yourself to opportunities as often as possible.

• **The screenings of future filmmakers** are held in Los Angeles. Quoting a *Variety* ad:

> New York University, Tisch School of the Arts, Institute of Film and Television. The 1996 Showcase of Award-Winning NYU STUDENT FILMS, DIFFERENT PROGRAM OF FILMS AND CHAMPAGNE RECEPTION EACH NIGHT, The Directors Guild of America Theatre Complex, Supported in part by grants from Chris Columbus, William Morris Agency, Creative Artists Agency, and International Creative Management.

• ***Back Stage West* writes an occasional column** about the hot talents in independent and student films. One of the things they reported on was one of the annual Student Academy Awards held by The Academy of Motion Picture Arts and Sciences. They honor student filmmakers from all across the country in four categories of filmmaking: alternative, animation, documentary and dramatic film. There were winners from Dartmouth, Rhode Island, NYU, Harvard, Stanford, Yale and Los Angeles. You can act in student films anywhere you live.

• **Academy of Television Arts & Sciences Foundation** recently held their Annual College Television Awards with a screening for the industry held at the Directors Guild of America Theater. Winners were from AFI, Brigham Young, NYU, Missouri, Florida, Columbia and Northwestern.

• **Ang Lee, the director of Sense and Sensibility and The Ice Storm,** did his graduate film at NYU, winning the school's annual competition. The film caught the eye of a William Morris agent, who signed him.

• **Actor Al Sapienza was advised not to work** for first-time directors for no pay. He didn't listen and acted in director Danny Cannon's first film, *Strangers.* Four years later, Cannon gave Al a co-starring role in his film *Judge Dredd.*

• **Quentin Tarantino** has optioned Reb Braddock's Florida State University thesis film, *Curdle.* Tarantino is planning on producing it.

• **USC student Laura Anne McCreary** turned in her senior thesis short film, "The Fourth John," to her professor, Carl Gottlieb, who wrote *Jaws.* He was so impressed he asked for a copy. When producer Ruben Hostka asked Gottlieb if he had any good scripts about young people, he gave him the tape. CAA is handling the script and Gottlieb and Hostka have become attached as producers. Will the actors in the piece get to do the feature film? Possibly, but at least they will be in the running.

• **Harvey Keitel** was studying at the Actor's Studio in New York in 1965. He answered an ad placed by film student Martin Scorsese, who was looking for actors to appear in *Who's That Knocking at My Door?,* a film he planned to make. Of course, they've gone on to make five feature films together. That student film was the turning point in Harvey's career.

• **At the 1991 Academy Awards**, Adam Davidson won an Oscar for his 1990 short film, *Lunch Date.* In his acceptance speech he said he was so surprised; he just did a 10-minute film for his film class and all "this" happened. He thanked the actors for contributing their talents.

• **Allen and Albert Hughes did a five-minute**, $250 short film that served as Albert's film school project at Los Angeles City College (LACC.) He used that as his demo reel. The 21-year-old twin brothers made their feature film debut co-writing and co-directing the $3 million New Line's *Menace II Society.* Suddenly every studio in town wanted to hire them as writers and directors.

• **Make it a priority** to gain experience by landing work in student films. Landing these roles can be just as competitive as any other part of the business. This is where networking can come in handy. Get on some of the crews, come to know the filmmakers. Ask them to keep you in mind when casting their next project. Hang around the campuses, find out what is going on, how you can get to be a part of what is going on.

Resources

Back Stage West/Drama-Logue lists the student films that are casting; answer the ads. But also, you might submit your picture and resume to each school, each semester on the chance that you would be perfect for a project a student may be casting.

The Art Center, Model Office, 626/396-2250. They will send you information on how to register in their film and print work files. Located in Pasadena, their students are always looking for subjects.

California Institute of the Arts School of Film & Video, 661/253-7825. 24700 McBean Parkway, Valencia, 91355. P&Rs are posted on the casting bulletin boards.

California State University Northridge (CSUN) Radio/TV/Film Dept., 818/885-3192. Send P&R, the school maintains casting files.

Columbia College, 323/851-0550. 18618 Oxnard St., Tarzana 91356. They maintain casting files. Actors receive a copy of their work.

Los Angeles City College (LACC) Radio/TV/Film Dept. Cinema Division, 323/953-4267. 855 N. Vermont Ave., Los Angeles, 90029. They maintain casting files.

The Los Angeles Film School 323/634-0044. www.lafilm.com. 6363 Sunset Blvd., Hollywood, 90028. This is the newest film school, opened in the fall of 1999.

University of California Los Angeles (UCLA) Film & TV Dept., 310/825-5761. 405 Hilgard Ave., Los Angeles, 90024. They maintain casting files.

University of Southern California (USC) Cinema School, Student Productions Office, 213/740-2235. University Park, Los Angeles, 90089. They maintain casting files.

STAND-UP COMEDY

• **Performing stand-up comedy** is a good way to be noticed in Los Angeles. Take a chance; hit all the open mikes at the many comedy clubs listed in *Backstage West/Drama-Logue,* and *L.A. Weekly.* Many comedians have been signed to development deals or cast as regulars on sitcoms because of characters they portray in their acts.

• **Some video stores have tapes** of stand-ups doing their acts. Study, watch the comedy channel. Read the books the comics have written. *SeinLanguage* by Jerry Seinfeld is the best that you can get. Figure out why you laugh on each page. His sense of language and vocabulary is extraordinary; he can turn a phrase better and funnier than most. Jerry just walking around is funny, his thought process is funny. One thing I like most about him is his loyalty to all of his stand-up friends. He looked for roles on the show where he could hire them, and then always appreciated their work.

• **Rita Rudner** analyzed the science of comedy by playing all of Woody Allen's albums from his stand-up comedy years, listened to Jack Benny albums and every comedy album she could get at the library. She tried to figure out what was funny. She would try a joke out on her friends and if they laughed, she would use it. "It's hard, yet you do feel a tremendous power."

• **Tom Dreesen** occasionally teaches comedy seminars. He tells of sleeping in his car in an alley in the Valley and hitch-hiking to the Comedy Store and begging for the chance to get on stage. He used to perform at The Show Biz. Some of the other comics there were Michael Keaton, David Letterman, Jay Leno, Robin Williams, and Debra Winger was the waitress. "Whatever the mind can see and believe it will also achieve. I used to go to that car every night and see myself on *The Tonight Show* and Johnny Carson laughing and telling me I was funny. Now I have a picture on my wall of that happening."

• **Eve Brandstein, who has managed several comics**, says, "You can develop characters or material in an improv, acting, writing or stand-up workshop. Work your material among your colleagues. Then go to one of the small clubs on their audition night, get up and try it. If it's for you, you'll know it; you'll get bitten by it. Bingo!"

• **Judy Carter, the author of *Stand-up Comedy: The Book*,** published by Dell Books, was nominated in Atlantic City as Entertainer of the Year, has appeared on four Showtime comedy specials, and her act is available on tape in video stores: *Paramount Comedy Theater with Howie Mandel, Part I.* She teaches stand-up comedy in Los Angeles, San Francisco, Big Bear, California and seminars around the country.

Q: Tell me about the book.

- **We have a complete listing of clubs, agents, and managers** in the appendix. No matter where they live in the country, there is a comedy club or a comedy venue near them.

Q: Do you have specific things to say about actors doing stand-up?

- **If you look at TV sitcoms, they are all using stand-up comics** because they know audiences don't lie. There's a certain confidence that stand-ups have to bring to a producer. They can make an audience laugh right there and then. Or an agent can bring an actor to a producer and say, "Yes, this person knows how to make an audience laugh. I saw it myself."

- **As a stand-up, it is much easier to showcase** your talents because when you have an act, you don't have to wait to be cast in a play. You can go to a showcase yourself. It's obvious why casting directors prefer to go to a club. At a showcase at the Improv, they'll get to see 20 people in two hours, eat nachos and drink. It's true. They talk, schmooze, mingle and maybe have sex with someone they've met when they are done. That rarely happens in waiver theater.

- **You can have a video of yourself** doing stand-up and get work that way. I can't tell you how many students I have with development deals because they sent a video tape to someone who showed it to someone else.

- **Create an act.** Decide what the sitcom would look like that you are in. For example, if you look at *Roseanne's* show and then you look at her first HBO special, you can see that everything was there. All the characters that she talked about and acted out in her stand-up act became real actors in the sitcom that she became the center of. Who are the people that are in your arena of life? What is your life like? Who is your family? If you look at Mary Tyler Moore, her family was the people she worked with. Her problems were due to being a single woman.

- **Back to *Roseanne***, it was her immediate family, trying to eke out a living and deal with men in this sexist world. If you put yourself in the center, who are the people that you have issues with? You start acting them out in your life and you start showcasing that. It's a great way to empower your career and hold the reins on your creative destiny. You're not waking up each day saying, "How can I get somebody to see me to give me a job?" You wake up each day creating material that will lead someplace.

Q: How do they learn to create material if it doesn't come naturally?

- **We have an audio tape workshop** that has four tapes. The first tape is "Creating your material," which asks a lot of self-help things like "It bugs me when my mother..." It bugs you with what isn't right with your immediate relationship. On tape two, we cover those "ranting and ravings," which all come from what bugs you about people that you are in relationships with. We talk specifically about how to arrange that material in stand-up material format. It's a very specific formula and structure that has to have a set-up to interest the audience and relieve itself in a laugh within 30 to 40 seconds because of the nature of television. You've got to keep people from channel surfing. Tape two goes into those techniques.

- **Tape three is "How not to bomb."** Once you've put your act together and you're going to go out and perform it, you need specific techniques to let go of fear. Tape four is how to go and market your act and start making money, which is a very separate issue.

- **CD Rom, Five Steps to Writing A Joke, comes with a little workbook.**

Q: What about the fear?

- **Actors that I speak to are dealing with fear**. "Oh, there's no one else on stage." What they find is the audience is their friend, and they become the other character in a scene. They learn that it's not about giving a monologue, but having dialogue with the audience. You just don't know how the audience is going to react. The same way in a play. You really don't know how the other actor is going to read a line, but you just have to be alive and respond.

Q: Do you have to be funny yourself?

- **Most people who make good stand-up** comics are people who aren't the center of attention but are the people who are watching. They are the ones outside of their family, the ones who have a crazy family and who aren't very involved, but watch and later, comment on what happened. It's the observers of life, but not necessarily the ones that are very funny, who are the stand-ups.

• **Bernie Young of the Bernie Young Agency** has managed many comics over the years. Currently, his only client is Rosie O'Donnell. He is her manager and the executive producer of her talk show.

Q: Do most comedians have a manager?

- **Yes. Certainly the person that is the self-motivator** and a very good organizer really can serve as his own manager. But most entertainers are so focused on their work that they don't have time to spend on those little things that make a difference in moving their careers forward. It's pretty important comedians have that other voice, that manager, who can give them career guidance and help move their careers in the right direction.

Q: Do you help comedians with their material?

- **If they are working on new material, I'll give them my input.** They respect my opinion and that I'll be objective in looking at that material. We always discuss what they intend to do, should and shouldn't do, but the final decision is theirs.

Q: What advice would you give for someone wanting to get started in stand-up comedy?

- **You need to have your own point of view, your own style.** Comedy is personal. My advice would be to understand who you are and develop your ideas around that. That's going to be the thing that sets you apart from everybody else. For so long, the industry didn't look at stand-up comedians as actors. The industry now realizes that these people are acting every night. They write their own material, perform it, and promote their own shows. It's perfect training for sitcoms and feature films.

Q: Then what do you do?

- **You have to get on stage, in front of an audience.** Wherever you are in this country, there's a comedy club somewhere close by. Work the material and the audience will judge whether or not it's good. In stand-up, today you can be "discovered" in any city in America. If you really want to get into TV and film, you need to be in Los Angeles or New York.

Q: How do stand-ups get their own television shows?

- **Thea Vidale was a classic example.** She's unique; she puts her own stamp on her material. As a stand-up comedian, she played in a lot of different cities in the country. Luckily enough, she was spotted from a videotape. Her point of view was a good premise to start a show. Being yourself can make all the difference in the world.

Q: On a typical day, what is your job?

- **It's really a matter of organizing** my artists' professional lives. I make sure that the publicist has the schedule of publicity that needs to be done. I follow up with the club and make sure that all the details of the venue have been taken care of. I also sit down with the artist and plan the future. We have to look down the road and see what steps we need to take to get there. I make sure the deals presented by the agents fit into our big picture.

- **I spoke with stand-up comic Thea Vidale.**

Q: How would you advise someone who wants to do stand-up in a comedy club?

- **Have a purpose and know what you're going to say.** When they have amateur night, you've got to suck it up and go, just go. Don't be drunk and none of that other stuff. Go to the comedy club. Get in touch with the owner or the manager of the club and ask him what you need to do to get up on his stage. Sometimes you have to sign a list, usually they'll say, "Well, you have to have five minutes of original material." How do you get original material? They never tell you what that is. Original material is stuff they haven't heard before. If they've heard it, you better be clever enough. It better swim.

Q: What does it feel like waiting backstage to go on?

- **It depends where you are in the line-up.** When you've got to go behind a lot of comics, you hope they're funny. You want them to be good, but you hope they won't be as good as you. It's nerve-wracking. It's a high anxiety point because you are next, and this guy was really, really funny. That means you better be funny, too. If the guy wasn't funny, you've got your work cut out.

Q: What does it feel like when you walk on stage?

- **For me, it feels like heaven.** It feels like here I am. I am in control, I will be in control. I'm really happy. It feels like I'm with a bunch of old friends.

Q: Even though they're strangers?

- **My concept is, these people are going to be my friends.** I'm going to make them love me, and we're going to have a good time. That's a strong place to be. When I first started going on stage, I was terrified and I needed the first laugh, a bunch of first laughs. Now, I only need one. I always need the initial first strong laugh. Sometimes it's terrifying when I don't get it, and that has happened. God has been good to me, because I've always been able to turn that around very quickly. I come out of it like a big fire. I'm coming to kill. I'm coming to take over. You have to be strong to do that.

- **You have to have a plan.** My plan was to be the most popular act, and one of the best of the best in every situation I was in. When I was the opening act, I wanted to be the best opening act there was. When I got to be a feature, I said I wanted to be one of the best features you can be. And when I was a headliner, I said I wanted to be the "baddest" headliner they ever have seen in the history of headliners. I want them to see that I am all that I say I am and believe myself to be.

Q: What was it like doing the *David Letterman Show?*

- **It was a dream. I was real nervous.** I was scared because I thought it was going to be a New York crowd and they wouldn't adjust to me like everyone else, like *Arsenio's* did. But the audience liked me. They were glad to see me and I was glad to see them. That's the whole thing. I'm always glad to see my audiences. David was very gracious to me. I had the best time. He was so sweet. He thinks I'm funny, a hoot.

Resources

Judy Carter, 310/915-0555. www.judycarter.com. She guarantees a performance at a comedy club and a video of your act. *Stand-Up Comedy: The Book* includes a test to find out if you're funny. She offers free class auditing. Call for her brochure. Advance class showcases every week. Call 1-800-4COMICS for a free subscription to her newsletter, which is published quarterly and is full of inspiring talks and tips and everything that goes on across the country. Private consultation for one-person shows.

Stanley Myron Handelman, 818/883-7175. Comedy workshop, comedy acting, stand-up comedy, writing, character development. Private and weekend classes.

Sandy Holt, 310/271-8217. She is a *Second City* alumni, has a looping group and teaches improvisation, character work and on-camera sketch comedy. I asked Sandy for advice for struggling actors. She laughed, "Marry a rich person so they'll pay for your classes. Be willing to do what ever it takes. I don't care what age you are or what you've been through; follow your dream." Private coaching to work on material, timing and stage persona. $75 an hour.

Harvey Lembeck Comedy Workshop, 310/271-2831. Scott Baio says, "The workshop broke the boundaries for me. It taught me how to be more creative, how to be more free." Robin Williams said, "I looked around the class and said 'I'm home, they can't hurt me now, forget therapy.' This is a home, someplace real special. I felt safe. It gave me freedom." Using improv as a method to teach comedy. Three levels of ongoing classes showing actors how to play comedy in scenes.

Mark Lonow, Improv co-owner 323/936-9550. 10-week classes that culminate with a performance at the Improv. Claudia Lonow is available for private coaching.

Paul Ryan's Comedy Studio at CBS Studio Center, 323/936-9524. All levels. Master comedy acting classes, sitcom character development, comedy improvising, comedy timing, sitcom auditioning techniques, cold readings, comedy scene work.

Cynthia Szigeti, 818/980-7890. Former head of the Groundlings' training program. She coaches actors and standups privately. $50-$75 an hour.

BOOKS

Order through Samuel French Bookstore, 323/876-0570 or 818/762-0535

Stand-Up Comedy: The Book by Judy Carter

How To Be a Stand-Up Comic by Larry Charles and Richard Belzer

SeinLanguage by Jerry Seinfeld

Successful Stand-Up Comedy: Advice from a Comedy Writer by Gene Perret.

Video West, 818/760-0096. 11376 Ventura Blvd., Studio City, 91604 . Second location, **Video West**, 310/659-5762. 805 Larrabee Street, West Hollywood, 90069. These video stores are the best! Bargain days Tuesday, Wednesday and Thursday, $1.29 a tape. Have them give you a tour of the store; they've got classics, independents, foreign, art house, comedies, stand-up comics. Just about anything you need to research. Fantastic!

THEATER AND THEATER GROUPS

• **Working in the theater is a way to keep acting**, networking and giving yourself the opportunity to be seen by someone who has the ability to hire you for film and television work. *Back Stage West/Drama-Logue* lists auditions for plays. The directors often put the notices through the Breakdown Service, too. Sometimes, agents aren't very interested in Waiver stage work because there is no commission for them. Perhaps they will let you drop in once a week to look through the Breakdowns for stage work. Go to all the play auditions you can; it gives you a place to practice your auditioning skills. *See Producing Yourself, page 215.*

• **After Robert Redford** had turned down the role of Benjamin in *The Graduate,* director Mike Nichols remembered seeing Dustin Hoffman in an off-Broadway play, playing a hunchbacked German transvestite, and flew him into Hollywood for a screen test. Dustin was cast to play his Oscar-nominated role. He was 30 and it was his first major movie role at a salary of $750 a week. He earned $20,000 in all and applied for unemployment benefits afterward.

• **Harry Belafonte told an understudy success story.** "In 1945, I worked as an assistant janitor; Sidney Poitier was a dishwasher. In our first play at the *American Negro Theater* in Harlem I had the lead and Sidney was my understudy. One day the young man covering my job called and said he couldn't work that night. I went off to haul garbage and Sidney went on to play my part. That performance turned out to be on the night a director from Broadway came to scout our company, saw Sidney in my part, and signed him on the spot for a role in *Lysistrata*, launching his brilliant career."

• **There are many theater groups**. Pick one that you feel at home in, a good way to find friends who are working together towards common goals. You'll usually need a short scene or monologue to audition. Certain companies may want a classical and a contemporary monologue. Go to the theater you are considering joining and see a production to find out if you like the acting and the production values.

• **Kelsey Grammer** (*Frasier)* tells this story: He was doing an off-off-Broadway show of *Lonely Hearts.* Opening night was the first blizzard of the season, there were three people in the audience. One of those people was the casting director who cast him in *Cheers!*

• **Beverly Long, actress turned commercial casting director**, was in R*ebel Without a Cause.* "Every actor in the entire city went on the auditions for *Rebel.* I had done a few TV shows and Corey Allen (now a director) and I were doing a play. The director saw us and cast us both. This is why I tell actors to do plays, you never know who is in the audience.

• **Chazz Palminteri** is a real inspiration to me. *A Bronx Tale,* directed by Robert De Niro, written by and starring Chazz was released in 1993. Five years before that, Chazz was a nightclub bouncer, TV bit player, living in a crummy North Hollywood apartment. "I was angry, I wasn't going anywhere. I went to Thrifty's, bought some pads of legal paper and started writing." He took his first five-minute bit and performed it at his theater company's workshop. Although it was well received, he kept writing and taking it back to class. Eventually he had a 90-minute one-man show he performed to critical raves at both the West Coast Ensemble Theater in L.A. and Playhouse 91 in N.Y. He was hot. Everyone wanted to buy his story. He held fast. He had $200 in the bank but he wouldn't sell unless he could write the screenplay and star in it. Robert De Niro had seen the play in L.A. and called him. They met and made the deal.

• **When you have landed a play for the first time**, throw yourself into rehearsals, learn your lines fast so you have more time to play with the words. Show up prepared to rehearse. Take care of yourself, your food and water. Provide yourself with the comforts you need so it frees you for the fun that rehearsals can be. The rehearsal time is often much more fun than the actual running of the play.

• **Stage managers are second-in-command** and often, after the opening night, are in charge. Show them every respect you can. Always let them know when you arrive. If there is a sign up sheet, as there will be at all Equity productions, sign it. When the play begins its run, the stage manager will give you half-hour, 15-minute and 5-minute calls. Always acknowledge that you heard them with a thank you or some verbal word to acknowledge that you heard it. This is proper etiquette. Stage managers can be your best friends if you get into trouble during the play. Be kind to them.

• **The last week before the play opens**, rehearsals are hard because you are into tech rehearsals with the lights, costumes, sound, curtains. The last dress rehearsal before opening will be awful. The second night is usually a let down from all the energy that went into opening night.

• **On your first dress rehearsal night**, set up your makeup space. You want to make it a safe place to return to between scenes. Take a box of tissues and a couple of lunch size paper sacks. You can tape one of the sacks to your dressing table in case there isn't a handy trash container. Use a hand towel to lay down in your place. Take paper cups, straws and a bottle of water. Share your water and cups. Lay your makeup out. I like to use a small glass for my makeup pencils, a regular pencil and a pen. Take a writing pad, post it notes and scotch tape.

• **When you get your opening night notes**, tape them up on your mirror. Also tape something that is special to you, a picture of someone who loves you, or a saying that gives you inspiration. Get little opening night gifts for everyone. It might be a rose, candy bar, bag of jelly beans, T-shirt with the play's name on it, helium balloon, balloon on a stick with something printed on it, a little miniature prop (kids' toys) that pertains to the person's role. Write a little personal note to the actors, director and tech people. This will make your opening night even more special. If you've received flowers, when they're near death, pour the water out and let them dry. They will still look good and you can keep them for the entire run.

• **Your curtain call is the last time the audience sees you**. Go out with great joy, no matter how you think your performance went. Often, you won't get many rehearsals on the curtain call. If you have any influence, insist on a well thought out and rehearsed one. You owe it to the audience so they can honor you. Bask in the applause, let yourself hear it, stay in the moment. It is what we act for, to hear the approval. Do not judge yourself; do that in your car on the way home. You can always improve and you will the next night, next week or the next play.

• **When you have a small part**, there is bound to be a let down after you open. In rehearsals the play seemed all about you, now you see it's really the people in the leading roles who carry the play. Keep making sure you find something new you want in your scenes. Bask in the glory when you are on stage, and next time maybe your part will be bigger. If you have a large role, don't let up. Keep putting all the energy into your acting choices. If the reviews are good, yeah! If they aren't, console yourself and make the reviewers eat their words. Many actors choose not to read reviews till after the run of the play or never because they feel if you believe the good ones, then you have to believe the bad ones.

• **Each time you have a performance** the audience is different and it is such an adventure. What holds you up is your acting technique. No matter how you are feeling or how you think things are going, you will take the audience on a journey if you keep concentrated and focused on your work and your acting choices.

• **Never whistle in the theater**. Develop little good luck charms for every run.

Resources

On The House, 310-399-3868. $149 a year for 2 tickets; many shows available every week.

Time Six, www.theatrela.org. This service provides up-to-the-minute information on what's playing where. You may also purchase half-price day-of-show tickets by phone. Tu-Sa 12-5. Mark Taper, Doolittle, Pantages, Pasadena Playhouse and other under-100-seat Equity houses.

Back Stage West/Drama-Logue prints an annual issue featuring all the theaters and theater companies in town. You can call them and get that back issue.

• THEATER COMPANIES

Actors Co-Op, 323/462-8460. 1760 N. Gower Street, Hollywood, 90028. Send a picture and resume. They audition twice a year. Bring in a three-minute monologue for a three person committee. On the call back you can do the same monologue or a different one, a cold reading with one of their company members and an interview for a seven person committee. This is one of the top companies in town. No initiation fee, dues are $20 a month. Janet Raycraft is one of the administrators.

Actors' Gang, 323/465-0566. 6209 Santa Monica Blvd., Hollywood, 90038. Artistic Director, Tim Robbins. Award winning theater. On the Board: Robert Altman, Annette Bening, Robin Williams, Susan Sarandon. Presents fine award-winning productions.

Actors' Forum Theatre, 818/506-0600, 10655 Magnolia Blvd., North Hollywood, 91601. Applicants can audition every last Saturday of the month from 12:30-1PM, or come to a workshop that meets on Tuesdays from 7:30-10PM. Dues $25 a month. No set season. Theatre looks for a variety of new plays. Workshop presentation on Thursday nights.

American Renegade Theatre Company, 818/763-1834. 11136 Magnolia Blvd., North Hollywood, 91601. Headshots and resumes are accepted, then actors are called in for an open audition every Wednesday at 5:30PM. Dues $40 a month. Requirements: four hours work per month are required in any area of expertise, plus one night of hosting or ushering during every production. The one-year intern program trades off membership status for tech work.

A Noise Within, 323/224-6420. Luckman Fine Arts Complex, California State University, Los Angeles, 5151 State University Dr., L.A., 90032.This theater presents classic American plays as well as Shakespeare. They have a 26 member resident company. New members are accepted by invitation only and not until you have worked a year with the company. They do audition for roles that cannot be filled within the company look in *Back Stage West.* They teach all levels of actors in their Shakespeare classes and have a summer program of the classics for teenagers.

Attic Theatre Ensemble, 323/469-3786. 6562½ Santa Monica Blvd., Hollywood, 90038. Pic/res are accepted for files; open auditions held every couple of months. Dues $50 a month. Six hours of theatre work per month. Exclusive casting policies within the company, access to credit union and dental plan.

Colony Theatre, 323/665-0280. 1944 Riverside Dr., Los Angeles, 90039. They audition two times a year. Send picture, resume and a self-addressed, stamped business envelope, c/o Denise. She will send you information on the company. If you are interested, call for an interview appointment. They hold a two-day marathon of interviews. Then they will notify you if they want you to audition for the company. Dues are $15 per month. Must work two mailings within four months of production, attend company clean-up weekend, usher six times and work a full running crew within first year of membership. Shows are selected with company members in mind. Industry comps are given to cast members. No workshops; they produce plays. Very prestigious company.

Company of Angels, 323/883-1717. 2106 Hyperion Ave., L.A. 90027. Send in your picture and resume, c/o Janet Aspers. They have auditions at least once a year. If you are called in they like to see two scenes, not over five minutes each and they may ask for a monologue. Initiation fee is $35, and dues are $35 a month. This is one of the oldest companies in town. They have many productions going on for the members to appear in. They don't have workshops but do have play readings; always looking for material.

Open Fist Theatre/Los Angeles Playhouse, 213/882-6912. 1625 North La Brea, Hollywood, 90028. They hold auditions two or three times a year. Send photo and resume c/o Scott, they will call you with details for the auditions.

Originals Only, 213/383-1650. Tom Hill is the founder and director. Established in 1948, this is the oldest theatre group. Directors, writers and actors; no dues, just a voluntary contribution and a willingness to work. They read screen, stage and television scripts and do staged readings and productions for the industry. Writers submit scripts and if accepted, the writer provides the scripts for the actors.

Theatre 40, 310/396-2325. 241 Moreno Drive, Beverly Hills, 90210. Located on the campus of Beverly Hills High School. "For more than 26 years, Theatre 40 has been one of this town's most stable and consistent actor-run professional theater ensembles." *Daily Variety.* Mail picture and resume c/o Robert Cohen, P.O. Box 5401, Beverly Hills, 90210. They will contact you if looking for members. They have workshops and company dues.

Theatre East, 818/760-4160. 12655 Ventura Blvd., Studio City, 91604. New members are by invitation only; interviews are held for 18-month apprentice program. Dues: initiation fee of $40, then $40 a month. Must have a union affiliation. Apprentices work crews and various other stage work instead of paying dues. Members, including apprentices, can participate in workshops, classes, seminars, industry showcases; productions cast exclusively from within the company.

Theatre West, 323/851-4839. 3333 Cahuenga Blvd. West, Los Angeles, 90068. You may submit your pictures and resumes to be considered for membership. A couple of months before the auditions, usually in the fall, the membership committee reviews the submissions received and on the basis of your experience you may be invited to audition for membership. Only the membership actors are in their productions. Initiation Fee is $66, dues are $34 a month. Free professional workshops are offered to their members: Monday night actor's workshop, Tuesday morning Shakespeare, Tuesday evening writer's workshop, Thursday evening musical comedy. The apprentice wing has their own acting workshop on Wednesday night for young directors.

West Coast Ensemble, 323/876-9337. Mailing Address: 2422 Wilshire Blvd., Suite A, Santa Monica, 90403. Theater located at 522 N. La Brea, Hollywood, 90036. Les Hanson is the artistic director. Auditions twice a year. Send a picture and resume, attention: New Members and they will notify you when the auditions will be held. You do a four minute scene for Les and then have an interview with the membership committee. Lots of workshops and productions to get involved in. Initiation fee is $100, monthly dues are $45. Plus you must donate five hours work time each month. You can reduce your dues to $35 by doing 10 hours a month. You must perform one production job a year. They offer a great intern program for beginners; if you are interested in that, mention it in your letter.

PRODUCING YOUR OWN PROJECTS

• **If you find it hard to break into the business**, or if it's been a while since you have acted, you have the power to generate projects for yourself. The people interviewed below are creating work in Los Angeles, but they all did it in their home towns before they got here. If you are not in Los Angeles yet, start at home. If you are in Los Angeles, start now. If you aren't familiar with how stage or performance art is produced, apprentice yourself to directors and producers. They are always looking for unpaid hard workers in exchange for the education they will give you. *Back Stage West/Drama-Logue* lists ads for technical and back stage people all the time.

• **Once you have found material** that suits your own personal style, honed, rehearsed, and performed it, you may want to professionally tape or film the production. A few minutes can be used for your audition tape, or perhaps you can find directors who need a 10, 15 or even 30-minute piece for their demo reels. Material is the hardest thing to develop. Once you have that, you may find all kinds of help from people who need to demonstrate their skills also.

• **Biff Yeager will make a movie starring you for $500,000.** Of course this is not for everyone but it's a very interesting idea. He produces the SAG project using industry writers, directors, a star name or two, dialogue directors and crew. He will make it any genre you want. **www.ultimatewishgift.com**.

• **Pamela Munro—actress, producer, producing coach**—studied, acted and produced theater in New York, London and Berkeley. She's been in Los Angeles for 10 years.

- **I was a member of St. Ambrose** church and the church hall wasn't being used. Our first play was *George Washington Slept Here* by Kaufman & Hart. We produced it for $500, which was loaned to us by the Church. We made $500 and paid them back.

Q: How could you produce for so little money?

- **We basically had costumes and set pieces.** An artist friend did the art work for the program; we sold advertising in it and that paid for the printing. We did a lot of deficit financing where people would buy things, keep their bills and get paid back from the box office. The money we had up front was mostly for printing, postage and royalties. I picked a play that was the high end of summer stock; a comedy. It had to be new enough that we didn't have to hassle with the costumes too much. I had a large cast so I had more resources to draw on.

- **I produced classical plays.** At the Pasadena Library, I found an ancient translation of Chekov's *The Boar* which did not require payment of royalties. We did friends' plays who were willing to forego the royalties and Cabaret things in which everybody did their own thing.

- **All deals do not involve money.** There are a lot of swaps in the non-profit sector. They call it Non-Cash Donations. We call it sweat-equity. It requires a tremendous amount of work. It's also contacts, contacts, contacts. Someone I know spent $15,000 and lost $10,000 on a show. I spent $1,000, and didn't lose any money. The same reviewer saw both shows.

- **When you have an actor's co-op**, you can do all kinds of things together that you can't do singly. In financing, they call it a syndicate. It's more sensible to produce as a syndicate and share in the profits and the losses, and everyone feels that they have a personal investment in what's going on.

- **I look for tech people** who are willing to be trained. For example, there was a film director who had just come into town and hadn't directed a play since college. He wanted his name all over the publicity and we said, "Sure." It gets the director's names out there. It's worth it to them.

- **I knew several women** who were doing one-woman shows, so I put together a compilation of excerpts from their shows for ANTA. I brought that in as a package. I've been piggy-backing other organizations, because the theater companies already have insurance and the spaces are sitting there.

- **The biggest expense is theater rental**, which really isn't necessary. You can produce little productions in a cabaret setting, a club. It's the high end of the poetry scene and you don't have to worry about the unions. They also do dramatic things and acoustic music. We did a show called *A Collage of Women's Moments* in the club and cabaret circuit. We worked at Highland Grounds, Natural Fudge, Pikmeup, the old Santa Monica Improvisation.

Q: How do you get people to see you?

- **There's the audience of the venue**, the audience of the friends and families of the actors, then there's the general public. If you're working for an existing venue, find out if they have a mailing list or a calendar and get yourself on it. Give all the people in the ensemble lots of flyers. If it's getting to the end of the week and the response is weak, get on the phone and paper the house saying, "This is the weekend that you can get all your friends in on two-fers."

- **To get industry people**, we put the flyers in the Breakdown Service. If you get seven people and it costs $70 to put the ads in Breakdowns, that's $10 a piece. It's more reasonable for actors to pay $10 each than pay for individual postage to the casting directors.

Q: What was the drive for you to produce?

- **My payment was that I had artistic control,** or artistic input. They were the kinds of things I wanted to do, the kinds of parts I wanted to work on. I didn't have the lead in every show, but there was always something there. Also, I kept myself working and learned a tremendous amount. Most of the things in L.A. are over-produced. I'm interested in getting results, not window dressing. You have a couple of well-placed chairs and some good actors; what else do you need?

- **Everybody should have an act.** I've developed a role for myself that's a combination of Renaissance and Celtic music, and I go to Renaissance Faires; there are a whole string of them. Sometimes I make money, sometimes I just pass the hat. My entourage and I get in for free; it's sort of like having a paid vacation. I work on my music and have a great time.

• **Anne Etue is a performer, director, producer and publicist** for the West Coast Ensemble Theatre and several other theaters and projects. Anne directs and helps produce performers Amy Hill's and Nobuko Miyanoto's one-woman shows.

Q: How did you get interested in one-person shows?

- **Amy had some material** that she thought would make a good one-person show, and asked me to direct it. Her first show, *Tokyo Bound*, had a theme of her at age 18 going to Japan to find her mother's roots. We put the ideas on 3x5 cards and she would go away and start writing. I was initially a sounding board for her on whether or not I thought the material worked and I did some editing for her. She also had a dramaturge involved in the process.

Q: What's a dramaturge?

- **A dramaturge is a person** who looks at the script and helps to shape it. It's common in most theater companies to help research the material or go through the material and give feedback on whether it should be produced. One mistake a lot of people make is not to have a director or someone outside the piece to formulate it. Amy was approached by the Japanese-American Cultural Center and that was the first booking.

Q: Was that for money?

- **It wasn't much, but we always had some kind of compensation.** We decided that we had a good half-hour of material. Then we workshopped it at West Coast Ensemble. We had maybe 10 people in to give us some feedback in preparation for a run at the East West Players. Amy applied for a $9,000 grant from the Cultural Affairs Department; that's how the first run was partially funded.

- **When you get a grant, they don't just hand you a check** but at least it validates the goal; it's the green light to keep on working on it. We had a run and it was a huge success. Sylvie Drake *(L.A. Times)* came and saw it, loved it and gave us the front page. All of the reviews were outstanding. At the 99-seat level, it probably was one of the most successful one-person shows. In the program I was listed as Hika Keltamaki, stage manager; Elizabeth Bennett, promotions; Anne Etue, director. It was basically me and Amy. We had a lighting designer, a set designer, a music designer. Amy felt very strongly about paying everybody involved.

- **Another fertile ground for these one-person shows is festivals** in Canada. We did the Montreal Fringe Festival. There is an entrance fee, maybe $200-$300, and you've got to get there. We had tons of frequent flyer miles to take care of that expense. They put you up at someone's house who's connected to the festival, then you keep the entire box office receipts every night. We did extraordinarily. Tickets are $7, seating 100+ people and every single night for two weeks we sold out. Each night they gave us $700 in Canadian money. Amy and I split it right down the middle and had a great vacation.

- **We could've gone all summer.** There were people that went from Vancouver all the way across Canada. We have been to Vassar College, Boston College, Arizona State University, Michigan State University, and a whole slew of schools.

Q: How do these colleges know about you?

- **Every year, there's a Western Arts Administrators Conference** called WAA. At the conference there are people who book for public venues, but the biggest number are people who book for the art centers. For example, UCLA has Royce Hall and the Wadsworth Theater, so the guy that runs that would be at the WAA Conference. We showcase a bit of the show at the conference; you get 15 minutes.

- **The college circuit has been a big thing for us.** We were at the Public Theater in New York. George Wolfe came to see *Tokyo Bound* when we did it at East West Players, and liked it. A number of theaters have solo performers' festivals. Louisville has a *Solo Performers Festival*; San Francisco has *O Solo Mio*. You don't make enormous sums of money, but they do pay. They'll be willing to subsidize your airfare and find you a place to stay.

Resources

Biff Yeager, www.ultimatewishgift.com. Produces your starring movie for $500,000. I've known Biff for years. He is a great actor and can really put things together.

Anne Etue, 323/669-0553. She is available for directing, producing and publicity work.

Pamela Munro, E. Duse Management, 323/467-1470. $25 an hour. Teaches small classes and is a private consultant. "Too many actors get ripped off. I tell people how to produce without spending a lot."

Back Stage West/Drama-Logue produces an annual edition with theater and spaces suitable for rent. You can call them and get their most recent back edition with the theater listings.

Women In Theater, 818-752-7466. A great organization, they have listings of people wanting to work on productions.

Theater L.A., 213/614-0556. Bill Freimuth's organization. Most all of L.A. theaters belong and they also take individual members. There is a monthly newsletter and you can keep up on everything that is going on in the theater in Los Angeles.

Public Access Cable Television

• **Anyone living in Los Angeles County** can produce their own 1/2-hour public access television show. Some studios charge $35 plus the cost of a 3/4" video tape, while other studios are free. If you provide a 1/2" tape, they will record the show on both formats at the same time for no charge. The best bargain in town!

• **It is possible to serve as a non-paid intern.** Most of the technical people are interns, thus the programs are not network quality. They give small workshops where you'll get actual hands-on experience with cameras, lighting, technical directing (TD) and even directing. You can apply by calling the cable company. I interned for about nine months when I first started producing my public access show so I would be familiar with all aspects of production. Many of the full-time employees at the cable companies started out as interns.

• **The cable companies offer classes for producers** in how to operate remote 3/4" camera equipment and how to use the editing bays. Century Cable charges $10 per hour for the use of their editing facilities and $50 per day for 3/4" remote camera, lighting, and sound equipment. At Media One, West Valley and TCI, there is currently no charge for editing or using remote equipment. Cable company rules change frequently but any amount they may charge will be reasonable.

• **I've been producing *Judy Kerr's Acting Workshop*** for 15 years. My students do cold readings, scenes and monologues; it helps them gain three-camera experience and exposure to industry people who may be watching. The tape can also be shown to agents and casting people if the actor has no other footage.

• **I also do talk shows**, interviewing prominent people in the acting business who have information for the acting community at large. My students present questions to the guests. Sometimes we have guest teachers designing exercises for the actors.

• **You can produce any type of show you wish.** Why not give yourself, your friends and associates an opportunity to do some acting or talk show work? For very little money, you can learn about the television industry from the inside out. All of the studios have day, evening and Saturday hours available in which to tape your shows.

• **When you're ready to produce a show**, you can rehearse in front of your home camera. In fact you can tape your whole show at home and use the cable facilities to transfer from your 1/2" or 8mm format to 3/4" tape and edit the pieces into a 28-minute show. After your tape airs with the cable company that recorded it, you can take the tape to each of the other studios and they will air the tape for no charge. You can even get a several-week regular time slot at all the studios except Century Cable.

• **All possibilities are open to you and your imagination.** I've coached many public access producers, working with them on-camera, guiding them and offering tips so they can avoid mistakes in their first few shows.

• **Here are a few studios to get you started.** Call and they will mail the guidelines, the producer meetings schedule, and provide information on the classes and intern programs. See you on TV.

Resources

Century Cable, 310/315-4444. 2939 Nebraska, Santa Monica, 90404. 2nd location: 213/255-9881. 3037 Roswell, Eagle Rock, 90065. $35 a show.

Media One, 323/993-8000. 900 N. Cahuenga, Hollywood, 90038. $35 a show.

West Valley Cablevision, 818/998-2266. 9260 Topanga Canyon Blvd., Chatsworth, 91311.

TCI of East San Fernando Valley, 818/781-1900. 15055 Oxnard St., Van Nuys, 91411. Free, you furnish the tape.

Private Coaching: Judy Kerr, 818/505-9373. $100 per hour.

STUNT AND ACTION ACTING

• **It is very hard to break into stunt work.** None of the stunt schools are recognized by any of the stunt coordinators who are the directors of the stunts on the set. Besides James Lew, I spoke with Steven Ho who was one of the Ninja Turtles. They agree it is who you know. Steven suggested getting the production charts and finding out where productions are working, go to the sets and try to see the stunt coordinators. Unless you have a real specialty—gymnastics, martial arts or your size is unusual—it's going to be very hard to break in. If you are an all around stunt person, the directors will not look at you as an actor for speaking roles. Stunt people are SAG and have all the benefits actors do. The stunt associations, Stuntmen's Association, Stunts Unlimited and International Stunt Association are also tough to join.

• **There are groups of stunt people** who work out together. Try to meet them and be invited to work out. It's a real networking feat to get to know and hang out with these people.

• **Actor James Lew** is a member of the Stuntmen's Association. His Martial Arts training began at age 14, first in Korean style Karate. He studied a combat style, developed by a member of the Green Beret, a Chinese style called "White Eyebrow" after the appearance of the original Grand Master, Kung Fu "Five Animals" style, the five animals being Tiger, Leopard, Snake, Dragon, and Crane. His favorite parts of the Martial Arts training were "the traditional weapons: spears, swords, many Chinese weapons; great for developing balance, speed, power, another extension to your body." James has successfully established credibility as an actor via the martial arts.

• **James is typically hired as a stunt coordinator** or martial art choreographer, which is somewhat like a dance choreographer.

Q: Tell me about your job.

- **I read the script and break it down.** The job is always to bring the vision of the director to life; he may want a certain feeling from the fight, a certain intensity, a certain drama. You try to choreograph moves accordingly. If it's a real brutal, intense fight, you want to use more of a street feel to it. Or if there is a bit of comedy, then you want to lighten it up. If things happen by chance, people fall or something breaks, you give it a different flavor.

- **When I was working** on *Undercover Blues*, with Kathleen Turner and Dennis Quaid, we had approximately two weeks time in pre-production for them to train. We worked on the basics first, to provide a foundation, footwork. Rather than trying to give them a general training program, we gave a concept of what the fight scenes were actually going to be so they could work on specific moves. Kathleen had a personal trainer so she was in great shape. I came in also as a physical trainer for Dennis, using weights and stretching. Both actors were very athletic so they picked it up easily.

Q: What training do you recommend for actors who want to do their own action work?

- **The only thing a production company** would allow an actor to do is fights; they won't allow them to be in a car chase or a high fall. A Martial Art program would be a very wise investment because it teaches you how to throw your body, how to fall down without hurting yourself. The styles vary with different schools, different instructors. It's best to audit a class and get a feel for it. Ballet is great for general movement. For stunts, gymnastics is beneficial; you need to experience rolling and tumbling. On *Buffy, The Vampire Slayer*, I trained Kristy Swanson in martial arts. She had dance training and enjoyed movement, so I had something to build on, a foundation.

Q: Is it hard to break into stunt work?

- **It's like getting a credit card without having credit.** People always want to know what you've done. If you haven't done anything, they don't want to hire you. Get some nonunion work; get some experience; get something on your resume. If you have a special ability, if you're a champion at something, it can open the door. Motorcycle riders, gymnasts, swimmers; doing something a little better than the normal person can do.

- **My first job** was on the original *Kung-Fu* series. They were looking for martial artists and I had that special ability. Then other projects came along, and I had a credit. Your last job is your audition for your next job. The stunt coordinator may have liked your work and will recommend you to someone else looking for someone with your abilities.

Q: What is the audition like?

- **The martial arts or stunt double audition** is the same as an acting audition. They're always looking for that spark, something special. So you want to come in with a lot of intense energy, to come across like you can really hurt the person that you're going to fight in the film. They'll ask you to do a demonstration. You need to get across in your body language and your eyes through sense memory or personalization that your opponent is someone that you really want to hurt, take care of, defend against. You've got to really sell it to the director. A routine is usually 30 seconds to a minute. If it is being taped, you play it directly towards the camera, as if that's the director or someone who would be watching it. If the director's in the room, you want to play it toward him and give him that impression personally. He can always watch it on the tape again.

Q: What advice do you have for martial artists or others wanting to break into action acting?

- **A lot of people make the mistake** of thinking that just because they are a martial artist, they can be in movies. It's a totally different field; it's movie making, so I recommend acting classes. That teaches you to hold a feeling while doing a fight. Also to be able to handle dialogue; not just kicking and punching and screaming. You have to be able to open your mouth and talk.

- **There's a bit of a difference** between film martial arts and real martial arts. It can be difficult to grasp. In real fighting you don't want to telegraph to your opponent, "I'm going to kick or punch you." In film, you need to show the audience: "This is the kick that I'm going to use," present it then go through with it. To make it a little more theatrical, you have to overemphasize certain moves.

- **To be successful, the key word is always "persistence;"** never give up. If you are a martial artist, you know what that means. If you want to do a certain kick, the only thing is to just do it over and over; be persistent about it. Finally, one day it comes. To be successful in the film business, it's the same thing; there's that big heavy door in front of you so you have to keep kicking, kicking, kicking until you kick it down. That's what I did for a long time.

Resources

Action Actor's Academy, 310/558-1143. www.wgn.net/~actiona. They are a company of actors learning to tell stories through physical movement and acting techniques for projects such as *Zorro* and *Hercules*. Classes include martial arts, European, Asian and Filipino weapons.

Westside Fencing Center and Center for Stage Combat, 310/558-1143. 8737 Washington Blvd., Culver City, 90232. The largest fencing center in the country. Classes and private coaching. Call for their brochure; there is a coupon for a free fencing lesson. Some former students are: Geena Davis (*Cutthroat Island*), Teenage Mutant Ninja Turtles, Robin Williams, Shelly Long, Keanu Reeves and Eric Roberts.

Beverly Hills Karate Academy, 310/275-2661. 9085 Santa Monica Blvd., West Los Angeles 90069. Emil Farkas teaches motion picture stunt fighting and all forms of martial arts stunts. He is a stunt coordinator and frequently casts stunt people from his classes.

Cold Reading and Scene Showcase Workshops

• **Showcase workshops give actors an opportunity** and a place to show themselves to people in the industry. Yes it does cost money, but so does everything else you do to promote yourself. If you don't have very many credits and don't know many casting people or agents, promotion is the name of the game. I was called in and cast for a situation comedy by a casting director I had met at a showcase a year-and-a-half before.

• **I believe the best showcases** to start with are the prepared scene showcases. Work a scene really well, audition, and then for about $20 each, you and your partner can perform it for the casting director or agent you choose. Go watch, see how they are run; the actors will appreciate having you in the audience. If you are low on funds this is a great opportunity to learn about different casting directors personally just by watching what they say to the other actors.

• **Good things do happen from these showcases,** but you can't count on anything except getting to act for a few minutes. That, in essence, is what you are paying for. If you are in a play, it is very hard to get a casting director or agent to come see the play. It will cost you to send out your flyers, do follow up calls and offer free seats that you often pay for. It seems like the unknown actor is always paying to be seen. It is one of the facts of our lives. I believe we must make peace with it or ignore the whole thing. It is not valuable to fight it or be angry over the situation.

• **The other type of showcases** are cold reading casting director or agent showcases and usually cost around $25 each. The casting director brings in sides (part of the script you will read from) for a show they've cast and assigns a part to you. You usually get to read for just one character. I personally don't believe you should do these until you are very good at cold readings; you can learn more about the acting of audition material from your acting teachers and then show yourself to a casting director at a showcase workshop. When you have acting experience, the casting director will have more to work with and will remember you as a good actor.

• **Sharon Lawrence of *NYPD Blue*** said when she first came to town she did a few casting director workshops. She chose the casting directors very carefully, picking shows she felt she would be right for. Sharon met casting director Junie Lowry Johnson's assistant, they called her and she booked a *Civil Wars* episode. When the part came up for a district attorney on *NYPD*, Junie remembered her and brought her in for the interview.

• **Rebecca McFarland was one of George's girlfriends on *Seinfeld*.** It was her fourth Los Angeles job; she had moved here the year before. A new friend asked Rebecca to audition with him for an agent he wanted—the agent took her and not him. She performs at a casting showcase each Tuesday night, sending a picture postcard in advance to the casting director she's meeting. Showcasing has helped her get auditions.

• **Casting director's jobs depend on bringing in actors that read well.** I think you get a good return for your money by attending a casting director's own workshop for a month or six weeks; they will remember you better because you worked with them over several weeks.

• **I know a lot of experienced actors**, including myself, who have landed roles from both types of showcases. Again—go, watch and decide for yourself where your showcase dollars will be spent most wisely.

• **A student of mine always sends a picture, resume and a short note** introducing himself to the casting director before he does the showcase. Typically, "I'm looking forward to meeting you at such and such showcase."

• **Beverly Nero, a hard working actor** friend of mine, wrote and rehearsed a four minute scene with her partner Clare Peck, that featured them in parts they could well be cast in tomorrow. They took the scene into Joan Darling's class several times for her direction. After it was honed to perfection, they took turns calling casting directors and asking if they could come into their offices to perform the scene for them. They did it in 111 offices over a three year period.

Q: Beverly, how did you accomplish this?

- **The scene was from a play I wrote** about a current and ex-wife meeting in an airport for the first time. It worked well in an office because it had virtually no requirements other than two chairs. It's just an office space, and casting directors can feel overwhelmed when there is a lot of movement or where they have to move their offices around to accommodate the scene. A five-minute scene can become 20 minutes if you have a set-up and a strike-down.

- **In order to build our confidence**, we took the scene to casting people we knew first. We were very straight-forward in our phone calls saying, "We have a scene that we're going to be taking around to casting people and we would love you to be among the first to see it and to have your input." The first couple of months we saw people that each of us knew well. After that we had to get a little more creative.

Q: Did you talk to the casting director or did you talk to the secretary or assistant?

- **We always asked for the casting director by their first name** and only used our own first names. I always felt very strongly, and I think that Clare did, too, that it's not that you don't respect the secretary, but you know that they're not the decision-maker. Why waste all your excitement on the secretary, and then they just write a little note and the person looks at it and throws it in the trash. I always felt that it was important to only speak to the person who is going to see your work.

Q. Did they talk to you after you did the scene for them?

- **We said, "We are going to be doing this play** and we'd love your feedback on the scene," so it took the onus and the pressure off of our performances. We made sure we were in our five minute time. We didn't wait for them to say go, we just set it up and went. If they wanted to talk, fine, if not, we were out of there. Clare and I were always told it was worth their time. I took pictures and resumes. Clare liked to follow up later with a note and her picture and resume.

Q: Did you ever do this when you weren't doing a play but just wanted to be seen?

- **My friend Gary Stein and I did 15 or 20 of them** within a two month period. It was a two-person talking scene we liked doing together. Very simple, *Love is a Time of Day.* We changed a few of the lines because it was outdated. We did the same thing. We called people and said that we had a five-minute scene and when could we come in? We got to go out, be seen, meet other people and exercise our chops. We had a blast.

• A theatrical agent talks about the value of cold reading workshops with casting directors.

- **When your agent sends your picture and resume to a casting director,** that casting director may have received 700-2,000 submissions for the same role. First, they bring in who their bosses told them to. The second group of actors are friends who could do the job. The third group are professionals who work all the time who they know can do that job. And the last person is the unknown picture in the pile that they have no knowledge of. My feeling is, you can jump from kindergarten to first grade if you can do the cold reading workshops with the casting director. I think they're extremely valuable for the good actor. Out of 16-20 people they see in a workshop, they're looking for the gem. If you're very good, they're going to remember you. You've now put yourself past the picture and resume that's been put across their desk by an agent. You're now a human being and they know a little bit about you.

• **Beware of scams when looking into showcases.** There are some unethical people who call actors that have submitted their pictures to casting directors. The actors are told, "You need to showcase with me in order to work." Do not accept phone calls from people you have not submitted to, who say they don't know how they got your picture or who gave it to them. *Please see Section Seven, Scams Page 451.*

Resources

• PREPARED SCENE SHOWCASES

Professional Actors Showcase, 818/754-4754. Produced by Live Actors' Society, www.liveactors.com. Richard Delancy Studio, 4741 Laurel Canyon Blvd. #100, Studio City, 91604. Tuesdays, 7:30PM, $20 each actor (a not-for-profit organization.) Prepared scenes, 3 1/2 minutes maximum. Auditions by appointment. Casting Directors, Agents, Directors, Producers.

SAG & AFTRA members are eligible for the union showcases. Usually several casting directors attend these monthly showcases. You can perform once every six months. For AFTRA, request the casting showcase registration card from the membership counter (10-4:30) or call 323/634-8100. For information on the SAG showcases call 323/ 549-6540.

• COLD READING SHOWCASES

These few have good reputations. Please investigate carefully; reputations can change. Check out others in Back Stage West *and* The Working Actor's Guide.

Casting Network, office: 818/986-3727. Free orientations & cold reading auditions. 818/788-4792. Showcases are at La Bella Center, 12500 Riverside Dr., #202 & #204, Studio City, 91607. $30 per session, discount when you buy a series. Many sessions a week. Directors, agents and casting directors. Call for their brochure. Strong acting background and/or union affiliation required.

Casting Break, 818/990-9994. 11965 Ventura Blvd., Studio City, 91604. Actors are given the choice of a cold reading, prepared monologue or scene. Casting directors, producers, directors and agents lead workshops. Individual workshops are $20 each; 6 workshops, $100; 12 workshops, $185; 18 workshops, $265; that's $14.72 a workshop. They only take trained actors; your first workshop is your audition.

In The Act, 310-474-7272. www.intheact.com. Organized workshop using casting directors, agents, directors and producers. Call for brochure and audition procedure. Casting 911 service.

One On One, 818/789-3399. Steve Duran. Average $28, special for series. Audition required, they are held each Wednesday between 1-4, 13261 Moorpark St., Suite 202, Sherman Oaks, no appointment necessary. Casting directors, agents, directors, producers.

Prime Time, Actors Studio. 323/874-4131. 3405 Cahuenga Blvd. West, Los Angeles, 90068. They offer showcases and classes, run by Mark Malis, former VP of Talent at Universal TV.

Reel Pros, 818/788-4133. "The Workshop for Professional Talent." They take great pride in the showcase and have a very careful audition process. Their brochure and networking guide is extremely helpful.

"To The Top" Workshops, 323/463-6885. www.tothetop.net. Hot line, 323/368-8160. The Taft Building, 1680 North Vine Street, #723, Hollywood, 90028. Jay Hastings runs the whole organization.They require everyone to audition. Showcases are $25-$30. Many of their actors have been called in to audition from the casting director workshops and have landed jobs. They focus heavily on bringing in independent projects. Union and nonunion. Over the Top Extra Casting operates out of there; no charge to join the extra casting agency.

• **A valuable class** might be the following. It gives an insight into the whole casting experience.

L. J. Lane, 310/826-0624. Five-weeks, $200. She is a Paramount casting associate. She takes actors through the actual casting process from the first meeting with a casting director to the producer's call back and then how to test for the part. This seems like a very worthwhile class.

• *For Cold Reading and Audition Material Teachers, see Section One, Page 30.*

DIARY: ACTRESS LIVING HER DREAM IN LOS ANGELES

• **This three month diary appears as it did in the eighth edition** of this book. I believe her activities are very typical of what a motivated person should be doing. Also see the epilogue and the current two-week diary, pages 236-238.

• **Jode Leigh Edwards, 20 years old, moved to Los Angeles** from Dallas, Texas. My daughter, Cynthia Kerr, met Jode when they were both attending KD Studios' Conservatory program. I saw Jode's work each semester when I taught a class for the Conservatory. Jode and Cynthia both worked hard and earned money acting while they were in school. Before graduation, Jode was signed by the Kim Dawson Agency, the top agency in Dallas. (See Jode's resume on page 114.) Although SAG eligible, she chose not to join until she landed her first SAG job here, so she could continue to work in nonunion independent films. She had the cash in reserve to join the union with a half-hour's notice.

• **Jode made an initial visit to Los Angeles** in January, with her parents and then in March with one of her agents to get a feel for Los Angeles. May 5th, she and her mother came to Los Angeles and rented an apartment in Studio City, furnishing it at Plummer Furniture. She was planning to move/drive out June 1st. But, she got a surprise audition and flew in on May 27th, while her dad drove her car to L.A.

• **When she finished my annual class,** which I teach during the television season hiatus, I suggested the Larry Moss Studio for Jode.

• **I asked Jode to keep a diary for me from the day she arrived.** She had a nest egg from her work in Dallas, some sponsorship from her family and a part time job that she does on her computer and fax machine. The only entries she included in her diary are the things she did for her acting career. She was well prepared for this move to Los Angeles.

Mon. May 27	Move to L.A. Private coaching with Judy to prep for Acapulco H.E.A.T. audition.
Tue. May 28	Acapulco H.E.A.T. audition - Sent thank you.
Wed. May 29	Met Tony at Judy's & picked up scene for Judy's cable show.
Thu. May 30	Dad drove into town with car and stuff. Rehearsed scene with Tony, Picked up Acapulco H.E.A.T. script for call back.
Sat. June 1	Appeared on Judy's cable show.
Sun. June 2	Sit in at Judy's workshop.
Mon. June 3	Phone gets hooked up. Call Michael at J. Michael Bloom (contact I made in Dallas).
Tue. June 4	Acapulco H.E.A.T. call back. Auditioned for casting director Beverly Long's commercial class.
Wed. June 5	Went to Samuel French, bought "*The Agencies.*" Left another message for J. Michael Bloom. Had pictures reproduced-Quantity Photo-they're really quick. Started writing cover letter for agent submission. Signed up for Beverly Long's commercial class. Sent thank you for Acapulco H.E.A.T. callback.
Thu. June 6	Lunch with Darren Wadyko (new agent @Cosden, I worked with him and he cast me in a National commercial in Dallas, also a KD Studio Alumni). Picked up photos at Quantity. Finished agent cover letter and mailed. "Actor's Network" Orientation - I joined. Submitted P & R to *Back Stage West/Drama-Logue* notices.
Fri. June 7	Met with Doreen at Jan's Video for consultation. Picked up "Actor's Network" Notebook. J. Michael Bloom returned my message and set an appointment for me to meet with LeAnne Fader. Called Eddie Winkler (agent with CNA, he was my agent in Dallas at Kim Dawson).
Sun. June 9	Judy's workshop. Drove by J. Michael Bloom and CNA (scouting trip).
Mon. June 10	Met with Eddie, Lori, & Patrick at CNA (commercial dept.).
Tue. June 11	Met with LeAnne Fader at J. Michael Bloom. Worked scene with Phil for Judy's workshop.

	Looked for new monologue. Called Larry Moss Studio for more information.
Wed. June 12	Edited demo reel at Jan's Video. Sent agent thank you notes. LeAnne Fader at J. Michael Bloom set up an appointment for me to meet casting director Linda Francis. CNA wants to sign me commercially.
Thu. June 13	Worked scene for Judy's workshop. Drove by Linda Francis' for tomorrow's general. Bought video tapes and covers for demos (Studio Film & Tape). Submitted for Back Stage West/*Drama-Logue* casting notices.
Fri. June 14	Met casting director - Linda Francis (sent thank you). Sent thank you to LeAnne for setting up appointment.
Sun. June 16	Judy's workshop.
Mon. June 17	Met with CNA's theatrical department. "Actor's Network" session.
Tue. June 18	Worked scene for class.
Wed. June 19	Met with Michelle Danner (acting coach) at Larry Moss Studio. Dropped demo tape off at Tyler Kjar. Last touch to demo tape at Jan's Video.
Thu. June 20	Met with Producer Russell Gray to intern pre-production (tip from Actor's Network). 1st commercial class with Beverly Long.
Sun. June 23	Judy's workshop.
Tue. June 25	Russell Grey's office - intern.
Wed. June 26	Worked scene for Judy's workshop.
Thu. June 27	Russell Grey's office - intern. Worked scene for Judy's workshop. Beverly's commercial class.
Fri. June 28	Back Stage West/*Drama-Logue* submissions. Script coverage for a script for Russell Grey. Submitted to more agents.
Sat. June 29	Audition for student film (Back Stage West/*Drama-Logue*). Work scene with Terry for Judy's workshop.
Sun. June 30	Audition for independent film (Back Stage West/*Drama-Logue*). Judy's workshop.
Mon. July 1	"Actor's Network" - met with acting teacher Kimberly Jentzen.
Tue. July 2	Interned for Russell Grey.
Fri. July 5	Saw play at Complex Theatre.
Sat. July 6	Saw "Moll Flanders" at DGA.
Sun. July 7	Audition for independent feature (Back Stage West/*Drama-Logue*).
Tue. July 9	Intern.
Thu. July 11	Intern.

	Rehearse scene with Tony for Judy's workshop. Beverly Long's commercial class.
Fri. July 12	Rehearse scene with Tony. Submit to *Back Stage West/Drama-Logue.*
Sat. July 13	Appeared on Judy's Cable Show.
Sun. July 14	Judy's workshop. Met agent Bonnie Howard in class - performed monologue.
Mon. July 15	Saw play reading at Canon Theatre.
Tue. July 16	Intern. Read screen plays. Booked commercial at Arts Center (*Back Stage West*).
Wed. July 17	Another actor approached me and asked me to join illegitimate managing group to get the breakdown service. I told him I wasn't interested.
Thu. July 18	Rehearse commercial. Met with Bonnie Howard again - she wanted to represent me. Beverly Long's Commercial Class. Submit *Back Stage West* casting notices.
Fri. July 19	Intern. Started taking technical acting classes with Michelle Danner at Larry Moss Studios.
Sat. July 20	Shot Arts Center Commercial.
Sun. July 21	Judy's last workshop.
Mon. July 22	Audition for independent film (*Back Stage West*).
Tue. July 23	Intern. Dropped tape off at Ann Waugh agency.
Wed. July 24	Saw a movie.
Thu. July 25	Met casting director Mark Tillman (Russell Gray set up). Class with Michelle Danner. Commercial class with Beverly Long.
Fri. July 26	I'm in San Francisco with parents and get a call from Schiowitz, Clay & Rose agency, they want to meet me next week (my own submission). Got a call - booked independent film.
Mon. July 29	Audition for independent feature (*Back Stage West*). "Actor's Network" meeting.
Tue. July 30	Intern.
Wed. July 31	Audition for independent feature (*Back Stage West*). Met student director to do scene for class at Arts Center.
Thu. Aug 1	Intern. Michelle Danner's class. Beverly Long's commercial class - met an agent.
Fri. Aug 2	Meeting with Schiowitz, Clay & Rose. Read thru for booked independent ("Roommates, Sex & Love").

Sat. Aug 3	Audition for independent feature - (*Back Stage West*). "Actor's Network" Summer Fling Party.
Sun. Aug 4	Rehearse scene at Arts Center for directors' class. Audition independent feature (*Back Stage West*) - "The Diary".
Mon. Aug 5	Audition/ independent film (*Back Stage West*) "Between Classes." Follow-up w/ Schiowitz, Clay & Rose - they like me, want to see a monologue. Michelle Danner's class.
Tue. Aug 6	Shooting "Roommates, Sex, & Love."
Wed. Aug 7	Reh. scene for director's class @ Arts Center.
Thu. Aug 8	Performed scene @ Arts Center - met a possible new cold-reading teacher. *Back Stage West*.
Mon. Aug 12	"Actor's Network" meeting.
Tue. Aug 13	Booked independent "Between Classes," met with director. Shot that evening "Roommates, Sex, & Love."
Wed. Aug 14	Michelle Danner's class.
Thu. Aug 15	Intern. CNA wants to meet with me theatrically again. Had 2nd meeting with Schiowitz, Clay, & Rose-they want to represent me. "Actor's Network" meeting. *Back Stage West* submissions to casting notices.
Fri. Aug 16	Rehearse "Roommates, Sex, & Love."
Sat. Aug 17	Call back for independent film "The Diary." Call back for independent film "What Do Women Want?"
Sun. Aug 18	"Actor's Network" meeting.
Mon. Aug 19	Filming "Between Classes."
Tue. Aug 20	Filming "Between Classes."
Wed. Aug 21	Started Kick Boxing classes. Called Eddie at CNA to set up appointment.
Thu. Aug 22	Intern (last day). Hooked up Voicemail/pager service.
Fri. Aug 23	Shooting "Roommates, Sex, & Love."
Mon. Aug 26	Filming "Between Classes."
Tue. Aug 27	Filming "Between Classes."
Wed. Aug 28	"Actor's Network" meeting.
Thu. Aug 29	Met Robert Costanzo at CNA - wanted to represent me. 2nd call-back for indep. film "What do Women Want?" Booked it!
Fri. Aug 30	Audition for independent film - (*Back Stage West*) Church's Chicken wants to reinstate National Commercial - I'm in negotiations.

Sat. Aug 31	Start rehearsal for "What do Women Want?"
Sun. Sept 1	Filming "Between Classes."
Mon. Sept 2	Filming "Between Classes."
Tue. Sept 3	Filming "Between Classes."
Wed. Sept 4	Rehearsal "What do Women Want?" Started learning sign language for role.
Fri. Sept 6	Filming "Roommates, Sex, & Love." Prepped for theatre audition on Saturday.
Sat. Sept 7	Audition for play in Santa Monica "Picnic." (*Back Stage West*) Rehearsed "What do Women Want?"
Sun. Sept 8	Filming "Between Classes."
Mon. Sept 9	Filming "Between Classes."
Tue. Sept 10	Filming "Between Classes."
Wed. Sept 11	"Actor's Network" meeting.
Thu. Sept 12	Met with Robert at CNA second meeting. Called Schiowitz. Clay, & Rose - decided to go with them theatrically.
Fri. Sept 13	Audition independent film (*Back Stage West*) Drama-Logue casting submissions. Filming "Roommates, Sex, & Love." Dropped pictures off at Schiowitz, Clay, & Rose.

• **Jode will be looking next for a commercial agent**; if she needs help or referrals, Beverly Long will help her. Jode is a very commercial type and has already done several commercials so she is a valuable client. It was important for her to pursue the theatrical agent first. Jode is ambitious and driven to be successful.

EPILOGUE

• **Jode wrote the above diary for the eighth edition** of *Acting Is Everything*, In June, two years later, I asked her to give me a copy of her next two week diary. As you will see she is busier than ever. She was writing this during the traditionally "slow time" in Los Angeles. Television shows are on hiatus, "grad films" are all finished waiting for the schools to start up again and commercial interviews are slow. Jode creates places to act when many actors are just complaining about how slow things are. She has had career ups and downs but stays determined to live her dream fully in Los Angeles.

Sun. June 6	9-10	Kickbox
	12:15-12:45	Audition for a SAG independent short film.
	2-4	Industry party in Malibu.
	5-8	Rehearsed showcase scene w/director at the Actors Network.
Mon. June 7	10-11	Made calls, returned messages, found out I booked the film.
	12-1:30	Rehearsed showcase scene in Santa Monica.
	1:30-2:30	Private w/acting coach Michelle Danner for audition.
	3:15-3:45	Audition for a USA MOW in Burbank.
	4:30-5:30	Called casting directors and faxed flyers for the showcase.
	7:30-9:30	Filmmaker's Alliance in Hollywood - every other Monday they have a screenwriting workshop, and they need/use actors to read their scripts.
Tue. June 8	8:30-1:30	Showcase tech rehearsal at The Coast Playhouse in West Hollywood.
	2:30-6	Called casting directors/faxed flyers for showcase.
	7:45-8:45	Therapy.
Wed. June 9	8:30-1:30	Showcase dress rehearsal.
	1:30-3	Getting last minute things together for show, stopped at laundry & picked up "good show" gifts.
	5:45	Call time for showcase.
	8:00	Showtime!! We had a packed house.
Thu. June 10		Spent most of day a vegetable after the show. The scene wasn't going as well as I'd hoped. I found myself pushing and not allowing moments to organically happen. I needed the day to regroup and figure out why.
	12:30-1:30	Kickbox.
	8-Midnight	Rehearsed the independent film.
Fri. June 11	12-5	Acting class, Larry Moss Studio, Santa Monica.
	8:00	Saw *Collected Stories* with Linda Lavin & Samantha Mathis at the Geffen, Westwood. Amazing show—I'm completely inspired by Linda Lavin's work. She is a lesson in specificity. I am so glad I didn't miss seeing it!
Sat. June 12		Day off!!!
Sun. June 13	9am-Midnt	Filmed all day. I had a lot of fun. It always feels so good to get in front of the camera.
Mon. June 14	1:45-2:45	Pick-up rehearsal with showcase scene partner.
	6:00	Call time for showcase.
	8:00	Showtime!! Another packed house! All of my agents' assistants came tonight and loved the show. The scene felt better too.

Tue. June 15	10:30-11:30	Therapy.
	12:30-1:30	Kickbox.
	2-5	Final calls/faxes to casting directors for showcase.
	8-10	Saw a show at The Space Theatre, Hollywood. Written & directed by acquaintances of mine. A friend I saw there is producing *Miss Julie* and asked me to look at the character Christine.
Wed. June 16	9:45-1:30	Voice Class/Santa Monica.
	6:00	Call time for the showcase.
	8:00	Final Show! Another packed house! My agents, acting teacher, friends including Cynthia Kerr and, of course, Judy Kerr were there for support.
Thu. June 17	9:30-10:30	Jogged around Lake Hollywood.
		Spent the day regrouping from show. I analyzed the feedback I'd gotten from my teacher, agents and Judy. Called people to thank them for coming. I cried a lot! Some people loved the show and my scene. Some hated it. What's the lesson? I guess you can't please everybody. In my heart I know I did the best I could under my given circumstances, and that makes the whole process a success.
	2:00-3:30	Read *Miss Julie*, decided to pass.
	4-5	Prep tomorrow's audition. A lot of it is going to be improv, so I wrote up a couple of scenarios just to be prepared.
Fri. June 18	9-10	Prep audition.
	12-3	Acting class/Santa Monica.
	3:30-4	Audition/new show on the Internet that reviews movies.
Sat. June 19		Day Off!

• **You must do something each day toward fulfilling your dreams**—there is plenty to do in this career you are creating for yourself.

SECTION FOUR

AGENTS

• **Many actors want to work theatrically** (films, TV and stage), in commercials and in voice-overs. Those are the three distinctly different areas of work. A few agencies handle all types of acting work; some handle just one area of the market. Many individual agents specialize in one field; some may handle actors across the board. An agency may have one or several agents working in each department.

• **Agents are protected by California law**; only they can solicit employment and negotiate actor's fees. They are franchised by the unions—SAG, AFTRA and AEA.

• **If you are a commercial type**, it can be easier to get a commercial agent first. They sign many more people than a theatrical agent; some agencies have several hundred actors on their rosters. A good theatrical agent would handle 30 to 50 actors alone; if there are three agents then perhaps 150 clients for one agency. These are very general figures just to give you an idea how it works. One of SAG's guidelines for agents is to accept only union actors—yet, if you have a great commercial look they will stretch the rules. If you are 22 or younger it is easier for an agent to accept you as a nonunion actor.

• **My advice is to read one of the several books** on agents which you can buy at a theatrical book store. Then design a short, unique cover letter. Enclose your wonderful 8x10 photo that looks just like you, and your resume. Mail it to specific agents within the agencies that use the type of actor that you are.

• **When agents are interested,** they will call you to come in and meet them. Go in dressed looking like your picture. Something in that picture attracted them. What you have to offer the agent is your good training, background, and the experience you have been able to get for yourself. They want hard workers because when you are first starting out, they are not able to devote much time to you; they concentrate on the actors who are making money for them. Agents make 10% of what you earn. They do 10% of the work and you do 90% of the work of obtaining employment.

• **I must caution you about certain scams.** *Never* sign with an agent who charges you any type of fee or insists you have pictures taken by a certain photographer or says you must study with certain teachers. Always call SAG to make sure the agency is franchised with the union. This must be strictly a business arrangement and it is your responsibility to get out of the office if things don't seem on the up and up. An agent's fee is 10% of what your gross salary is, period. They make their money when you work. When you terminate an agent, be sure to notify the unions.

• ***Back Stage West/Drama-Logue* have interviews on a monthly basis,** talking to agents. Cut these out, save them, learn more about the way the business is run. Agent Billy Miller of Michael Slessinger & Associates told this story.

> • **When Jenna Elfman (*Dharma and Greg*) was looking for an agent,** her husband read an article in *Drama-Logue* about agent Michael Slessinger. He said, "Jenna, this sounds like the kind of agent you'd want to be with." She asked her commercial agent to set up a meeting. There wasn't a lot on her resume except a couple of student films and commercials. She had scenes from her student films on tape and they were great, so we decided to give it a try. And that's how we started representing her.

• **Anne Archer** *(Fatal Attraction, Patriot Games)* advises, when you have landed your agent:

> • **Learn how to keep friendly**, positive communication with your agent—always telling them the good news—something positive someone said, a great project you heard about, etc. Make them feel like you're a team. Be helpful; take responsibility for creating a warm relationship with your agent.

• **Tom Cruise's** producing partner, Paula Wagner, at an awards dinner, remembered her meeting with Tom during her agent days at Creative Artists Agency 15 years ago.

> • **Tom wore a great sports coat** (borrowed) that covered a ripped T-shirt...he was living in and out of his car, and I was impressed with his

intelligence, presence, self-assurance, decency, capacity for good, and, as I came to know him, his curiosity, courage and conviction.

• **Theatrical agent Harry Gold,** of Gold/Marshak/Kiedtke Agency told Karen Kondazian in *Back Stage West,* what he thought an actor should know about this business.

- **There's so much more that you can do to get yourself work** besides waiting for your agent to call. The more you know about the business, the more empowered you are. The more you know your place within the structure, the better you can play the game. There's so much material to read to stay current with what is going on. Read the newspaper every day to keep up with current events, the trade papers to know who the principal players are that are making the decisions today. I find so many actors have no idea who, for example, is running ABC. You can be sure Al Pacino knows the head of every studio. He works the business as well as anybody. It's about understanding the business, about trying to look at the trends so you can follow them and be a part of them in some way.

- **The biggest stars in the world work the business.** It's a skill and it takes a certain kind of expertise. Seek to be in some kind of contact. You must be extremely resourceful in this business, even if you have an agent. The way you do it is by gaining a full understanding of the business and by networking well. If you can align yourself with good directors, good casting people that will help you get one extra little foot in the door, then you're playing the game a little bit.

• **Commercial Agent Merrill Jonas.**

Q: How do you get an interview with a commercial agent?

- **Get a friend to ask their agent** to see you. Always precede it with a picture and a resume. There's no sense in either of you wasting time if they are loaded with young moms, for example, and you're in that category. Agents see plays and showcases; they get referrals from managers, and actors submit their pictures and resumes.

- **During your interview**, the agent should have your resume—no matter how limited it may be. It's something they can make notes on and keep after you've left. They can see what you have done, if you water ski, speak fluent French, etc. Include height, weight, coloring and where you can be contacted. They may be looking desperately for a jet skier. If your resume says you're an expert jet skier, they have solved their problem; they say, "Get that guy in here."

- **When you get the interview**, don't come in all done up—they want to see the real you. You can't sit there like a lump nor can you dance on the desk. Auditions and interviews are like cocktail parties; be as charming and interested in other people as you can be—kind of up but not so energized that you wear the interviewer out. Don't get upset if they have to take a phone call. It might be a casting call that you're right for.

- **You will read some commercial copy** because they want to know what you do. They aren't just testing you; this will help them sell you more accurately and specifically. They want to hear the special quality you have. Some people are wonderful at sitcom style comedy, which is what commercials utilize and others can cry on cue and can do a heartfelt reading for AIDS prevention or something like that.

Q: What about phone calls to the agent's office?

- **Agents are busy** all the time so just make it quick and try to forgive them for being rude. When an agent is alone in the office and all the phone lights are lit up and one of those lights says "I sent in my picture 2 weeks ago," the agent says, "we'll call you" and hangs up.

- **Commercial agent Beverly Hecht.**

Q: How does the commercial agent's business run?

- **Let's say we're doing a Kellogg's commercial.** A whole breakdown of what kind of actors they want comes in to our office over the computer. We submit our people to the casting directors. They say who they want to see and we call the actors and tell them they have an interview. The two favorite words for an actor are "interview" and "booked."

Q: How should actors approach an agent for representation?

- **If someone walks into my office** and says, "May I leave a resume with you?" Fine. If they try to take up my time, it becomes annoying; I'm trying to get a job done. I will absolutely, positively look at pictures but will not call in people for interviews that are in conflict with my other clients. I don't believe in handling too many actors of the same type; then people are competing within the same agency.

- **Theatrical and commercial agent Bonnie Howard.**

Q: How can an actor get an appointment to meet with you?

- **A great 8x10 will attract attention.** By that I mean a ¾ shot from the knees up in a natural setting, looking very relaxed, and not posing. I like to see more in a picture than *generic nice guy.* Something a little more specific, perhaps *grandfather,* or *driving instructor.* Something a casting director could look at and say, "Yeah, he would make a great IRS collector." A ¾ shot has body language and tells you more about what the person is like. Leaning forward into the camera expresses more enthusiasm, more energy. If your picture is touched up, and you walk in with wrinkles that are not on the picture, it's disappointing and distracting. There's very little difference between commercial, theatrical and modeling pictures. I'm using them all for everything and getting good results. I look at every single picture that comes into my office because I'm interested in finding new talent.

- **A well put together resume helps.** Don't put any Extra work information on your resume. Instead of listing the type or name of the character you played, I would rather see the billing. If you were featured, costarred, or even starred in something, brag about it and put that on there. Commercials should not be on a theatrical resume. The reason for that is you might sabotage yourself unknowingly. Someone might want to call you in for AT&T. If you have Pacific Bell on your resume, they may say, "That's a competitor company, let's not call him in." Only include modeling if you've modeled for a top designer, like Dior, in Paris or New York. I would leave broadcasting off, unless you're going for a voice-over agent. Student films are good. You should list the school that you did the film for. The resume should be the same size as the picture. I don't care whether the resume is stapled or glued to the picture; *I do care very much about grammatical and punctuation mistakes.* Have a professional proofreader read the resume before you mass produce it.

- **I attend the UCLA and the USC student film screenings** and I find talent there. Showcases are also good. I strongly suggest doing Equity-Waiver plays.

Q: On a day-to-day basis, what exactly does an agent do?

- **I subscribe to the Breakdown Service.** It's a breakdown of every project in production. There's a description of each character that they need to cast. I get that delivered to my office every day. I represent about 65 actors—from the age of five to the oldest actor, who is 85. I submit the appropriate pictures to the casting directors; then I try to get auditions for the actors. The actor goes on the audition and hopefully gets a call back. Once the actor goes to the audition, it's out of my hands.

Q: What if the producer or director wants to hire the actor?

- **Usually the casting director calls me to make the deal.** The price of the job is determined by the prior history of the actor's work. It starts out union scale plus 10 percent for the agent. A good agent will always try to raise their actor's fee. Lately, the industry has been very tight-fisted. I like commercials a lot because I get to see my actors more frequently, and I get a great deal of pride from that. I also like it when the checks roll in. On national commercials, usually the actor works one day, and sometimes the checks come in for more than a year. Residuals are a big part of the business.

Q: If I have an agent, how can I help them to help me?

- **Don't bug them**. Don't call them frequently to say, "Why haven't I heard from you?" My pet peeve is, "I was just calling in to see what's new." If there is anything pertaining to that actor, the first thing we do is call them. Most agents represent a large number of clients, and it's very difficult if we get calls all the time. To help your agent, update your pictures; make sure your agent has a large supply of pictures and resumes at all times. I don't mind if my clients come in and check their supply themselves; it's a big help to me, but some agents may mind it. When you deliver your pictures and resumes, make sure your resume is attached to your picture.

Q: What about the actor's demo tape?

- **Demo tapes should be as short as possible**, and as high impact as possible. Just select the best work—nothing that's staged specifically for a demo; they are usually not great quality. Don't send it unless it is requested, because you probably won't get it back, unless you include an envelope with return postage.

• Theatrical Agent Jacqueline LeWinter.

Q: How do you find new actors to represent?

- **Through referrals from casting directors,** our clients and pictures and resumes we receive in the mail. When we see a play one of our clients is in, often there will be another talented actor who's looking for an agent. We always see casting director referrals.

Q: What do you like to see in an actor's submission package?

- **Funny letters!** A resume that's very direct and professional. The picture submitted should be interesting, intelligent and honest. We aren't interested in magazine layout head shots. What we look for when the actor comes in to interview is what the actor brings with them, their attitude, their commitment, and of course, their talent.

Q: What role do agents play in an actor's career?

- **First and foremost is the marketing of the actor**; making sure that the pictures and the resume are representative of what roles the actor will audition for. We try to send actors out on roles we feel are within their essence and range. That way they have a very good chance of, if not booking the role, at least getting called back and making a lasting impression on the casting director.

- **The only time** a **legitimate agent is paid money** is when an actor works. Most actors are paying their agents too much money. It's scale plus 10%, it's not 10% of the scale plus 10%, because then it becomes 11%. Agents sometimes take meals, mileage and per diem commissions, which they are not entitled to.

Q: What about agent scams?

- **There are people who say**, "For a fee, I can get you an agent." What the actor doesn't know is that this person has an arrangement with a SAG franchised agent and money changes hands. You think you have an agent and when you ask why you're not going out on auditions, the agent can give you all kinds of believable reasons. There are also photographic kickbacks, agents who insist their clients go to a specific photographer who charges a lot of money. They'll tell actors to get composites made because they cost more, even though composites are no longer used in the industry.

- **Theatrical Agent Richard Orr.**

Q: How does an actor make a living in this highly competitive field and a living for the agent too?

- **An agency takes 10%**; the agent doesn't actually get 10%, he gets less. Many agents make salaries and others get a percentage of that 10%. An agent never gets the full 10% unless he owns the agency.

- **To make a living**, the actor needs to either become a star in motion pictures, a regular on a TV series, under contract on a soap or a character actor who works all the time—normally in feature films because on television it's a little tougher for a character actor to make the same kind of living. There's another category that I'm not involved in, and that's commercials. Many fine actors are making over $100,000 a year in commercials. Anybody who becomes a star has a success-motivator inside them so strong that they go through tremendous uphill battles.

Q: How should an actor cultivate a relationship with an agent?

- **One of the most important things** for any actor is to be nice. Milton Katselas, a fine acting teacher in town, says, "There are a lot of great actors who are not nice that never work; there are a lot of actors who are not very good but are very nice that work all the time." Everybody has to work as a team, so nice people get hired in most cases. Be nice to your agent all the time. You're not their boss. An agent can fire an actor at any time no matter what their contract says. An actor cannot always do that with an agent. An agent is the keystone to your career.

- **Theatrical Agent Terry Lichtman.**

Q: How involved are you with your clients?

- **I think that you need to have a personal relationship with people.** You talk to them so much, you need to deal with lots of aspects of their life, not necessarily just getting a job. We know when they're working, when they're doing commercials, when they're studying and when they're doing a play. We're always on the phone with our clients.

Q: What kind of agent would you recommend for someone who is just starting out?

- **I don't think there is any one answer for everybody.** I think it's important to be with someone who believes in you, and that could be someone in a large or small agency. It should be someone who thinks you're talented, who you have a rapport with and trust.

Q: How do you meet new clients?

- **I don't see people without an appointment.** I don't have time. I certainly think that doing a showcase or doing theater around town is a good way to get people interested in you. We do look at pictures and resumes that come in, but frankly, I couldn't possibly see everybody. I do see a lot of plays, and that's probably where I get many of my new clients. I think that a good Equity-Waiver play is the best way to be seen.

Q: What about a cover letter included in the picture/resume submission package?

- **It's nice to put something in a letter** that you think will pique the interest of the person who's reading it. Something positive that you can say about what you've done. You've got to dig down and think about what might be of interest to the agent. Basically, they just look at the picture and resume.

Q: If more than one agent wants to sign you, how do you choose?

- **That is a tough choice.** If you know people in the business, ask their opinions. You should check and make sure the agents are SAG franchised. I would ask casting people; that's always a good source of recommendation. You can tell when you walk into an office; if it's busy, if the phones are ringing, business is being done.

Q: If an actor is working for a certain day rate, can they ask the agent to ask for more money?

- **Sure. We as agents represent your interests.** An actor makes more money by commanding more. You sort of know when there's an excitement about you; it's not really a secret. People are calling for you. You've got lots of interviews, getting lots of jobs, lots of choices. That's the time to adjust what you're getting. But when you're between jobs and you worked once this month, and you're going to work once again next month, it's not really the time to think about turning things down because the price may not be right, because there are so many good things that happen when you work.

Q: How would a day player escalate to being a regular on a series?

- **He must go for an interview that is for a series regular.** Go through the ranks. Go through the director, and eventually go through the network, and get the job.

Q: What kind of qualifications should actors have before they approach an agent?

- **You should think that you are ready to work**, that you can get the job if your agent sends you out. Sometimes actors overestimate whether they're ready or not. There are no requirements and there are many ways to work in this business. Some people work without ever taking an acting class. Some people work because they look right, because they're enormously talented, because they're lucky. There are a lot of reasons why people get work.

Q: How do you know when you need a new agent?

- **You need a new agent** if the relationship is not working for you. That could mean a lot of things. If you're not going out, if you are unhappy about the way the agent is handling the negotiations, if you feel that you are not being sent out for the right kind of roles. If you go out for an audition and you look around and you don't see anyone that looks the way you do and you feel that you don't belong there, you might decide that the agent is not seeing or not handling things correctly. But if you're going out to interviews, I can't see any reason why you need to change agents.

Q: How long are the contracts?

- **We sign for one year, initially**, then three years after that, just to keep the bookkeeping down. SAG has a 91-day rule. If you haven't worked in the prior 91 days, you may terminate your contract with the agent.

- **Patty Woo, Theatrical Agent, talks about the actor/agent relationship.**

  - **It's sort of like a romance...**your boyfriend hasn't been as attentive lately as you would like, so you call him more often, trying to push yourself on him. These actions make it harder for him to remember the wonderful reasons he's seeing you in the first place. Ditto for agents.

  - **Do tell me when you know a writer is changing the specs** on something. Do tell me when the producer has called you about an upcoming project. If you are new to my agency, do let me know when you have worked with the director before. I need tools all the time to get my clients work. If you can increase my arsenal, I'm grateful.

- **Jack Nicolson at the Acadamy Awards for 1998,** when excepting his Oscar thanked his agent. He has had the same agent his whole career.

Resources

BOOKS

Reference books date quickly; purchase only the latest editions. All of the following books may be purchased or ordered through Samuel French, 323/876-0570 or 818/762-0535, and other theatrical bookstores.

The Agencies: What The Actor Needs To Know by Acting World Books. They list each agent within the agency. This is the best book when you are looking for a new agent.

An Actor's Workbook: Get The Agent You Need & The Career You Want by K. Callan. She is a working actress and has written several books for actors.

Screen Actors Guild, 323/954-1600. Franchised agent's list available by mail or at the SAG office, $3 for nonmembers and free to members.

AFTRA, 212/532-0800. A national listing of AFTRA Franchised Talent Agents is available.

Personal Managers

• **You hire the services** of a personal manager to oversee and guide your career. A manager takes a percentage of the money you earn—usually 15%, but it could be much more, or even less. It is negotialable. You should walk away from someone who charges you a fee other than a percentage of what you earn.

• **I want to alert you** to some practices that I believe are not helpful to your career. Breakdown Services Ltd. over the years has sued and won judgements against many pseudo/fake management companies who go into business solely to charge actors $50 to $100 a month for access to the casting breakdowns.

• **Actors defend paying these illegal fees** by saying it helps them to know what roles are being cast. I believe there are legitimate ways to spend money that will indeed really help your career. The Actor's Network costs $40 a month and the return is of great value. Casting Showcases are a valid way to open yourself to casting opportunities; they average $25 to $30 a piece. Alicia Silverstone moved to Los Angeles when she was 14 to live with her acting coach Judi O'Neil. Soon afterward she was spotted at an actors' showcase by manager Carolyn Kessler. Within a year she was cast in *The Crush.* Her manager has shaped her successful career.

• **The best thing you can do for your career is to act** wherever you can make an opportunity for yourself. Submitting unsolicited pictures and resumes to casting directors is valid but one of the very least likely ways to be discovered. Doing showcases, student films and hosting or appearing on public access shows are legitimate ways of being seen.

• **When you have done enough work** and have enough experience to put together a five to seven-minute video reel of good acting, then you are ready to seek a manager. The exception would be if you are a gorgeous young man or woman able to begin your career on looks alone. Then you will want to go with a manager who has built careers for people like you.

• **An inexperienced manager** who has not built any successful careers will be counting on you to put them on the map. When you hire a manager, hire one who you honestly believe can help you achieve your personal career goals. This means you must have goals and educate yourself on who the respected managers are and how you can appeal to them. Value yourself. Don't be lazy. If you are lazy there is not much hope for your having a career no matter how much money you have to promote yourself. Without a solid work ethic—that means working every day on your acting craft—you probably will not have a career.

• **Being seen acting is the greatest and fastest way** to achieve success in an acting career.

• **Your personal manager** works in every part of your life. Managers have fewer clients than agents do and their clients speak with them daily. Anyone can be a personal manager, as they are not governed by state law. It is wise to choose one who belongs to a personal manager association. Before hiring a manager, check around to be sure he or she has a good reputation.

• **The manager is responsible** for the overall planning of the client's career. They sift offers, deciding which to pursue and which to turn down. They usually have the final say on the agent's negotiation with the casting director or producer.

• **Poppy Montgomery moved to Holllywood** from Sydney, Austrailia with no acting experience. She cold-called Julia Roberts's then-manager Bob McGowan to see if he'd help make her a star. She sent him pictures all the time. She says, "I think he thought I was kind of funny." Two months later he signed her. Two years later, by the time she was 23, she was working steadily, ABC's 1996 series *Relativity*, movies *The Other Sister*, *Life*, *This Space Between Us*, *Dead Man on Campus*, *Desert's Edge*, *Devil in a Blue Dress*, and her career continues to grow.

Arthur Toretzky, a theatrical agent, talks about managers:

- **If an actor wants a manager,** he must remember that he's putting together a team. If you're with an agent, it's not a good idea to go out and sign with a manager and then come to the agent and announce, "Oh, by the way, I just signed with so-and-so." What if the agent doesn't like so-and-so? If the actor is with an agency and wants a manager, they should come to the agent and say, "Give me a list of managers you enjoy working with." At our agency the list is very large and we can set up the meetings. Similarly, if an actor doesn't have an agent but has a manager, the manager is going to take the actor to those agents he enjoys working with. It's just so important to make sure that the actor keeps everybody involved in the process.

• **Jay Bernstein, who has generated big careers** for such people as Farrah Fawcett, Suzanne Somers, Stacy Keach and Mary Hart, says:

- **Look at the careers of actors you admire** and find out who their managers are, then try to attract them to you. You can find this out by reading the trades and making note of the managers who are mentioned in articles about their clients.

• **Tami Lynn, Personal Manager/Producer,** is past president of the Conference of Personal Managers (COPM) and became a lifetime honorary member in recognition of 30 years of personal management. She started the West Coast National Conference of Personal Managers and was executive director from 1986 to 1988. She and her husband, Kim Marriner, an Emmy Award winning journalist/anchorman, are producing films and documentaries through Tami Lynn Productions. She is co-producer of the NBC series *Jesse.*

Q: When is the right time to look for a personal manager?

- **When actors know that they need help,** they should seek representation whether they're just starting out or they are established.

- **A personal manager is one who guides** and gives direction to one's career.

Q: How does one look for a manager?

- **The best thing to do is to contact one of the organizations.** The COPM is based on the West Coast and the NCOPM is based on the East Coast. Contact the president or the secretary and explain that you're looking for a manager. We usually have actors mail their pictures and resumes and I will present them to the organization. If there is some interest, then the manager will contact the client. If you want to investigate someone, ask the appropriate manager organization to have them checked out.

- **Every manager should, like an actor, have a biography.** You can see who their current clients are and other clients they have represented, how long they've been in management, what their record is. I give my clients my full biography.

Q: Could you name some of the people that you've managed?

- **Valerie Bertinelli**, Adam Rich, Mary Beth McDonough from *The Waltons.* Currently, among others, I manage Katy Kurtzman, 36 running commercials, *Dynasty, Heidi* with Burl Ives and film *God, Sex and Apple Pie;* Christina Applegate, currently on the series *Jesse,* 11 seasons on *Married with Children* and films *Streets, Don't Tell Mom the Babysitter's Dead, Across the Moon, Vibrations, Wild Bill, Nowhere, Mars Attack, The Big Hit, Mafia, Claudine's Return* and *The Visitors.* We've been together since she was seven years old. I have my own son, Shane Butterworth, who was in the film *Vibrations* and on the *Bad News Bears* series, *Saved By The Bell.* I also represent writers for feature films.

Q: In Christina's career, before she got *Married with Children*, was she in that sexy mode?

- **Yes, she made many guest appearances on episodics.** She's a beautiful girl. At the age of 14 her career zoomed, which is usually a difficult age to hit. She had beautiful long hair which she cut all off like a punk hairdo. All the girls had long hair, and she would walk into interviews with this short, very unusual haircut. She got cast in *Heart of the City*, which really showed her acting ability. It was a wonderful hour-long series. She stood out. When the producers of *Married with Children* wanted to recast the role of Kelly Bundy, they came to us.

Q: What is the difference between a manager and an agent?

- **A manager is one who works with an agent**, because with the California laws, a manager may not negotiate work. An agent does that. We can assist in negotiations but we must have an agent with us. East Coast laws are different; they can negotiate deals there.

Q: Should an actor sign a management contract?

- **Once both people have done their homework** and the manager wants the actor and the actor wants the manager, most definitely there should be a three year contract. It takes a year just to put the whole thing together.

Q: What happens when a manager signs an actor?

- **The first thing is to evaluate their acting ability** and to make sure they are working with a good drama coach, that they have pictures that work. Most likely, they will need new pictures. Then get their resume together. A lot of times an actor doesn't realize that there are things that should be included. They think that school plays and things like that are not important. Anything they've done is important.

- **A manager will probably be in touch with a client daily** if they're working. If the actor isn't working, the two would be in touch to talk about something specific coming up or they would be sure the client is doing what is needed for themselves. If there is a problem on the set, the actor calls the manager, not the agent, because of the personal involvement that you have.

- **We can open up an interview for them.** Then the ball is totally in the actor's court.

Q: For a general interview, what kind of clothes are appropriate?

- **The simplest clothes are the best.** Casual clothes from jeans to simple skirts for girls, and for guys, just jeans and T-shirts. It should be a totally relaxed, simple situation unless there's a specific role that they're going for. Then they would most likely dress for that role. They shouldn't be investing in expensive clothing.

Q: What happens when the question of nudity comes up?

- **In advising the actor on what roles to take**, unless it's something like nudity, there's no role that should be turned down when you're starting out. Absolutely no role. I've heard actors say, "I'm looking for a particular role, or a particular path," or "I don't want to do this or that kind of role." That's insane. I think they should take the roles that are there whether it be feature films, television or cable, because you never know what you're going to get from that.

- **When you're talking about nudity, that's totally different**. There's nudity and then there's nudity. Pornography is an absolute no. It's the lowest type of work. All that does is to put you in the context of being a nude actor. It degrades you. I have actresses right now who will do nudity. That's fine as long as it's done in good taste and there's a reason for it. I will go in and say, for instance, both actresses are fine with their breasts but they do not want to show their butts. I will make sure in the contract, that whatever part of their body they do not want to show won't be shown.

- **I'm there whenever they do a nude scene.**

• **Steven Nash, head of Arts and Letters Management,** came to management after years as an acting coach and as a prominent producer/director in theatre and film.

Q: What sort of actors do you look for?

- **Talented, of course, but I need to feel that I can help the actor** to achieve an important career. I am always attracted to well trained actors who are marketable and appealing. I also look at the actor's ability to pursue a career aggressively in terms of time and resources.

Q: Would you consider taking on a client who is fairly new to the biz?

- **While the last actor I signed had extensive film and television credits,** if I see the potential of a "new" person, I could be interested. The time and effort that I put into each of my clients is quite substantial, so I have to be ready to commit.

Q: Where do you find clients?

- **Referrals of course. I go to theatre and showcases** and occasionally sit in on industry workshops. One of my clients I met at a party, then spotted in an independent film. His screen presence grabbed me.

Q: As a manager, what do you think it takes for an actor to get the job?

- **Getting the job in Hollywood is initially about things other than acting.** I believe casting directors, working efficiently in their high pressure job, have usually decided whether you are in the running before you even speak. This is particularly true in one of the many film/television auditions where your audition scene is three lines, and there is no event in the scene to sink your teeth into. In addition to having an appropriate look, I believe you need to have a carefully focused edge, an essence about you that is clear and instantly captures the casting director's attention. One can and should develop this edge intentionally. Figure out your unique traits, and choose the ones to put forward.

Q: Any advice for the young actor?

- **The cold reading, camera technique and result oriented classes** are important, but it is also significant to study basic acting. Learn how to interpret material. When you pick up a script, have a technique for making artistic choices into actable elements. On a business level, be organized and aggressive. Don't just wait for the phone to ring. There is always something you can do to progress. A good manager will certainly guide you.

• **Al Onorato, personal manager** with Handprint Entertainment Inc., was a casting director for 15 years and one of the founding members of the Casting Society of America (CSA).

Q: When, in your opinion, is it time for an actor to get a personal manager?

- **There are a couple of schools of thought.** One is that you start right from the very beginning, to discover people who have x quality or x amount of talent and direct them toward the right productions, films, projects, teachers, etc. I've always thought in this business you have to trust some people. I have to put trust in the people that I want to handle, and they trust that with my guidance they will avoid some of the pitfalls. Everything costs money, and so when you're going to spend the money, you want to put it in the right area so you're not just spinning your wheels.
- **On the other hand**, someone may have a career that's already started but has gotten blocked or typecast into one area of television or stage, and they can't make the move into the next area they want to be in.
- **When I read actors**, sometimes they may not have had a lot of training but they have certain instincts that work for them, and they are able to transcend all the training that other people have had for years.
- **There is a great demand right now for young actors and actresses**; so if someone has the right look their chances are greater of getting a shot. More than ever, actors who have been on successful television series are making the leap into leads in movies.

Q: Where do you find clients?

- **Everywhere. I go to workshops, showcases, watch television,** and see both big budget and small independent films. I travel across the country doing workshops and looking for talent. Along the way you find some people you think have a certain amount of ability and desire; those are the ones you encourage to pursue a career.

Q: When should actors move to L. A.?

- **If someone really wants a career** they have to go where the market is. That is Los Angeles for film and New York for theater. That old adage about "I'm not going to go there unless I have a contract" or "I'm not going to go there unless I have a job," well, that's really pie-in-the-sky thinking. Before someone gets a job there are numerous steps one must go through first: tapes, auditions, call backs, interviews. Before I encourage anyone to relocate, I try working with them long distance by requesting that they put themselves on tape for projects.

- **At the International Model & Talent Association** we found a girl from Ohio who we felt had great potential. We started working with her this way, on tape. Eventually she and her mom spent some time in Los Angeles so she could be seen in person. She did land a role in an Ang Lee film.

- **I did a workshop in Phoenix** and there was a woman well into her 60s who said, "My family's grown up, my husband's passed away, this is something I always wanted to do. What do you think about my coming to Los Angeles?" I told her she was going to be battling folks who have had a lot more experience. But you know something, I'm one of those people who believes if you want to do it, do it. Don't be discouraged; if you've got the guts, the wherewithal and the desire, go for it. She did it, she came out here. And she's been working.

Q: What do you do on a daily basis? What is your job description?

- **We try to keep apprised of all the projects that are going on,** whether it be television or movies and the various roles in the particular projects.

- **Most all our work is on the phone.** It's checking and dealing with agents. You deal with the studios, casting people at the studios and casting directors on various projects. We try to get our clients to where they have projects working for them. We're aiming to get into production so that we can find projects that we think our clients are right for and put together the writer, actor and director. We also handle producers, directors and writers and a very successful music division.

Q: Do you have any advice for actors?

- **Acting in this business is very much like athletics.** You have to do it. You've got to study. The best athletes and Olympic stars are people who have been nurtured and have had coaches along the way to help guide them and keep them away from bad habits and the wrong training. The people we revere in our business, Meryl Streep, Al Pacino, Anthony Hopkins and that calibre of actor, have trained and continue to grow as artists.

- **Don't believe people who say, "I'll make you a star."** It's not an easy process and if you want to be a star, hopefully you want to be an artist as well, not just somebody whose name is on a billboard but somebody who can point proudly to the work that they do. I think it's important to uphold dignity and principles. There are no guarantees.

- **What is so often the hardest thing for parents or loved ones of actors** to understand is that it doesn't happen overnight. Every time they say, "What have you done?" or "What are we going to see you on?" though it's done with love, it also puts the actor in a precarious situation, because they feel like they've got to prove something. Loved ones don't understand how long it takes.

• **Terrance Hines, personal manager, Hines and Hunt Entertainment,** acting coach and author of the best selling book *An Actor Succeeds, Career Management for the Actor.*

Q: What do you look for in prospective clients?

- **I look for honesty, a sense of humor and a passion that fills the room.** I like the actor to have good reasons why they want management. They should do their homework by checking out my company. They should have a support system in place and enough money to invest in pictures that look like them and enroll in excellent acting classes.

- **They should be open and honest** about who they are, with an understanding of how others see them. They should have a grasp on the business aspect of the entertainment world. Are they prepared to trust and listen to those guiding their career and are they able and willing to block out the voices that do not have their best interest at heart? Are they prepared for rejection? Do they understand that there are valleys as well as mountains in long careers? Above all, do they have a sense of humor to get them through the worst of times?

Q: How do you work for your clients?

- **Our company interfaces with a network** of producers, directors, writers, casting directors and executives. When you have clients on a series or in films, the casting directors or producers call to have lunch and discuss the show. This gives the manager the opportunity to discuss their client list.

- **I find that going with clients to an interview**, especially a producer call back or the network, has proven very fruitful. Discussing the choices of material, adjustments in the direction of the career, changing physical appearance and working on the acting tools take up much of the management day.

- **Management offers a landscape** where the actor can have a sounding board at his beck and call. Every artist needs to be encouraged to beat their head against the wall one more time.

• **Casting director Joey Paul.**

Q: What is your feeling about personal managers, working with them, etc.?

- **As a casting director**, I would love to spend more time finding new talent, but there are time constraints with the job that make that very difficult. Good talent that comes from the east coast or midwest regional theaters, who have their Equity and SAG cards but not a lot of TV credits, may have incredible difficulty just getting an agent. Smaller agents have difficulty getting their clients in to read for auditions. A personal manager who has both knowledge of the industry and certain relationships with agents, can get their clients representation. They can really make a difference in somebody's career when they're starting out.

- **Actors can benefit** from the manager's experience and relationships and save themselves a lot of time. The manager might steer them to a good teacher, a good photographer and help them to redefine their look into something that's marketable. Many actors come here thinking it's just about the acting or they hear it's all a look. They don't understand what a look is, what their look is. Many actors hear, "Well, you don't need a personal manager till you've got a career to manage." But there are personal managers who have developed careers right from the start. I think some of them are very worthwhile.

- **Theatrical and commercial agent Bonnie Howard.**

Q: How do you feel about personal managers?

- **I've found some managers who are great to work with.** The State of California is very clear about what a manager can and cannot do. They are not allowed to procure work. They also cannot negotiate a deal when they do get work. I feel it's not their place to do it. An agent goes through a lot of legal steps to become an agent. They have to be franchised, licensed, fingerprinted, bonded, and they're under constant scrutiny from the unions. A manager does none of the above, so I really don't feel that they are as qualified to be agents. I feel it's unnecessary for an actor to have a manager until they have a big career to manage. The manager's job is to help you choose your pictures, help you with your hair style or your hair color, help you get an agent. And then when you become a big star, help you decide which projects to turn down.

- **Theatrical casting director Clair Sinnett.**

Q: How do you feel about personal managers for newcomers who are having a tough time breaking down doors in the business?

- **Everybody has their own opinion,** but mine is a very positive one. I think that personal managers can help a newcomer get in the door because they have less clients and more time to devote to them. If a personal manager takes you on, you know it's because he feels he can make money with you. And a personal manager also thinks in terms of your career in the future. He's not just thinking of this moment and this job. However, a lot of casting directors are very opposed to personal managers because it doubles their work. If you have a personal manager and an agent both submitting pictures and both calling, that's double the effort and double the work. Just be aware that there's a real split camp. There are some managers who have a lot of clout. They even have more clout than some agents. It depends on the manager.

Resources

Academy Kids, TJ Stein and Bethany Constance, 818/769-8091.

Arts and Letters Management, Steven Nash, 7715 Sunset Blvd., #208, Los Angeles, 90046. They will consider mail submissions, from age 15 to 24 only.

Tami Lynn Productions and Management, 818/888-8264. Fax: 818/888-8267.

Handprint Entertainment, Al Onorato, 323/655-2400.

Hines & Hunt Entertainment, Terrance Hines, 818/557-7516.

Conference of Personal Managers, Inc. (COPM), 310/275-2456. This hot line gives detailed information of how to locate lists of personal managers.

National Conference of Personal Managers (NCOPM), 818/762-6276. Write for information at 964 Second Ave., New York, NY 10022.

The Actors' Network, "Where the Serious Actor Does Business." 818/509-1010. Kevin E. West, founder and president. They hold monthly orientation meetings where you can find out all about their organization.

Ross Report, Working Actors Guide, Personal Managers and *Hollywood Creative Directory* are among publications that list personal managers and are sold at Theatrical Bookstores.

Life Is A Contact Sport: Ten Great Career Strategies That Work, a book by personal manager Ken Kragen. Very inspirational, educating you on what a manager does for his clients. He talks about people and situations we all know of.

ENTERTAINMENT ATTORNEYS

• **It is an exciting time** in an actor's career when the future holds so much promise that an attorney is needed. Be certain that the finances and terms of your deals are properly in place so that you can calmly enjoy your hard-earned successes.

• **As actors' careers grow**, they must seek the best support people for their team. It is important to understand what an entertainment attorney can do for you before you need one.

• **Your attorney can advise you** of your rights in a given situation and negotiate a contract—money, billing and terms are complicated areas but it's vital they are handled to your best advantage. The ins and outs of an entertainment contract are so complicated and abstract that you need a specialist. It can be dangerous to your best interests to rely on a family attorney—or even your agent—who is not an experienced specialist. Attorneys usually charge by the hour and a good one will estimate costs for you. When seeking an attorney, ask your friends in the entertainment industry for their recommendations. We all hear the attorney-bashing jokes, but your personal legal matters are no joke and you need a caring, honest, loyal attorney. Interview several and then go with your well-tuned instincts as to who will work the best for you.

• **Chandler Warren, entertainment attorney**, began his career in New York representing the producers of *As the World Turns* and *Another World,* also dozens of stage productions on and off Broadway and over 50 independent feature films. Today he represents writers, directors, actors, producers and designers in all phases of film, television, stage and recording. He works extensively in low budget features in New York and Los Angeles, including the complicated area of film distribution.

Q: Under what circumstances does an actor need an attorney?

- **For example**, when an actor is required to sign a test option for a television series, it may bind him for the next three to seven years of his/her professional life. The agent can negotiate the basic terms of the deal, but it is important to have the fine points of the contract negotiated by an entertainment attorney.

- **When an actor is engaged for a series of commercials**, the agent will handle the basic negotiation but an attorney should review and negotiate the fine points. Otherwise, the actor could find his/her picture on the product's labels, billboards and cardboard cutouts in super markets and wonder what happened. Every phase of the use of the actor's name, likeness, voice, etc. has to be carefully spelled out.

- **When the actor is cast in a good role** in a motion picture, the producer may want additional options, etc. This should be reviewed on the actor's behalf. There are any number of things in most "standard" actor contracts that need to be negotiated.

- **When the actor is cast in a legitimate stage production**, often the producer will want options to take the actor along with the play as it moves. And there are billing considerations, housing, per diems, etc. to be negotiated. Or the situation may be reversed, where the actor wants the option to continue and this has to be negotiated so the actor is protected.

- **When the actor is also a singer** there are other pitfalls, as the music business is complicated and dog-eat-dog. Those contracts can tie up an actor and/or the actor's writing talents for many years. This is an area that must never be entered without an entertainment attorney at the actor's side.

- **When an actor signs with a manager**, a lawyer is essential. A management contract can be in effect for a long period of time and usually encompasses money from all sources of the entertainment business. An actor has to be sure the contract allows him/her to leave if the manager is not fulfilling the job. Remember, an actor must never rely on an oral promise.

Q: How do you feel about agents?

- **I am a strong believer** in both agents and managers. Most attorneys are not acting agents; they don't get the Breakdown Service, they aren't in contact daily with casting directors, etc. But if an actor doesn't have an agent yet and has been cast in a series, a soap, a major part in a motion picture, or gets a recording contract, the actor only needs the services of an attorney. From that job, the actor may then secure a top agent or manager.

Q: In what other situations might an actor need an attorney?

- **No one should direct a play** without a written contract, especially if the play is a new one by a new playwright. What is the director's future option to direct? What is the director's billing? Should the director agree to a royalty pool? And so on.

- **An actor who writes a play**, or has a unique idea, will need a copyright. No one reading this book should ever lose sight of the fact that a copyright is probably the most valuable commodity a person can have; yes, even better than residuals because it lasts longer. Also, the writer needs to negotiate royalties, travel and per diems, billing, subsidiary rights, option terms, etc.

- **Actors often produce** their own 99-seat waiver shows in order to showcase their acting talents. All of the many legal headaches which every producer must face will have to be dealt with. How do you raise the money and not violate the law? What is the vehicle you use to raise the money and produce the play? How do you prepare the budget? No producer should remotely consider going into the producing business without an entertainment attorney who is familiar with legitimate stage contracts, SEC filing requirements, limited partnerships, etc.

Q: Can you give me a ball park figure of what it might cost for certain contracts?

- **It is hard to answer specifically** because every situation is different. Certainly if the negotiations get very complex or drawn out it will increase the hours that an attorney will need to spend in reviewing and negotiating. An average television series or day time soap contract could cost $1000 to $1500 to review and negotiate, a management contract, usually $250 to $500.

Resources

Chandler Warren, 323/876-6400. 7715 Sunset Blvd. #208, Los Angeles 90046. Extremely knowledgeable, fair, and easy to talk to. His walls are lined with pictures of famous actors and posters of shows he's worked on.

Los Angeles County Bar Association, 213/627-2727.

California State Bar Association, 213/765-1000. Ask for information on several attorneys who are listed as specialists in Entertainment Law.

Working Actor's Guide (WAG), available at theatrical bookstores, lists many entertainment attorneys.

BUSINESS MANAGERS

• **As actors develop in their earning capacity** and start saving money, the next person on their *career team* will be a business (financial) manager. Some actors or spouses of actors may have an educated background in business and time to research, but most of us need to seek a professional to manage our expenses and investments. Business affairs become very complicated when the actor is working on remote locations.

• **When you have landed that role on a series or a big movie** that is taking you on location for months, it might be time to look for a business manager. Gayle Futernick, in her *Drama-Logue* column, gave some great examples of when you would need some help.

- **After 25 hours a day on a set spent learning your lines** and your marks, you aren't going to feel much like writing rent checks or doing budgets on Quicken. You need a new car, because you just can't drive to The Lot in your old, beat-up Chevy. Should you buy or lease a new car? Should you open a retirement fund? Maybe you should keep your bucks in a liquid, short-term investment just in case. Then again, the producer did smile and mention something about a starring role in the spin-off.

- **Maybe it is time to buy a house.** Who is going to help you get a mortgage? Who is going to refer you to a reliable investment advisor? Who is going to reconcile your check book? Who is going to be on hold with the bank for 20 minutes while they figure out why your service charge quadrupled last month? Who is going to remember to deposit your residual checks in the investment fund and the weekly paychecks in the household account?

- **Who has time to keep up with your paperwork? Not you!** You're busy getting to sets on time and interviewing with the press. They need you in wardrobe at 7AM for a fitting and you're supposed to lunch with your agent at Le Dome. Life is a bit hectic and right now you're spending your time shmoozing with the right people at the right parties.

- **Tax planning is not exactly your strong point** and you're not really sure how to build a spreadsheet that will remind you when to pay your bills. And mom lives too far away to help...

• **I love Gayle's writing and I think she makes her point very well.** As actors, we all hope and yearn for the predicament she outlines. Here are a few more of her thoughts on using the right business manager.

- **There are no generic answers.** These decisions depend on you and your lifestyle. If you tend to lose control with money, think about your future. Remember how hard it was to get this gig. Remember how many people are trying to become working actors. Unless you are an established mega-celebrity, be conservative with your finances and use your business manager as your money conscience.

- **While you need to be able to depend on your business manager,** it is not advisable to totally turn over the reins and never check his work. It is your money and your financial health that are important. Request and review periodic (monthly or quarterly) reports. You are paying them to provide services for you and to educate you about your financial matters. Trust is a mutual understanding.

- **There are no licensing procedures for business managers.** You may want to find one who is a CPA (Certified Public Accountant). The advantage is tremendous: CPAs have passed the CPA Exam and have work experience in the accounting field. They are licensed and regulated by the state, and must abide by professional ethics and complete 80 hours of continuing education every two years.

- **Business managers can charge hourly, a fixed rate or a flat percentage** of your gross salary earned as their fee. Typically, business managers charge five percent of gross income that is earned from your professional services as their fee. Thus their fee would not be based on amounts earned on investments.

- **If your annual income exceeds $100,000,** it is probably time to consider using the services of a business manager.

• **At the beginning of Oprah's success**, she had Bill Cosby on her show. When discussing finances, Cosby said, "In order to know where your money is going, always sign every check and investigate and approve each investment yourself." Oprah credits his advice for much of her prosperity. I'm sure Oprah has a business manager to keep everything in order, but she runs the ship.

• **Shaquille O'Neal**: "When you're dealing with money, you have to take half of what you make and put it away. Then take half of what you have left and put that away. So you've put three quarters of it away and you play with the one quarter that is left. If you invest wisely, safely and don't take too many risks, you'll be all right."

• **Some actors are not interested in handling their money**. If you are this type, be selective in choosing your professional advisor. There are no regulations for financial managers so they have free rein. You sign your money over and trust they will do the right thing. Your hard-earned money could be gone—we have all heard the horror stories of business managers running off with all of their clients' money. On the other hand, most actors with money have been guided by financial consultants and managers.

Personal Manager T.J. Stein had an article in his newsletter by business manager, CPA Scott Feinstein about whether or not to incorporate. I am quoting some of the article to give you an overall view. Keep in mind this is general information and tax laws change every year.

- **It comes down to one main issue, cost vs. benefit.** The costs of incorporation include initial one-time, out-of-pocket expenses plus on-going annual expenses such as legal and accounting fees and additional payroll and corporate taxes. On the other hand benefits of incorporation include the ability to establish a pension plan, the right to deduct medical expenses and the transfer of other expenses from your personal tax return to corporate tax return where there are no limitations and the financial advantages of fiscal year-end planning.

- **The benefits fall into three basic categories:** pension plans, medical and business expense deductions, and fiscal year-end planning.

- **As an employee of a production company/studio** and the recipient of W-2 income, the only retirement account you can voluntarily set up is an IRA. Unfortunately, if you are a member of a union, and although you have the right to contribute to an IRA, the contributions would <u>not</u> qualify as a tax deduction. With a loan-out corporation, you can set up a corporate pension plan and take a deduction from your gross income of up to $30,000 per year. This would obviously save significant tax dollars.

- **Your employee business deductions are included on Schedule A** of your personal tax return and, as such, are subject to several limitations. In fact, if your deductions are large enough you could be subject to what is referred to as an "alternative minimum tax." In simple terms, you could lose a significant portion of the tax deduction. With a corporation, there are no such limitations. The IRS generally respects the deductions of a corporation. In other words, the standards for proof can be greater on a personal tax return than on a corporate tax return.

- **As for medical and other personal expenses,** a corporation can adopt a medical reimbursement plan which allows the corporation to pay directly and deduct all medical expenses (less amounts paid by insurance) including expenses for mental health, eye care, chiropractic, etc.

- **Finally, a corporation can establish a "fiscal" year-end** as opposed to the required December 31 calendar year-end for individuals. This enables you to manipulate income by pushing back or accelerating income between calendar years, depending on your particular financial status each year.

- **Since there are no regulatory bodies** or other ways to check on financial/business managers, you must do some extensive research before making any financial decisions. Ask your accountant, attorney, agent, manager, successful actor friend or any other trusted friends in the business for their recommendations.

Resources:

Feinstein & Berson: Scott Feinstein, 818/981-3115. 16133 Ventura Blvd., #800, Encino, 91436. CPA and Business Manager, has a strong client list consisting almost exclusively of SAG, AFTRA, IATSE and DGA members.

California State Board of Accountancy, 916/263-3680. You can check to see if the business manager or accountant you are considering is licensed and in good standing.

Working Actor's Guide (WAG), available at theatrical bookstores, lists many well known business managers.

PUBLIC RELATIONS AND PUBLICISTS

• **No one knows who you are or what you are doing** without publicity. All the networks and most of the production companies hire publicists, formerly known as press agents. These publicists get the press to write about the TV shows, movies and the actors in the projects. Even so, many individual stars hire their own representative to handle their publicity.

• **Alicia Silverstone, Jenny McCarthy and Matthew McConaughey** are among the newest actors to became household names even before we saw the projects they were promoting. This is because a publicity machine had put their faces and names in front of the public with such repetition that we wanted to know who they were. A while ago it was Sandra Bullock and Brad Pitt.

• **A publicist's basic responsibilities** include preparing written biographies of their clients to send to the press, keeping contacts in the media aware of any favorable newsworthy developments in their client's lives, taking the requests from newspapers, magazines and TV talk shows that want to interview their clients, and pitching story ideas about clients to these same requesters. The publicist can also decide how the public should see their client and proceed accordingly to create that image.

• **Rosie O'Donnell** mentioned in a live interview at the 1994 Oscar ceremonies that she was out of town and her publicist picked her gown and jewels. She flew in from location that morning and had the final fitting. Publicists can design the way their artists are presented to the public.

• **Marisa Tomei's** successful nomination for the Academy Award for *My Cousin Vinnie,* was directly due to her publicity team. They took out trade ads and got tapes to all of the Academy voters. When she was nominated they doubled their efforts and she won the *Best Supporting Actress* for 1992.

• **Jason Alexander** of *Seinfeld* has been with his publicist for years because, he says, "she doesn't like publicity." She doesn't ask him to do openings and the type of things he doesn't want to do.

• **When selecting a publicist,** as in other business choices, choose by reputation, personality and a mutual agreement on the way you want to be represented.

• **Liria Mersini is a public relations consultant and life coach.** She coaches individuals and leads workshops on *Celebrity 101, The Power of Image and Creating Perfect Bios.*

Q: How do you help actors create PR?

- **My goal is to de-mystify the PR process and help my clients** create powerful packages. I work with actors before they are ready for representation, as well as established actors who are ready to make a change in their image. In both cases, I work to help actors understand the PR process and package themselves so that they can gain more control of the image they and their team put forward.
- **Understanding PR and the way it works can really help an actor** navigate the system and set reasonable expectations for their own PR campaign. Taking a workshop or interning at a PR firm is great exposure. It can take the mystery out of building celebrity and help a new actor think in terms of marketing.

Q: How does an actor start?

- **An important first step is to create a bio that reflects their essence,** especially before they've done a great deal of work. This is one tool that can clarify their whole package and set the tone for meetings with agents, casting directors, managers as well as publicists. The point here is to have your package of materials (you, your pictures, bio, resume, and tape) deliver a strong, consistent message. It is never too early to begin this process.
- **I work with actors on becoming experts on marketing themselves.** In this business there is so much pressure on actors to conform to someone else's idea of who they are when it is really their uniqueness that generates interest and builds celebrity.

Q: Where do you see actors getting stuck?

- **The biggest mistake I see, both in new actors and in celebrities,** is that they tend to abdicate their power to experts. Remember, a good publicist is an expert at the process of building celebrity. They have training, experience and, most importantly, contacts. However, you are the world's foremost expert on you. When an actor knows who they are and what they want from the publicist, they radically increase their chances for success.

- **Often, an actor will hire a public relations firm** because of the "A list" artists that firm represents. Sometimes this strategy pays off, but there are no guarantees. It is also common for actors to present themselves as blank slates and ask for guidance on how to be marketed. Either way, the whole power structure is off. The actor is only one of many clients on a talent roster and that can be disempowering, especially when there are bigger names on that roster.

- **The bottom line is, if you are an expert on you,** then you can really benefit from a good publicist's ideas and contacts. It can be a very exciting process. At $2,000 to $5,000 per month, it is definitely a costly one. Doing your homework can prepare you to get the most from this important relationship.

Q: Tell me about the Power of Image workshop you teach.

- **The basic workshop is a weekend PR/marketing boot camp.** There are really seven steps to understanding the process and creating your own powerful image. These steps are a roadmap that clients can then use to understand the industry and polish or revise how they're putting themselves out there. Once you have the basics, we provide support in creating a winning package. It's a powerful process!

• **Publicist Kelly Bush** of ID Public Relations works in entertainment publicity, representing actors, directors, composers and writers.

Q: Does an actor hire you on a regular monthly basis?

- **The publicist,** like the agent or manager, is part of the team. When an actor has a strong team supporting them, they are able to focus on doing great work while their team does its job. It is important the publicist, agent and manager are in constant communication.

- **I have an ongoing relationship** with my clients just like the agent or manager. People sometimes think a publicist can be hired only once in a while. When there is an opportunity to make something happen for someone, what happens if they are not "on" at the time? It is important to consider publicity for the entire career—not just for a particular project. For example, magazines work sometimes up to 4-6 months in advance.

Q: When you get a new client and you are the first publicist, what is the procedure?

- **If the client has worked** for 10 years and never had a publicist, they've probably done a mish-mosh of interviews based on what they were promoting at the time. I approach the entire career. I start with smaller things and work towards magazine covers. I look at all the photographs that have been taken and biographical information or feature stories that have been written. I write a new bio that is very straightforward. If necessary, I put together a photo shoot so we have something we're happy to send out.

- **It's about presentation** and packaging. If a client has never done any press, it's exciting because you can do it right from the beginning.

Q: Is there a great deal of expense for new clients?

- **The client doesn't pay** for the magazine or newspaper photo shoots; the publications do. If we're promoting a film or television show, usually the studio will pick up expenses associated with the publicity. The client only pays publicity fees and expenses.

Q: How are those fees determined?

- **It's a flat monthly fee.** Publicists charge anywhere from $2,000-5,000 a month. There are perfectly reputable publicists that charge less but in my opinion, you get what you pay for.

Q: How do actors shop for publicists?

- **Their agent or manager will know publicists** the client would get along well with and whose work they trust. I would take no more than three meetings, otherwise it gets very confusing. Ask the publicist about their approach to things, or what they feel are important types of publicity, and you will get a pretty good sense whether or not you agree with their ideas. If you trust your publicist, they can do their job and help take your career to a high level—which makes the agent's and manager's job easier. If a producer sees an actor in *Vanity Fair*, they may say, "If *Vanity Fair* thinks they're hot, then I want them in my next movie."

Q: When is it time to hire a publicist?

- **When the actor has something to promote.** A television show, a film, a theatrical production—with enough time in advance to do the proper job. Look at Rita Wilson from *Sleepless in Seattle.* She got a good amount of press with just a five-minute crying scene in the film. There have been a lot of small parts that stood out and received attention for the performer. A publicist can get your work in front of an editor, to convince them that your story is worth covering. The time to think about hiring a publicist is when you've done work you're really proud of.

- **My job is to educate** the magazine editors and television producers on who my clients are and why they should be on their shows or in their magazines.

Q: Does the publicist go to these interviews?

- **You accompany your client** on everything. For print interviews, I introduce the writer to my client and then I leave them. I'm there for every photo taken and every television appearance.

Q: Have you ever had a client who is really shy and publicity was difficult for them?

- **I don't put them in situations** where it's going to make them uncomfortable. I have clients that I would never put on *Letterman* or *The Tonight Show.* It's just not appropriate for them. There are a lot of other things you can do, though, that are more conducive for your client. If they're more comfortable with a one on one situation, everything they do is in print. They just don't do TV.

Q: How do you find clients?

- **The best way to get a client is to do a good job** for the ones you have and word gets out. Also, I go after clients. For example, at the film festivals you see movies before their theatrical releases. I hear about someone who is outstanding in a role, and I'll call their agent and say that I'm interested in meeting with this person.

Q: Do you have any advice for actors who don't have that movie or television project yet?

- **Do great work** and if you receive great reviews that gives you something to go on. I've met with people who wanted a publicist and once we had a meeting, I was able to tell them that it's not time for it yet. A person may have a supporting role in a successful television series and the media may have no interest in talking to them. The publicist really doesn't know what we can do for that person until we get out there and start working and see what kind of response we get.

Q: What advice can you give for actors who already have publicists? How can the actor help?

- **Doing press is almost like an audition.** You put on your acting hat and you're an actor. You put on your publicity hat and you're doing publicity. It's very different. You really have to know what you're doing. You really have to make an impression. The client can make a publicist's job easier by being good at it. It helped to see other people on TV shows like *Letterman*, read magazine and newspaper articles, see other actors doing press and the kind of impression you get after you read the article. You may say, "Do I like this person?" or, "This person sounded really arrogant" or, "This person I admire." You see someone doing *Leno* and you say, "That was really boring."

- **You can learn from that.** You see a great actress like Geena Davis who brings on her inventions. That makes for good TV. These TV producers want to get great ratings. They want people to stay up late and watch.

Resources

Working Actors Guide lists Public Relation Firms.

ID Public Relations: Kelly Bush, 310/204-6868. 3859 Cardiff Ave. Culver City, 90232.

Platform Public Relations, 310/360-7266. 816 S. Robertson Blvd., Los Angeles. Siri Garber's clients include cosmetics firm, hip-hop bands, heartthrob thespians. "We focus on artists who are trendsetters, not trend followers."

PR Consultant, Liria Mersini, 310/828-7670. www.lmersini@aol.com. Public relations consulting, workshops and personal coaching for creative artists and entrepreneurs. Call for workshop schedule or personal consultation.

Studio Fan Mail/Tamkin Color, 310/275-6122. 1122 S. Robertson Blvd., Los Angeles, 90035. When it is time in your career to have someone answer your fan mail. Jack Tamkin runs a wonderful business. They send out all color photos with authentic-looking autographs and personal messages. Their costs are lower than most black and white photos. They will send out an interesting, thorough set of samples.

CAREER AND LIFE COACHES

• **Career and Life Coaches** have come to be a very important part of actors' teams. I started this book in 1981 for my students because I felt they needed career coaching in order to compete at the highest levels. In the last several years many classes, seminars and workshops have been established solely to help people promote their careers. One of the largest areas of private coaching is now in building careers. Career building in no way replaces talent development, nor would any career coach of merit make that claim. I think career coaching is very valid and necessary in this competitive field. Each individual has to decide how much energy they want to put into art and how much into business. Sometimes we can do both at different stages of our lives. The truth of the matter is, it is always hard work. Perhaps the career coach can guide you in answering where best to focus your time.

• **Liria Mersini and Melissa McFarlane are life coaches.** They work as partners in moving you closer to your goals and dreams.

Q: How is having a life coach different from having a career coach?

- **A life coach helps your career within the context of your whole life.** We help clients gain a clear sense of who they are, what they want, and what ultimately matters to them in life. Then we work on a plan to get there. With this foundaton, actors are less likely to make choices based on their fears, on what others say they must do, or what they see another, more successful actor doing. Now the career is being developed on a strong foundation. Career development is much more successful and satisfying approached this way.

- **We all know that when one part of our life is out of balance**, the rest of our life is affected. Most people would agree that if they were offered both a wonderful life and a wonderful career they would take it. A life coach becomes your partner in making that happen.

Q: Why would an actor need a life coach?

- **Having a life coach is like having a personal trainer for your life.** This is a particularly important resource and relationship for actors. In an industry that requires you to take risks and face regular rejection, it is important to have ongoing support. A good deal of an actor's life is spent waiting between roles. It can be tough for even the most successful actors to stay focused. Part cheerleader, part task-master, part counselor and part mentor, your coach is there to support you in defining, refining and achieving your goals and dreams.

Q: What do you do as life coaches?

- **A coaching relationship is a business partnership** based on the client's desires and goals. We are committed to our clients and their own greatest vision of themselves. Coaching works whether someone wants to prepare for a move to L.A., book a sitcom, break into film, or balance personal and career development. We know our clients are capable of having lives of deep personal fulfillment and brilliant career success... if they can keep their eye on the ball. That's where we come in. Our relationship begins with an extensive intake process; from there we establish goals and deadlines and work weekly to achieve them.

Q: How does the coaching process work?

- **Most of our clients choose to work privately**, in half-hour sessions by phone; others prefer to participate in a supportive weekly class. Some clients enjoy both. There are times when a person must focus so deeply that others are a distraction. Sometimes, however, the input and support of a group can carry us further than we could go alone. Between us, we offer weekend workshops, six-week courses, 12-week courses, and ongoing groups on a variety of themes including business for actors, pitching workshops, and the power of image.

Q: How can someone determine if coaching is for them?

- **Try it! Most coaches offer a half-hour coaching session without charge.** Others hold free introductory classes or seminars. Generally, people know right away whether they want to continue. Our best advice would be: trust yourself; you know what is best for you. As with anything, if you feel pressured or uncomfortable, leave. If, on the other hand, you feel like a thirsty traveler who has just been given a huge glass of cool water, stay and enjoy the drink. Any coach worth their salt would say the same thing. Remember, coaches want you to win!

Q: You mentioned preparing for a move to Los Angeles. Could someone work with you over the phone while they are still living out of town?

- **One of the greatest uses of a coach would be preparing for the move.** Since this process is very effective by phone, an actor can have a strong support system in place before they arrive.

• **Carolyne Barry, commercial actress, teacher and casting director,** works with coaches Breck Costin, Barbara Deutsch and Laurie Johnson.

Q: Why do you like working with life coaches?

- **I've done therapy where you are dealing with issues** that are far in the past. This work deals with the present—how you are hearing things, how you are seeing things, how your perception is. If you get in tune with all that, it really cleans up the past as well, but it doesn't stress the past. It is all about reality and perception. I use what I have learned from my coaches in my teaching all the time; the clearer my perception is, the better my teaching is. I know, on a personal basis, it has transformed me.

• **Laurie Johnson is a life coach, as well as a working actress.**

Q: How do you know if you need a life or career coach?

- **There are two ways I approach it.** One is if you feel a block somewhere. If you feel like your shoe is nailed to the floor in a particular arena and there is some obstacle in the way. The second way is you are not feeling blocked but you don't know what the next step is. Everything is going great and I want to kick it to the next level. You can't quite see what that next level is or how to do that. One is handling an obstacle and one is a design conversation. The kind of obstacles I've dealt with are: trouble in auditions, fear, can't seem to move into action.

- **For some people it can be, "Am I in the right career?** Is this really my passion? Am I doing this because I told my high school friends and parents I going to do this, so now I have to?"

Q: Would a coach help them find what they should be doing?

- **Yes, to discover what their passion is,** and also to relieve them in knowing that they don't have to do this. There is no contract that says they have to do this. This business is a choice, it is not an obligation. Many times I have to remind people I work with that they chose this. They are the ones who have the say, nobody is doing this to them. There is no "industry" per se, there are just a lot of people. There is not a big monolith somewhere.

- **The other thing I work with people on are conversations** that they buy into in the industry that are disempowering. Like, "If you are over 40, you are not going to work very much." I don't buy that, I am on the court with them because I walk my talk. I work and I'm almost 50. I just got into the business seven years ago, so if I can do it, anybody can do it. It is not a product of talent; turn on television and you can see it is not talent. Talent is a nice icing on the cake but it is not the requirement to work.

Q: What is the requirement to work?

- **You really have to take a very strong stand for working** and you have to have a very strong stand on yourself. You have to be unstoppable. If somebody says no—you don't go down the tubes. If one person out of 10 says, "I don't think you've got it," and nine people think you do and you go to the one person, then we've got to have a talk about that. That's not healthy.

• **Breck Costin, of BCC & Associates,** conducts many different types of seminars.

Q: What led you into seminar coaching?

- **I noticed actors acted as if they were uninvited guests** crashing a private party. Meaning they would get into situations or auditions, and find themselves not able to come up with the goods. I take them from uninvited guests to host of the party—it really all has to do with their ability to belong.

- **I work on the inner dialogue that prevents people** from fully expressing themselves, having full permission for their talents and having more freedom in their choices and expressions.

- **I'm looking to see when pressure is put on,** where they break down. They may not know how to do an effective cold call, how to generate auditions or how to manage their representation. I work on those tools.

Q: With 150 people in a class, how can an individual be helped?

- **I work with individuals, but it impacts the whole group.** Most of them have the same concerns.

- **They have a homework assignment each week.** It's very specific tools and language, whether it be marketing, management, closing deals, negotiating, or even how to move from guest starring to starring or how to move from recurring to regular roles on TV series.

Q: How would you expect a beginning actor to be affected by a three month seminar?

- **I have a lot of beginners, people who have just gotten off the bus.** It probably saves them about a year and a half of time. Some of the people in the seminar are starring in features or have their own series, with strong agents or middle-of-the-road agents. The new actor has the entire lay-of-the-land, immediately. They are in a community of support where they can see the absolute possibility of beginning something, following through, and having something happen at the end. They have a much stronger sense of what it's going to take to produce in this town. They find out the inner workings so they don't have to go down blind alleys and spend a lot of money.

• **Mitchell Bank, Life By Design Consultants, Ltd.,** talks about how they coach actors.

- **We help actors recognize, realize and understand** that all the reasons they say that have been preventing them from success are not the reasons they are not reaching success. It is not who you know, your contacts, your connections, it's not your agent, head shot or acting classes. There are plenty of actors and, I can tell you from personal experience, (Mitchell produced sitcoms for 15 years) that have not had strong agents, or a lot of experience, did not have contacts and connections and still became successful.

- **The only common demoninator in everyone who has been successful** is their own belief in their success. When you have belief in your success you are inspired to do the action that brings success to you.

- **Actors who believe, "There is no point** in going on this audition anyway because I am not going to get it," are the actors that screw up in the audition, forget their lines, show up late, can't remember where to go. Things always go wrong because of a self-fulfilling prophecy. If one's dominate belief is, "This is a difficult business, it's all who you know, I'm not going to make it, it's all an uphill battle," then their inspiration comes from that place. This does nothing but perpetuate their own beliefs.

- **There are other actors who know, "I am going to make it."** When someone tries to tell them, "You can't, so why do you believe you can?" they say, "I just know." They are the ones who take the actions; they are the ones who are inspired to do the things it takes to reach success.

Q: How do you change your mind about what you believe?

- **The first key is to look for evidence to support that belief.** There is evidence all around. During seminars, we would have an actor in their 50s say, "I'm too old." I would turn on the television and flip through the channels and show them 20 people in their 50s that obviously don't believe they are too old. Someone will say they are too short and we will talk about Danny DeVito. Someone will say they have an accent and we'll talk about Arnold Schwarzenegger. There is enough evidence to support any positive belief. There is as much positive evidence as there is negative evidence to support a negative belief.

- **It is the set of beliefs you choose to ascribe to** that are going to determine your outcome.

Q: How do you work with people?

- **We work with people primarily in private consultation**. We get to the heart of what their beliefs are, what they believe their obstacles are. Then little by little we shift their belief to a new belief. The results have been tremendous. We have had amazing results with people who come out of sessions with us with an entirely new perspective, a new approach about how to go about this business. They are reaching new goals.

Q: How does an actor know when they need a coach?

- **Anytime they believe they are stuck.** For instance: actors move out here to Los Angeles and don't know the first thing to do. We would provide an enormous amount of help there. Next, is the actor who has been here a few years, has landed a couple of episodic parts, some call backs, maybe a commercial, but that is as far as they've gotten, they are stuck. They don't know why they are stuck, they see other people succeeding but they aren't. The next level of people have actually been series regulars or have been on a soap for years. We've had people with Emmy Awards come to us and say, "This is as far as I seem able to go. I'm stuck at this level." Stuck at $150,000 a year income level but for them, that's stuck. We provide the key to unlock being stuck, whatever that level may be for you.

• **Laurie Sheppard is a certified life coach.** I asked her how she works with the clients she coaches.

- **My work, individually and with groups, is about clarifying the dream** for the future and developing a particular action plan to get there.
- **As a life coach, I assist my clients in looking at the whole pie,** not just one piece—how their career and personal goals can integrate smoothly. But all of my clients hire me initially for their career development or career transitions. They are usually in four basic places: 1) they are clear and ready to up the ante in their productivity or results; 2) they are feeling overwhelmed and indecisive; 3) they have been working harder, not smarter and want to know how they can take a well-needed break, without losing ground; 4) they need to maximize their preparation time toward their dream, make clearer choices and prioritize their actions toward their goal.
- **I mainly work with entrepreneurs and professionals.** That is how I view the individual in the entertainment industry. They have a business; it is themselves they are selling and promoting. How to do it effortlessly and not lose the flame for their craft in the process is the key. Also, they are working with professionals and they need to know how to best communicate with those people.

Q: What else do you emphasize besides communication?

- **Change and Balance.** Balance includes the integration of all aspects of their lives and translating that into having their desired life. We are bombarded with distractions as well as opportunities; we need a discerning eye and a well-designed map to keep us on course. Understanding change, rather than being at the effect of it, gives us the necessary edge to expedite, as well as enjoy, the journey. My clients are more confidently accepting, more effortlessly maintaining their direction, and able to repeat the steps for the next challenge.

• **Sam Christensen's course is called Image Design Process.**

Q: Tell me about the unique course you teach.

- **The level-one class is an 18-hour course.** I have students that have just stepped off the bus two weeks ago, and I have people who have been at this for 30 years who are trying to focus. I begin with a basic introduction of how marketing works for any product, and then adapt it to acting. I then work on an image system, which allows people to figure out how they are perceived by other people outside of themselves. For example, with Greta Garbo, there was always mystery in her photographs: the clothes she wore, the publicity the studio did for her. The studios used to develop themes with an actor.

- **Suppose an agent represented Goldie Hawn.** Goldie Hawn thought she was a serious actress and she wanted to play Juliet. The agent took her because she's kind of a giddy blonde. Meanwhile, the photographer is attracted to her and he's trying to catch all the sexiness. Instead, if Goldie, the agent, photographer, and haircutter are all in agreement around the theme that Goldie is wacky, upfront, bright, lively and a little suspicious, if we've got those things going on, then everybody's talking the same language.

- **The actors come up with a set of words which are the primary** themes of what happens when they walk into a room—the stuff they bring to every part before they start making adjustments. It's the stuff that ought to be in a photograph of them.

- **For instance, from one of my classes,** there was an actress whose words are "urban, perplexed, genial, comic, direct, and impatient." Somebody else who is "tempered, amused, a tough-nut to crack, straight-shooting, embodied." Another person who is "hard-core, a mutt, motley, I land on my feet." Here's somebody who is "simmering, wild-eyed, mad-cap, conspiratorial, I know where the body's buried." These are not descriptions I give them. These are things that they choose through a rather involved process.

- **All of a sudden** the actor has a language and qualities to talk to the agent about so the agent can go out and use those same kinds of descriptions. When the actor comes in to meet the casting director, the actor is what the actor is comfortable in being, the actor is what the agent has introduced, what the pictures look like and everybody is in agreement. Improvements show up in all kinds of ways, not just in getting jobs.

Resources

Artist's Way Workshop, 310/839-3424. www.creativelife.com. Remove seemingly insurmountable barriers to artistic confidence and productivity. Based on best selling book. Empowering 12 week programs.

Sam Christensen, 818/506-0783. 10440 Burbank Blvd., North Hollywood, 91601. "I try to give actors the same thematic ability that the golden era studios used so well to define stars. The actor is their own studio and has the option to create an image based on the reality of how they are perceived and how they perceive themselves." Informantive free preview classes.

Breck Costin, BCC & Associates, 323/848-9665. www.bccfreedom.com. 8033 Sunset Blvd., #8000, Los Angeles, 90046. Private,$250 an hour. One month seminar series, $300. Call for his free periodic introduction seminar. Three-months, $900. Monthly *chat room* Mondays, $30 per night. "Come to be coached, get your questions answered and gain clarity about your life." During pilot season, Breck holds a special *Pilot Season Boot Camp for Actors.*

Barbara Deutsch, 818/508-9096. www.barbaradeutsch@inotherwords.com. She works with artists in front of and behind the camera. Private sessions, $125 an hour. Actors' workshops, $100 a month. *Breaking The Rules*, an ongoing workshop for actors in developing their careers. *In The Biz*, interactions and role playing with high level film and television agents. Many other titles, brochure available.

Lori A. Frankian, Individual Consultation for Actors, 617/437-0334. In Boston. I met one of her clients when he moved here from New England. She had really helped to get him ready for the move into the Los Angeles market.

Flash Forward Institute, 323/850-7392. www.flashforwardinstitute.com. Tools: How to get mentors, referrals, bookings and deals. Network with high-powered Flash Forward alumni from agencies, networks, studios, production and casting companies. They offer very inexpensive introductory courses: *One evening crash course!* $10. *The absolute scoop on how to get a great agent*, $10. The *Flash Forward intensive* is $425. SAG Conservatory had a two-hour session, which was informative and inspirational.

Laurie Johnson, 323/935-1528. Four sessions, $300. They are one-hour taped sessions. You walk away with a tape for life. "Once you finish the four sessions, that can be it or you can maybe come back for one. But if there is a new issue we do another set of four." Very non-confrontational, very direct and hands on.

Judy Kerr, 818/505-9373. www.actingiseverything.com. Private hour-and-a-half, one-time class for $100. I critique pictures and resumes, steer you toward services and teachers best for you, as well as guide you on long and short term goals. For people out-of-town, $50 half-hour phone consultation.

Life By Design Consultants, Ltd., Mitchell Bank and Hope Ingersoll, 310/281-7579. They work privately. "We offer a free 30-minute consultation. When there is a good fit we set up a personal appointment." $175 for 90 minutes. Custom packages available.

Life Skills, Liria Mersini, 310/828-7670. www.lifeskillbuilder@aol.com. "Give a call. Always glad to get to know you and let you get to know us by phone." Intensive six-session *break through* program for actors and entrepreneurs anywhere in the U. S., $150. Ongoing *troubleshooting* and *mastery* coaching in person, online or by phone. Empowering weekly groups in L. A. Call for topics. I really enjoyed my *Power of Image* weekend seminar with Liria and Melissa.

Melissa McFarlane, 323/697-0165. Certified life coach, with over 20 years as a professional actress, she brings a unique perspective to coaching. She holds workshops as well as private sessions in person and over the phone.

Laurie Sheppard, 310/109-3020. www.creatingatwill.com. Certified life coach, $45 for one-hour coaching introduction. Twelve-session rate for start up. Call for private sessions, current workshop or adult school instruction class information and availability.

Cat Williford, Winning Ways, 818/562-6851. Personal best coach and self-professed joy junkie. Her clients are on a quest for a more successful, satisfying and balanced life.

SECTION FIVE

HOME BUSINESS OFFICE

• **As a self-employed, self-motivated actor**, you are now in business and this requires an office, a private phone line (not to be shared with a roommate) and an answering machine, voice mail, or message service. One lost message could mean the loss of a career break as well as the loss of a day's income, which could pay for two years of phone service.

• **It's wonderful to have a separate room** for your office, but few of us have that luxury. So set aside an area devoted to taking care of business.

• **Your first order of business** is to get your pictures and resumes out to prospective buyers of your talent. Just as an employee shows up for work each day, you must make a commitment to look for acting work each day. It doesn't matter what that acting work is: big, small, paid, free; you are looking for experience in your new business. Free jobs are just as valuable as paying jobs in your career.

• **You need a desk or table** and file folder dividers or trays. Designate a folder or tray for each different head shot, a place for letterhead stationary, business envelopes, 8x10 or 8$^{1}/_{2}$x11 envelopes, postage scale, stamps, appointment book, acting notebook, networking card file, and bookshelf. You need a computer; until you can afford your own, some libraries and copy service stores have computers and printers available for your use.

• **Keeping track of incoming and outgoing phone messages** is an important part of every business. I find a valuable book for this is Avery's #50-111 In/Out Call Log, 100 pages. When I pick up my messages I write them in the book. My personal technique for checking calls off when I returned them allows me to use both pages for incoming calls.

• **When my book is full**, (about two years) I file it away. There have been times I've had to refer to old books for the phone number of someone I needed to reconnect with. This is a small community and we do run across the people we've worked with again.

• **Use a file box or file drawers to set up your files.** *Some suggestions for file folder titles are:*

- **Advertising/promotion**. Copies of any publicity about you.
- **Articles of interest**. Keep pieces on people you know, or would like to know; information on projects you'd like to work on; story ideas, etc.
- **Audition copy**. The sides and copy from your readings.
- **Bank statements.**
- **Cash receipts**. Keep for income taxes. Write any pertinent information on the back. Don't forget video rentals.
- **Commercial pictures**. Print work from magazines you could have done. Ideas of how to dress for commercials.
- **Correspondence**. Keep a copy of any letter you send out or receive.
- **Income statements of earnings.**
- **Manuals for equipment**. If you don't know how to work your VCR, hire someone who does for a private lesson. Part of your business is watching all the CURRENT TV shows so you will be familiar with the characters.
- **Master head shots and negatives**. Labeled in a folder, you never have to worry about where to find your negatives to run off new pictures.
- **Phone lists**. Keep every phone list you're given from acting classes and productions you've worked on. Over the years, these lists will be valuable when you want to make a networking call to someone.
- **Pictures**. I keep a few of each shot within reach.
- **Pictures of acting roles** I want to play or a characterization I think will help me.
- **Publicity, general**. I save copies of trade ads that I may want to copy; also publicity on my friends and students.
- **Receipts** from check and credit card purchases.
- **Resumes.**
- **Reviews**. Keep a copy of all reviews from every project you're in.

• **Create additional files** as the need arises for your developing career.

Phone Preference Service for people who do not want telemarketing calls. To register, write to Direct Marketing Association, Phone Preference Service, P.O. Box 9014, Farmingdale, NY 11735-9014. Include your name, address and phone number and request no telemarketing.

BOOKS

Working From Home, by Paul & Sarah Edwards.
The #1 Home Business Book, by George & Sandra Delany.
Small-Time Operator, by Bernard Kamoroff, CPA.

WEB SITES

iVillage www.ivillage.com/work. Find answers to questions about starting a home business and tax issues that may affect your venture.

Work-at-Home Success, www.workathomesuccess.com. This site posts listings of companies that hire home-based workers, plus discussions of important issues, including effective ways to communicate with your boss on the telephone.

Home-Based Working Moms, www.hbwm.com. This national association offers helpful information, including a new home-business checklist and suggestions on finding places to hold conferences and meetings other than your living room.

Mom's Village, www.wahm.com. Check out the Mom's Village web ring to find links to more than 200 web sites run by work-at-home-mothers.

USED OFFICE FURNITURE

Advanced Liquidators, 818/763-3470. 10632 Magnolia Blvd., North Hollywood. M-F 9-5; Sa, 10-4. From Geri Cook's Bargins Column in the *Los Angeles Times* Fridays, Valley Section.

CAREER TOOLS

APPOINTMENT BOOK/TIME MANAGEMENT

• **Always have your "book" with you.** Write every appointment down. It should have everything you do in it: classes, rehearsals, interviews, workouts, meditation, dates for movies, plays, etc. All your phone numbers and addresses, and a place to jot down notes, career goals and future plans should be included. When you schedule your days be sure to allow for driving time. Sunday night is a good time to plan for the week. Purchase a system that has a full page for each day and lists the time of day down the left side of the page; a place for a To Do List and a place to write down directions to locations. I use the *Day Runner* in a 5x7 *Filofax* book. The daily log is valuable for verifying your tax deductions. You can file the year's log in the same file as the year's copy of your tax returns. I use a computer program for names, phone numbers and addresses. I update this every few months and reprint the pages and replace them in my book.

• **Electronic Palm Pilot Systems are also good if they appeal to you.**

• **The important thing about having a system to keep appointments** is the time management aspect. Time management can make the difference in having a successful career. You can educate yourself; there are time management courses. I have worked privately with expert Dr. Jo Christner and have taken a course from Dr. Jackie Jaye-Brandt. It is fun to manage your time and it can relieve that feeling of being overwhelmed. It will help every segment of your career and life.

Resources

Most stationery stores have inexpensive systems and books.

A N B Discount, 818/760-0244. 12338 Ventura Blvd., Studio City, 91604. M-F 9-6, Sa 10-5. Office and entertainment industry supplies.

Bush's Stationers, 818/766-7117. 6440 Bellingham Ave. North Hollywood, 91606.

Mac Enerney's, 818/762-6566. 12202 Ventura Blvd., Studio City, 91604. M-F 9-5:30.

Office Supply, 818/506-1619. 10538 Burbank Blvd., North Hollywood, 91601. M-F 9:30-5:30.

Staples: many locations. 800/333-3330 www.staples.com

Office Depot: copy and print center, 888/463-3768. www.officedepot.com

Office Max: digital printing and copying, 800/788-8080. www.officemax.com

The following systems are more expensive and prestigious.

Franklin System, at Franklin/Covey Store: 818/884-7791 or 800/996-1492. www.franklincovey.com. In the Topanga Plaza Shopping Center on Topanga Blvd. in Woodland Hills, second floor next to Nordstroms. Also sold in many good stationery stores. $229 *What Matters Most* Seminar includes the book! $229, *What Matters Most for Palm Comupting Organizers* does not include the Palm. Many other seminars; call the store and they will tell you all about their classes.

Filofax System: Fred Segal, 8100 Melrose Ave., West Hollywood. 323/651-1298.

Time Design System, 11835 W. Olympic #450, West Los Angeles. 800/637-9942.

Jo Christner, PsyD., 310/471-2773. Offices in Encino and West Los Angeles. Teaches you how to manage your time and to organize you and your environment. She is excellent for setting you up in your acting business. If you have a problem being late, get it straightened out with her. She is a Member of the National Association of Professional Organizers.

Jackie Jaye-Brandt, M.A., MFT, Corporate Communications and Psychotherapy, 818/505-1664. 3575 Cahuenga Blvd. West, #213, Los Angeles, 90068. Stress management, communications training, time management, group workshops, couples groups and individual counseling.

Time Web Sites

Tardia: at www.kaska.demon.co.uk
AtomTime at www.atomtime.com/
Time RC at www.geocities.com/siliconvalley/lakes/7206/timerc
Time Protocol Servers, www.eecis.udel.edu/~ntp/
NTP source code from the university's FTP archive at ftp://ftp.udel.edu/pub/ntp/

ANSWER MACHINE / BEEPER / CELLULAR PHONE

• **You must have a private phone** and message device, not to be shared with a roommate. If you share a phone number and message device, you will lose an important message. When you buy a machine or choose a voice-mail service be sure it will respond to all push button phone tones when picking up your messages. There are machines that won't pick up the very short tones.

• **Be sure to choose a machine** that has a 12 second or less *outgoing message* length, or is voice activated. Keep your message short and to the point. People wanting to interview or hire you hate to wait through cute, long messages. It is important that your name or phone number, not both, be on your outgoing message so your callers know they have not dialed in error.

• **There are call-forwarding systems** that don't reveal they are pagers or voice mail. Investigate thoroughly before purchasing; the phone is your life line in this business. You can have phone relationships with people and not meet them in person for months. Always strive to be polite and take the other person's time into account.

• **Phone companies** have message center systems that function like an answer machine; you operate it with your push-button phone. Nothing to buy; the fee is added to your phone bill each month. Many actors swear by this system.

• **Many voice mail systems provide a beeper service too.** If you are planning on having both, they should be linked to the same number.

• **Another important feature** is a *voice-activated incoming message.* The machine will continue to record as long as the caller keeps talking. This will allow you to receive long messages such as casting information, including directions.

• **Check in every 60 or 90 minutes** during casting hours (10-6). You never know who may have a last-minute interview for you.

• **When you call someone** and get their answering machine, speak your name and phone number slowly and clearly first, as if someone is writing it down, then the rest of your message and then your phone number again. Machines and voice mail systems often cut off but if you have given your name and number first, they can call you to see what the message was. *Always leave your phone number*, even if you think they know it. Your calls will be returned faster! When I'm working on the set I have an hour to run home, eat lunch, pick up messages, return calls etc. If someone leaves a message without a phone number, I'll write their name down and maybe not call for a couple of days because I have to look the number up. Why not make it the easiest thing in the world to return your call?

• **Do not leave a pager number for someone to return your call.** If you do, say you can't be reached any other way today, but you will call later with a number where you can be reached if they prefer not to page. Over and over, I hear business people say they do not want to page someone who is trying to talk to them. It is rude. I think it is all right to say, "Please try me on my cell phone, with the number." They will at least think there is a possibility you will answer the phone. When someone calls me and leaves their beeper number or when I return a call and hear the sound of a beeper, I hang up. I don't want to wait for them to call back. I have moved on, returning my other messages. I don't want their return call to interupt me.

Resources

Vista Telephone, Jack the Phone Guy, 818/768-7541. Sharon Stone says, "He'll figure out every imaginable trick for special lines, intercoms, whatever.

Costco, Circuit City, Frys, Office Depot, Office Max, Staples and Target carry answer machines.

There are many ads in the trade papers for voice mail companies.

GTE Phone Company Personal Secretary: 800/483-4000.

Pacific Bell Message Center System: 800/675-9005.

Economy Answering & Beeper Service, 213/878-0680. 1335 N. La Brea, #2, Hollywood, 90028.

Voice Mail Depot, Inc., 800/309-8888. Starts at $5.95 a month.

BEEPER

• ***Beepers are necessary*** if you are not able to call in to your machine every hour. The beeper number should be reserved for employment and emergencies only. You must have a beeper that can notify you with a light or vibration. There's nothing more embarrassing and unprofessional than being on a set as your beeper goes off, ruining a take!

• **The beeper with a voice-mail attached** is a nice option. It will cost a few more dollars a month. The caller can punch in their number but if they are calling from a phone where they can't receive a call or they are on the run, they can leave a message. You will be paged with your own beeper number. You can call and pick up the message as soon as you are able. I find when working on the set it, is difficult to use the phone at certain times.

Resources

Tel Mart, 323/656-5555. Fairfax and Willowby, Hollywood. $72 a year with voice mail. The most you pay is $40 for a pager. You can use your old pager. Any area code, even more than one area code, can be used and that number can pass from pager to pager.

American Post' N Parcel, 818/761-3217. 11333 Moorpark Street, Toluca Lake, 91602. Pager and voice mail service, plus many other services for actors.

Beeper King, 818/752-3900. Ventura Blvd., just east of Laurel Canyon. They can link your beeper to the voice mail.

Mobil Cam, 800/437-2337.

VMI, (323) 850-1414 or (818) 766-5090.

CELLULAR PHONE

• **I believe you must have a cellular phone for emergencies.** You never know when you will be stuck in traffic or in a deserted neighborhood in the middle of the night. The service companies usually have free phones if you sign up for two years; the least you can pay a month is $20. I have one with a cord for the cigarette lighter, so I don't have to worry if the battery runs out of charge.

• **Roaming plan.** The technology is changing all the time. Check the ads, ask your friends. At this moment, I think AT&T is best. They have analogue and digital service. You need to be able to reach anyone at any time. Steven Eckholdt from *It's like, you know...* and I had a half-hour conversation about cell phones. He had just thrown one from Pac Bell out the car window and is totally happy with AT&T. Good luck!

AT&T Wireless Services, 800/603-2200. Phones, service and systems.

FAX MACHINE

• **It is great to have your own fax machine.** If you don't, you must have a place where you can receive faxes 24 hours a day. You never know when you will need your sides faxed to you for tomorrow's audition. I prefer my fax machine on its own phone line, although I also have a modem on the computer to receive faxes. I don't leave my computer on all the time so it isn't the best way to receive faxes. Fax machines can be purchased at all the usual electronic and office supply stores. Frys, Target, Costco/ Price Club, Office Depot, Office Max, Staples and Best Buy. A plain paper fax is worth the extra dollars.

COMPUTER / E-MAIL /INTERNET/ WORLD WIDE WEB/WEB SITES

• There is so much information and networking to do. If you love computers and like communicating with your fingers, this is another marketing opportunity. *See our Web and Internet addresses in Section Ten.*

www.mrwakeup.com. This is a way to get free wakeup calls. However, you do have to register and listen to some advertising during the call. For a fail-safe system, use a phone wakeup call in conjunction with an alarm clock.

• **Check into www/hollywoodreporter.com** for an immediate directory of most of the show business community.

• **Get into the computer age** if you want to be more competitive in your marketing strategies. There is so much you can do yourself; an alternative is to pay someone else to do the work for you.

• **If you are interested in your own website,** check out Sean O'Riordan, 323/858-4959. www.performersweb.com. He designed mine and my husband's websites. He offers classy and inexpensive designs and he completely understands "the actor's world."

BUSINESS AND PROMOTIONAL PICTURE CARDS

• **Keep business cards** in your jacket pocket, purse, wallet, glove compartment. They are an important networking tool. Whenever you meet someone, hand them yours and ask for theirs. There is nothing more awkward than looking for a pen and scrap of paper when someone asks for your phone number.

• **You can print 500 cards** for $15 and up. Start with a simple card with your name and phone number. As soon as it is possible, have your picture printed on the business card.

• **I took a picture of the hairdresser** on *Seinfeld* with Michael Richards, Michael held up his script next to his body. She uses this great picture of them that says it all. After all, Kramer is known for his hair. Be inventive, people will remember you for it.

• **File the business cards you receive.** Make a note of the meeting place, what the person looked like, your conversation. I keep mine in 8½x11 clear-plastic sheets designed to hold business cards. The sheets are kept in a one inch three-hole binder on my bookshelf, close to the phone and ready for instant reference. Your stationery store has different types of systems for filing business cards.

See Printers & Photocopying, page 118 and Picture Reproduction, page 103.

American Post' N Parcel, 818/761-3217. 11333 Moorpark Street, Toluca Lake, 91602. 500 Business Cards for $12.96, one-day service.

Color Business Cards, 800/772-9993. www.daicolocard.com. 21203A Hawthorne Blvd. Torrance, 90503. 1000 for $70. They don't require a negative, just a color photo. Ten-day turnaround.

Summit Trading Cards: 818/776-8273. New and different, they are two sided and professionally laminated. You choose the colors and the text. They will send a sample and price list.

MAILING LIST/CARD FILE

• **Start now and keep a 3x5 index card file of everyone** you come in contact with who is in the business. Include on the card where and how you met and something about them that will help you remember them 10 years from now. Also, if you read something about them or send them something about you, note it on the card with the date.

• **This is the beginning of your mailing list**; these are the people who will possibly help you get acting work. When you are doing showcases, you will get much more value from your money if you keep up with the casting directors you have acted for. When writing to them you can say: You saw me do a scene (give the name of it) at so and so showcase on (give the date).

• **I've heard it said**: it is best to mail your announcement, flyer, post-card, etc. on Tuesday or Wednesday because everyone else mails theirs on the weekend and the casting directors receive them on Monday or Tuesday. Yours will arrive on Thursday or Friday. Or better yet, mail them on your lucky day. I personally send a little spiritual wish with each one. Hey, we need all the edge we can get.

THOMAS GUIDE

• **The Thomas Guide is your absolute bible** for directions. This book is very clear and easy to use. If you don't know how to read a map, have someone teach you. Then buy the L.A./Orange County Edition of the Guide at Costco or any book store or newsstand. I cannot stress the importance of owning and knowing how to use this guide. You can't trust other people's directions and you *must* get to the job or interview on time. The Guide will help save your sanity. Most people who live and work in Los Angeles have a copy. Also, try www.mapquest.com.

LOCK BOX/EXTRA KEY

• **You must have a lock box on your car** with a house and car key in it. Even though all of my students are given this book and hopefully read it, some will invariably lock themselves out of their house or car. Several times they have missed jobs, appointments and been late for auditions. Put this book down and take care of this now.

• **After you have the keys** made, test them. Do not trust that they will work. This is worth the extra effort to test the keys!

• **I keep a regular car key in my wallet behind my drivers license,** and a house key in the glove compartment, as well as a secretly hidden house key outside the house. If your car has one key for the door and another for the ignition, I would take it to a locksmith and have it rekeyed in order to use one key. But you can just keep an ignition key in the glove compartment. Take care of your self.

• **When you belong to the Auto Club of Southern California,** they will make a free key for your wallet that is thin plastic and will last through a few uses. Additional keys are $2 each.

Raul's Key Service, 323/656-1738. 7879½ Santa Monica Blvd., West Hollywood, 90046. Located in the Alpha Beta Market Parking Lot at Fairfax. I make many keys and never has one of theirs failed in the 25 years I have been using this service.

AUTOMOBILE CLUB OF SOUTHERN CALIFORNIA

• **The Auto Club Road Service Policy** is another protection you need for yourself. They will arrive to start your car anywhere, fix a flat tire, unlock your car, bring gas and, if necessary, tow your car. About $55 a year.

Auto Club of Southern California, 323/525-0018 or 818/240-2200. Ask for the office that is nearest you.

PASSPORT

• **You may land a job** because you are the only actor who can leave the country immediately. Have an updated passport and be ready to go. In December, 1995 the Passport Office closed for two weeks and no one could get a new or updated passport. Be prepared for all emergencies as well as all opportunities. New passports are generally $60, renewals $40. To expedite a passport request, the cost is an additional $35. The expedited passport will be mailed within three working days.

You must provide two new 2-by-2 inch photos (with your head against a white or off-white background). To confirm identification, bring your drivers license. To demonstrate citizenship, they generally require a birth certificate, naturalization certificate or previous passport.

Resources

www.travel.state.gov. The Dapartment of State's Internet site, includes state-by-state listings of all post office passport acceptance facilities. The site also includes blank passport forms.

• **900/225-5674**, 24 hour recorded information of how to obtain your passport, 35 cents per minute. Operators there from 5am-5pm. 888/362-8668, costs a flat $4.95, payable with credit card number. They will mail the forms to you; it takes 4 to 6 weeks.

• **You can apply at some post offices** or the L.A. Passport Agency at the federal courthouse. Ask at your local post office where the nearest location is.

• **Federal Courthouse**, 11000 Wilshire Blvd., 13th floor, West Los Angeles, 90024. Office hours: M-F, 8-3.

ACTING NOTEBOOKS

• **After each acting class, make notes in an acting notebook** on what exercises you did and what the reports were from your teacher and the other actors; put your feelings down too. The exercises you learned in class will be helpful in choosing acting work for your scripts; they are your acting tools. When you are looking for a piece of acting work to help you interpret a script, you can look in your notebook to see if one of the exercises will help you.

• **Keep a copy of all monologues and scenes you do**. They will come in handy four or five years from now when someone asks you to bring in a scene at the last minute. You can go to your scene notebook and find something that has been received well in the past. It is good to write acting notes on the scenes too.

• **Try to keep your interview scenes** (sides) from your film and TV auditions and the copy from your commercial auditions. File them in your notebook. When you work on a project, keep the scripts; years down the line you will love having them. Maybe your career will someday be valuable enough for a library donation. We never know till it's over. When you run out of bookshelves, try cardboard file boxes.

AUDIO TAPE RECORDER/VIDEO TAPE RECORDER/VIDEO CAMERA

• **An audio tape recorder** can be used for learning lines, taping your teachers' feedback, or taping you and your acting partner rehearsing a scene. I like the kind that has a pause button on it, and that has a little speaker in it so I can choose to not wear headphones when listening to it.

• **A VCR is a necessary acting tool.** Use it to look at old movies, to tape TV shows you miss because you are out, to tape pieces with characters that you would be right to play. You save a lot of time looking at tapes sans commercials, as a half-hour show is actually 19 minutes and an hour show is actually 38 minutes. Two VCRs hooked together are great for keeping a copy of commercials and scenes you like.

• **I encourage my students** to see every movie available from their rental store. It is also advisable to see at least two episodes of every TV series. When you are asked to audition for a show, you will have a better idea of how to relate to the characters in the script. You are now in the film and television business; it pays to know as much about your business as you can. I have six VCRs, so at the beginning of the season and during sweeps, I can record everything.

See resources, next page.

VIDEO CAMERA AS A TOOL

• **Some actors find it quite difficult**, at first, to fall in love with themselves on camera. They will look at the playback and instead of looking to see how their acting tools are working or how believable they are as themselves or as a character, they will hate their nose, weight, hair, etc. If you will come to love or simply accept how you look, you can begin to look at yourself without any defenses. Then you can make the proper choices of how you uniquely want to look. You may decide to go to speech class, cut your hair, lose or gain ten pounds, get your nose done or learn to use makeup properly. That is okay. But leave the possibility open to love yourself just as you are.

• **While you are working on camera**, don't judge yourself. Lay down all your judgments. When you are finished working, they will be there anytime you choose to pick them up.

• **Court the camera** as you would a new person whose friendship you would very much value. When going to class, think about what you would like to learn about yourself. Be curious as to how you can look different or how far out you can go with a character. Be willing to fail; then when you are getting paid to work on camera, you will have an idea of how much freedom you actually have. Sometimes, it has seemed to me, there are rules that you can't break. *Break them.* It is where the excitement is in life. As actors on camera, we can break rules and see if it works. Yes, there is a chance of failure, but there is also a chance of *flying.*

• **Flying is having moments** when everything is working, as with Holly Hunter in *The Piano,* Anthony Hopkins in *Remains of the Day,* Jack Nicholson in *A Few Good Men,* Jodie Foster in *Silence of the Lambs,* Daniel Day-Lewis in *My Left Foot.*

• **Very few of us will get paid** to portray characters who are quite different from ourselves. We use those characters in acting class, in Equity-waiver productions or in student films, to stretch our acting muscles and to play parts that may feel closer to our hearts than the way the industry sees us and casts us.

• **I encourage you to prepare ahead** of time for class or a reading by pretending you are living that certain role. Hairdresser, gangster, nurse, waitress, young father, upscale man or woman, business executive, secretary, jock, etc. Don't wear a costume, but wear something to suggest the life-style of the character. The minute you walk into the office or you see your playback on the monitor, they or you can say yes, this person looks like a gangster, secretary, father, sweetheart, etc.

Resources

Tom Kelly, 818730-1076. Better prices than discount stores and he delivers, sets up equipment and does repairs. He specializes in custom-designed systems. When he sells you equipment he also trains you how to use it. Also good bargains on used equipment and trade-ins.

Target, Frys, Best Buy, Costco/Price Club and department stores, many locations.

PROFESSIONAL WORK HABITS

PUNCTUALITY

• **Over and over in this book**, people being interviewed talk about the importance of being on time. This habit can make or break a career.

• **Garth Brooks** tells the story about when he had been in Nashville for a couple of years. He and his wife worked in a shoe store to make ends meet. He was scheduled to perform at 11:30PM at a song writers' showcase. It was not a prime spot, as the record company reps usually left by 11PM. Suddenly at 9:30PM, the owner ran backstage and said, "You're up, Garth. Ralph Murphy, the second act, hasn't showed up yet." Garth jumped up on stage, sang his heart out, and Capitol Records signed him before the evening was over. Ralph is still looking for a deal.

• **Check in with someone** immediately when you show up for work or an audition to let them know you are there.

• **Practice being on time every day, for every event.**

ATTITUDE

• **In this business, if you get the job**, that means you are skilled and crafted in what you do. If you have to shoot a movie for the next 10 weeks, or do seven years on a television series, who do you want to work with? Most people will want to work with kind, helpful, considerate, gentle, warm, fair, fun, funny, professional actors.

• **There are all kinds of attitudes to adopt.** My daughter, Cynthia, tells my grandsons, Austin and Jackson, to change their attitudes when they are acting inappropriate. Their faces and tones of voice change. At ten and four, they already know all about attitude and how to fix theirs.

• **I believe attitude is your frame of mind.** I think attitudes can be willed to change by changing your mind. If you are on a set and observe a lot of bad attitudes going on, don't get caught up in it. Know the attitude you want to put across and stay true to it. On the day of an audition, you may be having a horrible day. Do not take it into the audition room with you; it is nobody's business. Keep your negativity to yourself.

HARD WORK

• **Oprah's week-day schedule** was described by *People Magazine.* Her success is a result of hard work. How hard are you willing to work for your success?

• 5 AM:	Four-mile run.
• 7 AM:	Breakfast, makeup, hair and prep for shows.
• 9 - 2 PM:	Tape two shows.
• 2 PM:	Lunch.
• 3 PM:	Business and staff meetings. Phone calls.
• 5:30 PM:	Four-mile run, Stairmaster, sit-ups.
• 7-9 PM:	Tying up loose ends of future shows. Dinner.
• 10 PM:	Prep next day's show.
• 12 AM:	To bed

PREPARATION

• **Always have a pen or pencil** with you. Without a "note taking mechanism," you are minimizing your potential, rather than maximizing it. We think we'll remember a person's name or a phone call we need to make. Keep notes throughout the day. Each night, process those notes: sort, file, transfer. Develop your own system of keeping track of valuable information.

• **Your success requires extraordinary, extreme actions.** The universe is giving us "whispers" all the time, many times a day. There are opportunities all around you; don't let them pass you by. Have your antenna up, your nose in the air, your ear to the ground, your sights on success.

• **Swoosie Kurtz**, a film, televison and Broadway veteran stage actress, in a *Women In Film* interview:

• **In television and film there's no rehearsal.** In a one hour television drama you do a different scene everyday and once you do the scene, you never do it again in your whole life. As far as preparation, if I have the time, I sort of do the same thing for film and TV as I do for the theatre, which is read the material over and over again, get as familiar with it as I can. I don't mean in terms of learning lines but just the overall picture of the piece. What is the theme? What is this writer trying to say? And what is my part? What does my character do? And does she change? And, if so, what changes her?

• **Anthony Hopkins** talked of his preparation for *Shadowlands.*

> • **I read a couple of C.S. Lewis' books:** a few of the Narnia books and *A Grief Observed.* But the text was everything that I needed to use. I sort of metabolize the text, ingest it, absorb it into myself. I read the script three or four times to get the overall impression, and then I take a day on each scene that I'm going to do and I go through it over and over and over—literally 150, sometimes 200 times. For me, 150 is a kind of lucky mascot. It represents that I know it and makes me feel very secure.

• **Joan Darling, Emmy award-winning director,** talks about preparing for auditions.

> • **Have pride**—don't do anything less than the absolute best you can do. Work on the "given circumstances," pick two strong pieces of acting work, decide what function your character has in this painting. Am I the comic relief? Am I the villain? Do I drive the plot? If you know those very bold strokes and you know how to act, you can come in and give a pretty damn good performance very fast.
>
> • **I was in a television movie** with Dustin Hoffman called *Trap Of Solid Gold.* He had a tiny part as an accountant. There was so much texture to the portrayal; he so filled himself as an actor that when he first appeared, picked up his head and just looked at his fellow actor, you knew everything about his character. It was from the amount of work that he did. If you want to be doing leads, why not do all the work you do as if it were a lead?

CONCENTRATION

• **Being able to focus and concentrate** are two of your most important functions as an actor. Anita Jesse gives exercises to develop these tools in her book, *Let The Part Play You*, available at book stores.

• **Anjelica Huston** talked of when she was working on *Prizzi's Honor*. Her father was directing and her then long time lover, Jack Nicholson was starring. She stayed in a different hotel on location so she could keep her concentration.

• **Linda Buzzell, author** of *How to Make it in Hollywood; All the Right Moves*, gave some phone hints in the *Women In Film* newsletter.

- **Lack of focus can create a reluctance** to get on the phone because you're not really sure what you're offering or what you're asking for, or whether you want it if you get it! It might help to put your Hollywood pitch (pitch for your talents, services, script, whatever) up over the phone where you can sneak a peek if you freeze up.

- **Start out by calling a few friends** just to break the ice and get the day rolling. By the time you punch in the number of that studio executive or agent, you're nicely warmed up and ready to schmooze. Make your calls standing up and use your body to gesture as if the person were in the room with you. And smile! Research has shown that callers can actually hear the change in your tone of voice and will be more responsive. Making job search calls is a numbers game, not a reflection on your personal worth as a human being. It's important to remember that it may take 100 calls to land one serious job interview.

DISCIPLINE

• **When actors aren't acting,** they must be cleaning up their lives, their habits, their house, their bills, always preparing to go to work. Because when you are working as an actor, even in a class scene, you don't have time to do much of anything else. You can let everything else go and let your role consume you. All your discipline will go into your work. You will have trained yourself to have discipline by all the things that you intend to do each day and that you actually do each day. We ask 90% effort in acting—maybe it takes that much in life too—if you want to make a living as an actor. Effort has to do with commitment, intention and discipline.

• **Intention is keeping your agreements.** I intend to be curious, not judgmental; I intend to do my laundry; I intend to send out my pictures; I intend to change my life into positive stories; I intend to eat well; I intend to be on time, etc.

• **Not keeping your intentions** gives you anxiety which leads to guilt, which leads to failure. Don't waste energy on *trying* to keep intentions—just keep them. There is time for everything. Being in business for yourself, as actors are, takes a great deal of *self*-motivation; it won't be coming from anywhere else.

• **Glenn Close spoke of her discipline** when doing *Sunset Boulevard* on Broadway. "It takes a great deal of stamina to do a play. We do five shows each weekend, which is brutal. I don't smoke or drink and I've been eating very, very healthy. I have this policy that I can have two Oreos per performance. One of the things that gets me through the weekend is that I know I can have four Oreos on Saturday and four on Sunday."

• **Phone etiquette is very important.** Return those calls promptly, before the end of the day. When you call and leave a message *always leave your number.* They will return your call quicker. Do not ask someone to return your call by paging you, it is rude. Why should they wait by a phone for you to call them back?

• **Using your acting tools is a discipline.** Make your acting choices, do your sensory work. If you do your acting work 90% of the time, it will be 100% effective for the audience.

• **Discipline becomes easier** as certain sets of behavior become habits in your life. It has been proven: it takes about 21 days to unlearn a bad habit or to form a new positive habit. In those 21 days, it takes conscious effort and vigilance; but then the new habit is yours.

• **It all boils down to how much** you desire something. I saw two tennis players at the Forest Hills Open. One of them appeared cool, collected, concentrated, never ruffled, willing himself to win. The other player raged at calls and spanked, yelled at, scolded, cussed and coaxed himself. They were both driving themselves to win in different ways. Whatever it takes to drive you to win, DO IT. Take action, keep your intentions. *Pay now* so you can *play later.* Time does pass and if you commit, keep intentions and create discipline in your life, the time will pass with less anxiety and stress in this very stressful business.

• **The chief cause of failure** is giving up what you really want for what you want at the moment.

ACADEMY PLAYERS DIRECTORY AND ONLINE CASTING

• **The Academy Players Directory is a set of books** with actors' pictures and where to reach them. Every casting director, agent, producer and director in town has a set. It is used 100% of the time by 100% of the casting community. They are also on-line, www.acadpd.org.

The categories are:

- Leading Woman
- Ingenue
- Character & Comedienne Female
- Leading Man
- Younger Leading Man
- Character & Comedian Male
- Child Female
- Child Male

• **Actors do get called in to read for roles** because their pictures are in the directory. There is absolutely no reason not to be in it.

• **A student of mine was called in to audition** to play Tom Hanks double from the Academy Player Directory. SAG scale plus 10% for four weeks, and an incredible experience.

• **Two friends of mine** were specifically cast from the directory. Ken Olfson, a long time character actor, was booked to do the *Jack Klugman Show* without an audition because John Stamos (also a regular on the show) remembered him from a similar character he had played on a *One Day At A Time* episode. John couldn't remember his name so he looked through the directory till he found his picture. Peter Scranton, an unknown actor, was called in to audition and ultimately film *Space Camp* because the director spotted him while searching the directory for new faces.

I CANNOT EMPHASIZE ENOUGH HOW IMPORTANT IT IS FOR YOUR PICTURE TO BE IN THE DIRECTORY. You could miss a job if you are not in it.

• **To qualify**, you must have a franchised agent, personal manager, or be in a union. (Another reason to join AFTRA.) You may register only three specific times a year—two weeks during January, May and September. $75 a year, for one picture, one category; two photos, $85; three photos, $95; or $25 for a single issue, one picture, one category. If you are a character actor who also does leading roles, or a leading person who plays characters, you should appear in both categories if you can afford it. They will need a black and white 8x10 picture, lithos are acceptable. I prefer a quality photo paper print.

• **When you go in to register**, or at anytime, pick up their free booklet containing actors listed in the business. The booklet is updated every three months. I always buy a set of old Players Directories and keep them available for my students to browse through. Two-year-old editions are around $10; nine month old about $30 or $35.

ONLINE AND CD-ROM CASTING

• **Computerized talent services** are charging actors to put their pictures, credits and sometimes a short video on CD-ROM or an Internet system. The CD-ROM system is put on a compact disc, which is readable by computer, and then distributed to casting people. It is a non-public system. The online service is on the Internet system and is public. Some systems may require a password to access how to locate the actor. Never post your home phone number or address.

• **Casting is still done in the most traditional way**, that is, between the agent and casting director. Chances are slim that you will be called in for an audition from a picture in the Directory or online, but it does happen.

Reources

Academy of Motion Picture Arts and Sciences, (310) 247-3000. Ask for Academy Players. 8949 Wilshire Blvd., Fourth Floor, Beverly Hills, 90211 (between Robertson and Doheny). M-F 9-5. Free parking under the building. During peak registration hours, you may have to park on the street. The Academy has many other services www.oscars.org. Sending a note to get on their mailing list for seminars. They have several events a month.

Breakdown Service, 310/276-9166. www.breakdownservices.com.

Castnet, 323/964-4900. www.castnet.com. You must join to receive this service, which includes: free sides, talent search, create-a-postcard, agent submissions, resume updating, casting director mailing labels, driving directions, professional actor's forum. $99 a year.

Players Guide, 212/302-9474. www.players-guide.com. 1560 Broadway, Suite 416, New York, NY 10036. Players' Guide Book, Players' Guide Casting on the Web, Players' Guide CD-ROM.

The Casting Workbook, 310/207-5660. www.castingworkbook.com. 11925 Wilshire Blvd., 3rd Floor, L.A. 90025. Basic membership is $42 a year which includes free sides.

AUDITION TAPES AND DEMO REELS

• **All actors need an audition tape or demo reel.** Always ask for a 3/4" or Beta-SP tape of any work that you do; if not a 3/4" or Beta, then a 1/2" VHS tape recorded on SP, standard play, speed. If you're in a film that is available on video, rent it and have an editing company copy your scenes, bypassing the anti-copy code. When you are copying shows from television to use for your reel, use a new high grade tape and record on SP, standard play, speed. This will give you the best quality for copying. You can pay to have a company record it on 3/4" or Beta tape for you; that is called an air check. *See Resources, pages 310, 311.*

• **Gather your pieces of tape**, find a good editor at an editing company, and have a smashing video tape designed. Five or six minutes maximum, with all the scenes featuring YOU. Don't worry about story points, only your acting moments. Your name should appear at the beginning and end of the tape. A label on the tape and the tape box design should feature prominently the phone number where you can be located.

• **For actors who don't have work** on film and television, you have to get creative. Most agents and casting directors say unless you have network quality tape, don't bother. I believe laws are to be broken. I've seen some beautiful short clip collage work created by camera operators and editors for actors who didn't have professional work yet. They used a Hi8 camera and shot the actor all over town, on Melrose, at the beach, on a hillside bluff, in the woods, on a motorcycle, whatever was appropriate for that actor. Then they edited-in music and quick cuts of the actor in action. At the end, the actor was doing a short monologue on location, kind of a personality piece, just talking to the camera. They used natural lighting and didn't have to worry about sound except for the monologue. You can rent a microphone that will plug into your camera and place it close to you for the monologue.

• **If you produce a project** like this you need talented, creative people with you; research it carefully. You could get several actors and hire an excellent camera and camera crew and split the expense. This is not cheap, but when a producer or director asks you for tape, you will have something of quality to show them. Of course, you have to look very good (lighting and makeup) and act well. See if you can get your acting coach involved in the project. Remember to keep this three to four minutes long—even two to three minutes, as long as it is 100% high quality.

• **Take your footage** to an editing company with a sharp editor and put your piece together using fades and all their goodies to enhance the production value. If you have some *extra* work where you are seen, you could mix that in too.

• **Label your tape boxes** *and* your tapes in bold letters with your name and phone number. Use a white or black tape box that has a full plastic cover over the whole box. Cut down a heavy piece of paper so it will fit into the whole plastic sleeve, both the front and back covers. You can then glue or double-stick-tape one of your 8x10s cut down to fit the front plastic sleeve of the box. Glue it to the paper so it will show on the outside front of the box. I glue (or double-stick-tape) my name on top of my picture. I like to use a cut down 8x10 because it ends up being mostly face. Glue a miniature (reduced photocopy) resume on the back outside of the box and below that, print *To Return Tape: Contact,* then your agent's or your phone number. Glue another paper strip with your name and contact number sideways on the paper so it will show on the spine of your tape.

• I measure and draw the dimensions or where I will trim the paper to fit in the tape box with little marks, then paste up my resume and *To Return Tape: Contact* on the back. I then computer-generate my name and phone number for the spine and paste it up. I photocopy a few of these at a time and then trim them, paste the picture on and slip it in the cover of the tape box. This is a great looking package for very little expense and some creative time. Packaging counts for a lot; you want to look very professional.

• **You can have an editor freeze a single frame** on your tape and take a still picture from it. This is valuable when you are in a scene with a star. These are good photos to show in interviews, if you don't have any production stills.

• **Bonnie Howard, Theatrical and Commercial Agent says, about tapes:**

- **Demo tapes should be as short as possible**, and as high impact as possible. Just select the best work. Don't use anything that is staged specifically for a demo, unless it is done by a professional, such as Allen Fawcett. *(See next page.)* Don't send out a tape unless it is requested, because you probably won't get it back, unless you submit an envelope with postage.

- **Until you have a tape of your work** that you are proud of, that can help you to get roles and shows a range of your talent, you are better off without one. Tapes are generally requested (a) if you are not available for a reading, (b) to see the range of your talent, (c) to show your work to a director who may be out of town, already shooting on location.

• **John Ingle**, Edward Quartermaine on *General Hospital*, tells how he landed this role, replacing the actor who retired from the show. He auditioned and was being considered. Eight weeks later, the casting director, Mark Teschner, happened to turn on *The Young and the Restless,* and there was John playing a judge. Mark called John's agent to see if it had been taped. It hadn't been because it was a flashback on the show and John wasn't aware it was going to be on. John called Jan's Video (they tape everything) and asked them to find his scene, record it and messenger it to the casting director, who took it to the producer and said, "This is our actor." They cast John right then, after a long search of auditions here and in New York.

Resources

Demo Tape Class, Sam Christensen and Tom Jourden, 818/506-0783. Sam Christensen Studio, 10440 Burbank Blvd., North Hollywood, 91601. $50. They teach a four hour seminar on making your demo count. "No matter how much footage you have, you'll learn how to design and supervise the editing of a video demo tape that will open doors and show you at your unique best. You'll walk away from this seminar with a step-by-step 'video demo' system that will eliminate frustration, save money and get immediate results." This is a great class; I highly recommend it. I have seen some of the tapes that Tom Jourden has edited and they are impressive. Sam Christensen is an Actors' Image and Career Planning Consultant.

Imagestarter, Video Tape Packaging, 310/854-0443. M-F 10-6. The packaging and marketing experts. Set up an appointment, bring in your photos, resume, reviews or any other information you think might be good on your tape box. They'll design a truly distinctive look with matching labels. They also do resumes, photoresumes, business cards, postcards and other promotional items. Very classy and reasonably priced.

Jan's Video Editing, 213/462-5511. 1800 N. Argyle #100, Hollywood, 90028. M-F 9-6. Make an appointment. They will give their recommendations and assign you an editor. $78 an hour for Paul and $66 an hour for the other editors. Doreen believes actors need 1½ to 2 hours for first time reels. You only pay for the actual editing time you use. All the editors are good but Paul is my personal favorite. Jan's Video will tape your shows for you from the air on ¾" or Beta tape, $15 for an hour show, $10 for ½ hour. Best of all, they may have a copy of a show you did years ago, which would be impossible to obtain from any other source. Jan's has the most extensive library of tapes anywhere—most network series and all movies of the week. They can take stills from your videos.

Tom Jourdan, 818/372-1248. www.greattape.com Demo tape designer and editing coordinator. Call and have him send you his brochure—it is an education. I've seen his reels; they are great.

Allen Fawcett, 818/763-7399. Gives a free seminar on: *See reels that agents love; get your own reel—now!* They say, "We shoot and edit tasty demo reeels that make agents drool." Check it out.

Demo Reels, 310/820-1772. 2050 S. Bundy Drive, #104, West Los Angeles. They do air checks. They shoot demo reels; check them out.

Dub-it, 323/993-9570 or 888/993-8248. 1110 N. Tamarind Ave., Hollywood, 90038. Video and CD-ROM duplication and conversion. VHS custom packaging, only orders over 2500. Minimum of tape copies is 50. When you are doing large quantities, this is the place to go.

EZTV, 323/462-3678. 6522 Hollywood Blvd., Los Angeles, 90028. M-F 10AM to 12 midnight, Sa 10-7. $75 an hour. Prepare actor's reels and all dubbing and copying. 10 minute tape with the full sleeve box, $3. No air checks.

Our Production, Inc., 213/465-4197. 6255 Sunset Blvd., Suite 2201, Hollywood, 90028. Will tape shows off the air for you on ¾" tape at $65 an hour. They will keep the tape for you or edit your scenes onto your reel. Editing is $65 an hour with an hour minimum. For a first tape, if you have a lot of material it will probably take two to three hours. They record everything on network television but only keep it for a month. You can leave your master there and for $15.50 they will run a copy off for you to pick up or they will deliver it for $5.

Pro-Star Media, 818/509-9316. 11366 Ventura Blvd., Studio City, 91604. At the intersection of Ventura and Tujunga. M-F 10-6, Sa 12-5. Editing and copying. 10-minute tapes sell for $2; full sleeve tape boxes $1. Air checks $45 an hour for 3/4", $20 an hour for 1/2". Avid-computer digital editing system; Beta sp, $80 an hour.

Reel Video, 323/466-5589. 937 N. Cole Ave., #8 Hollywood, 90038. Specializes in designing actor's demo reels. One-on-one attention. Air checks, effects, titles and fast duplication.

Ross Hunt Productions, 818/763-6045 or 818/980-3812. 12438 Moorpark, Studio City, 91604. Demo reels, inexpensive quantity duplication. Editing.

Speed Video Duplication SVD, 310/447-5525. 12113 Santa Monica Blvd. #201, West Los Angeles, 90025. Video copies from VHS, S-VHS, 3/4" Betacam SP, Betamax, 8mm. Hi-8 and VHS editing for demo tapes. Air checks.

Studio Film & Tape, 323/466-8101. 1215 N. Highland Ave. Hollywood, 90038. Cash, check or credit card with no penalty. 3/4" Sony 30-minute tapes, in 10 tape bulk packs, BRS $9.95, XBR $11.75. 30-minute 1/2" VHS bulk tapes are $1.45 and 1.57 a tape, cardboard sleeve is $.25 extra. 30-minute tapes in 10-tape bulk packs. 60-minute bulk tapes. Black and white tape boxes with full plastic sleeves, $.60. Tapes for any use available. Call ahead and they will have your order ready. Park next door at gas station.

The Actor's Image, 323/525-1225. Demo Reel Production, Headshots and Resumes. A student of mine attended their seminar and thought them very good. Check them out.

The Tape Company, (32ß∑3) 461-6868. 1014 N. Highland Ave., Hollywood, 90038. 8-8 M-F, 9-5 Sa. Bulk means 10 tapes in a package. VHS 1/2" 15-minute Sony tapes are $1.31 each in bulk. Sony 3/4" 30-minute BRS $12.21; XBR is $14.09; BRS in bulk is $9.48. Plastic sleeve box $.74.

VDI, 323/461-3726. 1220 N. Highland Ave., Los Angeles, 90038. 24 hours a day, 7 days a week. Any copying from any type of format. These are the top of the line machines, including film to tape. The best quality. No editing or air checks.

Video Tape Products, 800/851-3113. 1014 N. Highland Ave., between Melrose and Santa Monica Blvd. M-F 8-8. 3/4" Sony 30-minute tapes: BRS $12.21, XBR $12.57. 1/2" VHS Sony 30 minutes $2.82, includes sleeve and label. 50 Bulk tapes: Fuji 30-minutes $1.33 each. 40 bulk 10-minute tapes are $1.21 each. They have occasional blowout sales on bulk tapes.

Video Tech, 818/765-1778, in North Hollywood. $1.15 for duplicates.

World of Video, 310/659-5147. 8717 Wilshire Blvd., Beverly Hills, 90211. M-F 9-6, Sa 11AM-4PM. Editing and duplication for all formats, digital effects, film-to-tape and freeze frames. Avid editing, $129 per hour. Linear editing, $89 per hour. No air checks.

TRADE PUBLICATIONS AND NEWSSTANDS

BACK STAGE WEST/DRAMA-LOGUE

• ***Back Stage West/Drama-Logue* is a must-read.** You may reach a level in your career where you don't need to read it, but you may still enjoy the interviews and ads. Even when I am not actively seeking acting work, I still feel like it is part of my job to keep up with all of our trade papers. I sure want my doctors, dentists and plastic surgeons to keep up with their trades. For your information, *Drama-Logue* was the only paper of its kind in Los Angeles for about 20 years. *Back Stage West* came to Los Angeles (it is *the* paper in New York) and five years later *Drama-Logue* merged with *Back Stage West.* It is published by the same company that publishes the *Hollywood Reporter* and the *Ross Reports.*

• **If you are actively seeking acting work,** I advise subscribing on-line, then you have a bit of a jump on the people who buy *Back Stage West* on the newsstand Wednesday afternoon and evening. You will definitely have a jump on the people who subscribe and don't get it till Thursday. Several times a year it doesn't arrive in my mail until Friday. This is crucial when you are trying to have your picture and resume opened first.

• **One of my acting students, Mark McKeel,** has an extensive theater background but needed film experience. In just a few months of class and following the directions in this book, his evenings and weekends were jam packed with auditions, rehearsals and work from USC, UCLA and independent films—all from ads in the trades. He is very serious about a career and is making it happen for himself. At first he landed smaller roles and then leading roles in several student and independent films, even earning some money.

• When he had enough film experience and had a short audition tape put together from his work, I advised him to do a few month's extra work to get his three SAG vouchers so he could look for an agent. He was an extra on *Apollo 13*, and Bill Paxton got to talking to him and said, "Hey, I'll help you." He called over the director, Ron Howard, and said, "I think Mark here should ask me for my gum before I put my helmet on." Ron said okay and Mark got his first speaking role and his eligibility for Screen Actors Guild.

• **There are listings for every type of acting work** in *Back Stage West/Drama-Logue*. Some jobs pay, some don't pay, but you earn audition experience, credit and sometimes a tape copy. Read all the ads. Highlight or mark every possible acting job you could do—union, nonunion, film, TV, commercial, extra, student productions, stage, etc. As you send out each picture, write down the information in a notebook or on a sheet of paper that you keep in one of your file folders. Include the date and role description. I cut out the ad and glue it on a 3x5 index card, write the date on it, and put it in a card file, to be thrown away if I don't get a call from them. Don't call or deliver in person if the ad says not to. On student films, many times you may not be called in for three months. The producers and directors are always eager to get ideas of actors they may be interested in using.

• **Send out your pictures and resumes** and make your phone calls as soon as you get *Back Stage West/Drama-Logue*. There are some newspaper stands that get the publication on Wednesday afternoon. There is a 24-hour stand in Hollywood on Cahuenga just south of Hollywood Blvd., and another one in Studio City on Laurel Canyon Blvd., at Moorpark. For every job, hundreds of actors submit their pictures; as always, it pays to be early.

• **Put the name of the role** you are submitting yourself for on the envelope and attached to your picture with a *post-it* note. No need to include a cover letter, unless you have some pertinent information—the part is for a golfer and you are a champion, or you've worked with the director and you want to remind them of that. Just writing a cover letter to say you want the job is unnecessary.

• **The free jobs that give you the most value** for your time and effort are usually, but not always, Equity-Waiver plays and graduate school sync-sound films. If you need experience in auditioning, then audition for everything. One of my students, T. R. Richards, auditioned over 160 times in two years from ads in the *Back Stage West.* He's been in over thirty student films. Needless to say, with his studying and auditioning experience, he is moving his career right along. My career started from the first ad I answered (*Drama-Logue* cost 25¢ then), a USC student film, playing a waitress. The lead in that movie, Rick Davis, led me to my best friend, Samantha Harper, who led me to my mentor, Joan Darling.

• **If you are just starting out**, you can gain valuable experience working on crews. So if you have the time, look for those jobs too. The more you understand what goes into a production, the better an actor you will be.

• **Michael Lerner**, Oscar-nominated for best supporting actor for *Barton Fink,* said he owed his success to the *Drama-Logue.* He was living in a one-room Hollywood apartment with a pull-down bed. The phone was down by the gas station. He didn't have a car, lived on unemployment. He read about a play audition and got a part in *Little Murders.* Director Paul Mazursky came to see the show, put him in his movie, *Alice in Wonderland.* Director Michael Ritchie saw that and cast him in *The Candidate* and his career was launched.

• **New actor Robert Restraino** read an ad for a lead actor with intense eyes for a nonunion independent film, *Motor Psycho.* He ran a photocopy of his picture and erased the color of his eyes to lighten them. He landed the audition and the job.

• **Kevin Costner** credits his start from landing jobs he auditioned for out of the *Drama-Logue.*

HOLLYWOOD REPORTER AND *DAILY VARIETY*

When you have started a serious career, it is a must to read one of these every day. You decide which is best for you and subscribe. I couldn't do without either one because in the social columns, my favorite, the same gossip isn't repeated. It's nice if you can share the expense and paper with another actor. You can also read them at the Beverly Hills or Hollywood libraries.

This information can be valuable when meeting a producer or director; you will be able to discuss their projects with them because you are familiar with them. I keep files of articles that interest me or that may come in handy at a later time. I also have a file on types of publicity I like so I can refer back to it when I'm designing my own ads or mailings.

• **Jay Bernstein**, manager, writer, producer, publicist, taught a course called *Stardom, the Management of, the Public Relations for, and the Survival and Maintenance In.*

Q: Why should actors read the trade papers?

- **It's important to be educated** in anything you do. You're meeting people at parties. You may never know that you're meeting a director or a producer or who that person is unless you subscribe to the *Hollywood Reporter* or *Daily Variety*, read the *Los Angeles Times Calendar* section, and *People* magazine to get a feeling of who everybody is. You can spend a whole evening talking to someone and not connect their name or face to show business because a lot of people don't talk about it. You might have made a different impression if you had known. There are too many people, too many names. Also, learn the history of this business.

Resources

The Trade Papers can be purchased at almost any newsstand, 7-11 store or theatrical bookstore in the area.

Back Stage West, 310/474-6161, 800/458-7541. www.backstagewest.com 2035 Westwood Blvd. #210, Los Angeles, CA 90025. Six months, $45; one year, $75; two years, $125. $1.85 per single copy at newsstands and 7-11's in the Los Angeles area. Some newsstands receive it on Wednesday afternoon around 2PM. It's owned by the *Hollywood Reporter. Back Stage* has been the bible in New York for many years.

Daily Variety, 323/857-6600 or 800/552-3632. 5700 Wilshire Blvd., Suite 120, L.A., 90036. $280 a year, three and six month prices available. Television productions listed every Thursday, film productions listed every Friday, cable listed every Monday.

Hollywood Reporter, 323/525-2000. 5055 Wilshire Blvd., L.A., 90036. $280 a year for daily paper or $170 a year for Tuesday edition only. Film productions listed every Tuesday, television productions listed first and third Tuesday of every month. Their subscribers are affluent and trend setting: $180,000 average income; $659,000 average residence value; 26% are millionaires; 35% own real estate in addition to their primary residence. Sounds great doesn't it?

Los Angeles Times Newspaper, 800/LA TIMES. Every day, $15 a month; Sundays only, $8 a month. Another must. *Every morning,* read at least the Calendar Section. It will provide you with openings for conversation and again, more knowledge about the business and people in it. Much of film and television content, as well as style, relates to current events in the world. Your competition is reading the newspaper.

• NEWSSTANDS

Al's News #1, 370 N. Fairfax, Los Angeles.
Al's News #3, 1257 Third Street Promenade, Santa Monica.
Al's News #5, 226 N. Larchmont, Larchmont Village.
Book Soup (Bookstore and Newsstand), 310/659-3110. 8818 Sunset Blvd., West Hollywood, 90049. Hours: M-Su 9AM to midnight.
Bookstar, 100 N. La Cienega, Los Angeles.
Bookstar, 12136 Ventura Blvd., Studio City.
Daily Planet News, 5931 1/2 Franklin Avenue, Hollywood.
Encino Newsstand, 16720 Ventura Blvd., Encino.
Melrose News, 647 N. Martel, just south of Melrose, between La Brea and Fairfax.
L.A. Int'l News, 310 Pacific Coast Highway, Hermosa Beach.
L.A. Int'l News, 3127 Lincoln, Santa Monica.
Laurel Park Newsstand, 4346 Laurel Canyon Blvd. at Moorpark.
National News, Sepulveda and National, West Los Angeles.
Newsroom Cafe, 310/319-9100. 530 Wilshire Blvd., Santa Monica. Great reading material. Coffee drinks. Many celebrities come here.
Newsroom Cafe, Second Location, (310) 652-4444. 120 N. Robertson, Beverly Hills.
Newsstand Etc. #2, 2726 Main Street, Santa Monica.
Porter Ranch News, 18743 Devonshire in Porter Ranch.
Robertson Newsstand, 1414 Robertson Blvd. at Pico, 24 hours a day.
Samuel French Bookshop, 7623 Sunset Blvd., Hollywood between La Brea & Fairfax.
Samuel French Bookshop, 11963 Ventura Blvd., Studio City.
Sherman Oaks Newsstand, Ventura Blvd. at Van Nuys Blvd.
Studio City Newsstand, 12133 Ventura Blvd., Studio City.
What's News, 21900 Ventura Blvd., Woodland Hills.
Woodland Hills News, 19714 Ventura Blvd., Woodland Hills.
World Book and News, (323) 465-4352. 1652 N. Cahuenga, just south of Hollywood Blvd., Hollywood. 24 hours a day.
Worldwide News and Books, 1101 Westwood Blvd., West Los Angeles.

BOOKSTORES, LIBRARIES AND VIDEO RENTAL STORES

• **We are changing every second of our lives.** All knowledge gained is growth, even when some of the knowledge is rejected as not being valid. Just the act of making the choices of what is good for us is molding our unique selves. Below are a few books I have found to be valuable. There are so many books, I am just scratching the surface. Yes, more effort, energy and action to take!

• **Reading is an important tool for an acting career.** In *Dreams into Action,* Milton Katselas tells how reading can enhance your career. He gives exercises on how to improve your reading. I highly recommend this book from this respected director and teacher.

• **Sandra Bullock** when asked by *Vanity Fair* what book was on her reading table said, "*The Greatest Salesman in the World,* by Og Mandino. It was given to me by Matthew McConaughey on the set of *A Time To Kill.* It's really special."

• **John Singleton**, when living in South Central L.A., would catch the bus to Hollywood to go to the movies. "I'd hang out, spending hours in Larry Edmunds and Samuel French bookstores, read literature, wonder if I could ever be a part of the movie making environment."

• THEATRICAL BOOKSTORES

These stores are very important to your career. Besides all the plays, they have many reference books, including Variety's Who's Who In Show Business, seminar books such as How To Get An Agent, How To Publicize Yourself and videotapes on How To Make It In Show Business. Give yourself a treat and spend a few hours there getting acquainted with all the information that is available. Have fun, they don't mind. You can order by mail from any of these stores.

Samuel French's Theatre & Film Bookshop, 323/876-0570. 7623 Sunset Blvd., Hollywood, 90046. M-F 10-6, Sa 10-5. Second location: 818/762-0535. 11963 Ventura Blvd., Studio City, 91604 (1 block east of Laurel Canyon.) M-F 10-9, Sa 10-6, Su 12-5.

Larry Edmund's Theatrical Book Shop, 323/463-3273. 6644 Hollywood Blvd., Hollywood, 90028. M-Sa 10-6.

Performing Arts Books 818/703-7311. Outside Los Angeles County, 800/900-3949. 21530 Sherman Way, Canoga Park, 91303. M-F 11-7; Sat 11-5.

Elliot Katt's Theatrical Book Store, 310/652-5178. 8568 Melrose, L. A., 90069. M-F 11-5:30, Sa 11-4.

• BOOKSTORES

Book Soup (Bookstore and Newsstand), 310/659-3110. 8818 Sunset Blvd., West Hollywood, 90069. Everyday 9AM-12 midnight.

Bookstar, 310/289-1734. 100 N. La Cienega Blvd., across from Beverly Center. 9-11 Su-Th, 9-12 F, Sa.

Bookstar, 818/505-9528. 12136 Ventura Blvd., Studio City.

Bodhi Tree, 310/659-1733. 8585 Melrose Ave., West Hollywood, 90069. A spiritual bookstore. New and used books. 10-7 everyday.

Brentano's Book Store, 310/785-0204. In the Century City Mall, right next to the movie theaters. 10-10 Su-Th, 10-12 F, Sa.

Cosmopolitan Book Shop, 323/938-7119. 7017 Melrose Ave., Hollywood, 90038. M-Su 11-6. A wonderful used-book and magazine store. They will go to great lengths to find the publication you need.

Crown Books and **Super Crown Books**. Many locations. Most stores open M-Sa 10-9, Su 11-5. Discount prices on all books.

Heritage Books, 310/659-3674. 8540 Melrose Ave., West Hollywood. A special place.

La Cite, French Bookstore, 310/475-0658. 2306 Westwood Blvd., Los Angeles.

Psychic Eye Book Store, 818/906-8263. 13435 Ventura Blvd., Sherman Oaks. M-Sa 10-10, Su 11-8. New Age, metaphysical, candles, incense and crystals.

VIDEO TAPE RENTAL STORES

These are stores that specialize in unusual videos, including classic movies and old television shows.

The Continental Shop, all things British, 310/453-8655. 1619 Wilshire Blvd., Santa Monica.

Eddie Brandt's Saturday Matinee Video, 818/506-4242. 5006 Vineland Ave., North Hollywood, 91601. Tu-F 1-6, Sa 8:30-5, closed Su, M. Free catalogue, $2 by mail. 44,000 titles, from episodic TV *77 Sunset Strip* to Japanese sex epics *Notorious Concubine.*

Now Playing Video, 310/306-3336. 4718 ½ Admiralty Way, Marina del Rey. Old classic, $2 for five days. New foreign or domestic release, $3 for two weekdays, $3.50 for a weekend. The staff can really help you pick a winning selection.

Odyssey Video, 818/769-2000. 4810 Vineland Ave., North Hollywood, 91606. M-Su 9AM-12 midnight. More than 25,000 movies to choose from. Tu & Th, 99 cents each. Hong Kong section which offers karate action flicks normally available only in Asia.

Ross Hunt Productions, 818/763-6045. 12240 Moorpark, Studio City, 91604. M-F 10-7, Sa 10-3.

Rocket Video, 323/965-1100. 726 N. La Brea Ave., Los Angeles, 90038. 11-10 Su-Th, 11-11 F-Sa. Will find films by request. Huge foreign section.

Tower Video, 310/657-3344. 8844 W. Sunset Blvd., West Hollywood, 90069. Silents, B and C titles, cult, foreign and hard-to-find films.

Video Hut, 323/661-4680. 1864 N. Vermont Ave., Los Angeles, 90027. 10-11 Su-Th, 10-12 F-Sa. Also Asian films and will find special requests.

Video Journeys, 323/663-5857. 2730 Griffith Park Blvd., Los Angeles, 90027. 10-10 everyday. Library of 14,000 movies, 1,000 foreign films, and television series collections, documentaries.

Video West, 818/760-0096. 11376 Ventura Blvd., Studio City, 91604. Also 310/659-5762. 805 Larrabee Street, West Hollywood, 90069. 10-12 everyday. My favorite. These video stores are the best, bargain days Tu, W, Th, $1.29 a tape. Have them give you a tour of the store—they've got classics, independents, foreign, comedies, stand-up comics. Just about anything you need to research. Fantastic!

Vidiots, 310/392-8508. 302 Pico Blvd., Santa Monica. Eclectic offerings at this alternative-video store. Large TV selection.

Websites: B-Movie Theater, www.b-movie.com. Critics' Choice Video, 800/367-7765, www.vcatalogccvideo.com. Facets Video, 800/331-6197. Home Film Festival, 800/367-7765, www.homefilmfestival.com. Movies Unlimited, 800/466-8437, www.moviesunlimited.com. Reel.com. www.reel.com.

LIBRARIES

Academy of Motion Picture Arts & Sciences, 310/247-3020. 333 S. La Cienega Blvd., Beverly Hills, 90211. Closed Wednesday, open other weekdays, 10-5:30. Scripts. You can also look up actor's agents.

Beverly Hills Library, 310/288-2220. 444 N. Rexford Drive, Beverly Hills, 90210. 10-9 M-Th, 10-6 F-Sa, 12-5 Su.

Brand Library, 818/548-2051. 1601 West Mountain, Glendale 91201-1209, located in Brand Park, at the top of Grandview Ave. Tu 1-9, W 1-6, Th 1-9, F-Sa 1-5. A very valuable source for music and art books, records, tapes, and over 4,000 CD's.

Burbank Central Library, 818/238-5600. 110 N. Glenoaks Blvd., Burbank, 91502. Scripts for use in the library.

Career Transition for Dancers, Career Resource Library, 323/549-6660. SAG Building, 5757 Wilshire Blvd., Los Angeles, on the 8th Floor. Hours vary; call for appointment to use the library or computer.

Glendale Public Library, 818/548-2040. 222 E. Harvard Street, Glendale, 91205. Information from Kelley Blue Book for prices on new and used cars.

Los Angeles Central Library, 213/228-7000. 630 W. 5th St., between Flower St. and Grand Ave., downtown L.A. Largest public library on the west coast. Open every day; call for hours.

Los Angeles City Library, Goldwyn Hollywood Branch, 323/467-1821. 1623 Ivar Street, Hollywood, 90028. M-Th 10-8, F-Sa 10-6, Su 1-5. All aspects of the industry including scripts and books on acting. *Free Money for People in the Arts* is one of their most popular books on grants, loans, money for film and video projects.

Los Angeles County Library, Culver City Branch, 310/559-1676. 4975 Overland Ave., Culver City, 90230. M-Th 10-8, F 10-6, Sa 10-5.

Los Angeles Public Library, Fairfax Branch, 323/936-6191. 161 S. Gardner St., Los Angeles, 90036. M-Tu 12:30-8, W-Th 12:30-5:30, F-Sa 10-5:30.

North Hollywood Library, 818/766-7185. 5211 Tujunga Ave., North Hollywood, 91601. Large selection of plays; also books on acting.

Santa Monica Public Library, 310/458-8600. 1343 Sixth Street, Santa Monica, 90401.

Pasadena Public Library, 626/744-4052. 285 E. Walnut Ave., Pasadena, 91101.

MAKING A LIVING

• **An actor must have financial backing.** If you don't have a trust fund, supporting parents, spouse or angel, then you'll have to provide it yourself. Your "day job" will give you the cash flow to support you and your career. Like any other person in business, career expenses will always be a part of your life. At some point, the money you earn acting will be used to live on and to reinvest in your career. Most actors end up earning money in many different aspects of show business, adding hyphens to their names: directors, producers, writers, teachers, dialogue and acting coaches.

• **Some other jobs actors have had**: Jenna Elfman, clothing manufacturer. She put rhinestones on jeans and vests. Julianna Margulies: when people died, she would go in and pack up their belongings. Thomas Gibson worked in a bank vault, bagging coins. Tom Hanks, hotel bellboy (carried bags for Cher). Quentin Tarantino, video rental store. Ray Romano, washed trucks. Lucy Lawless, gold mining company, sawed rocks in half. Jack Scalia, construction. Grace Jones, director's assistant. Ellen Barkin, waitress in Greenwich Village. Dom DeLuise, baby photographer. Elayne Boosler, waitress. Robert Duvall, post office. Meg Ryan, grocery checker. Harry Belafonte, assistant janitor. Steve Martin, at Disneyland selling guides, then the Bird Cage Theater at Knotts Berry Farm, learning balloon tricks and the banjo. Sidney Poitier, dishwasher. Mary Steenburgen waitressed in New York for five years. Tuesday Knight, receptionist. Geena Davis, waitress. Danny DeVito, hair dresser Mr. Dan. Michael Caine, donut maker. Bob Saget, deli clerk (he financed his student films in college from his earnings). Warren Beatty, brick layer's helper. Bill Cosby, shoe salesman. Sean Connery polished coffins.

• **Gretchen Mol**, in 1996, was working as a coatcheck girl at a restaurant named Michael's in New York—a lot of agents dine there. She says, "One day an agent asked for my picture and resume." She was cast in Woody Allen's comedy, *Celebrity,* and hasn't stopped working.

• **Billy Bob Thornton arrived in Los Angeles struggling and broke.** He took a job as a waiter. First night on the job, as he worked a Beverly Hills banquet, director Billy Wilder, a many time Oscar-winner, walked up to him and said, "So you wanna be an actor?" Before Billy Bob could answer, the man said, "Look, I hate to disillusion you. You don't have the looks for a leading man. And I don't know if you even have the makings to be a character actor. So here's my advice. Learn to write. Then write your own movie—and write yourself a good part in it." Years later, after Billy Bob had learned to write, he wrote *Sling Blade* and was nominated for best actor and won the Oscar for best writer.

• **Ethan Erickson** worked at West Hollywood's Le Montrose. He worked his way from bellman to desk clerk. While on the desk, he was spotted by a casting director. Erickson is now in New York, starring on daytime's *Guiding Light.*

• **Jeremy Gursey, at 19, when working at a coffeehouse** in Studio City, noticed the lines for iceblended mochas. He decided to create his own version and take it to film and television sets. He saved $100 from three paychecks to buy a commercial blender and an ice chest. He said, "I figured if all else fails, at least I'll be able to whip up some damn good margaritas. At the time, I was charging $2 by the cup and I remember returning home with a fat stack of ones." One night, when watching *Seinfeld,* he scanned the credits for the line producer, called and worked his way in. We loved him; he had somehow memorized all of our favorite blends. He would bring mine to the set because most of the time I couldn't get away. Everyone loved him. Last time I saw him, at age 24, he figured his company, Mocha Kiss, had prepared more than 75,000 coffee drinks on about 100 films and TV shows. His assets now include thousands of dollars worth of large-scale commercial cappuccino machines, a van and his own office. He and four employees shuttle between 12 and 20 productions a week. What would he really like to do? "Direct." He has several film ideas percolating.

• **Marla Gibb** *("227")* **continued her airline job** on the weekends for the first three years she was a regular on *The Jeffersons.* The producers asked her to give it up. She said, "Fine, tell me how much my raise is." They gave her a healthy raise and a long-term contract. She has had a lot of experience in the ups and downs of this business—she kept her day job as long as possible.

• **Michael Landon was working at a gas station** across the street from Warner Bros. Studios when an executive suggested he join the Warner's Acting School. The class led to B-movies, which led to his breakthrough role in *I Was A Teenage Werewolf,* which led to *Bonanza,* then directing, producing, and writing *Little House On The Prairie, Highway to Heaven* and many other television projects.

• **Michael Jeter,** (*Evening Shade)* played Carnegie Hall. Three years before, he worked as a legal secretary just three blocks away.

• **While job researching,** a good exercise is to write down everything you love to do and see if you can possibly put them together in a job you would like. Another theory holds that you should pick something you *do not* like to do. The reasoning is, if you're unhappy with your job, you'll pursue your acting career with even more persistence. For myself, I try to be happy in everything I do. When you are on the job, you want to shine, to be the best at what you are doing. This will increase your chances to make more money, but most of all, you will be a champion at everything you do. This will raise your self-confidence and self-esteem; you will be contributing to a better work place. Striving to be the best that you can be is a valuable acting tool. You can train for it every day.

• **Keep your priorities straight.** If you are an actor, you need to be acting somewhere at all times. Pick a job that won't drain you physically or emotionally. It should give you some flexibility for auditions and the ability to take off for a few days if you land that one, two or three-day job. Generally, stage actors look for day jobs, and film and television actors look for night and weekend jobs.

• **It is in your best interest** to choose a job that is connected to show business or one that is in an area of town where people in the business will likely show up. There is the slim possibility that you will be discovered on your job—it happens all the time. At least you will make friends who are connected and interested in the biz.

• **Learn the skill of saving money** when you are working your "day job." An actor's paychecks can be few and far between. If you save your acting money and live fairly frugally, you can actually support yourself working relatively few days a year. *See Unions, pages 123-125 for pay scales.* Inexperienced actors will make a major purchase when they receive their checks for six week's work on a film, then have to scrounge next month's rent. We never know when our next acting job will be. Knowing how to manage money is one of the keys to an actor's success.

• **Here are some ideas for jobs** that have worked very well for people I know. Some of these jobs take research to find out where to apply for them.

- Fit Model. *(See page 184.)*
- A substitute teacher can make a good living/hours are great for our business.
- The airlines offer flexible hours, great benefits, trips to New York for auditions.
- Work in restaurants or upscale grocery stores (Whole Foods, Pavilions, Gelsons, Trader Joes, Ralphs) in Beverly Hills, Brentwood, Encino, Malibu, Santa Monica, Pacific Palisades, Studio City, West Hollywood or West Los Angeles.
- An actress I know works 20 hours a week, for 1-800-DENTIST, making $15 per hour. She can switch hours for her interviews.
- One of my students does Mystery Shopping, earning about $200 a month.
- A friend does "acting as if he was a patient" for doctor's tests.
- A dog walking and grooming company is a good way to be your own boss.
- Traffic school teachers work on weekends and make $100 a day, a good way to work on selling yourself to people, practice speaking and comedy.
- Work as a messenger or delivering food to offices and studios; landscaping or taking care of office plants; a mail clerk in a big theatrical agency; a secretary at a public relations firm; a limousine driver or a runner in an entertainment attorney's office.
- Auditions for the many stage shows at our local amusement parks are advertised in the trade papers.
- Many temporary agencies furnish the studios with office workers.
- Nude dancing, go to the place with a male friend, watch to see if you can do it.
- People who know computers can get jobs at night inputting information. The hourly rate is usually around $15.
- Construction.
- A teller at a Beverly Hills bank.
- Extra work. *(See page 190.)*

* **Dan Cortes (*Suddenly Susan*) began his show biz career** as a production assistant at MTV. He was going to be let go in a month due to cutbacks. He wrote a treatment, mailed a copy of it to himself and left it

sealed, for the postmark date. Then he pitched the concept for a sports show with him as the host. They said they weren't interested but in two weeks time they had developed the same show he pitched. The last day of his employment they were auditioning 15 guys for the host. One guy didn't show up on time, so they asked Dan to hop up on stage to hold the spot for the guy. Dan auditioned along with everyone else until the guy showed up. Two days later the producer called and offered Dan the job. I asked him, why didn't you say I was the one who conceived it? He said, "I was grateful to get the job and knew they wouldn't give me a piece of it. If they had gone with another host and been a hit, eventually I could have gone to court with the treatment I had presented." Landing the job of the host was his opening into becoming known as a personality.

• **Andi Matheny**, one of the members of my theatre company, works in the Universal Studio Wild West Stunt Show. They have two casts of five, and five or six alternates for each role. They trained her and she rehearsed for a month. The auditions are advertised in the trade papers. As third and fourth alternate last year, she made $22,000. You can always be available to take auditions because an alternate will fill in for you.

• **Mel Harris** made $85,000 in 1985 on the $100,000 Pyramid. She used the money to pay bills and finance her career. Five short years later, in her third year on *thirtysomething*, she was on the $100,000 Pyramid as a guest celebrity. So if you like game shows and are good at them, give it a try. They sometimes advertise for contestants in *Back Stage West/Drama-Logue, Daily News* and *Los Angeles Times.*

• **Craig Zisk,** a producer and director of *The Single Guy,* began his show business career as a production assistant (PA) on *Family Ties* during the summer of his junior year in college. After graduating, he held many different jobs. In 1995, he became the supervising producer on *The Single Guy.* After directing several shows in the first season, he became full-time director in the second season. He and Brad Hall, the creator of *The Single Guy,* met working on *Family Ties.* This is how networking friendships are made in this business. Always do a good job, no matter what that job is; you will be remembered.

• **Catering, bartending, waiting, valet parking** and limousine driving jobs allow you the opportunity of seeing how successful people party. The hours are flexible and the pay is good. Like most jobs, you have to prove yourself in order to get the best parties and hours; a good place to work on your personality skills. Work for the companies that cater celebrity show biz parties. Read the gossip columns in the *Daily Variety* and *Hollywood Reporter* trade papers; they often mention who caters the parties and parks the cars.

• **Many actors do audience recruiting** for movie screenings and marketing research for studios. *(See Resources)*

Resources

Hiring On The Internet: JOBTRACK: Computer proficiency, www.jobtrak.com.
The Working Actors Guide (WAG) has many listings of where to find jobs for actors in Los Angeles. Order through Samuel French Bookstores 323/876-0570 or 818/762-0535.
N.R.G., 213/228-1380. 5900 Wilshire Blvd. L.A. 90036. Audience recruiting.
Talent Search, 1-800-A-Job-Now, ext. 1416. Audience recruiting.
TV Audience Recruiting, 818/386-6605 Ext. 53.
Back Stage West, as well as the other trades, has weekly listings.

CATERERS

Along Came Mary, 323/931-9082.
Ambrosia Caterers, (310) 453-7007.
Craig's Crew, (323) 257-1920.
Scotty's Bartending & Waitress Service, (818) 247-9968.

PARKING SERVICES

Chuck's, (818) 788-4300 (The best).
Valet Girls, (310) 457-6657.

GENERAL AGENCIES

Friedman Personnel Agency, 310/550-1002. 9000 Sunset Blvd., #1000, Los Angeles, 90069. Jobs in the industry, fees paid by employer.
The Job Factory, 310/475-9521. 1744 Westwood Blvd., Los Angeles, 90024. Unusual jobs and flexible hours. They've been helping actors for 25 years.
Our Gang Agency, 323/653-4381. 825 N. Fairfax Ave., Los Angeles, 90046
Temps On Time, 818/845-3030. 403 E. Palm, Burbank, 91501.
Transcription Zone, 818/848-0575. www.transcripts.net. They transcribe video footage into scripts. If you are fast on the computer, this might be a good place to apply. 24 hours a day.
USC School Of Medicine, Dept. of Medical Education, 1975 Zonal Ave. KAM 200, Los Angeles, 90033. Actors portray actual patients to help train medical students. Strong improv skills a must. All ages, all types. Send picture and resume to Attn: Angela Atencio.
Hollywood Creative Directory: free job board: www.hcdonline.com.

BOOKS

Development Girl by Hadley Davis.
How to Be a Star at Work by Robert E. Kelley.
Survival Jobs by Deborah Jacobson.

INCOME TAXES AND ACCOUNTANTS

Since *Acting Is Everything*, many expenses you have are tax deductible. You don't necessarily have to be earning money acting in order to deduct expenses. A tax specialist will determine exactly what is right for you.

• **When you start filing your income taxes** as a full or part time actor, seek an Entertainment Accountant. They will be aware of all the current deductions. Your part is to save receipts and to mark everything you do in your appointment book. Should you ever be audited, you will need to justify every expense.

• **Jerry Zamarin, entertainment tax accountant**, financial consultant and finance manager, answers some income tax questions.

Q: Why should an actor hire an accountant to do income taxes?

- **The laws are very complicated** and change every day of the year. There are specific areas of deductibility for actors that are unique and an accountant has to be knowledgeable about them and must stay current on the changes in the law. In my experience, most actors are not knowledgeable about this and basically give the government excessive money in taxes every year.

- **In general, an actor can deduct anything** that has relevance to his career, the normal deductions relating to such things as union dues, use of their car for business purposes, subscriptions and books relative to their profession, going to theaters and movies where they can basically research current trends in acting, business travel, lessons as far as becoming an actor and numerous other specific items related to their unique career.

Q: Can you start deducting these expenses before you are earning money as an actor?

- **This is an area that is constantly changing** under the law. If the person is dedicated and exercising their efforts as an actor even though they are not earning money at this time, they can develop what is called business losses which they can utilize in one of the following ways: They can deduct those losses during the first two years of their profession and then accumulate any losses after that until they earn money. Generally this is not advisable because if they are not earning money the first two years the losses are not that beneficial.

- **I would recommend generally,** in the case of an actor whose career is accelerating, that they don't immediately utilize their beginning years' losses until they start to make better money because each deduction will create bigger tax savings. As they earn more money, they get into higher brackets. You list the losses on the year you spent the money but you put them into a reserve account that you can accumulate for future benefit. When you have future independent acting income, you can then extract those past losses and deduct them from your future income. It is necessary to list them in the year you spend the money, otherwise they are forever lost.

Q: How do you choose an accountant?

- **Usually clients pick an accountant on a friend's recommendation.** Then they decide to go with the accountant because they tell good jokes, have gone to the same college or for other wrong reasons. When actors are having a hard time deciding, I suggest they ask their potential accountant for three recommendations from current clients, three from former clients and the accountant's banker.

Q: How much does it cost to have your income tax done?

- **Accountants all have their own fees** based on the work involved. Minimum for a new client is $250; last year my average client paid around $280. When actors start taking business deductions, their returns are no longer simple. Many new actors go to a general accounting firm like H&R Block and pay a smaller fee because generally their associates are not as qualified as an independent accountant.

• **It is a joyous day when your income tax return says occupation: actor.** It is a time to take a moment and reflect on where you have come from, to acknowledge that some of your dreams are coming true. My return says occupation: actress/acting coach/producer/author; it has expanded over the years.

• **At tax time, the trades run articles** about actors' taxes and ads for accountants.

• **Some tax filing categories:** Advertising and publicity, pictues, resumes, audio/video tapes, Academy Players Guide, Castnet; commissions paid; professional fees, tax preparer, attorney, bank charges; office supplies and postage, pens, pencils, paper, business cards, postage; dues and initiation fees, unions, theatre groups; trade publications, including Breakdown Services Casting Directors; supplies for research, plays, films, scripts; career enrichment, workshops, classes, private coaching, video rentals, movies; wardrobe and makeup; telephone, long distance calls; equipment; auto, insurance, license, parking, gas, oil, repairs; business meals; business gifts, $25 and less.

• *Working Actor's Guide* has listings for accountants, deductions and business managers.

Resources

Feinstein & Berson: Scott Feinstein, 818/981-3115. 16133 Ventura Blvd., #800, Encino, 91436. CPA and Business Manager, has a strong client list consisting almost exclusively of SAG, AFTRA, IATSE and DGA members.

Pamela Price, 323-663-5727. 4527 Ambrose Ave., L.A. 90027. She used to be an actress and specializes in people who are in the entertainment business.

Scott Rubenstein, E.A., (323) 658-5271. 8350 Melrose Ave., Suite 204, L.A., 90069. Tax consultant. Scott has given seminars for SAG. He has many clients in the biz. Photographer Alan Weissman recommends him.

VITA, Volunteer Income Tax Assistance Program. M-F 9:30 to 3:30. From February through April 15. Union members help fellow union members with their taxes. They hold classes in January for those who wish to be Tax Assistors. If you pass the test, you are qualified to help other members prepare their own taxes. Every paid up SAG or AFTRA member can get this free help.

California State Board of Accountancy, 916/263-3680. You can check to see if the business manager or accountant you are considering is licensed and in good standing.

Working Actor's Guide (WAG), available at theatrical bookstores, lists many well known accountants.

Changing Your Name

• **There are two reasons to change your name.** One, you don't like it and feel it doesn't suit you. Two, your name is already taken in SAG (Rule 15). I stayed with Kerr, one of my married names, because it fit, I liked it and my children are named Kerr. A numerologist once told me I would have more luck if I added an E as a middle initial or spelled my name Judie. I tried to do it, but couldn't; it didn't feel like me. I like my name so I will have to make more of my own luck. Listen to all opinions and then make your own decisions based on what fits you. Part of developing self-awareness is following your own instincts; they are there to guide you.

• **James Bumgardner** was told by Warner Bros. to cut the bum off, thus James Gardner.

• **A friend of mine, viewed as a success** by everyone who knows her, was broke, though her creativity is extraordinary. She was told by her astrologer that the numbers in her name were very spiritual but not for success in material matters. The astrologer advised her to add an A as a middle initial to her name. She did so on all of her bank accounts and in six months the money started rolling in. She had the best year financially, last year, that she has ever had.

• **If you must change your name** because of SAG, then pick a name that means something to you or your family. I would consult a numerologist with a list of possible names you could live with and see what numbers may be the luckiest. Look for numerologists at psychic fairs and the Bodhi Tree Bookstore's bulletin board. (*See page 318.*) As with anything else, be cautious. Consultants will each have their own opinion based on their personal studies. It wouldn't hurt to get two opinions on this important matter. After you have two or three possible names, have a SAG member call the union for you and check to see if any of the names are available. You can check online at www.sag.com. You can also go to the Academy Players Directory office and check their books. (*See page 306.*) Not every actor is listed, but probably 80% of them are.

• **Jay Bernstein, personal manager, writer and producer**, taught a course called *Stardom, the Management of, the Public Relations for, and the Survival and Maintenance In.*

> • **A limousine driver/actor once asked me,** "Should I change my name? I've been worried about this now for a year—its Alexander Propapalis." I told him to change his name, because no one should have to get through your name to get to your talent. If no one is going to remember your name, they're not going to run down and say we have to get... They're just going to cut you.

• **Salma Hayek says ten years ago Hollywood producers shunned her** because of her nationality. "When I first started, they said, 'Just don't say you're Mexican. With your name and your looks you can pass for Lebanese. Work on your accent so that it sounds more Midddle Eastern.'" She refused. "I was born and raised in Mexico, I'm Mexican."

• **Michael Keaton's** real name is Michael Douglas. Of course, it was already taken. British actor James Stewart had to change his name to Stewart Granger.

• **Goldie Hawn** at age 20 worked on her first movie. The producer said, "Change your name, you sound like a stripper." Goldie said no!

• **Actress Samantha Harper** had to change her name from Harriet Harper. There was another actress in SAG with that name. She chose the name Samantha, because her fiancee at the time said he wanted to name a daughter Samantha. He said, "When we have a daughter we can name her after you." The minute she tried the name her heart sang and she knew it was for her.

• **Bill Macy** (*Maude)* had to change his name from William Garber and was very unhappy about that. He took his middle name for a last name. Later, William H. Macy had to add an initial in order to keep his name intact.

• **Joel M. Barkow from** SAG, wrote in the SAG newsletter about name changes on Social Security cards.

- **Applicants who have legitimate business needs** for using assumed names (such as performers using stage names) are allowed to request additional cards. Apart from filling out an SS-5 form, available at all Social Security offices, you merely need to submit documents at the time of application that show use of the old name and current use of your stage name. A driver's license or similar I.D. would suffice for the former, while the latter can be evinced from a signed contract or pay stub using the assumed name.

- **Since the employer submits only your Social Security number**—and not your name—you can wait to apply for the second card until you receive the initial pay check stub before filling out the necessary application. However, the transfer must be taken care of prior to tax time, when the IRS begins checking names against Social Security numbers. The second card is for ID purposes only—it is not a legal document and does not have the same effect as a legal name change.

• **In 1998,** SAG **approved changes** to its previously strictly enforced Rule 15. They are out of the business of being the final arbiter of name disputes. SAG officials say they will continue to "urge membership applicants not to join SAG with a professional name that duplicates or can cause confusion with that of an existing member. The Guild wishes it to be known that it shall not be legally liable or responsible if an applicant or member chooses to use a professional name that may cause confusion."

Resources

Legal Name Change, Los Angeles County, 213/974-5299. Call this line for recorded complete information of how to change your name legally. The cost is $192, plus a publication fee of $95.

Lying About Your Age

• **Honesty is always the best policy!** *However,* if you are 30 and look 22 and you are reading for a part that is 22, and *if* you are asked how old you are, give the age the part calls for. You can only do this if you are very comfortable with it. It is hard for a casting director to bring you in to meet the director and producer for a 22-year-old role if they know you are 30. Remember, you will be laughed at if you look 30 and claim to play 20 to 30. You must judge your age according to how those in-the-know in the industry perceive you.

• **On the other hand**, one of the stars I coach has been adding a few years to her real age because she's pursuing roles in an older category, where she has more casting potential.

• **It is usually best, around this issue, to do what your agent wants** you to do. They will be selling you at a certain age. When you are hired, someone in the production office will end up knowing your age because of the ruling that you must show your driver's license, passport, or birth certificate to prove your right to work. SAG has been trying to get this rule overturned.

• **Theatrical agent Terry Lichtman advises:**

- **I don't recommend lying**; I just recommend side-stepping the question because once you tell someone the age you are, they always think of you as that age.

• **Stuart K. Robinson, noted commercial acting teacher,** acting teacher, successful actor and director highly recommends that you never tell your age. He believes that if you are asked outright, "How old are you?" which is against the law, that you avoid answering. I love watching Stuart teach; he has the perfect body language and verbal language to avoid telling his age. Such as, "I don't tell my age." or "It is a long tradition in my family, we never tell our age." or "You tell me, do you think I look the right age to play this part?" or "Don't you agree, I'm in the age range to play this part?" or "I believe I look the age to play this part. If you disagree, I'm out of here." Stuart is a master at pulling this off with style.

• **I am one to always blurt out my age.** You really have to always play it as you see it. We can change our minds on how we see things. If you decide not to tell your age then you will have to keep it a secret from most everyone. Angelina Jolie has been pulling off younger for years. One of my students graduated from UCLA with her younger brother. My student was 25 and Angelina was still selling 22. Every article about her has a slightly different age. I'm not saying she isn't what she says she is, but she may not be.

• **There is no denying the fact, the younger you play** the more opportunities you will have to work. This will not change, so each of us has to make peace with this issue. There is no use in trying to change the business; you can only change yourself, your thinking, your age.

• **In legal terms, according to SAG,** a performer should never be asked their age or ethnicity. The only exception is if the producer needs to know whether or not the performer is a minor or if the actor speaks a certain language.

SECTION SIX

STYLE, IMAGE AND WARDROBE FOR ACTORS AND ACTRESSES

• **Angela Lansbury**, film, stage and television star, said, "I made peace with myself early and decided I was going to be a rare bird." She understood her style and image and capitalized on it. She started acting at age 16 and made all the transitions, carrying her image with her.

• **Much of who we are as actors** is how we look, what we wear, how we present ourselves. Some of us are born or raised with a sense of style and taste; others develop it. You must look successful. If you are not naturally talented in this area, you will have to learn how to dress yourself to present the image that you choose to project. You can cultivate taste and create your own *look.* Read books, consult a friend whose taste you like. Try different styles; decide how you want to uniquely present yourself. Always practice looking your best, whether your style is beach dude or conservative homemaker.

• **When you consider the thought** and money that go into film wardrobes, you realize how important dressing is. Costume designers receive Academy Awards. When you are working on a show, see what tips you can pick up from the wardrobe design people. When I was doing my first film on location in Oregon, Donfeld (nominated for an Academy Award for *Prizzi's Honor)* took me shopping to show me what styles would be good for me. I still use the information I learned that day; basic rules don't change.

• ***Felicity* wardrobe designs**, from an article in the *Los Angeles Times* Fashion Section interviewing costume designer Linda Serijan-Fasmer.

- **Felicity, a bit of a wallflower, isn't supposed to be too sexy** or adorable looking. But Keri Russell looked gorgeous in almost everything we tried on her. Body-conscious clothes showed off her enviable size 0 figure, so it became apparent that not only her legs, but also her waist would have to be off-limits. She's an extra small so we buy mediums. Everything is oversized. Flattering colors lit up her face, which meant that colors had to be restrained—navy, rust, olive, burgundy. Felicity's closet revolves around pants (Levi's 501s are her favorite, followed by Army surplus or Abercrombie & Fitch khakis and other straight-legged pants), cotton shirts and dozens and dozens of sweaters—textured, nubby cardigans, turtlenecks and crew necks in patterns and earth-colored solids.
- **We have every DKNY turtleneck made.** Man-style shirts from stores such as the Gap, Banana Republic and Nordstrom are usually not tucked in. Every single one is recut to look somewhere between fitted and baggy, but never with darts. Darts are too sexy. Her shoes are strictly utilitarian, either Converse navy sneakers or Birkenstock boots or sandals.
- **Keri is also a stickler for character consistency.** She won't wear anything with stretch or sheen. She doesn't like big, groovy collars. She won't wear anything in her hair, and she won't paint her nails. I bought her a stainless steel Swiss Army watch, but she doesn't think it's right. It's like, too much.
- **Resident advisor, Noel Crane (Scott Foley) wears Big Star,** Lucky and Diesel jeans because they are most flattering to the rear end.

• **When I've taken style classes**, I studied pictures of styles that were flattering to me and learned what types of clothing suited me best. I have hired stylists to go shopping with me to teach me the clothing style and color foundations I needed to build my wardrobe. It has been a great help to me professionally to be able to present the exact picture of myself that was right for the occasion.

• **If your funds are limited**, go to resale stores, discount designer stores, department store sales and factory outlets. I have listed a few. There are also countless books available with their locations. When buying clothes, the fabric and fit are most important. Recently, a student of mine, because she didn't have money to buy clothes, never shopped. She had no idea what her size was, what current styles were up to date. You can educate yourself. Do lots of shopping and trying on, no buying; when you can afford to buy, you will know what and where to buy.

• **See Photography Section**, Pages 77 and 79, for clothes to wear on your shoot.

•**Maude Feil, costume designer, wardrobe specialist** and sometimes with partner, Geraldine Dirks of Closet Queens, specializes in working with actors and actresses just starting to set their own style or in changing their style.

- **I can put a man or woman together for about $1,000.** That includes my fee of $60 an hour. I know all the places downtown, I know where to get the look for less money. I work on commercials all the time and I'm used to staying within a budget. There are just certain wardrobe pieces you have to have. I work with all shapes, sizes and ages. If a client needs special hair and/or makeup styling, I bring in someone from one of the network shows I work on, to consult with them. That would be an extra cost of around $150.

- **I don't work with color charts myself**; I find it too confining. But many times a client will give me their book of colors and I work within those colors for them.

- **One of my clients called me recently because he wasn't happy** with the roles he had been auditioning for, strictly senators. He wanted a broader range. He has an abundance of white hair and a very tailored conservative East-coast look. I went through his closet, picked out some things he could use, got rid of some of the Brooks Bros. shirts. We added some soft t-shirts and softer clothes, and I advised a buzz cut for his hair. He is very pleased, has new pictures and now he is auditioning for and landing a wider variety of roles.

- **When I start working with someone, I get an idea of the look** they want to achieve, I pull magazine pictures, put them in a book. I'll look at their closet to see what they have. There is shopping, fittings, alterations, returns. I work with the client like I do when I am working for a director of a show.

• **Tom Baxter, Emmy-nominated wardrobe stylist, costume designer,** winner of the *Aldo Award* for "Most Influential Costumer in Fashion on Prime Time Television."

Q: What about audition clothes for the actor?

- **Let the dialogue in the script guide you.** For auditions, the actor should get the breakdown of the character from their agent and dress close to the person they are playing. For example:

- **Preppie, upwardly mobile, young male professional**: Go for the stereotype navy blue blazer, gray slacks, maybe a sweater vest with a tie and shirt, perhaps a crest on the blazer. A more casual look could be khaki pants, an oxford button-down shirt and a V-neck sweater. Visually, you need short to medium hair. If it says preppy and you have long hair, you might as well stay home, or wear a ponytail and tuck it in the back of your shirt.

- **A tough, over-the-hill broad**: If it's a comedy and the actress is busty, take advantage of that; a V-neck sweater and a pair of slacks with a big wide belt. She would be the girl sitting on a bar stool, 55 trying to look 35, with a cigarette hanging out of her mouth and a pink scarf tied around her neck. We did this exact look for an actress in *Pennies From Heaven.*

- **Upscale, trendy patron at an art museum**: For a woman 30-50, a suit would be nice; '40s gabardine styles obtained at resale or vintage stores. Guys in this setting can do it with a suit or khaki pants and a cotton blazer.

- **When you go thrift store shopping** for your audition clothes, you can tell if it is a good store if it is organized: if the suits are all together and sized; if the shirts are sized and by color, style or period.

- **Men 21-50 with these few items can do anything.** A black blazer (sport coat), a navy blazer, one suit, a pair of khaki, grey, navy, black and white dress slacks. A business look with the suit, a nautical look with the blazer and white slacks (just stick a crest on the blazer on the pocket.) Put the black blazer with the black slacks and you have a black suit. The khakis with the black blazer and you have nice sporty look. Gray pants with the blue blazer you've got a nice business or preppy look.

- **Women's looks vary with their age.** 18-30 is one look, 30-50 is another look, and after 55 another look. Women need a rayon suit with a skirt. For the money, rayon looks and hangs the best and seems to be the easiest to alter. Make sure the skirt is a color that matches the jacket. Substitute a pair of slacks to make it more casual. A short or long black stretch evening dress for a young girl going up for sex-pot or modeling parts. Jeans, sweater or chambray shirt and sneakers. A sweat shirt for a housewife that lives next door. Secretary in a law firm, don't go in without a suit; you can always take the jacket off and put it on the back of the chair. It is a nice piece of business and something a secretary would do, unless you sit at the front desk—then it would stay on the whole time. Secretary in the car rental or super market manager's office: A skirt or a nice pair of slacks and blouse and cardigan or sweater vest. A tough secretary would wear jeans and sweater.

• **Illeana Douglas** (*Action TV series, Message in a Bottle, Grace of My Heart*) says she buys her t-shirts and sweaters in the children's department; "They fit much better."

• **The colors you wear** will determine how people perceive you: whether you look vibrant, washed out, cool or hot. This is valuable information when you are dressing to read for a specific role.

• **Have an expert or professional do your colors.** Your color consultant will hold different shades of all colors next to your face to see what looks best on you. Some color systems put people into four categories: fall, winter, spring or summer. Then there are variations within each season. (I'm a "gentle summer"; my husband is a "vibrant winter.") The expert will make an individualized color chart that you carry with you when shopping. If you stick to your color chart, you will be able to wear everything in your wardrobe mixed and matched; all your clothes will go together. This information will enable you to be a wise shopper and help minimize your expenses. Having your colors done is a one time expense.

• **Know what your colors are** even when being photographed in B&W. You can help your professional makeup artist: When you sit in the makeup chair, describe what colors look best on you.

• **Jennifer Butler, owner of Through Nature's Beauty,** has a unique way of achieving color and style harmony for her clients. She has created a system of personalized design and color analysis that draws upon her 4,000 swatch color system.

Q: Why are colors important?

- **How many times have you looked in your closet** and said, "I have nothing to wear!" even though you have a closet full of clothes. When you walk into a meeting, is your unspoken communication saying, "I'm approachable" or "Leave me alone!"? Do people think you are overpowering when your biggest challenge is overcoming shyness?

- **What may be a power color for one person** could signal romance in another. You can see what a dilemma this could cause. And if you send out the wrong messages, you may well be puzzled by other people's responses to you.

- **Have you ever noticed how one day** everyone you see tells you how great you look while on another day, you don't even get noticed? If you choose to wear clothes that are reflective of your personality and physical characteristics, you will experience more and more of those, "Gee, you look great" days. In fact, not only will those who see you notice how well you look but you, too, will see and feel the difference.

- **Color Consultant, Jill Kirsh, says:**

  - **People think having their colors done can be very limiting,** that they can only wear a few colors, but what you see when you have your colors done is that everyone can wear every color. It is just finding the shade of the color that works best for you.

- **You can create different characters with the use of color.** When you have your colors done, you find out what colors make you look vibrant and alive, say for commercial auditions, but you also can create different effects for characters by using the wrong shade for you. What would you wear for a character that is out of step with the real world? For a trailer park resident? For a druggie? For a socialite? Homeless? Rich?

- **Tina Lynne, wardrobe stylist,** takes into account the color of your hair, eyes and skin though she doesn't adhere to a strict color palette. She believes everyone can wear certain shades of all colors.

Q: Let's say there was a new actor, a guy, who comes to town. All he has ever worn in his life are jeans and a t-shirts. He's 22-30, good looking. He needs a couple of good outfits for interviews. What would it cost him to be "styled" including your fee and the clothes?

- **He will need a dressy look, a GQ look.** There is a great store called the Men's Warehouse. You can get a nice knock-off Italian suit that will make him look like a million bucks. Another basic sport coat, two pairs of pants, four shirts, four ties and one or two pairs of shoes, a nice belt, and he will look absolutely fabulous. The cost for the clothes might be $500. The cost for my services would be from $50 to $150 an hour, depending on where we have to go. For men, I also find the Beverly Center is a great place because they have hip looking, very Hollywood looking clothes. You don't have to get the name brands, you just have to know what looks good on you.

Q: How about an actress who has moved to Los Angeles, 22 to 30, who will be auditioning and doesn't know her image. She's thin, a size 2 or 4, and will be playing leading ladies. How would you get her together for auditions?

- **This is where my psychology background comes in.** When a woman walks into an audition, she should be dressed for the part and comfortable with the type of person she's trying to project, I coach them on how to wear the clothes and project the image that they want to project. Depending on the build, the coloring and whether they have a hard or a soft look will determine whether we create a floral or a very simple kind of look.

- **Looking finished, put together, color coordinated** is probably one of the biggest keys in landing a role. Look at soap operas. When they decided to spend a great deal of money on the clothing, accessories, hair and sets, daytime TV changed forever, the ratings became huge.

Q: What kind of investment would an actress need to get them a *look* and how long would it take for you to do that for them?

- **If somebody's on a budget,** I take them through Neimans, through Saks Fifth Avenue so they can see what is available and what they like. That takes half an hour. Then I take them to a store that is reasonably priced and we match the look. You start with two skirts, two jackets, four tops, two pairs of shoes. one pants suit and two bags. You have one black dress. You can do this at a place like Ross or Loehmann's for $500, versus one Armani jacket which is $1000.

- **Lohmans is a great place to start** because they have the more expensive clothing at a quarter of the price and you can get some basic, fabulous clothes there. Then at the Beverly Center, Jones of New York and Tahari make some classy stuff that looks like Armani but is a quarter of the price. Marshalls and Ross's are also good. You have to take the time to go through everything.

• **Dino Calabrese, clothing designer** and wardrobe, hair and makeup stylist, gives the following hints for actors with limited funds for clothes.

- **No matter how much you spend,** if you don't have a good guideline you're wasting your money. Learn textures, colors and prints. Study reference books and high fashion magazines, preferably European, because most fashions come from Europe. What makes clothing really work, instead of just sort of work, is when there is an element of your personality reflected.

- **Thrift store shopping is great.** You can take a vest and cover it with old jewelry and you're very voguish. Vests are in; color and texture are in; denim is always good.

- **Both men and women** should own a pair of black slacks, a nice denim jacket, oversize so you can layer it. A pair of jeans—not just a pair with holes. Nice basic blazer whether it's oversized or not; rayon, not wool. Something in black is good and primary colors are good too. Combine colors, layer tank tops and t-shirts. Keep the same types of textures in your wardrobe; mix and match silks with lighter weight rayons or cottons.

- **A basic skirt** should be gabardine or a light weight fabric to wear with silk. Wear a t-shirt with the skirt and thick obi belt and you have a nice casual look. Long scarves are good; you can wear them around your neck or double them around your waist or layer them around your neck so it becomes like a cowl neck. You can do an Annie Hall look.

- **Everyone should have a white shirt**. Plain form fitting t-shirts can be worn under the shirt. Women need an A-line black dress. A pair of colored hose makes one outfit, belt it for another look, wear it as a tunic over a pair of bell-bottoms or pajama pants. A string of pearls works with a dress, sweater or t-shirt. Plain black boots with a medium heel to wear with skirts and pants are a necessity. Same with men—basic black boot; wear with tuxedo or jeans. Always keep shoes cleaned and shined and clothes pressed.

- **Take t-shirts**, skirts, jackets all in the same fabrics but different colors to mix and match. Use blue, green and yellow and tie it together with a multicolored belt and you look great but if the texture's off, it doesn't work.

Image Makers

Wardrobe consultants and image makers are listed in The Working Actor's Guide (WAG) and trade ads.

Creating Your Audition Package: Carolyne Barry has put together this one of a kind, eight session workshop (separate ones for men and women), guides each actor to determine the primary roles that they should be auditioning for, then creates the complete physical audition package of colors, wardrobe, hair and attitude for each of their personal roles. Guest speakers are commercial and theatrical casting directors, color and wardrobe expert, TV and film hair and makeup stylists and an audition technique coach.

Jennifer Butler, Color and Wardrobe Expert Owner of Through Nature's Beauty, 323/931-2626. 20 years experience in the art of color and design. She offers extensive services and is an expert on your whole image. She has introductory free seminars each month. She does wardrobe consultations, color palette design, shopping excursions and wardrobe classes. She can send you a brochure outlining her many excellent services. Very highly recommended. Why not check out her free seminar, you will gain new knowledge.

Closet Queens, Maude Feil, 310/545-0882 or Geraldine Dirks, 310/374-8061. They rearrange your closets putting outfits together so you won't have to wonder what goes with what. They will go shopping with you; in fact they will shop and bring you the things to try on and return what doesn't fit or you don't like. It is more expensive that way, but working actors often don't have the time to shop. They work as a team or on a one on one basis.

Tina Lynne, Style Consultant, 323/939-9117. A specialist in the complete make-over. She can put you together from the inside out. She loves new actors and people new to town. She is willing to work within a fairly small budget. Says she shops all the time and knows what is out there in the stores.

Helene Mills, Grant's Pass, Oregon 541/474-0458. Helene does wonderful color charts, puts together clothing for you, sells makeup, clothing and very well priced jewelry.

The Color Company, 818/760-7798. Jill Kirsh uses the Spring, Summer, Autumn and Winter color formula. She drapes you with all the possible colors and picks out the colors that are best for you and makes a chart for you to carry with you. She works often with actors, helping them to choose the right colors for auditioning. For men she uses suit fabrics to show what works for best for them. For women, she tells which makeup colors are best. The price is $150.

Louis, owner Lou Melazzo, 310/659-3070. Sunset Plaza, 8635 Sunset Blvd., Los Angeles 90069. Charmaine Simons, the costume designer on *Seinfeld* recommends this store. Very high end, current, hip clothes for men. Lou will style you, at no charge. Call to make an appointment.

Books and Newsletters

Always in Style with Color Me Beautiful by Doris Pooser.
Best Bargains by Geri Cook, $40 a year, 310/203-9233. www.labestbargains.com. Her radio show is on at 10am on Saturday mornings, KIEV, 870AM on the dial.
Buying Retail Is Stupid: Southern California's Discount Guide To Buying Everything At Up To 80% Off Retail by Trisha King and Deborah Newmark.
Color Me Beautiful by Carole Jackson.
Color For Men by Carole Jackson.
Color Wonderful by Joanne Nicholson and Judy Lewis-Crum. Bantam.
Image Impact edited by Jacqueline Thompson. Essays on style.
Image Impact For Men edited by Jacqueline Thompson.
Looking Terrific by Emily Cho. Classic in the business.
Make-over Miracles by Michael Maron. You can be recreated through makeup and plastic surgery. He gives all the secrets.
Make-over Magic by Michael Maron is out of print but can be found in libraries. Make yourself glamourous.
Universal Style by Alyce Parsons & Diane Parente. Very current.

Services

• CLOTHING DESIGN

Shawnelle Eveningwear and Custom Dressmaking, 310/230-2032. She specializes in evening wear, award shows and costume design. Gowns average $800. She also does suits $300 to $800. By appointment only. Works for actresses Elizabeth Sung, Shelley Taylor Morgan, Crystal Carson and Crystal Chappell.

• ALTERATIONS AND CLEANERS

5 Star Cleaners & Laundry, 818/506-8960. 4356 Laurel Canyon Blvd., Studio City, 91604. M-F 6:30-8; Sa 6:30-6; Su 9-5. Great service and great prices! Alterations.

Suke at Beachwood Cleaners, 323/467-0021. 2699 N. Beachwood Dr. Hollywood Hills. Great cleaning, fast alterations and inexpensive.

International Custom Tailors, 818/509-9032. 12075 Ventura Place, Studio City. Good prices. He can just about alter anything beautifully. They are great people.

Golden Needle Tailoring, 323/666-3365. 2044 Hillhurst Ave., L.A., Expert tailor, can loosen trousers without making them baggy.

Studio Cleaners, 818/505-0828. Ventura Blvd. at Eureka, across from Bally's. $1.50 per item. Surprisingly good work. Very good alterations.

• EYEGLASSES

Westside Opticians, 213/653-0243. 817 N. Fairfax, Los Angeles, 90046. M,Tu,Th,F 9:30-6; W & Sa 9:30-1:30. The best styles and prices. Jeff can fix anything.

Happy Eyes, 818-246-2202. 114 E. Wilson Glendale. Recommended in Geri Cook's Best Bargains, Tony the owner is very helpful. Great bargains and great styles.

• SHOE REPAIR

Sunset Shoe Repair, Manuel Keshishian, 323/654-7743. 8036 Santa Monica Blvd., L.A., 90046. (Crescent Heights & Santa Monica) "We rebuild your shoes like new." There has never been a shoe or purse problem this man couldn't fix for me.

Garbo Shoe Repair, 310/394-6306. 1450 4th St., Santa Monica, 90401. Very reasonably priced. "If your shoes are uncomfortable, he won't let you out of here until he's got the pad just right."

• LUGGAGE REPAIR AND SALES

Beverly Hills Luggage and Gift Shop, 310/273-5885, 404 N. Beverly Dr., Beverly Hills. Expensive but great.

H. Savinar, 323/938-2501. 4625 W. Washington Blvd., L.A. Valley store: 818/ 703-1313. 6931 Topanga Canyon Blvd., Canoga Park. 30%-50% off Tumi, Hartmann, Boyt, etc. Also replacement hardware.

Langers Luggage Shop & Handbag Hospital, 323/469-6500. 6223 W. Sunset Blvd., L.A., between Vine and Gower. The best; they can fix anything. If you ever have luggage damage at the airport, report it, then take it straight to Langers; they take care of everything.

Luggage For Less, on Lankershim near Magnolia in North Hollywood. Do not buy luggage until you check this place out.

• WIGS

J & J Wigs of Hollywood, (men and women) 323/466-0617. 6324 Hollywood Blvd., 90028. Men or women can rent a wig for photo shoots for $25 or $29 and they will style it and put it on you. They have wigs to buy for as little as $35. You can get a good one for $60-$70. The real hair and hand-tied ones go for up to $250.

Trendy/Upscale/Resale/Vintage/Thrift shops

Geri Cook's Best Bargins Newsletter, 310/203-9233. www.LAbestbargins.com. $40 a year. This is a must for truly good shopping! Bargins on everything.

The Ultimate Consignment & Thrift Store Guide, www.consignmentguide.com. They have many links to other shopping information.

Aardvark's Odd Ark, (men & women) 323/655-6769. 7579 Melrose Ave., 90046. M-Th 11-7; F-Sa 11-9; Su 11-7. Other location: 310/392-2996. 85 Market St., Venice, 90291. Everyday 11-7. Vintage and regular clothes.

Age of Innocence, 818-980-0462. 11054 Magnolia Blvd., North Hollywood. 50's, 60's, and 70's clothes, plus original and eclectic designs. 12-6 M-Th, 12-7 F & Sa, 12-5Su.

Alice & Annie's, 818-761-6085. 11056 Magnolia Blvd., North Hollywood. Vintage, antique clothing. 1870's-1970's including couture-hats, gloves, gowns. 12-6 Tu-Sa, and sometimes open on Sundays.

Armani, 310/451-2277. 1126 Wilshire Blvd., Santa Monica.

Armani Wells, (men) 818/985-5899. 12404 Ventura Blvd., Studio City, 91604. M-Sa 10-10; Su 12-7.

American Rag, (men & women) 323/935-3154. 150 S. La Brea Ave., L.A., 90036. M-Sa 11-6; Su 11-5.
Baba's, (women) 310/360-9494. 517 N. La Cienega Blvd., West Hollywood. Custom couture, exquisite fabrics, and warm salon. Custom prices start at $350.

Becca's Chic Boutique, 818/703-0151. 21048 Ventura Blvd., Woodland Hills, 91364. T-Sa 10-6.

Cherie, (women) 818/508-1628. 12526 Ventura Blvd., Studio City, 91604. M-Sa 10-6. Very upscale designer clothes on consignment.

Cinema Glamour Shop (men & women) 323/933-5289. 343 N. La Brea Ave. (just north of Beverly), L.A. M-F, 10-4. Designer and vintage wear. Many stars donate their clothes; proceeds benefit the Motion Picture Home. They provide clothing to extras at affordable prices. They are having super sales on the last Saturdays of the month. Call first.

Claudia's Boutique, (men, women & children) 818/980-3473. 11930 Ventura Blvd., Studio City, 91604. M-Sa 10:30-7; Su 12-5. Really packed in tight, but she seems to know where everything is.

Concern's Closet, (men & women) 310/247-9827. 9327 W. Pico Blvd., L.A., 90035. M-Sa 10-5. Good prices. Managed by the Concern Foundation for Cancer Research. The clothes come from donations. They have a pickup service.

Collectible Glitz, 818/347-9343. 21435 Sherman Way, Canoga Park, 91303. One block west of Canoga Ave. M-Sa. 10-6; Su 12-4. The greatest vintage jewelry in Los Angeles. It is all sorted according to color. Most is old jewelry but some new that looks vintage.

Council Thrift Shops, (men and women) 310/477-9613, 11571 Santa Monica Blvd., 938-8122, 1059 S. Fairfax Ave., L.A., 90019. Also 818/997-8980, 14526 Victory, North Hollywood. Also 323/654-8516, 7818 Santa Monica Blvd., West Hollywood, 90046. This is one of my favorites, really good brands at low cost. Excellent men's sport coats and suits. They will pick up your donations. They provide clothes for homeless women and children.

Daddyo's, 818/769-8869, 5128 Vineland, North Hollywood. Cool vintage for hip cats. Late 1800's-1970's.

Fashion Institute of Los Angeles Scholarship Store (FIDM), (men and women) 213/624-1201. 919 So. Grand, Los Angeles. M-T 9-5, F 9-4, Sa 10-4. The institute operates a year-round fund-raiser to support their scholarship programs. Local manufacturers and retailers donate new merchandise, some quality, some irregulars and the public is invited for some excellent bargains.

Great Labels, 310/451-2277. 1126 Wilshire Blvd., Santa Monica. M-Sa 10-6.

Heaven 27, 323/871-9044. 6316 Yucca Street, Hollywood. Sofia Coppola, daughter of director Francis Ford Coppola owns this shop. she designs panty-camisole sets, knit caps, logo tees, hooded sweatshirts and other things. Prices range from $20 for a t-shirt to $150 for a denim jacket.

Happy Eyes, 818/246-2202. 114 E. Wilson, Glendale. Watch for sales where you can buy two pairs of glasses for one price.

Hubba Hubba, 818/845-0636. 3220 Magnolia Blvd., Burbank. Vintage 30's-60's clothing in good condition. Average selling price $50.

Iguana, (Men and women) 818/907-6716. 14422 Ventura Blvd., Sherman Oaks, 91403. Styles of the '40s, '50s and '60s. M-Th 11-7; F & Sa 11-8; Su 12-7. This is a huge store, very organized. Great shopping.

It's A Wrap! (men & women) 818/567-7366. 3315 W. Magnolia Blvd. Burbank, 91505. M-Sa 11-6; Su 11-4. Large busy store; they have a lot of clothes from the film and television industry. Definitely a place to take people visiting from your home town.

Jet Rag, 323/939-0528. 225 N. La Brea, Los Angeles. M-Sa. 11:30-8. They have everything from every era. For current and vintage styles. Winona Ryder, Juliette Lewis and Drew Barrymore have been known to stop in.

Junk for Joy, (men & women) 818/569-4903. 3314 W. Magnolia, Burbank, 91505. Tu-Sa 12-5. New and used vintage fashions, footwear & accessories. Kimonos, junk jewelry, gloves, bow ties, spats, hats and eyeglasses. Silly and ugly clothing of good and bad taste.

Kool Kats, (men & women) 818/505-1528. 5140 Vineland Blvd., North Hollywood. Tu-F 12-7; Sa & Su 12-6. They have 50's-70's collectibles & Hawaiian. Studio friendly.

Le Chateau Outlet Store, 310/203-0650. 1499 So. Robertson Blvd., Los Angeles. M-F 11-7, Sa 10-6, S 12-5:30.

Lisa's N.Y. Style Resale, 818/788-2142. 13541 Ventura Blvd., Sherman Oaks. M-Sa 10-6. The clothing is top quality, and leans toward the exotic.

Nena's Fashions, (over 40 crowd) 562/697-7885. 581 W. La Habra Blvd., La Habra 90631. M-Sa 11-5. The specialty at Nena's is the levi bend-over pants, the pants that fit most women's bodies and which are hard to come by. They mail these pants all over the country, but at the store, you can try them on. They also come in every color.

Past Perfect and Jean's Stars' Apparel, 818/760-8872. 12616 Ventura Blvd., Studio City, 91604. M-Sa 10-6, on Thursday till 8. Top of the line designer labels at about 1/3 the regular price.

P.J. London, (women) 310/826-4649. 11661 San Vicente Blvd., Brentwood, 90049. M-Sa 11-6; Su 12-5. Highest fashion, lowest prices for clothes.

The Paper Bag Princess, 310/358-1985. 8700 Santa Monica Blvd., West Hollywood. Very upscale, shoppers are said to be: Elle MacPherson, Shalom Harlow, Demi Moore, Elisabeth Shue, Parker Posey, Courtney Love, Madonna, Sofia Coppola, Jennifer Nicholson. Puccis, Pradas, Guccis, prices range from $25 to $6,000.

Pasadena City College Flea Market, 626/585-7906. Pasadena City College, 1570 Colorado Blvd. at S. Hill Ave., Pasadena. 8-3 on first Sunday of the month. Like garage sales, it's free and showcases a somewhat haphazard mix of merchandise, offered by established circuit dealers and casual sellers who strew goods on the ground. The market is in four sections, three along S. Hill Ave. side of the campus and the fourth, off Bonnie Ave.

Play Back, (women, children & gifts) 310/273-5673. 622 N. Doheny Dr., West Hollywood, 90069. Tu-Sa 11-5. They carry a wide selection of white lace clothing from 1900 to 1950, rayon dresses and unusual vintage hats. She also makes new dresses out of vintage material. Very interesting store. My daughters, Chris Kerr and Cathy Kerr, buy many things there.

Playclothes, 818/985-1306. 13045 Ventura Blvd., Studio City. Vintage fashions from the 30's to 60's. Some children's clothing. Good prices.

Ragtime Cowboy, 818/769-6552. 5213 Lankershim Blvd., North Hollywood. Vintage clothing & costumes. This is one of the first vintage clothing stores in No Ho.

Ragtime on Green, 626/796-9924. 1136 E. Green St., Pasadena. M, Tu, W, F 10-5; Sa 10-3. Jammed with inventory with low prices. Brand names, also.

Rebecca's Dream, 818/896-1200. 16 Fair Oaks Ave., Pasadena. Their specialty is Victorian-era apparel and accessories. By appointment only.

Repeat Performance, (men & women) 323/938-0609. 318 N. La Brea, Los Angeles, 90038. M-F 11-6. Fine vintage clothing and accessories in perfect condition. Specializing in '40s & '50s attire.

Rose Bowl Flea Market, 213/560-7469. Rose Bowl Dr., Pasadena. More than 1,500 vendors. Second Sunday of every month.

Sacks SFO, (men and women) New clothing with extraordinary deals. There are six SFO locations: 818/972-2797. 1421 W. Olive, Burbank; 818/506-4787. 12021 Ventura Blvd., Studio City; 310/559-5448. 9608 Venice Blvd., Culver City; 323/939-3993. 652 N. La Brea, Hollywood; 310/659-1771. 8936 Santa Monica Blvd., West Hollywood; 562/987-0099. 2101 E. Broadway, Long Beach.

Star Wares On Main, (310) 399-0224. 2817 Main Street, Santa Monica, 90405. M-Sa. 11-6. They only sell items that celebrities have worn or owned, movie wardrobe and props. This is not the usual resale shop.

Studio Wardrobe Services and Retake Room (men and women) (818) 508-7762. 12132 Ventura Blvd., Studio City, 91604. Just west of Laurel Canyon. M-Sa 10-6; Su 12-5. Clothes that are returned from film and television sets. I have good luck with men's clothes here.

The Address (women), 310/394-1406. 1116 Wilshire Blvd., Santa Monica. M-Sa 10-6; Su 12-5. Clothes from very wealthy women who can't be seen in the same outfit twice, plus new clothes.

The Place and Company, (men and women) 310/645-1539. 8820 S. Sepulveda Blvd., Los Angeles, 90045. (Half block south of La Tijera). M-Sa 10-6. 75% off the original price for suits worn by Jay Leno (44 long) and Pat Sajak. The best bargains.

Discount shops

Citadel Factory Outlet Stores, 323/888-1220. Right off the I-5, Los Angeles. From I-5 southbound, exit at Washington Blvd. From I-5 northbound, exit at Atlantic Blvd. North. M-Sa 10-8; Su 10-6. 44 stores. Ann Taylor, Geoffrey Beene, Bass, Eddie Bauer, Gap, Harve Bernard, United Colors of Benetton and many others.

Cooper Building, 323/622-1139. 860 S. Los Angeles St., near 9th St., downtown L.A., M-Sa 9:30-5:30; Su 11-5. Call their voice mail for excellent directions. Eight floors of little discount shops.

DNA, 310/399-0341. 411 Rose Ave., Venice. For jeans and t-shirts, everything from Calvin Klein to Point Zero, for less. Joseph jeans, normally $89, and Big Star jeans, $120, are only $14.99 and $39.99. Weaver's soft cotton loose-fitting t-shirts are three for $10.

Dressed Up!, 818/708-7238, 6000 Reseda Blvd., Tarzana. M-Sa. 10-5:30; Sun. 11:30-4:30. "L.A.'s only evening wear superstore."

Encore Sports, 818/985-2221. 4446 Forman Avenue, Toluca Lake. M-F 11-6, Sa 10-5. Clothing for: Golf, tennis, fitness, ski, equestrian. Up to 75% off retail prices. Track pants, bootleg pants, bike shorts, stretch tops, sweats, all discount priced. For ski & Equestrian or Maude Feil, 310/545-0882.

Foot Locker Outlet, 310/450-8178. 115 Lincoln Blvd., Venice. 30%-50% off Nike, Reebok, Adidas, K-Swiss, LA Gear and others.

Loehmann's, 310/659 0674. 333 S. La Cienega, 90048. Across from the Beverly Center. M-Sa 10-9; Su 11-7. This is where Tina Lynne brings her image clients that are on a budget.

Marshall's, 800/627-7425. Call for store locations and complete information.

The Nordstrom Rack, (men, women & children) 818/884-6771. 21490 Victory Blvd., Woodland Hills, 91367. M-F 10-9; Sa 10-8; Su 11-7. You can find real treasures here.

Rick Pallack, (men only) 818/789-7000. 4554 Sherman Oaks Avenue, Sherman Oaks, 91423. They dress all the stars and design movie wardrobes. Twice a year they have a huge sale. Take advantage of looking like you are a successful actor.

Sara's, 818/755-9070. 10216 Riverside Drive, Toluca Lake. The prices on women's apparel with a European flair are always reasonable. Great twice a year sale. A Wild Rose dress sells elsewhere for $160, at Sara's for $89 and during Sara's sale it would be $66.75. Very helpful sales staff.

Sichel Promotional Sportswear, 818/505-0361. 11730 Ventura Blvd., Studio City, 91604. They make many of the T-shirts, caps and jackets for film and TV crews. About two weeks before Christmas they put a couple of racks on the sidewalk filled with the left overs. They are a steal, relatives back home love to get these treasures.

TJ Maxx Stores, for locations 800/285-6299. In Culver City, 310/390-7944. Studio Village Shopping Center, West Jefferson Blvd. & Sawtelle Blvd., north of Fox Hills Mall. Also: 310/390-7944. Studio Village Shopping Center, West Jefferson Blvd. & Sawtelle Blvd., north of Fox Hills Mall.

Costumes and period clothes

RENTAL AND SALES

CRC Costume Rentals Corporation, Rental only 818/753-3700. 11149 Vanowen Street., North Hollywood, 91605. Huge! Uniforms/research library, check them out.

Glendale Costumes, 818/244-1161. 746 W. Doran, Glendale, 91203. Tu-Sa 10-6. Good prices.

Hollywood Toys & Costumes, 323/465-3119. 6600 Hollywood Blvd., Hollywood, 90028. 9:30-7 M-Sa; 10:30-7 Su. They have a huge selection.

Magic World Costuming, 818/848-8100. 10122 Topanga Canyon, Chatsworth. M-F 9-Sa 10-4.

Western Costume Co., Rental only 818/760-0902. 11041 Van Owen, North Hollywood, 91605. M-F 8-6. Probably the most famous and most expensive. They have everything you could possibly need.

MAKEUP AND MAKEUP ARTISTS

• **While women always need a full makeup** for their B&W photos, men seldom need full makeup, just a little help.

• **Men will need** translucent powder to remove shine and maybe an eyebrow pencil to fill in their brows. It is most important that a man doesn't look like he is wearing makeup in his photos. Other imperfections can be removed in retouching.

• **Makeup artist Lorraine Altamura tells men:**

- **For photo shoots**, 95% of Caucasian men can use Revlon's Love Pat in the Suntan tone found at any drugstore for about $6. It is a moisturizing powder and can be put on dry or wet. If you put it on wet, just dust off the excess when it dries. Don't put it on your lips. Joe Blasco's Natural Blue Neutralizer I, found at professional beauty supply stores, is a mild beard cover and great for eliminating dark circles under the eyes.

• **Robert Raphael, makeup artist, talks about eyebrows.**

- The many looks your brows can have would surprise you. Where your arch is placed can make close set eyes appear further apart and can help a heavy lid to appear lifted without cosmetic surgery. Your brows and lashes may need to be colored. Pale blondes look better with a deeper ash brow and redheads need a touch of brown. Men can really benefit from natural eyebrow grooming. Dark lashes will give your eyes a stronger expression when you are acting.

- **Dee Dee Altamura, makeup artist, talks about lips.**
  - **I use a product called Young Lips** to smooth on the lips first, this will keep your lip color from bleeding. Next apply lip pencil and then lipstick.

Rita Montanez, makeup artist, designer and teacher, tells actresses:

- **Makeup is incredibly important when it comes to photography**; the right makeup shows that you are professional. If you don't have a makeup artist for your photo session, make sure that you know how to do your own properly. In black & white photos you have to create a lot of contrast because normal makeup will not show up. You use more, concentrating on shading, using grays, browns and blacks. Color photography is different because it's more natural; something you can wear everyday.
- **Always take your own makeup kit on a shoot** so you're prepared if the makeup artist doesn't show up for some reason. In interviews, your makeup can be the same as for color photography. For commercials, you need to look natural. On soap opera interviews, you want a glamour look. If there's a little bit of chubbiness or excess chin area, learn how to contour in order to complement your face.

- **Lorraine Altamura gives hints on how to work with your makeup artist.**
  - **Come with your eyebrows tweezed or waxed.** Don't tweeze the top of the eyebrows—the natural shape duplicates the top line of the upper eyes. When you strip that line away, it takes away your personality. Do your eyebrow, mustache waxing and facials at least a week before the shoot. Your face goes into shock for three or four days after these procedures. Get your hair styled at least two weeks before the shoot to be sure the style works. If you want your hair to grow another inch, then wait; you want these photos to last for a long time.

- **Anne Archer** (*Fatal Attraction, Clear and Present Danger)* thinks actresses should learn to do their own makeup. She likes to do hers at home so she can leave for the studio a little later. She has two complete sets of makeup; one is set up at home and the other is organized in a portable bag she always carries with her.

- **Most makeup artists in beauty salons or department stores** will give free makeup lessons if you buy from them. Hold a mirror so you can watch what they do; ideally, they will draw a step-by-step chart for you. If you aren't buying products, a lesson is usually $35 to $100. Makeup by a professional artist for a photo shoot is between $25 and $150.

Rita did the following chart for my readers and students. Rita has listed commercial products but she has developed her own line of great products that are reasonable and can be purchased in person, by phone or on her web site.

MAKEUP CHART FOR WOMEN'S BLACK & WHITE PHOTOGRAPHS

by Rita Montanez 818/509-5733 www.webworksps.com/makeupbyrita.

- Use a makeup sponge or the back of your hand to blend colors like an artist's pallet.
- Use Joe Blasco's red neutralizer both #1 & #2 for lighter and darker red areas such as blemishes or age spots. You may need to blend them together. Don't use on upper lid; foundation and eye shadows go there. For dark circles under the eyes use Ben Nye's mellow yellow #1 or #2 as a concealer. Dab with ring finger.
- Creme foundation next. Start at forehead and work down, quite heavy to cover everything. Joe Blasco, MAC and RCMA (best) are all good brands.
- Powder. Use loose with a puff for best control to set makeup, then use a large brush to brush off excess. Always brush down so the facial hair will lay flat.
- Eyebrows. Brush them; then, with a little angle brush, use some light brown powder on them; blend well. Eyebrows should be waxed or plucked before shoot.
- A very soft beige powder goes right under eyebrow. This is to diminish the puffy look under the brow; it is lighter than the eye shadow.
- Brush yellow tone eye shadow over the whole lid.
- Dot on a dark brown eye shadow, high on the crease of the eye, using an eye shadow brush. Blend in well; use translucent powder to lighten; if it gets too dark, blend.
- Eye liner for top lid. To get as close as possible to lashes, lift lid then put on liner with a tiny angle brush and dark brown eye shadow, take it to inner eye very thinly so it covers the whole lid.
- Liner for bottom lid is light brown powder. Dot or dab, don't draw a line. Blend/smudge with a sponge.
- Curl eyelashes.
- Top eyelashes. Use a stiff fan brush to apply mascara; just take the mascara off the brush from your roll-on mascara. The fan brush will make each lash separate. Wait to do bottom lashes until these dry. The stiff fan brush comes big—you have to trim it down pretty short.
- Contour cheek bones in a slant from the notch in your ear to the corner of your mouth. Use a soft fan brush and soft beige powder.
- Brush your powder blush over the contouring, up and around the eye.
- Now the top lashes are dry; you can do the bottom lashes very lightly with stiff fan brush.
- Lips. Use a brownish sort of natural lip liner pencil, then a tawny, soft rosy beige type of matte lipstick.
- Check all of your makeup during the shoot. Use either powder/foundation on a puff or loose translucent powder on a puff for touchups. A great deal of attention and focus on your makeup will make a world of difference in your black and white pictures. Hint: a little Preparation H hemorrhoidal creme will take down puffy eyes.

- **Lorraine shares further tips:**

  - RCMA (Research Council of Makeup Artists) is the best creme foundation for B&W photos; mostly pigment and less grease for more coverage and less shine. MAC cosmetics have very good colors. If you can't go to a beauty supply store and get RCMA then MAC is a good choice. Actors and models get a 30% discount. The foundation doesn't have to go down the neck but put a little blush or contour powder in the middle of your neck, and to contour the décolletage line.

  - **We use three tones or shades** on the eyes and several tones on the face: foundation, highlight, contour and blush. Also use three tones on your lips. For instance: a deep rose, almost burgundy on the outer edge, a lighter rose to blend it all in together and a beige on the inside bottom lip to highlight and pucker the lips; it makes them more interesting. When you're touching up, use a creamy lipstick pencil that's just a shade or two darker than your lip color; filling in your lips with pencil color is the trendy thing to do. You can use just a tiny bit of foundation on the hot spot of the bottom lip.

  - **Put your lipsticks in little round pots** that screw together or in little plastic flip top pill boxes with several compartments. Buy the pots at the professional beauty supply and the pill boxes at the drug store. Scoop out the lipstick from the tubes with a plastic spatula or knife and put them in the containers, microwave them for a few seconds and the lipstick will quickly melt to the bottom of the containers. Use a brush to combine your own lipsticks for interesting looks.

  - **Cleanliness is very important**, especially for people who have sensitive skin. I sharpen all my pencils as I put them back. I use disposable mascara wands that go into the tube once and are discarded. Bring your own mascara; if someone has conjunctivitis and the wand goes back in the tube, the mascara is contaminated. Use clean sponges with the creme foundations. I use a spatula or side of the brush to take it out of the pot and put it on my pallet (hand) so the sponge doesn't go back into the pot. The Board of Health says the Hepatitis B Virus can stay alive on a piece of paper for eleven days. AIDS virus stays alive on cuticle snippers through general washing; it has to be killed in a 10 part water, 1 part Clorox solution.

- **Robert Raphael is a talented makeup artist.** I had my first makeup lesson from him almost 20 years ago. I still use the special brushes I bought from him. I found him again through photographer Nancy Jo Gilchrist. He talks more about makeup.

- **Makeup can make your best features pop.** When applying your own makeup, bring your best features forward first. Your so called flaws will diminish without much effort.

- **For Men:** Base makeup should always go two shades darker for black and white photo shoots and television and one shade darker for film. With this technique, their faces will never be washed out by the studio lights. A second base three shades darker for contouring the cheeks, chin and eye crease area. Concealer for under eye area should match skin tone. Medium to deep translucent powder to eliminate shine.

- **For Women:** Plan your brows a week before your photo shoot . If there are any areas of facial hair that appear to cause shadows, waxing can eliminate the hair for up to six weeks. You can also have the photo retouched.

- **Mascara:** From dark brown to black. Painting only the upper lashes is a more youthful look in photos, as well as omitting the liner from the bottom lid. When it comes to television and film this rule does not apply.

- **Eye Brows:** Fill your brows in with a powder shadow a shade lighter than your brow color. Match only your brow shade if there are no brow hairs, such as at the end of your brows. If the brows appear too dark when finished, simply apply ivory shadow or translucent powder over them.

- **Keep all shadows, blush and lip color matte, Avoid all frost colors.**

• **Rand Rusher, RN, CNOR** of Wilshire Aesthetics, A Dermatology and Plastic Surgery Group talks about the best way to take care of your skin.

- **Commit yourself to the basics.**

- **Water:** Drink eight glasses a day. Increase your intake during hot weather and heavy workouts. Skin is the largest organ of your body and it need to be well hydrated—if you want to look your best.

- **Cleanse:** Soap and water cleansing removes most substances from your skin. A cream based soap is better for removing makeup from a day's shooting. Your cleanser should match your skin type. Strong enough without drying your skin. Rinse thoroughly leaving no residual cleanser.

- **Sunscreen:** Use one everyday. The easiest way is to use a moisturizer with a SPF of 15 or higher already in it. If you are applying a separate sunscreen, put it on before moisturizing. The skin absorbs the sunscreen but leaves the moisturizer on the surface. If you do it the other way, the sunscreen will be useless.

- **Moisturize:** This is the easiest way of locking in water. Even oily skin can benefit from the light application of a non-greasy moisturizer. The primary purpose of moisturizers is to hold in your skin's moisture...that you won't have if you don't drink your water!

Resources

Eyebrow Specialists

Robert Raphael, 310/888-1800. The West End Salon, 9021 Melrose Avenue, West Hollywood.

Anastasia Soare, 310/273-3155. 430 N. Bedford, Beverly Hills.

Valerie Sarnelle of Valerie Beverly Hills, 310/274-7348. 460 N. Cannon Drive, Beverly Hills.

Fake Tattoos

Galerie Lakaya, 323/653-1724. 8360 West Third Street, Los Angeles. Mehndi tattoos, lasts three to five weeks. A way to try that tattoo you've always wanted or to freak out someone who doesn't want you to get a tattoo. Sharon Stone recommends Bakari as the artist she likes.

Makeup Artists

Photographers will usually have professional makeup artists they recommend.

- ***The following makeup artists sell makeup and give lessons at their places of business.***

Cinema Secrets, 818/846-0579. 4400 Riverside Drive, Burbank, 91505, in Toluca Lake. M-F 8-6, Sa 10-5. $75 to $150 per lesson for a one or two hour session. You can come in another time and practice the look and they will critique it for free.

Columbia Stage & Screen Cosmetics, 213/464-7555. 1440 N. Gower St., Hollywood, 90028, Near Sunset. M-F 8-6, Sa 10-3. $25 and up. They will do your makeup for specific looks such as your B&W photo look.

Naimie's Film & Television Beauty Supply, 818/655-9933. (Naimie's Beauty Center) 12640 Riverside Dr., Valley Village, CA 91607. This is where most of the studio makeup and hairstylists get their supplies. The regular retail store is on the top level. 10% discount with your SAG card. Second, smaller location, 818/763-7072 or 323/877-2230. 12801 Victory Blvd., North Hollywood, 91606. M-Sa 9:30-6.

The Color Company, 818/760-7798. From Geri Cook's Best Bargains (to subscribe 310/203-9233). Kirsh manufactures her own color coordinated line, has appeared on QVC.

Kit consists of eight eyeshadows, four blushes, two lipsticks, lip gloss, lip liner, eye pencil, mascara, three brushes, a color swatch booklet, a scarf and a miniature makeup version for travel, $89.95. *See the wardrobe section for more about her color charts.*

• ***The following professional makeup artists will go on your photo shoots to work with you.***

Alicia Ali, contact her through Rich Hogan at 323/467-2628. Hair, makeup and photo styling. She works mainly with Rich but is available for outside shoots. She also does private lessons and consulting starting at $25 an hour.

Alisa Chompupong, 323/935-0003, Pager 213/719-7790. Hair, makeup and photo styling, $100 and she stays the whole shoot. Makeup for special occasions, such as award shows and weddings. Also works in film, videos, print and television. *See Cynthia Kerr's theatrical photo that Alisha Tamburri took on page 92, and commercial photo on page 164.*

Laura Connelly, 310/285-9277. Makeup and hair. $50 and up, depending on time and locations, for a general photo shoot. She likes to stay the whole shoot to keep an eye on the hair and makeup for the photographer. If she has to do a complete hair style there is an extra charge. Makeup for a special occasion is $75. *Janice Allen's theatrical photo taken by Carrie Cavalier on page 89, commercial photo on page 166.*

Ivy Halford of Ivy's Skincare and Make-Up Garden, 310/451-7780. 522 Wilshire Blvd., Suite G., Santa Monica, 90401. Transformational Skincare and Makeup. Makeup Union Local 706. The art of corrective makeup to treat blemished skin and to cosmetically camouflage irreparable damaged surface tissue and scars. She has her own line of transformational skincare and makeup products. Written diagnostic skincare and makeup analysis and customized at home maintenance regimen. Eyebrow design and shaping, waxing lash and brow tinting. Helps you prepare for those auditions, headshots and special occasions.

Eryn Krueger, 818/414-1314. $150 for a 4 hour shoot, including hair and make up changes. $75 for an hour makeup and hair session at the photographer's. She'll leave you instructions on how to change for a more glamorous look. Eryn certainly knows the glamorous look; Emmy nomination for helping to create the "looks" on General Hospital. She works also in video, commercials, film, stage and print.

Anne Marso, 310/281-1904. $150 for hair and makeup. In the business for 15 years, she does B&W and color print; also videos, commercials, features, fashion and weddings.

Rela Martine, 323/878-0675, Pager 213/303-5122. $75 and up, makeup and hair depending on how many rolls and looks. Color and black and white print. Rela has traveled the world doing the fashion runways in Spain, France, Italy, Germany, etc. Member IATSE Local 706, doing film, TV and commercials. Available for private sessions showing you how to apply your makeup easily and makeup tips. "This industry is all about having fun!" She did Cynthia's makeup when she shot with Diana Lannes. *See theatrical photo of Cynthia on page 93 and in the Commercial Section on page 165.*

Deborah McNulty, 310/457-8391. $200 for a photo session, hair and makeup. Videos, features, B&W and color print. She is a soft, gentle person to spend time with.

Rita Montanez, 818/509-5733. www.webworksps.com/makeupbyrita. Hair and makeup: $75 for a general shoot. I've worked with her many times. Besides being available for your photo shoot, she gives seminars and private lessons in how to do your own makeup. Private lesson $75. She teaches color and B&W photography look, natural and glamour looks. $75 for a special occasion or bride's makeup. You get a 25% discount on her professional line of cosmetics. Puts your kit together for you. Rita works with many photographers. *See Alan Weissman's '40s look of me on page 85 and Sean McCall's picture of Janice in the photo section on page 88.*

Robert Raphael, 310/888-1800. The West End Salon, 9021 Melrose Avenue, West Hollywood, 90069. $125 hair and makeup when he is at the shoot with you. $40 at the shop. He does great eyebrows $15-$18. Makeup lesson is $55. I knew Robert years ago, he was in the first editions of the book. He gave me my first makeup lesson and I still use the basic brushes I bought from him. He carries a great line of makeup, still gives lessons and the salon has all the services. *See Nancy Jo's theatrical picture of me, page 84 in the photo and in the Commercial section on page 165.*

Laurel Wiley, 213/707-9726. Makeup and hair $75 and up, depending on how many rolls or looks. She owns Studio Makeup Academy at Sunset Gower Studios, training makeup artists for film, television, print and special effects. Sometimes the students use models. Call for information 323/465-4002. Private and seminar lessons are available, $100.

Sandy Williams, 818/752-2582. Pager: 818/327-9036. Makeup and hair for photography sessions, $85-$150. "I believe actors should have a real say in how they want to look, especially their hair, because they have to duplicate it. We go from looking very natural to upscale glamour." Special occasion, award show makeup, $300. She also does, film, rock videos, commercials, television. *See Mary Ann Halpin's theatrical photo of Cynthia Kerr on page 93 and commercial photo on page 164.*

Yolanda Frye Skin Care, 310/275-3981. 632 1/2 Doheny Dr, Los Angeles, 90069. Black and white photography and special event makeup, $50 at the shop. $75 at the photographers. See her special facials and notes about her full service skin and nail services, under the Age Defying Section.

Professional beauty supply stores

For regular or stage makeup and hair supplies, beauty supply stores are your best bet. All of these stores will give a 10% discount to actors. They also provide mail order service.

Cinema Secrets, 818/846-0579. 4400 Riverside Drive, Burbank, 91505, in Toluca Lake. M-F 8-6, Sa 10-5. Owner Maurice Stein has been in the business 30 years. Makeup artists and hair stylists work there part time, so you have professionals helping you.

Columbia Stage & Screen Cosmetics, 323/464-7555. 1440 N. Gower St., Hollywood, 90028, near Sunset. M-F 8-6; Sa 10-3. The salespeople are makeup artists; Doris Butler has been giving advice to actors for years.

Naimie's Film & Television Beauty Supply, 818/655-9933. (Naimie's Beauty Center) 12640 Riverside Dr., Valley Village, CA 91607. This is where most of the studio makeup and hairstylists get their supplies. The regular retail store is on the top level. 10% discount with your SAG card. Second, smaller location, 818/763-7072 or 323/877-2230. 12801 Victory Blvd., North Hollywood, 91606. M-Sa 9:30-6.

Frends Beauty Supply, 323/877-4828 or 818/769-3834. 5270 Laurel Canyon Blvd., North Hollywood, 91607. M-Sa 8 - 6, Su 10-4. Makeup and hair supplies, all brands.

Alcone Makeup Supply, (212) 633-0551. 235 West 19 Street, Manhattan, N.Y. 10011.

Special mail order

Alcone Makeup Supply, 800/466-7446. 5-49 49th Avenue, Long Island City, NY 11101. Call and ask Vinny for a great catalogue. They are the largest store and outlet on the East Coast. There is no sales tax for out of state sales, which balances the shipping cost.

Beauty supply stores with theatrical makeup

Bay City Beauty Supply, 310/393-3709. 320 Santa Monica Blvd., Santa Monica, 90401. M-Sa 9-8, Su 10-7. Good prices. Big inventory.

Diamond Beauty Supply, 818/761-1778. 12151 Ventura Blvd., Studio City, 91604. One block west of Laurel Canyon. Wonderful store, carries all the good products and they are very knowledgeable and helpful. Full service beauty shop in the back including an African-American specialist, hair extensions, facials, waxing and makeup.

MAC Make Up Store, 310/854-0860, 800/387-6707. 133 North Robertson, Los Angeles, 90048, across from the Newsroom Cafe. M-Sa 10:30-7, Su 12-5. They give a 30% discount to actors—bring an 8x10 or Union card. Also sold in the Beverly Center at the MAC store. Without discount, sold at Nordstroms and Macy's department stores. The creme foundation is wonderful, especially for your photos; covers everything. The powder colors and lipsticks are excellent; I see many makeup artists on the set using all their products.

M.P. Beauty, 323/934-7500. 6244 Wilshire Blvd., L.A., 90048. Corner of Wilshire & Crescent Heights in a strip mall. M-F 10-7, Sa 10-6. Denise does hair. A small store but packed with products.

Number One Beauty Supply, 310/656-2455. 1426 Montana Ave., #3, Santa Monica. They have all of the Hard Candy shades. Beverly Hills 90210 stars are regulars as are Jennifer Aniston, Courteney Cox, Holly Hunter, Michelle Pfeiffer, Robert Wagner, Mary Steenburgen, Anne Archer to just name a few. Body jewelry, a self-painting kit for tattoos is big with the celebs.

AN ACTOR'S MAKEUP KIT
by Rita Montanez

Foundation in your shade.
Concealer for dark circles.
Pencil concealer for other things to hide.
Finishing powder and puff.
Blush for healthy glow or
Bronzing powder for a natural tan look.
Eyeliner, soft taupe or gray pencil.
Mascara.
Carmex or lip balm on lips before liner.
Neutral lip pencil as lip liner.
Lipstick close to liner color.
Powder brush to blend all of the face powders.
A sponge and Q-tips for clean up.

Hair Stylists, Manicurists and Waxing

• **As an actor, how you look** has a great deal to do with getting your career moving. You need a hair stylist who can be trusted to deliver your hair the way you want it each and every time they work on you. Sometimes you are hired for a role two or three months ahead of time and the director expects you to show up looking the same as when they hired you. You want a hair stylist who will please you if you are maintaining a look, as well as contribute their own ideas on how to develop the unique you to the fullest. Cultivate your relationship with this most valuable person on your team of personal professionals.

• **Be sure to have your hair cut**, colored, permed or straightened at least a week before your photo session. The exception is the man's split session with the hair long and maybe a few days' growth of beard, then a shave and haircut before returning for more photos.

• **Fernando Dejesus of the West End Salon talks about hair:**

- **It is important to have the right look** when showing up for a casting call. Style, shape and color should be current with today's fashion world. The product you could sell or the series you could star in partly relies on your look. Updating your image can make the difference in a director casting you for the role that may have gone to someone else.

- **A step beyond the new haircut** is the color. Not only can it highlight your features but it can actually change your image from comic, to that zany redhead! You can be as subtle as going from mousey brown to golden brunette. Take a good look at who is making it and ask yourself. "Does their look play a big part in their success?" "Yes!"

Stan Vogel (aka Red), one of my favorite hair stylists, comments:

- **If there's anything constant**, it's the change on a man's head of hair. Whether he likes it or not it thins out, he loses it, the hairline changes, grey starts coming in. Men aren't that knowledgeable about what hair can do, so they need a lot more instruction. They might appear to be easier to deal with, but it's hard for them to accept change. Women are more adaptable. Culturally, it's cooler for women to color their hair, and we're getting there as far as men go; there is progress.

- **Attitude is everything. You can wear your hair the way you want,** as long as you have the right attitude about yourself. Barbra Streisand does all kinds of things with her hair and none of it is really right, but it's right because she's got the right attitude. If you're not satisfied within, it doesn't matter what you do on the exterior. All's fair in love and hair!

- **Edward Salazar, hair and makeup designer, says:**

  - **Whether you're seasoned or aspiring**, you must realize that your hair is the first thing people notice; it frames the features of your face. When your hair has an excellent cut and color, the overall appearance gives off a message of success and confidence.

  - **As an actor, the choice of how you want to be presented is up to you,** whether you are a leading man/woman or a character type. When working with a character actor, I generally keep the same hair style/design as a statement of their character type. I rarely try to change their image once it is established; I simply clean up the rough edges or encourage a subtle update or brighten the hair with color. When you commit yourself to a change in hair color, cut and/or perm, you need to consider the time and economics involved. The worst thing you can do is play your own hair dresser. You may think you look great but your potential employers will definitely be able to tell the difference. When you go to a casting call, the one thing that can give you that special edge is your fresh image; it makes you stand out from the crowd.

  - **As actors' careers progress, they have a tendency to get stuck** and safe in the same redundant style. Actors don't stop taking acting risks but they stop taking risks with their image. Seasonal changes should have an effect on your hair color. During the summer months, I brighten *Entertainment Tonight's* Mary Hart's hair, then come fall and winter, I begin warmer tones.

Q: How do you choose and communicate with a hair designer?

- **Find someone you trust** to guide your image. When you approach a truly talented and gifted hair designer, your objective is to get as much information and guidance as possible. When an actress or actor sits in my chair, I always ask how they see their image first. This gives me my perimeters and helps me to define their needs. I tell them all the options and considerations available. The worst thing you can do at this point is to become indecisive and insecure.

- **Allow your professional** to tell you everything from one extreme to the other and then pick out the avenues that seem appropriate. It isn't necessary to do everything at once. When you're working with your hair designer, you're developing a relationship. If your bangs were too long or you've decided to evolve into a new hair direction, it requires communication and patience. It's not unusual for me to take conservative steps until we develop a rapport, then evolve into all your hair and image possibilities as time progresses.

- **I believe that the true path** to success is knowing yourself, your direction and standing by your convictions and decisions. The only difference between an average person and a stunning model, actress and or beauty queen, is hair and makeup. There hasn't been a make-over person that, if all the features are roughly in place, I couldn't make gorgeous. The bottom line is, if you're not willing to maintain your fresh image and if you don't see yourself in your new image, you will always return to what makes you feel safe.

Q: Any special hair hints?

- **If your hair is dull and lifeless** before the camera, request highlights or a combination of highlights and tint between foils. Complement this with a vegetable clear gloss for shine. If your hair is frizzy from its own natural texture or because under that hair color is gray frizzy hair, get your hair relaxed straight. If your hair is soft and fine, get a body wave and learn to work with round brushes and/or rollers to get that great look.

Resources

The following professional hair stylists work with men and women.

Art Luna, 310/247-1383. 8930 Keith Ave., West Hollywood. Cuts $100-$200, color, $150 and up. Clientele includes Claire Danes, Kelly Lynch and Candice Bergen.

Borealis Holistic Artistry, Lisa Lowe, 310/262-7785. 1460 7th St., Santa Monica, 90401. For men and women. She is a very special stylist. Hair Balancing is the most sensitive and life-enhancing hair care system in the world. It is a holistic healing art that involves cutting the hair using the principles of Sacred Geometry, and is designed to achieve healthy, vibrant and beautiful hair. Each hair is balanced to every other hair on your head. The hair is cut vertically, horizontally and diagonally. With "hair balancing" you can expect these benefits: hair designs tailored to you, wash and wear hair, artful "grow-outs," reduces hair loss, hair grows thicker and faster, enhances curl and wave, maintains shape longer than other hair cuts. I love to have my hair balanced. Many people with thinning or unmanageable hair have benefited greatly. Also natural enzyme hair coloring.

Brenda Ferreira at Studio B, owner/stylist, 310/395-8025. 1512 11th Street, Suite 206, Santa Monica, 90405. All services. She can be very trendy, if you want that. For $75, she will spend an hour with you and show you several different ways to wear your hair (I got seven.) Her background is as an image consultant for men and women. She is good to talk to about how you look and how you would like to look. Great with men.

Jeremy at Aida Thibiant European Day Spa, 310/278-7565. 449 North Canon Dr., Bevery Hills. "In and out in 30 minutes." $50 for a blowout. Clients include Alicia Silverstone, Bette Midler and Annette Bening.

Linda Kammins' Aromatherapy Salon, 310/659-6257. 848 N. La Cienega Blvd., Suite 204, Los Angeles, 90069. "If you can't control your hair, how can you control your life?" Linda says, "Hair coloring and highlighting is all possible through choosing a more natural alternative and the results are preferred by comparison to traditional chemical applications." She sets a peaceful, tranquil and rejuvenating atmosphere. Services: Aromathearapy hair and scalp oil treatments; aromathereapy hair loss treatment, enzyme hair coloring and hair painting, herb coloring and texture developing, expert artistic hair cutting and styling, hair painting-botanical color, herbal facials, custom blended aromatherapy beauty products. My friend Mary Lu Chasteen loves her work. She brings thinning hair back!

Mauro, 310/273-0600. 425 N. Bedford Drive, Beverly Hills, 90210. Consultation on a new look, 30 minutes, $75. Restyling (first time clients) $80. Cut and blow-dry (existing clients) $65. Blow-Dry $50. Up-do from $75. Full Weave from $125, Partial Weave, $95. Color Correction (per hour) $80. My friend, Samantha Harper, has been following him from place to place for years. He does many celebrities as well as new actors just creating their individual "look." He has developed a great product line, as well. For information: 800/42-MAURO.

Object Beauty Shop, 213/852-0978. 8237 W. Third St., L.A., 90048, at Sweetzer. My daughters, long-haired Cathy Kerr and thin-haired Cynthia Kerr love Hiroshi; he never cuts too short and you don't have to wait a long time for an appointment. Cynthia loves his special highlights. They rave about the massage shampoos.

Rosiland Mitchell at Carlton's Hair Salon, 818/986-8750. In Fashion Square Mall, she also has good products. Highly recommended by makeup artist Rita Montanez.

Stan Vogel (aka Red) at Louis Michael Salon, 310/275-1322. 413 N. Canon Dr., Beverly Hills, 90210. A good guy, never runs late, never cuts too much, very talented in all areas of hair work, a color expert. I love the highlighting he does for me and when I was a red head, he kept it the perfect red. He blows hair really straight. Because I have curly hair, this is important to me; not everyone can do it. He's fun and easy to be with. *See his comments above.*

Susan's Hair Salon, 213/658-8760. 7823 Melrose Avenue, Los Angeles, 90046. Susan is long gone, the owners are Annie and Dan. Dan does great work with hair, especially blowing long hair straight, $15, also reasonable, simple color and cutting. Annie does hair color and cutting. It is fairly easy to get an appointment here.

Fernando Dejesus, The West End Salon, 310/888-1800. 9021 Melrose Avenue, West Hollywood, 90069. Fernando is from London, he specializes in corrective hair coloring. Beautiful custom stylized work. One of my students, took in a magazine cover picture of Elizabeth Hurley to match the color and style, she got beautiful results.

Vito at Capella Salon, 818/506-1450. 12816 Ventura Blvd., Studio City. His haircuts are normally $50 but for actors who mention *Acting Is Everything* he will give a $15 discount, $35. My friend loves his haircuts, raves about him. Color great, too.

Yuki's, 310/652-7474. 8640 Sunset Blvd., Sunset Plaza, L.A., 90069. Don Moran is very famous for color; he used to do Marilyn Monroe's hair. My daughter Chris Kerr swears by him. This is a very well known salon, lots of celebrities.

MANICURISTS AND WAXING

Bolo Salon's Courtney Upton, 310/247-1912. 636 N. Almont Dr., West Hollywood. Pedicures, she has been known to cure ingrown toenails otherwise destined for surgery.

Chinoiseri, 818-752-4347. 12246 Ventura Blvd., Studio City. Sharon Stone says, "Tammie Ly will create any nail color polish you want. She'll duplicate any shade you like."

Esfir Tselner of Esther's Place, 310/274-4552. Hair removal. legs and bikini lines, $40. "My customers tell me I don't hurt them as much as other people do."

Susan's Hair Salon, 213/658-8760. 7823 Melrose Avenue, Los Angeles, 90046. Annie does wonderful pedicures, $11 and natural manicures, $9 for french nails. She doesn't do any acrylic work, so the shop doesn't have that awful smell. She does "gentle as she can" reasonable waxing for men and women. It is fairly easy to get an appointment here.

Yolanda Frye Skin Care, 310/275-3981. 632 1/2 Doheny Dr, Los Angeles, 90069. She does manicures and pedicures and acrylics. Cathy and Chris Kerr love her weekly manicures. Cathy often has a manicure and pedicure when returning from a long exhausting business trip; it perks her right up. Waxing, men and women.

Age Defying and Beauty Enhancing Techniques: Facials and Massage

• **Your face is your billboard**; it's where the audience sees what you are feeling and thinking. The first time you see your face on a big screen it is awe inspiring.

• **When you are wearing makeup** and working in it for hours, you need a thorough cleansing. A facial every month or so is a wonderful way to relax and treat yourself well. Aging can be slowed down; our profession is so youth oriented that it demands we look as young as we can for as long as we can. Surgery is a last resort because when they cut into the skin you never know how your body will heal.

• **Medical doctors used to say that nothing** rubbed on the skin can penetrate and help stop aging; it has to come from the inside. Then Retin A, glycolic acid, and chemical peels came along. Now the doctors are using these products and admit that they do retard the aging process.

• **Christie Brinkley** is known for her beautiful young skin; she has made a living with it. It is said that she never turns on her heat or air conditioner, as they dry out skin. I have an actress friend who has to be in her late forties, though she never tells her age, with the most flawless skin. She has never been in the sun and during the winter, layers her clothing so she doesn't use heat. She did this even while acting on soap operas in New York. It has paid off, she looks like she is in her thirties and is still being cast as that. Women have to stretch their young years as long as possible. Men need to stretch their mid years.

• **Rand Rusher, R.N., C.N.O.R.** Botox and Collagen Specialist of Wilshire Aesthetics, shares the following information about suntans.

- **I'm afraid there is no such thing as a safe suntan**, no matter how carefully you want to "get some sun." Tanning is still a defense mechanism of the skin. With sun exposure, the skin produces more pigment to provide protection against the sun. The presence of a tan indicates there has been some degree of damage. This damage is responsible for 85% of aging.
- **If this is not going to stop you from getting a tan**, here are some tips that will help reduce the damage. *Tan the hide, hide the face.* Use a heavy SPF on your face, lower number on your body. Good face products are oil free, waterproof, SPF 30, paba free, non-communigenic sunscreens like Banana Boat, Neutregena and Coppertone. *Avoid becoming sunburned at all costs.* The damage may not show up for years, but it will. *Always wear sunscreen even when it is cloudy,* even if you have very dark skin. *Lips need sunscreen too.* Neostrata makes an excellent product for this. *Fake tans are great; use self action tanners.* The trick is to find one that complements your natural skin tone. Chanel smells great but is a bit greasy, California Tan has no smell and not greasy but can streak. You really have to try the products out on your own skin.

• **Sylvie Archenault, owner of Sylvie's Advanced European Skin & Body Care System,** has been doing facials for thirty years. She works with three chemists and two laboratories developing her cutting edge Sonäge skin products, importing the raw materials from Europe, Japan and Australia. Sylvie talks about the results people can expect from facials:

- **When you have a facial,** you should see a change right away; your skin will be glowing, energized, and cleansed. You are taking off all the makeup and grime, the skin is pure. If you have acne or a breakout, you should not be red when the treatment is over. A deep pore facial once a month is good for general cleaning and toning, but if there are skin difficulties or special occasions then you will need facials more often. The aesthetician can do things to make your skin beautiful for a photo shoot. Makeup responds beautifully when you have healthy skin underneath. The style now is very light makeup; you can't hide the imperfections so you must really clean your skin.

Q: How do you choose a skin care person?

- **Skin care is an art.** You will probably go to a facialist before the plastic surgeon and dermatologist. You want to choose a professional, first by their word of mouth reputation, then by the techniques they use and most importantly the results. Have a consultation or an over-the-phone interview. Finally, you must experience their facial. If it's too strong it can bruise the skin and leave you marked for a few days—that might interfere with your acting interviews. At Sylvie's we use the latest techniques and revolutionary ingredients; my goal is to fight aging.

Q: How can actors help their skin?

- **Drink a lot of water** because it provides energy, keeps the skin glowing and cleans up your system by drawing the toxins away from your body. Caffeine and smoking does a lot of damage. Exposure to the sun is damaging. It is easier to apply makeup on porcelain skin; you can not take off the tan if you need a white skin.

Facialist and natural product developer Leah Ruiz of The Vital Image gives some hints for skin care.

- **Don't touch your face**, unless you are going to be gentle. Don't rub your eyes if they itch. Use your middle fingers and pat to keep from stretching your skin. Use short, firm strokes to apply products.

- **In order to drink more water each day** make a pot of herb tea or add a splash of juice to your water and drink throughout the day.

- **Increase oxygen intake to relieve stress.** Oxygen bath: add a full 16 ounce bottle of common 3% Hydrogen Peroxide to a warm bath. Soak for 20 minutes. Oxygen break: make a point of taking ten deep breaths, ten times a day.

- **Acne skin is especially sugar intolerant.** Substitute a natural, sugar free sweetener such as stevia extract to sweeten drinks and food.

- **Be a fanatic** about your skin care routine at night before retiring. You will help your skin to rejuvenate itself by sticking to this good habit. Your skin is most actively regenerated between the hours of midnight and 4:00AM.

- **Don't sleep on your face.** Sleep on your back or side to avoid wrinkling and creasing your face while you sleep. It's easy for most people to train themselves into a favorable sleeping position. Satin pillow cases reduce friction that stretches and damages hair and skin. Look for pure silk rather than synthetic fabrics. To release tension around the eyes, put your head on the pillow, inhale deeply and with your thumbs, press upward toward the forehead on the eye socket—the sensitive area between the eyebrows. Exhale while applying pressure and relax the jaw, repeat three times. The results will amaze you.

- **Proper exfoliation can step up cell renewal.** You can use simple table sugar as an exceptional exfoliant. It has fine grains for gentle removal of dead surface cells, it is nondrying and rinses away completely. Wet your face and lather then add a half teaspoon or more of sugar to one lathered up hand. Dip the two middle fingers of your other hand into the sugar and gently wash your face using a circular motion. Rinse well and pat dry. Your face should look rosy but not irritated. After exfoliation, your skin will absorb more nutrients and moisture.

- **Perfume is okay but never directly on your skin.** It is best in your hair or on your clothes.

• **Tina Lynne, the creator of *The Lynne Technique*** answers the very important questions about how to look your best when you have overindulged.

- **Our motto is: if you've had a "marguerita and salty chips" night**, don't wear it on your face the next day; do the *Lynne Technique.* When you do the technique it helps to clean out the lymph system, which is a filtering system that removes toxic bloat in your body. Open your mouth into the "long O" which is like the men's shaving position, put on your cleanser then blot the face with a hot compress, working down towards the heart hitting some of the pressure points, press down, with your knuckles on your chest, two, three, pump. Then pushing the knuckles into the armpits, one, two, three, pumping. Next take some deep breaths, the breathing is really important to oxygenate the body.

- **You can continue to reduce swelling and puffiness** by pressing accupressure points while you're applying your undereye concealer and makeup, just by rolling your finger on the inside corner of the eye, out the side to the temple, walking your fingers out. This technique will help reduce dark circles and puffiness. Make sure you're never stretching the skin on your face.

Q: How does your technique done professionally help to defy aging and enhance beauty?

- **What I do is called the body clearing treatment.** It is the best part of a facial or traditional massage, which brings up circulation and carries away toxins. I clean out the lymph system. If your lymph system is clogged up it becomes inefficient. The analogy is: how poorly your dryer works when you don't clean the lint screen. You clean out the lymph system so your body is removing it's waste efficiently and quickly. A lot of massages swish around the toxins, but they don't end up leaving the body so people are still bloated afterwards. The treatment we do is to help dispose of the toxins though the kidneys, through both ends, so to speak. It's like a colonic without the machine.

Q: When working with facialists and makeup artists, how can we get the best results?

- **When you are getting a facial**, make sure you don't let the person squeeze the pores. The facialist must use an extractor, which is what the dermatologists use, or the facialist should be creating pressure in one direction only, with a piece of tissue.

- **If you have a pimple at home**, use hot water and a product designed to pull out impurities. (I have one called, The Mineral Infusion, its a "vacuum in a jar.") Then press in the direction of the pores so the impurity will pull out. If it's not ready, leave it alone. If you have an important event or photo shoot you can go to your dermatologist and they can inject the pimple and it will go away.

- **When a makeup artist is applying your makeup**, make sure they don't tug on your skin. You open your mouth into the "long O" and tell them "this is *The Lynne Technique* and if I don't open up my mouth for you, my skin gets stretched." It's actually easier for the makeup artist when you do open your mouth, because they can get into the contours more easily.

Facialist Margaret Tomaszewicz, who works at the Burke Williams Day Spa and Massage Center, talks about men's facials.

- **Men can shave in the morning**, if they're having a facial in the evening, but should not shave right before; it makes the skin too sensitive. Men tend to have good facial skin, but they break out on their backs due to sports and exercises. If there are just a few spots, an exfoliation treatment will be enough with an occasional maintenance. When there are a lot of problems, the client would have to come in every couple of weeks. I would also advise a topical medication for them to use. We do full-body facials for swimsuit and body photo shoots. It polishes the skin.

Q: Why is a massage valuable for actors?

- **Doctors in Europe** prescribe massages for health reasons. A massage gives oxygen to the muscles and the tissue, even more than exercise can provide. It gives life, circulation, and relaxation as well. When directions on bottles of creams say to massage vigorously into the body, it's not the creams that are good, it's the actual massage that breaks up the toxins in your body. In short, it's great for relaxation and for long term effects; it's very good for your health.

Resources

The Vital Image, 310/823-1996 or 800/414-4624. Leah has a studio in Playa del Rey. $50 for an hour facial. Guaranteed quick results. She does minimal extractions so there is no marking at all. She believes the products will pull most of the toxins out. The facials, special Chinese lamp and all natural products heal skin damaged from age, sun and deep abrasion or laser work. I've had terrific healing with these facials. The three products, Face & Body Wash, Skin Renewal Complex and Phytohydrator (liquid moisturizer) are all you need to deliver fabulous skin. Among their many other products, they have a special under-eye bag cure, it removed my daughter Chris's inherited bags, (from me, sorry Chris) she's thrilled. I love their Shaving Miracle liquid, I've never gotten such a close shave, men love it—no break outs. Newest is Lift & Firm, fights wrinkes and flaccid skin, eye lift, jawline and neck firming, it works! Sun Shield Moisturizer: amazing and 100% free of man-made chemicals, powerful nutrients. Call for their special product report.

***The Lynne Technique* for Face and Body Care by Tina Lynne**, 310/858-8886 or 323/939-9117. When actors overindulge she can get them ready for their close-ups by taking the toxins and swelling out of their faces and body. Some of the symptoms her technique helps fight are puffiness, dark circles, facial lines, acne, headaches and jet lag. She combines a regimen of acupressure massage with a balance of minerals, herbs and emollients to firm muscles, clear sinuses and revitalize skin cells by inducing detoxification and faster metabolism of fats and other wastes and nutrients thus stimulating cell renewal and growth. She works pre/postoperative plastic surgery treatment to maintain and enhance surgical results. She brought me through a major detoxifying in a short amount of time. Incorporating her own designed products and exercises, you can carry on the work at home. Many celebrity clients including International and Hollywood royalty.

Dermaglow at Beauty Body Wellness by Anna Marie Colavito, 310/858-8886. The Los Angeles Center for Healing, 1157 S. Robertson Blvd. Los Angeles, 90035. She has developed "Dermaglow" which is micro-dermabrasion, 30 minute treatment without laser or chemicals. Finely shaped crystals gently polish away dull and damaged skin. Reduces fine lines, wrinkles and pore size, painless, 0 down time, men and women, minimizes sun damage and acne scars, erases stretch marks, no peeling or dryness, immediate results. A series of six treatments is recommended, complimentary consultation. Many models, actors and celebrities flock to her.

Ivy's Skincare and Makeup Garden, Ivy Halford, 310/451-7780. 522 Wilshire Blvd. Suite G, Santa Monica, 90401. 22 years of clinical skills as a paramedical esthetician and makeup artist (Makeup Union Local 706). Transformational Skincare and Makeup. Immediate results to ready you for video, screen and photography work. Extensive specialty services, include micro-dermabrasion, glycolic peels, oxygen facials, the deepest pore cleansing in town, ("You can audition the same day, you won't leave red and marked up.") skin bleaching, hyperpigmentation treatment and makeup including products and design. Many of her clients are celebrities, models and actors

Yolanda Frye Skin Care, 310/275-3981. 632 1/2 Doheny Dr, Los Angeles, 90069. Her special beauty treatment is Oxiana a European skin therapy, "a fountain of youth for men and women's skin!" With Oxiana it is possible to apply highly concentrated Oxygen and skin enhancing nutrients where needed. Especially recommended after all laser resurfacing - as soon as bandages are removed; all skin peel recipients; acne conditions; following electrolysis, waxing and permanent makeup procedures; and in combination with deep cleansing facials. Her facials start at $50 to $150. Cathy Kerr especially loves her back facials, great for when you are wearing a low back dress, men love this too. Yolanda does lash and brow tinting, skin and body waxing, full nail service and makeup.

Sylvie's, 818/905-8815. 17071 Ventura Blvd., Encino, 91436. For men and women. Tu&F 9-5, W & TH 9-8, Sa 8-5. Deep pore cleansing facials start at $50. Modeling and toning $70, lifting $65, bleaching $35. They do skin and body waxing, lash and brow tinting, permanent lip, brow and eyeliner makeup. One hour body massage $60. Varied prices for several types of massage including lymphatic drainage, reflexology, anti-stress detox, PMS treatment, exfoliation, cellulite, hair removal by electronic tweezers, electrolysis and European waxing. Aromatherapy. Manicures and pedicures. All of the aestheticians are trained by Sylvie using her techniques and methods. Her Sonäge skin care products are healing, enhancing, concentrated, smell good; you see and feel a difference right away. Cathy Kerr's favorite. There is a discrete back entrance for clients who may not want to be seen.

Beverly Hot Springs, 323/734-7000. 308 N. Oxford Ave., L. A., 90004. Everyday 9-9. This is not a fancy place but many celebrities go there. Built over a natural hot spring they offer many services. Separate men and women pools, everyone is naked. Admission $25-$30.

Burke Williams Day Spa & Massage Center, 310/587-3366. 1460 Fourth Street, Santa Monica, 90401. Have a facial with knowledgeable Margaret Tomaszewicz. Four-and-a-half-hour packages like "Day of Beauty," & "Gentlemen's Choice" cost from $220-$270. Christian Parkinson, masseur. All sessions include sauna and whirlpool free.

Drew James, 310/395-1405. 13050 San Vicente Blvd., #208, Los Angeles, 90049. Facials $85 and up. Glycolic peels available. He's great at picking out your imperfections, without marking you. Waxing and lash tinting. Large clientele of men and women.

Nina Bard, PME, 310/589-5385, north end of Malibu. She does facials, waxing, eyebrow design and permanent eye liner, eyebrow and lip liner cosmetic tattooing, plus her well researched products.

Rand Rusher, R.N., C.N.O.R. Botox and Collagen Specialist of Wilshire Aesthetics, A Dermatology and Plastic Surgery Group, 323/936-1245. www.wilshireaesthetics.com. 5670 Wilshire Blvd., Suite 650, Los Angeles, 90036. He is a master with the needle. I love botox and collagen; they do help defy the look of aging. A good technician will make all the difference; if they get too much botox in your forehead, your eyebrows can sag. Great for lines around the eyes too. The collagen fills in lines, especially chronic frown lines, and those pesky lines around the mouth.

Spa Transcendental, 818/505-9511. 10645 Riverside Drive, Toluca Lake, 91602. They have many specialized services and spa packages. Massage Therapies, foot reflexology 30 minutes, $40, deep tissue and sports massage 60 minutes for $65.Body treatments and wraps. European Facial 75 minutes for $65. Waxing, lash and brow tinting. Agent Bonnie Howard says, "you feel like you have been on vacation."

Tova's Body, Mind & Spirit Salon and Boutique, 310/205-0511. 188A North Canon Drive, Beverly Hills, 90210. Facials, massage therapy, nails and products. I worked with Tova's husband, 80 year old Ernest Borgnine on *The Single Guy*. Take one look at him and you will want Tova's products and services; you would swear his skin looks 20 years younger. Many celebrities attest to great skin improvements. Tova's won international awards for her products. The full-service salon also offers half-day and full-day spa packages. Ming-Na Wen's (*The Single Guy)* favorite fragrance is *Tova*. She says, "I've never received so many compliments before from a fragrance I'm wearing." It smells wonderfully clean and subtle.

The Arcona Studio Holistic Beauty Therapy For Face and Body, 818/506-5192. 5505-5511 Laurel Canyon Blvd., Studio City. Men and women. $65 for nonsurgical face lift and facial contouring with essential oils. This treatment is what attracts many people to them; you can tell the difference. Many other treatments including glycolic acid peel and European deep-suction cleansing. Arcona is booked six months ahead, many celebrities including Sharon Stone, but she has trained assistants.

• MASSAGE & BODY WORK ONLY

Myrna Moss, M.T., 805/526-1636 or pager 818/372-9474. She is a massage therapist to the stars and regular folks too. $60, she brings her table to you. Deep tissue work, she is a healer. Massage lowers your blood sugar and enhances creativity and productivity. Many production offices and shows hire her to come in and give neck and shoulder massages to cast and crew. What a great Christmas gift or end of season present for a cast or crew member to give to their fellow workers.

See above for *The Lynne Technique*.

Workouts, Exercise and Dance

• **All actors need some type** of body movement class at least twice a week for body awareness, three times a week to change their bodies. The purpose of this is to become acquainted with every muscle and tendon. Acting is physical work, and if you don't know your body, you are denying a great many tools that could be available to you.

• **Working as an actor has a lot to do with how you look**, your weight, your health, discipline and stamina. There is no way to get around building your body and staying toned. If you don't have a steady, consistent work out program you will probably not be a working actor.

• **Glenn Close,** when talking about doing the stage play *Sunset Boulevard,* made these comments.

> • **It takes a great deal of stamina to do a play.** If I didn't do something physical every day, I wouldn't be able to make it through the show. You know those stairs you see me climbing? There are just as many stairs offstage that I climb to get to those stairs. I do a yoga class for forty-five minutes before each show. We do five shows each weekend. When working, I don't smoke or drink and eat very, very healthy. I have this policy that I can have two Oreos each performance. One of the things that gets me through the weekend is that I know I can have four Oreos on Saturday and four on Sunday.

• **Michael Richards** of *Seinfeld* introduced me to the practice of yoga. He is in such great shape, he can make his body do anything. In addition to his hour daily practice, he does a half hour of restorative yoga positions before each performance. Yoga enables him to do all of his physical comedy and not get hurt. He practices on his own, but when he takes a class it's at the B.K.S. Iyengar Yoga Institute.

• **Jerry Seinfeld** loves to exercise. Swimming, weights, treadmill, Nordic track and some yoga stretching before and after his workouts. During *Seinfeld,* he worked with a trainer at 6:30 AM. Jerry had a very tough schedule. Along with writing, casting, acting, editing, and promoting *Seinfeld* (of course with a talented, accomplished staff) he still got in his meditation and exercise.

• **Julia Louis-Dreyfus** of *Seinfeld* loves the treadmill and uses it most every day for an hour. She also has a trainer/physical therapist three times a week. She has a Pilates machine and a trainer to work out with her. She is tiny, yet very strong and looks great in whatever the wardrobe designers put her in. She always looks stunning in the spectacular dresses she wears to the award shows.

• **Jason Alexander** of *Seinfeld* trains in various ways. He does fight his weight so he was always looking for an exercise he enjoyed. He is proficient in Karate, he does the Stairmaster and his newest is the Pilates machine. He is so tough and strong, yet when you see him dance he looks like he's floating on a cloud.

• **So dance, fence, run, lift weights, practice yoga**, anything that requires precision movements. Going to classes and the gym are good places to meet other actors and people in the biz who might have information about acting jobs. Your VCR can help too. There are a lot of good exercise tapes for sale or rent. You can also tape workout television shows.

• **Personal trainer Pete Austria says:**

  • **You must look good** to work in this town. That is a truism that must be approached logically and intelligently. The human body is a miraculous machine to take care of. To have good health in our minds and bodies is all that really matters. In order to have lasting success and happiness, take care of yourself mentally and physically.

• **Personal trainer Carla Jones talks about how to burn fat:**

  • **The only way to achieve long term weight loss, decreased body fat**, a firm and shapely physique and a higher level of overall fitness is to address both sides of the fitness equation. In order to maintain your current weight, your caloric intake must equal your caloric usage. If you eat more than you burn, you'll gain weight. If you burn more than you eat, you'll lose weight. Burning fat calories is crucial for any weight management plan. However to burn fat most efficiently, you must work within your fat burning heart rate zone. Many people don't realize that there are five heart rate training zones in all. Each training zone is at a different level of exercise intensity and is best suited for a particular purpose. Training in one or all of these zones can play a crucial part in your overall training program.

- **Moderate Activity Zone** (50-60% Max HR): the heart rate training level, if you are primarily interested in weight loss, beginning a program after being sedentary, are in extremely poor condition, or are rehabilitating from a medical difficulty. In this zone, the fuel used for energy is about 85% fat, 10% carbohydrates and 5% protein.

- **Weight Management Zone** (60-70% Max HR): starting at this intensity level and upward, your body begins to reap the positive effects of aerobic exercise. In this zone, your heart is working hard enough to become stronger and ready for a steady, pain-free, moderate pace. The fuel used for energy in this zone is also 85% fat, 10% carbohydrates and 5% protein.

- **Aerobic Zone** (70%-80% Max HR): training within the aerobic zone benefits your cardiovascular and respiratory systems (heart and lungs). If your goal is to become fitter, faster and stronger, this is the zone for most of your concentrated efforts. This zone has been known as the "target heart rate zone" for years. The fuel used for energy is about 50% fat and 50% carbohydrates.

- **Anaerobic Threshold Zone** (80-90% Max HR): this zone brings you near the point where aerobic training crosses over and becomes anaerobic training. Primary benefits of training in this range is to increase your body's ability to metabolize lactic acid allowing you to train harder before crossing over into the pain of lactate accumulation and oxygen debt. This training benefits athletes interested in high performance training. In this zone you will burn about 15% fat and 85% carbohydrates.

- **Red-Line Zone** (90-100% Max HR): train at this level only if you are extremely fit from extensive training and have a working knowledge of the principles of high performance training. While in the red-line, you will have crossed over the anaerobic threshold and will be operating in oxygen debt (your muscles will be using more oxygen than your body can provide).

- **Fat Burning:** you will need to exercise three to six days per week at a low intensity level, long duration (35 minutes or more) and moderate pace.

- **Weight Training:** In addition to your fat burning work, which will serve to reduce your percentage of body fat, you will need a comprehensive weight training program design. It would be prudent to seek the advice of a certified personal trainer to ensure that you are working at a safe, practical level of intensity and utilizing proper weight training techniques.

- **Proper Nutrition:** maintaining a healthy diet plan can be much simpler than most people realize. First, keep in mind that calories are provided by four nutritional categories: protein provides four calories per gram, carbohydrates provide four calories per gram, fat provides nine calories per gram and alcohol provides seven calories per gram. A healthy diet should include a wide variety of foods.

Resources

Shelly's Discount Aerobic & Dance Wear, 310/475-1400. 2089 Westwood Blvd., Westwood, 90025. (Between Santa Monica Blvd. & Olympic) M-Sa 10-6, Su 11-4.

Encore Sports, 818/985-2221. 4446 Forman Avenue, Toluca Lake. M-F 11-6, Sa 10-5. Clothing for: Golf, tennis, fitness, ski, equestrian. Up to 75% off retail prices. Track pants, bootleg pants, bike shorts, stretch tops, sweats, all discount priced. Some resale items for ski & equestrian.

• PROFESSIONAL DANCE STUDIOS

Edge Performing Arts Center, 213/962-7733. 1020 North Cole Ave., 4th Floor, Hollywood, 90038. All ages, beginning through professional; jazz, ballet hip-hop and tap. $9 a class, SAG $8.

Debbie Reynolds Rehearsal Studios, 818/985-3193. 6514 Lankershim Blvd., North Hollywood, 91606. $9 a class, union $8. M-Sa 9-9. Adult and children. Jazz, ballet and tap, hip-hop, musical theatre, specialty classes in turning.

Jennifer Nairn-Smith, 323/938-6836. Private and small classes specializing in changing your body. Jennifer is from the New York City Ballet and danced in the film *All That Jazz.* She teaches all types of dance and choreographs for films, music videos and commercials. Fosse style original jazz.

Moro-Landis Studios, 818/753-5081. 10960 Ventura Blvd., Studio City, 91604. All ballet, jazz and hip hop dance single classes are $10 and $9 for union. Dance coupons are 5 for $47 and 10 for $87.

Pedro Montanez, 818/829-5195. Teaches privately ballroom, waltz, rumba, samba, salsa, fox-trot, hussle, hip hop, street dancing, ballet, jazz, and tap. He choreographs weddings and is hired to get people dancing at parties. He can be hired if you need to learn a dance step quickly for an audition. As an actor, you should know the usual dances for your resume.

Conjunctive Point Dance Center, 310/836-3962. 3631 Hayden Ave., Culver City. Stanley Holden formerly of the royal ballet is the master. This is the real thing for ballet. Reid Olsen great teacher. Classes $12.

The Dance Center, 818/980-3336. 11401 Chandler Blvd., North Hollywood, 91601. Ballet, jazz, tap, funk, hip hop and step aerobics. $9 a class, union $8. $42 for five classes in one month. $80 for 10 classes in two months. $145 for 20 for 30 classes taken within three months.

• PERSONAL TRAINERS

Pete Austria, 310/659-0416. Trains at several locations. He has a degree and is a certified personal trainer. He really takes his work seriously. He helped train athletes during the 1984 Olympics. When I worked with him, I really got tough and looked good.

David Brown, 323/957-9066. He is a great personal trainer, inexpensive, fun to be with and has a great looking body. He only trains at Gold's Gym, so you have to be a member there.

Body Concepts, Tommy Iacona, AFAA, IDEA, ACE Certified, 213/288-3844. $55 a session. Men and women, nutrition, weight management, body sculpting and toning. House calls available.

CD Body System, Cynthia Deziel, 818/985-4455. $70 an hour. Generally three times a week. She goes to the client's home, bringing everything; you just need sneakers. If you schedule a session, you pay for it. Her expertise is in sculpting the body by shaping the muscles. "My forte is women's shapes that are feminine with tone and building bulk on guys. I do everything."

Tony English Fitness, World Private Training Centers, 818/761-TONY. He is in Studio City. He has a small private gym or he will come to you.

Ron Fletcher Studio, 323/655-5084. 8330 W. Third Street, Los Angeles, 90048. The original Pilates technique studio.

Kenneth Golding, 323/655-4602. 8416 West Third St., L.A., 90048. Private and semi-private. $30 to $120 per session. Combines all the basic elements of physical fitness regimented activities: strength, flexibility, cardiovascular and endurance. His goal is for his clients to make progress with each workout and carry it to other activities in their lives. He does seminars for his clients such as nutrition and discipline. Dr. Theresa Gormly, D.C. recommends him.

Javier at Hotte Bodies Technique, 818/508-4545. 11634 Ventura Blvd., Studio City, 91604. Body sculpting, weight reduction, strength training away from the crowds. Javier's specialized services: Nutritional evaluation and guidance for weight loss and weight gain, cardiovascular conditioning, flexibility training, physical rehabilitation and stress reduction.

Carla Jones of Star Quality Fitness Training, 213/918-2906. Certified personal trainer. She distributes all natural supplements. My friend Mary Ellen Jones has had great success working one on one with Carla. Mary Ellen is a tennis jock but says she has never been in better shape since weight training with Carla. One-on-one sessions; personalized program designs; fitness evaluations; nutritional evaluations. Single session in the gym $45. In-home training single session $60. Body fat assessment, $15.

Tina Lynne, 323/939-9117. A specialist in the complete make-over. She does basic nutritional consulting. Instructs her clients in the proper exercises for posture lengthening and grace. Facial exercises for firming and toning. She teaches privately or in small classes. She also does facial and body massage.

Tawny Moyer, 323/650-0748. "With Pilates, we reshape the body for maximum strength and long, lean muscle." Specializing in women, focusing on muscle sculpting, strength training and flexibility. Recommended two to three times a week. Private sessions in her studio, $75.

Pilates, Donna Eshelman 310/475-6038. 10780 Santa Monica Blvd., #470, Los Angeles. She believes that training twice a week consistently is all you need for stronger muscles and a sleeker, more balanced body.

Rob Parr, 310/476-9172. Helped reshape Demi Moore, Maria Shriver and Tatum O'Neal after pregnancies. John Mc Enroe and Christy Turlington.

The Private Gym, 818/766-3035. 4419 Coldwater Canyon, Suite B, Studio City, 91605. Sherry Mandan, private trainer and owner. Body sculpting for muscle tone and definition, flexibility training for relaxation and strength, cardiovascular conditioning for body weight balance, strength training to prevent muscle strain and back injury.

Michael Thurmond's Six-Week Body Make-over, 800/639-2639. He advertises in L.A. Magazine. I met a mature actress on the set of Thea who had lost 40 pounds. She said she looked better than she had in years. She was working out with weights, said Michael's program really motivated her.

• WORKOUT PLACES

Adventure Fitness Training, 888/488-4AFT. 3027 Wilshire Blvd., #118, Santa Monica. Courses are geared to different skill and fitness levels. Pentathalon-like workouts—repelling, rope climbing, ocean swimming, mountain biking.

Angel City Yoga Center, 818/762-8291. 12408 Ventura Blvd., Studio City, 91604. Multi-method Hatha yoga, Sivananda Hatha; Iyengar; Astanga; Kundalini. $12 per individual class. 8 class card $85. Unlimited, $108 per month, $270 for 3 months.

Aquatic Masters Program, 310/451-6666. Clay Evans has designed this program to aid injury recovery, as well as overall fitness and swimming ability. You are videotaped during stroke-technique exercises.

B.K.S. Iyengar Yoga Institute of Los Angeles, 323/653-0357. 8233 West Third Street, Los Angeles, 90048. Individual 1 1/2 hour class, $14; the noon one hour classes, $12; series of 10, $120; monthly unlimited, $140. First class is free. I love this place; the teachers are great. There are three levels so you don't have to worry if you are new. For your first class I would recommend 7:30 Wednesday night, or Saturday morning 10:45 with Chris Stein or Tuesday morning 8:30 or Tuesday night at 7:30 with Leslie. I love the 8:30 morning classes; they are small and Leslie and Sue really have the time and inclination to make sure you understand all the moves. All the teachers are very highly trained and are very aware of keeping you from injury. Larry, Marla, Sylvie, Herb and Karin are great too. Alice teaches a special class at 9am on Saturday morning for people with scoliosis.

Body Sculpting, 310/657-4140. 624 N. La Cienega, West Hollywood. This is not a membership gym; the trainers pay to belong and then charge you for the workout. Many trainers.

Bally's Total Fitness, 323/461-0227. 1628 N. El Centro, Hollywood, 90028. M-F 5:30AM to Midnight, Sa&Su 8-8. Swimming pool, running track, many treadmills and bikes, TVs to watch. 818/760/7800. 11315 Ventura Blvd., Studio City, 91604. M-F 24 hours, Sa&Su 8-8. I love Bally's because I can always find a gym in another city when traveling. Not as fancy as others but the price is right.

Bodies in Motion, 310/264-0777. 2730 Santa Monica Blvd., Santa Monica, 90404. 310/836-8000. Also 1950 Century Park E., Century City. Kick Boxing, Boxing, Yoga, Aerobics, Free Weights, Treadmills. Jode Edwards takes kick boxing and says this is a terrific workout. "When you finish hitting that bag its like a release, you get all your anxieties out."

Critical Mass. 310/917-1199. 26th and San Vicente, Brentwood. Tori Spellilng, Harry Hamlin, Anne Archer. Owners/trainers David Kelmenson and Steven Kates.

Crunch, 323/654-4550. Corner of Sunset and Crescent Heights where the old Schwabs Drugstore used to be. Madonna's trainer Carlos Leon is there. Afro-Brazilian aerobics. Marisa Tomei, Julianna Margulies, Laura Dern, Brad Pitt, Jeff Goldblum, Julie Delpy, Jon Favreau, Debi Mazar, Ben Stiller.

L.A. Fitness at Warner Center Club, 818/884-1100. 6336 Canoga Ave., Woodland Hills.

Gold's Gym, 310/392-6004. 360 Hampton Drive, Venice. 323/462-7012. 1016 N. Cole, Hollywood. The Venice gym is filled with every big name from the world of bodybuilding plus the likes of Janet Jackson, Lisa Bonet and Jodie Foster.

Gymnastics Center, Santa Monica, 310/838-4228. 8476 Warner Drive, Culver City, 90232. For adults: Richie Salas, 310/837-3635. My daughter Chris Kerr swears by his workouts. She used to be a champion gymnast and returned as an adult to the sport she loves. Will Estes and Elisabeth Shue love this place.

Gymnastics with Bob Carreiro, 310/652-3060. 722 N. La Cienega Blvd., L.A. 90069. Bob can turn even the most uptight body into one that is lithe, strong and obedient. The risk is higher; so are the rewards. Private and small classes.

Easton Gym, 323/651-3636. 8053 Beverly Blvd. (near Crescent Heights.) 5AM to midnight. Cardio and strength training, personal training, complete locker facilities.

Karate, Simon Rhee, 818/224-3400. 22880 Ventura Blvd., Woodland Hills, 91364. Master Rhee is an action actor, *Best of the Best I & II,* and others. Cathy Kerr is a Black Belt—oh I hate to brag! Love my girls!

Karate, Jun Chong, 323/658-7570. 6401 Wilshire Blvd. L.A. 818/769-9308. 5223 Lankershim Blvd., North Hollywood. Danny Gibson is the manager here. Mr. Gibson is inspirational and keeps his students motivated. Cathy and Cynthia Kerr trained with him when they were teenagers. Masters Chong and Gibson are action actors. Third location: 310/449-1333. 2300 Santa Monica Blvd., Santa Monica, 90404.

Rock Climbing, 310/473-4574. After training you go to Stoney Point in Chatsworth to climb boulders 30 to 60 feet high. Equipment is provided.

24 Hour Fitness, 310/652-7440. 8612 Santa Monica Blvd., West Hollywood, 90069. Membership Gym. Weight lifting; all types of exercise classes. M-Th 5:30AM-11PM, F 5:30-10, Sa&Su 7AM-8PM.

Sports Club L.A., 310/477-7799. 1835 Sepulveda Blvd., West Los Angeles. Very expensive, but in!

Stair Climbing on the 4th Street Stairs, at 4th and Adelaide streets in Santa Monica, 189 steps.

Stairs, in Santa Monica. They ascent from the 400 block of North Mesa Road to Amalfi Drive, 201 steps. Less crowded then the 4th Street stairs and redwoods, wisteria and live oaks.

Southern California Boat Club, 310/822-0073. 1355 Fiji Way, Marina del Rey. Wide array of classes and boats for rent.

Westside Fencing Center and Center for Stage Combat, 310/204-2688. 8737 Washington Blvd., Culver City, 90232. The largest fencing center in the country. Classes and private coaching. Call for their brochure; there is a coupon for a free fencing lesson. Some former students are: Geena Davis (*Cutthroat Island*), Teenage Mutant Ninja Turtles, Robin Williams, Shelly Long, Keanu Reeves and Eric Roberts.

Workout Warehouse, 310/358-1838. 648 N. La Peer Drive, Los Angeles, 90069. Lots of celebrities. The gym's high tech resistance machines are known for flawless motion, Tectrix Bikemax stationary cycle gives a smooth ride. Great locker rooms, a staff massage therapist, rubdowns for a dollar a minute.

Yogatopia, 310/899-0047. Corner of San Vicente and 26th, Brentwood. Meg Ryan, Goldie Hawn, Dennis Quaid, Elizabeth Berkley, Jim Belushi, high-energy power yoga class. Also more meditative classes.

Working Actor's Guide lists many gyms and trainers.

HEALTH, DOCTORS, NUTRITION, THERAPY AND PLASTIC SURGERY

• **Choosing doctors, dentists, nutritionists, alternative treatments and therapists** are very personal decisions; what is perfect for one person may not work at all for someone else. I can only speak to you from my own and close friend's experiences.

• **I am inclined to investigate most everything.** I have received help and healings from many different types of traditional and nontraditional techniques.

• **As always, proceed with the utmost of caution.** By investigating and following your own instincts, I believe you will be led to the paths that are best for your life.

Physical Health

• **It is imperative to have your body in excellent condition** in order to be the best actor you can be; your body is your instrument. The following practitioners are all specialists in their fields. I hope you are never sick and only need to consult doctors in order to improve your life's condition. In my experience, holistic doctors allow me to take an active part in my recovery so I seek them out.

• **Dr. Cynthia Watson, Medical Doctor and Naturopath.**

Q: What are your recommendations for staying healthy?

- **Maybe the most important factor is life style.** Make sure that you try to eat a healthy and balanced diet, lots of fresh fruits and vegetables. Stay away from the junk foods and sugar. Smoking, drugs, coffee and alcohol really rob your body of nutrients. Important to take a good vitamin program on a regular basis. Many of the congestion problems in Los Angeles are related to the pollution. Take antioxidant vitamins, A, C, and E. These vitamins help your immune system and handle some of the heavy toxins we're dealing with. One of the first things that I do with patients who have postnasal drip problems is take them off dairy products. Enzymes are a very important part of what the body does to help break down toxins, chemicals and food. As we age, we make fewer enzymes. I've found that taking enzymes between meals can help with some of the congestion problems like allergies and some of the digestive problems that I see in my practice.

Q: How do you keep healthy and keep the energy up when you are working the long hours our industry demands?

- **Again, antioxidant vitamins** like vitamin A, C, E and Zinc are important. B vitamins are essential for the nervous system, the adrenal glands and the liver. There are also herbs that can help give you energy and keep your immune system strong. Siberian Ginseng is an herb that really helps; it can be taken over long periods of time and it helps to support those glandular functions. Echinacea is an herb that helps to support the immune system. It shouldn't be taken over long periods of time, but on a short term basis like those three or four weeks that you're on a shoot, is fine. There are products on the market that have Echinacea and Golden Seal root together that help fight infection. Start these herbs in the beginning, as a preventative, and you'll have a much better effect in keeping illness away. Eat well. You can substitute coffee with Siberian Ginseng or American Ginseng for women, the Chinese Ginseng for men. Bee pollen, royal jelly or B vitamins will give you a little extra energy.

Q: What about traveling on locations, especially to foreign countries?

- **One of the things that helps my patients** is to take a form of acidophilus. That is a product that you can buy in your regular drugstore. It's a culture that's in yogurt and various milk products, and is available in capsule form that doesn't need to be refrigerated. When you take these capsules while traveling, you're continuing to fill your intestines with the healthy bacteria that your body is used to. It helps to prevent traveler's diarrhea and stomach problems. You want to be really careful about your water supply. If you're on a long air flight, take a bottle of water with you on the plane; don't rely on the plane water—it's generally not very good. Flying is extremely dehydrating. A little atomizer bottle helps to spray your skin. For motion sickness there is a homeopathic remedy called Cocculus. There are other drugs, but they tend to make you sleepy and give you dry mouth; the homeopathic won't.

• Dr. Theresa Gormly, Chiropractor and Founder of the Los Angeles Center for Healing, offers additional information on staying healthy.

- **If people paid greater attention to their diet** they would not have as many physical complaints. I strongly recommend three meals a day consisting of 40% carbohydrates, 30% protein and 30% fat plus two small equally balanced snacks. The key is to eat high quality protein, lean red meat, turkey, chicken, fish and soy; low glycemic carbohydrates, vegetables, fruit, very little grain; and high quality fats such as raw nuts, cold pressed oils or avocado. For many people. it is also necessary to abstain from foods that they may be sensitive to. such as dairy and wheat.

- **Nutrition is one side of the triad of health** that I assess when it comes to staying healthy. It is highly beneficial to care for the physical structure of the body. The spine and extremities house our central nervous system, the brain and spinal cord. Chiropractic care and plenty of exercise are great ways to care for the physical structure.

- **Equally important is the emotional side of the triangle.** There are wonderful techniques that help clear the body of stored or toxic emotions such as Neuroemotional Technique (NET), Reiki and homeopathy. By paying attention to one's daily routine of nutrition, exercise, rest, work and play, it is easier to keep the triad of health in balance. EMOTION/ CHEMISTRY/STRUCTURE.

Q: What do you recommend for delivering one's best performance when working long hours under a great deal of pressure?

- **It is important to center one's mind** through meditation or attunement at the beginning of the day. The tool for long term *sustained* energy is blood sugar stabilization. This is done with the right choice and amount of food and no longer than four to five hours of time between balanced meals. This routine takes the stress off the adrenal glands and sustained energy and a clear mind will follow. A second 20 minutes of meditation or rest in the later part of the day will give the body a second wind for the evening hours. By combining rest or meditation with the appropriate food plan you can't miss.

Q: What about air travel? Is it a concern when traveling to locations?

- **Hobon Environs is a homeopathic remedy I recommend** for supporting the immune system during air travel and hotel lodging. This remedy helps prevent contracting airborne diseases that come through the ventilation systems. One capful per hour is recommended. It never fails. For jet lag, I recommend a Systemec Formula Gf to support the glandular system. It is to be taken at the beginning of the flight, mid-flight and every two hours on landing for about four to six hours. This helps the body handle the time zone changes.

Resources

Books: Working Actor's Guide, L.A. and **Hollywood Here I Come!** by Cynthia Hunter offer more doctors, dentists, alternative type treatments, nutritionists, mental health services, as well as medical insurance information.

Free Clinics: Los Angeles Free Clinic, 323/653-1990, 8405 Beverly Blvd., Los Angeles, 90048. Valley Free Clinic, 818/763-8836, 5648 Vineland Avenue, North Hollywood. Hours: M-Sa, 10-5. Appointments are given out daily from 9 to 11am on a first call basis. They offer free pregnancy and HIV testing.

Cynthia Watson, M.D., Family Practice, 310/393-0937. 530 Wilshire Blvd., Suite 203, Santa Monica, 90401. Covered by SAG and AFTRA insurance; you file your own forms. A family practitioner treating men, women (obstetrics, gynecology included) and children, she combines conventional medical therapies with herbs, homeopathy, and nutrition. She is a nationally recognized authority in immune disorders and chemical toxicity. Her main interest is preventative medicine and longevity. Her book *Love Potions, A Guide To Aphrodisiacs and Sexual Pleasures* is a best-seller. She continues to write books on nutritional supplements that have healing capabilities.

Harvey Abrams, M.D., Wilshire Aesthetics, *A Dermatology and Plastic Surgery Group*, 323/936-1245. www.wilshireaesthetics.com 5670 Wilshire Blvd., Suite 650, Los Angeles, 90036. Dr. Abrams (a true artist) and his associates are excellent. For procedures covered by insurance, they will file SAG and AFTRA forms for you. In addition to treating all skin diseases, they do wonderful laser dermabrasion work that takes years off your face. They use botox, collagen and the latest techniques to fill in lines, pump up lips and smooth out frowns. Rand Rusher is my special favorite for these needle treatments, he has a knack. Dr. Robin Schaffran is a very knowledgable, good dermatologist. Nina Bard's facials (only there on Tuesdays) will not leave you marked but she gets everything out, $75 for cleansing and toning. Maya does the facials on the other days and gives exceptional individual attention. They have vein and hair removal specialists, and laser resurfacing. Dana has 23 years experience in hair removal. Marilyn and the receptionists are all very helpful; they send you home with a piece of candy and a colorful bag of samples. *See Plastic Surgery Section, page 401.*

Uzzi Reiss, M.D., for women, 310/247-1300. 414 N. Camden Dr. #750, Beverly Hills, 90210. They will file SAG and AFTRA insurance forms for you. Obstetrics, gynecology, infertility. He's delivered many babies of famous people. Although an M.D., he will prescribe homeopathic remedies. Very thorough, explains in great detail. A wonderful man and Julia Louis-Dreyfus's personal favorite.

Vernon Erwin, D.D.S., Dentist, 818/246-1748. 620 E. Glenoaks, Glendale, 91207. They will file SAG and AFTRA forms for you. A homeopathic dentist, he will remove silver fillings and has all the equipment to test your body's reaction to what will be permanently put into your mouth. These type of dentists are hard to find. He does beautiful bleaching, repair and cosmetic work that looks like you have had nothing done, just beautiful teeth. He also treats TMJ. Theresa is the teeth cleaning person and she is excellent, very caring and is gentle but thorough.

Harry Aronowitz, D.D.S., 310-246-0100. 465 N. Roxbury Drive, #1011, Beverly Hills, 90210. Orthodontist, specializes in celebrity orthodonics including removable braces. He is gentle, quick and honest. One of the best in his field. Recommended by Tina Lynne.

J.Alan Bloore, D.D.S., Orthodontist, 310/277-9700. 300 S. Beverly Drive, #101, Beverly Hills, 90212. My daughter, Cathy Kerr, had her teeth straightened as an adult. She just had to wear a retainer for several months and now they are beautiful. She says, "He is the best."

Dr. Roberto Villafana, Tijuana, Mexico, 619/428-1262, in Tijuana, 011/52-66-84-09-55. This Mexican dentist was trained at USC, one of the finest dental schools. He does holistic and cosmetic dentistry, removing silver fillings and uses the finest of materials. His office is very "high tech." His prices are about one third of L.A. My friend, Leah Ruiz, and her husband of The Vital Image, had all of their work done there and just raved about his wonderful technique. Leah is on the cutting edge of all that is healthy for the body.

Conrad Sack, D.D.S., Orthodontist, 310/273-5775. 9201 Sunset Blvd., Suite 200, Los Angeles, 90069. He specializes in Crozat, a removable appliance to take the place of braces. He treats many actors.

William Dorfman, D.D.S., 310/277-5678. 2080 Century Park East, Los Angeles. Cosmetic dentist. He is the inventor of Nite White, the country's most popular teeth whitener. Used by the casts of *Friends, Melrose Place, Beverly Hills 90210, ER, Seinfeld.*

Dr. Huggins, D.D.S., Dentist, 800/331-2303. He is the author of the book *It's All In Your Head.* If you have some chronic medical problems that cannot be solved, you may be suffering from mercury poisoning which is caused from silver fillings in your mouth. This dentist is in Colorado but they will send you the book that lists all the symptoms.

Warren Reingold, M.D., 818/763-3937. 12139 Riverside Dr., Suite 101, Valley Village, 91607. Optometry, contact lenses, fashion eye wear, diseases of the eye. He is a very caring person and I find the office very friendly and helpful. Covered by SAG and Motion Picture Industry Health Insurance, they take care of the insurance for you. He also does all of the laser vision correction eye surgeries.

Caster Eye Center, Andrew I. Caster, M.D., F.A.C.S., 310/274-1221. 9100 Wilshire Blvd., Beverly Hills. Laser vision correction. Frances Fisher says "I see the world through new eyes!" "Best laser Eye Surgeon in Los Angeles" *Los Angeles Magazine.*

International Sportsmedicine Institute, Dr. Leroy Perry, 310/559-6900. 3283 Motor Avenue, Rancho Park. Chiropractic care, massages and beauty treatments, a rehabilitation swimming pool, saunas and steam rooms. Sharon Stone says, "Dr. Perry got me through a bad car accident."

Alan Rosenthal, D.C., Chiropractor, 818/591-8847. Community Chiropractic Health Centre, 23317 Mulholland Drive, Woodland Hills, 91364. Covered by SAG and AFTRA insurance; they file the forms for you. Chiropractic, Metabolic Typing, Herbal Therapy, Sports Medicine, Massage, Homeopathic, Applied Spinal Biomechanical Engineering. They will mail you a brochure with all their services.

Dr. Murray Susser, a homeopathic doctor, 310/966-9194. Also recommended by Sharon Stone told to reporter George Christy in *The Hollywood Reporter.* "He's created IV bags of vitamins and immune boosters, and when we were shooting *Casino* all night long I was never tired. Wonderful too for jet lag, you take it the day before."

Theresa Gormly, D.C., Los Angeles Center for Healing, 310/858-8886. 1157 S. Robertson, Los Angeles, 90035. Covered by SAG and AFTRA insurance; you file your own forms. She is wonderful for relief of pain, stress, nutritional problems, Candida, Epstein Barr and general balancing. Networking and Body Integration. I cannot begin to explain the wonderful treatment I have received over the last fifteen years from Dr. Gormly. Upon hearing my age, people are always surprised at how well I've held up—I owe the insides to her. Many, many celebrities and models go to her. Just a small percentage is covered by insurance but you can deduct the rest from your income taxes. She has cured me of the flu, sore throats, and a few cases of the "blahs" in a few hours with her homeopathic or flower remedies. For those of you into alternative medicine, she and her associates are a gold mine!

Noel S. Aguilar, Ph.D., HMD., The DNA Health Institute, "The Power of Advanced Natural Medicine at its Very Best." 310/858-8886, 1157 S. Robertson Blvd., Los Angeles, 90035. Part of the Los Angeles Center for Healing. Dr. Aguilar uses many tests for diagnosis including electroacupunture to screen the body. Using pen shaped metal rods (microcurrent probes) that are hooked up to a computer, he touches the probes to different acupuncture points, or meridians, on the hands and feet that correspond to specific organs or body parts. The machine measures the small flow of electricity through each meridian, the numbers show on the computer and he can tell where your weak areas are. Two of my friends have been going to him for years with remarkable results. I'm very happy with the work I've begun with him.

Jeffrey Rochford, D.C., Chiropractor, 310/859-0444. 9730 Wilshire Blvd., Suite 215, Beverly Hills, 90212. Covered by SAG and AFTRA insurance. He specializes in nutrition from a scientific standpoint.

Theresa Dale, Ph.D.., 805/962-6484 or 800/638-2404. In Santa Barbara. Very expensive. She is the holistic practitioner for someone who is not recovering from an illness. After seeing many medical doctors, I went to her when no one else could diagnose a medical condition I had fifteen years ago. She found it in twenty minutes; the cure took two years. I believe she saved my life. Alternative medicine and bioenergetic muscle testing. She's developed a type of therapy called Body Readiness and Remedies to release toxins from the organs.

Duong Huy Ha, C.A., Acupuncture. 310/394-9747. 1326 A 5th St., Santa Monica, 90401. Partially covered by SAG and AFTRA insurance. He started practicing in China at age nine. His phone number is unlisted; people come to him only through personal recommendation. He helped me quit smoking. Yeah!

Wing Hsieh, Acupuncture, 310/859-7618. 9400 Brighton Way, Suite 208, Beverly Hills, 90210. I have never been his patient but Lily Tomlin spoke of when she had a bad fall while doing a stage play, he helped her recover quickly and get back to work again.

Christina Marino, L.Ac., at Spa Transcendental, 818/505-9511. 10645 Riverside Drive, Toluca Lake, 91602. They have many spa packages and acupuncture for facial beauty. "When mind and body are in complete harmony, creating a perfect balance between the physical and the spiritual the result is a state of well-being which is the most natural condition of mankind."

John W. Davis, 310/398-9196. 12036 West Washington Blvd., Suite #1, Los Angeles, 90066. Healer, body work, Reichian emotional release work, based on the body armor theories of Wilhelm Reich. John's work helps actors find the true depth and range of their feelings; a center inside from which they can make the transformation into the character. Sees a lot of actors, directors, writers and producers, including my husband Ron, who has scoliosis, believes his monthly treatments help him to stay out of back pain.

Allred Technique, 310/390-5424. $65-$70. 11739 Washington Blvd. West Los Angeles. Colonics. This is where you go when you are really getting ready to look great or you have overindulged. Also anytime you need to get rid of toxins. Connie Allred is an amazing healer and has personally trained the other technicians working for her. She is recommended by many celebrities, doctors and healers.

• **Diana Lipson-Burge, R.D., nutritionist, has developed many new tools** to help with with weight management. She and her co-author Jackie Jaye-Brandt, M.A., MFT, have written *Finally Free,* a book that teaches people how to release their diet mentality, which then releases their excess weight.

- **I am struck by the enormous number of clients** who come to me for weight management tools and yet never apply the tools, or seem to be blocked when it comes to making a life style change for results. I find it is important to learn, first, who they are and what they are doing daily to take care of their needs prior to addressing their weight issues. The weight issue is a direct reflection of individuals not focusing on themselves and their own inner needs.

- **When working with clients, I find it impossible** to focus on the weight management tools (e.g. eating every three hours, listening to the hunger scale) when there may be so many other issues on the client's mind. By reminding them to daily observe their lives it provides a tool to place the responsibility in the hands of the client to really address other areas that may be causing stress; like a feeling of being out of contol or feeling overwhelmed.

- **Clients come to notice the difference** between physiologically and psychologically fed hunger. They choose food types and amounts to meet their needs and health desires that they decide upon themselves, not those dictated by others. Above all, they learn the pleasure that can be obtained from food and eating.

Nutritionists

Also see The Working Actor's Guide for Nutrition Counseling.

Weight Watchers, 800/651-6000, www.weightwatchers.com. They offer a very sound nutritional way of eating and motivational speakers.

Web Sites: Fitness Online: www.fitnessonline.com. **Rob Woods Home of Fitness Testing:** www.worldguide.com/Fitness/hf.html. **In Fitness and In Health Site:** www.phys.com/ **Nutritiously Gourmet Web Site:** www.nutritiouslygourmet.com/.

Erewhon Natural Food Market, 323/931-4074. 7660 Beverly Blvd. Los Angeles, 90036. Receive a complimentary 10 minute consultation with the staff nutritionist or personal trainer for healthy eating, natural food shopping, recipes and menu suggestions. Alternative foods kitchen restocking. Call for appointment.

Diana Lipson-Burge, R.D. Registered Dietitian and Director of The Energy Resource, 310/643-9016, Voice Mail 310/534-7867. Co-author of *Finally Free.* Owner and Director of the Energy Resource, and has been treating disordered eating for over 15 years. She is an active lecturer to professional athletes, the medical industry and the Motion Picture and Television Fund. Diana creates permanent solutions by supporting her clients to look at their underlying belief systems about nutrition and food. She helps them to understand that the deprivation involved in dieting only leads to a need to overeat, thus, never getting permanent results. Diana teaches the science of food, and how it works with the mathematics of calories and metabolism.

Kristin Lundstrom, D.C., at Los Angeles Center for Healing, 310/858-8886. 1157 S. Robertson, Los Angeles, 90035. Covered by SAG and AFTRA insurance; you file your own forms. She is wonderful for relief of pain, stress and nutritional problems. She really taught my husband and I about eating in The Zone. She tests different foods on you to make sure your body you can tolerate your prescribed nutritional plan. She uses contact Reflex Analysis (CRA) and Network Spinal Analysis to accurately determine the body's structural, physical, and nutritional needs. The root of the health problem is uncovered or it is used as a preventative technique to stop a problem from becoming a health issue. "Find it early and correct it."

Alan Ebling, D.C. and Danielle Thompkins, D.C., 818/788-8451. www.living in the zone.com. These chiropracters specialize in teaching people what to eat according to the "Barry Sears, Zone" books. They do an evaluation and provide sample menus utilizing the suggested protein, carbohydrate and fat ratios. They help you adapt this way of eating for a healthier, more energetic life.

Gabriella Juris, Ph.D., M.S., 818/501-1164. Internationally recognized expert in Physiology, nutritional medicine and anti-aging science. Author of the books, *Conquer Fat for Life* and *Fundamentals of Nutrition for Health, Beauty and Longevity.* Specializes in cellular nutrition; metabolic approach to reversing degeneration; mind/body medicine; antioxidants; herbal therapies and more.

The Vital Image, 310/823-1996 or 800/414-4624, in Playa del Rey. Call for their special product report. Power O2 Tonic +. This charged organic nutritional powder gives you enhanced focus, concentration and willpower and fuels your energy reserves and stamina. Great for those early morning set calls and the long extended working hours. *Also see their listing under Age Defying Techniques for all of their valuable treatments and products.*

Homeopathic Medicines

Santa Monica Drug, 310/395-1131. 629 Broadway, Santa Monica, 90401. M-Sa 9:30 to 5:15; parking south of building.

Capitol Drugs, 310/289-1125. 8578 Santa Monica Blvd., West Hollywood, 90069. Nice coffee and juice bar. M-F 9-9, Sa&Su 9-7.

Capitol Drugs, 818/905-8338. 4454 Van Nuys Blvd., Sherman Oaks, 91403. 9-9 everyday.

Mental Health

• **Knowing yourself can help you know the characters** you portray better; finding your own essence will help you find the essence of the character. As you learn to deal with your own anger, fears and anxieties you will probably become a better actor. Working with a therapist or a self-help program can bring you to a deeper self-awareness.

• **Dr. Sherie Zander** gives the following advice on shopping for a therapist:

- **Choosing the best psychotherapist** for your particular needs is of utmost importance. You will not only be spending time and money, but you will be talking about some very personal issues. The person you work with must be someone you believe you can trust. Base your trust on gathered information and an inner reaction or gut-level feeling about that person. If a therapist is recommended by someone whom you respect, that is a good place to start.

Q: What questions should you ask when interviewing a therapist?

- **Are you licensed** by the State? How long have you been practicing? What type of therapy do you practice? Do you have experience with my particular issues? Have you had positive results? Would you do in-depth work to get to the root causes or would you have a more immediate behavioral approach? What is your fee? How often would I need to come in?

- **As you gather information**, you will begin to get a feeling about the therapist and to form an opinion. It is important to trust that inner response you are having. If possible, interview at least three psychotherapists and compare the information you get and the ways you respond to each one. Based upon all of this, make a choice.

- **If, after several sessions**, you believe you have made the wrong choice, I would encourage you to tell your therapist that you are dissatisfied and then move on to someone else. It is far better to start over, than to continue in a situation that is not working for you.

Q: What do you most enjoy about your work?

- **It is a great source of encouragement** to me when I see someone move from a place of despair to a place of hope, when emotional pain is decreasing and wounds are healing, when someone begins to utilize new tools and techniques to handle old sets of problems, and when life is being viewed from a new perspective.

Resources

Sherie Zander, Ph.D., 310/472-9736. Very supportive. Private and group therapy; she also teaches a class in men/women relationships. She has been a guest on my cable show several times, discussing how she helps actors learn to deal with their anger, fears and anxieties. Call her to request a free guide she uses with clients to help them deal with anger. Dr. Zander also specializes in couple communications, family relationships, help with attracting a mate and addictive behaviors.

Jackie Jaye-Brandt, M.A., MFT, Corporate Communications and Psychotherapy, 818/505-1664. 3575 Cahuenga Blvd., West, #213, Los Angeles, 90068. Stress management, communications training, time management, group workshops, couples groups and individual counseling. Jackie has made a huge difference in my life. She teaches at the Wellness Program which is part of the Motion Picture Industry Health Plan. We've taken classes and many of them several times on Self-Esteem, Time Management, Couples Communication, Understanding and Transforming Anger and Tapping Into The Power of the Mind. She works with people privately for usually short periods of time. She wants you well in a timely manner. Along with Diana Lipson-Burge, R.D., she is the author of *Finally Free,* a book that teaches people how to release their diet mentality, which then releases their excess weight. *See Section Seven, page 403, for 20 of her valuable Self Esteem Builders.*

Pat Allen, 310/553-8248, 800/303-1902. Specializes in finding and keeping a mate. She gives private or telephone consultations and her books and lecture tapes are available. Monday evening seminars, 7- 8:30, are $5-$10. The location and price are subject to change; call for the latest information. A great place to meet singles. You will either definitely agree or disagree with her strong opinions. Author of the book is *Getting To I Do!*

Jo Christner, Psy.D., 310/471-2773. Offices in Encino and West Los Angeles. She specializes in helping you feel your very best so that you can have peak performances and a better quality of life. She has appeared on my cable show and has assisted many from the acting industry, from the novice to the renowned. Mood disorders (depression, anxiety and panic attacks,) eating disorders, stress management and geriatric services are among her specialities. Her services include confidential, individual and group psychotherapy as well as educational seminars.

I have not been to the following clinics but if you feel you need help and cannot afford a private therapist, these listings are available on an ability-to-pay basis.

Antioch Counseling Center, 310/319-2716. 13274 Fiji Way, Marina del Rey, 90292.

Bel Air Presbyterian Church Crisis Counseling Center, 818/788-0702. 16221 Mulholland Drive, Los Angeles, 90028. They will see you for six weeks then refer you to someone who will best fit your need. They ask for a donation only.

Gay and Lesbian Center, 323/993-7640. 1625 N. Schreder, Los Angeles, 90028.

Maple Center, 310/271-9999. 9107 Wilshire Blvd., Lower Level, Beverly Hills, 90210. Sliding payment scale for actors who live or work in Beverly Hills. Sometimes they will accept people out of the Beverly Hills area.

Open Paths, 310/398-7877. 12655 Washington Blvd. #101, Los Angeles, 90066.

Southern California Counseling Center, 323/937-1344. 5615 W. Pico Blvd., Los Angeles, 90019. I've known a few of the therapists and also know people who have received good help here.

Thalians, 310/855-3504 at Cedars Sinai Hospital, 8730 Alden Dr., Los Angeles, 90048.

AIPADA: 12-Step Programs - General Hot Line (800) 222-5465. Call the general hot line or use the phone book to find specific 12-step programs. Phone numbers often change; don't get discouraged if you can't reach the specific program you are looking for right away. There is no cost and many people have found recovery in these programs.

AIPADA-Alcohol & Drug Abuse Hot Line: (800) 756-HOPE
Take 12 meets every Friday at 8:30 p.m. in the James Cagney Room at SAG, 5757 Wilshire Blvd., Los Angeles. Closed meeting for union members only. Marijuana Anonymous, 323/964-2370; Adult Children of Alcoholics (ACA); Overeaters Anonymous; HOW/Overeaters Anonymous; Nicotine Anonymous; Anger Anonymous; Codependents Anonymous (CODA); Debtors Anonymous; Gamblers Anonymous; Sex Anonymous; and for people who deal with alcoholics or addicts in their life or addictions not listed here: ALANON 818/760-7122. Many meetings are held at the Crescent Heights Methodist Church, 1296 Fairfax Avenue, West Hollywood. Stop by and look at their posted schedules.

Plastic Surgery, Liposuction, Vein and Hair Removal, Skin Resurfacing

The most important thing you can do as an actor is to stay out of the sun; it is what ages you. If you have already done the damage before you knew you wanted a long career in front of the camera as a leading actor, then save your money. Unless you have fabulous genes you will need cosmetic corrections done. Be sure to also check the section on facials, age-defying and beauty treatments for things to be done before the knife, including resurfacing, botox and collagen.

When considering breast implants, understand that extremely large breasts will limit your casting possibilities. Yes, it will open up some roles but unless they call for nudity, you can do those parts with false breasts, even the nude ones can be done with body doubles. The problem is, there is no way to make your breasts look smaller. Even Pamela Anderson Lee removed her very large implants for just large ones. She still can't play a role that calls for a small breasted woman. Demi Moore and Teri Hatcher, I think, have the best breasts because sometimes they look small and other times big. The most requested size for women getting implants is a full B or a C cup.

Liposuction, noses, eyes and breasts seem to be the most popular procedures and I have found experts to discuss these and other procedures. Be conservative in your surgery decisions. I know it's tempting to have it all done at once because you save money, but wiser to not have plastic surgery decisions made because of cost. Not all doctors are the same; they all have different views of the same surgeries. Choose carefully.

Recently a new student of mine came for a private class after having just been to a plastic surgeon. This girl is adorable, 22, looks 16, ample breasts and lips, fashionably thin, attractive face, nice nose, cheeks. She went to a very notable plastic surgeon (a family friend) because she had a couple of small growths under her skin that needed to be removed. She was correct in seeing a plastic surgeon. But he met with her for an hour and showed her all the possibilities of improving her face and body. When she arrived at my house she was feeling ugly and asked me for advice of what to do first. I said leave yourself alone, you're unique and beautiful. Earlier that day I had been talking with an agent on the phone about meeting one of my very talented students. He said "I hate her picture, looks like she's had her lips all pumped up." What could I say; she had. I relayed this to my new young student and told her to please let her good acting talent beam through her natural good looks.

Plastic surgeons are also sales people as are most doctors. Our goal should be to have as few surgeries as possible. Follow your instincts.

Joan Rivers, says:

- **Every woman on TV over the age of 25** has had something done, whether it's cheek implants, breasts, chin augmented, or nose altered. Plastic surgery is like a tool in an actor's tool box.

- **Hair and Makeup Stylist Edward Salazar wrote in his newsletter:**

    - **Your surgeon of choice is "a human being" not "God."** Ask questions, get clear answers and make sure costs, procedures and recovery are involved. If you're one of those "awkward in the face of authority types" then bring along a friend for moral support. Pay attention to the surgeon's attitude, temperament and responsiveness to questions. Ask for recommendations, photos or videos of befores and afters. Check the American Medical Association for negative reports. Remember that when getting a face lift, incisions will be made into the hairline. The skin removed in this area contains hair follicles and could mean a possible decrease in hair. Tell your concerns to your surgeon; discuss each procedure whether it's a face lift, upper or lower eyelids, forehead lift, liposuction, acid peel, etc.

- **Dr. Harvey Abrams, the founder of Wilshire Aesthetics, A Dermatology and Plastic Surgery Group, talks about what liposuction can and cannot do.**

    - **Thanks to recent technological developments**, especially the development of smaller, more refined instruments, liposuction is much improved. It can be offered to many more patients for whom I am able to remove larger amounts of fat safely and with minimal risk. In addition, the recovery process is much shorter and more comfortable.

Q: Who performs liposuction, how do you choose a surgeon, and how much does it cost?

- **Liposuction does not belong to any particular surgical specialty.** Board certified physicians, especially Dermatologists, Cosmetic and Plastic Surgeons who have performed many liposuctions and have an interest in liposuction, are the best choices.

- **Word of mouth is the best possible endorsement.** Get referrals from people who have had the procedure and are satisfied with the results and the care they received. It is important the physician is board certified in their area of specialization. It is best to find someone who has performed this type of surgery on a regular basis for many years.

- **Fees vary greatly** but generally range from about $3,000 to $7,000.

Q: Is this a good way to lose weight and does the fat come back?

- **Liposuction is not for weight loss.** It changes the shape of the body by removing unwanted fatty bulges. It is a very successful way of contouring for individuals who are within 10% of their ideal body weight.

- **Scientific evidence indicates** that fat cells removed do not grow back. If a person maintains a weight close to their normal body weight through proper diet and exercise, there is every reason to believe the body changes achieved will be permanent.

Q: Dr. Abrams, what can you tell me about laser hair removal techniques? Does it work on everyone? Is it permanent?

- **The whole field of laser hair removal is very new.** It doesn't always work, that is why you have to go to someone who knows whether it will work for you or not. There are a lot of variables; it depends on the thickness and color of the hair and on the color of the skin. Not everybody is a good candidate. Go to a technician who has had a lot of experience and will level with you. Dana, in our office, has had 23 years experience in hair removal. Hair can be removed from every part of the body and it can be expensive. There are many "so called" bargains, that turn out not to be bargains because the technicians can't deliver on their promises. New lasers are being developed all the time, it is an evolving field. You want to go to someone who keeps up with the latest research and owns the latest proven equipment.

Q: What can be accomplished with laser skin resurfacing?

- **Lasers are used to irradicate many different flaws on the skin**, blood vessels, wrinkles, sun spots and other signs of aging. Wilshire Aesthetics has a full range of laser services including removing tattoos. The success rate depends on the tattoo, the ones that are a blue/black are very successful. The ones that have many intricate colors; blues, reds, yellows and greens are much more difficult, and require many more treatments. It doesn't usually leave a scar, but sometimes you can't get out all the pigment. So don't start unless you are committed to finishing. It can take anywhere from eight to twenty treatments. A small tattoo could cost $1000, a large one could be several thousand dollars.

Dr. Guy Massry, the director of cosmetic surgery at the Sinskey Eye Institute, specializes in reconstructive and cosmetic surgery of the eye, eyebrows, forehead, and mid-face lifting. I asked why some doctors choose to specialize.

- **I think when a doctor specializes in a specific area** their experience will be greater, the surgical results superior and, most importantly, complications are minimized. For instance, in facial cosmetic surgery, a poorly done nose or eyes can cause significant disability to patients, as breathing and vision can be affected. It is vitally important that the surgeons performing these procedures are well versed and have vast experience in order to avoid postoperative problems.

- **The way I developed my practice** is to combine the expertise of surgical subspecialists, thus creating a cosmetic team, in order to provide the best service and attain excellent results. A common example is the patient who desires a browlift, eyelid surgery and a rhinoplasty (nose job). I will evaluate the patient for, and perform, the brow and lid surgery, while my associate, who specializes in rhinoplasty, will address that portion of the patients concerns. The patient gets the best of both worlds.

- **A significant part of my practice is revision surgery**. This refers to patients who have had previous surgery who need further correction or are unhappy with the results. Typical problems are eyelids that won't completely close, lower lids that are pulled down or turned out, a "wide eyed" appearance, or residual puffiness or skin. These are complex problems that truly require a specialists care. For instance, when lower lids are pulled down, lifting the cheek to supply skin to the lower lids is often times necessary. Thus, to correct these problems, an understanding of midface surgery is essential.

Q: What about cheek implants?

- **You can lift the cheek without an implant**; the implant just brings the cheek out. Lifting the cheek is a procedure which brings the thicker cheek tissue higher and makes the cheek more prominent. If I can avoid putting foreign material in someone's face for life, I will. I'm very cautious about a foreign substance. When necessary, we will put it in.

• **Dr. Garth Fisher is a board certified Plastic and Reconstructive surgeon**. He specializes in aesthetic/cosmetic plastic surgery of the face and breasts. His practice has predominately included entertainers, celebrities and executives from around the world.

Q: When doing breast implants, do you make the incisions around the nipple for actresses that do not want any noticible scars?

- **A large majority of the Playmates are my patients.** They often work with their clothes off, so I am very careful with the scars. I close the incisions carefully so that the scars are difficult to find. That is taken into account on a daily basis here.

Q: Is silicone still available?

- **Primarily, for first-time patients, we use saline implants**, unless there are mitigating circumstances, then we can use silicone. For reconstructive patients, I often use silicone.

- **There is an inclusion criteria set up by the FDA** and implant manufacturers. If the client fulfills the guidelines, then I use silicone. There are advantages and disadvantages to silicone implants. They are especially helpful for patients that have very thin skin.

- **There are different types of implants.** Teardrop shaped implants are mainly used on top of the muscle. Round implants can be used on top or below the muscle. The implant that is used depends on the person's body.

- **The important thing is having the implants look natural,** small or large, you want to make them look like natural breasts. I find that is what most patients want. They don't like the round, hard, beach-ball look.

Q: I understand that you often have to do reconstructive surgery when **a patient has had bad surgery elsewhere.**

- **They are challenging cases and I've have a lot of experience with them.** I've done over 4,000 breast implants and associated reconstructive procedures. We try to convert people to a more natural look, a softer look. It depends on what particular problem they have.

Q: Is there any advice you would give people when interviewing doctors for breast implants?

- **Bring in pictures, show the doctor exactly what you want.** Communication is very important. Let the doctor know exactly what you are trying to achieve. Hopefully, he'll be honest enough to tell you whether he can deliver it or not. In our office, a patient will bring in a Playboy magazine. We know most of those girls, so we know what they are trying to accomplish. Look at before and after pictures, review some of the results of the doctor's work. Does he get the results that the patients are after?

Q: Is there any way a person can try out breasts before they actually have surgery?

- **They can fill ziplock bags with saline or rice** and put them in their bra if they want to approximate sizes. It is not real reproducable and exact, but it may help.

- **Dr. H. Edward Sterling talks about breast improving surgeries.**

Q: What material do you use in breast implants.

- **I prefer saline implants.** If I have a patient that has silicone implants and wants to have them exchanged for whatever reason, I try to talk them into saline implants. They give a very natural look and feel. I place the implant in front of the muscle. The results, I think, are much better; you don't have any deformity when you contract your pectoral muscles. I don't believe in going in through the areola, I go in through the mammary fold, which hides the scar.

Q: What type of procedure do you use if a woman wants her implants totally removed?

- **We remove the breast implants** and do a mastopexy or a breast lift without removing the breast volume but tightening the skin bra. There will be a scar around the areola and a vertical scar in the six o'clock position down to the mammary fold. That scar is usually very well tolerated.

- **If a woman has large pendulous breasts** with a history of back and neck aches, that calls for a reduction of the breast volume. That is a reduction mammoplasty. The location of the scars will be the same as when removing breast implants.

- **Respected plastic surgeon Dr. Gregory Mueller talks about facial surgeries.**

Q: What kind of corrective facial surgeries are popular?

- **Eyes are the most common surgery** done in people's thirties. That's when you tend to get bags under the eyes; it is very nicely corrected with surgery. Sometimes the upper eyelids will have excess skin. Removing the skin gives you a more refreshed look.

- **Laser resurfacing is great for fine little wrinkles** around the mouth. Sometimes we can also do liposuction of the neck at an early age, that can help to sharpen up the jaw line and neck.

Q: At what age should someone consider a face lift?

- **Face lifts are good for removing excess skin and excess fat,** so it really depends on your genetics and how you age. When people notice they are beginning to get jowls around the jaw border area. Or if they notice that underneath their neck they may be getting a little band almost like a turkey gobbler neck. Those are good candidates for a little face lift. Certainly lifts can be done in all varying degrees, from a major face lift where you make the incision from the temple area all the way around the ear and back into the hair by the neck, that is where you are lifting everything. Some patients just need a lower face lift, to just sharpen up the jaw line and the neck. That is less surgery and there is no problem in repeating it in eight or ten years.

Q: How do you hide the scars?

- **The scars are very well concealed.** There is no way you can do surgery without scars, but the way we make incisions, they are right along the front of the ear. We actually pull the front part of the ear forward and we are able to make the incisions almost on the inside of the ear and then we bring it right around the ear where the earlobe attaches to the head and then back behind the ear in the little crease where the ear meets the side of the head, and then along the hair line, or sometimes in women, we will go up in the hair. Done this way, it allows us to hide the scars within the natural contour of the ear. The face, because of its great blood supply, heals incredibly well. The scars are very hard to see after several months. It usually takes two to three months for the scars to completely heal, but even after two weeks by putting on cover-up makeup, you can conceal the scars.

Q: How do you keep from having a pulled, artificial look?

- **That is something that every surgeon has a judgement on.** How hard and how much tension they are going to place on the skin. So you want to make sure you go to someone who has the same sort of aesthetic idea that you don't want to look pulled, you just want to look rested. Certainly you can do the pulled look. You have to rely on your surgeon to have good judgement on what looks good.

Q: What if you want to lift your forehead or raise your eyebrows?

- **There's a couple of different treatments for foreheads.** Probably the newest and the most popular is botox. Botox helps people who have wrinkles on the forehead. It is a medicine that you inject, an office procedure that takes about ten minutes. It basically makes the muscles so that they are unable to lift the eyebrows. What happens over a few weeks is, it will soften the wrinkles that run horizontally along your forehead. It will also improve frown lines and the laugh lines around your eyes.

- **Some patients have very low eyebrows**, so they aren't candidates for botox which could actually cause them to have a further drop of the eyelids. They would be a better candidate for a brow lift. I did a brow lift on a 25 year old male model from Germany with very low set brows. Botox wouldn't work but the brow lift gave him a nice result.

- **There are two types of forehead lifts.** There is one where we make an incision that crosses all the way across the head from ear to ear. You basically take out a strip of scalp and then just pull everything up backwards and sew it together. That is sort of the traditional brow lift, the new one is probably the most popular especially with men, because of receding hairlines, it is called an endoscopic brow lift. We do a series of five small incisions in the front of the scalp. We use a scope on a digital camera system to visualize the operation with the skin still remaining on the forehead. We are able to release the eyebrows from underneath and then by using little anchors or screws we are able to suspend the forehead. We wrap the forehead in an ace bandage for a week to ten days and the forehead will then stick and that allows us to raise the eyebrows.

Q: How long after a face procedure does is take to look presentable?

- **I tell my patients to have two weeks of down time** if they don't want people to know. With makeup, you can pretty much conceal most of the scarring. You'll still have swelling but the majority of it is usually gone. We'll send men to a department store ahead of time to find a cover-up that will work for the bruising. Usually, most of the bruising is lower on the neck so a high collar will conceal a lot. After five to seven days you can return to work if the appearance doesn't concern you.

Resources

I give you the names of the following MD surgeons as a place to start your research, but you must rely on your own medical advisors before taking drastic surgical steps. Interview three plastic surgeons for any procedure you are thinking about. Some surgeons I've listed may have specialties in one area, others may do all types of surgeries.

Liposuction & Laser Skin Resurfacing

Dr. Harvey Abrams, of Wilshire Aesthetics, a Dermatology and Plastic Surgery Group, 323/936-1245. www.wilshireaesthetics.com 5670 Wilshire Blvd., Suite 650, Los Angeles, 90036. Dr Abrams is the founder of the group and has been developing instruments and procedures for liposuction work for many years. He also teaches his procedures to other doctors. Dr. Abrams, in my mind, is "the artist of liposuction." The results depend on the artistry as well as the technique of the doctor.

American Society for Plastic and Reconstructive Surgeons

American Society for Plastic and Reconstructing Surgeons, 847/228-9900. When you call they will refer you to their web site for information, www.plasticsurgery.org. You can put in the name of the doctor and they will tell you whether or not they are certified. The web page also has other links. If you are not on line, call 800/635-0635, give them the names of the doctors and they will mail you a printout with the information.

American Board of Plastic Surgeons, 215/587-9322. You can call them and they will look up three doctors per phone call.

Plastic and Reconstructive Surgeons

Dr. Gregory Mueller, of Wilshire Aesthetics, A Dermatology and Plastic Surgery Group, 323/936-1245. www.wilshireaesthetics.com 5670 Wilshire Blvd., Suite 650, Los Angeles, 90036. Dr. Mueller's practice involves all areas of plastic surgery, including plastic surgery for men. Excellent bedside manner and aesthetic good sense. A famous retired plastic surgeon when asked who would replace him, said, "Dr. Greg Mueller is the most talented, up and coming surgeon in Los Angeles." Great, supportive staff. Laser skin resurfacing.

Dr. Garth Fisher, 310/273-5995. www.garthfisher.com. 120 S. Spalding Drive, #222, Beverly Hills, 90212. Board certified. *Los Angeles Magazine's* "one of the best plastic surgeons in L.A." *Best Doctors in America* Review choose him as "one of the top facial cosmetic and breast surgeons." How I am most personally impressed is by his "tear drop" silicone breast implants. One of my students had implants that were too large replaced by Dr. Fisher. He went in through the nipple and performed a miracle. This actress needs to have invisible scars. I saw them after only three months, amazing! International clientele. Very helpful staff. Laser skin resurfacing.

Dr. Guy G. Massry, Director of Cosmetic Surgery at The Sinskey Eye Institute and Aesthetic Laser Center, 310/453-8911/800-258-8989. 2232 Santa Monica Blvd. Santa Monica, 90404. Dr. Massry specializes in reconstructive and cosmetic surgery of the eye, eyebrows, forehead, and mid-face lifting. He worked a miracle on my eyelids, they had already been through three surgeries, he cured my tearing problem, plus (yeah!) they look better. He also does laser skin resurfacing, treating skin that is sun damaged, wrinkled, pigmented and scarred. His staff, Diana and Jody, are very helpful. Dr. Massry loves fixing other doctors' mistakes.

Dr. Harry Glassman, 310/550-0999. Very large celebrity clientele.

Dr. Glowacki, 310/540-0144. Torrance Blvd., Hawthorne. Board certified. One of my students had implants that were too big for her body, saline double Ds. He replaced them with saline Ds and she was very happy with the outcome. Very reasonably priced at $2000.

Dr. Steven Grifka, 310/204-4111. Board certified. I have received glowing reports from readers of past editions on his work.

Dr. John Joseph, 310/859-7193.

Dr. Bernard Koire, 310/247-8577.

Dr. Ronald Matsunaga, 310/659-2660. Face, Eyes, Nose, Face lift. Stylist Edward Salazar has been recommending him highly for 20 years. Edward works with many beautiful, glamorous personalities; he knows what he's talking about.

Dr. Toby Mayer, 310/278-8823. He did my girlfriend's face/brow lift 15 years ago and it is still holding up well. He specializes in hair transplants for complete baldness.

Dr. Paul S. Nassif, of The Sinskey Eye Institute and Aesthetic Laser Center, 310/453-8911. 2232 Santa Monica Blvd. Santa Monica, 90404. He specializes in rhinoplasty, the surgery of the nose, and facelifts.

Dr. Sheldon Rosenthal, 818/981-3333. 16633 Ventura Blvd. Encino. Board certified. I met a woman in Dr. Gormly's office who had researched everyone and she was happiest with him. $7,000 for the lower neck and jaw lift along with laser wrinkle remover.

Dr. Edward Sterling, 714/871-2683. 2720 N. Harbor Blvd., Suite 230, Fullerton, 92835. Board certified. He is known for his artistic placements of implants and restructuring of stomachs (much more than just liposuction) and breasts. He also does all of the facial surgeries, including resurfacing. His prices are generally lower because he is in Orange County.

Dr. Harvey Zarem, 310/315-0222. Board certified.

Dr. Steven Zax, 310/553-1511.

Breasts Boost Without Surgery: BodyLines: Curves, 800-528-7837. Soft, but very durable, the large size increases you by 1 1/2 to 2 cups, x-large by 2 to 2 1/2 cups. $130. They claim super models and actresses on more than 100 television shows, soap operas and films wear them, as well as over 200,000 women worldwide.

Hair Transplants

Dr. Lee Bosley, Bosley Hair Instutite, locations all over the country.
Dr. Peter Goldman, 310/855 -1160 at Cedars Hospital in Los Angeles.
Dr. Toby Mayer, 310/278-8823. He specializes in hair transplants for complete baldness.
Dr. William Rassman, The New Hair Institute, 1-800-NEW-HAIR. 9911 West Pico, Los Angeles. Probably considered the number one hair transplant surgeon in the United States.

SECTION SEVEN

Psychotherapist, Jackie Jaye-Brandt is generously allowing me to include her important list of self-esteem builders. I have taken many of her classes and they have made a profound impact on my life. She works with people privately and in classes. Because she was in show business before she found her true calling, she fully understands our needs and insecurities. She, along with Diana Lipson-Burge, R.D., are the authors of "Finally Free," *a book that teaches people how to release their diet mentality, which then releases their excess weight.*

SELF-ESTEEM BUILDERS

© BY: JACKIE JAYE-BRANDT, M.A., MFT
818/505-1664

1. **Begin by De-emphasizing Material Possessions:** They don't love you, comfort you or bring you great joy. They are just *things.*

2. **Stop Comparing Yourself To Others:** Comparing sets you up to feel like you're not enough. If you must compare yourself, compare yourself to yourself (as you were last year, ten years ago, etc.).

3. **Resolve to Accept Yourself Unconditionally:** If you have some cleaning up to do, get to it. Unresolved stuff stays with you forever. Then, after an inventory and the appropriate amends or completion work, no matter what you've done, forgive yourself and move on. You are the only *you* in the world. Accept that you are also the *best* you—you can be, and, as such, a work-in-progress. Accept your weaknesses, as well as your strengths.

4. Forgive Others for all the Things You're Still Holding Onto: Forgiveness does NOT mean: It was okay, it was right, the person shouldn't be punished, you are condoning their actions, you are reconciling the relationship. It simply means that you are choosing to let go of your feelings of resentment and revenge, forever, in favor of moving forward.

5. Find your Gift/Passion and Pursue it: Everyone has a gift or gifts. It can be singing, art, candy-making, teaching children, etc. Find out what it is that gives you passion, and pursue it.

6. Set Goals: First get clear on your value system. From there should spring your goals. Goals give us direction, purpose and reason to celebrate ourselves. They also allow us to have our dreams come true. Give up the *failure mentality.* It doesn't really exist, except in our minds.

7. Celebrate your Accomplishments, the Attainment of your Goals & your Successes: Learning to acknowledge yourself is vital. We've certainly learned how to beat ourselves up!...only acknowledgment actually moves us forward.

8. Reset your Goals: Many people, once they've achieved a goal, sit back and decide to now rest, relax, and say "okay, I did it." Unfortunately, you will soon feel hollow. Keep at least one goal in front of you at all times. The more goals the better. A good rule of thumb is at least 101 goals...only work on a few at a time, to avoid overwhelm.

9. Find a Way to Take Responsibility for all your Actions and Consequences: Understand that until you accept this, you will find yourself constantly feeling victimized, out of control and burdened. Responsibility gives us *control* over our lives. It is understanding that we always have *choice.*

Give up, forever, the notion of being a victim...of your circumstances, your relationships, your career, etc. Being a *victim* is a state of mind that needs to be replaced with being a *creator.*

10. Get and Polish your Communication Skills: Otherwise you will stuff your emotions, gather up and store anger, and question what is and isn't real. Communication skills allow you to turn criticism into requests and to express yourself without alienating others. This must also include SETTING BOUNDARIES...*we teach people how to treat us!*

11. Personal Integrity: Everyone's sense of what is right and wrong is personal, but your body will tell you as well. Start tuning into what is right for you, so that your actions are congruent with who you are (your values).

12. Start Investigating and Questioning Belief Systems: Those who know it all have nothing they can learn. Give up sentences like "I've always been this way," "I can't do...(i.e., math)," or "I wish I was someone who..." This simply *locks* in your belief system. *You become what you believe... You attract what you believe is possible, and you always get what you expect!*

13. Learn to have the Proper Conversations with Yourself: These are usually manifestations of your belief systems. Speak positively and visualize positively, rather than being worried about failing or the "what-if's". Have conversations like "I love to exercise," "I am adept at everything I do," "I love to risk."

Be grateful - This is switching yourself from thinking about what you don't have, and bringing yourself to the reality of what you do have. It's not Polyana thinking, but rather directing your mind to a place where good feelings reside. Feeling grateful takes *practice,* especially if you're more inclined to notice what's *missing* in your life.

14. Create and Nurture Love and Support Systems: If you have toxic family members or don't have solid, loyal friends, it is important to create them. Everyone needs people to talk to and trust (in addition to their spouse). As we get older it seems harder to create friends, and it's not...it just takes effort and trial and error. It is also important to have good advisors, since none of us are experts at everything.

15. Take Care of Yourself: This includes vigilant exercise (#1), proper nutrition, stress education and yearly physical exams. Make sure your body supports your mind.

16. Challenge Yourself/Take Risks/Grow: Part of creating self-esteem is feeling adept. When you try something new, challenge yourself to something difficult, keep going after you miss the mark a few times, you build your self-esteem enormously. Each of these experiences builds on itself, so that you can *call it forth* to reinforce yourself at any time.

17. Press Through Fear: (Similar to "Challenge Yourself" above). Each time you *have* your fear and do it anyway, you build self-esteem. Fear is simply a signal that you're truly alive and moving. Every time you press through fear, it means you've exhibited courage. Courage builds self-esteem.

18. Become Aware Of, and Take *Action* on, Your Incompletions. *Action* can include (1) Education/Classes/Growth Groups; (2) Therapy (individual or group); (3) Promises (i.e., "I'll return to school when the kids start high school").

19. Be Willing to Give up Being Right: Needing to be right is a full-time job, and a needless waste of energy. It's also very lonely.

20. Laugh at Yourself: Since we have already given up being right, the next step is to accept ourselves and our human-ness. It is utterly silly to take life so seriously when none of us get out of here alive. Laugh as much as possible every day, especially at yourself. The less seriously you take yourself, the less seriously you'll take everyone and everything else.

ACTORS' SECRETS

• **"Talent is: never using two words when one will do."** Thomas Jefferson.

• **Actors, as a rule, are great talkers**; they spend time and energy talking about what they are *going* to do, giving away all their secrets. In fact they talk so much to so many people, they don't do what they were talking about because they've expended the energy through the talking.

• **Learn to focus your conversation** on what you are actually doing, not on what you are going to do. If you decide you're going to send out 20 pictures and resumes to agents, don't tell a soul until they are in the mailbox. When you have an audition, don't tell anyone but your acting coach. If you're planning on getting a night job so you'll have your days free for auditions, get the job then talk about it. So much energy will build up from your career plans that you'll be bursting to carry your plans out! When you take action, the payoff is: you can talk about what you are really doing. You become interesting to listen to, an inspiration.

• **Condense your stories**—get to the bottom line fast. You needn't go into boring details; assume the person you're talking with understands what you are saying. You can teach your mind to think in a concentrated form like a writer. The practice of conserving words can be developed without a loss of communication; in fact there should be an increase in communication. People (casting directors, agents, directors, loved ones) will want to hear more; they will ask you to explain if they don't understand. Don't give away more of yourself than is absolutely necessary. Mystery is an important asset.

• **When you have spoken a word**, it reigns over you. When it is unspoken, you reign over it. There's no point in speaking unless you can improve on silence.

• **In acting**, you may be thinking a paragraph or two in your mind but have only one line of dialogue to convey your thoughts. Dialogue is concentrated because a play, television show or film is limited in time. The writer knows the actor can portray much more than just the words and assumes that the audience will get the message.

• **By controlling the content of your conversation**, people will be more attracted to hiring and spending time with you. Be *responsible* for all of your words. Negativity is death to creativeness. Guard yourself! Talking about illness, everyone's flu, the car accident you just saw, the horrible interview, the awful casting person, smog, this town, lack of money—robs you of energy. When you hear this going on with yourself or the people around you, don't say anything about it or point it out; simply change the subject to something positive. It is difficult to drop old habits but change brings an *awareness* of self. Awareness is what actors are constantly searching for.

• **Finally, do not allow yourself** to make excuses or to blame someone or something else for your reality. Take responsibility for the words you speak and the deeds you do. If this is a new concept for you, there are many self-help books available at libraries and bookstores on creating your own reality.

• **Secrets are very valuable acting tools.** They give you energy, power and mystery; they draw dramatic, wonderful attention to you. I have heard it said: "Very good actors never talk about their art; very bad ones never stop."

• **Albert Einstein** said, "The most beautiful thing we can experience is the mysterious. It is the source of all true art and all science. He to whom this emotion is a stranger, who can no longer pause to wonder and stand rapt in awe, is as good as dead: his eyes are closed."

LOVE OF YOUR CAREER AND SHOW BIZ

• **I decided I had to live my life as an actor**—that I could be nothing else—in January 1975, sitting in my car at the corner of Hollywood Blvd. and Vermont. That decision, ambition, drive, has guided my life every day since. If you can be anything else but an actor, be it. But if you can't, then forge ahead, and love your choice. It is great to learn to have fun in life.

• **Tom Hanks says,**

- **Acting is one cool gig.**

• **Kate Winslet said,**

- **Because of the person I am I won't be knocked down—ever.** They can do what they like. They can say I'm fat, I'm thin, I'm whatever, and I'll never stop. I just won't. I've got too much to do. I've too much to be happy about.

•**Timothy Hutton said the most important lesson he learned about acting** was from his actor father, Jim Hutton. When Jim was working and things were going well, he was happy; when things weren't going well, he was still happy because he had such a great appreciation for just being in the business.

• **James Woods said,**

- **Acting per se has never been a struggle for me** because I enjoy it so much. I enjoy the other actors, being on the set, the excitement and the tension of going for the gold.

- **Janine Turner** said, before she got *Northern Exposure,*

  - **I was very depressed.** I had been auditioning for something like 11 years. I was wiped out. I couldn't even get a job as a waitress. So I went down to the jewelry district with the ring. (At one time she was engaged to Alec Baldwin.) I didn't know who to trust and I ended up walking away–I just couldn't do it. I had $8 in my checking account and wasn't able to make the rent. With nowhere to go but up, I tried for the part of Maggie.

- **Life can turn around on that phone call for an audition.**

- **We plant many seeds. It is important not to dig the seed up** to see if it is growing. We trust and have faith that it is indeed growing and it will manifest itself at the perfect time.

- **Ed Marinaro says,**

  - **If you can understand the reality of the business** and find a logical way of approaching it, your chances of being successful are going to be a lot better. There's nothing fair about the business. It's all about luck. The only thing you can count on is being prepared. You have to know what you're doing, train and become as good an actor as you can. What you can't count on is getting a break. But if you do get a break, you better be prepared; and that's true for every actor that's ever been successful. They got lucky. If you're really emotionally down and feel like the world's dumping on you, the next day you might get a shot and you're not going to be prepared. You're gonna blow it.

- **When we use acting tools, we cannot go for results.** We have to *make the effort* and then be willing for nothing to happen. The results will take care of themselves. It is hard to trust this, but by filling our hearts with love it is easier to trust.

- **When we read 12 plays to find one scene** that we want to do in class, when we audition for 20 plays and finally get a walk-on role, when we send out 200 pictures and get one response, when we have 10 different odd jobs just to support our career, when we go on 20 interviews before getting one line on a television show, when we have 50 commercial interviews before landing one, we are *making the effort* and we will reap the benefits. All of these endeavors are our careers. "Happiness is found along the way, not at the end of the road."

• **Discouragement is a killer**—a heart killer—don't give it a chance to grab hold of you. Yes, there are the times of discouragement and depression, but we must emerge from those times with even more determination and faith that the efforts will bring forth the results.

• **William Hurt says,**

- **There's nothing about being an actor that isn't silly.** That's one of the attractions. It is very important to focus on this side of the work or else life can become tedious. So much of the effort we put out does not seem to get immediate results. One of the important bonuses is that the work is fun.

• **Farrah Fawcett says,**

- **No matter what the experience, good or bad**, I think in the long run it strengthens your character and furthers your career.

• **Be willing for the results to be different than you imagined.** Usually they will surpass your wildest dreams—that's why it is very important to dream big, bigger, biggest. Do not limit your dreams. Who do you know who is more worthy of their dreams coming true than you? I trust your answer is "no one." When your dreams come true, you can help others attain their dreams as you have been helped to attain yours.

• **Susan Ruttan said,**

- **On New Year's Eve I make a list of what I call "revolutions."** My own tradition. Things I am going to change or bring out. I make them very specific. On New Year's Eve prior to getting the pilot for *LA Law,* I wrote down that I wanted to be on a television series. One that was sold for at least 13 episodes and in which I had a regular part and that made me happy and brought satisfaction and not just for the money. It's not that it's magic, but it helps me to visualize it.

• **Matthew Broderick said,**

- **Actors have this desperate need to get in front of people** and do something. I don't know where that comes from, I have it too. Sometimes I think about it and I find it totally embarrassing, it's some kind of exhibitionist quality that we all have.

• **Visualization is a valuable tool. See yourself driving to the studio,** saying hello to the guard and pulling into your parking place with your name on it. Hear those magic words on the phone, "You got the job." Watch yourself driving in your new car to your dream house with all the worldly goods that would represent your monetary success as an actor.

• **Most of us are daydreamers living in fantasy worlds.** Put your dreams to work for you; instead of dreaming negatively—worrying about future problems—dream positively. Guard and treasure your fantasy world: it is the key to your future. If you can *picture* yourself doing something, you can attain it. Your dreams will show you how to fulfill your desires.

• **Mary Steenburgen,** at a tribute for Jack Nicholson, told of working as a waitress in New York for five years while dreaming of an acting career. She heard of a casting call for *Going South* which Jack was directing. When she went by the office, the casting director told her, "We're only seeing well-known actresses or very beautiful models." Mary says, "Shy as I was, I did insist on seeing the script. Suddenly I hear this unmistakable voice, which said, "Are you waiting for me?" And I answered, "No, I don't have a script." After he gave me a script, he promised he'd see me for 10 minutes the next day." Several days later, Mary got the call to go to Hollywood for the screen test, and we know of the great career that audition fostered.

• **Julian Myers,** a Hollywood publicist, wrote a column years ago that I keep as an inspiration. Here are some of the ways he suggests to keep happy working in Hollywood.

- **Be individualistic. Be different. Have outside interests.** Entertain, even if necessarily modestly. Master the Internet, and use it. Attend many industry doings, including dinners and forums. Eat, drink and have your hair done where your colleagues do. Drive a more expensive car than you can afford, and keep it shiny. Keep in touch with prospective employers every few months, preferably by mail. Dress attractively. Work long hours if they are leading you upward. Set aside savings for when you are unemployed. You will be. Cheerfully fill special requests. Have time, interest and advice for those not yet up to your career level. Attend movies and abserve what audiences react to. Try to see all important TV shows, and each series at least once. Average less than six hours sleep a night. You're in a tough race and you have to make each hour count. Read new books. Decide this is your industry and you'll always be a part of it, even when between jobs. Try to like almost everyone in the industry—and almost everyone will like you. Look for the good in Hollywood and defend it.

WORKING ON THE SET AND THE LAST DAYS OF *SEINFELD*

• **Katharine Graham said it best, "to love what you do and feel that it matters...how can anything be more fun."**

• **First and most important, you have the job**. It is yours. You might as well act on that instead of thinking, "Oh no! Someone is going to take this away from me." As a dialogue coach I have seen actors replaced quite a few times and in several of my acting jobs, actors have been fired: Lisa Eichhorn from *All Night Long* replaced by Barbra Streisand; Raquel Welch from *Cannery Row* replaced by Debra Winger; and Roslyn Kind (Barbra Streisand's sister) from *One Day At A Time.* From what I could tell about these projects, the actors were replaced because after casting, someone (producer, director, etc.) changed their concept of the character.

• **One day on *Seinfeld*,** we were all (actors and crew) on New York Street rehearsing a scene. A guest actor was back on the stage complaining, wondering how long he was going to be there, generally pestering the 2nd AD. Jerry happened to hear over the walkie talkies that there was a problem. He called the line producer asked her to fire the actor and call casting to bring in someone else. The next season this actor was the star of his own show and all the gossip was how horrible he was to work with. His show lasted just one season.

• **So yes, your worst fears are possible**—you can lose the job. But the odds are in your favor that you will do the job. Let go of the idea that somehow you won't live up to the role and that you can't deliver what is necessary. You can do it like no one else in the world can. So to say it again:

The job is yours. Use your energy in *how* to do the job, not in fear of not being able to do it. Make that role come to life through you.

• **Fear starts with a "what if" thought**. You can stop making up the fear thoughts. Create thoughts of how wonderful you are going to be. "I'm going to be totally satisfied with my performance." Fear is a misuse of your imagination. Wait till the bad things happen, then worry.

• **Jerry Seinfeld told a good/bad story on the set one day.** The first sitcom he was hired as a regular on was *Benson*. When he came to the set for the table reading of the fourth show he would be shooting, the assistant director called him over and said they had forgotten to call him and tell him he was fired. He had to leave the stage. He said, "That is when I knew I had to have my own show, so that could never happen to me again."

• **When doing a situation comedy** there will always be a table reading, if you have a significant role you will be at the reading. Prepare for it, like you did for your audition. If you can't get the script the night before, see what time you can pick it up from the office. Go sit in your car or the commissary and mark your script and rehearse your role. The writers need to hear you deliver the lines so they can see what works. Dress close to what you wore for the audition and look like you looked when they gave you the job. You are the guest; you want everyone to see why you were cast.

• **In order to study the finest of sitcom acting**, tape *Seinfeld* reruns. Each of the characters have a different form of comedy. Study how they deliver the lines, notice how it is not about the line, but the delivery. Of course, *Seinfeld* did have brilliant writers also.

• **Bobbie Eakes, *The Bold and the Beautiful,* was a student of mine** when she first moved here. She had been Miss Georgia. Being cast on the daytime drama was one of her first acting jobs. She has now been on the show for 10 years, she talks about when she first started.

> • **The main thing for me, when I was starting out and still very green,** was you fake it. You try to let them think you are completely confident even if you are nervous because they just want to know that you are going to be able to take the ball and run with it and do your job. Just try to be confident or exude confidence even if you are not.

• **For your first time working on a set**, here are a few hard and fast rules that cannot be broken:

• **If you accept a job, you must show up on time** and you must stay there until you are told you can leave or at wrap time. Always report to the Assistant Director when you arrive and when you leave the set for any reason. Sign out with the A.D. at the end of the day.

• **Being on time can be a chore.** Make a trial run before the first day if possible. Check out where the parking will be. If you are going on location there should be a map attached to the call sheet. If you are not on the set, have them fax it to you or your copy service where you receive faxes. You will probably have a ten or fifteen minute walk to the set from your car—wear comfortable shoes to get there. You may be delayed checking through security at the studio gate. Allow yourself the longest time it could take to get to the set, not the shortest.

• **Never look directly in the camera**; never talk or move when they have called "rolling" unless you are in the scene. Talk very quietly on the set, even when the camera is not rolling.

• **Never walk through a door** when a red light is on; it means the camera is rolling/shooting.

• **If you have an injury**, do not leave the set without reporting it to an assistant director. This happened to me. My finger was broken. I didn't realize it because I had been acting and the adrenaline was going. Luckily, the makeup person insisted I report it. Surgery was required to correct the break, which would have been very expensive if I hadn't reported it on the job.

• **When you are shooting you must focus** all your concentration on your acting work. You will be getting direction of where to hit your mark, you have to keep track of an activity you are doing to make sure you do the same thing on every take so the editor can cut in and out of takes. This may be your toughest assignment, there is usually so much activity going on around you.

• **Buy the book *The Camera Smart Actor*** by Richard Brestoff, read it the night before every new job. Take it with you, if you get scared and feel like you don't know what you are doing you can read it in your dressing room.

• **Michael Richards, Kramer on *Seinfeld*,** in an interview with the *Los Angeles Times* said,

- **It is hard work. Deep down I always enjoy the process**, but I find you have to work very hard to get to the moments where you surprise yourself—spontaneous moments where something comes through that wasn't in the script, the table reading or any discussions. That's always exciting. It feels holy.

* **Mira Sorvino said in an interview,**

- **I was absolutely neurotic doing *Mighty Aphrodite*.** Every night brought a new nervous breakdown. I'd cry and talk to God, I was so nervous. Then the next day, I'd show up and do my scenes.

• **In an interview in the *Hollywood Reporter*** the three following actors talked of what it takes to deliver on the set.

- **Robbie Benson**: At a moment's notice, you can be transformed into another world. Ten seconds before the director says "Action!" you are yourself, yet with that one word, you put your entire soul into what you're playing. It becomes an obsession, especially when it works and you know that it's working. You realize that your performance contributed to the film in that one moment. Even if they cut it, you think about that one moment that works. That moment carries you through all the bad moments. It's like baseball and that one perfect crack of the bat. You're going to keep swinging to hear that crack once more.

- **Rutger Hauer**: Actors make films for the same reason people go to see them—it's a chance to share the dream, the drama, the comedy, the horror, the fantasy of life. The audience wants to buy it and we want to give it. The key element is "Don't act." The moment the camera comes on, the moment it starts to roll, the actor's third eye goes into focus and he or she begins to live the part.

- **Susan Blakely**: Besides knowing your craft, there should be the ability to be spontaneous, to be intuitive, to feel how much you are projecting in front of the camera compared to what you project in real life. The spontaneity is so important, especially in television because you don't do much rehearsing, if any. You need to be open and loose so you can change things and react at the right moment. The best actors are able to be creative on their feet.

• **When you are the star of a project you will set the tone** for the whole on-set family. If you are a supporting player and the star acts like a jerk, don't go along with it. A friend of mine works on a show where some of the actors have contests to see who can be the last on the set. Two of the actors in a six actor ensemble show up on time prepared to work. They know the other actors won't be there and will keep them waiting. I admire the actors who are ready to go; it is rude to be late, to keep sixty people waiting for you.

• **In television there will be times** when, as a guest, you won't be able to rehearse with the star because they don't want to work that hard any more. Give it your all, when rehearsing with the stand-ins. Don't let a situation like this hurt your shot on that show.

• **On *Seinfeld*, the actors were all respectful of each other**, they were there when called and had a good time. They seemed to love to see each other each day and liked to gossip and catch up. They were always most concerned with delivering their best each week. On *Single Guy,* it was the same way; Jonathan Silverman has such an easy, calm attitude, even when problems arose and, on all shows, they do come up. He never seemed to be angry and kept his focus on the work to be done.

• **Speaking of gossip, the crew is full of it,** and when you are a guest you will be the target of some of it. There is so much empty time to pass and people who have been together for a long time have talked about everything there is to talk about so they are looking for anything new. Try to be a welcome addition to every set you go on.

• **Members of the crew often don't understand the way actors work.** They can't understand why you don't hit your mark and say your lines perfectly every time so they can go home. Don't look to them to judge how your acting truly is. The director and other actors can be trusted much more, although you may not get feedback.

• **Director Jim Burrows,** who's directed *Cheers, Frasier, Friends, Caroline in the City, 3rd Rock Form the Sun, Will and Grace,* and many others, is said to hug everyone before the shooting of every show.

• **Director Robert Altman** was interviewed by Bob Costa, who mentioned that Altman is famous for using people in his films who haven't acted before. To mention a few: Cher, Shelly Duval, Lilly Tomlin, Lyle Lovett. When Bob asked Robert Altman how actors act, he responded:

> • **They bring their personality to it**. Anybody can do this; it's just if they will. They can act if they get past that barrier of self-consciousness. All the experience you need is in your head. If they have the opportunity to do it and they have the confidence, they can break that shell and let the truth of themselves show. It's all in everybody's mind, it's in everybody's computer. We all sit there and say, "I'd do this or I'd do that"...that's all it is.

• **Steven Spielberg asked Dee Wallace Stone** why actors get so weird on the set. She gave him this explanation:

- **Actors are like race horses**; they are trained to get in the starting gate and go. When in hair, makeup, and wardrobe, they are getting ready and when the gate doesn't open for five hours, they get worn out.

• **William H. Macy** told *Back Stage West* when asked if there was such a thing as over-preparing said:

- **Perhaps not over-preparing, but useless preparation.** I've been guilty of it, and I think many actors are. You're going to play the Pope, and so you start trying to figure out, What does it mean to be the Pope? What does the Pope read? What was the Pope's childhood like? What does the Pope do when he prays? And I think the mature actor ultimately realizes, There's no way I can know any of that, and even if I did know it, there's no way I can act on it. I *am* the Pope—end of story. So that ends my preparation. Sure, you've got to figure out how Catholics do the service and all of that stuff. But that ain't about acting; that's about physicalizations and anybody can do that. Who is the Pope? You are the Pope. Quit auditioning. You've got that role.

• **The set is the most grown-up place to be.** At first appearances it seems that there are a lot of people to take care of you. Wardrobe, Makeup, Hair, Script Supervisor, Dialogue Coach and the Director. Make friends with these people; they are your allies. But these people will not necessarily always know what you need. You must take care of yourself.

• **The costume designer and wardrobe assistants** can really help you. Your wardrobe is so much a part of your character, you have to be comfortable in your clothes. Do not settle for just anything; keep pushing nicely till your clothes are right for you. If the director is dead set on a certain outfit you can't stand, get the designer to help you become comfortable in it. Within limits, you can help design your makeup; it will depend on the look of the film, but you do have a say.

• **Costume designer Tom Baxter suggests:**

- **If you are a visitor on the set**, guest starring or supporting, treat everybody the way you would like to be treated. If a wardrobe person asks you if you have clothes to bring in, tell them honestly what you have and if you think it will work or not. A lot of times they will think, "They said they had that so I don't have to cover that." Then you get there the next day and you find out they did have a white shirt but it was short sleeved and looked like a rag. It wasn't a white shirt you could use as a dress shirt. For the smaller parts you are always going to be asked to bring in your wardrobe, unless the show needs something specific or it's a period piece. When you get in and out of the clothes, hang them up. The wardrobe people aren't there to be maids; they are there to do a job. It's really quite a complicated one.

- **Be someone everyone likes.** If you have an bad attitude, it doesn't work. The most successful people I've seen in television are the people who have that spark about their personality.

• **On one of the films I worked on,** I had to ask for a different makeup person. He was so negative; every morning I spent my energy warding off the negativity. One day, he got drunk in the afternoon and started making sexy remarks. I had a week's work left and knew I couldn't go through that turmoil anymore or my acting would suffer. I went to the head of the makeup department and he put me with someone else. The makeup person is the one you will spend your first hour with each morning—he or she is important. On a situation comedy, I like to be one of the first to be made-up.

• **Handle hair the same way.** You know what your hair will and will not do. My hair is curly so I know if they are straightening it out with hot rollers they can't keep them in too long or it will go even curlier. I have a friend who goes to the set in her own hot rollers because her hair is really straight and it takes longer to curl.

• **The script supervisor** has your lines and can help you match lines for other takes if you happened to change a word or two. Assume you are giving directors what they want unless they say otherwise. If it isn't *your* scene, you may not get much attention; learn to give it to yourself. Don't rely on the outside world to tell you that you're wonderful; assume you are. After you assume you are wonderful, then see what else you can find. It may be another acting choice or something special to do with one of the props. Diane Ladd is a genius at this. I've worked with her on two different projects and she makes every tiny little thing count. Keep adding things you would do in your real life; some will work, some won't—take the chances. All kinds of surprises can happen in the editing room. Because of the master or a change in the concept of the scene, they may need to use your close-up because you were the most interesting and had the most life about you.

• **Your dressing room is your home** away from home. Bring with you things that make you feel comfortable. There is usually an abundance of time so you need things to fill the time. Depending on your type of dressing room, you can expand what you may need to feel safe and content. It's the place to prepare your acting work first and foremost. It is also the place to rest and conserve your energy, meet with other actors, work on your scenes, go over lines, have someone in to share lunch, make your phone calls and check your service. I try to keep most of my outside life away from me unless I'm having a real easy shooting day.

• **Jennifer Grey,** ***Its like, you know...***, the first week we were back from summer break went to Pier One and bought some great tables and a rug. She covered the ordinary couch with a lovely blanket and pillows. She brought in some pictures and favorite lamps. She made the rather drab place adorable and homey. She also snuck her little dog, Lu Lu, into her dressing room everyday for company.

• **I bring any little snacks** I need that I won't be able to get on location or at the studio. I bring incense because I like to make the room smell like me. I bring my own makeup (just in case) and, of course, a hairbrush. I always bring a book to read that I am loving at the moment—something to look forward to get back to reading. I bring a good tablet to write on. Sometimes I use it as a kind of journal; other times to just simply write over and over "I can do this role," "Everything is working perfectly," or any other affirmation I may need at the time. Usually there is a bed or couch to lay down on; if not, bring an air mattress the next day so you can stretch out. I always bring an inspirational book or two. Sometimes, if I'm feeling insecure, just by opening a positive book a passage may catch my eye and make all the difference. Be careful of eating meat or sugar; it gives your body too much work to do and can take away from your acting energy.

• **When on location**, there is the additional burden of finding something to do because you don't go home at night. You go to a hotel room that you have had to make into a safe, homey place. A camera can really get you involved with everyone else. I like a Polaroid because you can give pictures to the people right away. If you do this, you must ask the still photographer and cameraman for permission to shoot. Also ask if there are any rules you should know about—when or where not to shoot.

• **Sally Field** said that the first time she worked with Burt Reynolds she filled books writing "I am worthy for Burt to like me" and other such affirmations. Obviously it worked; they had an affair that lasted several years and films.

• **You are the star in your own life** and you are the star in the role you are playing. When it comes right down to it, you are the one who the audience sees on the big screen, little screen, or stage. So treat yourself in the best way possible. There are no don'ts. Make your own rules for taking care of *you.* Your instincts are there to guide you. Keep your mind open, take in all the information anyone has to offer and then make your own decisions as to what is best for you.

• **No one can act your role for you**. Your job is to be prepared and to make yourself comfortable or uncomfortable, whichever appeals to you.

• **If you do get scared trying to figure out a script** or getting a handle on the character, pick up a phone—call your coach or another actor and talk about it. Joan Darling tells a wonderful story about a role she was in a panic over. She couldn't see what the part was about. She went to see her old friend and teacher, Walter Beakel and raved on for the whole evening about not knowing what to do. He finally said "It's easy—she is a Jewish mother." Joan saw immediately what he meant. She went out and bought a big mommy purse and filled it with things Jewish mommies have in their purses and she was home free.

• **I worked with Sharon Farrell** on a pilot where she was playing a ditsy social reporter who was very interested in how she looked. The part was flimsy, so the day before shooting she went out and spent $100 on makeup. When she came on the set, she had all these new things to play with that ended up making the part very funny.

• **So don't panic: there are solutions to every acting problem.** Just ask the universe for the answer and you *will* come up with the solution. And after all, this is the fun part of acting, solving the problems.

• **Now you have the job**: wardrobe, makeup, hair, director and best of all, the other actors. The best thing that can happen is you can play totally *in the moment.* This is where acting is at its easiest; it feels like flying.

No matter how you may have prepared, leave yourself open for the wonderful surprises that happen when the camera starts to roll or the curtain goes up. Playing in the moment is what creates the real magical moments in any performance.

• **I talk so much about acting work** because when you are in trouble your work is your insurance. Just like life insurance, hopefully you won't need it. All your work is there if you need it, but it is okay to have everything going beautifully.

• **When I was coaching Dennis Erdman** (now a very accomplished director) in *Friendly Fire*, he called me from location. He said, "I don't know what happened; everything is gone. I was wonderful and then today I couldn't do anything." As we talked, it came out that he had been shooting for seven days and it was easy and fun. All the emotions were there, and he hadn't done anything but relax and hit his marks. Of course he wanted it to be that way, as we all do, but sometimes something happens for whatever reason (doesn't matter) and we *run dry.* All he needed was to start using the acting work. Well, he went back on the set the next day, used his work and came up with the same great acting he had been delivering. After that he had days when he would *fly* and days when he needed to call on his craft every moment he was shooting. Both ways work for the audience.

• **The more acting jobs you do**, the easier and simpler they get. If you are not feeling scared, that is okay. Yes, you may miss the feeling but you will get over it.

• **On every project** there are an abundance of ego trips, power plays, and politics. Ideally, the actors won't be involved in them. The director usually tries to keep these undercurrents away from the actors so you can do your job better. Of course, the gossip is always interesting and I am not saying not to listen to the stories going around. Sometimes they can be the most entertaining part of the job. But learn to not look at these trips personally. Don't get emotionally involved. If something is going on between some of the actors or even between you and another actor, it is most difficult to keep your personal emotions under control. But do it. Let's say, for example, you must insist on something you need to be able to perform and you can't get it—let it go. You will gain somewhere else. I'm not saying not to fight for what you want; but if you lose the fight, lose it and forget it. That way it can't really harm you. Feel good about the times you win and even let go of those too and move on to the next event.

• **Hopefully, your set will be a happy one** and a *family*. All sets end up being families but not necessarily the type of family we want. Whatever you can do to turn the people around you into the family you want, do it. Sometimes you may have to shield yourself from this family and other times you will die and cry when the project is over and you have to leave this family.

• **This is not your last job;** it is just a job and there will be another one. Try to collect good, funny, entertaining stories to tell on your interviews for your next job. They will also be good for any publicity you do, and there is always *Jay Leno's Tonight Show, David Letterman's Late Night* show or all the other talk shows.

• **When it was a wrap for *Seinfeld*, it was especially sad.** I had never been on a hit, a number one show, before and it actually took me quite a few months to let go of the loss. *Seinfeld* was the end of a television era, it was the end of those kind of ratings and that kind of language identification. Everywhere I go, people have certain sayings from the show that they have incorporated into their language. Thank goodness for the writing on *Ally McBeal*, I still have a fun show to watch actors really taking chances.

• **While we were on Christmas break**, in fact the day after Christmas, the news broke that we would not be back. Jerry was so sweet, he left a message on my machine, saying he had wanted to tell the crew first but the news had leaked. The last day of shooting before the Christmas break we always had a holiday party on the set. At the party the cast was missing for a while and we all figured they were making their decision. Jerry would have done another if the other three had insisted, but they were ready to let it go. When I saw Michael's face after the meeting, I knew. But as we often do, I tried to kid myself. Michael said, "I can't tell you," but his face said it all.

• **Jerry really wanted to leave in the ninth year** because nines figure very prominently in his life. An astrologer once told him she had never seen such a lucky chart, full of nines. Jerry does believe he is lucky and he is such a hard, industrious worker, that combination brought him his success. Most importantly, as Jerry explained to me several months before, he wanted to go out on top. He said as a comedian he knew what it was like to stay on stage too long and it was awful. He wanted to end the show when the audience was still screaming for more. He did achieve that, we had the highest ratings ever. So he got his wish. I was glad for him because I thought with all he had given me personally and the cast, crew and audience, he deserved what ever he wanted.

• **Working on the last two shows was a blast,** there were so many feelings, laughter one moment and then hidden tears another. Jerry wanted to go out with laughter and we did.

• **The show sent the crew off in a great way,** the cast gave us Tiffany designed gold class rings, that say *"Seinfeld"* on top and on one side "1989" and on the other side, "1998." Inside it says, "Thank you, Love, Jerry, Julia, Michael & Jason." I wear mine all the time. The producers gave us a fabulous year book chronicling our times together. Jerry gave digital video cameras to a few of the crew he was most closely involved with. I use mine all the time when I'm teaching classes and to record all family events.

• **I miss the cast tremendously**. Many *Seinfeld* people are a part of the show I currently work on, *It's like, you know...* and we often laugh over shared experiences.

• **One of the things I liked best about Jerry Seinfeld** was he was able to really feel and experience his feelings when they were happening. I saw him get angry a very few times and I saw him get his feelings hurt a couple of times. He dealt with it in the moment and didn't seem to carry any resentments. On the last day of shooting the show, I asked him how he felt. He said when he started driving to the studio that morning he had cried the whole way in. He then let it go and had a great day and evening.

• **Relaxation. Keep relaxing and feeling all your feelings.** Don't cover up fear, anger, tears, frustration, joy, ecstasy. Relax and experience all of yourself. Then go out and use all of it. If you are feeling joy and the scene is about sadness, then let the joy be there over how sad you can be. If you are feeling angry and the scene is about ecstasy, be in ecstasy over being able to feel such anger. Most of the time after your relaxation and full experience of your feelings, you will come through to the perfect emotions for the scene. Do not censor or cover up your feelings from *yourself*. Sometimes it is very appropriate to not let others see your feelings. You can have all your defenses up off-camera but never on-camera.

• **We usually get what we intend to get**. Intend to have a good time doing your job.

• **When it's a wrap for the day,** find some way to entertain yourself and be good to yourself. We all have our own unique ways; use yours. Again, there are no rules to follow except your own.

• **Drugs and alcohol** will shortchange you and the people you're working with. *STAY IN REALITY.* Actor Kelsey Grammer, in the middle of the television season, went to the Betty Ford Center. While that is good for him, there are seventy or eighty crew members who are without jobs because all of the television jobs are filled for the season. There are probably an additional 20 employees the production will continue to pay until he can work again because they are too valuable to let go.

• **Safety, safety, safety**. Actor Kenneth Steadman was 27 years old; he had moved to Los Angeles to pursue acting five years before his death. His career seemed to have great promise, he had been on *NYPD Blue* and *Baywatch* and the day of his funeral, guest star on the premiere episode of *Maloney.* He died while guest starring on *Sliders* when a dune buggy he was riding in overturned. The dune buggy had seat belts, but he wasn't using his. Take care of yourself on the set, wear the seat belts, let the stuntmen do their jobs.

• **Firearms Safety:** After actor Brandon Lee's death, SAG put out some guidelines for using prop guns on the set.

- **Use simulated or dummy weapons whenever possible.** Treat all guns as if they are loaded and deadly. Unless you are actually filming or rehearsing, all firearms must be secured by the prop master. Never engage in any horseplay with firearms or other weapons. Do not let others handle your gun for any reason. Never point a firearm at anyone, including yourself. Always cheat the shot by aiming to the right or left of the target character. If asked to point and shoot directly at a living target, consult with the property master or armorer for the prescribed safety procedures. If you are the intended target of a gunshot, make sure that the person firing at you has followed all these safety procedures. If you are required to wear exploding blood squibs, make sure there is a bulletproof vest or other solid protection between you and the blast packed. Check the firearm every time you take possession of it. Blanks are extremely dangerous. Even though they do not fire bullets out of the gun barrel, they still have a powerful blast that can maim or kill. If you are on a set where shots are to be fired and there is no armorer or qualified prop master, go to the nearest phone and call the Guild. A union representative will make sure proper procedures are followed.

• **Whoopi Goldberg** comments on winning awards.

- **It's never a slam if you don't win** because I always say to people the idea that you are one of five in any year makes you part of a very elite club. From now until the end of your life, you are an 'Academy Award nominee' or 'Academy Award winner.' Not everybody can have that. It's a title. So it's a no-lose situation. It's the greatest.

• **Reviews can be killers**. If you decide to read them, do you believe the goods ones and discount the bad ones? Glenn Close says she can't read them because even if they are good for her but mean to another cast member, it hurts her. I know many actors, myself included, that have gone to bed for days over bad reviews.

• **I want to encourage you to think of acting as a life-long career**. Brenda Blethyn did six films in the year following being nominated for an Oscar for *Secrets & Lies*. She did *Secrets & Lies* when she was 50 years old, it was the third movie of her career. Some actors do work in their older years, don't buy into, "your career is over at 40."

• **To read the TV ratings:** The first figure is the number the show comes in (right now out of 131 shows); the next figure is percentage/share: for instance: *Seinfeld* one week was #2 with 22.0/34. *The Single Guy* was #7 with 16.3/26. A single ratings point equals 970,000 households, or 1% of the nations 97 million TV homes in the Nielsen Media Research universe. Share is the percentage of sets turned on at a given time that are tuned in to a particular show.

• **To obtain the overnight television ratings** call 818/954-3482 after 7AM. The nationals come in at 1PM. You can be the first on the set to know how your show did last night.

Resources

Studio Fan Mail/Tamkin Color, 310/275-6122. 1122 S. Robertson Blvd., Los Angeles, 90035. Jack Tamkin runs a wonderful business. They send out all color photos with authentic-looking autographs and personal messages. Their costs are lower than most black and white photos. They will send out a very interesting, thorough set of samples.

The Vital Image, 310/823-1996 or 800/414-4624, in Playa del Rey. Call for their special product report. Power O2 Tonic +. This charged organic nutritional powder gives you enhanced focus, concentration and willpower and fuels your energy reserves and stamina. Great for those early morning set calls and the long extended working hours. *Also see their listing in Section Six, Age Defying Techniques for all of their valuable treatments and products.*

DIALOGUE AND ON-SET COACHES

• **Whenever someone asks me what I'm doing** and I say I am the dialogue coach on *Its like, you know...*, they ask, "What does that mean?" Or they think it is a dialect coach, who corrects speech or teaches accents or dialects, which it is not.

• **Cherie Franklin, actress and acting coach,** is a well known dialogue and acting coach on feature films and television.

Q: What do you do as a acting/dialogue coach on a set?

- **I try to isolate each actor's individual problem.** They might be frightened or lacking information or knowledge. I get to know the actor in order to find what might be stopping him from really nailing a script or understanding the emotion of a character and being able to use his own emotions to fuel that particular character's life. Our tools are our emotions and our facility to call those emotions up and down easily at 2:15 in front of 75 people and 50 crew members. It's my function to get the actor comfortable with being able to use his emotions. I build up a safe bed of trust where the actor can tell me his needs, can admit his flaws, can state his fears so that we can eliminate them. I am working with the director's vision, supporting the actor in his ability to take direction and to execute the director's request in performance efficiently.

• **Each dialogue coach** may give you a different job description. On other shows, I have been the acting coach where I actually prepare the actor or actors for the director, rehearsing with them and helping them to make their acting choices.

• **On the show I currently work on**, and in the recent past, I am there to run lines and rehearse with the actors, to help them memorize their lines and incorporate any line changes or new scenes that suddenly arise.

Typically on sitcoms, there are changes each day and even while shooting, there may be changes between takes. Sometimes I just read the cue lines flat; other times I read the full lines of the other characters, close to the way the characters will be saying their lines so the actor I'm reading with can work out their moves, timing and reactions.

• **Sometimes we will have non-actors as guests on a show.** I usually work very intensely with them to not only help them to learn their lines but to help them sound real. We had Los Angeles Mayor Riordan on *Its like, you know...*, he had all of his scenes with A.J. Langer who plays Lauren. As I was running the lines with them, the Mayor said about himself, "Oh that didn't sound real.". A.J. gave him such a great tip. She said, 'Try and make each line just a little different, have a different attitude on each one." That was such an easy way to think about the lines. He understood what she meant and really gave a good performance and got laughs.

• **Each actor has their own personality** and their own way of working. The coach must try to be very sensitive to their needs because there is much more that goes into the acting process than the words. Some actors like me to be close by all the time; (Jerry Seinfeld, Olivia d'Abo and Jennifer Grey) others prefer to work mostly on their own and ask me to run lines with them occasionally. Still others may like to just sit down and go over a difficult scene or some may just want to go over the line changes.

• **Jason Alexander, George on *Seinfeld,* has a photographic memory**; it seemed like he could look at the lines once and have them down. Before he shoots a scene, I will hang around, available to run lines with him, although I know it isn't necessary. I'll run the lines with the guest actors as many times as they want, then I'll ask Jason to run them once with the guests. It would be tedious and unnecessary to run them more than once with him. I don't know how Jason made the despicable George likeable, but he did. Jason received a lot of fan mail from women because they thought he was adorable, which Jason is in real life.

• **Julia Louis-Dreyfus was a blast to work with.** Maybe because I have three daughters around her age; maybe its her curly hair (I also have curly hair); it certainly was her sense of humor and talent. I loved it best when we had a new script or were blocking and shooting and taking one scene at a time out of sequence. She would come into the makeup room and say, “I don’t know the lines, I haven’t looked at this.” So for the next hour while she was getting her hair done, she would get the entire script down and have an idea of how she wanted to play each scene. She learns very fast and starts out running her lines flat and then, about the third time through, she follows her instincts and begins to flesh out her role. When she went on the set, she turned it up another 100 degrees and nailed it.

• **It seems to me Julia can make any line work.** I remember in one script Elaine had the line, “Tim Whatley.” Jerry says he’s talked to Tim Whatley and she responds, “Tim Whatley!” with so much emotion and body movement, the audience got it that she is nuts about him, he is adorable and she would do anything to get him, loose woman that she is.

• **Michael Richards (Kramer) is so very talented and funny.** He was my first buddy when I started on the show—he had the flu that week and really needed my help. I think he may have worried more than anyone about his lines but he always got them. He had so much to figure out besides the lines—the timing of his physical humor is so precise. It looked easy, natural and truthful, but he planed it meticulously. When he had a complicated scene to work out, we would go over it many times. Yes, there are surprises, like when he jumped out of a window while chasing Newman and just about ended his sex life. I think the most important thing for him is to be truthful; he was always working to achieve that.

• **In one scene, Kramer was supposed to be taking pictures** of George to impress the girl at the one-hour photo place. We were shooting the scene without an audience so Michael hadn’t had any rehearsal. He had many props in the scene, supposedly lights to set, a fan to move and turn on, pictures to take from different angles and George to convince to relax and loosen up. Very precise movements, lines to be said and marks to be hit all at the same time, so the four cameramen shooting the show can each get their shots. Since there had not been a rehearsal, I had to run lines with Michael, anticipating the pace that Jason might use. It was so entertaining watching Michael work out the crazy stuff he does and fun to be a part of his acting process.

• **Jerry Seinfeld was very particular** about getting each line exactly as it was written. Because he had the final decision of each word in each line, he liked to have the lines rewritten just the way they would be spoken. Each week I would pick out my favorite line in the show; most often it was one of his lines and wasn't really a joke line, it was a payoff or an attitude he had. Before each show, we would run through his scenes and then before each scene was shot, all the actors ran through as much of the scene as time allowed, as they were getting touched up with hair and makeup on the set. I tried to keep track of any problem lines and point them out to them before shooting.

• **Jerry is a "money player;"** he was great in rehearsal but when the cameras rolled a whole new energy and dimension came out. When he was acting, he was also producing the show, deciding on how the scene was to be played. I don't know how he did it, he had control of it all and yet, he seemed to have a very good time working. One of my favorite things about Jerry is, he didn't mind looking like a fool. He could write the show so he always looks good but it's funnier if his character looks shallow. On show days he likes to have a precise schedule which includes light meals. His assistant, Carol Brown, made sure he had everything he needed to be comfortable. He meditates before each show. Jerry seems to have endless energy— I never saw him look tired on the set, except the second to last show. He got sick and lost his voice, it was the first time in nine years we had to postpone the shooting for one day.

• **On *The Single Guy,* we had a good time**; the pace wasn't as fast and there weren't as many scenes as *Seinfeld.* Jonathan Silverman started working as a teenager and has never stopped. He is great on the set and is concerned about all of the cast and crew. When we did the pilot, he had *Single Guy* hats made for all of us, which is unusual for an actor to do on a pilot, but it made us all, cast and crew, a family.

• **Ernest Borgnine was so much fun**, he loves to laugh and has a thousand stories to tell. He used the script cover he's had since *Marty,* the movie he won his Academy Award for. He brought in his Oscar to the set one day so we could see it. His chair that he uses was made in Mexico for him when he was working on *The Wild Bunch.* At his age, he had plenty of energy, loved to work and was able to keep up with everyone on the set. He is always prepared with his script, we just ran lines a few times.

• **Shawn Michael Howard**'s first regular role on a series was *Single Guy.* He liked to run all of his lines in the script from the beginning to the end. He would get his lines down perfectly and then when we were shooting he would throw in some lines that he thought might work for his character. The producers encouraged him to do this because they were still developing the character.

• **Ming-Na Wen just fascinated me**. *Joy Luck Club* was one of my favorite movies and the serenity and mystery of the character she played was so beautiful. But on *Single Guy* she was snappy, hip and New York sarcastic. It is interesting watching her listen. There is always so much going on in her mind; she listens actively.

• **Joey Slotnick (Sam on *Single Guy*) had a great amount of energy**, he had sort of an engine running inside. He always had some activity, something that was going on in the scene. He was in the movie *Twister,* a small role but every time he came on the screen, he was full of where he had been and where he was going. The same was true for *Blast From The Past,* he was so funny as that religious hippy, intense and that engine was running inside.

• **Olivia d'Abo (*Single Guy*) was great to work with**; she loved to rehearse so I got to spend a lot of time with her. She was always working out her activities and because she was new in the second season, she was trying to discover more things about who her character was. In one scene we were shooting late at night, she had to fly in the door, find out Jonny wasn't going to stop a friend's marriage, hit several marks as she was all over the room, tell a long story filled with emotion and then flop into the chair. The scene was playing too long so the producer decided to cut part of the dialogue. They cut a chunk out from the top and then a piece out of the middle of the monologue which changed the blocking. It is hard to remember cuts like that but Olivia tackled it like, "Oh, boy here we go; this is a challenge and fun." Each take was hilarious, it was always like it was the first time she was doing the scene, whether it was a different turn of her head or inflection in her voice, she kept discovering new things each take. Actors must develop discipline, concentration and focus.

• **I work with all of the guest stars on the shows**, which I hope all of you reading this book will be sometime. Almost all the guest stars are good, have great respect for the shows and are happy to be there. It is important to remember that, as a guest star, you are there just for that show, so always check out the set, the cast and crew, figure out where it is designed for you to fit in. There is always a chance, if they like working with you, that you could be called back to do your character for another show.

• **If you get scared, just keep breathing** and there will probably be someone who senses it and will help you, though you don't want to seem needy. Occasionally actors have had panic attacks. They put so much pressure on themselves, they sort of short circuit. I don't think anyone else on the set has been aware of it and that is how I like to it to be. I will hang out with them, keep coming back to them, run their lines, laugh at their jokes, assure them that they can get through it. They always do.

• **It is important that you do your rehearsals at home** because you never know what your shooting day is going to be. On *Seinfeld* an actor was doing one scene on a no-audience, block and shoot show. He was playing a repair guy making a telephone call to Kramer; working half a day, doing one scene and leaving. This was a show shooting on location all over the studio lot. I ran lines with the actor and we rehearsed where he would be shooting until he felt comfortable with the hard hat and the phone on the pole. He was a big fan of the show and was fighting his disappointment at not being able to work with the cast. The scene played great, just what the director wanted. There were two takes and then the crew moved on, so anti-climatic for the guest.

• **It helped this actor immensely that he came in prepared**, he had done his acting work, figured out who, what, when and where. If he had been planning on discovering his character during rehearsal, he would have been caught short.

• **The actor who played the cable guy** on that same show was wonderful. He had several long monologues outside Kramer's door, in the last one there was quite a dramatic emotional change; he convinced Kramer to open the door and they hugged. He almost cried, yet he was funny. The preparation, talent and guts to do that take after take was remarkable. I must have rehearsed those monologues fifty times with him so he could try a lot of different acting work he was thinking of. The crew applauded at the end of his last take—it is unusual to move the crew.

• **When you are a guest on a show, come in absolutely prepared**,. We had one actress who could hardly tear herself away from other stuff she was doing (reading a magazine, eating, talking) to rehearse. She would have a wad of gum in her mouth, casually go off her lines like they didn't matter, and just think she was so cute. Of course, this drove me nuts. I would try to work with her but she always wanted to get back to me later. Finally, right before the show she was ready to work with me. Well, my policy is to take care of the guests first so I can be fully available for the members of the cast who have so many scenes and a story line to think about. This girl had given many of us— trying to do our jobs—a hard time. When you come to play on a team, jump in and be a team player.

• **One actor had fully prepared his work,** but in rehearsal he was completely flat. I knew he would be replaced if he didn't deliver the character. I took him aside to run lines and encouraged him to do all the stuff he had worked on. He said he was afraid of being too big. I said, "Go for it, they will tell you if you're too big." Well he did, and was so funny, they brought him back to do another show.

• **I love working as a dialogue coach**, I work closely with the script supervisor who, among other things, is in charge of making sure any missed or muffled lines are reshot so they don't lose a line or word the writer or producer wanted. Not everything can be fixed in the editing room. If a show doesn't have a dialogue coach, the script supervisor will run lines with the cast, in addition to their other work. I'm happy to say the script supervisors I've worked with are always glad I'm there to help the actors.

NUDITY, SEXUALITY AND THE CASTING COUCH

• **The so-called casting couch still exists.** There are people who will promise actors roles in film and television in exchange for their bodies, and there are actors who will go for it. There are also actors who will make the offer first. Sometimes it works—the actor gets a job, but most often the actor gets no job, possible exposure to disease, loss of self-respect and loss of reputation (a fragile commodity when you're trying to build a career.) I've seen actors waste enormous amounts of time trying to take this way to a career that resulted in one or two minor jobs and loads of broken promises.

• **Be honest with yourself**—have a fling if you choose because you think it might be fun and worth the risks, but don't fool yourself. With very few exceptions, the "casting couch" has not been a winning journey.

• **There are SAG regulations regarding franchised agents** or sub-agents which make it a violation as a condition of representation "to request of an actor a nude or semi-nude interview, or to request that an actor engage in sexual activity." Any breaking of this regulation should be reported immediately to SAG.

• **Three actors accused a former writer** for *The Arsenio Hall Show* of fondling their buttocks and genitals during an audition. These men had been called in for a skit spoofing Thighmasters. They claimed in a Superior Court lawsuit the writer fondled their buttocks after each removed his pants and underwear during one-on-one auditions.

• **Agent Bonnie Howard of Howard Talent West** received a package addressed to "Mr. Howard." In it was a pair of new sexy panties, a piece of candy, a condom and a letter requesting an interview.

• **Talent agent Wallace Kaye was tried**, found guilty and sentenced to five years and four months in jail for sexual attacks on eleven aspiring actresses and models ranging in age from 20 to 35. He would engage them in various improvisational scenes that were sexual in nature. The "auditions" were scheduled in the early morning or late evening behind locked doors. At a certain point in the scenes, he would force himself on them, putting his tongue in their mouths, fondle and kiss their breasts, grab their buttocks—all while they were physically restrained. One of my older woman students, Dolly Thompson, was represented by him and thought he was wonderful until the scandal broke. He had never tried anything with her.

• **The law says that sexual harassment exists** when attention is unwanted or unwelcome. The moment your relationship with someone changes for you, and you say so, you are a victim of sexual harassment if that attention continues.

• **Christine Lahti**, the *Los Angeles Times* reported, turned down the sexual advances of a director who was considering her for a role early in her career. He told her, "You're a fool—you're not gorgeous, you're not special, you have no connections."

• **Gregory Harrison** said he was propositioned by a female casting director at the beginning of his career and since turning her down 15 years ago, has never been offered a role at the network where she still works.

• **Sidney Poitier** advised Denzel Washington at the beginning of his career: "Be very careful of how you start in Hollywood. The first two, three or four movies will determine how the town looks at you. The choices you make then will affect the rest of your career."

• **Eve Brandstein,** producer, former casting director and author of *The Actor: A Practical Guide To A Professional Career,* was a guest on my cable show. One of my students at the time, Cynthia Geary *(Northern Exposure),* asked:

Q: Does the casting couch exist?

- **There is something like that going on all the time.** The casting couch exists in life, not just in a casting director's or producer's office. This particular profession you're involved in is a very seductive profession. I believe what an actor brings to the audition or to the interview or movie is a certain amount of sexual energy, the creativity, charisma, beauty, the specialness of the person. You have to use that to make your work great, and that is sexy and at the same time you're trying not to be seductive. So you're doing two things—you're sending the message "pay attention, hey how do I look, do you notice me." So there is something confusing; some people get mixed messages. Then there's the good old fashioned: you're attractive to somebody or you find them attractive. By the way, the casting couch goes both ways; it can be a two way experience. Nobody is an unwilling victim.

- **Bottom line, it's a personal decision.** I recommend you walk out of the room if somebody's putting the make on you as an actor. I don't think it's worth the risk. A lot of times it turns out to be a very bad thing for the actor. The person in power is certainly less at risk. If you feel you're being harassed or asked to do something that is obviously inappropriate for that interview or that audition that deals with your sexuality, I say get out of the room as politely and nicely as you can. Do not be offensive, leave. You are dealing with someone who has problems you do not understand, and it could possibly even turn against you. Leave, but follow it up. Make sure your agent knows. Report it to someone.

• **A young actor I know arrived in town from Texas** with a list from his teacher of a few people to look up. I was one of them. We met and he enrolled in class. Three days later I got a call from him. He was ready to leave town. He had met with a casting director who was on his list and the man was very nice and helpful. He asked the actor to pick him up at his home to go out to dinner to talk further about his career. The actor was very pleased to be having dinner with this well-respected person in the industry within his first week of hitting town.

• **During dinner, the casting director** spoke of specific actors he knew who were not gay but had sex with male casting directors in order to land their roles. My friend was shocked at the conversation and revelation and said he could never do anything like that. When they arrived back at the casting director's home, he invited the actor in to pick up some scenes to practice with. When they got inside, the actor stayed for a time talking, still reveling in being in this man's company. Eventually the man put on a porno tape and tried to seduce him. The actor fled, didn't sleep that night and called me early in the morning. I pointed out that perhaps he had been too nice during the dinner conversation when his instincts sensed it was going in a sexual direction. I also pointed out the casting director was wrong to take advantage of his profession in trying to seduce him. To give the casting director a break (a very big break), perhaps he felt the actor was hanging around waiting to be hit on.

• **It's been ten years since this incident** and the young actor has gone on to a very nice career in all areas of our business and maybe is on his way to stardom. I'm sure he smiles now at his naivete.

• **Make the decision as to how far you will go sexually** to land a part before you are in the situation where you must decide in the moment. Many actors have never faced a casting couch situation; I hope you never do. I hope it's always your talent, look and personality they want.

NUDITY REQUIRED

• **You may need to decide if you will do nudity** in your career and under what circumstances. Jenny McCarthy has built a career using her Playboy centerfold as a launching pad. (Although now she says she won't do nudity.) There are always low budget "B" movies. Darryl Hannah and Jamie Lee Curtis both made the transition from nudity-required "B" movies to big budget mainstream films. In Debra Winger's first movie, she had her top off *(Slumber Party '57)*. Sylvester Stallone was nude in *The Italian Stallion*, a low-budget soft-porn movie. There are mainstream movies where actors who have appeared nude, yet they haven't hurt their careers—in fact they may have propelled them. Minnie Driver in *The Governess*, Camryn Manheim in *The Road To Wellville,* Tim Curry in *The Rocky Horror Picture Show,* Isabella Rossellini in *Blue Velvet,* Natassia Kinski in *Cat People*, Glenn Close in *The Big Chill*, Kim Bassinger in *9 1/2 Weeks*, Sharon Stone in *Fatal Instinct.* Academy Award-winner and 1993 double-nominee Emma Thompson was nude in the 1989 British comedy, *The Tall Guy.* Heather Graham, in *Boogie Nights* and others. Holly Hunter won the 1993 Oscar for *The Piano* where she had a beautiful nude love scene and Harvey Keitel exposed his penis. There are some roles where a body double was used. In *Coming Home*, Jane Fonda requested a body double for her nude scenes.

• **There are the low-budget**, teen-exploitation, horror or comedy movies. Often, an actress' career can get locked in this genre and—because they have done one or two—that's how they will be cast. The producer will say, "You did it for that movie, so you have to do it for mine."

• **If you never want nude pictures of your body on the internet**, then never allow yourself to be photographed nude. Alyssa Milano, Pamela Anderson Lee and Dr. Laura Schlessinger went through law suits because old boyfriends had sold shots of them nude. Leonardo DiCaprio sued *Playgirl* because they used frames of his nude butt from his movie *Total Eclipse.* Charlize Theron's pictures ended up in *Playboy* because she had signed a release for pictures taken for her portfolio before she was famous.

• **Once you consent to work nude**, it is very difficult to take the decision back. Matthew McConaughey posed with his girlfriend in the nude in exchange for a few roles of headshots for acting pictures. When Matthew became a big hit, the photographer threatened to sell the photos. Beginning bids were half a million dollars. Remember the Vanessa Williams scandal—losing the Miss America crown because of the *Penthouse* magazine pictures? She survived and has gone on to become a major singer-actress. Also, Suzanne Somers, when at the height of her sitcom success with *Three's Company*; *Playboy* ran the pictures that she had modeled for when she needed money to raise her son. What is there to consider in making the decision? If it's a strong moral dilemma, don't compromise yourself. If it is not a moral issue, discuss it with your agent or manager in relation to your career. If you choose to do it, the things you have to consider are:

- Are you able to be nude in front of the cast and crew of a movie set?
- Will the scenes be shot in a tasteful way?
- Is the nudity important to the story line or there just for the sake of nudity?
- The videotapes of the movies will live forever.
- The time it will take to keep your body looking great.
- Be honest with yourself; come to a decision you can live with.

• **I was director Joan Darling's assistant** when she directed William Katt and Susan Dey in their first nude love scenes in *First Love.* Joan, a wonderfully sensitive director, discussed the design and choreography of each move. After the first day of shooting, the actors seemed to get used to it. They were both beautiful and in full body make up. After a week, cast and crew were all very bored and eager to get them out of bed and on to the rest of the shooting.

•**Olivia d'Abo** discussed her role with Armin Muller Stahl in *The Last Good Time.*

- **After the film was edited**, the director asked me to reshoot the scene of me walking out of the bathroom and this time actually dropping the towel so the audience could see what Armin was reacting to. I decided that it was important to the film. When nudity is totally organic and motivated by the scene and the actor is comfortable within their own skin and vulnerable in that moment, it works.

• **I asked Olivia about having love scenes with such an older man.** She said, "He's got baby's eyes, it made me want to mother him, to take care of him." She also talked of her deep respect for him as an actor. These feelings also parallel the plot of the film.

• **Winona Ryder, Meg Ryan, Julia Roberts and Alicia Silverstone** have always refused to work nude.

• **Liv Tyler removed her top in *Stealing Beauty,*** but declined to do so in *Onegin.*

• **Leonardo DiCaprio *Total Eclipse* and *The Beach.*** "Nudity is really tough but you have to do it if it's part of the film."

• **Mira Sorvino was nude in *At First Sight.*** When asked about it on Entertainment Tonight she said, "Have a sense of humor about it. Trust the people you are working with and have a generally good atmosphere on the set."

• **Daryl Hannah hid behind hair extensions in *Splash.*** She said, "If there was a role I really wanted to play and that was the only way I could get it, hell, I'd do it. Though I would really rather not."

• **Nicole Kidman and Iain Glen were both naked on stage** in New York doing the play *Blue Room.* Iain did nude cartwheels. *People* magazine asked Iain, "How did the decision to appear naked come about?"

- **We shook hands and said, "I'll do it if you do it."** And that's when we went for it, really. It's a very strange feeling being naked. It does make you feel vulnerable. But the thing that grounds us is trying to be inside the scene so that it's not about a thousand people watching you but one person—the character—watching you.

• **Bridget Fonda's first film was a NYU film,** ***Aria.*** There were 10 different directors directing 10 minute segments based on opera arias. There was no dialogue, just nudity and death. She "went for it all, first time out."

• **Gwyneth Paltrow says she used a body double** in a brief strip scene in *Great Expectations* because, "I would have had to not wear a bra, and I just didn't want to do that in front of the crew."

• **Angela Bassett says she was asked to undress** for *How Stella Got Her Groove Back.* She decided to keep her private parts private. That way, the audience "can put their own ideas of love and sensuality into it."

• **Halle Berry**, was lying facedown naked in *Introducing Dorothy Dandridge.* When asked if it was a body double or her body she said, "I'm not really comfortable with nudity in films. I doubt I'll do it again, but because that is how Dorothy was found dead, to stay true to history, I had to do it."

• **Sally Field** said in an Actors' Studio interview: "What is the big deal about taking your clothes off? Its about the acting work."

• **Holly Hunter** in an Actor's Studio interview, when asked what was it like to do the sex scenes in *The Piano.*

- Very easy. The sex scenes became integral to the story. It was necessary to the movie to see the unveiling of those characters. No big deal—by then the crew were all family.

• **Julianne Moore was asked** in the *Los Angeles Times* how her family dealt with the many times she has done nudity, especially in *Boogie Nights.*

- **My mother has always said, "I'd much rather see you naked than dead."** It's funny, but it's true. What's really disturbing, when you look at a movie, is seeing a dead body. But how scary is it to see your daughter walk across a room with no clothes on? Not very. But if you see her shot up a million times or have her head cut off, that's scary.

- **You just hope you're in a situation that's safe.** I did a nude scene in *Body of Evidence* that was just awful. I was too young to know better. It was the first time I'd been asked to get naked and it turned out to be completely extraneous and gratuitous. Ugh. It was a terrible film and a terrible performance by me. It was about nothing, and I didn't need to be doing it.

• **Ashley Judd** said that she won her applause prior to filming a lengthy nude scene. She arrived on the set in a robe and blithely announced, "Hi, I'm Ashley and I'm going to be nude for the next 12 hours. I'm not embarrassed and I hope you won't be either." The actress then dropped her robe and said, "This is my body." The ovation swelled.

• **Faye Dunaway,** in an Actors' Studio interview.

> • **What is really difficult is to reveal your soul**, your pain, your vulnerability. That's what has to happen, no matter whether you have clothes on or not. Nudity comes with the territory of movies. The actual clothes on or off is less important than the emotional nudity. In bed usually exposes moments of extreme vulnerability and openness—that's what is difficult.

• **Jennifer Jason Leigh says:**

> • **I don't have a problem with nudity** if I think it moves the story forward and says something about the character. But no matter how truthfully and honestly it's portrayed, it still seems to bother people.

• **Kate Winslet, when asked how comfortable she was** with her first nude scene in *Jude,* said:

> • **Not at all! No way! Oh, it was awful.** I was so nervous, I starved myself for a month beforehand. I went through all the paranoias: "My bum's massive. My breasts are saggy. I've got a spotty back. Chicken arms. I can't do it." I just had to keep remembering that the scene was a real turning point in the story and to get on with it. At the end of the day, you forget that you're completely naked.

• **Teri Hatcher** will take a role with nudity but then will try to get it changed. In *Two Days in the Valley,* a scene was topless and she asked if she could wear a T-shirt or a tank top because the scene seemed exploitative, she won. In *The Big Picture*, her first feature, she was also able to get them to change the nudity scene.

• **Stephanie Stephenson**, after landing a choice role in the touring production of the Broadway musical *Les Miserables*, quit the next day when she learned she would al*s*o have to play a prostitute in an ensemble scene.

• **I have a friend who is very cute.** His first day on the set in his first starring role in a Showtime movie, he was required to be completely nude, making love with Laura Boyle. They didn't know each other and, right off the bat, they were both totally nude and in bed. He said it was uncomfortable but got on with the task and was proud of his work. Incidently, he is gay so he really had to act.

• **Nudity can be a perfectly wonderful part of artistic expression,** or it can be in poor taste and a career risk. It is such a personal decision—I suggest you search and follow your heart. Trust your educated instincts. *See personal manager Tami Lynn's remarks on page 253.*

GAY ACTORS

• **I'm not here to comment on homosexuality.** I believe in freedom of choice in matters of personal sexuality. However, if an actor is perceived as gay due to certain types of mannerisms, this can be limiting to the actor's castability in certain types of roles.

• **On my cable show, an actor asked Eve Brandstein:**

Q: How do you advise actors who are gay in how honest they should be with their agents and casting directors?

> • **It depends; I certainly don't think it's something you have** to bring up since it's a personal issue in a very professional circumstance. If an actor has heard that they are perceived as gay, it may create a closing-in (of how they'll be cast). If you don't want your casting possibilities perhaps narrowed, it's perfectly okay to make a decision and adjust to how you are perceived.

• **I would like to add to Eve's comments** that an actor must always be working on their image and must understand it is important to learn how you are being perceived. It's hard to look at ourselves honestly, but it's necessary. Needless to say, a casting director is not always fair or reasonable.

• **An actor once came to me for private coaching** because he had accidently overheard the people in his theater group laughing and talking about him, saying he would be foolish to think he would be considered for a certain role because he was so obviously gay. The actor didn't understand what this meant. When he told me the story, he was choking back his tears. He had left the company and had been off sulking for a few weeks but then decided to face the truth of how he was being perceived.

• **When I met him, he did display mannerisms** that were probably inappropriate for the wide range of roles he was physically "right" for. The fact that he actually was not gay had nothing to do with his image problem. When we got on camera, he talked and walked and did some of his stand-up comedy act. Then I played back the tape so he could observe himself. He quickly developed an understanding of his own body language and appearance and was able to adjust his physical expression to create a more effective image. I saw him a few years later. He was fine and had gone on to a wonderful working career. While gay actors certainly play powerful, masculine roles, no actor can get such specific roles without the appropriate image.

• **Another actor was sent to me by a commercial casting director** who said "The actor is wonderful but with his mannerisms, he will never land a commercial." This actor happened to be gay, but the concern to me was not sexual orientation, but rather the actor's physical believability playing certain types of characters. After studying and analyzing the way he came across, he made some adjustments which improved his castability in a wider range of roles for his physical type. Within a year, he had landed eight commercials and continues to have a very lucrative commercial career.

• **What about playing a homosexual?** You and your agent must decide what's best for your career. You must decide if you can be comfortable showing affection in or out of bed with a person of the same sex if the script calls for it. Also, you must consider the idea of being typecast. Tom Hanks won the Oscar for *Philadelphia,* playing a gay man dying of aids. Hal Holbrook played a homosexual father in *That Certain Summer*; Matthew Broderick in *Torch Song Trilogy,* Aidan Quinn in the television movie, *An Early Frost.* William Hurt won the Academy Award for *Kiss Of The Spider Woman.* Will Smith *(Fresh Prince)* played a gay man in *Six Degrees of Separation,* but refused to do the sex kiss as it was written in the script, so they used a camera angle that looked like they kissed. These roles certainly didn't hurt the actors, but all of them had previously played roles as straight men.

• **More roles are opening up for men and women gay characters**. Ellen "came out" on her show. *Will and Grace* is a hit.

• **Agent Bonnie Howard went to a play, *Bar Girls,*** in which all the characters were lesbians—very sexually explicit. One of the women was seeking representation and asked to meet her. Bonnie assumed she was gay. She said, "No, I'm an actress." Bonnie signed her on the spot because she had been so convincing.

• **Sir Ian McKellen is the first openly gay man** to be knighted by the Queen of England. In a *Los Angeles Times* interview he talked about gay actors in terms of social conformity.

- **Acting at its best is of course about disguise** and not being yourself, about pretending to be somebody else. But if that pretense is going to work, the character has to be absolutely rooted in the imagination and experience of the actor.
- **So for a closeted gay to be an actor is a rather congenial situation.** He can disguise the fact he is gay, which is what society is encouraging him to do, but at the same time he can have an emotional release, using the absolute honesty of his own feelings within the performance. And he can do it in public. At the same time the public is saying, "Don't tell me about yourself, I don't want to know." The gay actor goes out and tells society everything and yet disguises it.

• **You do not have to divulge your sexual preferences;** it is nobody's business. You are an actor, and if you wish to play gay and straight characters, it is your choice.

ACTORS WITH DISABILITIES

• **Otto Felix**, an able-bodied actor, is the founder of Handicapped Artists, Performers, Partners, Incorporated (HAPPI), the largest non-profit theatrical group for diasabled performers in the country. Otto has done over 300 commercials, has been a regular on three TV series plus many guest-starring roles and worked in over 20 feature films.

Q: Tell me about HAPPI.

- **I created HAPPI in 1986.** There are actors, musicians, comedians and athletes. HAPPI includes partners who are all able-bodied people that also have the same aspirations, and they work side by side. We have a 10 piece band made up of able-bodied and disabled people. We have workshops Tuesday and Wednesday nights, and it's been going strong.

- **The honorary chairman is Fred Dryer** (*Hunter*). The students elect a president of HAPPI. Right now its Demott Davis. He's the fellow who broke his neck playing football at Harvard. The vice-president is Chris Warfield who wrote and produced his own movie, *Blind.* Pretty incredible, huh?

Q: How much does it cost to join the organization?

- **Everybody pitches in and helps** pay for the space that I rent over in West L.A. which usually comes to $40 apiece a month. The space costs $400 a month. It's a voluntary thing. We have an agency that we started that's called the H.I.T. Agency, that's HAPPI International Talent. We help people get jobs. They give us 10% of what they do; and the money goes back into HAPPI's account, which is a full non-profit association. I use it for buying stamps when I send their pictures out and make calls for them. It's not a big powerhouse agency by any sense of the imagination.

Q: How do you get work for your people?

- **I get calls from agents for work.** I got a call today for three blind guys that jog, and I've got three of them all lined up. The casting people know who HAPPI is. It's either Richard Wright, my partner, or myself. We have 180 or so people signed up.

- **Every other year, I do a showcase** at the Director's Guild. Last year it was hosted by Brea Walker and Jim Lamphrey. She is disabled, of course, and her husband, Jim Lamphrey is not. There you have a disabled and a non-disabled working side by side. The musicians sang. The governor, the mayor, Keith Carradine, Carl Weathers, etc. were there. I had celebrities give out little Ottos. Jon Voight calls them little Oscars. We give them out to handicapped people who did outstanding work in the previous year. We're growing; it was a great show.

• **My thanks to Terry Correll**, an actor/producer in a wheelchair, who told me about Otto and HAPPI. Terry is a wonderful, sensitive actor. He did a showcase scene on my cable TV show and had a leading role in a play I directed. His chair never made a difference. We didn't have to make any adjustments. He took care of everything.

Resources

HAPPI, Handicapped Artists, Performers and Partners, Inc., 310/394-6625. P.O. Box 24225, Los Angeles, 90024. Workshops and classes to assist talented, disabled artists seeking careers in film, television, radio and other areas of show business. Interviews and auditions are held on a continuing basis by appointment.

Otto Felix Film Acting Workshop, 310/470-1939. Actor/writer/producer/coach. He teaches disabled actors in both his regular cold reading classes and for HAPPI. A special rate of $50 a month.

PATH, The Performing Arts Theatre of the Handicapped, 818/503-3555. Weekly training programs. 72 casting directors saw the last showcase.

Deaf West Theatre Company, 323/660-4673. 660 N. Heliotrope Dr., L.A., 90004. Performed in American Sign Language with voice interpretation for the hearing audience. Resident theatre productions, also childrens theater. Workshops and scholarships available.

Writing and Directing Workshops

WRITING

• **If you have a talent for writing,** it can indeed be one of your greatest career assets. You should certainly develop it.

• **We have all heard of Sylvester Stallone's** *Rocky* script. He was living penniless in New York but refused to sell his script unless he could act in it. It could happen to you.

• **Actors** Matt Damon (*School Ties*), and Ben Affleck (*Geronimo*), decided, "If you want a good role, write it yourself." They sold *Good Will Hunting* to Castle Rock for well over a half a million dollars and both starred in it.

• **Copyrighting and/or registering your script is a must.** There are two ways to do it; some writers do both. The federal copyright office costs $20 and they keep the script for 75 years. The Writers Guild of America West is $20. They keep the script for five years, which means you must re-register every five years. You do not have to be a member to register. *(Phone numbers, addresses and websites next page.)*

• **Wannabe producer Heath McLaughlin solicited scripts** with an ad in *The Hollywood Reporter.* He found one he wanted to produce, *Just Write.* It stars Sherilyn Fenn, Jeremy Piven, JoBeth Williams, Alex Rocco and Wallace Shawn. The low-budget film is being financed by a limited liability corporation, a consortium of business investors from Wisconsin.

Writing Resources

American Film Institute, 323/856-7600. 2021 N. Western Avenue, Los Angeles, 90027. Professional Seminars and Workshops, Advanced Technology Computer Programs. Call and get on their mailing list to receive both catalogues.
Robert McKee's Story Seminar, 310/312-1002. $475, 3 days 9;30AM to 8:30PM.
Truby's Writers Studio, 310/575-3050. Classes, videos and tapes. Very popular among studio people.
UCLA Extension courses, 310/825-1901.
Computer programs widely used: Dramatica Pro; Scriptor. The Writers Computer Store, 800/272-8927 or 310/479-7774. 11317 Santa Monica Blvd., Los Angeles, 90025.
For Copyrighting: Register of Copyrights, Library of Congress, Washington, D.C. 20559. $20 fee. Forms and circulars hotline, 202/707-9100. The U.S. Copyright Office web site: www.lcweb.loc.gov/copyright Find answers to questions regarding copyright and download copyright forms.
For Copyrighting: The Writers Guild of America West, 323/762-8100.$20 fee. www.wga.com. 8955 Beverly Blvd., West Hollywood, California, 20559.
Saturday Sitcom Writing Workshop, 818/752-9566. The Kindness of Strangers Cafe, 4378 Landershim Blvd. Free, actors and writers.

• BOOKS ON SCREENWRITING

Dramatists Sourcebook and Writers Market
Fade In: The Screenwriting Process, by Robert A. Berman.
From Script to Screen: The Collaborative Art of Filmmaking, by Linda Seger and Edward Jay Whetmore.
Making A Good Script Great and others by Linda Seger. She's the premier "script doctor."
Making a Good Writer Great: A Creativity Workbook for Screenwriters, by Linda Seger.
How To Write A Movie In 21 Days, by Viki King.
Plots and Characters: A Screenwriter on Screenwriting, by Millard Kaufman.
Screenwriting, by Syd Fields.
The Screenplay: A Blend of Film Form and Content, by Margaret Mehring.
The TV Scriptwriter's Handbook; Dramatic Writing for Television and Film, by Alfred Brenner.
The Script Is Finished, Now What Do I Do? The Scriptwriter's Resource Book and Agent Guide, by K Callan.
The Complete Guide to Standard Script Formats, Part 1: The Screenplay, by Hillis R. Cole, Jr., and Judith H. Haag. Also Part 2: **Taped Formats for Television.**

• PLAYWRIGHTS' GROUPS

Asian Theatre Workshop/Mark Taper Forum, 213/972-7267.
A.S.K. Theater Projects, 310/478-3200. Readings, seminars, workshop productions.
BlackSmyths/Mark Taper Forum, 323-972-7539. Open to black playwrights.
First Stage, 323/850-6271.
Pasadena Playwrights Workshop, 626/577-4956.
West Coast Ensemble Playwrights Unit, 310/449-1447.

DIRECTING

Director Jim Pasternak teaches a professional 16-week film directing workshop during which time 12 people direct and shoot three to four scenes from different feature films. Participants include film or theater directors, actors, screenwriters, producers, cinematographers, editors, composers, production designers, lawyers and an occasional studio head.

Q: What do you do in the workshop?

- **The class members all want to refine skills** they already have or cross-over, reinvent and empower themselves. I create an environment where they can make mistakes, stretch, really grow. I'm like an old-style movie producer; I've got, on any given week, 36 different directors working or shooting. I like to think of myself as the "producer from heaven" because all of my efforts go to support and nurture the director.

- **Actors are my favorite students** because they are the most victimized and least enfranchised of the artists in the movie business. They tend to focus on one thing, which is being an actor, when they should function as writers, designers, musicians, dancers, producers and directors. To survive and create their own acting opportunities they must learn to become Renaissance personalities.

- **I teach the directors** how to read and analyze screenplays from a film director's point of view and how to prepare for shooting through the preparation of blocking diagrams, storyboards and dramatic workbooks. They learn to read in terms of actions, adjustments, activities, and images. They learn what the characters in the scene are doing, how they are doing it, and how they can do it non-verbally through the use of activities. I teach them how to see the scene and how to know when the events in the scene occur, and that if a scene doesn't have an event, it's their responsibility as a director to create an event. An "event" is a turning point; a discovery; something that happens to advance the action or advance the character. That happening can be the key to the photographic style of the film; for how you shoot a scene has to do mostly with how you see its catalytic moments. I teach directors to help actors understand what they want (their intention, their objective, what they're doing, what they're fighting for); how to use language that is actable; how to inspire and relax actors; how to ease them past the greatest acting problem of all, which is fear.

- **They learn where to put the camera.** You have to see with your right brain and you have to begin looking through a lens; you need to know about photography, to suddenly see the actor in that space.

- **They redirect through editing** and continue to direct through postproduction, still writing and shaping the movie, still creating actor's performances.

Q: Why should actors learn to direct?

- **When actors learn to direct they're better actors** because it helps them take responsibility for their own performance, to bring the director choices that the director can shape and nurture and be inspired by. It helps the actor to understand the craft requirements of lenses, of camera movement, and lighting. It helps actors to do their homework; it's not just their part they must focus on, but their part in relation to other parts. It helps them to find activities that are physical, cinematic equivalents for the words of the text. These are things directors think about when really they are things that actors should think about. Studying directing makes you a better actor because it makes you a fuller collaborator in the filmmaking process.

Resources

Filmaker's Boot Camp, 800/775-4330, www.guerrillafilm.com. Guerrilla Film Institute

Pasternak's Film Directing Workshop, 310/455-0165. Also available for consulting and preparing first time directors.

New York Film Academy, 212/674-4300, www.nyfa.com. Eight and four week workshops start the first Monday of every month, all year round.

Take the Director's Journey Workshop with Mark W. Travis, 818/508-4600.

Books on Directing

Actors Turned Directors: On Eliciting the Best Performance from an Actor and Other Secrets of Successful Directing, By Jon Stevens.
Directing the Film: Film Directors on Their Art, by Eric Sherman.
The Director's Journey: by: Mark W. Travis
The Film Director's Team, by Alain Silver and Elizabeth Ward.

SCAMS

• **In the years I have been writing this book** the number of scams has risen sharply. I started writing for my students so I could lead them in the right direction; they would find the right people and not be separated from their money and good reputations.

• **If someone says they can make you a star or get you work** and you have no training and no experience, run! They want money or sex from you.

• **There is a scam going on where certain agents and casting directors** sell or make available to showcases or pseudo acting schools the pictures that are submitted to them for employment. You will get a phone call from a salesperson who will say that you have come highly recommended from a casting director or agent. They won't know how they got your number but they want you to come in and audition for possible work. An actress told me she did a charity showcase with 80 people there from the industry. Each of the 20 actors received a call with this scam. One of the industry persons had sold or given away their folders that contained the actors' pictures and resumes.

• **Keep track of who you submit your pictures and resumes to.** Many producers receive thousands of submissions—they might throw them in the trash or they might pass them on to someone who has a scam going on. Actors are vulnerable because they want to act and are eager for the opportunity to do so.

• **There is a nonunion casting director** who has a showcase company. When you submit to the casting director for casting you may get a call from the showcase company asking you to come in and audition for the showcase. They usually say they don't know how they got your number, you will know how they got your number. It is fine if you contact the showcase yourself. I object to their practice of soliciting students in this way. I am not mentioning the showcase because they seem to present good showcasing opportunities and they are **not** a scam operation.

• **If anyone calls you out of the blue**, do not talk to them. If you have an agent or manager tell the caller to speak to them and get off the phone. I know it is tempting but there are no short cuts; you are not the exception. Do not trust anybody who has not come to you through your own thorough research or a personal introduction. Even then you have to be cautious.

• **Reported in *Back Stage West*,** a 17 year old victim said he paid $25 to be given access to casting director Randy Callahan's casting "hotline" after being referred to him by photographer Bud Stansfield of Western Images Photography. When he called, the jobs were always for over 18. Nevertheless, Callahan did let the boy come in for a purported audition for a *Playgirl* video that would feature frontal nudity and simulated sex. The actor took a couple of friends to the casting director's house for the audition. Callahan told him he needed three nude pictures of him—one from the back and two from the front, with one depicting him in a state of arousal—to show the video's director. The friends waited outside near a window so they could hear everything.

• **The actor said the first two pictures** made him "very uncomfortable," but it was the third that made him most nervous. "Callahan took off his shorts and then he started playing with himself. He said, 'Look, you do it, too." The actor followed the casting director's instruction and let him take the third photo.

• **When the police came in to search,** they found the actor's pictures in a drawer along with a stack of similar pictures of other men. Callahan had never sent them to the so-called director. A spokesperson for *Playgirl* said that the magazine did not produce the videos that Callahan claimed to be casting for.

• **Video Scam, a pitch given to a *Back Stage West* reader** from a manager who somehow got her number to see if they could work together. The meeting took place in his apartment. He said he was putting 24 actors on video to be sent to selected agents and casting directors. Each actor got two minutes on the tape. The cost to each actor is $175 and $40 a month for the term of the contract. He talked for two and a half hours saying he needed a decision right away because he was shooting the next video in a few days. Look out for video scams!

• **Premier Casting, an extras' casting company** also known as Universal Casting, charges $89 for a registration fee. They say you will work within a few days. Thomas Mills, "Tombudsman," a weekly columnist for *Back Stage West,* asked in his column for information. He was overwhelmed with complaints. After paying Premier, the actors had obtained no work or received a few post-midnight phone calls offering work early the following morning in faraway areas. They were promised a shot at small speaking roles if they signed up for $280 classes at Hollywood Way Pictures. The Better Business Bureau has logged 1,136 inquiries and 36 complaints against this company. Other names for the same company are Matthews Casting, Charles Matthews Casting and Take Five Casting.

Durkin Artists Agency, Debbie Durkin and On-Camera L.A. have been luring actors from out of state as well as in Los Angeles. She was a state and SAG franchised agent. She insisted potential clients study at On-Camera, her company, and have pictures taken by a photographer she got kick-back from. It is illegal for an agent to charge anything or to insist you study at a particular place or have photographs from a certain photographer. She finally lost her SAG franchise when she negotiated a commercial reinstatement for a former client and failed to turn over his residuals earnings of $3,500 for more than a year. Debbie Durkin is now a personal manager and not under the watchdog of the state or SAG. You are holding a book in your hands that recommends plenty of legitimate photographers and teachers. Do not get ripped off by these type of promises. It take a lot of violations and complaints for an agent to lose their SAG franchise. Don't even trust the list, investigate.

Kirk Owens was arrested for sexual battery of two actresses and probably more. He advertised for a 20-30 Caucasian, slender, blond, attractive actress for a one day nonunion shoot with pay. He used the name Tony Wilson, met one actress in a public place, then ask her to come to his apartment where the script was. He then ask her to take off her clothes down to her underwear because that would be how the scene would be shot. You are reading this and thinking, "Why would an actress do that?" but unfortunately they do. This is not the way to have a career—please hear me loud and clear.

• **Glamour Models** was reported to me by a reader of the 8th edition. She said they bragged of all the careers they had developed. They wanted to represent her, and there would be a fee of $500 for color pictures.

• **When auditioning for a "nudity required"** role you are never required to take your clothes off for the audition. You will have to do that after you have your contract which will spell out exactly what type of nudity will be expected.

• **West Coast Talent Ltd. Inc., Alexander Zafrin and David Leroy Harris** were convicted and sentenced to 30 days in jail for grand theft in connection with a scheme in which parents were entices to pay thousands of dollars for promotional materials and acting classes for their children. These crooks are probably already operating again, look out!

• ***Back Stage West/Drama-Logue*** goes to extreme measures to make sure their notices are legitimate, but you still have to be extremely careful with independent, nonunion projects. There is no one to protect you. If you are the least bit suspicious, take someone with you to the audition location. If anything seems odd, leave. If you are asked for money for anything, even a $10 picture, leave. Report them immediately to *Back Stage West.*

• **Do not submit your picture and resume to any publications** other than the trades. The ads in other publications, such as free papers like *New Times* and *L.A. Weekly*, are paid ads and will come to no good.

• **Entertainment Studios** say they are a management company; they charge people $495 for a seminar.

• **O'Brien/Rottman Talent Consultants** hold open call auditions for would be actors/models. A friend of mine went, they were interested in her child. She wrote them a check for half of the $1600 fee. The next day she changed her mind and called them; they said there was a $100 cancelation fee. Luckily, she had cancelled the check at the bank.

- **Stalkers and their Victims** (published by Screen Actors Guild.)

The Stalkers:

47%	Simple obsession: Stalker, usually male, knows target as an ex-spouse, ex-lover, or former boss, and begins a campaign of harassment.
43%	Love obsession: Stalker is a stranger to the target but is obsessed and mounts a campaign of harassment to make the target aware of the stalker's existence.
9.5%	Erotomania: Stalker falsely believes that the target, usually some one famous or rich, is in love with the stalker.

The Victims:

38%	Ordinary Citizens.
32%	Lesser known entertainment figures.
17%	Highly recognizable celebrities.
13%	Former employer; other professionals.

Resources

Gavin de Becker, 818/505-0177. A large staff of security people. Home-security systems, crowd, background checks. He is the author of *The Gift of Fear,* also an expert stalking consultant.

AFTRA Sexual Harrassment Hotline, 323/549-6644.

SAG, Affirmative Action, 323/549-6644 and **Legal Affairs**, 323/549-6627.

Bunco Squad, 213/485-3795, if you are confronted by a dishonest operation.

Threat Management Unit of LAPD, 213/485-7227. Handles cases of stalking.

Vice Squad, 213/485-2121. Deals with cases of immoral or lewd nature.

L.A. City Attorney's Office, 213/485-4515.

L.A. County Dept. of Consumer Affairs, 213/974-1452.

Actor Information Service @ Acting World Books, 818/905-1345.

Actors for Actors, Scam Alert Hotline, 800/304-4074. They are regarded as the entertainment industry's Better Business Bureau, working closely with SAG and AFTRA. Free actor hotline, 800/304-4070. Pre-screened referrals.

***Back Stage West/Drama-Logue* Casting Line**, 323/525-2358. If you have any suspicious occurrences during the auditioning process, call immediately.

SECTION EIGHT

CHILD ACTORS

• **If your child really wants to act**—really wants to work—it can happen with your help. This is the consensus of all the experts I have interviewed. Children, as well as adults, need dedication, talent and luck to make it.

• **In the writing of this ninth edition, my 10-year-old grandson, Austin Tovar**, has moved back to California. We had always promised him when he moved here we would help him get into acting. He has been around the entertainment business all his life, spending time with me on studio lots when I was coaching and visiting friends on television sound stages. He enjoyed sitting in the stands and watching scenes from *Seinfeld* being rehearsed and shot. He loves the physical comedy of Michael Richards. My daughter Cynthia and Austin joined me on my cable show, *Judy Kerr's Acting Workshop,* where we interviewed experts Hettie Lynn Hurtes and T.J. Stein on how to help children get started in show business. I am incorporating this new information with the other valuable interviews from the eighth edition.

• **Subsequently, we followed all the steps in establishing** Austin's career. He now has an agent and has shot three commercials (he is Jack Jr. on the Jack-In-The-Box commercials—yes, he is wearing the big head). He's had around 10 commercial auditions and four theatrical auditions. He loves his acting classes and has acted in two skits for his school's talent shows. He is active in soccer, baseball and karate, so he is not always available to audition. His parents opened a bank account for him and he pays for his pictures, classes and other career expenses from his own earnings. He gets to spend $5 to $20 from each paycheck he receives, depending on the amount of the check. He receives money for the days he works and residuals and holding fees when the commercials run. We hope they run for a long time.

• **Scams abound in the children's field.** We all think our children are fabulous. We can get swept away by the praise for our children and the promise of stardom. I have heard horror stories of families losing thousands of dollars after paying money up-front to illegitimate talent companies or acting schools for services that were promised but never provided. Throughout this section, I have quoted respected professionals in the business. Please read it carefully. Do not get ripped off.

• **There are expenses involved in getting any business started.** Your child will need classes, pictures and a working wardrobe, but you only pay for these at the time of service, not before. Agents and managers get paid commissions only after the child gets paid for working. At the end of this section I list teachers, photographers, agents and managers that I know personally or who were recommended by friends. Check these resourses out, do your own research, find out what you are paying for and follow your own intuition.

• **I have professional picture examples** and very good shots that my son-in-law, an amateur photographer, took. Snapshots cost almost nothing and even black and white shots are not that costly. Do not pay high fees for classes. Check out the classes listed here and then compare with the classes you are investigating to see if they are in the same price range. Nothing should be so outrageous that you question the fee.

• **Hettie Lynn Hurtes**, actress, broadcast journalist, author of *Backstage Guide to Casting Directors,* writes a column in *Backstage West* called Showbiz Kids. She has also produced a tape about how to get your children into the business. She manages her two children who are actors.

Q. Why did you get your children into the business?

- **Because they wanted to get into it.** Forcing them to be in show business is not going to be valuable to them. You have to make sure that your children want to do it. I hesitated at first because it is a tough life but not if you do it the right way. My daughter started at nine and my son at five. They are not doing a lot, but the projects I allow them to do are appropriate and I think they are very good experiences.

• **T.J. Stein and his partner Bethany Constance own Academy Kids Management and Training Center** in North Hollywood. They were both child actors themselves and then evolved into management representation and training.

Q: What is the first step to get your child into the business?

- **I think the first step would be enrolling your child in an acting class.** Basically to get in front of the camera, get an idea of where the camera is and what to do, following directions and to see themselves on TV. They will learn about being creative and using their imagination.

- **Most children really have no idea what to do** when they first walk into a room to interview with an agent or to audition. In class they get the experience of what is going to be asked of them. Class for kids is really a training and a practice ground for them to go into the audition.

• **When the child gets to know how to work with the camera,** feels comfortable and wants to pursue acting professionally, it would be time to look for an agent. A SAG franchised agent makes 10% of any fee your child is paid for work. There is never any up-front charges for you to pay to the agent.

• **Manager Diane Hardin of Hardin/Eckstein Management,** along with her partner, Nora Eckstein, manages careers of some of the top working young actors in town. Diane owns and teaches at the Young Actor's Space in Van Nuys, California.

Q: What is the best way to find an agent for your child?

- **If the parent doesn't know any agents** they can go to the Screen Actor's Guild and get a copy of the SAG franchised agents. It will say which agents handle children. Take some good color snapshots of the child, close-ups and full body shots. The children should look like real kids wearing play clothes, like they've just come from school or the playground. Get 3x5 or 4x6 copies made and send them with a cover letter listing their birthday, interests and skills to all the franchised agents.

- **Have a meeting with the agents** who call you. Look at their track record, at the other clients they represent. What sort of a reputation does the agent have? They should sign with the agent who shows the most enthusiasm for their child.

• Austin asked Hettie Lynne Hurtes, "On my interview with the agent, what will we talk about?"

- **It is important to know you will be going into the agent's office alone.** Your parents will be waiting for you in the front office. The agents want to find out if you are open to talking to strangers, to people you are not familiar with. This can be a difficult situation for young actors because they are used to their parents telling them not to talk to strangers. The parents will have to tell the child, "This is an atmosphere where your mom is right outside the door and you can feel safe talking to these business people."

- **The best thing you can do is to be yourself** and talk about anything you want to, if they let you. Sometimes they will have specific questions like, "How old are you? What school do you go to? What grade you are in? What is your favorite subject?"—things that they know you know. The way they find out about your personality is to ask questions about your everyday life. They want to see if you are an out going kid. That is very important in a child actor. The kids who are gregarious and precocious are the ones who usually work. If you are shy and quiet you will not be interesting to the agent.

• **Agent Judy Savage of the well-respected Judy Savage Agency, represents children and very young adults.** She started with her own three children, then opened the agency when her youngest son was 14. The children she represents work in commercials, movies, television and stage.

Q: When you get a picture in the mail and you are interested in that child, will you call?

- **I look at all the pictures that come in.** One Saturday a month, we set up a time where the children come in and do a monologue for me if they're old enough, or I have them read something. I spend about 15 or 20 minutes with them and also with the parents. Usually out of a Saturday where I'll see 15 or 20 kids, I'll find maybe three or four new ones. You always have to build from the bottom up in an agency. You've got to get new little ones.

Q: At what age do you start them?

- **In California, the legal age to work is six.** I do start interviewing at three years old, but I prefer not taking them until they're old enough. When producers hire children under six, they usually want twins or they want a six year old to play four so they can work them more. It's a business. If they can save money, then that's what they're going to do.

Q: How would you advise parents?

- **Make sure that they're with an agent who cares about children.** There are some agents and acting classes that make the kids cry. Protect them. Make sure the team around them supports, loves and nurtures them. When they go on an interview, it's a really special time for a mother and a child. They should play games in the car or whatever they can think of to make it fun. If you make it fun, they're going to do better. When my children were little, I used to take all kinds of toys. When you get to the interview, take them aside, teach them the dialogue, make sure that they know it, and then relax and have a good time. Don't hound them to death by combing their hair, etc. When they come out of the interview, don't insist on knowing everything that goes on. The kids hate that.

• **Agent Arletta Proch of the Kelman/Arletta Agency** has been in the business over 25 years.

Q: How do you get children and parents started?

- **We talk to them about the business**, the good and bad points. This business is very good for children, especially those who are extremely intelligent or have a lot of energy, even children who have a bad time in school. Some wanted to be in this business so badly they have gone from F's to straight A's, because in order to get and keep a work permit, you have to maintain a C average. The parents are astounded.

Q: How do the children deal with rejection?

- **There should be no rejection**. It's never to be taken personally. It's strictly what they are buying. The person choosing the actors actually has someone in mind; the actor walks in the door and that's it. So it's today we're buying apples and tomorrow we're buying oranges. There's a lot of matching going on in show business—flashbacks of the adults as children growing up, or families being matched together.

• When you have interviewed and signed with an agent, you will need your career tools. T. J. Stein of Academy Kids Managment talks about pictures, resumes and work permits.

- **The picture is the calling card for the child.** It is important to research the photographers you are thinking of using. Agents and managers have photographers that they will recommend. The Screen Actors Guild requires that an agency recommend at least three different photographers. The parents can base their choice on which photographer's work they like and how the photographer works with the child. Pictures cost $100-$250, depending on the photographer and how many rolls you will get. I would not pay anything over $250 for a child getting a head shot.The pictures should be taken after you have signed with an agent so that the agent and or manager can help you choose which picture to blow up into an 8x10. The commercial shot will tend to be a smiling shot because commercials are always happy. The theatrical shot shows a more serious side of the actor.

- **Resumes are attached to the back of the 8x10.** On the resume you have the child's name, birthdate, unions, a list of the projects the child has worked on, name of the show, the part played. List the child's special skills and the acting classes they have taken.

- **It is necessary to have a work permit for the child.** It allows them to work in the entertainment industry. Go to the Department of Labor Standards—there is one in Van Nuys at 6150 Van Nuys Blvd. Fill out the application; if the child is of school age there is a section for the child's teacher to complete. During the summer, a current report card will take the place of the teacher's signature. The parent can do all of this without the child being present. Each time you work, the permit will be stamped. The child must maintain a C average in order to be eligible and the permit must be renewed every six months. It can be renewed through the mail and must be kept current or the child can lose a job.

• **When your child is on an audition** they are not covered by the state's strict laws because they apply only when your child is actually employed. So you must be on guard that there is never a situation where your child is in danger. If you have any misgivings, remove your child immediately.

• **More from Diane Hardin:**

Q: What is required of the parent?

- **Constant vigilance.** The parent has to be ready at a moment's notice to run on interviews and to sit on a set. A parent, grandparent or somebody who is really connected to that child should be with them. Children have to attend three hours of school every day and maintain a high grade average in order to keep their work permit. There are a lot of wonderful experiences and nice people involved, but it's also a lot of pressure.

Q: How old do you think a child should be before they start?

- **I wouldn't do it before six.** Children may be asked to be in uncomfortable situations and they don't understand the difference between an angry scene on the set and an angry scene in real life.

Q: When is it time to put your child in the business?

- **Only when your child is constantly begging you** to be in the business. It should come from the child's saying, "Oh, I can do that. I want to do that." And if the child wants to try out for all the school plays and really seems to have a need to do it, then I think that they should have every encouragement in the world, just like you would encourage someone who wanted to play Little League or the violin.

Q: How do the young actors take rejection?

- **My main suggestion is to make it about the work**, about doing the best acting job every time they go out and not about getting the job. When they land the job it's a nice surprise.

Q: How should a parent interview acting schools?

- **There's only one reason for a child to take acting classes**, and that's because it's fun. I don't think it should be too psychological or too critical. I am very strongly based on positive reinforcement, rather than the negative. I will be quick to tell them what I believed in their work, rather than what I didn't believe. You can't build your confidence if you're constantly being torn down. If it's a chore and it makes them feel bad about themselves because somebody is tearing them down, then that's not the right place to study acting.

- **You can't really teach someone to act**. You can just give them a way to discover how to be real in the moment—how to listen and react. They have to learn to make very quick decisions and strong choices.

- **At the Young Actor's Space** we help these young people discover what it feels like after they've made strong choices about who they are, where they are, and what they want in the scene. They read it, make those choices, relax, listen and react within the given situation.

- **Every class at the Young Actor's Space** is based on improvisation. The first hour is improv warm-ups, improv scenes of different kinds. They have scenes to do every week. I tell them the scenes have to look like an improvisation, like this is happening for the first time, every time they do it.

• T.J. Stein talks about acting classes.

- **Money spent on classes is never wasted.** Your child will build self-esteem and develop their personality. Having your child in an acting class will help you to decide whether your child has the stamina and talent for an acting career. Any type of acting class will be helpful. The kids may be involved with theater games, working with a camera or in scene or improv classes. It is important for young performers to work on their craft on a regular basis. It is a very competitive marketplace. Young actors need every advantage they can develop.

• Agent Judy Savage:

Q: How do the kids turn out as adults?

- **I think I've known every child actor since Jodie Foster and Ron Howard** when my kids were working. It is absolutely, positively the family structure that makes the difference. If they have a good family, ethics, morals, some sort of spiritual background and the work is treated like a hobby they get paid for, they turn out just great.

Q: What is the pay off for parents putting in all this time and energy in their kids?

- **The pay off is their children get famous** and earn a lot of money. 25% of the money goes into a trust fund. The other money makes for a better life for all the members in the family. As they get famous, there are trips all over the place. When Jodie Sweetin had been on *Full House* and Terryn Smith on *Home Improvement,* I made a deal with Toys R Us where the two of them went to New York to see a Broadway show, to Bloomingdale's and Serendipity and then shot a cover for a catalogue and got paid a few thousand dollars. They were 9 and 12 years old.

Q: What about scripts with violence or sexual abuse? How do you deal with that?

- **We are alerted by the casting directors.** They'll call us, or they'll have on the breakdowns, "This is really sensitive material, make sure you alert the parents." We get the material ahead of time. We let the parents look at it and decide if they think their child is able to handle it. Some do and some don't. I've had people turn down major work. I believe these children have to have a life first because show business can come and go but they have to have a life afterwards.

Q: Anything you think parents should know?

- **It is very, very competitive in this business**, and there are many, many, many rejections. You may go on a hundred interviews before you get something. People are almost never discovered overnight. Some people think that they can come to Hollywood and get work in three months. My experience in working with really talented kids who are in training every week has been it takes about three years to get somebody started. There are twice as many parts for boys than there are for girls, yet there are probably 10 times as many girls in the business. If you're a 6-year-old, there are maybe 10 other kids, and by the time you are 14, there are 400, and by the time you are 18, there are 2,000.

- **It's a myth that child actors make all this money** that their parents spend. When a child works, 25% of their money goes into a trust fund, 10% goes to the agent, 15% goes to the manager, if they have one. Because they are making a high amount of money each week, they are in a 40% tax bracket. When a child actor works, their check is about 10% of their salary but they do have a nice trust fund when they turn 18. Usually their mother has to give up a job and work full-time as a driver. By the time you're on a series for eight years, you may be making $30,000 an episode, so even if you take home 10%, that's $3,000 an episode. Actors making their first movie usually earn scale plus 10% for the agent, even for adults. By the second movie, they make $40-$50,000; by the fourth movie, $100-$125,000. They may make $200,000 if it's a lead part, unless they luck out and it's a hit movie, like Macaulay Culkin did. Macaulay is the only child since Shirley Temple that's received a million dollars a film. Everybody thinks, "I want to do movies so I can make money like Macaulay." *Home Alone* was Macaulay's third or fourth movie. He made $100,000.

- **Agent Arletta Proch:**

Q: Have you ever had a child or parent who was distraught over losing a role?

- **Yes. I have suggested that they take a break from show business** or just get out of it entirely. The parents have a harder time than the child; if they can't deal with it, I have suggested that they get a manager for the child who can handle the career on a management level. The parent can then be a parent. It's worked for some problems we've had.

- **Manager Diane Hardin:**

Q: What are the manager's duties?

- **My partner and I are, perhaps, a little different than some managers**; we meet our clients on every single audition and give them hands-on coaching. We also coach them when they get the job. If they get a series, we coach them on their weekly scripts. Nora and I feel our main job as managers is to nurture their talent through coaching, exposing them to theater, recommending books for them to read, such as Uta Hagen's *Respect for Acting,* insisting that they take acting classes and that they stay in class. We do offer our clients as many acting classes as they care to take at the Young Actor's Space. It's all part of the management fee.

Q: What is the manager's fee?

- **We take 15% of their salary**. We take 5% of commercials, because we don't go with them on commercial auditions. But we do know that the good training does affect their commercial potential.

- **Manager T.J. Stein**

Q: When do you think is the right time to look for management?

- **I think that you really need the guidance and support right away.** Some people say, "Well, what do you have to manage if you are brand new?" You have a lot to manage. You need to get to the right people, you need to make sure that I, in my position, open the right doors. A child is a child for a very short period of time. There is a lot of competition.

- **Diane Hardin**

Q: Can you talk about Kellie Martin's career?

- **Kellie came to study at the Young Actor's Space** when she was eight years old. We knew right away she was a special little talent. Her mother asked, "Would you manage her?" We took Kellie on, and she started hitting everything she went on. She did some movies of the week and a recurring role on *Hogan's Family.*

- **She was offered two pilots at once,** *Life Goes On,* an hour drama and *Mars Base One,* directed by Dan Ackroyd. We had to choose between the two.

- **Kellie's mother, the agent, my partner and I were a team.** I like to think of it like a circle. Kellie's in the center, and we're all working for her, to keep her safe. The highs are so high and the lows are so low.

- **She was on *Life Goes On* for four years.** When it was over, she did a movie, *Matinee,* and the series *Christy.* She went to Yale, and was cast on *ER* when she graduated.

- **Debbie Martin, Kellie Martin's mom.**

Q: Did your younger daughter feel slighted because Kellie had so much notoriety?

- **When Kellie was at home**, she was not treated any differently than anybody else. Heather I'm sure was jealous at times, but it was always exciting to go to shows and meet celebrities. The drawbacks would be that I wouldn't be home quite as often as I'd like to be.

Q: Kellie's working was really a full-time job for you, wasn't it?

- **Yes. Kellie started working when she was seven**, and I taught school until she was 11. The first time she got something that lasted for a month, I quit working and never went back.

Q: Why did you put her in the business?

- **She was an outgoing child.** She did a play at school where she had to memorize tons and tons of pages. Her teachers thought that she was wonderful, and I thought why not give it a shot.

- **She played with Michael Landon's children**. My sister was their nanny. Kellie would tell Shawna, his daughter, that she wanted to be on her dad's show. Shawna called her dad and said, "My friend wants to be on your show," and he said, "Okay, have her come in and talk with me." She went in and two days later he called Shawna and said, "Tell your little friend I found her a part."

- **She got an agent** and we said we'd give it a shot for a year. At the end of the year she had done six or eight commercials. One of the product companies was having a convention and they took us all to Hawaii for her to be introduced before they showed the commercial. It was really exciting and fun.

Q: What are the drawbacks?

- **For us, there were no drawbacks**. We always took it one year at a time. Up until Kellie was a freshman in high school, she went to a regular school and our life was regular. She just happened to go on interviews, or she just happened to work once in a while. It was not disruptive; it was just something she did. She got the series and we were very excited. For Kellie, there was never a drawback.

Q: Any advice for parents?

- **My advice would be to only do it for as long as it makes your child happy**. My younger daughter went on interviews when she was six for about three months. At one point, I heard them call her name for her to come in and she turned white, like a sheet. I looked at her and she said, "I don't want to do this," and I said, "You don't have to do this." It wasn't her. She didn't like to go in front of people that she didn't know.

• **Agent Arletta Proch:**

Q: How do you protect the kids in working situations?

- **The production company wants to have a happy set.** They will give the actors the best facilities possible. I'm not in the desert, South America or Europe with them when they are shooting, but if they call me with a complaint, I'll handle it with the people at this end. Children in this industry are not mistreated.

- **The working children who grow up to have problems** are the children whose parents did not give them a family life outside of show business. Most of our children go on to college and don't become adult actors.

Q: What should people living out-of-state do about getting their children into show business?

- **They have local agents in their area** and they can send in a snapshot, not a professional picture, with all their vital statistics. Height, weight, color of hair and eyes, any sports they like, if they are old enough to have a sport, if they like to sing and dance, birth date.

Q: At what age do you start children?

- **We start babies.** Babies have to be 15 days old to work. Most of our babies come from referrals. Twins, or course, are much more needed because of the time on camera. You get that exceptional little child who comes in at the age of three, winds up on your lap, and reads a book to you.

• **Al Burton, executive producer for Al Burton Productions:**

Q: What are some of the shows you've done?

- **My list of shows that children worked on would include** *One Day at a Time,* which introduced McKenzie Phillips and Valerie Bertinelli, *Diff'rent Strokes* with Gary Coleman, Todd Bridges and Dana Plato, *Silver Spoons* with Ricky Schroeder. In that show, we introduced Jason Bateman when he was 12. I worked with Michael J. Fox in *Palmerstown, U.S.A.*, a Norman Lear show that predated anything Michael had done in the U.S. The cast of *Square Pegs* was Sarah Jessica Parker, Jamie Gertz, Tracy Nelson, all teenagers, varying in ages from 15-19. Molly Ringwald started at age 12 in *Facts of Life.* She was a regular in the first year, then she got *The Tempest* with Mazursky, which shot her into a movie career.

- **Then *Charles in Charge* and *The New Lassie*.** Wendy Cox is now at UCLA and Will Estes whom I'll mention later. In *Charles in Charge* we had Josie Davis, Nicole Eggert, Alexander Polinsky and Christina Applegate, very early in her career; Erika Eleniak who went on to become Ellie May in *Beverly Hillbillies* and starred in *Baywatch,* and Pamela Anderson who played the girlfriend of Charles for several weeks. I recommended both Nicole and Pamela to the *Baywatch* people and they became *Baywatch* stars.

Q: When you were casting *Facts of Life* and *Diff'rent Strokes,* you saw a lot of kids, didn't you?

- **Yes. I was not satisfied until I felt I had cast the very best actors** in the United States. We sent casting people to New York, Atlanta, Dallas, Denver and Boston to look for kids.

Q: How would they find kids in other states?

- **They start with little theater people.** If they had cast six kids in the previous year, we would see every one of them. We would put many on tape. I remember a casting director who went to Chicago, was told by somebody he ought to see a little kid in Zion, Illinois. He went up to Zion and found Gary Coleman. I got the tape when it came back and I looked at this little pair of eyes and this little nose peering over the desk. I ran and showed the tape to Norman Lear, he agreed and we brought Gary out and signed him to a contract from just the first meeting. He was perfect. His delivery was fabulous from day one.

Q: You seem to understand working children.

- **I feel very protective about children.** I have conversations with my directors and writers where my argument is, "Protect the kid." Don't ever say, "the kid can't act" or "the kid is bad." Your material needs to be fixed or your directing needs to be fixed. I often show a documentary on Steven Spielberg directing a 13-year-old boy in *Empire of the Sun* to directors. Spielberg gives direction that shows he unconsciously cares for, works with and has respect for the kid. I admire him a lot.

Q: If a child has that desire, what should they do to be discovered?

- **There are ways to get exposure** in Sheboygan, Dallas, Atlanta, etc. Acting is acting, whether it be in school, community theater or church, and I think experience in acting gives you the wherewithall to begin having a career. I began my career in Columbus, Ohio. By the time I was 15, I had engineered every opportunity I could find, which included producing shows for the boy scouts and local radio shows, just to give myself a part. It turned out that I liked the producing better than the acting, but it didn't start out that way. I created my own opportunities every step of the way.

- **In my heart of hearts**, I always want to say that if you're a parent and you see your child wants to be in the entertainment world, encourage it, and then get them close to a production center. What does it do to change your life? It may change it for the better!

Q: How did you cast Will Estes on *The New Lassie* series?

- **Will was just a terrific 10-year-old.** We made him come back, I think, seven or eight times to audition because we weren't quite sure. He was littler and younger than we wanted in that part and, other than Lassie, it was the starring role. He kept having something that we didn't want to let go of. He never lost his cool or got disgusted. He just came and was the same sunny Will he always was. I've known him for 10 years now and we remain friends.

Q: What is it that makes you pick the kids that you pick?

- **I'll use Will Estes, as an example.** His engine in the office worked very well. He's a dynamo, and yet he's not hyper. He had something in him that was very, very good, and it looked to me very promising. When it was Jami Gertz or Sarah Jessica Parker or Tracy Nelson, they had a package that was great. It wasn't just a voice or just acting or timing. It was everything: great eyes, great presence. They were interesting and had a totality. Norman Lear used to say, "They have to have television eyes." I think everybody I have liked did have eyes that could give a great close-up.

Mary Lu Chasteen is the mother and manager of her 21-year-old son, Will Estes.

Q: How old was Will when he got into the business?

- **He started when he was nine.** Friends of ours referred us to the Kelman/Arletta Agency who had been in the business for years representing all but one of the kids on *The Brady Bunch.*

- **Arletta said, "Yeah, we'd like to sign him."** He has an All-American look they liked. Within the first month he booked a print ad for Lee jeans. Then he got his first commercial, Fruit of the Loom. It was real exciting for us. From that point on it just kind of snowballed.

Q: How did you know what to do?

- **Well, the agent tells you but it's learn as you go.** The agent would call and give us the interview, the time, what he should wear, what he should take with him like a skateboard, skates or anything, and then we'd go on the audition. In a few days if they were interested they'd call him back. Then sometimes he'd book the commercial.

- **Within the first year** she started sending him out for theatrical things. He tried out for a part on *The New Lassie.* There were eight call backs over a few month's period.

Q: How long did he work on that series?

- **It turned out to be one of the greatest experiences we've had.** We did 48 shows. He was there nine-and-a-half hours a day, five days a week. To this day he still keeps in touch with some of the friends he made on the set, people he worked with and the owners of *Lassie;* it was really like a family situation for him. I think that's hard for kids as they get older, when the show stops, the family stops. Will did tell me, not too long ago, that he was glad he was old enough to have his own self-identity before he started this business.

Q: What about his schooling, grades and outside activities.

- **Some of the money Will made went for his private schooling.** It was a half day, straight academic school. When he worked, they prepared his lessons for the set. If he missed, they would tutor him to catch him up. Because of the concentrated studies he skipped a grade and graduated one year early with honors.

- **All the things he's interested in** seem to stem from things he did on jobs. He's really into gymnastics, and that came from a job he did on a commercial where he had to use a trampoline. They had a coach from UCLA work with them. He got the bug for gymnastics and is still taking classes. When he worked on *Lassie,* the guys on their lunch hour would ride bikes; they took him and now he's into mountain biking. Karate is something he initiated on his own. But the agent said parts come up that call for karate. So he has enhanced his ability to get jobs.

- **I made sure the teachers on the set** were accredited and able to teach him what he needed. The thing I was always most concerned with was that his educational needs were met. I don't want to jeopardize his education with the business. I don't want to compromise anything for him. That's why parents really have to watch out for the kids.

Q: How do you pass the time on the set?

- **When you are on the set there is observing to do.** For instance, one time when Will was younger, he was inside an airplane prop where I couldn't hear him so I was listening to him on the headset. I heard him say to the guest actress that she had a mustache. I knew I had to tell him that you aren't supposed to say that to women.

Q: How are the finances and show-biz life style for you?

- **You put a percentage of the child's earnings away.** When he works we usually let him buy something like a skateboard, video game or something to reward him but not all the time. The busier he got, the less I could work. My job is pretty much taking care of Will, of what he needs as far as getting to auditions, taking care of his finances, going with him when he works on the set. We've had to travel to different areas. So we have to be ready at a moment's notice to go wherever.

- **I love spending time with my kid**, being with him, going places; we do a lot together. It's been exciting, to say the least. I'm really proud of him. It's changed my life because it enables us to do things we would probably never do. When we went to Miami, we saw the Everglades. We've been to Hawaii twice, Vancouver, New York, Texas and Chicago.

- **If children want to work**, I think it's important that the parents are supportive and helpful. Having the support of their families helps them get through the tough times.

• **Will Estes has appeared in 40+ commercials** and as a regular on four series, *The New Lassie, It Had To Be You, Kirk* and *Kelly Kelly,* plus guest starring television and supporting film roles. Now as a young adult he already had four starring roles in the films, *Terror Tract, U571, Blue Ridge Fall* and *The Road Home.* *See his resume on page 116.*

Q: What about rejection?

- **I've never really had a problem with rejection**, it never bothers me. There are other things I have a lot of fun doing. I go to an audition and then head on down to gym class. I'll get in the car and it'll just leave my mind; I don't even think about it.

Q: What is it that your mother does that helps you in your career?

- **Well, before I could drive, she took me to all my auditions.** She would sit in the waiting room and I would go into the actual audition by myself. She would read the other characters lines in the script to help me memorize my lines. Sometimes she gives me suggestions; that's cool. I like having her opinion.

Q: What do you do on auditions?

- **If there are lines, I'll look over those.** If I have my lines down or there are no lines, as the case with some commercials, sometimes there'll be people there I know, I can talk to them and hang out.

Q: What about young actors getting on drugs?

- **I don't see that acting relates to drugs.** I've never even come across it.

Q: Do you have any advice for kids?

- **If you really want to do it, then give it a try.** Don't take it too seriously, when it comes to an audition. What's the big deal if you don't get the job? It's not worth being stressed over.

TAKING BLACK & WHITE HEADSHOTS AT HOME
by Hank Tovar

• Be prepared to shoot through a few rolls of film until you find a shot that works. There is black and white film that you can develop at your local one-hour photo store. Several manufactures make the film—Kodak Black and White + Select, Ilford XP2 or Ilford XP2 Super. All are 400-speed film. 400 speed film is very forgiving, versatile and can be used in a variety of different settings, lighting, and has good overall contrast. If the box says C-41 processing, then you can *only* develop it at the one-hour photo lab, not at a a black and white custom lab. If the C-41 film has been developed at a one-hour store, you can take the negative to a black and white lab to have the master made.

• Choose an outdoor area with indirect light, but bright. Choose a non-busy background, one that has contrast or texture like a wood fence, stone wall, barn door, etc. Make certain your camera is focused squarely on their face and head and their eyes are looking directly into the lens at all times. The head can be turned, but those eyes *must* be focused directly on the lens. The more open the eyes, the better. Talk to them, ask for something so they can react to it. Give me a funny look; show me excitement; react like they were on a rollercoaster; jumping off the high dive. Have their eyes speak to the camera lens.

• Once you're done, bring the rolls to a one-hour lab. If they print the shots on color paper, you will get a tinted, cibachrome look. If they print on black and white paper, you should get the right results. When you find a shot you like, take the negative to a custom black and white photo lab to have them make your master 8x10 print that will be used to make the reproductions. The masters cost $5 to $10 dollars and should be printed on fiber, not rc or glossy paper; it does make a big difference. If you don't have a lab near you, mail the negatives to Isgos or one of the photo labs on page 101. Have fun and save your receipts. *See Hank's photos of Cynthia, Jackson and Austin on Page 167.*

Resources

TURN TO PAGE 167 TO SEE THE CHILD ACTOR PHOTOS!

• PHOTOGRAPHERS

Rich Hogan, 323/467-2628. One roll, one 8x10, $125 shot in studio. *See theatrical shot on page 86 and commercial shot on page 166.*

Sean Kenney, 800/505-7698. One roll with two 8x10s, $175; for two rolls, two changes with four 8x10s, $250. Sean is recommended by many top children's agents, including Austin's agent, Kelman/Arletta. *See Austin Tovar's picture on page 169, commercial shot on page 166 and theatrical shot on page 87*

Diana Lannes, 213/427-8096. One roll, $120 includes one 8x10; two rolls, two 8x10s, $165. She has experience shooting the little ones and really enjoys the kids. *See Jackson Tovar's picture on page 168,* the first ever shot by a professional photographer. *Theatrical shot on page 93 and commercial shot on page 165.*

Schultz Brothers Photography, in Los Angeles 323/634-7004, in Orange County 714/540-6544. One roll, $215, three or four wardrobe changes; two rolls $315, one 8x10 retouched master per roll included in price. Additional retouched, 8x10s, $16.

Doreen Stone, 323/876-2636. Ages 3 to 21, $140, one roll. 8x10s are $15. T.J. Stein of Academy Kids says, "She catches the child's personality and energy in the way that really sells the child; triple A rating!" Doreen tells parents, "Keep it simple; simple clothes. And don't worry, a child can't do it wrong." *See the pictures of Austin on page 169 and Jackson on page 168.*

Linda Van Off, (310) 550-8430.

• CHILDREN'S ACTING CLASSES

Academy Kids, 818/769-8091, www.academykids.com. 4942 Vineland Ave., North Hollywood. Children's managers T.J. Stein and Bethany Constance, along with Lynn Marx, head of talent development, offer ongoing on-camera commercial, theatrical, improvisation and agent showcases, as well as a special Tiny Tots program for kids aged three to five. Private coaching is available. They have an extra casting company for children. Therre is a charge to join and you pay a percentage of the child's earnings. My grandson, Austin, loves his commercial and theatrical classes at Academy Kids. The teachers are very encouraging and the classes are fun. My daughter, Cynthia, and I attended a showcase produced for the industry. We were very impressed with their clients and the spectacular production.

A Noise Within, 323/224-6420. Luckman Fine Arts Complex, California State University, Los Angeles, 5151 State University Dr., L.A., 90032. They have a seven-week *Summer With Shakespeare* program for teenagers 13-19.

Pamela Campus, casting director, 310/398-2715 or 818/897-1588. Has cast over 3,000 commercials and taught over 10,000 adults and children. Children starting at age three. They are always taught personally by the casting directors. Very highly recommended by agents.

Divisek Casting, casting directors, 818/506-6868. Always taught personally by the casting directors. Very highly recommended by agents.

Beverly Long, 818/754-6222. Casting director teaches a kids only commercial class. Beverly was a child actor and so were her children. She has cast hundreds of kids in commercials.

Kevin McDermott's Center Stage L.A., 310/837-4536. He is also an on-set children's coach. "Acting classes provide the young actor with an opportunity to practice their craft in a safe and creative environment" They offer theatrical workshops ages five to 20, scene study, cold reading, improv, character development and interview techniques. Private coaching with Kevin is $45 per half-hour. A friend of mine, Lee Alexander, has her son Tyler enrolled here and is very happy with the approach.

Terrance Hines, 818/557-7516. He teaches a block of six classes for $235. Monday, Tony Gregory, 6:30-9pm (8-12 year old); Tuesday 6:30-9:00PM (13-18 years old); Wednesday, Justine Hunt, 6:30-9PM (13-18 years old.). His associate Eretha Lopez teaches 4, 5, 6 and 7 year olds on Saturday afternoon. Besides acting and improvisation, they cover the pilot season, the audition, the interview and dealing with rejection. Terrance is also a personal manager and author of *An Actor Succeeds.*

Tracy Martin is Koaching Kids & Teens, 818/752-8487, VM: 213/240-8771, mstracyco@aol.com. Highly recommended by agents and parents. Classes held in Hollywood and Toluca Lake. Audition coaching $50 an hour. Private lessons, rates depend on how many lessons booked. Four week, four student, audition technique classes $145. Eight week, eight student, acting technique classes with a showcase included, $295. Free career coaching for parents who have children in her classes. "We have fun every week in class and the students show great growth in their work."

Komedy For Kids, 323/936-9524. CBS Studio Center, 4024 Radford Avenue, Studio City, 91604. Bill Margolin, artistic director, Saturdays $175 a month.

Young Actor's Space, 818/785-7979. 5918 Van Nuys Blvd., Van Nuys, 91401. You can audit a class for free but they encourage people to take one class for $35 to see how they like it. They have regular showcases for people in the industry. Diane Hill Hardin developed these supportive classes. She was a student of Joan Darling and her husband and daughter are actors. She also manages a few lucky young actors. I have attended several of their presentations and was very impressed with the talent I see in their classes.

The Young Actor's Studio, 310/281-7545 or 818/766-9958. The Ventura Court Theatre in Studio City. Kids and teens 7-17. They have a brochure for all their classes.

Young Filmmakers Academy: Kids Filmmaking Workshops: www.youngfilmmakers.org. 310/259-1906. Film Workshop for ages 9-12 and 13-15. Four-day summer filmmaking instensive. Other programs offered througout the year.

• VOICE AND DANCE TEACHERS

Conjunctive Point Dance Center, 310/836-3962. 3631 Hayden Ave., Culver City. Stanley Holden formerly of the royal ballet is the master. This is the real thing for ballet. Reid Olsen great teacher. Classes $12.

Claire Corff, 323/969-0565. $35-$45. She is an associate of the very famous Bob Corff, specializing in children and young adults, beginners through advanced. Singing, speaking and accent reduction. Austin Tovar (my grandson) loves working with her, he's learning to slow down and to be easily understood. He loves the exercises she gives him.

Godeane Eagle, 310/450-5735. She has an M.A. combination in music, theatre and clinical speech. $50 to $75 an hour. Specializing in speech defect correction, projection and accent reduction, she has worked with many children over her long career.

Singing and Piano: Jennifer Haworth, 310/557-1939. $40 an hour, teaches good habits for singing any style of song, helps with performance skills. Also teaches beginning piano. She is available to come to the child's home if you have a piano.

Dance at the Outback Studio with Jennifer Narin-Smith, 323/938-6836.

• AGENTS

• *A few children's agents out of the many listed by SAG.*

Screen Actors Guild—SAG, 323/954-1600. 5757 Wilshire Blvd., Los Angeles, 90036 (between Fairfax and La Brea.) M-F 9-5.
SAG **Child Actor Hotline**, 323/549-6030.
SAG **Franchised Agents List**, 323/549-6733.

Tyler Kjar Agency, 818/760-032l. 5116 Lankershim Blvd., North Hollywood, 91601.

The Savage Agency, 323/461-8316. 6212 Banner Ave., L.A., 90038. Judy Savage.

Buchwald/Talent Group Inc., (TGI), Youth Division, 323/852-9555. 6500 Wilshire Blvd., 22nd Floor, Los Angeles, 90048.

Herb Tannen and Associates, 323/782-0515. 8370 Wilshire Blvd., Suite #209, Beverly Hills, 90211. Commercials.

Howard Talent West, 818/766-5300. 10657 Riverside Dr., Toluca Lake 91602. Bonnie Howard.

• *Consult your State Film Advisory Board for agents in your area.*

• BOOKS AND TAPES

• **By Kids for Kids**, by Catherine Gaffigan. Monologues for children 6-18 years old.

• **It's a Freeway Out There**, $30 by Judy Belshe. Agent Bonnie Howard insists all of the parents with new kids in the business read this book. It is easy and fast to read and really gives parents the answers they need.

• **Launching Your Child in Show Business,** by Dick Van Patten. He should know how, having started on Broadway at age seven, as did his sister Joyce. "My mother was a real stage mother. On the other hand, it's terrible if a stage mother pushes a child into the business. People berate stage mothers—but how about mothers who push their kids to become doctors or lawyers?"

• **The Parents' Guide To L.A.**, $19.95, in bookstores. "Over 650 pages of detailed information that puts everything you need right at your fingertips."

• **Your Kid Ought To Be In Pictures:** A How-To Guide For Would-Be Child Actors and Their Parents. By Kelly Ford Kidwell and Ruth Devorin.

• **The trade papers put out annual special issues** for Show Business Kids with many agencies, managers, photographers and teachers listed.

Mail Order Tape: Lights, Camera, Kids! How to Get Your Child in TV Commercials, 323/654-2212. Carolyne Barry, Actress/Commercial Coach, produced this very informative tape and booklet.

Mail Order Tape: Show Biz Kids: The ABCs of Getting Your Child in the Biz, 310/275-5755. Special price for mentioning this book, $19.95. This award winning video will help you avoid getting ripped off.

SCAMS

West Coast Talent Ltd., Inc., WCT, Screen Artist Talent, Alexander Zafrin and David Leroy Harris illegally operate an employment counseling service enticing parents to pay thousands of dollars for promotional materials and acting classes for their children. They've been charged with many crimes, including making false and misleading statements and making false and deceptive representations. By the time you read this, these to men have probably changed the name of their business and continue to steal from parents. Be your child's watchdog!

Obrien/Rottman Talent Consultants hold open call auditions for would-be actors/models. A friend of mine went; they were interested in her child. She wrote them a check for half of the $1600 fee. The next day she changed her mind and called them; they said there was a $100 cancelation fee. Luckily, she had canceled the check at the bank.

SECTION NINE

THE RIGHT TIME TO MOVE TO LOS ANGELES AND THE SCOUTING TRIP

• **This section of the book was inspired** by an interview I had with Tony Shepherd. At the time he was Vice President of Talent for Aaron Spelling Productions, overseeing the casting of all of their television series such as *Beverly Hills 90210, Melrose Place, The Heights, The Love Boat, Colbys, Dynasty, Hotel, Family.*

• **Tony gives back to the acting community** by traveling all over the United States presenting his acclaimed Seminar, *An Approach For Actors On Acting.* More than 125,000 actors have participated.

Q: When do you think it's time for an actor to consider moving to Los Angeles?

- **If an actor** wants to earn a living in motion pictures or television other than doing commercials, they have to be in Los Angeles. You can't live in New York, Chicago or Dallas; the work isn't there.

- **It may be time to think of moving** to Los Angeles when you've outgrown the market you're in. That means if you're getting callbacks 20% of the time and you're getting 5% of the jobs, you're not ready yet. But if you're in Chicago and you're pulling 60-70% callbacks, booking 35-40% of the jobs, you're ready.

- **If you've never been** to Los Angeles, make a trial visit before you decide to pick up and move. L.A. is the circus without the tent. It's a tough city to live in; it's expensive. Take a look around. Go to Beverly Hills. Take the Universal Studios Tour; it may be the only studio lot you'll ever get on. When someone is moving to L.A., it's not the actor, it's the person. You are ready to be in Los Angeles if you've got the background and the ability. It's a question of whether you want to pick up stakes. To move to L.A., you need talent, marketability, desire, time, money and patience.

• **I agree with Tony. Make a trip to Los Angeles** and check out the town; see if you could live here before you move. You'll need a good running car, money, plan on two or three month's spending money, and an adventurous spirit. Do not count on a public transportation system to get around, you will be sorry. In your home town, buy a Sunday *Los Angeles Times* newspaper or order it mailed to you, 800/966-2450, $4. You will find lots of information, possible survival jobs available and the costs of rents. When you get here, pick up the *L.A. Weekly* newspaper. It's free and can be found at most 7-11s, liquor stores, newsstands, theaters, restaurants and many other locations.

• **You will have this book with you** and you should purchase *The Working Actor's Guide* and *The Thomas Guide* (street map book). The *Los Angeles Times* newspaper puts out a book of places to see, *Curbside LA., which* you can order on the phone, 800-246-4042. The *Working Actor's Guide*'s Living Section is very good for the best housing areas, with maps and detailed information about the areas, referencing the zip codes and page numbers in *The Thomas Guide.* Many rentals will expect first and last month's rent, a deposit and a six month or one year lease. There are bulletin boards and rental services where you can look for a roommate. Be careful, don't trust too easily.

• **When you are thinking of moving here** you must be close in to town, do not live in Orange County, Riverside or Oxnard. These areas are all an hour away from Los Angeles early on a Sunday morning, but any other time, count on two hours. This is not close enough to be a part of the show biz community. If you are making the move, give yourself as many advantages as possible.

Jay Bernstein, manager, writer, producer, taught a course called *Stardom, the Management of, the Public Relations for, and the Survival and Maintenance In.*

Q: What is your advice for actors who are moving here from out of town?

- **They should be studying the town.** It's very tricky with a lot of roads and some of them look like freeways. You have to be very careful where you're going. I tell people to spend a year like you were in college. If your parents paid for your college, they may pay for a year here. If you worked your way through college, then work a year here. Get a feeling of what's going on. Weigh every decision. There's plenty of time. Get that career team together.

• **Teri Hatcher** (*Lois and Clark*) was a student of mine for a year when she first came to Los Angeles. She lived in San Francisco and had taken some acting classes at ACT, her teacher was Annette Bening; she wasn't really planning to be an actress. Her friend wanted to audition for one of the dancing girls on *The Love Boat* and wanted Teri to come with her. As stories go, of course, she ended up landing the job.

•**Teri dropped out of college and came to Los Angeles** with the idea that she would do this for the one-year *Love Boat* contract and then go back to school. Once she got here she landed an agent and started to build a career. In class she always worked hard. When I was coaching Finley Light for a screen test for the new James Bond, I used her as his acting partner. She really had a talent and loved to work hard; she threw herself into every scene and gave full out performances, she didn't have any fear in her acting.

• **If you are new, visit or call the local Police**, crime prevention section and ask if where you are planning to stay is in a safe area. Call Information for the telephone numbers.

• Always be on the lookout for film and television personalities. You will see them.

• HOTELS & MOTELS

There are many hotels and motels here. You can probably pick up a guide book at your local bookstore. The ones below are mentioned to give you an idea of some acceptable areas.

Banana Bungalow Hollywood Hostel, 213/851-1129. 2775 Cahuenga Blvd., Hollywood. Behind the Hollywood Bowl. On the road between Hollywood and the Valley. hwres@bananabungalow.com

Best Western Farmer's Daughter Motor Hotel, 213/ 937-3930. 115 S. Fairfax Ave., L.A. $65 single, $69 double. Across the street from Farmer's Market and CBS Studio City, where shows are taped.

Beverly Garland's Holiday Inn Hotel, 818/ 980-8000. 4222 Vineland, North Hollywood. Right off the 101 Freeway but nowhere to walk. Moderately priced. Paradise Cafe is a favorite. $84-$164. Special rates for AAA, entertainment cards.

Beverly Laurel Motor Hotel, 323/651-2441. 8018 Beverly Blvd., Los Angeles. Near the Beverly Center Shopping Mall. $69 single, $73 double.

Beverly Terrace Hotel, 310/274-8141. 469 N. Doheny, Beverly Hills, 90210. Basic but in a safe, central spot across from a great little market. Single $95 a night or $550 weekly. Double $105 a night or $650 weekly.

El Patio Motel, 818/980-2176. 11466 Ventura Blvd., Studio City, 91604. Near Universal and CBS Studios. AAA recommended. $59 single, $79 double.

Holiday Lodge, 818/843-1121. 3901 Riverside Dr., Burbank, between Hollywood Way and Pass Ave. off the 134 Freeway. Very near Warner Bros., N.B.C., Disney and Universal Studios. $65 single, $75 double.

Holloway Motel, 213/654-2454. 8465 Santa Monica Blvd., West Hollywood. $75 to $85 a night. Weekly rates are less. www.hollowaymotel.com

Olive Manor Motel, 818/842-5215. 924 W. Olive, Burbank, at Victory and Olive. Close to Burbank; not too far from Hollywood and freeways. $46 single, $50 double.

Ramada West Hollywood, 800/845-8585. 8585 Santa Monica Blvd., West Hollywood. Great location. $149 a day includes breakfast. To get a corporate rate, sign up for their free RBC club when you arrive to check in.

Sportsman's Lodge, 818/769-4700. www.slhotel.com Ventura Blvd. and Coldwater in Studio City. $93-$130 a day. Resturants and shopping.

The Standard Hotel, 323/650-9090. 8300 Sunset Blvd., West Hollywod. $95-$200. On the strip.

• CAR RENTALS

Very valuable web site: **www.lawa.org** *LAX airport parking lots, rates and locations, car rental agencies, hotels, busses and shuttle vans, a map of the airport and nearby streets.*

All the national companies are here in Los Angeles. You generally get a better deal renting at either LAX airport (Century and Sepulveda) or at the Burbank airport (Hollywood Way between Victory and San Fernando.)

Avon, 323/850-0826. 7080 Santa Monica Blvd., Hollywood. Open every day.

Enterprise, 323/654-4222. 8367 Sunset Blvd. West Hollywood.

Both have many locations. They will pick you up if you are in the vicinity of their location. Good standby rates for the weekends.

Bob Leech's Autorental, 800/635-1240. 4490 W. Century Blvd., L.A., very near the airport. They will pick you up from the airport. Big drawback is they are only open 8AM-9PM weekdays and 9-5 on weekends so you have to arrive in that time frame. Only five reservations a day are taken for Toyota Tercels at $25 a day, 150 free miles a day then 10 cents a mile. The other cars are $30 a day with 200 free miles a day.

• STREETS TO KNOW ABOUT

Beverly Blvd. and Beverly Drive. Beverly Blvd. runs east and west, the same as Melrose and Sunset. It starts in downtown L.A. and ends up dead ending at Santa Monica Blvd. in Beverly Hills. Beverly Drive runs north and south in the middle of Beverly Hills shopping.

Cahuenga Blvd. and Cahuenga Blvd. East and West. *(ca-weng-ga)* Cahuenga begins near Melrose and runs north through Hollywood and through the Cahuenga Pass (Hollywood freeway in the middle), turns into Cahuenga Blvd. West and disappears for a little bit at Lankershim near Universal Studios, then picks up after Universal on your right. So if you are told Cahuenga, find out what part of town and a cross street.

Sepulveda Blvd. *(seh-pull-va-da)* is a great street. It runs from the San Fernando Valley alongside the 405 freeway over the hill past the LAX airport to Long Beach.

La Cienega. If you arrive at L.A. Airport, rent your car and take Century Blvd. to La Cienega and turn left (north.) La Cienega dead ends at Sunset Blvd. Turn to the right to go to Hollywood or to the left for the Sunset Strip scene and keep driving west and Sunset ends at the beach.

• THINGS TO SEE

Universal Studios, 818/508-9600. Make your first stop here. It is an actual studio lot with an amusement park-like tour for $39. Plan to stay all day so you can take the tram out to the back lot. I've worked on many shows produced here and I still get excited driving on the lot.

You enter from either Cahuenga Blvd. West or Lankershim Blvd. Take the 101 Freeway to Barham or Lankershim, then the signs will lead you. Don't miss City Walk, if you can't afford the tour, at least check out the movie theater and night life. You can park on Cahuenga Blvd. West and walk over the bridge and not pay the $6 parking.

Warner Bros. VIP Studio Tour, 818/954-1744. 9-3 weekdays, 12 people a tour, $30. Reservations are required. One of a staff of six will lead you on a two-hour informal drive-and-walk jaunt around the studio. You will even get to go on some working sound stages and see the faux streets. You will most likely see famous faces. Enter at gate #4 where Hollywood Way ends at Olive.

Disneyland, 714/999-4565 or 213/626-8605. 1313 Harbor Blvd, Anaheim. From Los Angeles take the 5 Freeway South to either Harbor Blvd or Katella Ave. Turn right. Mickey Mouse lives here. Open M-F 10-6, Sa Su 9AM-midnight. One day, $39; two days, $72; three days, $99.

See tapings of TV shows. It doesn't cost anything and you will see the actors working. For a half-hour sitcom, plan at least three hours. Eat first because you'll have a long evening of sitting.

Audiences Unlimited, 818/506-0067. The ticket office is located on the Van Ness Street side of the Fox Television Center Building, 5746 Sunset Blvd. between Gower and 101 Freeway. M-F 8:30-6. There is recorded information for all the shows they have tickets for. Write for their monthly newsletter of current shows. Send stamped, self-addressed envelope to Audiences Unlimited, 100 Universal City Plaza, Bldg. 153, Universal City, CA 91608. Tickets available for more than 40 sitcoms, game and talk shows.

Fox Television Center, 5746 Sunset Blvd., Hollywood. M-F 8:30-6 and Sa Su 11-6. Tickets are offered on a first-come basis starting on Wednesdays for most shows scheduled for the following week. Tickets are sometimes available the day of the show, but early arrival is advised. Also: Paramount Visitors Center 213/956-1777. 860 N. Gower St., Hollywood. Weekdays 8-4.

Beverly Center, on La Cienega between Beverly Blvd. and Third St. This is really state-of-the-art cool. See-and-be-seen MTV generation.

Getty Museum, 310/440-7300. www.gett.edu. Closed Monday, $5 parking, museum is free. You have to call for parking reservation.

Griffith Park Observatory. 213/664-1191. Take Hollywood Blvd. east to Western Avenue then go north or toward the mountains. Just past the American Film Institute (on your left) will be a curve in the road where Western turns into Los Feliz Blvd. The next street is Ferndale; turn left and follow the signs. Great hiking and picnicking there too.

Hollywood Bowl, on Highland near 101 freeway.

Hollywood Fantasy Tours, 310/326-8279. 6715 Hollywood Blvd., Hollywood.

Hollywood Sign, From the 101 Freeway or Hollywood Blvd., go north on Gower, right on Franklin and left at the next street: Beachwood. As you drive up Beachwood, look up and there you are. **Beachwood Canyon** is a lovely area. There is a small cafe where many locals eat. There's a great bulletin board outside for rentals, roommates and other stuff.

Lake Hollywood, where earthquakes and floods are filmed. From the 101 Freeway, take Barham Blvd. north. Turn right at Lake Hollywood Drive. Follow around until you see the lake. It's about 3 1/2 miles to walk around it. Drive past the lake, continue on Canyon Lake and you will get a real close-up of the Hollywood sign. Continue down to the Beachwood area.

Los Angeles Sports Teams (star spotting at the Lakers Games)

Main Street, Santa Monica and Venice Beaches. Shopping and eating. Santa Monica Freeway west to Fourth Street, turn left to Pico, then right to Main St., then left and that's it.

Montana Avenue in Santa Monica between 17th and 9th streets, celebrities!

Third Street Promanade in Santa Monica, begins at the 4th Street Mall and runs north for several blocks of shopping, eating and people watching.

Mann's Chinese Theater on Hollywood Blvd. between Highland and LaBrea. Go and put your feet in the foot prints of the stars!

Tackiest souvenirs are on Hollywood Blvd. around the Mann's Chinese Theater.

FOR RESTAURANTS & HANGOUTS

See the L.A. Scene/Hangouts page 487.

• **Now we begin your scouting trip.** Refer to this section and the L.A. Scene section for locations.

If I were planning your trip for you, I would say bring your best friend, at least $2,000 and drive in to your hotel or motel on Thursday afternoon. If you are flying, rent a car at the airport.

Day One - Friday

3 mile walk around Hollywood Lake. Find your way in the Thomas guide through the hills. You will drive very close to the Hollywood Sign.

Breakfast at the Village Cafe on Beachwood, 323/467-5398. Then down Gower to Santa Monica Blvd. Turn left then right into Hollywood Cemetery, drive slowly; lots of stars buried here. Come out, turn left and left again on Gower past Paramount Studios, right on Melrose then an immediate left on Larchmont for two blocks; cross Beverly Blvd. and park.

Coffee at Starbucks and shopping in Larchmont Village. Back to Melrose, left to several blocks past La Brea; park and walk both sides of Melrose Ave.

Lunch. Plenty of places to eat here. In car, east on Melrose, turn left on Cahuenga follow over the hill to Barham, turn right. Barham turns into Olive and the gate to Warner Bros. will be on your right.

3:30 Prearranged reservations for Warner Bros. Tour.

Hotel/motel/friend's or relative's. Rest and get ready for a movie in Westwood, Century City, Santa Monica or Burbank, depending on where you are staying.

Movie

Day Two - Saturday

Breakfast at Patricks Roadhouse in Santa Monica, then walk the beach-walk from there to the Santa Monica Pier, then past the pier south to Venice Beach. At the end of the merchants on the boardwalk, turn left and walk a few blocks inland to:

Main Street in Venice and walk back to Santa Monica along Main Street.

Lunch on the Third Street Promenade. Blocks of shopping and people watching.

See a play in a little theater. Pick up Sunday's *L.A. Times* (early edition.) The Calendar section will have a complete listing of plays in little theaters. Choose a play that is recommended; see pick of the week. There are also plays listed in *Back Stage West/Drama-Logue* .

Day Three - Sunday

Disneyland all day and evening, till it closes. Get there early. If you have breakfast at the Disneyland hotel, you get into the park an hour earlier .

Day Four - Monday

Breakfast at Good Neighbor Restaurant on Cahuenga Blvd West.

Universal Studios, till it closes. Go on a week day when possibly you will see some shooting on the back lot.

Dinner at Universal's City Walk.

Day Five - Tuesday

Jerry's Deli on Beverly Blvd. for Breakfast..

Farmer's Market on Third Street and Fairfax.

See a television show's taping or filming, maybe *Its Like, You Know...;* we shoot on Tuesday or Wednesday. Check with Audiences Unlimited for other shows. If you are going to a show at CBS at Radford, go to a late lunch/early dinner at Dupars. Afterwards go to Jerry's Deli, west on Ventura Blvd. If you are seeing a show at Paramount, go for a late Mexican dinner at Lucy's on Melrose.

Day Six - Wednesday

Breakfast at Dukes on Sunset Blvd.

Research (during breakfast) areas where you might want to live and map out a plan for looking at as many as you can tomorrow. Now head east on Sunset to Stanley, turn left and right in the first driveway to park in the Samuel French Bookstore parking lot.

Samuel French's at 10AM. Plan two hours to hang out and look at all the information.

Free afternoon and evening.

Day Seven - Thursday

Breakfast at Rose Cafe, 310/399-0711. 220 Rose Ave. in Venice.

Look all day at areas you think you may like to live; start on the West side.

Movie and check out Mann's Chinese theater on Hollywood Blvd., in Hollywood.

Dinner at Hamburger Hamlet across the street. Shop for souvenirs.

Day Eight - Friday

Breakfast at Hugo's in West Hollywood, Santa Monica Blvd.

Griffith Park Observatory.

Lunch at Musso & Franks, 323/467-7788. Take Cahuenga over the hill, turn right on Barham, go past Warner Bros. Studio, left on Hollywood Way, right on Magnolia.

Visit "It's a Wrap." 3315 W. Magnolia. Used clothes from films and current TV shows.

Castaways Restaurant, 818/848-6691, in Burbank, for cocktails. Continue East (toward mountains) on Magnolia until it ends. Turn left onto Sunset Canyon. Right on Harvard all the way to the top of the hill. Valet parking free.

Night spots you think you'll enjoy.

Day Nine - Saturday

Walking tour of Beverly Hills. Park at the two-hour free parking lot just south of Santa Monica Blvd on Canon or Beverly Blvd.

Lunch at Barneys department store on Wilshire. Then drive east on Wilshire to La Cienega, turn left to Beverly Center.

Spend afternoon at the Beverly Center.

Movie and nightclubbing

Late, late night. Canters Deli after 2AM.

Day Ten - Sunday

Whatever you have been dying to do.

Day Eleven - Monday

Return home.

• **This is not a vacation** for relaxing; this is the type of pace it takes to work and live here. If you follow this plan, you will cover many of the areas that are part of a Los Angeles actor's life.

My cousin and three friends (dancers) came to Los Angeles, rented an apartment in La Brea Towers. I thought they spent too much time sleeping and fixing their hair to go out. It could take two or three hours to get out of the house. When you arrive be prepared to go; you can party when you get home. Your time is very precious here.

Things nice to fit in:

La Conversation, 310/858-0950, 638 N. Doheny Dr., West Hollywood, 90069. Lovely food, sit outside near corner of Santa Monica. Have a facial at Yolanda's next door. This is the way to live!

Beverly Hills Hotel's poolside Cabana Club Cafe, 800/283-8885. 9641 Sunset Blvd. Beverly Hills. Expensive - pay cash so you don't have to explain you aren't staying there.

360 Degrees, 323/871-2995. 6290 Sunset Blvd., Hollywood, the corner of Vine. At the top of a 19 story building - lovely view - dinner or late drinks.

L.A. Scene / Local Hangouts

• **You have moved here to seek your fame and fortune.** Here are places you may wish to check out that will put you in the neighborhoods where some of the action is. I've picked places that are known to be hangouts for people in show-biz. Places of business have a way of disappearing, but find your own. Have fun finding your favorite hangouts. *L.A. Magazine* and the Calendar Section of the *L.A. Times,* Sunday and Thursday editions will keep you up on the latest happenings.

The L.A. Weekly and New Times are free local newspapers. Pick them up at newsstands, 7-11s, liquor stores and businesses.

• COFFEE HOUSES

The Abbey, 310/289-8410. 692 N. Robertson Blvd., West Hollywood. Cappuccino and dreams of Tuscany midst all the fountains.

Bourgeois Pig, 323/962-6366. 5931 Franklin, Hollywood, 90028. Good coffee and desserts. Light stuff - bagels etc.

Coffee Bean & Tea Leaf, 310/453-2093. 1426 Montana Ave., Santa Monica. Ice-blended mocha drink, no fat, no calories, but fabulous.

Cyber Java, 323/466-5600. 7080 Hollywood Blvd. L.A.'s first Online coffeehouse. Cruise the Web for $9 an hour.

Lu Lu's Beehive, 818/986-CAFE. 13203 Ventura Blvd., Studio City, 91604. Los Angeles Magazine says "Best coffee scene in the Valley."

Highland Grounds, 323/466-1507. 742 N. Highland Ave., Hollywood. Live avant garde music and readings every night.

Hollywood Hills Coffee Shop, 323/467-7678. 6145 Franklin Avenue. A scene from Swingers was filmed here. Celebs. Great for breakfast or lunch.

King's Road, 323/655-9044. 8361 Beverly Blvd., West Hollywood. Always packed.

Library, A Coffee House, 562/433-2393. 3418 E. Broadway Blvd., Long Beach. Carries thousands of titles on metaphysics, psychology, etc. nothing over $5.95. More than cappuccino. Ted Danson and Mary Steenburgen stop every week for the chili.

Lulu's Alibi, 310/479-6007. 1640 Sawtelle Blvd., West L.A. Open till 2AM.

Newsroom Cafe, 310/319-9100. 530 Wilshire Blvd., Santa Monica. Great coffee, sweets, sugar-free desserts. Many celebs.

Van Go's Ear, Restaurant and gallery, 310/396-1987. 796 Main Street, Venice. 24-hours.

• RESTAURANTS, UPSCALE

360 Degrees, 323/871-2995. 6290 Sunset Blvd., Hollywood, the corner of Vine. At the top of a 19 story building - lovely view - dinner or late drinks.

Alice's on Malibu Pier, 310/456-6646. 23000 Pacific Coast Highway. Watch surfers. Cathy Kerr's favorite beach.

Cabana Club Cafe, 800/283-8885. 9641 Sunset Blvd., Beverly Hills. Pool side dining at the Beverly Hills Hotel. Live large and pretend you are staying at a $700 per night bungalow.

Cafe 8 1/2, 310/652-2048. 201 South Robertson, Beverly Hills. Sharon Stone recommendation.

Cafe de Paris, 310-358-0908. 650 North Robertson, West Hollywood. Another Sharon Stone favorite.

Cafe Med, 310/652-0445. 8615 Sunset Blvd., West Hollywood. Keanu Reeves favors the spaghetti Bolognese and James Woods enjoys the pasta with olive oil and garlic.

Dan Tana's, 310/275-9444. 9071 Santa Monica Blvd., West Hollywood. Northern Italian food in a busy restaurant. Celeb hangout. Great New York steak.

Divino, 310/472-0886. 11714 Barrington Court, Brentwood. Clientele ranging from Diana Ross to Billy Crystal.

Four Oaks, 310/470-3623. 2181 N. Beverly Glen Blvd. Bel Air. Secluded garden, great.

Geoffrey's Malibu, 310/457-1519. 27400 Pacific Coast Highway, Malibu, 90265. Power place in Robert Altman's *The Player.*

Georgia, 323/933-8420. 7250 Melrose Ave., Los Angeles. Southern cooking—Norm Nixon is a co-owner.

Ivy, 310/274-8303. 113 N. Robertson, L.A., south of Beverly. If you can afford it, minimum $25 for lunch. Eat here at least once.
Ivy at the Shore, 310/393-3113. 1541 Ocean Ave., Santa Monica.

La Pergola, 818/905-8402. 15005 Ventura Blvd, L.A. Marlon Brando comes often for the pastas and Italian cuisine.

Lavande, 310/576-3181. 1700 Ocean Avenue, Santa Monica. A favorite place of Goldie Hawn, Steven Bochco and Sharon Lawrence.

Le Dome, 310/659-6919. 8720 Sunset Blvd., Sunset Plaza, West Hollywood. Big music business hangout.

Kate Mantilini, 310/278-3699. 9101 Wilshire Blvd. at Doheny Drive, Beverly Hills. Many celebrities. Great for power breakfast. Jerry Seinfeld sightings.

Mr. Chow, 310/278-9911. 344 N. Camden Drive, Beverly Hills. Prices are high, cooking is good and celebs go there.

The Grill, 310/276-0615. 9560 Dayton Way, Beverly Hills. Power lunch for agents.

Osteria Romana Orsini, 310/277-6050. 9575 West Pico Blvd. near Century City. Agents, producers, and studio executives from MGM and Fox hang out here. Italian menu which has fed Sean Connery, Michael Douglas and Cameron Diaz.

Polo Lounge, Beverly Hills Hotel, 310/276-2251. 9641 Sunset Blvd., Beverly Hills. Have breakfast in the coffee shop and look around.

Spago, 310/385-0880. 176 Canon Dr., West Hollywood, just north of Sunset Blvd. Sit at the bar for dessert and experience this world-famous restaurant.

Sushi Roku, on Third near LaCienega, very popular, many celebrities. Calista Flockhart comes in once a week. Has a glass of water and half of a cucumber roll.

Trattoria Amici, 310/858-0271. 469 S. Doheny Dr., Beverly Hills. "Friends" buddies Jennifer Aniston, Courteney Cox and Lisa Kudrow are served delicious pastas. Elizabeth Hurley and Hugh Grant often lunch on the patio.

Typhoon, 310/390-6565. 3221 Donald Douglas Loop South (off Centinela). Oriental influenced dishes with a view of the airfield at Santa Monica Airport. Lauren Bacall orders the salmon with ginger poached in banana leaves. Robert De Niro, Al Pacino and Harrison Ford dine here.

• RESTAURANTS, MEDIUM TO LOWER PRICES

The Apple Pan, 310/475-3585. 10801 W. Pico Blvd., West Los Angeles. Open Friday and Saturday until 1AM, other days except Monday until midnight. Great burgers and apple pie. All counters; people stand behind you and wait. Great after a late movie at Westside Pavilion.

Amazon, 818/382-6080. 14649 Ventura Blvd., Sherman Oaks. Three blocks west of Van Nuys Blvd. The atmosphere is not to be missed.

Art's Delicatessen, 818/762-1221. 12224 Ventura Blvd., Studio City. Favorite of the Hollywood community that resides in the Valley. Best Black & White cookies!

Aunt Kizzy's Back Porch, 310/578-1005. 4325 Glencoe Ave., Marina Del Rey. Southern cooking. Actors and athletes love the fried chicken and baked ribs.

A Votre Santé, 310/314-1187. 1025 Abbot Kinney Blvd., Venice. Also 310/451-1813. 13016 San Vicente Blvd., Brentwood. Also 213/857-0412. 345 N. La Brea Ave., Hollywood. Gourmet vegetarian.

Back Door Bakery, on Silver Lake Blvd., in Silver Lake, great breakfast.

Barney Greengrass, 310/777-5877. 9570 Wilshire Blvd., Beverly Hills. Great fish straight from Barney's in New York.

Birds, 323/465-0175. 5925 Franklin Ave., Hollywood. Perched in the shadow of the Hollywood sign.

Cafe Brazil, 310/837-8957. 10831 Venice Blvd., Culver City. Excellent food, also vegetarian. Most dishes under $8.

Cafe Luna, 323/655-8647. 7463 Melrose Ave, Hollywood. 8AM-3AM. Outside seating (you can draw on the tablecloths.) Great for people-watching. Mick Jagger and Christopher Lloyd like this place.

Caffe Capri, 323/644-7906. 2547 Hyperion Ave., L.A. Lunch and dinner Wednesday through Monday. Italian food served in a cute, diminuitive restaurant.

Canter's Fairfax Restaurant, 323/651-2030. 419 North Fairfax, L.A. Open 24 hours. Folksy by day; underground by night. In the old Jewish neighborhood. Great for the middle of night after play rehearsal. Bakery open all the time.

Carney's Restaurant, 323/654-8300. 8351 Sunset Blvd., West Hollywood, 90069. Restaurant is in an authentic railroad car. Also on Ventura Blvd. in Studio City.

Chin Chin, 310/652-1818. 8618 Sunset Blvd., Hollywood. Indoor and outdoor seating; watch the crowd go by! Other locations. I love the light chicken salad.

Dimples, 818/842-2336. 3413 W. Olive Ave., Burbank. Lunch and dinner, continuous Karaoke 6PM-1:30AM. Cheap, fun.

Duke's, 310/652-9411. 8909 Sunset Blvd. Big breakfast place, served all day, parking in rear.

DuPar's, 818/766-4437. 12036 Ventura Blvd., near Laurel Canyon. Robert Urich recommends the great pancakes and strong coffee.

El Coyote, 323/939-7766. 7312 Beverly Blvd, Hollywood. Popular with the twenty-something crowd.

Formosa Lounge, 323/850-9050. 7156 Santa Monica Blvd. Long time old movie star hangout.

Good Neighbor, 818/761-4627. 3701 Cahuenga Blvd. West, Studio City. Great place, near Universal. Look for my picture on the wall. Breakfast & Lunch closes at 4.

Gladstone's 4 Fish, at the end of Sunset Blvd., at the beach.

Greenblatt's, 323/656-0606. 8017 Sunset Blvd. Parking in rear. Next to the Laugh Factory. The best deli in town. Open till 2:00AM.

Hamptons, 323/469-3038. 1342 N. Highland, Hollywood.

Home, 323/665-HOME. 1760 Hillhurst Ave. Breakfast, lunch and dinner daily. Homey dining room with a jukebox, romantic patio.

Hugos, 323/654-3993. 8401 Santa Monica Blvd., just east of La Cienega, West Hollywood. Power breakfasts, many celebs.

Jerry's Deli, 818/980-4245. 12655 Ventura Blvd, Studio City, 91604. 24 hrs. Huge menu.

Jerry's Deli, 310/289-1811. 8701 Beverly Blvd., West Hollywood. Very "in" especially late at night.

Light House, 310/451-2076. 201 Arizona, Santa Monica. All you can eat Sushi, under $10 at lunch time.

Lucy's El Adobe, 323/462-9421. 5536 Melrose Ave., Hollywood. Across from Paramount Studios, lots of celebs. Very casual.

La Conversation, 310/858-0950. 638 N. Doheny Dr., West Hollywood. Adorable open weekdays late breakfast and lunch. My daughters love, love the soups and great pastries.

Mel's Drive In, Sunset Blvd. 24 hours, 2 blocks West of La Cienega. Great outdoors and in, good people watching on the Sunset Strip.

Musso & Frank Grill, 323/467-7788. 6667 Hollywood Blvd., Hollywood. Old time hangout. You must check this place out!

Nate 'n' Al's, 310/274-0101. 414 N. Beverly Dr., Beverly Hills, 90210. When you're in Beverly Hills this is the deli! This is a power breakfast spot for the film industry.

Original Pantry, 213/972-9279. Figueroa & 9th Streets, downtown L.A. 24 hrs. Known for their breakfasts and long-time waiters.

Patrick's Roadhouse, 310/459-4544. 106 Entrada Dr., Santa Monica. Lots of celebrities for breakfast. Patrick is a legend, is gone now but his son is carrying on the tradition.

Pink's Hot-Dog Stand, 711 N. La Brea, just north of Melrose. Sean Penn proposed to Madonna there.

Red Eye, on Beverly at Martell, West Hollywood. Great for Breakfast.

Roscoe's House of Chicken & Waffles, 323-466-7453, in Hollywood. It is the best in the middle of the night. Down home food. Another Sharon Stone favorite.

Russia, 323/464-2216. 1714 Ivar Avenue, Hollywood. A Hollywood version of a Russian style restaurant. Within walking distance of the Pantages and Doolittle theaters. Live music and dancing on the weekends.

Smoke House, 818/845-3731. 4420 Lakeside Drive, Burbank, very near Toluca Lake. The best garlic-cheese bread in the world. Steaks and chicken, music in the bar.

Sittons Coffee Shop, 818/761-3341. 11329 Magnolia, N. Hollywood. 24 hour coffee shop. Good food and prices.

The Rose Cafe, 310/399-0711. 220 Rose Ave., Venice. Simple cafe and patio where the locals do breakfast and lunch.

Village Cafe in Beachwood Canyon, 323/467-5398. On Beachwood about one mile north of Franklin Avenue in Hollywood. Look up and see the Hollywood sign.

Vitello's, 818/769-0905. 4349 Tujunga Ave., Studio City. Great Italian food.

• HANGOUTS

Alligator Lounge, 310/449-1844. 3321 Pico Blvd., Santa Monica. Cover varies, rock & blues.

Bar Marmont, 323./650-0575. 8171 Sunset Blvd., Los Angeles. No cover. At this moment, it is the place to be.

Key Club, 310/274-5800. 9039 Sunset Blvd., West Hollywood. This is the site of the old very famous Gazzarri's and Billboard Live. Cover varies. Call for bookings.

Diane Bennett's Personal Introductions, Hot line: 310/859-6929. She plans parties at hotels for singles. Upscale, $12 fee.

Dome Billiards, 323/650-1886. 7901 Santa Monica Boulevard, West Hollywood.

Doug Weston's Troubadour, 310/276-1158. 9081 Santa Monica Blvd., West Hollywood. Singer-songwriter based shows. $5-$20 cover.

Dragonfly, 323/466-6111. 6510 Santa Monica Blvd., L.A. Hollywood club with a different type of music each night.

Father's Office, 310/451-9330. 1018 Montana Ave., Santa Monica. Excellent foreign draft beer.

The Garage, 323/662-6802. 4519 Santa Monica Blvd., Silver Lake. Devotees include celebs Jennifer Aniston, Brad Pitt and Jennifer Love Hewitt.

Harvelle's, 310/395-1676. 1432 Fourth Street in Santa Monica. Smokey blues bar.

HMS Bounty, 213/385-7275. 3357 Wilshire Blvd., Los Angeles. Across the street from the Ambassador Hotel. Free jukebox.

Hollywood Athletic Club, 323/962-6600. 6525 Sunset Boulevard, Hollywood. Young industry types.

Hollywood Billiards, 323/465-0115. 5504 Hollywood Blvd., Hollywood. 35 tables, video games, snacks, open all night.

House of Blues, 323/848-5136. 8430 Sunset Blvd., West Hollywood.

Miceli's, 323-466-3438. 1646 N. Las Palmas Ave, Hollywood. Scripted, spontaneous, interactive, tribute to the Vegas-style variety shows of early '60s.

Molly Malone's, 323/935-1577. 575 South Fairfax, Los Angeles. High spirited bar band.

Maloney's Sports Bar, 310/208-1942. 1000 Gayley Ave., Westwood. 14 TVs and drink specials. Near UCLA but all ages go there.

Sunset Marquis Hotel Bar, 310/657-1333. 1200 Alta Loma, West Hollywood. Young, hip, celebs and music industry folk.

The Roxy, 310/276-2222. 9009 Sunset Blvd. West Hollywood. L.A.'s major showcase, rock, pop and jazz artists, call for bookings.

Viper Room, 310/358-1880. 8852 W. Sunset Blvd., West Hollywood. Johnny Depp's place. Where River Phoenix died.

Whiskey a Go Go, 310/652-4205. 8901 Sunset Blvd., West Hollywood. Loud; world famous in the '60s and '70s.

Woody Harrelson's O2 bar and restaurant, 310/360-9002. www.o2bar.com. $13 to inhale 20 minutes' worth of pure, canned oxygen.

Yankee Doodle's, 310/394-4632. 1410 Third Street Promenade, Santa Monica. 29 table billiard parlor.

• JAZZ

Baked Potato, 818/980-1615. 3787 Cahuenga Blvd. West, Studio City. 7PM-2AM.

Bel Age Hotel, 310/854-1111. 1020 N. San Vicente, L.A., off Sunset Blvd.

Catalina Bar & Grill, 323/466-2210. 1640 Cahuenga Blvd., Hollywood.

Gardenia, 323/467-7444. 7066 Santa Monica Blvd., Hollywood.

Jazz Bakery, 310/271-9039. 3233 Helms Ave., Los Angeles, off Venice Blvd. Call for bookings, jazz in a smoke-free environment. Tickets $10-$20.

LaVeLee, 818/980-8158. 12514 Ventura Blvd., Studio City. Tu-Su 8PM-1AM. Specializes in Lebanese dishes. Latin jazz and R&B.

Lunaria, 310/282-8870. 10351 Santa Monica Blvd., West L.A. Happening jazz scene in Westwood.

Peninsula, Beverly Hills Hotel, 310/551-2888. 9882 Santa Monica Blvd. Many stars come by to hear pianist-vocalist George Bugatti.

• PLACES TO DANCE

Salsa dancing, www.salsaweb.com. Do a city search for clubs in Los Angeles.
Swing dancing, www.nocturne.com. This is for Los Angeles clubs.

Cava, 323/658-8898. 8384 West Third Street, West Hollywood.

Cherry at the Love Lounge on Fridays, 213/896-9099. 657 N. Robertson Blvd., West Hollywood. Good music focusing on '80s new wave, glam and metal.

Coconut Club at the Beverly Hilton, 310/285-1358. 9876 Wilshire Blvd., Beverly Hills. Open Fridays and Saturdays. Full dinner menu. A supper club with dining, dancing and a cigar lounge. Visitors include Victoria Principal, Loni Anderson, Esther Williams and Mickey Rooney. Private booths, 900 square foot dance floor. A special place for a special occasion.

Crush Bar Continental, 323/461-9017. 1743 N. Cahuenga, north of Hollywood Blvd. Big dance floor.

The Derby, 323/663-8979. At Louise's Trattoria, 450 Los Feliz Blvd., Los Angeles. Swing dancing , cool place.

Good Bar, 310/271-8355. 9229 Sunset Blvd., West Hollywood.

Harvelle's, 310/395-1676. 1432 Fourth Street, Santa Monica. Oldest blues club.

Jack's Sugar Shack, 323/466-7005. 1707 N. Vine Street, Hollywood. Pool and dance.

Moonlight On The Blvd., 818/788-2000. 13730 Ventura Blvd., Sherman Oaks. Big bands.

In The Pink (Pinks), 310/392-1077. 2810 Main St., Santa Monica. Sean Penn's hangout. $10 cover, alley entrance, open Th, F and Sa.

Sportsmen's Lodge, 818/769-4700. 12825 Ventura Blvd., Studio City. Call for info. Latin, ballroom and country-western nights.

St. Marks, 310/452-2222. 23 Windward Avenue, Venice. Swing and Latin night, call first. Dance Lessons. No cover if you eat there.

Sugar, 310/899-1989. 814 Broadway, Santa Monica. Different DJs and themes 5 nights a week.

• GAY AND LESBIAN SCENE

Big scene in West Hollywood, Santa Monica Blvd., between La Cienega, and Doheny Blvds. Many street festivals.

Gay and Lesbian Community Services, 323/993-7400.

Gay Theater, Celebration Theatre, 310/289-2999. 7051 Santa Monica Blvd., West Hollywood.

A Different Light Bookstore, 310/854-6601. 8853 Santa Monica Blvd. Free publications in front.

Michelle's xxx Topless Revue, Club 7969 on Tuesday night. 7969 Santa Monica Blvd., West Hollywood. Tastefully sexy midnight strip show for the ladies, by the ladies.

• COMEDY CLUBS

Acme Comedy Theater, 323/525-0202. 135 N. La Brea Ave., Hollywood. Call for times and reservation.

Laugh Factory, 2323/656-8860. 8001 W. Sunset Blvd., Hollywood. Thanksgiving and Christmas dinner free to people in the biz.

The Improvisation, 323/651-2583. 8162 Melrose Ave., L.A. Top comedy acts. Talent nights and open mike nights.

The Original Comedy Store, 323/656-6225. 8433 Sunset Blvd. Many actors have been discovered here. Open mike nights.

Groundling Theatre, 323/934-9700. 7307 Melrose Ave., Hollywood. Improvisational group doing consistently good work.

• ACTIVITIES

Backbone Trail. Three-mile hike in Malibu Creek State Park, which takes you to the old *M*A*S*H* set.

Barbra Streisand's former Malibu estate, 310/589-2850. Now part of the Santa Monica Mountains Conservancy, the nearly two hour tour offers a thorough look at the estate, including three of the five houses. $30.

Bowl-A-Rama, 323/254-2579.

Canoga Park Bowling, 818/340-5190. 20122 Vanowen Street, Winnetka. Open 24 hours, 32 lanes, billiards and video arcade.

Coldwater Canyon Park. Just east of the intersection of Coldwater Canyon and Mulholland Drive. Five miles of marked trails.

Culver City Western Hemisphere Marathon, 310/253-6650. Early registration, $25, race day, $35. Expansive views oft the Pacific Ocean above Dockweiler Beach.

Dodgers Adult Baseball Camp, 800/334-7529. $4,000

Equestrian Center, on Riverside Drive in Burbank. This is our horse country. Many stables, restaurants, ice skating rink.

Fairfax Cinemas, 323/653-3117. 7907 Beverly Blvd. L.A. Inexpensive movie theater. Any seat, any show for $2.50.

Glendale Batting Cages, 818/243-2363. 620 East Colorado Blvd., Glendale. Softball or hardball batting cages.

Hiking: Mount Hollywood Trail, Griffith Park. Enter Griffith Park from Los Feliz Blvd. and turn onto Griffith Park Drive. Parking lot next to the carousel. 800-foot uphill trek from the carousel to the planetarium. There are also easier trails.

Hollywood Bowl rehearsals, 323/468-2332. 2301 N. Highland Ave., Hollywood. During the Hollywood Bowl season from June to September, mostly Tuesday, Thursday and Fridays, you can see the program scheduled for that evening for free.

Hollywood Boxing Gym, 323/845-1420. 1551 La Brea Avenue, L.A.

Hollywood Star Bowling Lanes, 323/665-4111. 5227 Santa Monica Blvd., L.A. Open 24 hours, 32 lanes, video and pinball arcade.

Los Angeles County Museum of Art, 323/857-6110. 5905 Wilshire Blvd., Los Angeles.

Los Angeles Downtown Walking Tour, 310/470-4463. $12.50 plus $3 in transit fares. Two-hour Angel City Tour starts at Union Station and Olvera Street, then via subway to Grand Central Market, Angel's Flight, Central Library and the Bradbury Building. Greg Fischer is an inexhaustible fountain of facts.

Indoor Climbing at Rockreation, 714/556-ROCK. 1300 Logan Ave., Costa Mesa. 10,000 sq. ft. of sculpted artificial rock.

J. Paul Getty Museum, 310/440-7300, www.getty.edu.. They are completely redoing the one in Malibu. Both museums are a "must see." 17985 Pacific Coast Hwy., Malibu. Reservation for parking a must. Spectacular!

Laser Storm, 310/373-8470. 22535 Hawthorne Blvd., Torrance or 818/999-3150, 20929 Ventura Blvd., Woodland Hills. Laser tag venue lets you shoot at one another or at electronic objects in an arena filled with black and neon lights. Everything glows in the dark.

Mar Vista Bowl, (310) 391-5288. 12125 Venice Blvd., Mar Vista. Call for open bowling times.

Melrose News, 323/655-2866. 647 N. Martel Ave., L.A. Celeb newsstand. Eddie Murphy allegedy stopped by the night of his infamous adventure with a transvestite.

Merchant of Tennis, 310/855-1946. 1118 S. La Cienega Blvd., Beverly Hills. 9-6. $15 per hour, per group. Lessons 6:30AM-1PM, $45 an hour.

Moore-N-Moore Sporting Clays, 818/890-4788. 12651 N. Little Tujunga Canyon Road, San Fernando. Practice your marksmanship skills with clay pigeons. Celebs John Milius and Charlton Heston have been spotted here.

Poetry Readings, Beyond Baroque, 310/822-3006. 681 Venice Blvd., West Los Angeles.

Natural History Museum, 213/744-3466. 900 Exposition Blvd., Exposition Park, Los Angeles.

Paramount Ranch, 805/370-2301. Free, this location has played the role of colonial Massachusetts, ancient China and countless Wild West towns. Take 101 Frwy west to Kanan Road, south on Kanan half a mile to Cornell Way. Follow Cornell three miles to Paramount Ranch Road and turn right into the parking lot.

Power Pools. Swim in the pools if you buy lunch at Mondrian, Chateau Marmont, Regent Beverly Wilshire, Hollywood Roosevelt, Sunset Marquis. Takes a great body and nerve.

Runyon Canyon Park. Franklin Ave., 1 blk. East of La Brea, on Fuller. Past old Errol Flynn estate; foundations, old swimming pool still visible. At top a bench and view.

Santa Monica Pier, at the end of Colorado Blvd. in Santa Monica. Historical carousel and a whole amusement park, rides open on weekends, but plenty to do during the week. Bands play on the pier during summer early evenings.

Shatto 39 Bowling Lanes, 213/385-9475. 3255 W. 4th Street, L.A., 19 pool tables, bar and coffee shop.

Sports Center Bowl, 818/769-7600. 12655 Ventura Blvd., Studio City. 32 lanes. Lots of industry clientele.

Stair Climbing on the 4th Street Stairs, at 4th and Adelaide streets in Santa Monica(189).

Stairs, in Santa Monica. They ascend from the 400 block of North Mesa Road to Amalfi Drive (201). Less crowded then the 4th street stairs and redwoods, wisteria and live oaks.

Sunset Beach, one of the best surfing spots. Take Sunset Blvd. west and park on Pacific Coast Highway, just south of Gladstone's 4 Fish.

Sunset Ranch Hollywood Stables, 323/464-9612. 3400 N. Beachwood Dr., Hollywood. Friday night rides in the Griffith Park Hills on horseback in the Griffith Park Hills.

Train Ride, Fillmore & Western Railway, 800/777-TRAIN or www.fwry.com Two-and-a-half-hour excursion between Fillmore and Santa Paula. Barbecue dinner and dancing.

• AREAS

Beverly Hills, between Santa Monica and Wilshire Blvd., Cañon on the east and where Santa Monica and Wilshire cross on the west.

Farmers Market, 323/933-9211. On Third and Fairfax, Los Angeles. M-S 9-7. Su 10-6. Great shopping and eating.

China Town, in downtown Los Angeles, Hill and Broadway. Experience a dim sum tea breakfast for an unusual treat.

Fairfax Avenue, from Melrose to Sixth Street. The heart of the old Jewish district.

Koreatown, Olympic Blvd. from Vermont to Western. The Korea Plaza mall on Western features designer clothing, housewares, a bakery and large Korean grocery store.

Larchmont Blvd., between Melrose and Beverly Blvd. and Rossmore (Vine) and Gower. Old world village shopping and dining district.

Little Tokyo, 1st and 2nd streets between Los Angeles Street and Alameda in downtown L.A. Check out the new national Japanese American Museum. The Japanese Village features shops and restaurants. Also visit Yaohan Plaza at 4th and Alameda to see an incredible Japanese super grocery store, restaurants and an extensive Japanese bookstore. There's also a karaoke lounge where you can book private karaoke rooms by the hour.

Melrose Avenue, between La Brea and Fairfax. Underground chic shopping, eating and looking.

Montana Avenue at 16th St. in Santa Monica. Great place for shopping and eating; a little town, lots of celebs live close.

Mulholland Drive. Enter from Cahuenga Blvd West (off Barham and the 101 Freeway.) On a clear day you can see the ocean, downtown L.A., and Century City Towers. 20-min. drive to the 405 freeway. Take in the Valley and the City. If it is not a clear day, you'll be above the smog.

Old Olvera Street, by Union Train Station in downtown L.A., off the 101 Freeway at Alameda. Permanent Mexican street festival.

Old Pasadena, 134 Freeway off at Colorado. Check out Green Street and Fair Oaks. Antiques, dining, hot night time scene, very in!

Third Street Promenade, 3rd Street between Colorado and Wilshire Blvd. in Santa Monica. Pedestrian mall with restaurants, movie theater and live street performers. A fun evening of strolling and browsing.

Santa Monica, Malibu, Zuma, Laguna, Newport Beaches!

Venice Beach Boardwalk, great shopping, walking, looking. Take Venice Blvd. west. Funky and crowded.

• Books

The Underground Guide to Los Angeles, by Editor, Pleasant Gehman.
Curbside L.A.: From the Pages of the Los Angeles Times, by Cecilia Rasmussen.

Novels about L.A.

The Big Sleep by Raymond Chandler.
What Makes Sammy Run by Budd Schulberg.
Ask the Dust by John Fante.
The Day of the Locust by Nathanial West.
City of Quartz by Mike Davis.
A Red Death by Walter Mosley.
Maps to Anywhere by Bernard Cooper.
Golden Days by Carolyn See.
I Should Have Stayed Home by Horace McCoy.
Sad Movies by Mark Lindquist.
Armed Response by Ann Rower
Los Angeles Without a Map by Richard Rayner.
L.A. Is the Capital of Kansas by Richard Meltzer.

CITIES OUTSIDE OF L.A.

• **Many of you reading this book** are as yet outside of Los Angeles and thinking and wondering how you will make the leap into the Industry. Here are some ideas to speed you on your way.

• **Al Burton gives an excellent interview** in The Child Actor section about the work you can do in your hometown. Throughout the book the information can be used to gain your training and experience to help you achieve a satisfactory artistic life where you live. If you can become a big fish in a little pond, you can gain a great sense of accomplishment.

• **My daughter, Cynthia Kerr**, moved to Dallas, Texas. She had been an accomplished actress as a teenager; and after marriage, motherhood and a successful real estate career, she wanted to return to her first love, acting. When her husband was transferred to Dallas, she thought she would go to a State University, study and perform.

• **The first week**, I visited and we checked out the town. Actors from Dallas had studied with me and I asked them where to look. KD Studio was mentioned by several. We met with them and knew we had found a home. They gave us information on everything that was happening. They spoke of *STAGE, Society for Theatrical Artists' Guidance and Enhancement*, a support group for the large number of actors in Dallas. They have showcases, productions and casting information. *KD Studio* and *STAGE* are also casting facilities.

• **Cynthia enrolled in KD Studio Actors Conservatory** of the Southwest. Photographer Suze Lanier from Los Angeles, on one of her trips to Dallas, took excellent pictures of her. Cynthia interviewed with four agents; one offered to take her on the spot. Because of the excellent schooling and networking at KD Studio she was in two plays, three industrials and a McDonalds' national commercial during her first year. At the time of her graduation, she had paid for her education and expenses from her acting work, plus the residual payments continued. She then moved to Nashville had another baby and now, at last, they have been transferred home, to Los Angeles. Read about how she launcher her out-of-state career into a Los Angeles commercial career. *See Commercials, Section Three, page 160.*

• **Janine Turner** of *Northern Exposure,* originally from Dallas, was whisked into the acting world in 1980 by a producer who met her in a hotel gift shop and landed her three episodes in a bikini on *Dallas.*

• **Photographer Sean Kenney** works in Phoenix several times a year.

• ***Back Stage West*** lists casting notices and local resources in Northern California as well as occasionally other states, 323/525-2356. Call to see if they have a back issue for your State or area.

• **Judy Carter, the author of *Stand-up Comedy: the Book,* published by Dell Books.** "We have a complete listing of clubs, agents, and managers in the appendix. No matter where the readers live, there is a comedy club or a comedy venue near them. If they call us at 1-800-4COMICS, www.judycarter.com, they'll have a free subscription to our newsletter, which is published quarterly and is full of inspiring talks and tips and everything that goes on across the country."

• **The Actor's City Sourcebook** by Andrea Wolper, published by Back Stage Books is very valuable. She gives a complete rundown on working and living in 11 cities: Boston, Chicago, Dallas, Los Angeles, Miami, Minneapolis/ St.Paul, New York, Philadelphia, San Francisco, Seattle and Washington, D.C. Order through Samuel French Bookstore, 323/876-0570

• **Contact your state's Film Advisory Board** for agents, films and extra casting agencies that will be casting in your area.

• **See Internet and World Wide Web listings, *Section Ten***

I have the following resources for your information. These numbers have not been checked for accuracy, that will be up to you. Make a name for yourself where you live and then bring yourself here.

Resources

California Film Commission, 323/860-2960.

Northern California: Boom Models & Talent, 415/626-6591; Callboard 415/957-1557; Covers Model & Talent Agency, 707/539-9252; Marla Dell Talent, 415/563-9213; The E.S. Talent Agency, 415/543-6575; Film Theatre Actors Exchange, 415/433-3920; The Frazer Agency in San Jose, 408/554-1055; Generation Model & Talent Agency, 415/777-9099; Laura Folger Casting, 415/749-7666; Look Model & Talent Agency, 415/781-2341; Mitchell Talent Management, 415/395-9475; Ann Montgomery Talent & Model Agency, 925/417-7480; Panda Agency, 707/576-0711; Quen Casting, 1911 Douglas Blvd., #85230, Roseville, CA 95661; Claudia Quinn Associates, 650/615-9950; San Francisco Top Models & Talent, 415/391-1800; Stars, The Agency, 415/421-6272; Talent Plus/Los Latinos Talent Agency, 408/443-5542; Tonry Talent Agency, 415/543--3979; Film Arts Foundation, 415/552-8760; Theaters:The ArtRise Theatre, South San Francisco, CA, 650/873-2442; Broadway West Theatre Company, Fremont, CA, 510/683-9218; Contra Costa Musical Theatre, Walnut Creek, CA, 510/932-5064; Exit Theatre, San Francisco, 415/666-0786; Mira Theatre Guild, Vallejo, CA, 707/642-2152; The Pleasanton Playhouse, Pleasanton, CA, 510/462-2121; This Side of the Hill Players, Half Moon Bay, CA, 650/728-5827; West Coast Broadway Productions, University of San Francisco, CA, 510/339-7750; Woodland Opera House, Woodland, CA, 916/666-9618; Z Studio Space-Annual Afro Festival, 415/346-9344.

Southern CA: Ahmanon Theater, Downtown LA, 213/628-2772; Arts Council for the Humanities 916/322-6555, Theatre L.A. 213/614-0556.

Orange County: Artist Management Agency, 949/261-7557; Berzon Talent Agency, 949/631-5936; Burkett Talent Agency, 949/830-6300; Express Entertainment Talent Agency, 714/557-8423; The Morgan Agency, 949/574-1100.

San Diego: Agency 2 Model & Talent Agency, 619/291-9556; Artist Management, Talent Agency, 619/233-6655; Elegance Talent Agency, 760/434-3397; San Diego Model Management, 619/296-1018; Shamon Freitas & Co., 619/549-3955; Nouveau Model Management, Talent Agency, 619/456-1400.

All The Other States and Cities

Alabama Film Office, 800/633-5898.
Alaska Film Office, 907/269-8137.
Arizona Film Commission, 602/280-1380; Agencies: Act, Tucson, 520/795-4615; Action Talent Agency, 520/881-6535; Danis Agency, Phoenix, 602/263-1918; Ford Robert Black Agency, Scottsdale, 602/966-2537; Fosi's Talent Agency, 602/795-3534, Leighton Agency, Inc., 602/224-9255; Signature Models & Talent, 602/966-1102.
Arkansas Film Office, 501/682-7676.
Boston, Maggie, Inc. 617/536-2629; Model Group, 617/426-4711.

Colorado, Agencies: Donna Baldwin Talent, Denver, 303/561-1199; Mattas Talent Agency, Colorado Springs, 719/577-4704; Maximum Talent, Inc., 303/691-2344; Voice Choice, 303/756-9055; Jeffrey Talent, 313/663-6398; Talent Shop, 810/644-4877; Film & Television Office, 303/620-4545; U.S. West TheatreFest-submit original plays to: Denver Center Theatre Co., 1050 13th St., Denver, CO 80204; The Francesca Primus Prize offered to Women Playwrights, 303/893-4000.
Connecticut Film, Video & Media Office, 860/270-8084.

Delaware Film Office, 302/739-4271.
Florida Entertainment Industry Council, 305/673-7168.
Georgia, Atlanta Models & Talent, Inc., 404/261-9627. Burns Agency, 404/299-8144; Georgia Film Office, 404/656-3591.
Hawaii, ADR Model & Talent Agency, 808/524-4777; Extras: 808/995-6511; Kathy Muller Agency, 808/737-7919; Hawaii Film Office, 808/586-2570.
Idaho Film Bureau, 208/334-2470.
Illinois Film Office, 312/814-8874; St. Nicholas Theater Co., Steppenwolf Theatre Co.
Indiana Film Commission, 317/232-8829.
Iowa Film Office,515/242-4726.
Oregon, Rose City Talent, Portland, 503/274-1005.
Kansas Film Commission, 913/296-4927.
Kentucky Film Commission,502/564-3456.
Louisiana Film Commission, 504/342-8150.
Maine Film Office, 207/287-5703.
Maryland Film Office, 410/767-6340.
Massachusetts Film Office, 617/973-8800.
Michigan Film Office, 517/241-0593.

Minnesota Film Board, 612/332-6493; The Playwright Center in Minneapolis produces Playlabs, to help produce original plays, 619/332-7481.
Mississippi Film Office, 601/359-5757.
Missouri, Branson Theatre Association, 417/334-0076; Missouri State Film, 314/751-9050; SAG, St. Louis, 314/231-8410; Kansas City 816/753-4557; Wright/Laird Casting, 816/531-0331; Talent Unlimited, 816/561-9040; Premier Talent, 816/756-1600; Film Commission, 573/751-9050.
Montana Film Office, 406/444-3762.
Nebraska Film Office, 402/471-3680.
Nevada Film Commission Hotline, 702/486-7373. Recorded casting information and schedule of free workshops. For referral to services, 702/486-7150; J. Baskow & Assoc., 702/733-7818; Classic Models, Ltd., 702/367-1444; Creative Talent Agency, 702/737-0611; Lenz Agency, 702/733-6888; The Talent Group, 702/365-8720; The Wauhob Agency, 702/733-1017.

New Hampshire Film & Television Bureau, 603/271-2598; Motion Picture Division, 702/486-2711.
New Jersey Motion Picture/TV Commission, 973/648-6279.
New Mexico, Aesthetics, Inc., 505/982-5883; Applause Talent Agency, Albuquerque, 505/262-9733; Cimarron Talent Agency, 505/292-2314; Eaton Agency, 505/344-3149; Film Office, 800/545-9871; Flair Modeling & Talent, 505/881-4688; The Mannequin Agency, 505/266-6823; The Phoenix Agency, 4121 Cutler Ave., NE, Albuquerque, NM 87110; South of Santa Fe Talent Guild, Inc., 505/880-8550.
New York Film & Television, 212/803-2330.

North Carolina Film Office, 919/733-9900.
North Dakota Film Commission, 800/328-2871.
Ohio, Cleveland, AFTRA, 216/781-2257; Film Commission, 614/466-2284.
Oklahoma Film Office, 918/581-2660.
Oregon Film & Video Office, 503/229-5832; Cusick's Talent Agency, 503/274-8555; Erhart Talent, Inc., 503/243-6362; Ryan Artists, Inc., 503/274-1005.
Pennsylvania Film Commission, 717/783-3456; Philadelphia: Reinhard Agency, 215/567--2008; Claro Modeling, 215/925-7795; Philadelphia Festival of World Cinema Screenwriting Competition, 800/969-7392.
Rhode Island Film Commission, 401/273-3456.
South Carolina Film Commission, 803/737-0490.
South Dakota Film Commission, 605/773-3301.

Tennessee Film Commission, 615/741-5829; Nashville: AFTRA 615/244-4108; Actor & Others Agency, 901/385-7885; Box Office Talent Agency, 615/256-5400; Creative Artists Agency, 615/383-8787; William Morris Agency, 615/385-0310; Talent & Model Land, 615/321-5596; Talent Trek Agency, 615/977-8735.

Texas, Agencies: Acclaim Partners, Austin, 512/323-5566; Actors, Etc., Houston, 713/785-4495; The Campbell Agency, Dallas, 214/522-8991; Mary Collins Agency Talent, 214/559-520; Kim Dawson Agency, 214/746-7920; Double Take Talent Agency, 972/404-4436; Neal Hamil Agency, Houston, 713/789-1335; The Horne Agency, Inc., Dallas, 214/350-9220; Intermedia Talent Agency, 713/622-8282; Marquee Talent, Inc., 214/357-0355; Quaid Talent Agency, 713/975-9600; Ivett Stone Agency, Irving, 972/506-9962; Peggy Taylor Talent, 214/651-7884; Tomas Agency, 972/687-9181; Sherry Young Madhatter Model & Talent Agency, 713/266-5800; Film Commission, 512-463-9200.

Utah Film Commission, 801-538-8740.

Vermont Film Commission, 802/828-3618.
Virginia Film Commission, 804/371-8204.
Washington, Agencies: Actor's Group, 206/624-9465; E. Thomas Bliss & Assoc., Inc., 206/340-1875; Classic Promotions, Inc., 1800/344-8731 or 206/720-1110; Dramatic Artists Agency, 206/442-9190; E L Vogue International Models & Talent, 425/688-8183; Entco International, Inc., 206/670-0888; Carol James Agency, 206/447-9191; Topo Swope Talent Agency,206/443-2021; Seattle Casting Directors: Walker & Co: 206/622-9646; Casting Real People 206/322-5855; Complete Casting, 210/441-5058; Dixon Walker Casting, 206/622-9646; Callies/Levine Casting, 206/447-9318; On Location Casting, 206/292-7010; Rothfield Casting, 206/448-0927; Heather Terzieff, 206/789-4417. The Actor's Handbook & Producer's Guide, edited by Ellen Taft: Capitol Hill Press, P.O. Box 12222, Seattle, WA 98102, $24.95. The Play's The Thing Drama Bookstore, 514 E. Pike Street; Film Commission, 206/464-7148; A Contemporary Theatre (ACT), Seattle, 206/292-7676.

Washington, DC, The Erickson Agency Movies Commercials, 703/356-0040; Office of Motion Picture & Television, 202/727-3787.

West Virginia Film Commission, 304/558-2234.
Wisconsin, Milwaukee Aftra, 414/291-9041; Film Commission, 608/267-3456.
Wyoming Film Office, 307/777-3400.

Summer Study:

A Noise Within-Summer with Shakespeare, Glendale, CA, 818/546-1449; ACTeen Summer Academy, New York, NY 212/391-5915; Acting for Camera, New York, NY, 212/247-2011; Acting for Television/Film/Theater at Weist Barron, New York, NY, 212/840-7025;The Actor's Center, New York, NY, 212/447-9688; The Actor's Conservatory, Hollywood, FL, 954/925-1380; Stella Adler Conservatory of Acting, New York, NY, 212/260-0525; Elaine Aiken's Actor's Conservatory, New York, NY, 212/764-0543; American Academy of Dramatic Arts, New York, NY, 212/686-9244 or Pasadena, CA, 626/798-0777; American Conservatory Theater Summer Training Congress, San Francisco, CA, 415/439-2350; American Musical Theater Artists Institute, San Jose, CA, 408/453-7100 Ext.145; American Stage Festival, Nashua, NH, 603/889-2330; American Theater Dance Workshop, Locust Valley, NY, 516/759-0282; Applause Performing Arts Center, Ramsey, NJ, 201/236-9027; Art of Choreography, Santa Monica, CA, 310/392-0689; Artistic New Directions-Improv., Musical Theater, and Playwright's Retreat, New York, NY, 212/857-1857, Email: ArtNewDir@aol.com; Atlantic Theater Company Six Week Intensive, New York, NY, 212/691-5919; Audrey Cohen College, New York, NY, 212/343-1234 Ext. 5001; Ballet Academy East, New York, NY, 212/410-9140;

The Barn Theater, Augusta, MI, 616/731-4545, Email: Barntheatr@aol.com; Bay Street Theatre, Sag Harbor, NY, 516/725-0818; Berkshire Theater Summer Training Program, Stockbridge, MA, 413/298-5536; Boston Conservatory Summer Dance, Boston, MA, 617/912-9157; British American Drama Academy, New York, NY, 212/749-0120; Collaborative Arts Project 21, New York, NY, 212/807-0202; California State Universiy Summer Arts, Long Beach, CA, 562/985-2064; Children's Acting Academy, New York, NY, 212/860-7101; Circle in the Square, New York, NY, 212/307-0388; Columbia Gorge School of Theater, White Salmon,WA, 800/405-3450, email: info@egst.com; Conservatory Ensemble Performance Program, New York, NY, 888/277-GATE; Denver Center Theater Company, Denver, CO, 303/446-4897; Edna Manley College Summer Dance, Kingston 5, Jamaica, 876/968-0027; Elaine Aiken Lily Lodge Actors Conservatory, New York, NY, 212/764-0543; Ensemble Studio Theater Conference, New York, NY, 212/581-9409; Eugene O'Neill Theater Center Cabaret Symposium, New York, NY, 212/864-3349; Exiles Theatre, Cork, Ireland, 212/591-1251;

Flat Rock Playhouse, Flat Rock, NC, 828/693-0731; Liz Fleischer School for Music and Dance, New York, NY, 212/501-3360; Fordham University in Orvieto, Italy, 212/636-6338; Gallatin School of Individualized Study (NYU), New York, NY, 212/998-7370; Gateway Playhouse, Bellport, NY, Fax: 516/286-5806; Gregory Abels Training for Monologue Preparation, New York, NY, 212/689-9371; Gene Frankel Theater, New York, NY, 212/777-1767; Gushee-Anania Studio, "Out of your head, Into your body," New York, NY, 212/353-0114; Gwyn Gilliss Communications Career Coaching, New York, NY, 212/595-9001 or in L.A., 310/798-3322; Hangar Theater Lab Company, Ithaca, NY, 607/273-8588, Email: info@hangartheatre.org; Hartwick College Acting Workshop, Oneonta, NY, 607/431-4416;

Hippodrome State Theatre, Gainesville, FL, 352/373-5958; Improvizational Theater with Paul Sills, Baileys Harbor, WI, 920/854-5072, Email: paulsills@dcwis.com; KD Studio Career Acting&Film Camp, Dallas, TX, 214/638-0484; Kids Love Acting At the Weist-Barron Studios, New York, NY, 212/874-1081; Lee Strasberg Theater Institute, New York, NY, 212/533-5500; Lessac Training & Research Institute, Fredonia, NY, 716/673-3597; Liz Caplan Vocal Studios, New York, NY, 212/246-2552; London Academy of Performing Arts Shakespearean Acting, London, England, 011-44-171-727-0220; Lynette Sheldon Actors Studio, New York, NY, 212/477-0171; Maine State Music Theatre, Brunswick, ME, 207/725-8769; Manhatten School of Music, Musical Theater Workshop, New York, NY, 212/749-2802 Ext. 474;Michael Howard Studios Summer Conservatory, New York, NY, 212/645-1525; Mount Holyoke College Summer Theatre, South Hadley, MA, 413/538-2632; Mountview Arts Centre-Shakespeare's Text in Action, London, England, 011-44-181-889-8110; Muhlenberg Summer Music Theater, Allentown, PA, 610/821-3335; National Stage Combat Workshop, University of Nevada, Las Vegas, 702/895-3662;

Neighborhood Playhouse, New York, NY, 212/688-3770; New Actors Workshop, New York, NY, 212/947-1310, http://admnet.com/naw/; New London Barn Playhouse, New London, NH, 603/526-6710/4631; New York City Dance Alliance, New York, NY, 212/686-5678; New York School of Cinematic & Theatrical Combat, New York, NY, 212/227-3069; New York State Theatre Institute, Troy, NY, 518/274-3295; New York University Music & Performing Arts Professions, New York, NY, 800/771-4NYU Ext.R79; New York University Tisch School of the Arts, New York, NY, 212/998-9175; NJ Shakespeare Festival, Madison, NJ, 973/408-3278; Noh Training Project, Bloomsburg, PA, 570/387-8270, Email: learnto@csrlink.net; North Carolina School of Drama, Winstom-Salem, NC, 336/770-3235; Peninsula Players Theatre, Fish Creek, WI, 920/868-3287; Pennsylvania Renaissance Faire Internships, Cornwall, PA, 717/665-7021 Ext. 124 or 135; Peridance, New York, NY, 212/505-0886;

Pittsburgh Civic Light Opera, Pittsburgh, PA, 412/281-3973; Playwrights Horizons Theater School, New York, NY, 212/529-8720; Pre-College Summer Institute, Philadelphia, PA, 215/875-3355; Donna Reed Festival and Workshops for the Performing Arts, Denison, IA, 712/263-3334, Email: dreedfpa@pionet.net; Royal Academy Course, London, England, 011-44-171-636-7076; Royal Theatre of Great Britain Atlantic Overtures, Omaha, NE, 402/453-3872; Sande Shurin Acting Studio NY/LA, New York, NY, 212/262-6848, Email: shurinacting@hotmail.com; Saratoga Intl' Theater Institute, Saratoga Springs, NY, 518/580-5590; School for Film & Television, New York, NY, 212/645-0030 Ext. 108; School of Russian Art Theatre, 888/635-7536;

Second City Improvization, Chicago, IL, 877/2ND CITY; Shakespeare & Co., Lenox, MA, 413/637-1199 Ext. 114; Shakespeare Summer Workshop, London, England, 011-44-171-373-9883; Shakespeare Theatre, Washington, D.C., 202/547-5688; Simon Studio Professional Lab, New York, NY, 212/704-0488; Singers on Stage on Broadway, New York, NY, 888/746-4692; Skidmore College Theater Institute, Saratoga Springs, NY, 518/580-5590; South Coast Repertory, Costa Mesa, CA, 714/708-5577, Email: www.scr.org; Stage Combat Workshop At Pace University, New York, NY, 212/330-6868,

Email: Kleemcchin@aol.com; Stanislavsky Summer School, Pittsburgh, PA, 412/422-1115, Email: stanschool@aol.com; Steps on Broadway, New York, NY, 212/874-2410; Theaterfest Apprentice Program, Upper Montclair, NJ, 973/655-7071; Trinity College Abroad Performance Program, New York, NY, 212/598-3058; University of the Arts, Philadelphia, PA, 215/875-3355; Vassar & NY Stage & Film's Powerhouse Theater Training Program, Poughkeepsie, NY, 914/437-5473, Email: www.vassar.edu/powerhouse; Video Associates Studio, New York, NY, 212/397-0018; Webber Douglas Academy of Dramatic Art, London, England, 011-441-71-370-4154; Will Geer's Shakespeare Seminar, Topanga, CA, 310/455-2322; Williamstown Theatre Festival, New York, NY, 212/228-2286; Williston Northampton Theater for Teens, Easthampton, MA, 413/529-3203, Email: info@williston.com; Youth Theatre of New Jersey, Newton, NJ, 973/579-5734, Email: youththeatreallyn@yahoo.com; David Zema Voice of Success, New York, NY, 212/473-6448.

Regional Theaters:
The Broadway Palm Dinner Theatre, Ft.Myers, FL, 717/898-1900; Actors' Playhouse At The Miracle Theatre, Coral Gables, FL, 305/444-9293; Apple Tree Theatre, Highland Park, IL 847/432-8223; American Musical Theatre of San Jose, CA, 408/453-7100; Arkansas Repertory Theatre, Little Rock, 501/378-0445; Bristor Riverside Theatre, PA, 215/785-6664; Caldwell Theatre Company, Boca Raton, FL, 561/241-7380; Carousel Dinner Theatre, Akron, Ohio, 330/724-9855; Chanhassen Theatres, Chanhassen, MN, 612/934-1500; Charlotte Repertory Theatre, NC, 704/333-8587; Cleveland Signstage Theatre, OH 216/229-2838; El Portal Center for the Arts, North Hollywood, CA, 818/508-4234; Ensemble Theatre Company of Santa Barbara, CA, 805/965-6252; Florida Stage, Manalapan, FL, 800/514-3837; Helen Hays Performing Arts Center, Nyack, NY, 914/358-2847; Hippodrome State Theatre, Gainesville, FL, 352/373-5968; Human Race Theatre Company, Dayton, Ohio, 937/461-3823; Living Stage Theatre Company, Washington, DC, 202/234-5782; Mill Mountain Theatre, Roanoke, VA, 540/342-5740; North Caroling Black Repertory Company, Winston-Salem, 910/723-7907; North Carolina Theatre, Raleigh, 919/831-6941; Paper Mill Playhouse, Millburn, NJ, 201/379-3636; Pennsylvania Centre Stage, University Park, PA, 814/863-7327; Playhouse On The Square, Memphis, TN, 901/725-0776; PlayMakers Repertory Company, Chapel Hill, NC, 919/962-1122; San Jose Repertory Theatre, San Jose, CA, 408/291-2266; Studio Areana Theatre, 710 Main St., Buffalo, NY 14202.

SECTION TEN

INTERNET AND WORLD WIDE WEB ADDRESSES

• **There are many sites to search involving show business** and acting and there are new ones coming on line every day. You can meet actors, casting directors, directors and producers in Los Angeles or in your area. The computer and internet will open your world to many possibilities.

• **Following are many websites,** where you'll find links to related websites. This is a fast moving world and some addresses may have already fallen by the wayside, but there will be many to explore. You can find scripts of your favorite shows too.

• ***Variety* reported the following account of an actor being discovered:** Producer Gene Corman was surfing the Internet one day when he decided to enter Actors World, where he was met with scads of actors' photos and resumes. One picture intrigued him: Donald Hoffman, an unknown living in Bismark, N.D., who was a dead ringer for the elderly Orson Welles. He was flown to L.A. to read and subsequently cast in the role for a four-hour miniseries project "Orson Welles: The Later Years." Corman marveled, "It's amazing what you can do on this Internet."

• **If you are interested in your own website,** Sean O'Riordan, who designed mine and my husband's, offers classy and inexpensive designs and he completely understands "the actor's world." Call or write, 323/858-4959. www.performersweb.com

Judy Kerr, author of *Acting Is Everything: An Actor's Guidebook for a Successful Career In Los Angeles:* **www.actingiseverything.com**

Internet Addresses

Academy Kids: Child Actors: www.academykids.com
Academy of Motion Pictures Arts and Sciences: www.oscars.org Also the official site of the Academy Awards.
Academy of Television Arts and Sciences: www.emmys.org
Academy Players Directory: www.acadpd.org
Act Now!: www.icorp.com/actnow/actnow
Acting Classes: www.candacesilvers.com for Candace Silvers Studios.
Acting Coach Howard Fine: www.howardfine.com
Acting-L Mailing List: www.albany.net/~danorton/acting-l/index.shtml
Acting.net: www.acting.net
Actorsite, Resource site for actors: www.actorsite.com
Actors Access - Breakdowns for Actors: www.breakdownservices.com
Actors for Actors: www.actors-for-actors.com
Actors Studio, The New School University www.newschool.edu
Actors Equity Association, AEA, also called Equity, www.actorsequity.org
Actor's Web: starone.com/actorsweb
Actor's Worldlink: members.aol.com/aworldlink/
Actresses@Work: www.geocities.com/~anotherhat Encourages the entertainment industry to recognize the potential of women representing the expanding "Baby Boomer" era.
Airport Information/Car Rentals/Hotels - great web site: www.lawa.org
Aisle Say: www.escabe.com/~theanet/AisleSay.
Alexander Technique, Bruce I. Kodish, www.transmillennium.net/brucekodish/; www.alexandertech.com
American Federation of Television and Radio Artists: www.aftra.com
American Film Institute: www.afionline.org
American Women in Radio and Television: www.awrt.org
Artist Rights Foundation: www.artistsrights.org
Artist's Way Workshop: www.creativelife.com
Ask Theater: www.primenet.com/~askplay
Auditions Online: www.auditions.com
Awesome List: www.clark.net/pub/journalism/awesome
Back To One: Hollywood Extras' Guidebook: www.cullenchambers.com
Backstage West: www.backstagewest.com Includes casting notices, articles, reviews, performing arts directory and more.
Best Bargins in Los Angeles, www.labestbargins.com.
Best Books Online: www.speaking.com
Biff Yeager: Making a Movie: www.lbc.com/silverpenny
Book Wire for book lovers: www.bookwire.com
Box Office News: www.enidata.com
Breck Costin, BCC & Associates: www.bccfreedom.com
Canada Film Commission: www.canadafilm.com
Career/Life Coaching: www.lifeskillbuilder@aol.com
Cast Online: www.castonline.com
Casting: www.castingnet.com Lists what is casting.

Casting Connection: members.aol.com/rlshelly/rlshelly.htm
Casting on the Web: www.actors.it/defe.htm
CastNet: castnet.com
Chat board for professional actors: www.InsideTheWeb.com/messageboard/mbs.cgi/mb93217
Child Actors: www.academykids.com
Cinewomen: www.cinewomen.com Dedicated to promoting women in the film industry.
Comedy with Judy Carter, www.judycarter.com
Comedy on the Lot: www.onthelot.com
Commercial Casting Director, Lien/Cowan: www.liencowancasting.com
Consumer Information Center: www.pueblo.gsa.gov
Cosmetics:www.clinique.com,www.cosmeticscounter.com
www.bobbibrowncosmetics.com/home
Coupons: www.valpak.com Thousands of on-line coupons are available that you just print and use. Other sites include: www.coolsavings.com, www.valuepage.com, www.hotcoupons.com, www.directcoupons.com and www.ralphs.com
CPI Model/Talent Exposure Service: www.cpimodel.com
Daytimer: www.daytimer.com Free stuff.
Directors Guild of America: www.dga.org/dga
Discounts: www.umdn.com Union Members Discount Network. Discounts at over 200 businesses in the L.A. area for members of the entertainment industry.
Episodic guide: www.xnet.com/~djk/main page.shtml Guide to episodic TV.
Extra Work on Hollywood Sets: www. cullenchambers.com
Film Festival on the Web: www.reeltimefilm.com An online festival of indie shorts available in the RealVideo format.
Filmmaking for Kids Workshops: www.youngfilmmakers.org
Film, TV & Commercial Employment Network: www.employnow.com
Film School: The Los Angeles Film School, www.lafilm.com
Fitness Online: www.fitnessonline.com **Rob Woods Home of Fitness Testing:** www.worldguide.com/Fitness/hf.html **In Fitness and In Health Site:** www.phys.com/
Nutritiously Gourmet Web Site: www.nutritiouslygourmet.com/
Geri Cook's Best Bargins Newsletter, www.LAbestbargins.com.
Getty Museum: www.getty.edu
Getting The Job, An Audio Tape, www.carolynebarry.com
GNN's Whole Internet Catalog: www.gnn.com/gnn/wic
Health: www.healthyideas.com, www.onhealth.com, cgi.pathfinder.com/drwell
Hollywood Actor's Network: www.hollywoodnetwork.com/hn/acting/index.html
Holllywood Creative Directory: www.hollyvision.com
Hollywood Film Institute: www.hollywoodu.com
Hollywood Mall: www:hollywoodmall.com/
Hollywood Network: www.HollywoodNetwork.com
Hollywood Radio & Television Society: www.hrts-iba.org
Hollywood Reporter: www.hollywoodreporter.com Then go to the Hollywood Hyperlink area where you will find hundreds of addresses revolving around show business, including all of the Film Commissions, Unions, Casting Tools & Actor Resources, Scripts & Screenwriting, Production & Equipment Rentals.
HollywoodWeb: www.hollywoodweb.com
Independent Feature Project North: www.mtn.org/ifpn
India, Entertainment: www.redifindia.com
Industry Labor Guide: www.laborguide.com
Interactive Talent Network: www.talnet.com

Internet Movie Data Base: www.imdb.com
Internet Resources: www.brandonu.ca/~ennsnr/Resources/Welcome
Jobs: www.jobtrak.com
Judy Belshe Casting: members.aol.com/JBelshe412
L.A. Actors List: www.geocities.com/Hollywood/Set/1194
Life/Career Coach: Breck Castin, bbc & Associates: www.bccfreedom.com **Barbara Deutsch:** www.barbaradeutsch@inotherwords.com
Load Media Network: www.loadmedia.com Pilot testing on the web.
Los Angeles Film School: www.lafilm.com
Makeup: Rita Montanez, www.webworksps.com/makeupbyrita
Maps and driving directions: www.mapquest.com
Mark Taper Theater: www.tmn.com/Oh/Community/ctgtaper/home
Memorization, Vicki Mizel, "Brainspouts," www.artnewmedia.com/brainspouts
MGM's Video Savant: www.mgm.com/savant/index.html
ModelBase: modelbase.com
Modeling: www.howtomodel.com
Models-Net: www.models-net.com
New World Order Theater: www.yurope.com
News Sites: www.cnn.com,www.msnbc.com
Newsgroup for actors: alt.acting. USENET Newsgroup for actors.
New York Wooster Group: www.escape.com/~philbus/wooster
Nutrition, www.living in the zone.com
Office Depot: www.officedepot.com
Office Max: www.officemax.com
Onstage: www.geocities.com/Broadway/1444
Oregon's CoquilleTheater: www.presys.com/ohwy/c/coqcomth
O'Reilly Web Review: www.gnn.com/gnn/wr
Photographers: Raffi Alexander: Spiderbox Photography, www.spiderbox.com; see photo section. **Carrie Cavalier** of Cavalier Photography Studio: www.cavalierphotography.com. see photo section: **Alan Weissman:** www.alanweissman.com.see photo section: **Mary Ann Halpin:** www.goddesshood.com *See photo section, 73.*
Plastic Surgery: www.garthfisher.com *See page 401.*
Plastic and Reconstructing Surgeons, American Society: www.plasticsurgery.org
Playbill: www.playbill.com. World-wide theatre information.
Professional Theater Resources-Theater around the world: www.fleethouse.con/fhcanada/western/bc/van/entertan/net-link
Publications: www.backstage.com, www.hollyvision.com, www.hollywoodreporter.com, www.reelwest.com, www.variety.com, www.latimes.com
Publicity Consulting: www.lmersini@aol.com
Quickcast Network: www.quickcast.com
Resource Center for Actors: www.caryn.com
Resumes: www.Imagestarter.com
Reviews of movies, including film festivals: www.filmscouts.com
Screen Actors Guild: www.sag.com
Screen Actors' Guild Health Directory: www.sagph.org
Dallas/Fort Worth AFTRA/SAG: www.entertainment.com/org uns/dfwactor/asdfw
San Francisco: www.aftrasf.org
Seattle: www.aftra.com

Scripts, Barbarians: www.pages.ripco.com:8080/~bbb/scripts
Scripts, E.M. Archives: www.ccn.cs.dal.ca/Recreation/EMA/scripts/scripts
Search services: www.altavista.com, www.beaucoup.com, www.dogpile.com, www.excite.com, www.google.com, www.hotbot.com, www.infoseek.com, www.lycos.com, www.northernlight.com, www.webcrawler.com, www.yahoo.com
Shopping, Thrift Stores: www.consignmentguide.com. **Buy from chains supporting social causes:** www.shopforchange.com. **QVC Shopping Network:** www.qvc.com/
Showcase: www.liveactors.com
Sides Faxed: www.actorfax.com
Showfax: www.showfax.com
Stage Presence, www.sikehealth.com; www.alexandertech.com; www.transmillennium.net/brucekodish/
Stars' Driveways: www.driveways.com
Starring Role In A Movie: check it out at: www.ultimatewishgift.com
Sundance Institute: cybermart.com/sundance/institute/
TalentBank International: www.talentbank.com
TalentWorks: The Online Csting Source: www.talentworks.com
Television Shows: www.infoweb.magi.com/~datakes/index
Theatre Central: www.theatre-central.com
Time Management Systems: Franklin System: www.franklincovey.com
Traffic Conditions: www.maxwll.com/caltrans. Real-time driving conditions from Los Angeles, Orange County and San Diego.
Train Ride, Filmore & Western Railway, www.fwry.com
UCLA Extension, www.espa.unex.ucla.edu
UCLA School of Theater, Film and Television: www.tft.ucla.edu
Union Member Discount Network: www.umdn.com
Unions: www.actra.com, www.aftra.org, www.dga.org, www.actorsequity.org, www.sag.com, www.wga.org
Video Sellers: www.reel.com
Virtual Headwork: www.xmission.com/~wintrnx/virtual.html
Voice: www.mnusa.com.corff
Voice Overs: National Voice Database, www.voicedatabase.com
Wake Up Call: www.mrwakeup.com This is a free way to get wakeup calls. You do have to register and listen to some advertising during the call. Worth it, I think, for that double way to wake up. Alarm and phone call.
WannaBe's Talent Discovery & Development: www.rain.org/~wannabe
Weight Watchers, www.weightwatchers.com.

Web Site of Your Own: www.performersweb.com

Wilshire Aesthetics, Dermatology & Plastic Surgery Group: www.wilshireaesthetics.com
Women In Film: www.wif.org
Woody Harrelson's O2 bar and restaurant, www.o2bar.com
World Wide Stars: www.worldstars.com
Writers, Scripts. Usenet discussion group: www.misc.writing.screenplays

Acknowledgments and Conclusion

NEW YORK STAGE ACTORS' PRAYER

Oh Lord, Give me successes that are not just successes, but contain just enough quality to let me feel I haven't wasted my life. Give me long enough runs to pay my bills, and then when I am rich, get me into Repertory. Let me make wise decisions with regard to my career but when I cannot be wise, let me be undeservedly lucky. Let me be praised, let me be paid, let me be proud. Give me the strength never to announce my plans beforehand, give me the grace to get through interviews safely, give me the fortitude to survive my collaborators. Humbly, I ask all this...and Sardi's (Spago's, for L.A.) too. Amen.

Please wave "hello" to me as we
pass through the studio gates.

THANK YOU

Ron Gorow, my husband. I could not have written this book without the encouragement and hours of reading, editing and input. You are the best.

Morgan Ames, proof reader, editor, friend. Thanks for being a stickler.

Bonnie Howard, proof reader, business consultant, agent and friend.

Robin Gee, my dear friend, for her organizational skills getting me started on the ninth edition and then updating the Web Addresses and the Cool Places To Go In Los Angeles; she knows cool.

Marlene Hajdu, for inputting the additional material in the Cities Outside of L.A. Section, and the help with the vintage stores.

Janice Allen. Thanks for scouting the scouting trip and adding more fun, and for your help and support as my class assistant.

Jode Leigh Edwards. Your diary is an important, interesting part of the book.

Cullen Chambers and Rich Hogan for keeping the Extra's Section current.

Amber Baldwin, for updating all the phone numbers. Not an easy task, I know.

Liria Mersini, my life/publicity coach, who came on board during the last crucial month of writing.

Hank Tovar. Thanks for your contributions in the Child Actor Section.

Austin and Jackson Tovar for your help in the Child Actor Section and for your great contribution to my life!

Thomas Cobb, my son-in-law, for the perfect cover. This is your fourth one and the lights are really shining. You are a genius!

Cynthia Kerr, my daughter, my dear. I can't say thank you enough for the Commercial Section and for your help in the Child Actor Section. It is such a pleasure to have you on board. Maybe the 10th edition will come from you. I can turn it over gratefully!

IN CONCLUSION

I BELIEVE...

- That we can fulfill our dreams.
- It takes accepting responsibility for our actions and choices.
- We choose our paths daily and are offered many opportunities.
- It takes extreme focus and clear intentions to fulfill our dreams.
- We need tenacity not to give up and to see adversities as opportunities.
- It takes extreme curiousity.
- We must use time and organizational skills to our advantage and respect them for the power they give us.
- If we operate from poverty thinking, we will always be lacking.
- Without a developed spiritual life and fundamental values/beliefs, we will not experience real joy and are likely to feel empty.
- Having fun is the most important goal in life.

I have written this book for you.

With love,

Judy Kerr

ON THE SET • GLOSSARY

ABBY SINGER: The last shot, sometimes called the "Martini shot", named after the Assistant Director who always claimed it was the finale and inevitably called for one more set-up.
ACE: A 1000 watt spotlight.
ACTION: What the director calls out to begin all principal acting on a set.
A/D: see DIRECTOR, ASSISTANT.
ANIMAL HANDLERS: They handle the animals and are responsible for transportation, feeding, grooming and general care.
APPLE BOX: A wooden box approximately l'W x 1'6"D x 8"H. These boxes are used for actors to stand on to raise their height. They are also used to prop up different items, lights, etc. There are also half-and quarter-apple boxes.
ASSISTANT CAMERAMAN: see CAMERAMAN, ASSISTANT
ASSISTANT DIRECTOR or **A/D:** The First A.D. hardly ever leaves the director's side. They yell "quiet on the set" and tell the camera person to start rolling. The A.D. is in charge of the set.
ASSISTANT DIRECTOR, SECOND: This is the person who you will most likely report to when you arrive on the set. 2nd A.D.s are responsible for daily call sheets, talent and extras' time sheets and vouchers. They will phone you with your call time for the next day. They also direct the extras or background players on the set. There can also be a 3rd A.D. Always report to the 2nd A.D. when you are leaving the set for any reason.
ASSOCIATE PRODUCER, see PRODUCER, ASSOCIATE
AVAIL/FIRST REFUSAL: Not legally binding and no compensation is involved: you are being asked whether you are available for future engagement.
BACKGROUND: Extras are referred to as background. In a scene background refers to the action that the extra will need to make.
BACK TO ONE: All actors and extras are to go back to their first position of action in the scene. This means you will be reshooting the scene and are to perform the same action unless told differently.
BARN DOORS: These are black metal gates on lighting equipment used to direct and control the light.
BEST BOY: Is an assistant to the gaffer—helps handle all equipment.
BLOCKING: The director plans where the principal actors will move and the 2nd A.D. will set up the extra's movement in the scene.
BOOM: An overhead microphone, usually held on a long pole.
BOOM OPERATOR: Person who handles the boom mike and stays out of the camera shot.
CALL SHEET: A printed schedule of the day's work that is to be filmed and the people, place, and things needed. Keep a couple from each shoot that you do along with your saved script.
CALL TIME: The time you are to report to the set. When you get there, check in with the A.D.

CABLE OPERATOR: Ensures the physical safety of the actors and the equipment.
CAMERAMAN / CINEMATOGRAPHER / DIRECTOR OF PHOTOGRAPHY: They are directed by the director as to what to capture on film or video.
CAMERAMAN, ASSISTANT: Keeps track of and records everything that's shot, loads and unloads the film, and keeps the camera and lenses clean.
CAMERA LEFT & CAMERA RIGHT: The direction to look or to proceed when facing the camera. Camera Left is your right.
CAMERA OPERATOR: Responsible for the actual operation of the camera and lenses. They load and unload the camera, set the lens, take measurements, and check the focus.
CARPENTERS: Primarily for the purpose of assembling sets and building props.
CATERING: When on location, meals must be provided every six hours. The catering truck will usually fix hearty breakfast, lunches and dinner.
CINEMATOGRAPHER: see CAMERAMAN.
CLAPBOARD / SLATE / STICKS: A mini chalkboard that has the name of the production, director, and cameraman. It is used to keep records of what scene is being filmed and makes a clapping sound to tell the person who edits the film where to start sound.
CONTINUITY: Matching everything you did in a previous scene so it looks exactly like it happened the first time you did it.
COOKIES: camera operators use to break up light and produce a softening effect.
CRAFT SERVICE: This is the person responsible for keeping the craft table neat, clean and supplied with drinks and food items.
CRAFT TABLE: A table located near the set, with coffee, water, sodas, snacks and fruit for the actors and crew. When there are a lot of extras on the set, there will usually be two craft tables, one for the actors and crew and the other specifically for the extras.
CROSS: The movement the actor or extra makes from point A to point B in front of the camera when the scene is being filmed.
CUE: A signal (nonverbal or verbal) from the director to start your action.
CUT: Yelled out by the director to stop the action, camera and sound.
CUT & HOLD: To stop the action, camera and sound, and tell all actors and background to hold their places.
DAY PLAYER: An actor hired by the production to play a certain role generally for a day only.
DEUCE: A 2000 watt spotlight.
DIALOGUE EDITOR: Ensures that production tracks are technically good; also locates alternate tracks/takes that could augment background dialogue.
DIRECTOR: Makes every decision and has the last word on how each scene will be shot. It is the creative vision of the director that will bring a scene to life. Sometimes the producer will take some of this power back—that's why directors like to be the producer too.
DIRECTOR, ASSISTANT: see ASSISTANT DIRECTOR
DIRECTOR OF PHOTOGRAPHY: see CAMERAMAN.
DOLLY: When they move the camera toward you or away from you during a shot, that's called "dollying."
DOLLY GRIP: They specialize in moving the camera with a smooth steady action.
DOWNSTAGE: This is in front of you as you are standing on the set or stage. If you're told to move downstage move toward the camera or audience.
DRIVERS: They move equipment vehicles from location to location. They transport performers and perform stunt and standard driving in the scenes.
DROPPING THE FLAG ON THE PLAY: when the crew stops their present activities.
86: Forget about it.
EDITOR: Cuts the film apart and reassembles it in the order and method dictated by the director. A lot of it is done on computer now; videotape is edited digitally.

EFFECTS EDITOR: Provides all incidental sounds, from footsteps to fist fights to doors slamming to lovemaking and cars screeching. Records or replicates the sounds, or designs a new combination.
ESTABLISHED: Person or prop having been filmed in a certain position in a previous scene.
EXECUTIVE PRODUCER: see PRODUCER, EXECUTIVE.
EXT: Exterior, a scene shot outside.
EXTRA: These are the men, women and children who give realism to a motion picture, television program or commercial. Background movement players commonly referred to as background, background artist, atmosphere.
FDR: means next shot is a "new deal" or a different setup.
FIRST TEAM: Principal actors.
FOLEY ARTIST: The person who makes the sound effects that aren't replicated by other methods by using voice, hand props, gadgets or tools. Actually performs to picture on the screen.
FOREGROUND: The area in front of the camera lens, between a principal actor, actress or thing.
GAFFER: Chief electrician on the set; responsible for the lighting of the set.
GEL: A diffuser made of a gelatin type material for softening lights or changing colors of a light.
GOLDEN TIME: This refers to overtime after the 16th hour. It's golden because your pay is usually doubled.
GRIP: Member of the crew that physically moves equipment on the set and from location to location.
GROUCHO: Cameraman wants the actor to imitate Groucho Marx's bent walk so that everything fits in the shot—actor and background.
HICCUP: In 4 camera shows, this is where the cameras move in the middle of a scene.
HOLD: Legally binding and requires that payment be made to talent since you are being told to schedule a specific day of your time for use by that employer.
HONEYWAGON: Mobile trailer used for dressing rooms and toilets for cast and crew on location.
HOT SET: Hands Off! This is a set that has been used or has been prepared to use and is NOT to be Disturbed.
IATSE and **NABET:** The two unions that represent editors, camera people, electricians, set designers, and other crafts workers on the set.
INT: Interior, a scene shot inside as opposed to outside.
KEY GRIP: Sets up the camera as well as the dolly it sits on. Works with the director and gaffer to make sure things get done as intended.
LOCATION: Any place where there's a set if not on a studio sound stage.
LOOP: Watch film of yourself in a recording studio and replace damaged dialogue in sync with your lips—looping or ADR, automatic dialogue replacement.
LOSE IT: This is usually yelled out by the director or assistant director when he or she wants something out of the way.
MARK: These are pieces of tape placed in various areas on the ground as designation points where an actor is to stand for the camera. These are very specific, if you aren't on them you won't have your best light.
MOS: "mitt out sound" from an obscure German director. Scene shot without sound.
MUSIC EDITOR: Designs music tracks to fit with dialogue and sound effects. Helps define and design proper levels.
OBIE LIGHT: Named after actress Merle Oberon, is a 250 watt lamp which adds a twinkle to the actor's eyes and reduces wrinkles!

ON A BELL: A request by the Director to the sound man to sound a bell to alert everyone that filming is about to begin; silence must be maintained.
P.A. / PRODUCTION ASSISTANT: Fancy word for gofer. Usually an entry-level position for people who want to work for a production company. Sometimes they work as interns (for free) or for a pittance.
PAN: A camera shot which sweeps from side to side to follow the action.
PANTOMIME: Mouthing words in a scene when there is dialogue being recorded as the action takes place.
PER DIEM: Fee paid to you when on location to pay for your meals.
PHOTO DOUBLE: To be photographed as the principal actor in a scene when the actor is not needed, usually long distance shots.
PICK UP: When a take gets botched, you can do a pick up for just a portion of the scene, starting and ending anywhere.
PRINCIPALS: The people who have speaking lines or special bits or stunts in a scene.
PRINT: The director was happy with the scene and wants to keep it. This usually means they will be moving ahead to the next scene.
PRODUCER: Oversees everything in the production including the hiring of the cameraman, crew, actors and director if they have not been hired. The producer may be the writer and/or director of the project and at times may have his own money involved in the production. If no executive producer involved, the producer will develop the entire production from scratch.
PRODUCER, ASSOCIATE: Someone who contributed to the management of the production. Other times may be a key executive or major investor. Performs one or more producer functions as delegated by the producer.
PRODUCER, EXECUTIVE: Person usually responsible for financing or securing the financing for a production. They usually have acquired and/or developed the script or story at some point. After financing is in place, they will the hire the Producer and Director. Supervises one or more producers in the performance of their duties on one or more productions.
CO-PRODUCERS: Two or more producers who perform the producer functions as a team.
COORDINATING PRODUCER: To achieve a unified result, coordinates the work of two or more producers working separately on single or multiple productions.
LINE PRODUCER: Supervises the purely physical production aspects of a motion picture or television production and is supervised by another producer who handles all other duties.
SEGMENT PRODUCER: Produces one or more individual segments of a multi-segment production.
SUPERVISING PRODUCER: Supervises one or more producers in some or all of their functions either in place of or subject to the overriding authority of an executive producer.
PRODUCTION/UNIT MANAGER: An executive hired by the producer to coordinate and supervise all financial and technical details of the production. They *must* keep the production budget in line.
PROPERTY MASTER: Heads the prop department and is responsible for the acquisition, storage and placement of props. They also have the candy bars hidden in the trucks to bring out in the afternoon.
PUP: A 500 watt small spotlight.
REHEARSAL: Running through the scene without the camera actually filming the action to work out any mistakes or movement of last second directions.
REVERSE: To move the camera around to shoot the other actor's point of view.
ROLLING: Camera and sound are in motion and the action is ready to be filmed.

SANDBAG: Small burlap or plastic bag filled with sand, used to temporarily hold pieces of equipment in place.
SCRIPT SUPERVISOR: Monitors the script as the film is shot to assure that everything scripted is properly spoken. If a line is missed or an error made, they maintain the appropriate notes to allow the editor to correct the problem later. They also note any new lines the director or actors might add during the shooting.
SECOND A/D: see ASSISTANT DIRECTOR, SECOND.
SECOND TEAM: see STAND-IN.
SET: Where the actors do their work—on the set.
SET DESIGNER: Hired early, long before actual shooting, to design the sets or to prepare plans to modify existing locations.
SET DRESSERS: Actually select and place decorations and detail items on the set to provide authentic realism. Such items can be salt shakers on a table, mail in a mail slot, statue in a foyer.
SET-UP: When they move the camera, lights, etc. from bathroom to bedroom. That change is a new set-up.
SINGLE: One person in the shot.
SLATE: (see CLAPBOARD).
SOUND DESIGNER: The team's manager responsible for the development and augmentation of all soundtrack material.
SOUND STAGE: A soundproof building in which the action is shot.
SPEED: Speed is announced from the soundman to the director when the audio tape is running at proper speed for recording in sync with the film.
SQUIB: These are used in scenes to give the effect of bullets hitting walls, cars, and people.
STAND-IN / SECOND TEAM: The people who substitute for the principal actors when principals are not needed such as when lighting or camera blocking is being done by the production crew. It gives the actors a chance to rest. This is a premium extra position!
STAY WITH THE MONEY: is an instruction to keep the camera focused on the star.
STICKS: see CLAPBOARD.
STUNT COORDINATOR: They decide when and where to substitute stunt performers for the actors during dangerous scenes.
TAKE: The time between "action" and "cut" that the camera is actually rolling.
TRACK: Metal tracks laid down so the camera can dolly smoothly.
TURN AROUND: The number of hours between dismissal one day and call time next day.
TWO-SHOT: Two people on camera.
UNDER FIVE: An actor who is hired to speak fewer than five lines.
UPSTAGE: Behind the actor as he stands on the stage or set facing the audience or camera. When someone "upstages" you, he is doing something behind your back while you are facing the audience. It draws attention to them.
WRANGLER: see ANIMAL HANDLERS.
WRAP: What the Director calls out when the day's filming is completed. Yeah!

SCRIPT GLOSSARY

C.S.	Close shot.
C.U.	Close up.
CUT	Immediate change of location or point of view.
CUT TO INT.	Cut to interior.
CUT TO EXT.	Cut to exterior.
DISS.	Dissolve.
E.C.U.	Extreme close up.
E.T.	End title.
F.F.O.	Full Fade Out. End of act or end of picture.
F.I.	Fade In.
F.O.	Fade Out.
F.O. to COMM.	Fade out to commercial.
F.S.	Full shot.
L.S.	Long shot.
M.L.S.	Medium long shot.
M.S.	Medium shot.
M.T.	Main title.
O.S.	Offstage. (dialogue or sound)
PAN	Panning shot, horizontal or vertical movement of camera.

Index

ACTING IS EVERYTHING

WORKSHOPS

• To arrange an *ACTING IS EVERYTHING* workshop in your area, please contact me through my website at www.actingiseverything.com or via fax at 818/505-9311.

• Current plans include workshops in Manhattan, San Francisco, San Diego, Seattle, Dallas, Miami, Vancouver and Switzerland.

• If you would like to be notified about seminar workshops in your area, send your name, address, phone number and e-mail address to Judy Kerr via fax at 818/505-9311 or the website at www.actingiseverything.com

Telephone Consultation With Judy Kerr

For Out of Los Angeles Area Actors

818/505-9373

• If you are in the Los Angeles area and are interested in scheduling a career coaching appointment or a private acting session, call 818/505-9373.

• To be put on the mailing list for the once-a-year group class, contact Judy Kerr via phone, fax or web site.

• Order more copies of *Acting Is Everything: An Actor's Guidebook for a Successful Career in Los Angeles* at the web site or in bookstores everywhere.

ACTING IS EVERYTHING WORKSHOPS

• To arrange an *ACTING IS EVERYTHING* workshop in your area, please contact me through my website at www.actingiseverything.com or via fax at 818/505-9311.

• Current plans include workshops in Manhattan, San Francisco, San Diego, Seattle, Dallas, Miami, Vancouver and Switzerland.

• If you would like to be notified about seminar workshops in your area, send your name, address, phone number and e-mail address to Judy Kerr via fax at 818/505-9311 or the website at www.actingiseverything.com

Telephone Consultation With Judy Kerr

For Out of Los Angeles Area Actors

818/505-9373

• If you are in the Los Angeles area and are interested in scheduling a career coaching appointment or a private acting session, call 818/505-9373.

• To be put on the mailing list for the once-a-year group class, contact Judy Kerr via phone, fax or web site.

• *Order more copies of Acting Is Everything: An Actor's Guidebook for a Successful Career in Los Angeles* at the web site or in bookstores everywhere.